NOW
city guide

MW00478514

Produced by **NOW Ink Inc.**

Edited and designed by
NOW Communication Inc. (NOW Magazine)
189 Church Street
Toronto, ON
Canada M5B 1Y7
Tel **416-364-1300** Fax **416-364-1166**
www.nowtoronto.com

Editor Barrett Hooper
Art Director Stephen Chester
Photography* James Pattyn

Editorial
Associate Editors Michael Hollett, Susan G. Cole
Food & Drink Editor Steven Davey
Copy Editors/Proofreaders Fran Schecter,
Katarina Ristic, Crissy Boylan
Indexer Emily Schultz

Contributing Writers
Benjamin Boles, Susan G. Cole, Evan Davies,
Enzo DiMatteo, Graham Duncan, Julia Hoecke,
Michael Hollett, Barrett Hooper, Jon Kaplan,
Sarah Liss, Tim Perlich, Andrew Sardone, Glenn
Sumi, Kevin Temple, Adria Vasil, Joseph Wilson

Editorial Assistant Mary Zondanos

Design
Design Consultant Bryan Gee
Maps Nabil Elsaadi
Photo Coordinator Karen Chapelle

Sales & Marketing
Vice-President Sales & Marketing Grant Crosbie
Sales Operations Manager Rhonda Loubert
Promotions Manager Brian Francis

NOW Communications Inc.
Editor/Publisher Michael Hollett
Editor/CEO Alice Klein
General Manager David Logan
Art Director Troy Beyer

*except where otherwise indicated.

Copyright © NOW Communications Inc., 2006
Published by **ECW Press**
2120 Queen Street East
Suite 200, Toronto, ON
Canada M4E 1E2
www.ecwpress.com

LIBRARY AND ARCHIVES CANADA CATALOGUING IN PUBLICATION
Toronto : the essential guide to the best of the city / NOW magazine.
Includes index.
ISBN-10: 1-55022-745-9
ISBN-13: 978-1-55022-745-1
1. Toronto (Ont.)–Guidebooks. I. Title.
FC3097.18,T665 2006   917.13'541045   C2006-904106-7

Text typeface: Thesis. Display typeface: FF Cocon.
Printed and bound in Canada by Transcontinental Printing
Printed on 100% recycled (20% PCW) paper stock

Distribution
Canada: Jaguar Book Group, 100 Armstrong Avenue, Georgetown, ON L7G 5S4
United States: Independent Publishers Group, 814 North Franklin Street, Chicago, Illinois 60610

ECW PRESS
ecwpress.com

Toronto

the essential guide to the best of the city

Toronto in a box.

If it's happening in T.O., it's in NOW.

NOW Magazine crams the city's best film, theatre, dance, comedy and concert listings into every issue. Best of all, it's free. Look for the NOW green street boxes or find us at most shops, restaurants and bars across the city. Read us online at nowtoronto.com.

Everything Toronto. Every Week.

contents

City Hall and Nathan Phillips Square

welcome

to the second edition of **Toronto: the essential guide to the best of the city**, a book that gives you an insider's view of one of North America's most vibrant cities – seen through the eyes of the people at NOW Magazine, who know the city best.

Every week for 25 years (and counting), NOW Magazine has published the lowdown on what's really happening in Toronto. Our comprehensive arts and entertainment coverage – from film and music to theatre and dance and everything in between – makes NOW the first place people turn for essential information on what's going on in and around Toronto. But NOW isn't just an entertainment guide – it's also Toronto's most trusted source for news about the people and events that mainstream newspapers often ignore. We're proud of NOW's long-standing reputation for reporting stories that take on the powerful, that challenge public opinion and that open debate on important local and international issues.

The NOW City Guide continues this tradition of exploring and explaining the city from a fresh viewpoint. Both first-time visitors to Toronto and longtime residents will find the guide an invaluable handbook on the best places to eat, party, dance, shop and generally have fun in the city. Whether you're here for a weekend, a month, or the foreseeable future, you can rely on the NOW guide to show you a side of Toronto that goes beyond tourist traps and picture-postcard places. Journey through the best Toronto has to offer, neighbourhood by neighbourhood.

And for the latest up-to-date info on what's happening in Toronto, check out the NOW Magazine website at www.nowtoronto.com, or pick up your free copy of NOW Magazine, available every Thursday at over 2,000 locations – including restaurants, clubs and retail outlets, as well as our distinctive green street boxes.

Michael Hollett
Editor/Publisher

Alice Klein
Editor/CEO

toronto now

No matter how you look at it, Toronto – T.O., the T-Dot – is one of the coolest places on the planet to live. That also makes us one of the coolest places to visit, and this book is the ultimate resource for surviving and thriving in Canada's biggest, baddest, boldest metropolis. The NOW City Guide has everything you need to navigate the city: where to eat, drink, sleep, shop, play and party. Why would you want to go anywhere else?

Okay, let's come clean. There are certainly prettier cities to put on a postcard. Sure, from the right angle and in the right light at the right time of day, when the sun and the clouds and the snow and the rain and the smog co-operate Toronto's kind of picturesque, a slouching lakeside metropolis of neatly arranged office towers and condominiums and construction cranes (to build the office towers and condominiums).

There's a barely noticeable necklace of islands across the harbour. There's a wind turbine – part of T.O.'s growing green efforts – spinning lazily like the propeller on some kid's beanie. And of course, there's the CN Tower, a 553-metre-high phallus with the SkyDome (it might have suffered the indignity of corporate rebranding, but the home of the 92 and 93 World Series champs is no Rogers Centre) hanging off it like a single, lonely testicle half-buried in concrete.

But we lack the defining character possessed by other great cities, the arrogant majesty of New York or the historical grandeur of Paris or London, or even the cheesy pop culture familiarity of Los Angeles. We may boast the world's longest street – Yonge Street splits the city into east and west starting at the lakeshore and doesn't end for 1,896 kilometres – but it ain't the Champs Elysées or Broadway. Although, again, from the right angle in the right light, it could be. Which is part of the reason Hollywood shoots movies like Chicago and Cinderella Man here, cuz we can be dressed up to look like everywhere while never actually looking like anywhere.

Not that we lack significance. We're the fifth-largest city in North America, after all. Only Mexico City, New York, L.A. and Chicago are bigger. Our more than 5.3-million residents – 41 per cent of whom were born outside of Canada, doncha know? – speak close to 150 languages and dialects,

introduction

which the United Nations says makes us the most multicultural metropolis in the world.

The current City of Toronto is an amalgamation of six prior municipalities, but really, we're a city of neighbourhoods, from the lakeside Beaches to the boho Annex to ritzy Rosedale, Little India to Little Italy, Greektown to Cabbagetown to Koreatown to at least two Chinatowns. And with all this ethnic diversity, there's no better way to explore the city than by eating your way around the globe at any of our countless great restaurants.

The Toronto Stock Exchange is North America's third-largest exchange by value traded. In fact, Toronto is the very heart of the Canadian economy, even if the soul stretches from St. John's, Newfoundland to the Queen Charlotte Islands, British Columbia to Cape Columbia, Nunavut. And we have our fingers wrapped around more than our share of the country's political strings, although we're not the capital of Canada (that would be Ottawa, dammit!).

When it comes to culture, Toronto is no couch potato. It's home to the world's third-largest English-language theatre scene, where internationally renowned productions – like Lord Of The Rings – have received their world premieres. There's the National Ballet Company, the Toronto Symphony Orchestra and the Canadian Opera Company. The Toronto International Film Festival, one of about 40 film festivals the city hosts each year, is the world's biggest, but, appropriately, not the world's most glamorous. And while we're talking about movies, we wouldn't be Hollywood North if we didn't have a few famous actors and directors of our own, including Keanu Reeves, Sandra Oh, Sarah Polley, Mike Myers, Jim Carrey, Christopher Plummer, Catherine O'Hara, David Cronenberg and Norman Jewison.

Our gay population is the biggest in Canada and the Pride Week celebration is one of the three largest in the world (along with New York City and Sydney, Australia). Likewise, Caribana is the largest Caribbean festival north of Jamaica, attracting close to 2 million partiers each summer. A million more stop by for the International Dragon Boat Festival. And those are just a few of the hundreds of festivals held here each year.

We've got a vibrant music scene and Toronto is the hometown to the likes of the Barenaked Ladies, Blue Rodeo, Broken Social Scene, Neil Young, Rush, k-os and that dude with the 'tude who won the job as lead singer of INXS.

Our favourite sport is hockey, naturally, and we love our Maple Leafs as much as the rest of the country hates 'em. We also spill our beer (and the occasional tear) over the Blue Jays, Raptors, Argos and Rock.

We erected the world's first permanent AIDS memorial. We invented the world's first alternating current (AC) radio tube, which allowed radios to run on household current. We discovered insulin and created IMAX. M.A.C. Cosmetics was founded here, for chrissake!

Mick and Keef and the rest of the Stones love Toronto. They recorded a live album here, they prep for all their world tours by rehearsing in our local clubs, and when SARS delivered a stinging bitch-slap in 2003, they came to our emotional rescue with an all-day concert that drew 800,000 fans and reminded everyone that Toronto is a really great place to be.

Now, all of this might seem like bragging, and to some degree it is. It's part of the reason why the rest of the country sees us as confident to the point of arrogance: we believe we're the centre of the country, if not the entire universe, which is kind of funny when you consider that while one-third of Canada's population lives within 160 km of Toronto, the actual geographic centre of the country is just south of Yathkyed Lake' in Nunavut, somewhere near the Arctic Circle.

We're a big fish in a small pond at home, but it's perhaps not surprising that we're a little unsure of ourselves on the international stage, striving for acceptance like someone's kid brother. We're still a young city in a young country, and we have a lot of growing up to do.

And we're doing it. Sure, we have crime and pollution and social problems like any city, but we're already far safer, cleaner and greener than most urban centres our size. Even the picture on our postcards is changing. Our buildings, long staid and rather plain, are getting a makeover thanks to some of the world's most acclaimed architects. The Toronto-raised Frank Gehry is currently overseeing a redesign of the Art Gallery of Ontario while Daniel Libeskind has sketched out a funky crystalline addition for the Royal Ontario Museum. English architect Will Alsop's controversial Sharp Centre for Design building has turned some heads while the understated Four Seasons Centre for the Performing Arts, home of the Canadian Opera Company and National Ballet of Canada, is perking up more than a few ears.

But after all that, what do visitors think about Toronto? It's clean. Yup, cleanliness is our claim to fame, along with friendliness. Sure we're proud of our clean streets and environmental initiatives and the fact our mayor drives a hybrid and that people will smile and wave and say please and thank you and help you with directions if you ask. But these aren't exactly things to trumpet from the rooftops – "Toronto. So clean. So friendly. So dull." – when it's so obvious we're so much more than that.

We were once called Muddy York – ironic given our current reputation as one of the cleanest cities around – until we paved the hell out of everything. When we had the largest pork yards in North America, they called us Hogtown and that still stings a bit. Then, when churches stood on almost every corner and booze was banned, we were Toronto the Good. But somehow even that's never been good enough. Because, as anyone who's lived here awhile already knows, no matter what angle you look at us from, we're really more like Toronto the really fuckin' great!

Don't believe us? Just drop by for a visit. We'll show you around.

history lesson

From the Ice Age to the rock age – how a city swindled the natives, burned the White House, pissed off Charles Dickens, sparked a rebellion, broke up the Beatles and still earned a reputation as Toronto the Good.

TORONTO ARCHIVES F1231 IT2011

Track to the future. The view looking west along College, at Spadina, 1927.

In prehistoric times – before the CN Tower was the world's tallest TV antenna, before the forging of the Stanley Cup and the brewing of Labatt Blue, before gay marriage and hydroponic pot, back 10,000 years ago when the world was still flat and Toronto was a frozen wasteland 24/7 – hungry Leafs fans armed with foam fingers and stone-tipped spears scavenged Lake Ontario's northern shores. They hunted for bear and elk and woolly mammoth and complained about the cold.

Fast forward to the 17th century. The ice was gone – for nine months of the year, at least – and agri-minded Iroquois Indians had settled the region to grow corn. Archeologists have since discovered the remains of close to 200 Iroquois villages in and around Toronto.

French and British fur traders brought firearms, firewater and disease to the natives in exchange for beaver pelts and a prime piece of New World real estate.

And on September 9, 1615, explorer Étienne Brûlé accompanied a Huron war party to Toronto (the Huron word for "meeting place") to become the first European in the region to complain about the cold.

For the next 100 years, the British and French engaged in a cold war buildup of forts and block-houses. The French established a trading post in Toronto and, perhaps recognizing a sweet spot to set off fireworks, built Fort Rouillé in 1750 on what is now the Canadian National Exhibition grounds.

Nine years later, the Brits captured Toronto ("capture" being a relative term as the French forces fled before there was bloodshed). The American Revolution brought fleeing United Empire Loyalists with their tricorne hats and bonnets northward.

In 1787, the Brits took ownership of the 250,000 acres in and around Toronto from the Mississauga Indians in exchange for 2,000 gun flints, 24 brass kettles, 120 mirrors, a bale of flowered flannel, 96 gallons of rum and some walking-around money.

John Simcoe, the first Lieutenant-Governor of Upper Canada (now Ontario), named the town York in honour of the Duke of York, in 1793. The name drew unwanted comparisons to New York and led to it being derogatorily referred to as Little York.

By the War of 1812 – when the United States declared war on Britain and sought to "liberate" Canada from colonial rule whether the Canadians liked it or not – Toronto was a less-than-thriving town of 700. After an American fleet with 1,700 troops blew up Fort York, Toronto retaliated by setting fire to the president's home in Washington. The building was later painted white to cover up the charred wood and has since been known as the White House.

On March 15, 1827, King's College – the precursor to the University of Toronto – was granted its royal charter by King George IV. U of T opened its doors 16 years later.

When the town was incorporated and renamed Toronto in 1834, the population of 10,000 was pretty pale – mostly Brits and Scots. But the groundwork for Toronto's current multiculti makeup was soon laid with the arrival of thousands of famine-fleeing Irish, Jews from Eastern Europe and blacks escaping slavery south of the border via the Underground Railroad.

One of Toronto's earliest black settlers was William Peyton Hubbard, who became a founder of electric company Toronto Hydro, the city's first black politician and acting mayor. The black community newspaper the Provincial Freeman was founded in 1853 with the help of Mary Ann Shadd, the first black woman journalist in North America, while the city's first black businessmen, Jack Mosee and William Willis, operated a toll road in 1799.

Despite the growing diversity, Toronto's ruling class continued to be composed of the well heeled and well connected: doctors, lawyers, judges, church officials, politicians and sundry land-grabbers and entrepreneurs, a group so tightly knit through business dealings and intermarriage that it became known as the Family Compact.

Charles Dickens visited Toronto and commented on the city's conservative bent: "The wild and rabid Toryism is, I speak seriously, appalling."

Pissed off by the Family Compact's political stranglehold, newspaper baron William Lyon Mackenzie published anti-Conservative rants, so Conservative rowdies tossed his printing presses into the lake.

But Mackenzie's popularity only grew. In 1834, he won the mayoral election. When his party, the Reformers, failed to topple the provincial government, losing a crooked race that saw the Conservatives offer free booze for votes, Mackenzie organized a rebellion. On December 5, 1837, Mackenzie and 700 supporters gathered outside a tavern at the intersection of what is now Yonge Street and Eglinton Avenue, intent on seizing City Hall and its cache of guns. The rebellion was quashed by the local militia, and Mackenzie fled to the U.S., only to be pardoned in 1849. He was later elected to the provincial legislature.

In 1867, Canada officially became Canada when it gained its independence from Britain, and Toronto became the capital of the newly created province of Ontario (although it's still referred to as Uppity Canada by people outside the province, especially those on each coast).

In the early years of the 20th century, the city's arts scene began to come to life. The Art Gallery of Ontario, the Royal Ontario Museum and the Toronto Symphony Orchestra were established even as Toronto rebuilt itself following the Great Fire of 1904 that levelled 122 buildings in the downtown.

During World War I, doomed aviatrix Amelia Earhart, then a nurse in Toronto, was inspired to fly while watching fighter pilots train here.

By 1925, the city's population had risen to 500,000.

The numerous Gothic and neo-Gothic church spires poking at the skyline, coupled with the city's strong puritanical leanings (Prohibition, a ban on Sunday shopping), earned it a reputation as Toronto the Good.

As the population neared 1.2 million, the Toronto Transit Commission built Canada's first subway system in 1954. It ran north-south beneath Yonge Street and consisted of just 12 stops. The TTC is now the second-largest public transit system in North America.

Over the next 20 years, close to 30,000 buildings were torn down to make room for apartment buildings and office towers.

The St. Lawrence Seaway connecting the Atlantic Ocean to the Great Lakes opened in 1959 and the city became a shipping centre.

By the hippie-dippie 60s, Toronto shook loose from its puritanical past. The bar and club scene thrived and flower power held sway as Joni Mitchell and Neil Young and Leonard Cohen spread the message of peace and love throughout Yorkville's coffee houses, darkened only by the haze of spliff smoke and the creeping shadows of skyscrapers.

On September 13, 1969, John Lennon performed for the first time with Yoko Ono and the Plastic Ono Band as part of the Toronto Rock 'N' Roll Revival at Varsity Stadium, effectively ending the Beatles. Also in the lineup were the Doors, Eric Clapton, Chuck Berry, Little Richard, Jerry Lee Lewis, Bo Diddley and a little-known Alice Cooper, who reportedly bit the head off a live chicken during his performance.

By the 70s, European immigration took a back seat to the arrival of people from Africa, Asia, the Caribbean and Latin America. For the first time, people of British descent were in the minority.

In 1976, Toronto officially became Canada's largest city, edging out Montreal by just 1,000 inhabitants. The city became a criss-cross of highways, freeways and expressways dotted by shopping malls, strip malls and super-malls.

By the mid-90s, the push was on to reorganize and downsize municipal government in the Greater Toronto Area. On January 1, 1998, Metro Toronto officially amalgamated with its five member municipalities (Etobicoke, York, North York, East York, and Scarborough) to form a new City of Toronto. In 2001, more than half of the city's 2.5 million residents were born outside Canada. One million residents were members of visible minority groups, and close to 150 languages and dialects were spoken.

Today, Toronto continues to grow. Condos are popping up on every corner, it seems, and the downtown is being revitalized by a wave of innovative architecture, leaving a lot to experience, both old and new.

sightseeing

downtown

After you've seen the CN Tower – and seen the city from the CN Tower – and wandered through the Royal Ontario Museum and the Hockey Hall of Fame and Casa Loma, then what? Toronto has a lot more to offer the serious urban adventurer, from smart museums to fine galleries to globe-spanning ethnic neighbourhoods. So go explore.

Waterfront

Once a wasteland of warehouses, freight sheds and old warves, this stretch of downtown has slowly been clawing – and construction-craning – its way back into the city's good graces. Now high-priced condos with great views of Lake Ontario scratch away bits of the skyline as the area transforms itself into a popular residential and cultural nabe, with museums, galleries, parks and restaurants.

Exhibition Place

This large waterfront park – really more of a parking lot when not hosting some event – offers historic buildings, amusements, cultural and sporting events and craft and trade shows, from the **Canadian National Exhibition** and the **Royal Agricultural Winter Fair** (see **Festivals**, page 162) to the **Champ Car Grand Prix** (see **Sports**, page 194). A just completed stadium on the site is the home of Toronto's new soccer team Toronto FC.
■ *Lakeshore W between Strachan and Dufferin, 416-263-3800, www.explace.on.ca.*

Harbourfront Centre

A lakeside playground with blocks of boutiques, antique markets, outdoor recreation facilities and free exhibitions and events. The centre's **Concert Stage** offers a great view of the lake. Weekend multicultural festivities happen throughout the summer, and a small pond provides public skating in winter.
■ *Queens Quay W from York to Bathurst, 416-973-4000, www.harbourfront.on.ca.*

Historic Fort York

If you want to see men playing soldier, this is the place to go. Founded in 1793 by Lt.-Governor John Graves Simcoe to guard the newly formed town of York, Fort York really only saw military action during the War of 1812, when it was sacked by the Americans (an event which actually took place in 1813). The fort has been restored and depicts early military life in Upper Canada, complete with guards in period regimental uniforms who conduct tours and re-enactments. Site of large Canada Day celebrations.
■ *100 Garrison, off Fleet near Bathurst, 416-392-6907, www.fortyork.ca.*

Open Victoria Day to Labour Day daily 10 am-5 pm, rest of year wkdays 10 am-4 pm, wknds 10 am-5 pm. $6, stu/srs $3.25, child $3. Guided tours on the hour.

Ontario Place
Easily recognized by its giant golfball-like IMAX Cinesphere, this amusement park on three man-made islands includes a kids' village, dinosaur exhibit and mega-maze, wilderness adventure and raft rides, bungee jumping, pedal boats, mini-golf, shops and restaurants. During the summer, the park's **Molson Amphitheatre** is an ideal venue for taking in a concert.
■ *955 Lakeshore W, between Aquatic and Newfoundland, 416-314-9900, www.ontarioplace.com.*
Open daily 10 am-10 pm. $10-$15, play-all-day pass $20-$32, srs/child age four-five $10-$17.

The Power Plant
A non-collecting exhibition facility located next door to **Queens Quay Terminal**, the Power Plant (once a generating plant, as evidenced by its distinctive smokestack) is Canada's leading public gallery devoted exclusively to contemporary art, including painting, sculpture, photography, film, video, installation and other media. Public programs designed to complement the year-round exhibitions include gallery tours, lectures and artist/curator talks.
■ *231 Queens Quay W, 416-973-4949, www.thepowerplant.org.*
Open Tue-Sun and holiday Mon noon-6 pm, Wed noon-8 pm. $4, stu/srs $2, children/members free; Wed 5-8 pm free.

Queens Quay Terminal
This former warehouse has been transformed into a complex of upscale shops, restaurants and galleries. It's also home to the **Premiere Dance Theatre** (416-973-4000, www.harbourfront.on.ca), which presents the World Moves dance series, featuring contemporary dance with an international flavour.
■ *207 Queens Quay W, foot of York, 416-203-0510, www.queens-quay-terminal.com.*
Open daily 10 am-9 pm.

Redpath Sugar Museum
An entire museum devoted to the sweet stuff, this former sugar warehouse is home to a collection of memorabilia from the history of the Canadian sugar industry. And best of all, it's free – sweet!
■ *95 Queens Quay E, between Yonge and Lower Jarvis, 416-933-8341, www.tateandlyle.com.*
Open Mon-Fri 10 am-noon, 1-3:30 pm. Free.

Scadding Cabin
Located adjacent to the **Fort Rouillé Monument** in the shadow of the city's lone wind turbine, this squat wooden one-room house built in 1792 and originally owned by the clerk to the first lieutenant-governor of Upper Canada, John Graves Simcoe, is the oldest building in the city. Today costumed guides explain its history and demonstrate 19th-century crafts like spinning.

■ *Canadian National Exhibition grounds, Lakeshore West between Strachan and Dufferin, south of the Dufferin Gates, 416-494-0503. Open Sat-Sun and holiday Mon 10 am-4 pm. Free.*

Toronto Music Garden
Simply serene. Inspired by Johann Sebastian Bach's Suites for Unaccompanied Cello, the garden was designed by renowned cellist Yo-Yo Ma and landscape designer Julie Moir Messervy as a means of interpreting in nature the music of Bach's first suite. Each dance movement within the suite corresponds to a different section in the garden. Free concerts are offered during the summer, as are guided and self-guided tours.
■ *475 Queens Quay W, on the water's edge between Bathurst and Spadina, 416-973-4000.*

York Quay Centre
Part of the Harbourfront Centre complex, this converted terminal building houses a cinema, theatre and galleries, as well as exhibition and performance space. The Brigantine Room hosts the **Harbourfront Reading Series** and the **International Festival of Authors** (see page 165). Bounty Contemporary Canadian Craft Shop (416-973-4993) sells one-of-a-kind items in glass, textiles, metal and ceramics by resident artists at the centre's craft studio (416-973-4963) and other Canadian artisans.
■ *235 Queens Quay W, 416-973-3000, www.harbourfrontcentre.com.*
Open daily 7 am-9 pm.

top ten
things to see and do in T.O.

1 Save your money – skip the CN Tower. For the cost of a cocktail, check out the view from the rooftop **Panorama Lounge**. See page 124.

2 Visit the mummies at the **Royal Ontario Museum**. See page 24.

3 Take the ferry to the **Toronto Islands**. See page 15.

4 Get your game face on at the **Hockey Hall of Fame**. See page 17.

5 Rent a bike and explore Toronto's diverse neighbourhoods. See pages 35 and 41.

6 Claim your 15 minutes of TV fame at Citytv's **Speaker's Corner**. See page 16.

7 Go boho in **Kensington Market**. See page 21.

8 People watch from the patio of the **Black Bull**. See page 130.

9 Picnic in **High Park**. See page 38.

10 Satisfy your foot fetish at the **Bata Shoe Museum**. Seriously. See page 24.

WALTER WILLEM

We do like our beer,
Steam Whistle Brewing.

Entertainment District

Depending on your age, this area is also known as **Clubland** (for obvious reasons) or the **Theatre District**, Toronto being the third-largest theatre centre in the English-speaking world.

The Entertainment District is where the city has come to play for more than 200 years. In the 1800s, it was home to music halls and theatres. Today you'll find some of the city's best theatres, restos and nightclubs. Located only a block apart on King West, the **Royal Alexandra** and **Princess of Wales** theatres are home to lavish Broadway-calibre productions and form the heart of the district. The area also includes such attractions as **Roy Thomson Hall**, the **CN Tower**, the **Rogers Centre** (home of the Blue Jays), **Canada's Walk of Fame** and the future home of the Toronto International Film Festival Centre.

Air Canada Centre

The $265-million hangar-shaped home of the NHL's Maple Leafs and NBA's Raptors, the state-of-the-art ACC also hosts concerts and events year-round.

■ *40 Bay, south of Front behind Union Station, 416-815-5982, www.theaircanadacentre.com. Tours Sep-Jun, Wed-Sat hourly 11 am-3 pm, Jul-Sep daily 10 am-4 pm, event scheduling permitting. $12, stu/srs $10, child $8.*

Canada's Walk of Fame

A somewhat less-star-studded version of the famous Hollywood walk – just who is Jim Elder anyway? – it stretches along King West from Simcoe to Duncan, from Céline Dion to the cast of SCTV. Have fun stepping all over a variety of home-grown celebs, from Paul Anka to Bryan Adams to John Candy to Jim Carrey, and Mike Myers to Rush to Donald and Kiefer Sutherland to Fay Wray to Neil Young.

■ *www.canadaswalkoffame.com.*

CBC

Headquarters of the Canadian Broadcasting Corporation – a.k.a. the Mothercorp – Canada's internationally respected national public radio, television and news media broadcaster. Tour the CBC Museum and watch old news footage and children's shows, check out the garden mini-set, wardrobe and set design displays and the set of The National evening news program. The CBC is also home to the 340-seat **Glenn Gould Studio**, named in honour of the late great Toronto pianist, one of the top venues for concert-goers. It's home to CBC Radio's flagship live concert series OnStage, which presents everything from jazz and world beat to classical and pop music performances. (Sep-May; ticketline 416-205-5555, http://glenngouldstudio.cbc.ca, box office Mon-Fri 11 am-6 pm.) The studio also doubles as a state-of-the-art recording facility for the CBC.

■ *250 Front W, at John, 416-205-8605, www.cbc.ca. Open Mon-Fri 9 am-5 pm, Sat noon-4 pm. Free.*

CN Tower

At a height of 553.33 metres (1,815 feet, 5 inches), it's the world's tallest free-standing building. Actually, it's a radio tower with tourist trappings: glassed-in elevators offer a spectacular view of the city en route to three observation levels (a plexiglass floor on one gives a dizzying view of the streets below), Horizons nightclub, the completely skippable 360 revolving restaurant (the quality of the cuisine seems to go up and down as often as the elevator), motion-simulation rides, virtual-reality games and gift shops. A bit pricey, sure, but it's something everybody has to visit at least once, and the view – day or night – can't be beat.

■ *301 Front W, 416-868-6937, www.cntower.ca. Open Sun-Thu 10 am-10 pm, Fri-Sat 10 am-10:30 pm. $19.99, srs $17.99, child $13.99.*

Rogers Centre

Formerly and better known as SkyDome, this turtle-shaped white sportsplex beneath the CN Tower was the first sports stadium with a retractable roof and is home to the Toronto Blue Jays (baseball) and Toronto Argonauts (Canadian football) as well as numerous concerts and events.
■ *1 Blue Jays Way, 416-341-2770 for schedules, www.rogerscentre.com.*
Walking tours daily 11 am, 1 or 3 pm, event schedule permitting. $12.50, stu/srs $9, child $7, age two and under free.

Steam Whistle Brewing

There's no denying it – we love our beer. Barley and hops are in our blood (often literally). It's part of our national identity. So why not treat yourself to a taste of some of our finest brew? Located in an old railway roundhouse tucked between the ACC and the CN Tower, this is one of Ontario's most popular micro-breweries, dedicated to brewing just one beer: an exemplary European-style Pilsner. Tours are offered every hour on the hour and always end with a pouring of Pilsner – a good deal at four bucks.
■ *255 Bremner, at Spadina, 416-362-2337, www.steamwhistle.ca.*
Open winter Mon-Thu noon-6 pm, summer Fri-Sat noon-6 pm, Mon-Thu noon-7 pm. Tours on the hour. $4.

Union Station

Sure, this mammoth building, completed in 1927, is the city's hub for rail, subway and commuter travel. But the really cool thing about it is the top-secret – and very exclusive – gun club and shooting range hidden away behind an unmarked door.
■ *65 Front, between Yonge and Bay.*

Queen West

Queen Street West from University to Bathurst is one of the city's hippest shopping districts (see **Shopping**, page 168). Equally popular with gold-card-carrying scenesters and change-scrounging hipsters, the area features trendy restaurants, cutting-edge fashion boutiques, galleries, antique shops, dance clubs and bars.

Art Gallery of Ontario

The eighth-largest art museum in North America, the AGO's permanent collection comprises more than 36,000 works, representing 1,000 years of European, Canadian, modern, Inuit and contemporary art, including the must-see **Henry Moore sculpture exhibit**, totalling more than 900 works. A three-year expansion project is under way, resulting in reduced hours.
■ *317 Dundas W, 416-979-6648, www.ago.net. Open Wed-Fri noon-9 pm, Sat-Sun 10 am-5:30 pm (call for holiday hours). $8, stu/srs $5, fam $20, under five free, Wed after 6 pm free.*

Campbell House

The authentically restored home of William Campbell, chief justice of Upper Canada (1825-

toronto islands

Ask any local – they'll tell you that short of hightailing it to cottage country, the best way to escape the one-two punch of humidity and smog (a Toronto summer tradition since 1991) is just a 20-minute ferry ride from downtown.

Formed in 1858 by a violent storm that severed the spit of dirt connecting it to the mainland, this necklace of islands across Toronto's harbour offers a serene and picturesque sanctuary from the heat-shimmering hustle of city life.

Probably the cheapest day vacation around, the islands are all connected by scenic walking and bike paths that lead to secluded – and occasionally nude (but not pretty) – beaches perfect for sandcastles and bonfires. There are also picnic areas with public barbecues, tennis courts, paddleboats, a pseudo-19th-century town and enough open field space for a few hundred games of catch or Frisbee. Baseball historians take note: the long-gone **Hanlan's Point Stadium**, named after famed Canadian rower Ned Hanlan, is where Babe Ruth hit his first homer before joining the majors back in 1914.

The kid-centric **Centreville** amusement park and children's farm on Centre Island offers rides, carny games and greasy, sugary food stalls. Open daily 10:30 am-6 pm in June, Jul-Aug till 8 pm. Free (pay as you play).

And the **Olympic Island Festival** held each June has become a great rock showcase, with past performers including Sam Roberts, Sloan, Broken Social Scene, Feist and The Arcade Fire.

Feel free to prance around the islands with the abandon of a wood nymph cuz the rule is No Cars Allowed!
■ *Accessible year round via a 20-minute ferry ride. Scheduled departures leave daily from the foot of Bay and Queens Quay. Return trip $6, stu/srs $3.50, child $2.50. 416-392-8193.*

1829), is the only remaining brick residence from the original town of York. Guided tours daily. Events and exhibits during July and August.
■ *160 Queen W, at Simcoe, 416-597-0227, www.campbellhousemuseum.ca.*
Open Tue-Fri 9:30 am-4:30 pm, from Victoria Day to Thanksgiving Sat-Sun noon-4 pm. $4.50, stu/srs $3, child $2.50, fam $10.

Citytv

Just west of University stands the very large Victorian **CHUMCity Building**, complete with a mandatory photo op for gawking tourists in awe of the smashed-up pickup truck hanging halfway out the building's eastern exterior. Located at the corner of Queen and John, Chum is the TV broadcaster behind MuchMusic, Citytv, Bravo! and Space, among others. Its open-concept ground-floor studio is a welcoming environment for curious passersby wanting a behind-the-scenes look at daily local news tapings as well as live broadcasts hosted by a revolving door lineup of beautiful if slightly vapid MuchMusic on-air personalities. Why not drop by during MuchOnDemand, an audience-friendly weekday show where eager teenagers can scream and cheer for their favourite new songs? If you've got something to get off your chest, or you just want to show off, the iconic Speaker's Corner TV recording booth on the southeast corner offers you your 15 minutes of fame. For a dose of media history, check out the **MZTV Museum of Television** next door, with the world's largest collection of TV sets, then wait patiently outside the Queen entrance for one of the many special concerts and celebrity drop-ins. Complete your Chum experience by picking up an Ed the Sock T-shirt in the MuchStore gift shop.
■ *277-299 Queen W, 416-591-7400 ext 2870, www.chumlimited.com.*
Tours weekdays 2 and 4 pm. Adults $6, stu/srs $4, fam $18, groups $4/person.

Graffiti Alley

The alley running along Queen West from Spadina to Portland has been dubbed Rush Lane or Graffiti Alley. It's a rush taking in the walls covered in dreamy spray-painted images. Each summer, a group called Style in Progress (www.styleinprogress.ca/SIP05.php) takes over Graffiti Alley for a 24-hour period of legal painting. But the object that most intrigues the odd tourist floating by to admire the artwork is a lone swing on chains tucked behind iron bars in a narrow space between two buildings. The bars are bent back to permit entry, but only the brave dare venture in – the tight confines and garbage piled beneath make a ride a shoulder-scraping proposition. It's the work of local artist Corwyn Lund, who erected the swing in 2003 as part of a group show on guerrilla projects at YYZ Artists' Outlet. He also produced a video documenting how he had to make like a rock climber to install the swing's anchor high above the alley floor.

Osgoode Hall

This has been the historic home of the Law Society of Upper Canada since cows roamed free on

Capturing the old within the new at **BCE Place**.

Queen – hence, the unique fence that surrounds Osgoode, built in 1868, to keep the bovines out. Osgoode was also the first law school in Canada, although it's since relocated to York University in the north end of the city.
■ *130 Queen W, at University, 416-947-3300, www.osgoodehall.com.*
Open from Canada Day to Aug 30, guided tours weekdays 1:15 pm. Free.

Textile Museum of Canada

A Trading Spaces fantasy museum, this is the only museum in Canada devoted exclusively to the collection and exhibition of textile art from around the world. Among the more than 10,000 items in the collection are fabrics, carpets, quilts, garments, ceremonial objects and other artefacts from Canada, India, Pakistan, Africa, China, Japan, South East and Central Asia, South and Central America, Europe and the Pacific. It'll make that cheap wallpaper and shag carpeting back home seem a little less fabulous.
■ *55 Centre, at Dundas, 416-599-5321, www.textilemuseum.ca.*
Open daily 11 am-5 pm, except Wed 11 am-8 pm. $10, stu/srs $6, Wed after 5 pm pwyc.

Financial District

Like Wall Street in Manhattan, Bay Street – the north-south-running street through the Financial District – is synonymous with business, home

the history of the TSE and how it operates.
■ *130 King W, at York, First Canadian Place, 416-947-4676, www.tse.com.*
Open Mon-Fri, call for hours.

BCE Place and Heritage Square

BCE Place consists of two high-rise office towers as well as architect Santiago Calaltrava's 25-metre-high **Allen Lambert Galleria**, which boasts the historic Bank of Montreal building and the **Hockey Hall of Fame** (see below). It also envelopes 11 heritage buildings under its expansive roof, as well as various shops and restaurants.
■ *161/181 Bay, www.bceplace.com.*

Design Exchange

Once the 1930s art deco home of the TSE, it now houses a non-profit gallery showcasing Canadian and international innovations and achievements in furniture design, packaging and architecture by emerging artists. Guided tours available.
■ *234 Bay, 416-363-6121, www.dx.org.*
Open Mon-Fri 10 am-5 pm, Sat-Sun noon-5 pm.
$5, srs/stu $4.

Hockey Hall of Fame

A must-see for any hockey fan (and really, only for hockey fans), this rococo shrine to Canada's unofficial national sport (lacrosse is the official sport) has an unrivalled collection of artefacts, memorabilia and media on display, from old game footage and photos to sweaters, sticks, pucks and equipment worn by the top players in the biggest games. Interactive games let you test your sniper and goalie skills. The highlight is the trophy room, where the Stanley Cup is on display alongside the wall of engraved plaques honouring each Hall of Famer.
■ *BCE Place, 30 Yonge, switchboard 416-360-7735, infoline 416-360-7765, www.hhof.com.*
Open Sep-Jun Mon-Fri 10 am-5 pm, Sat 9:30 am-6 pm, Sun 10:30 am-5 pm; July-Aug Mon-Sat 9:30 am-6 pm, Sun 10 am-6 pm. $13, stu/srs $9, child three and under free.

to blue-suited biz-nobs with briefcases and bad haircuts. The centre for Canadian banking since the 1800s, the four corners at King West and Bay hold the headquarters of four of the five major Canadian banks, while the surrounding 'scrapers house brokerage houses, law firms and insurance companies. Warning: the following information is strictly for Alex P. Keaton types and those with a skyscraper fetish: The 34-storey Canadian Imperial Bank of Commerce, a.k.a. **Commerce Court North** (25 King W), has an interior hall modelled after the baths of Caracalla in Rome and was the tallest building in the British Commonwealth when it was built in 1931. Check out the carved figure of Mercury, the banker's god, looking down upon a flock of bees, bears and squirrels around the impressive entrance. A new 57-storey CIBC designed by famed architect I.M. Pei was built nearby, while the three Mies van der Rohe-designed towers of the **Toronto-Dominion Centre** dominate the landscape at the southwest corner of King and Bay. The **TD Gallery of Inuit Art** (79 Wellington, 416-982-8473) is located on the ground level of the TD's Maritime Life Tower, while a herd of seven life-size bronze cows sculpted by Joe Fafard contemplate a bull market from a patch of grass in the towers' central plaza.

Stock Market Place

Thanks to computers, there's no trading floor at the Toronto Stock Exchange, Canada's largest. But the Stock Market Place learning centre explains

St. Lawrence

When this area – now quaintly referred to as the Old Town of York – was established in 1793, Lake Ontario lapped at the back of huge warehouses along Front, allowing ships to off-load. The area between Front and the lake has since been filled in and built upon, and many of the warehouses have been converted into residences, stores, restaurants and pubs. The highlight, however, remains the old **St. Lawrence Market**.

St. Lawrence Market

There's a reason why this market – consisting of two buildings on either side of Front – has been named one of the 25 best farmers markets in the world by Gourmet magazine. The **North Market** building (92 Front, at Jarvis) is open only on Saturdays and features fruits, vegetables and fresh meats and fish, often sold by the same farmers who produce them. Be sure to get there early; the farmers set up by 5 am and pack up by 1 pm. On

The **Gooderham Flatiron** is one of T.O.'s top photo ops. Page 23.

Sundays, the North Market is transformed into a popular antiques and flea market, offering everything from vintage clothes to old records.

The red brick **South Market** (95 Front, at Jarvis, 416-392-7219, www.stlawrencemarket.com) dates back to 1905 and incorporates the remains of the original City Hall into its structure. In the 1970s, the former council chambers on the second floor were transformed into a civic art gallery (see **Market Gallery**, below), which presents an ongoing photo exhibit on the development of Toronto. The building also houses dozens of permanent vendors – butchers, bakers and candlestick makers – over two floors who operate Tuesdays through Saturdays. Be sure to arrive early on weekends as it can be pretty crowded by 8 am. (See **Shopping**, page 178.)

■ *Open Tue-Thu 8 am-6 pm, Fri 8 am-7 pm, Sat 5 am-5 pm. Free.*

Market Gallery

Displays paintings, photos and documents from the city's archives as well as rotating art exhibits.
■ *St Lawrence Market, 95 Front, at Jarvis, 416-392-7604.*
Open Wed-Fri 10 am-4 pm, Sat 9 am-4 pm, Sun noon-4 pm. Free.

Toronto's First Post Office

Entering this perfectly restored 1833 building is like stepping into history, as posties in period costume take visitors back to the days of the Pony Express. At this full-service community post office, visitors can write and post letters in the manner of the 1830s, using a quill pen and sealing wax.
■ *260 Adelaide E, 416-865-1833, www.townofyork.com.*
Open wkdays 9 am-4 pm, wknds 10 am-4 pm. Free. Self-guided and guided tours available.

Toronto Sculpture Garden

This small urban park hosts exhibits of contemporary sculpture and installation art, changing two or three times a year.
■ *115 King E, at Church, www.torontosculpturegarden.com.*
Open daily 8 am to dusk.

Yonge-Dundas

Yonge-Dundas Square

Across from the **Eaton Centre** shopping megaplex at the intersection of Yonge and Dundas, Yonge-Dundas Square (www.ydsquare.ca) just might become as electric a city centre as New York's Times Square or Tokyo's Shibuya – if it ever gets finished. The Metropolis, a long-delayed retail and entertainment complex overlooking the square's north side, is set to open in 2007 and will include the Canadian Music Hall of Fame, a 12-cinema AMC Theatre and home electronics chain Future Shop.

You'd never know it by day, when it seems as anonymous and grey as any corner in the core, but come nightfall, the electronic advertising towers that soar overhead come alive like some sci-fi cityscape straight out of Blade Runner.

top ten
things to do with kids

1 Feed the animals at the **Toronto Zoo**. See page 44.
2 Eat french fries and candied apples, ride the Zipper, then puke off the ferris wheel at the **Canadian National Exhibition**. See page 162.
3 Eat french fries and candied apples, ride some roller coasters, then throw up at **Paramount Canada's Wonderland**. See page 44.
4 Indulge your inner nerd at the **Ontario Science Centre**. See page 34.
5 Take an amphibious tour of the city aboard the **Hippo Tours** floating bus. See page 245.
6 When in doubt, take 'em to a movie at the arcade-like **Paramount Theatres** (see page 152), but...
7 The live performances at the **Lorraine Kimsa Theatre for Young People** might be more enlightening. See page 154.
8 Take in a **Blue Jays** game. Tickets are cheap and easy to come by, and games at the Dome are never rained out. See page 194.
9 Check out the animation course at the **NFB**. See page 152.
10 Slap on some sunscreen and hit **Riverdale Farm** before cooling off in the wading pool. See page 26.

Pretty bleak during the winter – but, then, what part of T.O. isn't? – in summer, the square hosts frequent open-air music performances and film screenings, while arts and crafts fairs take over the platz on weekends. When it's really hot, the dancing water jets offer a quick way to cool off. It's also where you'll find cheap theatre tickets (see **T.O. Tix**, page 155) and nab a seat for a bus tour of the city.

The area around Yonge-Dundas Square is a popular shopping district. In addition to the Eaton Centre, there are numerous clothing stores, home furnishings and electronics shops, cheap jewellery vendors and record emporiums. And if you're looking for a Leafs jersey or an I Love Toronto T-shirt, every other doorway seems to be in the tacky souvenir business. Also nearby are the **Elgin and Winter Garden Theatres**, the **Canon Theatre**, the venerable **Massey Hall** and **Ryerson University**.

City Hall

Built in 1965, Toronto's fourth city hall was considered an architectural marvel, a sci-fi inspired saucer-shaped building cupped by two curved office towers that overlook **Nathan Phillips Square** (see next page) to the south.
■ *100 Queen W, at York, 416-338-0338, www.city.toronto.on.ca.*
Self-guided tours Mon-Fri 8:30 am-4:30 pm.

Eaton Centre

Located at the heart of downtown, the Eaton Centre is a shopper's delight, with a glass galleria to bring in the daylight, more than 285 shops, restaurants and services that attract more than 1-million visitors each week. A **Tourism Information** booth is located on level 1.

■ *220 Yonge, between Dundas and Queen, 416-598-8700, www.torontoeatoncentre.com. Open Mon-Fri 10 am-9 pm, Sat 9:30 am-7 pm, Sun noon-6 pm.*

Mackenzie House

Once the home of William Lyon Mackenzie, a newspaper baron and Toronto's first mayor who led the Rebellion of 1837 against the province's corrupt conservative government (see **History lesson**, page 9). The historic home offers walking tours and features a print shop with a working flatbed press.

■ *82 Bond, south of Dundas, 416-392-6915, www.city.toronto.on.ca/culture/ mackenzie_house.htm. Open Tue-Sun noon-5 pm. $5.50, srs/yth $4, child $3.50.*

Nathan Phillips Square

During the summer, this large open space hosts cultural events, concerts, art exhibitions, dance performances, farmers markets and on July 1 – Canada Day – a large outdoor party with fireworks. In winter, the fountain becomes a skating rink (skates are available for rent), and on New Year's Eve the square's rammed with drunken revellers trying to keep warm while the clock counts down to the start of another year.

■ *100 Queen W, at York, 416-338-0338.*

Old City Hall

A designated National Historic Site, OCH (one of four city halls in the city's history) is a Romanesque Revival-style gingerbread building with stained-glass windows and faux marble columns. It is now used as a provincial court.

■ *60 Queen W, www.toronto.ca/old_cityhall.*

Trinity Square

The labyrinth in the middle of this little-known green space tucked behind the Eaton Centre is a great place for curiosity seekers. The "walking meditation" was inspired by the 13-century stone labyrinth at Chartres Cathedral in France and designed to resemble an urban medieval park. Go any time of day and you're bound to find everyone from Yorkville types in high fashion to punks with nose rings contemplating the twists and turns of life in the dozens of hairpins that make up the maze.

■ *Dundas and Yonge, behind the Eaton Centre, 220 Yonge.*

You will never see the **St. Lawrence Market,** Toronto's most historic market, this empty. Page 17.

Chinatown

Toronto is home to more Chinese people (some 300,000 and counting) than anywhere in Canada, making them one of Toronto's largest and most visible ethnic communities. As a result, two distinct Chinatowns have grown up in the city's core, along with at least three others in the ever-expanding suburbs. But when locals refer to Chinatown, this is the one they're likely talking about. (Toronto's second, smaller Chinatown is at Broadview and Gerrard; see page 34.)

Old Chinatown, on Dundas between Bay and University, was once home to more than 300 Chinese hand laundries. Now occupying the area around Dundas West and Spadina, just a few blocks west of its original location (where the new **City Hall** now stands; see page 19), Chinatown is a noisy, crowded nabe with a definite Hong Kong feel. Sidewalks are crammed with open-air food stalls and fruit and vegetable vendors, and shops selling everything from Asian knick-knacks to phone cards and bootleg DVDs spill from every nook and cranny. Street signs are written in English and Chinese, and there are two large shopping malls, Chinatown Centre and Dragon City, on Spadina south of Dundas.

But the real attraction is the row upon row of traditional Asian restos. No day-old fried rice and sweet-and-sour chicken ball combos here. The cuisine's authentic – Szechwan, Hunan, Mandarin, Cantonese, Vietnamese, Thai – and so are the ingredients, fresh from the surrounding stalls. Just don't be put off by the barbecued pork and duck hanging in the windows, bathed in a soft neon glow. (For more on Chinatown dining, see page 48.)

Baldwin Street

A tiny tree-shaded enclave nestled in the shadow of the **Art Gallery of Ontario** (see page 15), just a couple of blocks east of Chinatown between Beverley and McCaul, this boho nabe is an old fave among locals, although it's often overlooked by tourists. The area's main attraction – indeed, its only attraction – are the trendy-but-not-too-trendy cafés and patios that line the street (see **Restaurants**, page 46).

Kensington Market

During the 1920s, Kensington Market was known as the Jewish Market, and the area had as many as 30 synagogues. The Jewish population began to thin out in the 50s – Bathurst from Eglinton to Steeles in the north of the city is now the prime Jewish area – but there's still evidence of the Market's Jewish past. The **Kiever Synagogue** (25 Bellevue, 416-593-9702, http://kievershul.tripod.com), built in 1927, and the **Anshei Minsk Synagogue** (10 St. Andrew, 416-595-5723, www.theminsk.com), built in 1930 and the last fully Orthodox shul in the downtown, continue to play an important role in the community. They're frequent stops for tourists thanks to their religious and historical significance and Byzantine architecture.

Today, Kensington Market is a bohemian enclave of densely packed houses and storefronts where cultures from around the world mix. You'll find Jamaican patty shops, Middle Eastern and Latin American grocers, Chinese vegetable markets and dim sum shops (the area borders Chinatown). While there are a few notable bars and restos in the area (see **Bars**, page 117; **Patios**, page

sightseeing

129; **Restaurants**, page 46), Kensington Market is famous for the trove of vintage and second-hand clothing shops that line the streets (see **Shopping**, page 167).

University of Toronto

Founded in the late 1800s from the amalgamation of several liberal arts colleges (including King's College, established in 1827), today's ivied St. George Campus is dotted with ornate neo-Gothic and Romanesque buildings and Victorian mansions renovated to house offices and classrooms, all scattered around numerous courtyards and quads. Famous U of T alumni include director Norman Jewison, actor Donald Sutherland and the guy who helped invent the frickin' laser, Arthur Schawlow. Marshall McLuhan taught here. Free walking tours of all seven U of T colleges, led by students, depart from the **Nona Macdonald Visitor Centre** weekdays at 11 am and 2 pm.
■ *25 King's College Circle, 416-978-5000, www.utoronto.ca.*

Gerstein Science Info Centre
The GSIC is a U of T undergrad centre, but if you pose as a student you can take a sneak peek.
■ *7-9 King's College Circle, 416-978-2280.*

Hart House
Named in honour of old-money patriarch Hart Massey, this former men's undergrad centre (now co-ed) is full of old English-style Beaux Arts Gothic arches, vaulted ceilings and bay windows, and is also home to the Justina M. Barnicke Gallery.
■ *7 Hart House Circle, 416-978-8398.*
Open Sep-Jun Mon-Fri 11 am-7 pm, Sat-Sun 1-4 pm; Jul-Aug Mon-Fri 11 am-6 pm, Sat 1-4 pm. Free.

U of T Art Centre
Also worth checking out is the Art Centre, located in the Laidlaw wing of University College, one of the oldest buildings on campus and easily recognized by its single asymmetrical spire. This little-known museum houses the private collection of noted New York psychoanalyst Dr. Lillian Malcove, whose tastes ranged from Picasso to Matisse to a rather nice collection of Byzantine and medieval art.
■ *15 King's College Circle, 416-978-1838, www.utoronto.ca/artcentre.*
Open Tue-Fri noon-5 pm, Sat noon-4. $5.

Eric Arthur Gallery
Also at U of T, the Eric Arthur Gallery, part of the Faculty of Architecture, Landscape and Design, is named for the local architect whose book, Toronto: No Mean City, is a bible of historical architecture in the city. The tiny gallery is a must-see for architecture and design buffs.
■ *230 College, at St. George, 416-978-5038, www.ald.utoronto.ca.*
Open Mon-Fri 9 am-5 pm, Sat noon-5 pm. Free.

building

From Libeskind's ROM redux to the sci-fi inspire

Toronto's oldest building, the drab and squat **Scadding Cabin** (see page 13), located at Exhibition Place, was built by the Queen's Rangers for a government clerk in 1794. Architecturally speaking, for a city with a lot of buildings, surprisingly little worth mentioning has happened since. Until recently, that is.

While it's not exactly an architectural renaissance, things have been starting to look up – and so have pedestrians – with a number of innovative buildings either recently completed or in the works. As the aw-shucks city learns to overcome its modesty and showcase its thriving cultural activity, money has flowed into inspired (and inspiring) projects, such as the Daniel Libeskind-led reno of the **Royal Ontario Museum**, Frank Gehry's **Art Gallery of Ontario** updo and the long-awaited new ballet and opera house. From the historic to the euphoric, here's a look at the buildings worthy of architectural admiration.

ART GALLERY OF ONTARIO
317 Dundas W, at McCaul.
Also undergoing a facelift, the AGO's massive makeover – due to be finished by 2008 – includes the addition of a block-long glass facade that looks like a sneeze guard and a blue titanium-encrusted tower all designed by world-famous Toronto-born architect Frank Gehry who grew up nearby.

City Hall is where the aliens parked their flying saucer.

blocks

...Sharp Centre, our architecture is looking up.

CITY HALL
100 Queen W, at Nathan Phillips Square.
The curved concrete towers and low, clamshell centrepiece, designed by Finnish architect Viljo Revell, still impress after four decades. Out front there's a nice big square with benches and water fountain that becomes a skating rink in the winter to relax on, but don't get too comfortable – a shameful local bylaw prevents the homeless from enjoying the civic centre.

FLATIRON BUILDING
49 Wellington E, at Church.
Located just west of St. Lawrence Market where Wellington forks off from Front, the wedge-shaped Gooderham Building (a.k.a. the Flatiron) is, at five storeys, significantly smaller than other flatirons. While Toronto has traditionally been a follower of architectural trends, this red brick number with the copper-topped spire – built for just $18,000 in 1892 by the whiskey baron behind the Distillery (see page 36) and designed by David Roberts Jr. – was the first of its kind and is now one of the most photographed buildings in the city. It's also home to some of the city's most expensive office space.

FOUR SEASONS CENTRE FOR THE PERFORMING ARTS
Queen W and University.
Opened in the summer of 2006, architect Jack Diamond's long-awaited $181-million opera house also serves as the new digs for the National Ballet of Canada, and boasts exquisite acoustics.

THE GRANGE
Beverley, south of Dundas.
Once part of a row of Georgian mansions belonging to Toronto's elite, the Grange is the last one standing. Donated in 1910 to the Art Gallery of Ontario, it also served as the first home of the Ontario College of Art and Design. Open Tue, Thu-Fri 11 am-6 pm, Wed 11 am-8:30 pm , Sat-Sun 10 am-5:30 pm. Free with Art Gallery of Ontario admission.

ONTARIO LEGISLATURE BUILDING
Queen's Park, at College and University.
Predictable Romanesque Revival, true. But it's still the seat of provincial government, and the park itself is a good place to gather with friends to get tear-gassed by police while attending Ontario Coalition Against Poverty rallies, or, you know, to just lay around, maybe have a picnic.

R.C. HARRIS WATER TREATMENT PLANT
2701 Queen E, at Victoria Park.
Michael Ondaatje dubbed this Depression-era building the "palace of purification" in his novel In the Skin of a Lion. With its long, low fortress-like profile and art deco design, it looks more like a museum than a filtration plant that purifies 1-million cubic metres of Toronto's tap water a day. Unfortunately it's closed until spring 2007.

ROBARTS RESEARCH LIBRARY
130 St. George, at Harbord.
Designed to look like a peacock, the building's innate, fascinating ugliness makes a lot of people sick, but it's still a work of genius. With over 5 million volumes and plenty more on microfilm, the University of Toronto's largest library can deliver books from all 14 floors mechanically to faculty and students. Rumour has it the building is slowly sinking due to the weight of the books.

ROYAL ONTARIO MUSEUM
100 Queens Park Crescent, at Bloor and University.
The original Romanesque Revival building has slowly been engulfed by architect Daniel Libeskind's massive aluminum and glass crystalline expansion, jutting from the north side.

SHARP CENTRE AT THE ONTARIO COLLEGE OF ART AND DESIGN
100 McCaul, south of Dundas.
Like a prop from War of the Worlds made by a three year old, Will Alsop's astounding checkered-table-on-coloured-stilts addition to the college – featured on the cover of this very guide book – appears to be either fucking or feeding off the original building. As a bonus, you can picnic in the park between the structure's legs.

Illicit
There are parts of buildings designed for you to enjoy and then there are all the areas that aren't, the ones that are marked Off Limits or Employees Only. The latter make for more interesting adventures if you know how to find them.

Late Toronto explorer Ninjalicious (a.k.a. Jeff Chapman) not only wrote extensively about his forays into off-limits storm sewers and abandoned subway stations, he even coined the term "urban exploration" for a growing number of enthusiasts across North America.

The basic idea? Trespassing is not a crime as long as you don't litter, vandalize or steal. If you want to see a relatively unknown side of Toronto, check out Ninj's site, **www.infiltration.org**, where you can read about the time he let himself into City Hall. There's also plenty of good advice on how to get in and how not to get hurt in his book, Access All Areas, available at Pages bookstore (see page 185).

midtown

Toronto is a city of neighbourhoods, and nowhere is that more evident than here. From tony Rosedale to historic Cabbagetown to über-chic Yorkville, it's the perfect place to eat, drink, shop and explore.

Bloor Street

More than just the main east-west thoroughfare (and subway route) through the city, Bloor Street is a destination in its own right, connecting cool nabes like the boho **Annex**, **Koreatown** and **High Park**. As Bloor crosses the Don Valley east of Yonge, its name changes to Danforth Avenue and things take on a distinctly Hellenic flavour (see page 34).

Bata Shoe Museum

It might sound hokey but the BSM is actually one of the city's cooler museums. It traces the history of footwear, from sneakers to stiletto heels, cowboy boots to Birkenstocks. The 10,000-strong collection includes shoes worn by European kings and queens, Elton John's platforms and African and Asian rubied royal slippers. And admission is free Thursdays 5-8 pm.
■ *327 Bloor W, at St. George, 416-979-7799, www.batashoemuseum.ca.*
Open Tue-Wed, Fri-Sat 10 am-5 pm, Thu 10 am-8 pm, Sun noon-5 pm. $8, stu/srs $6, child $4, fam $12, under five free.

George R. Gardiner Museum of Ceramic Art

First there was the textile museum. Now there's this, the only museum specializing in ceramics in North America, just recently renovated spectacularly. The permanent collection includes 18th-century European porcelain and figures from Italian comedy, 17th-century English delftware and slipware, Italian Renaissance majolica, Chinese porcelain, pre-Columbian artifacts and international contemporary ceramics.
■ *111 Queen's Park, at University, 416-586-8080, www.gardinermuseum.on.ca.*
Open Mon-Thu, Sat-Sun 10 am-6 pm, Fri 10 am-9 pm. $12, srs $8, stu $6, under 12 free.

Ontario Legislature Buildings

In the same architectural style as **Old City Hall** (see page 20) – that is, overwrought – the provincial parliament buildings sit in the middle of Queen's Park like last Christmas's gingerbread house.
■ *Queen's Park, at University north of College, 416-325-7500.*
Tours wkdays 8:30 am-6 pm (tour schedule varies, call for details). Free.

Royal Conservatory of Music

Originally the Toronto Baptist College, the Royal Conservatory of Music is one of the foremost schools of music in North America. Passersby can often hear piano and violin classes practicing. Currently undergoing renovations, the **Telus Centre for Performance and Learning**, set to open in 2007, will restore the conservatory's historic Victorian-era home. The expansion will include a 1,140-seat concert hall, rehearsal space, classrooms, a public café and broadcast facilities.
■ *273 Bloor W, www.rcmusic.ca.*

Royal Ontario Museum

Canada's largest museum of decorative art, archaeology and natural history, with over 6-million

Bata Shoe Museum is a foot fetishist's delight.

objects on display. Among the many highlights are the world-renowned **T.T. Tsui Gallery of Chinese Art**, containing priceless Ming and Qing porcelains. Upping the cool factor are mummies, knights, dinosaurs and bats, which fill galleries devoted to the Ice Age, ancient Egypt, the Roman Empire, Canadian history and natural history.
■ *100 Queen's Park, 416-586-8000, 416-586-5549, www.rom.on.ca.*
Open Mon-Thu, Sat-Sun 10 am-6 pm, Fri 10 am-9:30 pm. $15, srs/stu $12, child $10, four and under free. Free Fri after 4:30 pm and Sat-Thu one hour before closing.

Toronto Reference Library
The largest reference library in Canada, it's worth a visit whether you're looking to peruse a book or not. Watch for great deals on books when the library periodically culls the stacks for its regular sales. And the library's Answer Line is like an old-school Google.
■ *789 Yonge, 416-395-5577; Answer Line 416-393-7131.*
Open Mon-Thu 10 am-8 pm, Fri-Sat 10 am-6 pm, Sun Sep-Jun 1:30-5 pm.

Yorkville
Originally its own city, established in 1853, Yorkville was a quiet residential nabe in the 50s and a rockin' hippie enclave in the swingin' 60s, when the likes of Joni Mitchell, Neil Young, Rick James and Gordon Lightfoot headlined the coffee house scene, guitars in hand and goodwill at heart. Now, this sliver – bounded by Bloor, Davenport, Yonge and Avenue Road – is the city's chic-est retail address. Dubbed "Rodeo Drive without the palm trees," it's home to some of Toronto's most exclusive and expensive designer boutiques, boîtes and hotels. The parallel main drags of Cumberland Street and Yorkville Avenue are pedestrian-friendly if you don't mind dodging the occasional Ferrari or Rolls-Royce, while a warren of laneways links the area's cobblestone courtyards, complete with rustic lampposts and wrought iron park benches. A great place for a Sunday afternoon stroll. Or a Friday night stroll, for that matter, as you'll never know what celeb you'll stumble across, especially during the **Toronto International Film Festival** (see *Film*, page 151) in September.

Hazelton Lanes
Once owned by the father of Seinfeld star Julia Louis-Dreyfus – get out! – Hazelton Lanes is no ordinary boutique shopping complex. Built around a series of inner courtyards, it offers everything from home decor and haute couture to wholly organic Whole Foods. It's as much about lifestyle as about shopping. What other mini-mall keeps track of celebrity shopper sightings on its website?
■ *55 Avenue Road, at Yorkville, 416-968-8604, www.hazeltonlanes.com.*

The Mink Mile

The strip of Bloor West between Yonge and Avenue Road is lined with luxe upmarket indulgences, from Louis Vuitton to Hermès, while homegrown additions include the casual Canadiana of Roots (remember those über-popular Olympic po' boy hats?) and upscale clothiers Harry Rosen and Holt Renfrew.

Church & Wellesley

The Church Street Village. The Gay Village. The Gaybourhood. Boystown. Or simply Church Street. A nabe by any other name would smell as sweet.

In the heart of downtown, bounded roughly – but not too roughly – by Gould to the south, Yonge to the west, Charles to the north and Jarvis to the east, with the intersection of Church and Wellesley Streets at the centre, the Village is home sweet home to one of North America's largest queer communities (along with a healthy population of students – gay, straight and otherwise – from nearby Ryerson University and U of T). Forget San Francisco – the Village is the hottest, coolest, hippest LGBT-friendly nabe in the world (see **Queer**, page 215).

Prior to the 1970s, the gay scene was mostly underground. **Allan Gardens** (see page 216) was cruise central (and now hosts the annual **FFN** fetish fair; see **Festivals**, page 162), and the most notable bar was the St. Charles Tavern on Yonge, near the **Glad Day Bookshop** (see page 220), Canada's first gay-oriented bookstore, which opened in 1970.

And of course, there's the **Pride Week** celebrations each summer, climaxing with the spectacular Pride Parade. The crowd of nearly 900,000 who watch the more than 90 floats go by are as much a part of the party as any of the drag queen divas and bondage boys who march through the city's downtown. (See **Pride**, page 218.)

Maple Leaf Gardens

Built in 1931, the Gardens, like the old Montreal Forum, was one of professional hockey's oldest and most-cherished homes. In addition to Leafs games, it also hosted concerts by everyone from the Rolling Stones and the Beatles to U2. Now the Leafs play at the **ACC** (see page 14) and the Gardens has become a piece of history. Rumours persist that some smart developer could transform this heritage-protected site into condos although a mega-grocery store seems more likely. Even though the ice has long been melted and the seats have literally been sold, it's still worth a walk past for Leafs faithful.

■ *60 Carlton, at Church.*

Cabbagetown

Old Cabbagetown, at the intersection of Parliament (where the parliament buildings of Upper Canada once stood) and Carlton, was originally known as East of Parliament, then Don Vale. It takes its current name from the main crop grown in the tiny front-yard gardens tended by the earliest residents, thousands of working-class Irish families fleeing the potato famine in the 1840s. Though there's lots of history here, there aren't many historic landmarks worth checking out. But that doesn't mean the area isn't worth visiting. If you've got an afternoon and feel like stretching your legs, Cabbagetown, bounded by the Don Valley and two of the city's oldest cemeteries, is one of the city's most picturesque areas. Once a nabe of fixer-uppers, its narrow, tree-lined streets and laneways are now filled with charming, restored Victorian homes and postcard-worthy gardens.

Riverdale Farm

Located in **Riverdale Park** on the west side of the Don Valley north of Gerrard, this operational turn-of-the-century farm (once the site of the Toronto Zoo) is home to cows, sheep, pigs, chickens and more, and a nearby wading pool makes it a kids' paradise.

■ *201 Winchester, at Sumach, 416-392-6794, www.city.toronto.on.ca/parks/riverdalefarm.htm, www.friendsofriverdale-farm.com.*
Open daily 9 am-5 pm. Free.

Rosedale

Little more than a subway stop on the Yonge line to most Torontonians, Rosedale is a quiet, tony nabe of Victorian, Georgian, Tudor and Edwardian homes where many of Toronto's WASPy well-to-do park their Benzes and Beemers after a hard day making another million.

Rosedale Park

As well manicured as a Rosedale socialite's toenails, this park (at Schofield and Edgar) was the site of the first Grey Cup football game between the

CONTINUED ON PAGE 28

top ten

ways to act like a local

1 Watch a **Leafs** game at a sports bar (cuz Leafs tickets will cost you a kidney).

2 Dine on dim sum in **Chinatown**. See page 48.

3 Go ice skating in **Nathan Phillips Square**. See page 20.

4 Party during **Caribana**. See page 163.

5 Party harder during **Pride Week**. See page 218.

6 Sate your inner cinephile at the **Toronto International Film Festival**. See page 151.

7 Feel hip and cool over cocktails at the **Gladstone** and **Drake** hotels. See page 141.

8 Partake in the all-time classic Canadian breakfast – peameal bacon on a kaiser roll – at **St. Lawrence Market**. See page 17.

9 Check out a rock show at the **Horseshoe Tavern**. See page 141.

10 Find somebody with a car and a cottage, beg them to take you with them, then spend the next nine hours in gridlock.

toronto the good

Proof of Toronto's puritanical upbringing is easy to spot – it's in the Gothic spires, stained-glass windows and cobblestone steps of its many churches.

Church Street might be one of two main drags through the **Gay Village** (see page 216), but a little further south, near Dundas and down to Queen, you'll find numerous reminders of how the street got its name.

There's the octagonal **St. George's Greek Orthodox Church** (115 Bond, near Gould, 416-977-3342), adorned with a beautiful mosaic of its eponymous dragon slayer and interior paintings by Pachomaioi monks from Greece.

Across the street is the **First Evangelical Lutheran Church** (116 Bond, 416-977-4786), established by German immigrants in 1898. The Gothic **St. Michael's Cathedral** (65 Bond, 416-364-0234, www.stmichaelscathedral.com), established in 1845, is the main church of Canada's largest English-speaking Catholic archdiocese. Next door is the renowned St. Michael's Choir School (66 Bond, 416-393-5518).

The world's largest pipe organ – 8,000 pipes, the longest of which is 10 metres – and 54 church bells can be found at the **Metropolitan United Church** (56 Queen E, 416-363-0331, www.metunited.org). A little further south is the Anglican **Cathedral Church of St. James** (65 Church, 416-364-7865, www.stjamescathedral.on.ca). The English Gothic Revival-style home to Toronto's first Christian community also has the tallest spire of any church in Canada.

Other notable Toronto churches:

ST. JAMES-BOND UNITED CHURCH
1066 Avenue Road, no phone.
Noteworthy because 007 author Ian Fleming worked for British intelligence during the second world war at the nearby Department of Defence. Now closed.

ALL SAINTS CHURCH
315 Dundas E, 416-368-7768.
Opened in 1874, this Victorian church has a 3,000-pipe organ, stained glass windows and a mosaic chancel floor.

CHAPEL OF ST. JAMES-THE-LESS
635 Parliament, 416-964-9194.
Opened in 1844, this small funeral chapel overlooks the grounds of the city's oldest cemetery.

CHURCH OF THE HOLY TRINITY
10 Trinity Square, 416-598-4521.
The Tudor-style towers were originally used by ships in the harbour to navigate. The Cowboy Junkies

Metropolitan United Church

recorded their breakout album The Trinity Sessions in the church.

CHURCH OF THE REDEEMER
162 Bloor W, 416-922-4948.
A classic example of Gothic Revival architecture.

HOLY EUCHARIST UKRAINIAN CATHOLIC CHURCH
515 Broadview, 416-465-5836.
A modern Byzantine-domed church serving a parish established in 1937.

ST. ANDREW'S PRESBYTERIAN CHURCH
115 St. Andrews, 416-593-5603.
Built in 1849, this is the oldest church in Scarborough.

ST. ANNE'S ANGLICAN CHURCH
270 Gladstone, 416-536-3160.
This 1907 Byzantine church has been declared a National Historic Site and houses a series of murals depicting the life of Christ painted by members of the Group of Seven and others.

ST. FRANCIS OF ASSISI CHURCH
101 Grace, 416-536-8195.
Little Italy was once an Irish nabe, as depicted in the stained glass windows of this 1914 church.

ST. PATRICK'S ROMAN CATHOLIC CHURCH
141 McCaul, 416-598-3269.
This cruciform-shaped church with the domed sanctuary was built in 1908.

ST. PAUL'S BASILICA
83 Power, 416-364-7588.
Built in the Italian Renaissance style and designated as the only minor basilica in Toronto by Pope John Paul II.

University of Toronto and the Parkdale Canoe Club in 1909. (The Grey Cup is now handed out to the top team in the Canadian Football League each season.) It now offers private tennis courts, a ball field and skating rink.

Forest Hill

There are trees here – a 1936 bylaw required every property to have one planted in front – but it's hardly a forest. And the most notable landmark is the snooty private school **Upper Canada College** (200 Lonsdale, 416-488-1125), where Canada's bluebloods have been preparing to inherit their families' fortunes since 1829. Famous alumni: NHL architect Conn Smythe, Eaton department store founder Timothy Eaton, actor Brendan Fraser, humourist Stephen Leacock, novelist Robertson Davies, one of the writers of TV's Lost and the guy who discovered stem cells.

Casa Loma

Located on the top of a hill in the middle of the city, this hundred-year-old medieval-style castle – yes, castle, complete with towers, turrets and secret tunnels – sticks out like a sore thumb. It would be a great place to play Clue (perhaps in the conservatory, with its Italian stained glass dome) and is not without its charms (the lavish gardens surrounding the property, for example). Built by Peter Pa... uh, Canadian financier Henry Pellatt as a bit of childhood wish fulfillment, Casa Loma is one of the city's top attractions, with more than 275,000 visitors each year.

■ *1 Austin Terrace, 416-923-1171,*
www.casaloma.org.
Open daily 9:30 am-5 pm. $12, stu/srs $7.50,
child $6.75. Multi-language self-guided audio
tours.

Spadina Museum Historic House & Garden

Built by businessman and financier James Austin in 1866 on six acres of parkland, this 50-room mansion boasts one of Toronto's finest restored Victorian and Edwardian garden (free to explore, whether you visit the museum or not).

■ *285 Spadina Road, 416-392-6910,*
www.toronto.ca/culture/spadina.htm.
Open Sep-Jan Tue-Fri noon-4 pm, Sat-Sun noon-5 pm (hours vary at other times of year). $6.75,
stu/srs $5.75, child $4.75, under six free. Guided
tours every hour from 12:15 pm.

City of Toronto Archives

The archives consists of a large warehouse and exhibition hall with rotating exhibits devoted to the

Not every city has its own castle. **Casa Loma**.

a tomb with a view

Anyone with a taste for the macabre should find Toronto's ever-expanding wealth of cemeteries a morbid treat. In addition to tombstones and plastic flowers, they offer plenty of walking terrain and bike paths, as well as examples of classic architecture, flower gardens and wildlife (the black squirrel being the most common).

Those looking for the prominently passed-away should check out **Mount Pleasant Cemetery** (375 Mount Pleasant, 416-485-9129, open daily 8 am-8 pm). Founded in 1876, the grounds boast tombstones for Canada's 10th prime minister, William Lyon Mackenzie King (December 17, 1874 – July 22, 1950), and world-renowned pianist Glenn Gould (September 25, 1932 – October 4, 1982), as well as one of North America's finest arboretums (you know, tree collections).

The very Buffy-sounding **Necropolis** (200 Winchester, 416-923-7911, open daily 8 am-6 pm) has some of Toronto's finest high Victorian Gothic structures. Among the deceased are Globe and Mail founder George Brown (November 29, 1818 – May 9, 1880), who was shot and killed by a disgruntled employee and Ned Hanlan (July 12, 1855 – January 4, 1908), the world's first professional rowing champion who was portrayed by Nicolas Cage in the 1986 film The Boy in Blue.

More cool Gothic architecture can be found at **St. James' Cemetery** (Parliament, north of Wellesley, 416-964-9194, open daily 8 am-5 pm). One of the oldest dead zones in the city, St. James has been around since 1844, with a magnificent Catholic cathedral housing some exquisite stained-glass windows and wood panelling.

city's urban history and geography. It has plenty of dusty old maps, blue prints, photographs and historical documents for the serious urban researcher. Check out the fascinating online photo archive.

■ *255 Spadina Road, near Davenport, Public Info 416-397-5000, Research Hall 416-397-0778, www.toronto.ca/archives. Open Mon-Fri 9 am-4:30 pm, Sat 10 am-4:30 pm (closed Sat in summer). Free.*

Wychwood Park

Founded by landscape artist Marmaduke Matthews in the 1870s, Wychwood is one of Toronto's earliest planned communities. Matthews intended the area to be an artists' enclave, an image it has struggled to maintain, and it's been designated as an Ontario Heritage Conservation district. The park's wooded ravine is also one of the city's most-exclusive – and least-known – neighbourhoods, with 60 or so Heritage-designated homes dating back as the late 1800s. Nestled in the south end of the park is Taddle Creek, home to swans Felix and Oscar, as well as snapping turtles, goldfish and ducks. In winter, the pond is used for ice skating.

■ *South of St. Clair W, west of Bathurst, between Alcina and Davenport.*

The very Buffy-sounding **Necropolis**.

north

While the area north of St. Clair is a far cry from the excitement of downtown Toronto, it's also a far cry from the urban wasteland some might make it out to be. After all, this is where Prince lives.

Corso Italia

In recent years, many Italians in the city have migrated northward to the Corso Italia area along St. Clair West between Lansdowne and Westmount, and some farther still to the suburbs of Woodbridge, Richmond Hill and Mississauga. Unlike Little Italy, Corso Italia is home to more fashionable (i.e. European-style) boutiques, gelaterias, cappuccino shops and, of course, authentic Italian eateries.

Yonge and Eglinton

A.k.a. Young & Eligible. Or Yonge and Eg (pronounced "Egg." This area of condos, multiplexes, restos and bars offers everything the young, single and successful could want.

Little Jamaica, mon

Toronto is the world's third-largest Caribbean city after Kingston, Jamaica, and Havana, Cuba, and more than half of the city's black population can trace its roots to any of the dozens of sun-blessed islands, from Barbados and the Bahamas to Cuba and Dominica and Jamaica and Haiti. The early Caribbean community set up shop at Bathurst and Bloor, but it has since moved northward, to Eglinton West around Oakwood, where Little Jamaica has established itself as a Caribbean shopping mecca, home to reggae, roti and r'spec.

our home, on native land

Every day we quite literally stomp all over what was once native land. But few sites of significance are memorialized like the **Tabor Hill Ossuary Memorial Park** (Bellamy, north of Lawrence), two pits excavated in 1956 that hold the remains of about 470 natives, believed to be 15th-century Iroquois. Archaeologists from the ROM who discovered the site say the graves show signs of being part of an ancient ceremonial reburial that followed the relocation of a native village. Some area villages date back to the 14th century. The bones were reinterred in 1961 in a special ceremony held by the city of Scarborough attended by several First Nations representatives. It's also one of several stops in the semi-annual Great Indian Bus Tour, organized by the **Native Canadian Centre** (16 Spadina, 416-964-9087, www.ncct.on.ca).

North York

Amalgamated in 1998, North York was once one of Canada's largest cities. It's too big and decentralized to explore on foot unless you're on some kind of Gump-like urban walkabout.

Bathurst Jewish Community Centre

In addition to numerous recreational, educational and cultural programs, the centre houses the **Koffler Gallery**, the **Leah Posluns Theatre**, which offers performances in English and Yiddish, and the Family Place at the **Jewish Discovery Museum**.
■ *4588 Bathurst, 416-636-1880, www.bjcc.ca.*

Black Creek Pioneer Village

There never was a Black Creek Village, but that didn't stand in the way of a recreation of 19th-century frontier life on this old German farmstead. More than 35 carefully restored 1860-era shops and homes are staffed by costumed hosts, from blacksmiths to cabinetmakers, who guide you through Canadian history.
■ *1000 Murray Ross Parkway, at Jane and Steeles, 416-736-1733, www.blackcreek.ca. Open May-June wkdays 9:30 am-4 pm, wknds/holidays 11 am-5 pm; July-Labour Day wkdays 10 am-5 pm, wknds/holidays 11 am-5 pm; Labour Day-Dec 31 wkdays 9:30 am-4 pm, wknds/holidays 11 am-4 pm. $12, stu/srs $11, child $8, under four free.*

Earl Bales Park

This park contains a Holocaust monument by Toronto sculptor and Holocaust survivor Ernest Raab. Another Raab monument commemorates Raoul Wallenberg, a Swedish diplomat who saved the lives of thousands of Jews in Budapest, Hungary.
■ *Bathurst, south of Sheppard, 416-661-1800.*

Edwards Gardens

Acres of gardens, paths and creekbeds. Includes the **Toronto Botanical Garden**, which has an amateur gardeners' info booth, gift and book shop and Canada's largest horticultural library.
■ *777 Lawrence E, 416-397-1340, www.civicgardencentre.org. Open wkdys 9 am-5 pm. Free.*

Funstation

Canada has a lengthy rail history. This railway-themed park is not part of it, but it does have go-

A taste of island life in
Little Jamaica.

karts, and who doesn't love pretending they're an Indy car racer, even if they're folded into a glorified lawnmower? There's also mini-golf (for those PGA fantasists), batting cages (to feed your inner Babe Ruth) and an arcade (in case you forgot your PSP at home).

■ *5 York Gate, York Gate and Finch W, two blocks east of Hwy 400 north of Finch, 416-736-4804, www.funstationfunpark.com. Open June wkdays 1-9 pm, wknds 10 am-9 pm, July-Aug daily 10 am-10 pm, April-May wknds (weather permitting). Free (pay as you play).*

Gibson House

The restored Georgian Revival-style 1851 farm home of David Gibson, local politician and partic-

ipant in the pitchfork-equipped Rebellion of 1837 (see page 10), is located behind the North York Rose Garden. Underpaid summer students dressed in period costumes act as guides and demonstrate such 19th-century skills as spinning and butter churning.

■ *5172 Yonge, 416-395-7432, www.toronto.ca/culture/gibson_house.htm. Open Tue-Sun holiday Mon noon-5 pm (closed Sep). $3.75, yth/srs $2.25, child $1.75.*

Holocaust Centre of Toronto

This education and memorial centre contains audio-visual presentations and memorabilia dedicated to the 6-million Jewish victims of the Holocaust.

sightseeing

■ *4600 Bathurst, group reservations 416-635-2883 ext 153.*
Open Mon-Thu 9 am-4:30 pm, Fri 9 am-3 pm, Sun 11:30 am-4:30 pm. Free.

Mel Lastman Square
Named for and by his Melness, the former mayor of North York and later Toronto, who was one of the driving forces behind amalgamation in 1998 and a national joke thanks to his propensity for malapropisms. The **North York Civic Centre** (formerly the City Hall) is located at the west end of the square.
■ *5100 Yonge, 416-338-0338.*

Toronto Aerospace Museum
Strictly for wing nuts, the former Downsview Air Force Base is now a park, sometime movie set and museum where volunteers restore old planes, including the Avro Arrow and Lancaster Bomber. U of T's experimental light plane, the Ornithopter, is also on display.
■ *65 Carl Hall, 416-638-6078, www.toron-toaerospacemuseum.com.*
Open Wed 10 am-8 pm, Thu-Sat and holiday Mon 10 am-4 pm, Sun noon-4 pm. $8, srs $6, stu $5, child under six free, fam $20. Self-guided and guided tours.

Toronto Centre for the Arts
This venue houses three theatres, including the **George Weston Recital Hall** (see **Music**, page 143) – considered by many as having the best acoustics of any building in the city.

■ *5040 Yonge, 416-733-9388, www.tocentre.com.*

York U. Astronomical Observatory
Other than the Toronto International Film Festival, this is the best way to see stars.
■ *4700 Keele, NW corner of the campus, 416-736-2100 ext 77773, www.yorku.ca/observe.*
Open for public viewings Wed from 9 pm. Free.

Richmond Hill
David Dunlop Observatory
A multi-domed observatory set in a park in the burb of Richmond Hill, it's home to the largest optical telescope in the country.
■ *123 Hillsview, 416-724-STAR, www.astro.utoronto.ca/DDO.*
Tours every Fri and Sat at sunset. $5, child/srs $3.

York
Beth Tzedec Museum
Oy vey, another museum. You need that like a loch in kop. But this smallish museum is notable for two things: it's located in the Beth Tzedec Synagogue, the country's largest, and it houses the largest Canadian collection of Jewish historical artifacts.
■ *1700 Bathurst, 416-781-3514 ext 32, www.beth-tzedec.org.*
Open Mon/Wed-Thu 11 am-1 pm and 2-5 pm, Sun 11 am-3 pm (closed Sun Jul-Aug). Free. Tours by appointment.

where the rich folks live

Forget the high-priced condos downtown. These nabes are where you'll find the city's ritzy rich — including Prince — kickin' back in their mega-bucks mansions.

Named for the riding trail used by the area's emerging estate classes in the 1930s, the **Bridle Path**, a forested enclave north of Lawrence has long been one of Toronto's most exclusive upscale neighbourhoods. The sidewalk-less tree-lined streets and manses on oversized lots recall the area's past equestrian charm – there are still riding stables at nearby Sunnybrook Park and the circa-1941 Cape Cod-style house built by Hubert Page, the first in the area, still sits off Bayview.

Beyond the gates and fine trimmed lawns, "millionaire's row" has given way in more recent years to the nouveau riche – among them, reclusive rock star Prince. Alas, media mogul Conrad Black, Lord of Crossharbour, remains.

But these days, the establishment of Toronto – government ministers past and present, university deans – reside further south and west amid the greenery of **Rosedale**, southeast of Yonge and Summerhill which borrows its name from the abundance of wild roses that once graced the hillsides that still roll and weave

through its numerous parks and ravines. A favourite destination for the protests of anarchists and anti-poverty activists, it's also here that the Rosedale Golf Club and lacrosse grounds that played host to the Canadian Football League's first Grey Cup in 1909 once stood. The tastefully turned-out manors still standing from that era are a sight to behold.

It's further west, north of St. Clair in the meandering streets of **Forest Hill**, however, where some of this city's most spectacular architecture can be found. The art deco classic built by Group of Seven artist Lawren Harris (2 Ava Crescent), the princely Barker house erected by industrialist E.G. Baker (135 Dunvegan) and the turn-of-the-20th-century Gothic masterpiece built in honour of department store tycoon Timothy Eaton – the Timothy Eaton Memorial Church (230 St. Clair W) – are only a few of the architectural marvels. The steeply rising Russell Hill Road at the foot of Forest Hill was once a Six Nations trail.

east

The west end might get all the good press for its hip, arty attitude, but this more laid-back side of town – sandy beaches, Greektown, a second Chinatown – is quickly earning a rep for its own brand of cool.

A typical day of blading at the **Beach**.

The Beach

Never mind "the Beach" versus "the Beaches" debate (it seems to depend on whether or not you live there and for how long). This fashionable nabe was once a summer getaway for 19th-century monied types. But it's looking less and less like a resort community as more and more condos overshadow the cute clapboard cottages.

Just 15 minutes from downtown and extending several blocks northward from the lake, the **Beach** is a charming (and expensive) place to live. It's also a great place to visit, particularly on summer weekends when the slow trek to cottage country is out of the question.

The main drag – Queen East – is a laid-back stretch of quirky stores and quaint antique and art shops separated by a cool collection of bars, restaurants and ice cream stands. But the real attraction is the stroll-worthy beachside boardwalk that stretches from Balmy Beach in the east to Ashbridges Bay Park in the west. There's also a path ideal for biking or blading, and the wide, sandy beach is perfect for building sandcastles, playing volleyball or just soaking up some rays. Sadly, water pollution makes swimming an iffy – and itchy – prospect, despite the city's best efforts to clean things up.
■ *Queen East, between Coxwell and Victoria Park.*

Kew Gardens

Kew Gardens, a large public park between Queen East and the boardwalk, is home to the Queen Ann Revival-style **Gardener's Cottage**, a bandstand and a lawn-bowling green, and is worth a visit, especially if the park is hosting one of the neighbourhood's many festivals, craft shows, concerts and exhibitions, including the **Beaches International Jazz Festival**, held every July (see **Festivals**, page 162).

Sculptor Shane Clodd, whose works include a sculpture garden carved from recycled hydro poles in nearby Pickering, got the idea to carve the three Fates of Greek mythology – Clotho (past), Lachesis (present) and Atropos (future) – in Kew Gardens Park (Queen East and Lee) after the city was forced to fell 25 oaks for safety reasons. Clodd thought the oaks should be transformed into works of art "to compensate for the loss of these great trees and to enrich the experience of attending Kew Gardens." The result is a detailed masterpiece incorporating mythological signs, symbols and figures into the faces of the Fates.

Chinatown, the sequel

The intersection of Broadview and Gerrard is where you'll find the city's second Chinatown, although other Southeast Asian cultures – Vietnamese and Cambodian, notably – have also moved in over the last couple of decades. A lot like the Chinatown at Spadina and Dundas, with markets, food stalls, bakeries, grocers, herbalists and discount shops, except the prices may be a little cheaper, if that's possible, and the nightlife a little less lively.

Corktown

Named for the original Irish settlers, many of whom were originally from County Cork, who populated the area in the 1800s, this east side nabe's current boundaries are Berkeley Street to River and South Shuter to the lakeshore. Notable stops include the historic **Enoch Turner School House** (see below) and the former **Gooderham and Worts Distillery** (see page 36).

Enoch Turner Schoolhouse

This restored 1848 schoolhouse offers a glimpse of education during pioneer days – bet there was a lot less history back then – and is a common field trip

for local school kids. Maybe they'll let you clean the erasers or wear a cone-shaped dunce cap. Various prices.
■ *106 Trinity, near Parliament and King, 416-863-0010; www.enochturnerschoolhouse.ca. Open Mon-Fri 10 am-5 pm.*

The Danforth

A hundred years ago, there were just 20 Greek names in Toronto's city directory. Now, the city is home to more than 150,000 Greeks, making it the fourth-largest Greek city in the world. And five or six blocks of resto- and ouzeri-lined Danforth Avenue, from Donlands Avenue in the east to Broadview in the west, make up what we call **Greektown**.

Street signs in English and Greek, blue-and-white Greek flags and the classical architecture of the National Bank of Greece and other buildings, coupled with the smells of souvlaki and moussaka, lend the area a decidedly Mediterranean atmosphere. The bars and restos are open late into the night, especially during the summer, when patios are packed and glass walls are flung wide.

Eat your way through Greektown during the annual **Taste of the Danforth** festival (see **Festivals**, page 164) in early August. The street is closed to traffic and turned into the city's biggest food court, with kiosks and food carts offering an outstanding opportunity to sample the various delights offered by local restaurants.

Don Valley

The Don River was once an important waterway through the city. Then came industrialization and urbanization. Pollution followed and the natural ecosystem suffered. The occasional three-eyed fish was hooked. But let's not forget what's important: the river still looks great! Walking and bike paths follow its course, and efforts are being made to restore some semblance of a natural balance.

Ontario Science Centre

The OSC isn't strictly for the nerd herd. Forget boring old display cases and stuffy narrated filmstrips – participation and hands-on are the name of the game. Through more than 800 exhibits and Toronto's only planetarium, the centre lets you explore rainforest and ocean ecosystems. Try hands-on scientific gizmos, games, simulations and visit the Omnimax movie theatre.
■ *770 Don Mills, 416-696-1000, www.ontariosciencecentre.ca. Open daily 10 am-5 pm. $14, stu/srs $10, child $8; Omnimax films $7-$11.*

Todmorden Mills Heritage Museum and Arts Centre

Buildings harkening back to the olden days in the Don Valley include the Don Train Station, a brewery museum, two of T.O.'s oldest homes and a newly refurbished paper mill and gallery.
■ *67 Pottery, 416-396-2819, www.toronto.ca/culture/todmorden_mills.htm. Open Jun-Aug Tue-Fri 10 am-4:30 pm, wknds and holidays noon-5 pm; times vary at other times of year. $3.50, stu/srs $2.25, child $1.50, five and under free (more for special events).*

on the cheap

It's easy to drop a few hundred – or a few thousand – exploring the city. A single afternoon in **Yorkville** will melt the black strip off your credit cards. But you don't need to spend a lot to enjoy the Toronto experience.

Window-shopping and people-watching in Toronto's trendier nabes – Queen West or College Street, for example – don't cost a dime. There are plenty of cool parks to enjoy, and many city-run facilities – swimming pools and ice rinks, for example – are also free (for listings, see **Recreation**, page 196).

And Toronto only looks like a slab of concrete poured over broken glass. If you feel energetic, there are miles of walking paths, bike trails and green spaces throughout the core (see **Green Toronto**, page 204).

Cheap eats are easy to find if you know where to look (and if you don't, check out our suggestions starting on page 59 and 70). If museums are more your bag, the Museum Passport ($25, children $15) provides access to 10 museums and historic sites, available from the Royal Ontario Museum (see page 24) or TicketKing (416-872-1212; www.ticketking.com). There's also the Toronto CityPass (416-868-6937), which gets you into six attractions – CN Tower, Art Gallery of Ontario, Royal Ontario Museum, Casa Loma, Ontario Science Centre, Toronto Zoo – for $55, available at participating venues.

bike trip east

Toronto is one of North America's most cycle-friendly cities. To see the sites from the saddle, try this route that begins at Union Station. For bike rentals, see page 212.

The streets around Union Station (Bay and Front) are packed with cabs and lost tourists, so get away from here ASAP. Southeast of Union (off Yonge) is the Esplanade, an ideal street to work your way east. Check out the **Bier Markt** (58 the Esplanade, 416-862-7575, www.thebiermarkt.com) for a great sampler of ales from around the world.

To the north, you'll see the **St. Lawrence Market** (see page 17). It comes alive with a farmers market Saturdays and an antique market Sundays. Farther east along the Esplanade is tiny Parliament Park, the site of the original parliament buildings of the city of York, destroyed by American troops in 1812 (don't worry, we got them back by burning down the White House).

Follow the path through the park and take Mill Street into the heart of the **Distillery District** (see page 36), once the largest distillery in the British Empire and now a multi-use space for artists and businesses. At the east end of the Distillery District, take Cherry Street north to King. Follow King east until it meets Queen and ride the bridge over the Don River beneath the quote from Eldon Garnet, "The river I step in is not the river I stand in."

A great cruise down Queen takes you through the neighbourhood on the east side of the river, **Riverdale**. Turn north before you ride under the railway bridge, though, and follow Degrassi to Dundas. Every Canadian who grew up in the 80s recognizes this as the setting of Degrassi Junior High, the TV teen drama of choice for school guidance counselors everywhere.

Turn east along Dundas until you hit Greenwood and make a left. At Gerrard, turn right and you'll soon find yourself in **Little India** (see page 36), amidst delectable aromas of curry and incense. Little India ends at Coxwell, so turn left on Coxwell and go under the railroad bridge until you hit Felstead, where you can turn left to ride past Monarch Park.

When you get to Greenwood, turn right and you'll see the ginormous TTC yard, designed to service the trains on the Bloor-Danforth subway line. A left on Chatham and then a right on Euston takes you to the **Danforth** (see page 34), synonymous with Toronto's **Greektown**, one of the world's largest diasporas of Greek people.

Refuel with some souvlaki before continuing west on Danforth, crossing the Don River on the **Bloor Viaduct**, adorned with the artistic installation the Luminous Veil by Derek Revington, locally known as the suicide barrier. The traffic here is pretty nuts, so when you get to the other side, stop at the lights and cross to the south side to make your way down.

On the west side you'll see **St. James' Cemetery** (see page 29), where you can float around on a bike looking at the headstones from the 1800s. Farther south is the **Necropolis Cemetery** (see page 29) in

Saris and rice and all things spice are what **Little India**'s made of.

the heart of the historic streets of **Cabbagetown** (see page 26), an early settlement of Irish immigrants. This neighbourhood also boasts the kid-friendly **Riverdale Farm** (see page 26).

As you make your way out of Cabbagetown, go right (that would be west) on Gerrard. At Sherbourne, you'll see **Allan Gardens** (see **Queer**, page 216), home to the glorious Allan Gardens Conservatory and a remarkable selection of trees, plants, ferns, cacti and flowers. Not just a spring and summer stop, in the winter, Allan Gardens feels like you're in a rainforest.

Farther west along Gerrard you'll see Church Street, the home of the **Gay Village** (see page 26; **Queer**, page 216), one of the largest queer nabes in North America. Make a left to work your way south along Church. Just below Dundas on the east side at Shuter is the **NOW Magazine** head office (189 Church, 416-364-1300). While you're in the neighbourhood, drop in, have a drink and a bit of lunch at the first-floor **NOW Lounge** and pick up the latest issue of NOW – it's free.

Farther south, you'll see the **Metropolitan United Church** (see page 27) and **St. James Cathedral** (see page 27), two of the oldest and more picturesque churches in the city. At the foot of Church, turn right (west) on Front and make your way back to Union Station. **For a westerly route, see page 41.**

sightseeing

Little India

Toronto's growing population of immigrants from India, Pakistan, Afghanistan and Sri Lanka – some quarter-million and counting – has resulted in one of the city's most vibrant and visible ethnic communities, centred on the Indian Bazaar on Gerrard between Greenwood and Coxwell, better known as Little India. It's east of **Riverdale**, which faces **Cabbagetown** (see page 26) across the DVP, and north of Leslieville. Saris, silk, scarves and spices are the order of the day, and a walk through the nabe reveals fine Indian restos, grocers and shops.

Scarborough

Sometimes called "Scarberia" because of its relative remoteness from the downtown core and the rather unpicturesque number of low-rises, strip malls and industrial buildings that dot the area, if nothing else Scarborough is famous for producing Mike Myers and the Barenaked Ladies.

Cedar Ridge Creative Centre and Botanical Gardens

This 1912 manor fronted by English-style gardens hosts art classes, a gallery space, pottery studio and woodcarving shop.
■ *225 Confederation, 416-396-4026.*
Open Mon-Thu 9 am-10 pm, Fri 9 am-2 pm, Sat-Sun 9 am-4 pm.

Guild Inn Gardens

Aha! Not just a botanical garden, but also a sculpture garden preserving works that ornamented now demolished city buildings. In a park-like setting, no less. And it also provides historical info on the area, from early pioneer days to a Depression-era artists' colony. Guided tours by appointment.
■ *191 Guildwood Pkwy, 416-338-8798.*

Scarborough Bluffs

Stretching for 14 kilometres along Lake Ontario (from the foot of Victoria Park in the west to the mouth of Highland Creek in the east), the escarpment rises some 65 metres above the water at its highest point. On top of the bluffs, a large meadow offers an excellent view of the sandstone cliffs and the lake. **Bluffers Park**, created from 2.6-million cubic metres of fill and jutting from the cliffside into the lake, offers a beach and picnic area as well as a public marina.
■ *Brimley Road, south end.*

Scarborough Historical Museum

A museum dedicated to the history of a nabe of strip malls and warehouses known locally – and somewhat affectionately – as Scarlem.
■ *Thomson Memorial Park, 1007 Brimley, 416-338-8805, events 416-338-3888, www.toronto.ca/culture/scarborough_historical.htm.*
Open Victoria Day to Labour Day Wed-Sun noon-4 pm, Sep-mid-Dec Mon-Fri 10 am-4 pm. $3, stu/srs $1.50, child $1, wknds pwyc.

whiskey a

Gangster Al Capone once walked the cobblestone streets of this former booze factory turned upscale arts community, which has appeared in such films as Cinderella Man, Chicago and X-Men.

Founded in 1832, the **Gooderham & Worts Distillery** (55 Mill, between Parliament and Cherry, 416-364-1177, www.thedistillerydistrict.com) was once the largest in the British empire, producing more than 2 million gallons of whiskey every year. Now, it's a slightly more sober pedestrian-only arts community consisting of 44 revamped Victorian buildings, the largest restoration project in Canada. More than 100 shops and services – galleries, performance studios, restaurants, boutiques – call its brick-lined streets and European-style piazzas home, and it also plays host to the annual **Distillery Blues Festival**, a farmers market

A booze factory turned upscale arts community. **Distillery District.**

90-90

(building 57, 416-682-3498), photography at the **Pikto Gallery** (building 59, 416-203-3443), and a mixed bag of paintings, ceramics, glass, textiles, metalwork, jewellery and clothing at **distill** (building 56, 416-304-0033).

For something less arty, more crafty, sample the handmade furniture, decorative objects and textile products at **Bookhou Design** (building 74, 416-368-0342) or **Akroyd Furniture** (building 74, 416-367-5757). Pick some flowers at über-florist **Elizabeth Munro Design** (building 9, 416-214-4760) or pimp your pooch at **Mona's Dog Boutique** (building 53, 416-361-9381). The automobilia on sale at the **Auto Grotto** (building 32, 416-304-0005) will turn the crank of any gearhead. Grab an engagement ring at **Corktown Designs** (building 54, 416-861-3020), which offers one-of-a-kind handmade jewellery, or a wedding band at goldsmith **Leif Benner** (building 74, 416-861-1282).

If you've built up a thirst, quaff a cold one at the **Mill Street Brewery** (building 63, 416-681-0338) before settling into one of the Distillery's many restaurants: there's the chophouse-style **Boiler House** (building 46, 416-203-2121), with its 22-foot wine rack, handcrafted timber tables and free live jazz (Thu-Sat nights and jazz brunch Sun), pizza and pasta at **Archeo** (building 45, 416-815-9898), seafood at **Pure Spirits Oyster House & Grill** (building 62A, 416-361-5859), or, for something more experimental, gather round the large open kitchen at **Perigee** (building 59, 416-364-1397), where the French- and Mediterranean-influenced mystery menu is based on the Japanese concept of "Omakase" (trust me).

Building 74 is home to some of the finest performing arts companies in the country, including **Dancemakers** (see **Dance**, page 156); **Native Earth Performing Arts** (416-531-1402), Canada's oldest professional aboriginal theatre company; **Nightwood Theatre** (416-944-1740), devoted to original Canadian and international plays by women artists; and the **Queen of Puddings Music Theatre** (416-203-4149), which offers an offbeat approach to classical opera.

Meanwhile, the jewel of the Distillery District is the 50,000-square-foot state-of-the-art **Young Centre for the Performing Arts** (building 49-50; 416-866-8666). Making use of two old rackhouses where barrels of booze were once stored, it's the result of a unique partnership between the conservatory-style **George Brown College Theatre School** (416-415-5000) and the **Soulpepper Theatre Company** (see **Theatre**, page 153), an artist-founded classical repertory theatre company.

Obviously, there's a lot to see. Thankfully, the Distillery offers guided walking tours. Or, if you're feeling hobbled by the cobbled streets, glide about the grounds on one of the two-wheeled Segway tours, departing from the **Distillery Visitor Centre**, although, like a lot of things in the Distillery, it's a bit pricey – 59 bucks for 90 minutes. (For information or to reserve a tour, call 1-866-405-TOUR, or visit www.segwayofontario.com/distillery.htm.)

(every Sunday throughout the summer) and numerous other events and exhibitions.

A good place to start exploring is at **Balzac's Coffee** (building 60, 416-207-1709). A cup of their house-blend roasted coffee in hand, pop over to the traditional English-style **Brick Street Bakery** (building 45a) to sample the all-organic breads and pastries before embarking on a morning of gallery hopping and gift shopping. A haven for both serious art aficionados and weekend gallery gawkers, you'll find regular exhibitions of emerging and established painters, sculptors and photographers at **Arta Gallery** (building 9, 416-364-2782) and **Brush** (building 55, 416-214-1226), contemporary Canadian and international artwork at **Artcore/Fabrice Marcolini** (building 62, 416-920-3820) and the **Blue Dot Gallery** (building 47, 416-487-1500), blown glass at **Catherine Hibbits Glass**

west

Everybody knows the west is hip and fashionable, with all the cool restaurants, bars, shops and galleries. But it's also got some of the greatest green spaces of any city anywhere, like shouldn't-be-missed High Park.

The Annex

Just a few blocks west of **Yorkville** (see page 25) and the **Mink Mile** (see page 26) sits this lively little student-friendly multiculti nabe of tall, narrow homes on long, narrow streets. The strip along Bloor West is home to curio shops, cafés, a handful of decent clubs and bars, some of the best (and cheapest) sushi in the city, old-school rep theatre the **Bloor Cinema** (506 Bloor W, 415-516-2331, www.bloorcinema.com) and famous eclectic discount department store **Honest Ed's** (581 Boor W, 416-537-1574; see **Shopping**, page 167).

Miles Nadal Jewish Community Centre

In addition to numerous sports, recreational and special group activities, the centre houses the Al Green (no, not that Al Green) Theatre, which hosts film screenings and live performances.
■ *750 Spadina, at Bloor, 416-924-6211, www.milesnadaljcc.ca.*

Bloor West Village

Bordered by High Park and the Humber River on the east and west and bisected by Bloor West, this quaint nabe has a strong eastern European presence, with shops, bakeries, grocers and cafés clearly reflecting the community's Ukrainian, German, Polish, Lithuanian and Macedonian roots.

Dufferin Grove Park

Technically not in Bloor West Village, only bordering on it, Dufferin Grove Park has a clay-and-straw structure built by locals and a newsletter that rivals the neighbourhood papers. Dufferin Grove Park is one patch of green you can chalk up to community spirit. So much is going on here, from bread rising in the communal oven to the weekly organic farmers market, that you can easily forget it's right across the road from a mall. Besides a grassroots open-air theatre, it has the sort of playground we all wish we'd had as tots, including a huge sandpit with toys for anyone to use and running water perfect for creating miniature Casa Lomas. The Grove is like the Internet with trees – it connects to everything.
■ *875 Dufferin, 416-392-0913, www.dufferinpark.ca.*

Colborne Lodge

This Regency-style cottage, built in 1837 on a plot of land overlooking Humber Bay, was the first home in the city to have an indoor toilet. Original period artifacts and furnishings are on display.
■ *Colborne Lodge, north of the Queensway, SW quarter of High Park, 416-392-6916, www.toronto.ca/culture/colborne.htm. Open May-Aug, Tue-Sun noon-5 pm (hours vary at other times of year). $4, srs/yth $2.75, child $2.50.*

College Street
Little Italy

When Italy won soccer's World Cup in 2006, more than 200,000 people celebrated in the streets of Via Italia. Many shops display photos, sun-faded and scratchy, of the impromptu party. The area's seen an increase in Portuguese and Hispanic influence: Little Italy begins to blend in with Little Portugal as it extends westward, while the area around College and Bathurst is a major Hispanic centre, with tapas bars and nightclubs. Many of the city's 650,00 Italians have migrated a little farther north to St. Clair West (see **Corso Italia**, page 30) and the suburb of Woodbridge, but this remains the spiritual home of Toronto's Italian community. Settled by seasonal labourers in the late 19th and early 20th centuries followed by another wave after the Second World War, the area along College between Euclid and Shaw is lined with trattorias, restos and cafés crowded with people sipping espressos, especially on summer weekends.

High Park

Lookin' for green space in the big city? High Park is a true park in the tradition of NYC's Central Park. Wander through, stop and smell the flowers at the park's gardens and bone up on their genus and species at the **Nature Centre**, an outdoor experiential learning facility (440 Parkside, 416-392-1748 ext 6). Adding some fauna to the flora is a small zoo. Located south of Bloor, west of Keele, the park is open dawn to dusk and closed to motor vehicles on Sundays. To the west of High Park is **Bloor West Village**, one the city's oldest and most successful business improvement areas that's transformed itself into a fashionable shopping and dining district.

Koreatown

Wander westward toward the outskirts of the Annex on Bloor between Palmerston and Christie and the street begins to take on a distinctively Asian attitude. Korean, specifically. Toronto is

Get a great buzz off the natural beauty of **High Park**.

home to 45,000 Koreans (80 per cent of the city's small groceries are reportedly owned by Koreans), many of whom spend time in the restaurants, karaoke bars and shops along this strip.

Parkdale

A bit farther west sits Parkdale, a former beach town cut off from the beach by the construction of the Gardiner Expressway in the 1950s. The area's heavily Polish-influenced, but with a strong taste of the Philippines – many of T.O.'s 60,000-strong Filipino community make the area home. The stretch of Roncesvalles between **St. Casamir's** **Church** (156 Roncesvalles) and **St. Vincent de Paul Roman Catholic Church** (263 Roncesvalles) is sausage central, with meat shops, bakeries and restos.

But it's not all kielbasas and klopsy, as the area is experiencing a resurgence of sorts. Real estate is still relatively affordable and the true neighbourhood feel has led many young families to move into the area, bringing with them numerous cool shops, organics stores and bakeries, like the pastry paradise **Queen of Tarts** (283 Roncesvalles, 416-651-3009).

West Queen West

Once merely a more eclectic extension of Queen West, this stretch of Queen west of Bathurst is coming into its own as a neighbourhood. The bars are brazen, the cafés cool, the eateries idiosyncratic and the boutiques bizarre (from one-of-a-kind shops to second-hand clothes and third-hand junk).

It's also begun to take on an arty air thanks to the newly reno'd loft and studio condos looming over the strip of art galleries, restos and shops, anchored by the duelling hipster hotel bars of the Drake and Gladstone.

For a little green space, there's **Trinity Bellwoods Park**, once the site of Trinity College, which opened in 1852. The college gates at Queen West and Strachan are all that remains.

Etobicoke

Humber Arboretum

Arboretum (noun): a place where an extensive variety of woody plants are cultivated for scientific, educational and ornamental purpose. Humber Arboretum (noun): an urban ecology centre on the West Humber River in northwest Toronto that offers garden tours, pond and insect studies, nature walks, camps and a biodiversity and climate change research program.

■ *205 Humber College, 416-675-5009, www.humberarboretum.on.ca.*

Centennial Park

Do you own plants? Do you water them regularly and make sure they get lots of sunlight? Do you talk to them? If you answered yes to any of these questions, these 12,000-square-foot greenhouses may be of interest.

■ *151 Elmcrest, 416-394-8543, www.toronto. ca/parks/parks_gardens/centennialgdns.htm. Open daily 10 am-5 pm. Free.*

Montgomery's Inn Museum

A bit of a trek just for afternoon tea served with 19th-century porcelain, but this former Georgian inn (1847-1850) does its best to preserve the life of a 19th-century innkeeper (which can't be that different from a modern innkeeper, can it?).

■ *4709 Dundas W, Etobicoke, 416-394-8113, events 416-338-3888, www.montgomerysinn.com. Open Tue-Sun 1-5 pm. $4, stu/srs $2, child $1.*

Neilson Park Creative Centre and Gallery

Two galleries and four studios offer a variety of classes and exhibitions throughout the year. Check the website for updates.

■ *56 Neilson, 416-622-5294, www.neilsonparkcreativecentre.com. Open Mon-Fri 9 am-4 pm, Tue evenings 7-9 pm. Free.*

Our **Chinatown** is like a little bit of Hong Kong in the middle of the city.

bike trip west

One of the best ways to see the city is from the seat of a bicycle. Try this westerly route that begins at Union Station. For bike rentals, see page 212.

York Street runs north from Union Station on the west side of the historic **Royal York Hotel**. This will take you through the **Financial District** (see page 16), until you hit Queen. Turn right for a great view of **Nathan Phillips Square** (see page 20) and our modernist jewel, Viljo Revell's **City Hall** (see page 19), which was ignominiously blown up in Resident Evil: Apocalypse! To the right, on the other side of Bay is **Old City Hall** (see page 20), which now functions as a courthouse.

Work your way north through Nathan Phillips Square until you hit Dundas. This stretch of Dundas is nasty for biking, but if you head west (turn left), it'll take you past the **Art Gallery of Ontario** (see page 15) at McCaul and the main intersection of Toronto's **Chinatown** (see page 21) at Spadina. Just past Spadina, you'll hit two streets, Augusta and Kensington, that'll take you into the eclectic **Kensington Market** (see page 21), which is closed to cars on summer Sundays. **Casa Acoreana** (235 Augusta, 416-593-9717), on the corner of Augusta and Nassau, is a great place to stop for a coffee, and if you're lucky, a soccer game will be on the telly. North of Kensington Market, turn right onto College.

Just past Spadina, turn left on the well-groomed St. George Street for a tour through the heart of the **University of Toronto** (see page 22). At Bloor, make a left, to work your way west through the **Annex** (see page 38), home of late urban philosopher Jane Jacobs and many of Toronto's literary elite. After you cross Bathurst, turn right (north) on Clinton until you hit Dupont. At Dupont, make a left and continue until you hit Shaw, where you can turn right up to Davenport. One of the few streets in the city that isn't on a strict north-south or east-west grid, it follows the ancient coastline of Lake Iroquois. Take Davenport west to Oakwood, where you can ride north to St. Clair, one of the main arteries of midtown Toronto.

Once you turn left onto St. Clair, you'll find yourself in **Corso Italia** (see page 30), an Italian outpost that expanded after downtown's Little Italy became gentrified with college students. On the south side of St. Clair, at Lansdowne, try some of North America's best gelato at **La Paloma Gelateria** (1357 St. Clair W, 416-656-2340). The ice cream, made from scratch in the back of the shop, comes in innovative flavours like basil-pineapple and green apple. Eat here. (Warning: this might spoil your appreciation for lesser ice cream.)

Go left on Lansdowne (south) until you cross the railway tracks, then turn left on Lappin. This turns into Hallam, which will take you to Shaw, a nice street to take south, so make a right. At Harbord, turn left (east) and then right (south) onto Palmerston under the mature tree canopy. At College, turn right (west) into **Little Italy** (see page 38), with its many bars, bookstores and requisite Italian restaurants. When you hit Crawford, make a left and pedal south until you hit the beautiful **Trinity-Bellwoods Park** sprinkled with lounging West Queen West residents. Wind through the park until you hit Queen, and take Strachan south. Strachan goes straight toward the lake, passing the new residential outpost of Liberty Village, over the railway tracks and past **Fort York** (see page 12), where the Battle of York was fought during the War of 1812.

At the foot of Strachan there's a nasty intersection with Lakeshore, so cross the street (somehow) and find the **Martin-Goodman Trail** into Coronation Park by looking for the blue and green lines painted on the pavement. Go left on the trail (east) until it spits you out at Queens Quay, where you can continue east for a scenic view of Lake Ontario. When you hit Rees, turn north to cross Lakeshore and check out the **Steam Whistle Brewing** (see page 15) on the right in the roundhouse, a structure designed to house and repair the original steam trains that ran on the tracks through Toronto. Turn right and along Bremner, and on your left you'll see the iconic **CN Tower** (see page 14). Keep going until you hit York Street, just south of your origin at Union Station. **For an easterly route, see page 35.**

beyond the city

You could spend days, even weeks, trying to take in everything that Toronto has to offer. But if you've got the time – and the energy – then there are few places that should be on every visitor's must-see list.

Algonquin Provincial Park

Itchin' to get in touch with your inner Grizzly Adams? While there are countless campgrounds scattered around cottage country north of Toronto, for a true wilderness adventure a trek to Algonquin Provincial Park is in order. Established in 1893, Algonquin is the oldest, and fourth-largest park in Ontario, covering roughly 7,725 square km of wilderness between Georgian Bay and the Ottawa River some three hours north of Toronto. Consisting of deep forests, picturesque hills and valleys, and more than 2,400 glacier-formed lakes and 1,200 km of streams and rivers, Algonquin is popular year-round with both weekend backpackers and seasoned survivalists. Home to a bounty of wildlife, from moose and deer to beaver and black bear to the protected eastern red wolf, it's little wonder the park was popular with artists such as Tom Thomson and the members of the Group of Seven, who drew inspiration from the landscape. There are eleven designated campgrounds along the edges of the park, especially along Highway 60, which runs through the south of the park. It's also possible to camp further inside the park at sites accessible only by canoe or foot (or by ski or snowshoe, in winter). In addition to fishing, mountain biking, horseback riding and cross country skiing, Algonquin is also home to an interpretive centre, logging museum and wildlife-centric **Algonquin Art Centre**, as well as the Natural Heritage Education program, which includes weekly "wolf howls" on Thursdays in the month of August (weather and wolves permitting).

Park staff maintain portages between many of the lakes, and interior campsite reservations must be made through the main Ontario Parks reservation system (888-668-7275).

Kleinburg

An hour north of downtown Toronto, this sleepy village within a city – Kleinburg is an unincorporated community of 900 or so people located within the city of Vaughan – is home to numerous galleries and boutiques, as well as the **Binder Twine Festival** held every fall to celebrate Kleinburg's agricultural history.

But the real reason to visit is the **McMichael Canadian Art Collection**, an ongoing exhibition of Group of Seven landscape paintings and contemporary First Nations and Inuit art, including paintings and sculptures, highlighted by the bold designs of painter Norval Morrisseau.

■ *10365 Islington, Kleinburg, 905-893-1121, www.mcmichael.com.*
Open 10 am-4 pm daily. $15, srs/stu $12, fam $30, child under 12 free.

Niagara Falls

Rarely has the world's natural beauty and humankind's crass sense of commercialism collided so colourfully.

Undoubtedly, Niagara Falls is a natural wonder on the same scale as the Grand Canyon. The sight – and sound – of half-a-billion gallons of water plummeting off a 177-foot cliff every second is truly breathtaking. (Although it's hard to understand why anyone would want to go over the falls

DIANNE DAVIS

in a barrel, as 63-year-old school teacher Annie Taylor, the first to take the plunge, did successfully in 1901.)

The falls, which actually moves upstream about one foot every decade due to erosion, are part of the Niagara River, connecting Lakes Erie and Ontario, and straddling the border between Canada and the United States. There are two bridges in Niagara connecting to the U.S. – Rainbow Bridge and Whirlpool Rapids Bridge – although the best view of the Horseshoe Falls is from the Canadian side.

There are numerous picnic and observation areas above and below the falls, but by far the most impressive is from **Table Rock**, where you can stand on the lip of the falls and watch the water rush by your feet (from the safety of a fenced-in platform, of course).

The nearby Table Rock Complex offers a restaurant, snack bar and souvenir shop as well as Journey Behind the Falls, which takes you behind the falls itself as in Last of the Mohicans, only with yellow rain slickers.

In addition to being the number one tourist destination in Canada, Niagara Falls is also one of the top honeymoon destinations in the world,

with more than its share of heart-shaped hot tubs. Diminutive dictator Napoleon Bonaparte's little bro, Jerome Bonaparte, honeymooned here in 1803.

See the falls properly on the **Maid of the Mist** tour boat (5920 River, 905-358-5781, www.maid-ofthemist.com). The boat takes you right under the falls and we mean it – you get outfitted with a raincoat to protect you from the spray – and the sound of water pounding down is stunning.

The city of Niagara Falls, however, leans rather heavily toward the tacky. Just take a jaunt up **Clifton Hill** (www.cliftonhill.com), which starts from the boat launch for the Maid of the Mist, and you'll pass such family friendly attractions as Ghost Blasters, Mystery Maze, the Movieland Wax Museum of Stars, Ripley's Believe It or Not and a Burger King with a giant green Frankenstein holding a whopper sticking out of its roof. And a little further up the hill is **Casino Niagara** (5705 Falls Avenue, 905-374-3598, www.casinoniagara.com), taking gamblers' money 24 hours a day, 365 days a year. Nearby **Marineland** (7657 Portage, 905-356-9565, www.marinelandcanada.com) is popular with people wanting to get up close and personal with killer whales and dolphins, while the

Enjoy the natural wonder of **Niagara Falls**. Barrel not included.

MICHELE PETERSON

Up the creek at **Algonquin Provincial Park** is never a bad thing. Page 42.

lovely **Niagara Parks Butterfly Conservatory** at the Niagara Parks Botanical Gardens (Niagara Parkway, 905-358-0025, www.niagaraparks.com) offers a similar yet more serene commune with nature.

The whole place would be a total tourist trap if it weren't for the fact that the falls are so damn impressive.

Niagara-on-the-Lake

Tear a vino-soaked page out of Sideways with a tour of the Napa of the North: Niagara-on-the-Lake and its surrounding region.

Located at the base of the Golden Horseshoe that wraps around Lake Ontario from Toronto to Niagara, this area is the grape-stained centre of Canada's wine industry – yes, we drink more than just beer – with over 20 wineries, including Inniskillen, Hillebrand, Jackson-Triggs and Pillitteri, many of which offer tours and tastings (see www.wineriesofniagaraonthelake.com for details).

Of course, there's more to Niagara-on-the-Lake than riesling-fuelled fun. Established in 1792 as the first capital of Upper Canada and later Ontario, this quaint community of Georgian and Victorian-styled buildings along the lake was once the scene of fierce battles with American forces during the War of 1812. Today, tourists can visit **Fort George National Historic Site** (Queen's Parade, 905-468-4257, www.niagara.com/~parkscan) once a British stronghold that now operates as a museum with fully costumed guides. Nearby **Laura Secord Homestead** (29 Queenston, Queenston, 905-262-4851, open mid-May to mid-September) is the home of the War of 1812 heroine who hiked 32 km through enemy lines to warn the British of an impending U.S. invasion.

When not wining and dining (or shopping in one of the many boutiques), many choose to take in a play at the **Shaw Festival** (see **Theatre**, page 155), one of Canada's premier theatre fests (April to December).

Paramount Canada's Wonderland

Ever been to Disneyland? Well, this is kind of like that, only not as big, or as kitschy-cool. But if you want to ride rollercoasters, which is really the only reason anyone over the age of 10 would want to go to Wonderland, this is the top – and pretty much only – spot to get your scream on in the country. More than 200 attractions, 65 rides, including 14 rollercoasters, a 20-acre water park, Hanna-Barbera Land and the Mission Impossible Stunt Spectacular. Need we say more? It's about 45 minutes from downtown Toronto and the Wonderland Express GO buses run regularly from Yorkdale and York Mills subway stations.

■ *9580 Jane, Vaughan, on Highway 400, exit at Rutherford Rd, 905-832-8131.*
Open early May to early October, hours vary throughout the season.
Admission individual season pass $104.57, season pass parking $28.50, 2 or more season passes $82.56 each, regular single day ticket $42.87, $30.73 srs/child.

Toronto Zoo

Home to 5,000 animals representing over 460 species from across the world, including lions and tigers and bears (oh my!), the 710-acre park includes over 10 kilometres of walking trails and eight pavilions. It's divided into six zoogeographic regions: Indo-Malaya, Africa, the Americas, Australasia, Eurasia and the Canadian Domain. Animals live indoors in tropical pavilions and outdoors in naturalistic environments, with viewing at many levels. Be sure not to miss the Gorilla Rainforest, the African Savanna and Discovery Zone, featuring a Kids Zoo, Splash Island and Waterside Theatre.

■ *361A Old Finch, Meadowvale, north of Hwy 401 (Exit #389), Scarborough, 416-392-5929; www.torontozoo.com.*
Open in summer daily 9 am-7:30 pm (winter hours vary; check the website). $19, srs $13, child $11, children 3 and under free.

Wild Water Kingdom

Water-fun theme park with wave pools, water wall and slides, giant hot tubs, bumper boats, batting cages, miniature golf and more.

■ *7855 Finch W, Brampton, 416-369-9453; www.wildwaterkingdom.com.*
Open June-Sept, hours vary, check website. $29, srs/child $21, under 4 free.

food & drink

restaurants

Fine dining might not be the first thing that comes to mind when you think of Toronto. But as the world's most multicultural city, exotic and enticing eats are par for the course, from Indian to Korean to Moroccan to Persian to Chinese to Nepalese. For the latest restaurant reviews, pick up NOW Magazine every week or visit www.nowtoronto.com.

Restaurants

🌐 = NOW Pick

☼ = Patio

Ⓛ = Open Late

		PER PERSON
$	=	$10 & under
$$	=	$11–20
$$$	=	$21–40
$$$$	=	$41–75
$$$$$	=	over $75

Downtown

Baldwin Village

Café

ART SQUARE
334 Dundas W, at McCaul, 416-595-5222.
Compared to the chaos of nearby Chinatown, busy Baldwin Village is an oasis of calm. Part gallery, part creperie, this casually elegant space across from the AGO offers a short card of expertly executed crepes both savoury and sweet. Best: the Blue & Sea crepe, a thin folded and quartered flapjack tiered with shrimp and gently roasted garlic in mild blue cheese cream; others topped with grilled chicken and Mayan organic chocolate, melted mozzarella and assertive garlicky tomato pepper purée or breaded veal parmigiana, both impressively sided with grilled zucchini and eggplant lavishly dressed with quality olive oil; another with smoked salmon and creamy chèvre tossed with raw red onion rings and briny caper berries, accompanied by organic greens in balsamic vinaigrette; for dessert, the Serendipity Aphrodisiac pistachio crepe for two spread with organic honey, bee pollen, ginseng and 30-some other allegedly stimulating herbs and spices as well as splashes of chocolate, sugar-free caramel and edible gold and silver. *Open for breakfast, lunch and dinner. Closed holidays. Unlicensed. Access: four steps at door, washrooms in basement.* $$ ☼

CAFE LA GAFFE
24 Baldwin, at Henry, 416-596-2397.
For foodies of a certain age, this former Kensington Market cantina holds many a fond memory. Since its move a few blocks east, the colourful room has retained its charm and competent kitchen, but the special alchemy that made La Gaffe such a find in the first place is long gone. *Open daily for lunch and dinner. Saturday and Sunday for brunch. Licensed. Access: three steps at door, two and a half to washrooms.* $$$ ☼

MANGIACAKE
**160 McCaul, at Elm, 416-260-5156,
www.mangiacake.ca.**
Housed in a well-worn Victorian, this Milan-inspired panini shoppe offers stylish northern Italian sandwiches sided with terrific soups, dependable salads and first-rate pasta specials. Warning: a laid-back and lovely luncheonette during off-hours, but come lunch its self-serve scene can get chaotic. Best: the eponymous Mangiacake panini piled with smoked turkey, smokier provolone, lettuce, tomato and spicy pesto pipotto sauce on sandwich-pressed calabrese brushed with herbed olive oil; a tribute to Ed Sullivan's favourite singing mouse, the Topo Gigo with melted Brie, sun-dried tomato and arugula on grilled rustic ciabatta; vegetarian calzone stuffed with wilted lettuce, eggplant, plump seedless tomato, bell pepper and lotsa mozzarella; robust daily pasta specials of penne drenched in Parmesan, good olive oil, fresh spinach and red chili-spiked tomato concassé; on the side, nicely executed soups like creamy sweet potato purée or a commendable Caesar salad; at brunch, cheesy zucchini pancakes. *Open for breakfast and lunch. Closed Sunday, holidays. Unlicensed. Access: four steps at door, washrooms on second floor.* $$ ☼

Chinese

EATING GARDEN
43 Baldwin, at Henry, 416-595-5525.
This long-time favourite seafood spot offers the usual two-for-one lobster special, but there's much more on the menu that makes this pleasant place a foodie find. Best: first-rate hot-and-sour soup brimming with shrimp, barbecued pork and pink tofu; meaty steamed Atlantic salmon in black bean sauce; shredded filet mignon in crisp bird-nest basket; retro egg foo yong frittata with veggies or shrimp; whole shrimp and sweet dwarf banana spring roll. Delivery, too. *Open for lunch and dinner. Licensed. Access: seven steps at door, washrooms on same floor.* $$$

YUNG SING PASTRY
22 Baldwin, at McCaul, 416-979-2832.
Although some crowd around its small stand-up counter just inside the door, when weather permits most of this perennially popular Chinese bakery's customers make a beeline for the picnic tables on its makeshift curbside terrace out front. Bonus: weekend-only dim sum! Best: favourites since the 70s, baked buns stuffed with savouries like curried beef, sweet 'n' sticky barbecued pork or chicken with crunchy bamboo shoots; braised bean-curd rolls loaded with minced seafood; earnest vegetarian

Asian Legend brings a touch of cool to neon-bright Chinatown. Page 48.

spring rolls and chow mein; rice-papered wraps filled with shredded shrimp, snow peas, scallions and Chinese celery dressed with chopped garlic; on the weekend, translucent har gow modestly brimming with sizable shrimp or tiny pinched pork siu mai knotted with red chili. *Open for lunch and dinner. Closed Monday. Unlicensed. Cash only. Access: barrier-free, no washrooms.* **$** ⁛

Indian

JODHPORE CLUB
33 Baldwin, at Henry, 416-598-2502.
Located in a Spartan space that once housed a hippie sandal shop, man, this small 30-seat chaotically decorated room gets packed out for its wallet-friendly weekday $8.99 Subcontinental lunch buffet. After dark, the kitchen turns up the heat on reasonably priced and assertively spiced northern and western Indian fare. Best: from the à la carte lineup, oven-grilled Pudhina lamb chops Kabuli-style slathered in yogurt-mint purée; splayed Hyderbadi baingan, baby eggplant simmered in a tomato-onion-ginger reduction zapped with licorice-like fennel seeds; tandoor-charred vegetable paneer tikka, freshly made cheese cubes skewered alongside onion, cauliflower and sweet bell pepper; Portuguese-inspired Goan fish curry, sole fillets steamed in banana leaves, topped with rich tamarind 'n' coconut sauce; from the lunch buffet, buttery chicken korma and moist tandoori chicken; rogan josh, slow-stewed lamb on the bone in delicious cinnamon and shallot gravy; rib-sticking yellow lentil dahl and puréed eggplant with green peas worthy of second trips; for dessert, warm seviyam vermicelli pudding sweetened with milk and soured with whole cardamom seeds. *Open for lunch and dinner. Licensed. Access: two steps at door, washrooms on same floor.* **$$$** ⁛

Pan-Asian

MATAHARI
39 Baldwin, at Henry, 416-596-2832,
www.mataharigrill.com.
Once the only exclusively Malaysian spot in town, this intimate bistro on downtown's busiest restaurant row is all dark hardwood floors, long green UltraSuede banquettes and blinding white walls embellished with inspiring messages like, "The heart is wiser than the intellect." Possibly so, but the menu remains a mix of Malay, Thai, Indian and Chinese flavours. Best: to start, addictive Shrimp Wonton with spicy peanut dip; achar-achar, a fiery salad of lightly pickled cabbage, green beans, carrot, and pineapple; Eggplant Malay, grilled Asian eggplant with garlic, shallot, and fermented shrimp cake on a banana leaf, sided with English cuke and orange slices; mains like slow-cooked Malaysian Rendang Beef in garlicky coconut gravy; Char Kway Teow, wide shredded rice noodles with grilled shrimp, garlic chives, bean sprouts, sweet molasses kicip, and sambal oelek garlic-chili sauce. *Open for dinner. Tuesday to Friday for lunch. Closed Monday, holidays. Licensed. Access: barrier-free, washrooms in basement.* **$$$** ⁛

Turkish
BALKAN BISTRO
126E McCaul, at Dundas, 416-913-0729.
This cheerful, unassuming boîte near the AGO and Baldwin Village offers an eastern Mediterranean menu that stretches from southern Italy to Turkey with stops in between. Nothing to get celeb chef Susur piqued – instead, straightforward plentifully portioned and modestly priced Old World mains and panini combos. Best: Hunkar Begendi, a slow-cooked Ottoman-style veal-and-tomato stew over creamed eggplant, sided, like most entrees, with roasted potato and grilled eggplant, bell pepper and broccoli; sizzling weiner schnitzel, a massive pounded veal steak in light, crisp batter; traditional eastern Turkish ground beef 'n' rice Kadinbudu Köfte – Ladies' Thighs Meatballs (!) – in eggy batter or plain, wrapped in thin ribbons of Italian eggplant; simple but tasty olive-oil-and butter-drizzled rotini tossed with grilled veggies and nutty basil pesto; thick slices of sautéed eggplant Parmesan in smoky cheese sauce. *Open for breakfast, lunch and dinner. Closed holidays. Licensed. Access: half-step at door, washrooms in basement.* **$$**

Vegetarian
VEGETARIAN HAVEN
17 Baldwin, at McCaul, 416-621-3636,
www.vegetarianhaven.com
Relocated from Etobicoke to Toronto's alterna-restaurant row, this pleasant generic bistro – narrow mirrored room, exposed brick, jazz Muzak – specializes in the kind of hippie vegan health food that first blossomed with flower power. When this earnest kitchen rises above that era's stereotypical brown rice and lentil cliché, the results are often nutritious if not that delicious. Warning: bring your own garlic. Best: starters like tofu faux turkey drumsticks complete with sugar cane handles, or Fried Crispy Tofu tossed with sesame seeds, both dunked in atomic red sweet 'n' sour sauce; charbroiled organic tofu burger topped with grilled bell pepper on a whole wheat bun plated with blue corn chips and fire-free kimchee-style cabbage salsa; loosely wrapped Thai Garden Rolls in raw rice paper stuffed with vermicelli, soy-marinated tofu, bean sprouts and mint; such seasonal soups as silky tofu in hearty vegetable stock swimming with pureed cauliflower, carrot and potato; humongous meal-in-one Souper Bowl noodle soups in very good broth with Chinese veggies, slurpable rice noodles, baby bok choy and faux pastrami that tastes just like the real thing. *Open for lunch and dinner. Closed holidays. Unlicensed. Access: two steps at door, washrooms in basement.* **$$$** ☺

Chinatown
Chinese
ASIAN LEGEND
418 Dundas W, at Beverley, 416-977-3909.
A downtown outpost of the suburban northern Chinese chain, this modish, elegantly appointed space is easily Chinatown's most deluxe digs. Lacking the contrasts of Cantonese or the heat of Szechuan, Legend's soothing Old World northern Chinese grub delivers home-cooking-style comfort, not fireworks. Bonus: all day every day dim sum till close. Braised ducks' tongues, anyone? Best: crisp pan-fried House Special Crispy Pancake stuffed with shredded shrimp, Chinese chives and scallions, or Onion Pancake Roll layered with lightly five-spiced beef; soup dumpling purses bursting with broth and minced shrimp; velvety deep-fried tofu sided with crushed marinated garlic and fiery red chili sauce; barely spiced Chinese meatballs with bamboo shoots. *Open for breakfast, lunch and dinner. Licensed. Access: 11 steps at door, washrooms in basement.* **$$$** ☺

BRIGHT PEARL
346-48 Spadina, at St. Andrew, 416-979-3988,
www.brightpearlseafood.com.
This cavernous second-storey banquet hall in one of the most garish buildings on the avenue offers old-school dim sum served from carts pushed by staff in green aprons. Point and it's yours. Bonus: deep dim sum discounts after 1:30 pm weekdays. Warning: come early or reserve unless you want to stand in what seems like an endless queue. Best: from the dim sum cart, feather-light steamed shrimp siu mai and wonton-wrapped minced pork topped with fish roe; plump pan-fried pork dumplings with sweet dipping sauce; crisply pan-fried squares of smooth daikon and taro cake; steamed rice noodle stuffed with shrimp; steamed snow pea shoots; steamed beef short ribs in starchy black bean gravy; bundles of sticky rice wrapped in lotus leaf. *Open for breakfast, lunch and dinner. Licensed. Access: barrier-free.* **$$**

⬤ CHINESE TRADITIONAL BUNS
536 Dundas W, at Kensington, 416-299-9011.
Featuring the street snacks of northeastern China, this subterranean snack shack downstairs from Sang Ho offers explosive light bites and full-course feasts. Bare-bones, fluorescent-lit, plastic-on-the-table decor gives way to smiling chef Jin Linda Liu's spectacular grub. Her fiery food doesn't just pick you up, it levitates you, then knocks you across the room! Best: although listed as a drink, think of Jellied Bean Curd as an ethereal tofu soup slammed with chili oil, raw garlic, salty dried shrimp, crunchy preserved vegetable pickle and fresh coriander leaf; cold noodles lashed with nutty tahini-esque sesame paste, sweet black rice vinegar and crisp scallion rings; lengths of cool Asian eggplant doused with sesame-oiled garlic chili; a Sino salad of smoky sweet pork belly and contrasting cucumber crunch; sides like deceptive-looking assorted vegetables – cellophane threads, slivered carrot and daikon – in blow-your-head-off mustard oil, or sweet-and-sour radish with Thai chilies, or Tianjin-style steamed buns stuffed with pork, raw ginger and green onions, dipped in chili oil, vinegar and sweet garlic sauces. *Open for breakfast, lunch and dinner. Unlicensed. Cash only. Access: 12 steps at door, washrooms on same floor.* **$**

GOLDEN LEAF
307 Spadina, at Dundas W, 416-597-1000,
www.goldenleaf.sites.toronto.com.
Slightly low-rent sibling of King's Garden in the Theatah District brings fancy digs and a mainstream if somewhat pricey Chinese card to the avenue of plastic table linen. Nearby Lee Garden should watch its back, cuz once this spot catches on with Toronto Lite readers, Lee's legendary lineups will dwindle *Open for breakfast, lunch and dinner. Unlicensed. Access: two steps at door and tight tables.* **$$**

GOLDSTONE NOODLE
266 Spadina, at Dundas, 416-596-9053.
Chinatown's most popular noodle joint jumps from early morning till well into the morning of the next day. Rock-bottom prices and a 400-plus Cantonese card guarantee a full house, but remember to KISS – keep it simple, sinophile. Best: from the window display, barbecued meat – non-fatty five-spiced duck, succulent pork and tender goose – over al dente mein and barely cooked greens in grease-free chicken broth; Soya Sauce Chicken, an alarmingly moist whole steamed bird with mild black bean gravy and incendiary raw garlic 'n' chive accompaniment; 20-some Shrimp Szechuan Style with sweet green bell pepper; seriously tasty pounded, peppered and pan-fried Steak with Spaghetti Hong Kong Style (really!). *Open for breakfast, lunch and dinner. Bar till close. Licensed. Access: barrier-free, but crowded space, washrooms in basement.* **$$**

HAPPY SEVEN
358 Spadina, at Cecil, 416-971-9820.
An unofficial offshoot of Swatow (see page 51), this Cantonese seafood haven is one of several Chinatown spots that stays open every night till 5 am. Nighthawks can expect a bright, mirror-lined room furnished with high-backed chairs and polyethylene-topped tables. Warning: before ordering, make sure to ask for both menus: the white offers standard Spadina fare, the pink far tastier stuff. Best: aquarium-fresh tilapia with fermented black bean sauce; zaftig sea scallops in deep-fried taro nest on a bed of decorative kale and edible broccoli 'n' shrooms; as veggie sides, stir-fried stalks of Chinese broccoli or garden-fresh Malaysian-style tung choi rich with oyster sauce; definitive hot-and-sour soup chockablock with fermented red tofu, crunchy lily buds and textured slivers of silver and black tree ear mushrooms; for the adventurous, honey-skinned mahogany-fleshed fried pigeon, French Southeast-Asian-style deep-fried frog legs, or stir-fried chicken with apple. *Open for breakfast, lunch and dinner. Licensed. Access: barrier-free, washrooms in basement.* **$$$** ⏱

HOUSE OF GOURMET
484 Dundas W, at Spadina, 416-217-0167.
Ever wondered about the mysterious dishes written in Cantonese on the walls of Chinese restaurants? This brightly lit space in Chinatown answers those questions with its 700-odd-item menu that goes from bacon 'n' egg sandwiches served with Ovaltine to Deep Fried Crispy Intestines downed with Grass Jelly. Best: crispy chow mein House Special Fried Noodle with barbecue pork, sliced scallops, chicken chunks, squid, shrimp, baby bok choy and 'shrooms; all-day breakfast congee with chicken and mushrooms, garnished with scallions and kicked with hoisin and sesame paste; Beef Tenderloin with Black Pepper Sauce; retro Chop Suey and Moo Shu Pork; Shrimp with Thai Chili and Peanut; scrambled-egg-like Crispy Milk Special Style with shredded seafood. *Open for breakfast, lunch and dinner. Licensed. Access: four steps at door, washrooms in basement.* **$$** ⏱

JING PEKING
404 College, at Lippincott, 416-929-5691.
Although its decor won't win any design awards (fluorescent-lit ceiling tiles hung with plastic vines, sheets of white polypropylene on the tables, past-it carpeting underfoot), Jing Peking has much to celebrate: an extensive Szechuan and northern Chinese card containing some of the cheapest grub in town. Tasty, too. Bonus: daily all-day dim sum. Best: Braised Spicy String Bean, twice-cooked Szechuan-style long beans stir-fried with minced pork; electric purple Asian eggplant and ground pork in garlicky chili sauce; sweet 'n' fiery slow-roasted Sliced Pork Doubly Sauteed in Chili Sauce; Premier's Beef (or chicken, shrimp, scallops or squid) in peppery soy gravy tossed with roasted peanuts; bountiful Cantonese noodles; from the dim sum lineup, pan-fried pork potstickers, soup-filled dumplings, onion-flavoured biscuit and House Special Crispy Pancake with scallions. *Open for breakfast, lunch and dinner. Licensed. Access: one step at door, washrooms in basement.* **$$$**

KIM HOA
332 Spadina, at Glen Baillie, 416-971-9719.
Old-school Cantonese cuisine with Szechuan specialties in new-style Spadina digs: friendly staff; bright,

Chinatown's most-popular noodle joint, **Goldstone**. Page 48.

clean and stylish decor; extensive menu and a large selection of in-house barbecue. Best: to start, Kiwi-style mussels or snails in Thai peanut sauce; sublime hot-and-sour soup studded with whole shrimp, tofu, carrot and green pepper julienne; myriad noodles in house broth topped with duck or pork; massively portioned Cantonese chow mein thick with roasted pig, squid, shrimp, beef tenderloin, baby corn, straw mushroom, snow peas, water chestnut and broccoli; Szechuan Kung Pau jumbo shrimp or sweet black cod in garlicky soy; schnitzel-style crispy chicken with minced seafood, sided with pickled scallions 'n' garlic purée. *Open for breakfast, lunch and dinner. Licensed. Access: barrier-free, washrooms in basement.* **$$$** ⓘ

◈ KING'S NOODLE
296 Spadina, at Dundas, 416-598-1817.
This long-standing Spadina shop is all gleaming glass and dark wood, although the stadium-bright lighting, communal tables and chaotic atmosphere remain. Barbecued meat dangling in the window and big bowls of noodle soup are the foundations of King's culinary house. Bonus: two menus and an additional specials list lets you go deep into the Cantonese repertoire. Best: barbecued duck and wonton noodle soup, a balanced bowl of shimmering broth, sweet tender duck, translucent shrimp-stuffed wontons and luminous bok choy in a mass of noodles; Salt-and-Pepper King Mushroom, Tofu and Pork Chops, a lightly battered plate of various textures spiked by aggressive Cantonese seasoning; barbecued pork with steamed noodles bold with ginger and green onion; perfectly wokked sautéed pea shoots with garlic. *Open for breakfast, lunch and dinner. Licensed. Access: barrier-free, but washrooms in basement.* **$$**

MR. GREENJEANS
Restaurant • Lounge • Bar
Toronto Eaton Centre

Tel: 416 979-1212 • www.mrgreenjeans.ca

LEE GARDEN
331 Spadina, at Baldwin, 416-593-9524.
Count on a half-hour wait at the door for a table at this beloved restaurant. For the area, Lee's is a rather formal joint – three rows of tables for four, and carpeting! As usual, order off the specials listed on bristol-board placards: minced quail in a lettuce wrap, stir-fried sliced pickerel, sticky rice with Chinese sausage, garlic shrimp served in a hollowed-out pineapple. A neon sign in the window announces that there's no MSG in anything. *Open for lunch and dinner. Licensed. Access: One step at door, washrooms in basement.* **$$$$**

NEW HO KING
416 Spadina, at Nassau, 416-595-1881.
Late-night Cantonese spot with friendly service, better than average decor and lower than usual prices. Best: spicy Hunan Beef, pounded meat with al dente green pepper and onion; Moo-Shu Vegetables with Pancake, a pile of shredded napa cabbage, onion and mushrooms to be folded into crepes along with raw scallion, English cuke and a squirt of hoisin; Dry Sautéed String Beans Szechuan-Style, the dish that made nearby Peter's Chung King famous back in the 70s; Ho King's Special Fried Rice, a humongous serving of short-grain strewn with baby shrimp, barbecued pork, fluffy scrambled egg and forgivable frozen corn. *Open for breakfast, lunch and dinner. Licensed. Access: one step at door, washrooms in basement.* **$$** ⓘ

PETER'S CHUNG KING
281 College, at Spadina, 416-928-2936.
When flame-thrower-strength Thai food swept through town 20 years ago, Szechuan cooking seemed tame in comparison. But this austere room – grey carpet, beige walls, ceiling fans, linen-topped tables – continues to fly the flag for the incendiary south-central Chinese cuisine that's been popular locally since the 70s. It's not you: indifferent-to-hostile staff continue to give everyone the same cold shoulder. Bonus: autographed photo thumbs-up from Chris "Lady In Red" DeBurgh as well as Sharon, Lois and Bram in the front window! Best: house Special Noodle, thick lo mein in slick, sweet soy and a kitchen sink of fixin's – beef, chicken, barbecued pork, cocktail shrimp, water chestnut and strips of raw scallion; twice-cooked dry-sautéed long green beans with stir-fried minced pork; puréed garlicky Asian eggplant mixed with finely diced bamboo shoots; not particularly fiery but definitely vinegary hot 'n' sour soup thick with bamboo shoots, bean sprouts, cubed tofu and oyster mushrooms. *Open for lunch and dinner. Licensed. Access: one step at door, washrooms in basement.* **$$$** ⓘ

ROL SAN
323 Spadina, at St. Andrew, 416-977-1128.
Retro Cantonese cuisine in a pleasant space a notch above the usual for the nabe. But don't get stuck in the front room with the tourists and first-timers. Past an open kitchen, a second more spacious room reminiscent of an 80s Hong Kong disco handles the overflow for all-day dim sum. Gruff, indifferent service. Warning: count on a wait at the door especially once the bars close. Best: from the dim sum card, pan-fried turnip or scallion pancakes; deep fried battered shrimp with Miracle Whip (really!); multi-textured soup dumplings stuffed with shrimp and mushroom in briny broth; beancurd skin wrapped around minced pork in oyster sauce; sticky rice in lotus leaf; shrimp har gow; deep-fried shrimp with chive cake; beef short ribs in black bean sauce; from the regular menu, steamed live sea bass in black bean sauce; ground pork with Chinese long bean. *Open for lunch and dinner. Licensed. Access: barrier-free.* **$$$** ⓘ

Ask for both menus at **Happy Seven**. Page 49.

SANG HO
536 Dundas W, at Spadina, 416-596-1685.
Don't even think of getting a dinnertime table on the weekend at this spotless Cantonese seafood stalwart unless you want to join regulars enduring a lengthy wait on the steps out front. The lure: crystal-clear aquariums holding live shrimp and tilapia just waiting to be doused in garlic 'n' black bean sauce. And like most everywhere in Chinatown, the best stuff is advertised on signs announcing house specialties. Best: straight-from-the-tank shrimp complete with flavour-rich shells, antennae, beady-eyed heads, furry legs and tails garnished with spring onions and garlic; tilapia or red snapper gingerly steamed, then deboned tableside and served with a light garlicky black bean sauce; off-the-wall-menu razor clams, mussels and snails in a thicker black bean sauce; mango chicken with carrot in five-spice; Lo Hun Bean Cake Hot Pot – one of only a few strictly vegetarian options – brimming with Chinese greens, baby corn and cloud ears, a satisfying meal by itself; inexpensive meat 'n' veg with rice lunch specials, too. *Open for lunch and dinner. Licensed. Access: seven steps at door, washrooms on same floor.* **$$$** ⓘ

SWATOW
309 Spadina, at Dundas W, 416-977-0601.
Steaming bowls of mein in soup rule at this no-nonsense noodle house named for the province in eastern China. Traditionally less fiery than the well-known Szechuan, dishes here are consistently well executed and generous, the menu's extensive, and extended weekend hours accommodate both insomniacs and clubbers alike. Warning: lineups at peak hours, especially Friday and Saturday nights. Best: namesake Special Fried Noodle, wide rice noodles in a smoky syrupy sauce studded with shrimp and chicken, dressed with raw scallions and sprouts; Shrimp Dumpling Soup, six plump dumplings filled with shrimp, ginger, green onions and shredded black fungus in a clear broth with a fragrant sesame oil finish, paired with Chinese broccoli; Swatow Roasted Duck with Special Sauce, crackling duck breast off the bone cut into 12 sizable pieces served on a bed of canned pineapple chunks, sided with six inflated shrimp chips and thinned plum sauce; Fried Noodles with Beef and Black Bean Sauce, a heaping portion of vermicelli tossed with slivers of tender beef, green pepper 'n' onion chunks in black bean sauce; incendiary chili sauce to garnish. *Open for lunch and dinner. Unlicensed. Cash only. Access: one step at door, washrooms in basement.* **$$** ⓘ

⚙ XAM YU
339 Spadina, at Baldwin, 416-340-8603.
Want proof of the popularity of chef Ken Fong's card of Cantonese-style seafood? The entire Cantonese

catalogue is translated into Vietnamese as well as English. Posher looking than most but still reasonably priced, this friendly family-run eatery attracts everyone from superstar chef Susur Lee to the local cops on the beat. Best: to begin, jumbo broiled oysters with gingery scallions or salty black bean garnish; for the gang, steamed Vancouver crab over perfect shrimp fried rice wrapped in aromatic lotus leaf; super two-for-one deep-fried lobster served two ways; generously plated Seafood Fried Egg Noodle — Cantonese Chow Mein, to most — with grilled shrimp, calamari and mussels; boneless chicken breast with fresh mango; a few veggie choices like guy choy with whole garlic; deer meat with XO sauce, and frog legs, too. *Open for lunch and dinner. Licensed. Delivery. Access: one step at door, washrooms in basement.* **$$$** ⓘ

Chinese Vegetarian
BUDDHA'S VEGETARIAN FOODS
666 Dundas W, at Denison, 416-603-3811.
Possibly the bleakest eatery in town – think Beijing, 1957 – this austere white and grim grey room comes staffed by smiling servers in green smocks. Despite its satanic address, the sterile space decorated with only an incense-burning shrine to the Buddha and some travel posters slings sizable Chinese-style veggie noshes on Pyrex pie plates that are nutrition-conscious and consciousness-raising. Best: three kinds of mushrooms – meaty 3-inch Chinese, slivered button and whole straw – show up alongside Chinese broccoli and carrot, mixed with thick rice noodles, in veggie broth alongside rubbery hair seaweed and with Asian greens and wheat noodles; toasted cashews add crunch to a stir-fry of pressed tofu, celery, bamboo shoots, water chestnuts, red pepper, baby corn and fresh garden peas; greasy-good deep-fried spring rolls and burrito-sized bean-curd-skin rolls stuffed with bamboo shoots, wood ear fungus and carrot; deep-fried wontons wrapped with gluten and dipped into old-school sweet 'n' sour sauce. *Open for lunch and dinner. Closed Tuesday, Christmas. Unlicensed. Cash only. Access: three steps at door, washrooms in basement.* **$**

Japanese
EDO NOODLE HOUSE
374 Spadina, at Baldwin, 416-597-1610.
No relation to the 43 similarly named eateries in town, this bright modern space was the first to bring something new to Spadina – sushi! Count on introductory bento combos, the requisite sashimi roundup and a more-skilled-than-most chef. Sleek decor, student friendly prices. Best: tempura shrimp bento combo of flavourful blond miso soup, exquisitely carved carrot, purple cabbage 'n' wakame salad with psychedelic pickles, three delicately battered tiger shrimp and sweet potato as well as thimble-sized veggie maki, minced chicken gyoza and barley tea; starters like panko-crusted deep-fried soft-shell crab or golden sushi pizza topped with tobiko and nori strips; Yaki Nasu, broiled eggplant dusted with bonito flakes; Kaki Age, tempura-battered oysters; the Spadina roll, a spiral of sticky rice lashed with coral roe, English cuke, ersatz crab and miniature egg roll. *Open for lunch and dinner. Licensed. Access: two steps at door, washrooms in basement.* **$$**

SIMON SUSHI
409 Spadina, at College, 416-977-2828.
Does downtown really need another cheap sushi joint? The answer's emphatically "yes" if owner Simon Au is wielding the knives at this remarkably chic spot (well, considering the neighbourhood) offering skillfully executed and amply portioned seafood-dominated mains. Attentive service varies in fluency. Bonus: $5.99 lunch combos! Best: the massive Sushi

A quiet evening in **Chinatown**.

Bento Box Special starts with regulation miso soup and freezing iceberg salad, follows with a six-pack of nigiri, a slab of teriyaki chicken, tail-on-shrimp and veggie tempura, minced beef gyoza, stir-fried carrot and sticky rice; the house chirashi set, a generous trawl through the day's freshest fish; stir-fried beef udon noodle with sesame beef and broccoli; cucumber salad roll, ribbons of English cuke wrapped around avocado and faux crab dolloped with miso mayo. *Open for lunch and dinner. Licensed. Delivery. Access: one step at door, washrooms in basement.* **$$**

Vegetarian

CAFÉ 668
**668 Dundas W, at Denison,
416-703-0668, www.cafe668.com.**
Named NOW's 2002 best new restaurant regardless of genre, this modestly decorated 20-seat storefront continues to deliver innovative pan-Asian vegetarian fare that's not only healthful but damned tasty, too. Self-taught chef Ngoc Lam draws on her Southeast Asian heritage for a unique spin on Vietnamese, Thai and Chinese vegetarian cuisine that travels far beyond its Buddhist roots, especially when she gooses the garlic. Best: to start, 668 Salad with shredded deep-fried tofu, cucumber, carrot, peppers and grilled cashews, or cold rice-paper-wrapped Summer Rolls stuffed with slivers of deep-fried tofu, carrot, cellophane noodles, wood ear and Thai basil; king mushrooms with faux sirloin over stir-fried mixed peppers, snow peas and baby corn in satay; Spicy Tofu – large cubes of silky-centred deep-fried tofu in a chili-spiked coconut cream thick with julienned carrots, bell peppers and snow peas; Vegetarian Curry with tofu "pork," carrots, chewy Chinese mushrooms, cauliflower and napa cabbage in tasty yellow gravy; for dessert, deep-fried bananas in yummy coconut cream. *Open for lunch and dinner. Closed Monday, some holidays. Unlicensed. Cash only. Access: two steps at door, washrooms on same floor.* **$$**

Vietnamese

KIM ASIAN CUISINE
6 St. Andrew, at Spadina, 416-977-9922.
Situated just a few doors west of the popular Pho Hung (see next listing), this Viet-Thai restaurant could easily survive on its neighbour's overflow. Yet Kim's is a destination in its own right and deserves to thrive as such. Pleasant staff serve delicate Vietnamese dishes with spicy Thai accents amid spotless, comfortable decor. The house special of fish in seven dishes for two ($28.95) is an excellent way to get acquainted. Bonus: $3.50 Tsingtao! Best: Sweet and Sour Fish Soup, a light broth with large pieces of mild fish, pineapple chunks, celery, Chinese chives, bean sprouts and tomato; Mango Fish Salad, a mound of finely shredded young mango with red and green peppers, cashews and red onion sprinkled with tiny dried fish, the crunchy equivalent of bacon bits; cold spring rolls bursting with Thai basil, barbecued fish and more tart mango; puffy shrimp chips topped with rice noodles, lightly fried unidentified fish, red roe and chopped peanuts; Thai-style red curry with coconut milk, snap peas and that same white fish with plain vermicelli on the side. *Open for breakfast, lunch and dinner. Licensed. Access: seven steps at door, washrooms in basement.* **$$**

PHO HUNG
**350 Spadina, at St. Andrew, 416-593-4274,
other locations.**
Toronto's mad for pho, the brilliant soup-that-eats-like-a-meal that perfectly showcases the complex cuisine of Vietnam, and the Hung does it better than most. True foodies will dig the weird stuff. Best: thin strips of lean sirloin cooked two ways – rare and well

Foodie friend **Pho Hung**.

done – in fragrant lemongrass-scented broth swimming with slippery rice noodles and garnished with crushed peanuts and mint leaf; Saigon-style escargot – snail vermicelli soup in spicier-than-most broth; grilled quail "roti" on fresh greens; cold spring rolls studded with pink shrimp and satay pork; beware curried eel in coconut sauce. *Open for breakfast, lunch and dinner. Licensed. Access: Spadina barrier-free, washrooms in basement; Bloor: 25 steps, washrooms on same floor.* **$$**

Clubland

Burritos

BURRITO BOYZ
120 Peter, at Richmond, 416-593-9191.
This tiny subterranean take-away in the heart of Clubland has inspired not only several copycat competitors but a second and much larger operation at Adelaide and Simcoe complete with first-time tables 'n' chairs. But fear not, hungry office drones and late-night party people – the Boyz' distinctive San Francisco Mission-style burritos remain as remarkable as ever. Bonus: Friday and Saturday the sombrero-outfitted joints stays open till 4 am! Best: hefty 10- and 7-inch grilled flour tortillas stuffed with tasty strips of grilled chicken, steak or battered halibut as well as creamy tomato rice, smooth refried beans, melted Monterey Jack and optional submarine-shop toppings like spice-spiked mayo, guacamole, chopped iceberg lettuce, ripe tomato and hellaciously hot jalapeños; and if that's not fiery enough, intensify the heat with the Boyz' off-the-Scoville-scale habanero hot sauce. *Open for lunch and dinner. Unlicensed. Access: six steps at door, washrooms on same floor.* **$** ⓘ

Diner

EAT ME
504 Adelaide W, at Portland, 416-703-3669.
Downtown's greasiest spoon is a diner with a difference – its all-day menu rocks from early in the morning till 5 am Friday and Saturday nights. Best: the house burgers, a beefy ground chuck patty, or grilled 'shrooms, eggplant and zucchini, properly topped with ripe tomato, a solitary raw red onion ring and a handful of mesclun, upgraded for a buck with either melted cheddar or crunchy bacon, sided like most mains with serviceable fries and/or designer greens in balsamic vinaigrette; burrito-style wraps stuffed with fajita-style strips of sirloin, more portobellos and sour cream; straightforward pasta specials and very good daily soups. *Open for breakfast and lunch. Closed Saturday, Sunday and holidays. Unlicensed. Access: one step at door, another to washrooms.* **$**

Spanish

CAYO COCO
304 Richmond W, at John, 416-593-9000,
www.clubcayococo.com.
A cozy converted Victorian in the heart of clubland, this darkly romantic Spanish cantina offers a modestly priced 40-item tapas menu from lunch until very late in the evening, 3 am on Friday and Saturday. While some items verge on cocktail-party canapés, most are robustly flavoured and a perfect accompaniment to a long night's drinking. Bonus: 2-ounce martinis are $3.99 Thursday and $4.50 Sunday. Best: pink-centred lamb chops in a luscious lemony sauce sweetened with pineapple chunks and Spanish paprika; Papas à la Diabla, spicy spuds in garlicky tomato sauce; emerald-hued spinach tossed with toasted pine nuts, sultanas and cracked black peppercorns; Homestyle Meatballs, meaty ground beef nuggets in red wine gravy, topped with sliced almonds; silken Spanish omelette layered with potato and onion; stuffed mussels on the shell draped with tomato, molten mozzarella and sweet mango purée. *Open for lunch and dinner. Closed holidays. Licensed. Access: six steps at door, 18 steps to second-floor dining room, washrooms on first floor.* **$$$** ⋮ ⊙

Downtown

Café

AVENUE CAFE & BISTRO
480 University, at Dundas W, 416-979-0500,
www.avenuecafe.ca.
Although there's little original about this swanky yet reasonably priced lunch 'n' brunch spot – think MBCo if it came to its Senses – it offers an impressive setting and often deftly executed sandwich-and-salad combos for less than 10 bucks. Warning: a potential zoo at noon hour. Best: huge, incredibly fresh sandwiches like roasted salmon salad on grilled Ace Bakery black-olive sourdough, sided with a crisp

Greek salad of mostly sweet bell pepper and crumbly feta, or shaved rare roast beef with caramelized onion and horseradish with house-made slaw; the Classic, an exemplary Patachou croissant piled with ripe Roma tomato, Black Forest ham and Brie with marinated fruit salad; egg-white omelettes stuffed with spinach and ricotta, served with grilled and olive-oiled Ace whole wheat baguette. *Open for breakfast and lunch. Closed Saturday, Sunday and holidays. Unlicensed. Access: barrier-free.* **$** ⋮

B ESPRESSO BAR
111 Queen E, at Mutual, 416-866-2111,
www.bespressobar.com.
With its ultra-chic Cecconi Simone design, this Milan-inspired coffee house turns a once dreary east-side stretch into downtown's hippest zone. The food's not bad either. Best: dense slices of chocolate jalapeño loaf, chocolate Tuscan-style brownies and chocolate cherry squares; super salads like roasted pear with bitter frissée and toasted walnuts or crostini splashed with olive oil, or fresh basil with ripe Roma tomatoes; rustic sandwiches like the Crudo with prosciutto, bocconcini, arugula pesto and truffle oil, and the Catullo, with chicken breast, thick lengths of grilled zucchini and mild fontina. *Open for breakfast and lunch. Closed Sunday, holidays. Licensed. Access: four steps at door, washrooms on same floor.* **$**

⟱ MORNING GLORY
457 King E, at Gilead Place,
416-703-4728, www.morningglory.ca.
The unofficial offshoot of Aunties and Uncles (see page 70) offers a similar all-day breakfast slash soup 'n' sandwich lineup but focuses more on the first meal of the day. Quality ingredients and first-class attention to detail make this diminutive diner the biggest thing to hit Corktown since the Great Fire of 1904. Bonus: read all about MG's daily specials – as well as the off-the-wall ruminations of its staff – at www.morningglory.ca/news.html. Best: on pre-proofed house-baked breads, regular sandwiches like sweet tuna salad with tart green apple on ciabatta, or Bavarian-style Mennonite ham and sharp cheddar on chewy baguette, or one-offs such as curried chicken breast on Italian roll; Asian-inspired soups like spicy squash purée with crushed Szechuan peppercorns, or complex lentil with lime; whopping omelettes wrapped around havarti 'n' leak or Brie paired with pear; more than competent cappuccino and retro raspberry crumble. *Open for breakfast and lunch. Closed Wednesday. Unlicensed. Cash only. Access: two steps at door, washrooms in basement.* **$$** ⋮

PETITE MARCHE
33 University, at Wellington W, 416-955-0302.
Claustrophobic coffee 'n' sandwich shop in the core. Lots of organic options and dirt cheap, but fast food this ain't – bring a magazine. Bonus: Wi-Fi! Best: thick slices of owner Rosemary Gallagher's Friday's-only old-school but non-organic pot roast in soy-accented jus sided with roasted potatoes and big green salad; Thursday-only meatloaf; inexpensive maki Mondays; beefy and cheesy rigatoni casserole à la Chef Boyardee; low-carb breakfasts like three eggs, organic bacon or sausage, fruit salad and thin whole-wheat toast; grilled organic veggie wraps; hefty daily sandwich specials like smoked turkey with Provolone on dark rye sided with raw carrot sticks. *Open for breakfast and lunch. Closed Saturday, Sunday. Unlicensed. Access: barrier-free, but tight space and tall counters, no washrooms.* **$**

Caribbean

COCONUT GROVE
183 Dundas W, at Chestnut, 416-348-8887.
This fixture is good but nothing fancy: place your order at the counter and grab a table, or hightail it to

Morning Glory is the hottest thing to hit Corktown since the Great Fire of 1904. Page 54.

a nearby park bench. Some of the cheapest global eats in the downtown core! Bonus: $2.50 lunch and dinner specials. Best: authentic curry-gravied rotis like cabbage, carrot with potato, or eggplant and spinach; jerk chicken dinners with rice 'n' peas, minimal salad and a free pop. *Open for breakfast and lunch. Closed on the weekend. Unlicensed. Access: one step at door, washrooms in basement.* **$**

Chinese

 LAI WAH HEEN
108 Chestnut, at Dundas W, Metropolitan Hotel, 416-977-9899, www.metropolitan.com/lwh.
Considered one of Toronto's top Chinese restaurants since the day it opened more than 10 years ago, this luxe hotel eatery is certainly one of the most lavish, all blond wood, beige walls, deep carpets, formally attired servers and not a plastic tablecloth in sight. Chef Terence Chan's pricey Hong Kong card can be equally over the top, a far cry from his low-rent Chinatown competition. Best: from the dim sum line-up, dumplings of marinated alligator loin with shrimp, bamboo shoot and garlic; Steamed Mousse Ball, a diaphanous shrimp dumpling in oyster-infused broth; Crystal Butterfly Dumplings, a delicate duo stuffed with buttery chopped scallop and shrimp, garnished with parsley stalk antennae; to finish, three tiny puff pastry tarts filled with creamy custard and dusted with subtle swallow's nest; at dinner, a casserole of braised Mongolian-style goat with shiitake. *Open for lunch and dinner. Licensed. Access: barrier-free.* **$$$$$**

SPADINA GARDEN
114 Dundas W, at Bay, 416-977-3413.
While this old Chinatown room is snazzier than most – and one of the busiest rooms in the core at lunch – its mainstream menu rarely ventures beyond familiar Cantonese and Szechuan fare. Warning: unless your idea of dinner music is the Bee Gees' Saturday Night Fever soundtrack, you might want to dine elsewhere. Best: deliciously deep-fried and battered Manchurian-style Crispy Beef flecked with red chilies in a sweet, honeyed sauce; greasy-good house Special Noodle (menu-described as Hakka-style but more Hakka lite and closer to Swatow in execution) – rice noodles thick with baby shrimp, chicken, beef and bean sprouts; Hot Spicy Peanuts (sic) Chicken, tender chunks of thigh accented with roasted nuts and fiery red pepper flakes in sweet soy gravy; shared Beijing-style starter of slippery cold noodles in sesame oil; shredded beef spring roll. *Open for lunch and dinner. Closed holidays. Licensed. Access: one step at door, washrooms on same floor.* **$$**

Contemporary

GEORGE
111 Queen E, at Mutual, 416-863-6006, www.georgeonqueen.com.
NOW's 2005 resto of the year! Lorenzo Loseto, formerly Susur Lee's sous at Lotus, is deservedly Toronto's hottest new chef, even if he has been around for more than 10 years. Working in a formally cool warehouse setting on the ground floor of an

There's more than primo plonk on the menu at **Jamie Kennedy Wine Bar.**

exclusive women's club, he's come up with a regional card that will delight adventurous diners of all sexes. Can't afford the big bucks? George does lunch come spring on a gorgeous courtyard patio. Best: chef's five-course tasting menu of sorts, a series of visually stunning dishes that challenge the taste buds like smoked beef tenderloin offset with truffled squash terrine, or sea scallops poached in olive oil; seared foie gras over rosemary shortbread and peppercorn-glazed pork belly; rack of venison in kumquat jus paired with chestnut-and-foie-gras-laced mash; Tasmanian trout with warm fingerlings; intermediary cheese course; to finish, bittersweet chocolate crème brûlée with coffee meringue. *Open for dinner. Closed Sunday, Monday. Licensed. Access: four steps at door, washrooms on same floor.* **$$$$$**

🔴 JAMIE KENNEDY WINE BAR
9 Church, at Front, 416-362-1957, www.jkkitchens.com.
One of Toronto's top chefs triumphs again at this casual contemporary 50-seat bistro that offers mix 'n' match tapas-style plates of upscale comfort food at surprisingly low prices. And, yes, that's Kennedy in full view in the intimate room's very open kitchen. Bonus: each dish has a suggested sommelier-selected by-the-glass wine pairing. Understandably, these are some of the hottest tables in town, and reservations are only accepted at lunch. At dinner, it's first come, first served, so if there are no vacancies and the tiny bar is full, leave your cell number with the door, go around the corner for a drink and wait till you're called. Ridiculous? Not for 10 bucks a plate! Warning: obscure signage. Best: though the menu changes almost daily, anticipate signature dishes like Kennedy's deservedly acclaimed Yukon Gold frites – now labelled fries but exactly the same as the originals – served in a logo-stamped brown paper cone on Jasper Conran china, sided with lemony mayo or topped with

free-range chicken breast, shards of sharp pecorino cheese and poutine-gravy-like lamb jus; black cod braised in crab broth with escarole; for dessert, chocolate brownies topped with chocolate mousse. *Open for lunch and dinner. Licensed. Access: two steps at door, washrooms on same floor.* **$$$**

LAIDE
138 Adelaide E, at Jarvis, 416-850-2726, www.laide.ca.
Romantically lit sex-themed lounge-cum-resto featuring chef Sam Gassira's often impressive parade of plates. Too big for tapas, too small for mains, consider them a variable series of starters. It's more bar than beanery, and most of the tiny tables are sized for a martini and not more than one oversized plate. Reservations required Friday and Saturday. Best: Thai-style red curried vegetable noodle soup; ravioli stuffed with blue crab, fresh basil and mascarpone sauced with burnt butter; wild sole tourneod poached in olive oil; braised coq au vin paired with "frigid weather" root veg; hoisin to glazed baby back ribs; pan to fried lamb 'n' cashew potstickers with hot and sour dip; blue corn nachos topped with vegetarian chili, Monterey Jack and salsa fresca; to finish, Kensington Market organic ice cream, and chocolate caramel tarts dressed with sour cherry compote. *Open for dinner. Bar till close. Closed Sunday, Monday. Licensed. Access: three steps at door, washrooms on same floor.* **$$$$**

🔵 ORO
45 Elm, at Bay, 416-597-0155, www.ororestaurant.com.
The $600,000 Maybach limo parked illegally out front of this elegant Italian-inspired trat is the first clue that Oro attracts some of the highest rollers in town. Call chef Dario Tomaselli's oeuvre Canadian cuisine – classical cooking with a contemporary streak based on locally supplied product. Bonus: those of us with bicy-

cle budgets can get the same luxe experience at lunch for slightly less dosh. Best: to start, at dinner, foie gras and terrine with gooseberry and apple preserve, truffled honey and a warm cinnamon bun; secondi like seared veal tenderloin paired with scallop mousse and sweet breads, braised red cabbage and potato Dauphine laced with creamy Brie; braised short ribs with parsnip purée and Brussels sprout quenelles; sweet carrot risotto with duck confit frothed with chive brown butter; to finish, spectacular house-baked desserts like lavender raisin brioche bread pudding with cloudberry compote and spiced pumpkin foam. *Open for dinner. Monday to Friday for lunch. Closed Sunday, holidays. Licensed. Access: three steps at door, washrooms in basement.* **$$$$$**

TOBA
243 King E, at Sherbourne, 416-367-8622, www.toba.ca.
After stints at Ellipsis, Mildred Pierce and Zucca, Tony Barone's laid-back east-side eatery comes by its pedigree legitimately. Pair chic decor – Chinese red walls, black panelling, Hockneyesque paintings of shimmering pastel pools – with a mainstream Cal-Ital card and it's obvious why this hot spot endures while others fade away. Best: from the dinner mains, seasonal dishes like super-moist pan-roasted Chicken Supreme stuffed with Spanish manchego cheese over buttery scallion mash; old-school gnocchi with spicy Italian sausage, pulpy tomato sauce and fontina garnish; 10-ounce Black Angus strip loin with horseradish cream and matchstick frites; at lunch, beefy bison burgers stuffed with more manchego and dressed with sun-dried tomato, basil aïoli and crispy onion sprouts; for brunch, Peking duck crepes slathered with hoisin, or corned beef hash thick with shredded potato and sweet onions, layered with a pair of expertly poached eggs sauced with hollandaise and chipotle purée. *Open Tuesday to Thursday for lunch and dinner. Friday and Saturday for dinner. Saturday and Sunday for brunch. Closed Monday. Licensed. Access: barrier-free, washrooms in basement.* **$$$$**

French
LE PETIT DEJEUNER
191 King E, at George, 416-703-1560, www.lepetitdejeuner.ca.
Although it's had many handles (anyone remember Triple X?), this funky laid-back east-side storefront with the sparkly naugahyde booths has evolved from its beginnings as a first-rate all-day breakfast spot into a low-key cantina with a Continental card created by Belgian-born owner/chef Johan Maes (Innocenti, Rosewood, Windsor Arms). Bonus: nightly three-course $30 prix fixe. Warning: it's so busy at weekend brunch, Belgian waffles are limited to two per table! Best: at dinner, steak frites with haricots verts; duck confit with balsamic shallots, roasted potato and mesclun in French dressing; at lunch or brunch, super Croque Monsieur, buttery grilled challah with layered ham and melted Gruyère, sauced with subtle Dijon-nipped béchamel and broiled till bubbly; Toast Champignon, a halved and toasted bagel tiered with grilled 'shrooms, bacon, onion and a runny poached egg, sided with rosti timbale and slightly pickled veggies over apple; to drink, hot house-made apple cider. *Open Monday to Friday for breakfast, lunch and dinner. Weekend for brunch. Closed holidays. Licensed. Access: barrier-free, washrooms in basement.* **$$$** ⬚

Greek
KATHY'S CORNER
139 Dundas E, at Mutual, 416-367-0645.
Long-popular with local beat cops, Kathy and Gus Nikopoulos's modest take-away offers steam-table-style but flavour-packed Greek grub to go or eat in.

You'll kick yourself the next day for not ordering more — all this Old World home cookin' gets even tastier as leftovers. Best: every-day whole roasted rotisserie chicken sided with boiled-then-baked Danforth-style spuds; Monday's carb-loaded ground beef lasagna or Thursday's moussaka – ground lamb layered over scalloped potatoes and sweet grilled peppers topped with creamy mashed potato – both sided with rice or salad; Tuesday's spectacular lima bean casserole in tomato sauce and olive oil kicked with dill. *Open for breakfast and lunch. Closed on the weekend, holidays. Unlicensed. Cash only. Access: barrier-free.* **$**

Indian
SPICES
4 Temperance, at Yonge, 416-364-6276.
Despite its low-budget decor and limited menu, this charming hole-in-the-wall delivers some of the tastiest and most health-conscious North Indian spreads in the core. Fear not, pyrophobes: even when ordered spicy, most everything arrives pleasantly mid-range. Bonus: come spring, a quiet patio with skyline view. Best: Chicken Biryani, baked boneless chicken tikka on basmati, sauced with a sweet tomato and onion cream studded with unpitted apricots and a spice chest full of aromatics, garnished with raw ginger threads and a solitary if-you-dare Thai bird chili; rich butter chicken and two vegetarian versions (Paneer Makhani and Tofu Makhani); Spicy Fruit Salad, tart green apple, strawberries, banana and mandarin orange dusted with black pepper and laced with maple syrup; terrific samosas – potato 'n' pea, nutty ground goat, smooth panneer – paired with fiery coriander raita. *Open for breakfast and lunch. Unlicensed. Cash only. Access: one step at door, washrooms on same floor.* **$$** ⬚

Italian
MERCATTO
15 Toronto, at King E, 416-366-4567, www.mercatto.ca/.
The downtown business crowd loves the in-your-face ambience of these brash sibling Italian trats for good reason: professionally prepared pasta, pizza and panini that won't break the expense account but will be sure to impress clients. Bonus: in-house gourmet boutique. Warning: closed weekends. Best: folded ciccio pizza over grilled veggies, herbed chèvre and ripe tomato; specials like sweet-potato-stuffed ravioli in pesto cream with peppers; potato gnocchi with grilled mushrooms in tomato basil pesto; calzone stuffed with artichoke hearts, black olives, ham and mozzarella, all slathered with onion-studded sweet tomato sauce; hearty seasonal soups – fibrous carrot or pumpkin purée, Mediterranean bean – combined with such panini as rare roast beef with caramelized onion and horseradish mayo on crusty ciabatta; to take back to the office, double chocolate pistachio biscotti and Gryfe's bagels. *Open for breakfast and lunch. Closed on the weekend, holidays. Licensed. Access: barrier-free.* **$$$** ⬚

MUSTACHIO
Lower level, St. Lawrence Market, 95 Front E, at Jarvis, 416-368-5241.
Forget Carousel's skimpy back bacon on a bun – the best sandwich in the St. Lawrence Market is in the basement. Though weekday lunches can overwhelm this bustling take-away, it's an extremely efficient operation and the line moves quickly. Better yet, show up early and have the joint to yourself. Best: though the prices have increased somewhat of late, the massive breaded Italian eggplant on fresh focaccia is still the best deal in town, 3 inches of lightly fried veg loaded with old-school tomato sauce, fried onions, hot or sweet peppers and mushrooms; a very competent California-style veal sandwich on a kaiser

with the same fixin's; old-school meatballs and daily pasta specials, too. *Open for breakfast and lunch. Closed Sunday, Monday. Unlicensed. Access: barrier-free.* **$**

Japanese

HIRO SUSHI
171 King E, at Jarvis, 416-304-0550.
For years a favourite on Church, Hiro Yoshida goes downtown in a monochromatic room punctuated with amaryllis and shoji screens. Sit at a table and savour tempura and teriyaki, but true dinner theatre happens at the sushi bar. Warning: apart from Hiro himself, there's likely to be a language barrier. Best: striped salmon sashimi nigirizushi; cone-shaped temaki hand roll with spicy scallops or toasted, smoky salmon skin; translucent toro – fatty tuna belly – with a wasabi depth charge; subtly delicious silver-skinned aji mackerel; live, then shucked razor clams and al dente asparagus tied in seaweed ribbons. *Open for dinner. Tuesday to Friday for lunch. Closed Sunday, Monday and holidays. Licensed. Access: one step at door, washrooms in basement.* **$$$$**

IZAKAYA
69 Front E, at Church, 416-703-8658,
www.izakaya.ca.
High-concept Westernized Japanese fast food for those afraid of sushi and sashimi. In their place, big bowls of noodle soup topped with quality ingredients and a short card of East-meets-West tapas. Noisy and chaotic when crowded, and hard backless benches and communal seating with strangers won't make you want to hang around. Bonus: unisex washroom. Best: moderately spicy Chili Chicken Ramen brimming with Sapporo-style noodles, red Anaheim pepper and Cumbrae free-range chicken, topped with

raw sprouts and coriander; Tokyo Beef Ramen swimming in meaty miso with medium-rare sirloin, scallions and minty shiso leaf; Kinoko Udon, a surprisingly meaty vegetarian broth topped with sliced raw 'shrooms that cook while you slurp; Duck Gyoza, garlicky potstickers filled with shredded bird and Chinese veggies; Seaweed Salad, rubbery threads of wakame, dulse, kombu and hijiki mixed with sesame seeds and pickled baby lotus root in rice wine vinaigrette over buttery Boston lettuce. *Open for lunch and dinner. Closed holidays. Licensed. Access: barrier-free.* **$$$** ⏱

JAPANGO
122 Elizabeth, at Dundas, 416-599-5557,
www.japango.net.
Famous among sushi-philes, this diminutive Tokyo-style resto offers the usual combos 'n' sets but ups the ante with first-rate fish. Just be prepared to pay for it – prices are appreciably higher than the Sushi on Bloor crowd are used to paying. Warning: at lunch, go early or forget snagging a table without a considerable wait. Best: from the sushi bar, uni sea urchin or delightfully crunchy masago smelt roe, both served battleship-style topped with quail egg; the house chirashi, an artfully carved sample of the day's catch that borders on sculpture; Deluxe Bento Box with California roll and a trio of nigiri, shrimp tempura, and teriyaki-glazed salmon – soup, salad and rice included. *Open for lunch and dinner. Closed Sunday, holidays. Licensed. Access: two steps at door, washrooms on same floor.* **$$$$**

Pakistani

KING PALACE
105 Sherbourne, at Richmond, 416-504-8188.

Neither royal nor palatial, this Pakistani take-away offers cabbies and club kids filling and fiery curries from modest digs in a downtown gas station. Ignore the signs advertising kebab 'n' pop specials and point and take your chances with the extensive but unnamed East Indian comfort-food curries and aromatic stews on the steam table, some just weird – unidentified hoof in bitter, gelatinous gravy? – but much of it downright delish. Bonus: open seven days a week till 5 am! Best: near-tagine of gorgeous on-the-bone lamb with chickpeas in spice-spiked tomato sauce; roti-style bones-and-all lamb in curried cream; cauliflower and potato garnished with fresh coriander stalks and mild green chili pods; al dente yellow lentils fired with green chili, or bitter kale with yellow split peas; moist basmati biryani rice flecked with curry leaf; for dessert, smooth rice pudding in sweet condensed milk, an ambrosial ambrosia dusted with crushed green pistachios. *Open for breakfast, lunch and dinner. Unlicensed. Cash only. Access: barrier-free.* **$$** ⓘ

Somali
LIBAN
211 Queen E, at Sherbourne, 416-214-5901.
Despite its barred facade, this modest Somali spot in a former greasy spoon is one of the friendliest spots on the lower east side. Popular with cabbies and really adventurous foodies, its short all-inclusive lineup of East African-style grilled meats coupled with East Indian basmati hallmarks a collision of cultures and cuisines. Warning: unless you're a fan of boiled supermarket spaghetti in barbecue sauce, pass on the pasta. Best: every meal begins with a small bowl of buttery goat soup, innocuous iceberg salad, a side of veggie stew, bottomless glasses of mango Freshie and a choice of bread – flaky French roll, Ethiopian injera or muffin-like muufu; mains include tender on-the-bone roast goat mixed with peppers, onion and tomato; pounded and grilled chicken steak with lemon and dried coriander; alarmingly red chicken thighs; at breakfast, smokey foul squirted with lime, fried liver 'n' onions or a dish called oödkac, finely diced beef mixed with dates; the whole lot blasted into orbit with the not-to-be-missed house hot sauce; in case you're wondering, the banana that accompanies everything on the card is a mid-meal respite from the heat, and not dessert. *Open for breakfast, lunch and dinner. Unlicensed. Cash only. Access: one step at door, washrooms in basement.* **$** ⓘ

Thai

SALAD KING AND LINDA
335 Yonge, at Gould, 416-971-7041, www.saladking.com.
Downstairs, the formerly dreary cafeteria has been replaced with a sleek stainless-steel-appointed room complete with table service. Upstairs, a more formal room decked out in chic chinoiserie and named for the wife offers fancier fare. Fear not, pyrophiles, as most of the Thai card, complete with its notorious 20-chili scale, is exactly the same as it was pre-renovation and, better yet, just as inexpensive. Best: at both, cashew chicken with sweet peppers and steamed rice; kaffir-scented lime chicken with snow peas, red peppers and chilies; vegetarian fare like Golden Curry with deep-fried tofu and veggies in a mild Thai spice blend, or Evil Jungle Prince – Asian veg in garlic chili sauce; from Linda, Fish Curry Hot Pot, turbot fillet in turmeric-tinted coconut sauce thick with okra and plump tomato in rice-paper papillote, or steamed pomfret wrapped in banana leaf. *Open for lunch and dinner. Closed Sunday, holidays. Licensed. Access: one step at door, washrooms on same floor.* **$$$**

9 under $10

Buddha's Vegetarian Food (666 Dundas West, 416-603-3811) serves up vegan vittles like pressed tofu, celery, bamboo shoots, water chestnuts, red pepper and fresh garden peas tossed with toasted cashews for $6.95. Large enough to be shared.

Caffe Brasiliano (851 Dundas West, 416-603-6607) offers affordable Portuguese daily specials – 6-inch squares of lasagna layered with minced beef, sweet tomato sauce and gooey mozzarella sided with non-designer greens, or old-school roast beef with superb roasted spuds, olive-oil-doused Brussels sprouts and buttery fava beans – for 6 bucks inclusive.

Long-time west-side fave **Café Bernate** (1024 Queen West, 416-535-2835) continues its tradition of wallet-friendly sandwich combos like ham, avocado and provolone on a Dijoned baguette with retro greens tossed in poppy-seed lemon mayo for $8.95.

They don't come any quirkier than **Vicky's Fish and Chips/Sue's Thai Food** (414 Roncesvalles, 416-531-8822), which gets it right when it sticks to Southeast Asian dishes like butterflied jumbo shrimp with cashews, red pepper, tart green apple and onion ($6.99).

Tacos el Asador (690 Bloor West, 416-538-9747) delivers Mexican street food with an El Salvadoran bent. Don't miss the namesake snack stuffed with lime-marinated chicken, steak, pork or chorizo, topped with crisp iceberg, ripe tomato and sharp crumbled queso ($2.20 each/vegetarian $1.85).

Across the street, Korean eatery **Buk Chang Dong To Fu** (691 Bloor West, 416-537-0972) features a short lineup of fiery kimchee-fuelled tofu casseroles served in clay pots, all $5.95, but only one strictly vegetarian.

Tucked under the Bloor Theatre's marquee, long-running **Ghazale** (504 Bloor West, 416-537-4414) offers Middle Eastern salads like chickpea with parsley, cabbage and ripe tomato, chili-oiled cauliflower and huge lemony chunks of carrot mixed with waxy potato, starting at $1.99.

As its name suggests, **Salad House** (24 Roy's Square, 416-920-4964) specializes in things leafy and green such as baby arugula with shaved parmigiano in a citrus 'n' shallot vinaigrette ($2.99), or a multi-tiered slab of lemony eggplant, sweet pepper, carrot and zucchini terrine ($4.34) served with mashed sweet potato. Finish with delish blowtorched crème brûlée ($1.99).

Housed in a gas station (hence its popularity with cabbies), **King Palace** (105 Sherbourne, 416-306-8188) goes one better and stays open till 5 am every night of the year, serving up a 16-ounce container of astoundingly tender and fat-free Pakistani halal lamb with chickpeas in a thick tomato gravy spiked with chili oil, curry leaf and slender slips of ginger, for just 6 bucks.

restaurants

Vegetarian

NATURALLY YOURS
100 King W, at Bay, 416-368-0100, www.naturallyyours.ca.
In the food court of First Canadian Place, this terrific take-away devotes itself exclusively to vegetarian and vegan guilt-free snacks and lunches. Though several other eateries found along the subterranean PATH have appropriated the concept, Naturally is the true original. Bonus: vegan pizza! Double bonus: check out its website (www.naturallyyours.ca, what else?) for daily specials. Best: garlicky lentil loaf with carrot and onion, topped with tofu-whipped mashed potatoes; remarkably flavourful Mediterranean-style Greek tofu tart on phyllo, thick with spinach, basmati rice, potato 'n' onion; whole wheat tortilla-wrapped yam burrito with additional kidney beans, salsa, cheddar, cumin and lime juice; whole-grain salads like Couscous Carnival – finely diced mango, apple, technicolour peppers and dried cranberries in a mango vinaigrette; zero-fat salads like artichoke antipasto or roasted eggplant, zucchini and carrot in honey mustard dressing; to complete, organic honey-bran muffins or gluten- and dairy-free cheesecake topped with Ontario blueberries, virtually as rich as the real thing. *Open for breakfast, lunch and dinner. Closed on the weekend, holidays. Unlicensed. Access: barrier-free.* **$**

Kensington Market

Burritos

BIG FAT BURRITO
285 Augusta, at Oxford, 416-913-7487.
This Burrito Boyz clone succeeds where all the eateries that have occupied this oddball Kensington space before have flopped; after several months, it's still open and every indication is that it will remain so. The secret? Good Cal-Mex grub and downright swanky digs – for the Market. Best: generous fajita-style strips of sirloin in a foil-wrapped flour tortilla oozing gooey cheese, house sauce and crunchy raw diced veg; the unique yam burrito, loaded with lots of sugary-sweet potato and salad-like fixin's. *Open for breakfast, lunch and dinner. Unlicensed. Cash only. Delivery. Access: barrier-free, one step to washroom.* **$**

Café

 IT'S ALL GOOD
68 Wales, at Leonard, 416-504-0222.
Tucked away behind Toronto Western, this obscure café on the fringes of Kensington Market won't be unknown for long. A small takeaway with a two-seat lunch counter, this foodie find deserves the spotlight, if only for its fabulous tomato soup and tacos. Bonus: Taco Tuesday – three for six bucks! Best: simply the best tacos in town, thick blue corn tortillas generously stuffed with ground steak 'n' peppers, chicken breast with caramelized onion, or grilled veggies, all layered with block Jack, organic lettuce, guacamole, sour cream and kick-ass house-made salsa; made-to-order organic tomato soup, thick with cream, ripe veggies and more garlicky salsa; Lucy's Chicken Sandwich, pounded breast paired with Italian-style peppers and old-school tomato sauce on grilled ciabatta; Malaysian fried rice topped with shrimp, beef, chicken or veg on an impressively sized bed of short-grain strewn with garlic, onion and dried chili pods; smoothies and retro blueberry pie. *Open for breakfast and lunch. Closed Monday. Unlicensed. Cash only. Access: four steps at door, no washrooms.* **$** ☼

Chilean

 JUMBO EMPANADAS
245 Augusta, at Baldwin, 416-977-0056.
When Irene Morales first dished out her authentic Chilean street food more than 10 years ago, she did so from a vending cart located on a sidewalk in Kensington Market. Now that she's moved indoors to modest digs a block away complete with awning-covered curbside patio, the savvy cook is Toronto's undisputed queen of the Latin American turnover. Want proof? She supplies several local upmarket cantinas that simply heat them up and sell them at nearly twice the price. Best: two-fisted empanadas overstuffed with either chicken (with red pepper, black olives and hard-boiled egg), beef (as above but with the addition of raisins) or veggies (spinach, red pepper, mushroom, onion and basil pesto); vegetarian tamale-esque humitas filled with mashed corn and onion, wrapped and tied with corn husk; take-home specialties like the house's relish-like homemade hot sauce and caramelized sugar-crusted pastel de choco, fabulously sweet upside-down pie of cornmeal mush thick with chunked beef, chicken, black olives, hard-boiled egg and raisins. *Open for breakfast and lunch. Closed holidays. Licensed. Cash only. Access: four steps at door, washrooms in basement.* **$$** ☼

Contemporary

 SUPERMARKET
268 Augusta, at College, 416-840-0501, www.supermarkettoronto.com.
From the crew that gave you Tempo and the defunct Lava comes this down-market – it makes nearby Planet Kensington (see page 115) look like Planet Hollywood – boho cafeteria/performance space furnished with cast-off wobbly tables and vinyl stacking chairs. Bonus: terrific, reasonably priced globe-trottin' grub from eclectic chef Manh Nguyen. Warning: friendly if casual service, so chill. Best: slow-braised oxtail and veal shank topped with an incendiary chiffonade of multicoloured bird chilies and Thai basil; generously portioned steamed PEI mussels in lemongrass and Caribbean hot sauce; panko-crusted salmon cakes with smoky chipotle sauce paired with Asian slaw in gingery sesame dressing; one of the best versions of poor old pad thai this side of Bangkok; grilled chimichurri calamari; Laotian spring

It's standing room only at Thai cafeteria **Salad King**. Page 59.

rolls with sweet 'n' sour dip; vegetarian yaki soba with tofu, carrot, scallion, cabbage 'n' sprouts; to finish, green tea crème brûlée. *Open for dinner. Bar till close. Closed Sunday. Licensed. Access: three steps at door, washrooms on same floor.* **$$$** ☼

French

⬤ LA PALETTE
256 Augusta, at College, 416-929-4900.
Here's a much-loved low-key boîte serving no-nonsense café standards that just happens to be French. Add suave service and a former Le Select chef who's got a deft touch with grilled meats and the sum is an unpretentious spot that defies food fads. Bonus: one of the largest imported beer selections in town! Best: superb 10-ounce triple-A Black Angus sirloin topped with sun-dried tomato and brandy butter, with hand-cut Yukon Gold frites; grilled wild boar, ostrich, venison or caribou wrapped in bacon with an oatmeal stout and black currant veal jus, sided with buttery roasted potato, beets, pearl onion and snap peas; Roulade Végétarien, garbanzo pâté, avocado, corn, roasted red pepper and grilled zucchini wrapped in Swiss chard served with a curried corn and cilantro coulis and carrot chips; for dedicated meat-eaters — and not listed on the menu so it doesn't frighten the faint-hearted — the Quack And Track, duck confit and horse (!) tenderloin with rosemary roasted spuds; daily $30 three-course prix fixe specials. *Open Monday to Saturday for dinner. Weekend for brunch. Licensed. Access: three steps at door, washrooms in basement.* **$$$$** ☼

Lebanese

AKRAM'S
191 Baldwin, at Kensington, 416-979-3116.
Akram Dow's Lebanese take-away proves that all falafels ain't created equal. Besides making one of the best wraps in town, this Kensington Market grocery store also carries baked goods — whole wheat pita! — from acclaimed Scarborough Middle Eastern bakery Arz. Bonus: organic ice cream. Best: freshly deep-fried falafels made with fava, mung and soy beans — Dow considers chickpeas "too gassy" — topped with tomato, purple cabbage, tahini, strong onion and even stronger homemade hot sauce; mackdouce salad with house-pickled eggplant, garlic, pinenuts and crushed walnuts; savoury spinach 'n' onion or feta 'n' black olive spanokopita-style turnovers; for the sweet tooth, an ever-changing assortment of premises-baked baklawa; from the shelves, jars of pickled eggplant spiced with walnuts, pinenuts and garlic; pomegranate molasses; 18-inch-diameter lavash flatbread; pistachio-studded halwa. *Open for breakfast and lunch. Unlicensed. Cash only. Access: four steps at door, no washrooms.* **$**

Mexican

EL TROMPO
277 Augusta, at Oxford, 416-260-0097.
Since its original owners split, this casual Kensington cantina has become more popular; a new liquor license might have something to do with it. But the room's former charm fades next to indifferent service, smaller portions and higher prices. *Open for lunch. Tuesday to Saturday for breakfast and dinner. Closed Monday. Licensed. Access: one step at door, washrooms in basement.* **$$** ☼

Portuguese

AMADEU'S
184 Augusta, at Denison Square, 416-591-1245.
Despite its seemingly endless luxe makeover, this charmingly off-kilter Kensington Market local remains a restaurant of two halves: one a traditional coastal Portuguese seafood eatery with formal, family-friendly decor suitable for a christening, the other a dodgy dive complete with cheap suds, top-notch pub grub and mythically rowdy clientele (Keith Whittaker RIP). Warning: those on a low-sodium diet should ask that their food be unsalted. Best: to start, velvety Caldo Verde soup thick with kale, cranberry beans and potatoes paired with rough-crusted cornbread; at lunch, daily seafood specials like grilled

veg out

Toronto offers plenty of options for hardcore veg-heads, starting with **Bo De Duyen** (254 Spadina, second floor, at Sullivan, 416-703-1247). Pronounced Bo-day-dween, this incense-scented Chinese/Vietnamese resto serves some of the best grub on the avenue, vegetarian or not. **Café 668** (668 Dundas W, at Denison, 416-703-0668) was named NOW's 2002 best new restaurant regardless of genre for its innovative pan-Asian veggie menu, while the verging-on-luxurious lounge **Fressen** (478 Queen W, at Denison, 416-504-5127) serves herbivorous cuisine that shows more innovation than places with meat in their repertoire.

Located in the Hare Krishna Temple, the vegan cafeteria **Govinda's** (243 Avenue Rd, at Roxborough, 416-922-5415) offers a tasty ever-evolving lineup of South Indian curries, rice dishes and salads. (If you're afraid you'll be inducted into a cult, there's no proselytizing.) **Kissan** (1411 Gerrard E, at Hiawatha, 416-466-9771), meanwhile, serves up an all-vegetarian lineup that incorporates the rich sauces of the north and the fiery chilies of the south. And don't be put off by the way the sparse **Narula's** (1438 A Gerrard E, at Ashdale, 416-466-0434) looks – this Indian vegetarian kitchen's inexpensive spice-intensive snacks pack a punch.

If you're into playing the percentages, **Kensington Natural Bakery** (460 Bloor W, at Brunswick, 416-534-1294) is a 99.8 per cent all-natural vegetarian cafeteria – no dairy, egg, refined sugar, artificial colouring or preservatives – with a large selection of pastries, breads, salads and casseroles. **Naturally Yours** (100 King W, at Bay, 416-368-0100) is a terrific take-away devoted to vegetarian and vegan snacks and lunches.

The tiny no-frills storefront **Salad House** (24 Roy's Square, at Bloor E, 416-920-4964) is one of the busiest lunchtime destinations in the area thanks to a good selection of garden-fresh salads and a rotating roster of comfort-food specials with a slight Middle Eastern accent. Don't knock the mock at **Simon's Wok** (797 Gerrard E, at Logan, 416-778-9836) – Buddhist temple cooking rarely gets this palatable or deftly executed.

Sunny Café (322 Bloor West, 416-963-8624) is an unpretentious spot with an extensive lineup of Mediterranean-influenced mains, some macrobiotic, while **Tre Fontaine** (486 Bloor W, at Howland, 416-535-1818) is Toronto's only Italian vegetarian all-you-can-eat buffet.

An offshoot of Fressen, **Urban Herbivore** (64 Oxford, at Augusta, 416-927-1231) is a completely vegan café serving a short card of salads, sandwiches and super takeout soups. And for those who eat – rather than do – lunch, **Wanda's Pie in the Sky** (7 Yorkville, at Yonge, 416-925-7437) is an affordable, kookily quaint cubbyhole that just has to be the best deal in Yorkville.

For a listing of organic restaurants, see page 210.

whole sardines sided with collard greens and Lisbon-style deep-fried potatoes; at dinner, grilled codfish topped with red onion and accompanied by steamed veg 'n' spuds ladled with lemony garlic olive oil; Pork Alentejana, seared cubes of pork tenderloin mixed with fresh clams, peppers and potatoes; to share, the Amadeu's Revolution, an upscale take on paella piled high with grilled lobster, crab, clams, mussels, shrimp and calamari mixed with rapini in garlicky lemon butter. *Open for breakfast, lunch and dinner. Bar till close. Licensed. Access: one step at door, washrooms in basement.* **$$$** ⠿ ☉

Salvadoran

EMPORIUM LATINO
243 Augusta, at Baldwin, 416-351-9646.
Tucked away in the back of this Kensington Market El Salvadoran grocery store is a terrific takeaway serving first-rate Latin American fast food. At the store's front, there's also a small lunch counter that opens to the passing parade when weather permits. Piñatas, too! Best: crisply fried Chiles Rellenos, mild green poblano peppers coated in omelette-like batter, stuffed with either sharp and smooth cheeses, shredded chicken or nicely spiced house chorizo, rice and beans sided with tangy coleslaw, tortillas, crema fresca and pulpy jalapeño hot sauce; five varieties of tamales in banana leaf, including cornmeal mush studded with boneless chicken, bell peppers, chickpeas, olives and capers; caramelized plantain dusted with cinnamon as dessert or dolloped with crema fresca as a side to the chiles rellenos plate; Pan con Pavo, a Latin-accented hot turkey sandwich slow-cooked in mole sauce, served with lettuce and slaw on Italian ciabatta. *Open for breakfast and lunch. Unlicensed. Cash only. Access: eight steps at door, no washrooms.* **$**

Spanish

⬡ TORITO
276 Augusta, at College, 647-436-5874.
With owners whose CVs include names like Latitude, Xango and El Cid, this terrific tapas bar can't help but be lo verdadero. Throw in informed servers, romantic lighting and the sensational Iberian card from chef Carlos Hernandez and no wonder this compact cantina is one of downtown's hottest boîtes. Warning: no reservations, so come real early or very late. Best: sharable plates like arugula dressed with manchego, toasted almond and quince vinaigrette; eggy potato tortilla topped with watercress; smoky chestnut and spicy chorizo soup; butterflied and grilled shrimp al ajillo drenched in butter and garlic; crab cakes dolloped with lemony parsley aïoli; quail glazed with pomegranate over sweet calabaza pumpkin mash; tongue 'n' cheeks – beef – slow-braised with classic mirepoix; to finish, chocolate flan or fresh honey-kissed figs paired with blue Cabrales cheese. *Open for dinner. Bar till close. Closed Sunday, Monday and holidays. Licensed. Access: five steps at door, washrooms on same floor.* **$$$$** ⠿

Thai

CHIENG MAI THAI
147 Baldwin, at Spadina, 416-813-0550.
This pint-sized eatery on the fringe of Kensington may not be the fanciest room in town (dig those plastic flowers!), but it more than makes up for its budget decor with well-prepared and moderately spiced Thai-style dishes. Best: to start, cold spring rolls stuffed with mint leaf, crisp carrot, cuke and red pepper, scrambled egg and deep-fried tofu; incendiary mains like curry pad thai with cauliflower, broccoli, peppers, pressed tofu, napa cabbage and wide wheat noodles in mild coconut-curried gravy; spicy beef salad with thinly sliced steak, shallots, mint, roasted

rice and tangy citrus dressing kicked with chilies; addictive General Tso-style breaded chicken with peanut sauce and stir-fried cucumber, pineapple, red pepper and tomato; lunch specials like lemon chicken soup, a faux pho rich of tamarind-tanged rice stick garnished with sprouts, slivered scallion and crushed peanut. *Open for breakfast, lunch and dinner. Unlicensed. Cash only. Access: five steps at door, washrooms in basement.* **$$**

Vegetarian
KING'S CAFÉ
192 Augusta, at Baldwin, 416-591-1340, www.kingscafe.com.
Since this Kensington Market ovo-lacto vegetarian eatery launched, it's ditched its oddball lineup of mock meat dishes (nigirizushi topped with chocolate sprinkles? we think not) in favour of a card that most will recognize. Friendly uniformed servers break into Happy Birthday – in Mandarin – when occasion arises, and at the back of the bright, high-ceiling room there's a small shop carrying the café's prepared entrees. Bonus: sides of ultra-nutritious steamed brown rice. Warning: bring your own wasabi. Best: King's Noodle Soup with thick, slippery rice noodles, broccoli and deep-fried tofu; crustless quiche, an ingenious blend of sun-dried tomato and cheese (feta, mozzarella, cottage), couscous, spinach and eggs served with organic greens in yogurt dressing; from the special spring and summer menu, Jasper rolls, sheet rice noodle spirals wrapped with al dente asparagus, carrot, crispy bean curd crumbs and soy "ham" dipped in sweet teriyaki sauce; Lettuce Wraps, iceberg lettuce leaves loosely folded around diced 'n' curried carrot, peppers and corn. *Open for breakfast, lunch and dinner. Unlicensed. Cash only. Access: barrier-free.* **$$** ⬚

URBAN HERBIVORE
64 Oxford, at Augusta, 416-927-1231, www.fressenrestaurant.com/herbivore.
An offshoot of wildly successful Fressen, owner/chef Stephen Gardner's completely vegan café at the top of the Market offers a short card of salads, sandwiches and super takeout soups. There are a few whoopee-cushion-like stools set up around a butcher-block table, but most do take-away. Bonus: besides being dairy-free, most everything's organic to boot. Double bonus: cooking classes. Best: to quench thirst, sensationally flavoured fresh iced lemonade mixed with wild raspberries one day, pucker-intensifying cucumber or winter-chillin' hot chocolate; a revolving lineup of memorably massive muffins like raspberry with pineapple, or a wheat-free spelt version with contrasting almonds, dates and sweet potato; salads such as baby spinach in cranberry vinaigrette with shiitakes, grape tomatoes and broccoli; enormous veggie sandwiches like roasted red pepper and sliced yam on multigrain spread with spinach-walnut pesto and olive-date tapenade; for home, returnable Mason jar-stored soups like cumin-kicked Mexican black bean loaded with garlicky legumes, carrots, corn and celery. *Open for breakfast and lunch. Closed holidays. Unlicensed. Access: four steps at door, no washrooms.* **$**

Queen West
Burritos
NEW YORK SUBWAY
520 Queen W, at Ryerson, 416-703-4496.
Forget the Big Apple and write off the subs. This East Indian-inspired take-away from the family responsible for nearby Ghandi (see page 64) and Babur fuses mild-to-wild roti-like curried veggies with Mexican tortillas and calls them burritos. Then they add cheese to the wraps, grill 'em and dub them California Rolls although they have nothing to do with sushi. And the only thing remotely NYC about the modest room is a poster of the Brooklyn Bridge. Best: so-called burritos stuffed with curried cauliflower mash, slightly bitter spinach or ground chicken, and grilled versions loaded with eggplant and spinach, satay chicken or jumbo-esque shrimp; quesadillas – real ones! – lined with cheese, ham, roast beef and/or onion; grilled curried potato subs studded with mustard seeds. *Open for lunch and dinner. Unlicensed. Cash only. Access: one step at door, washrooms on same floor.* **$** ⊙

Caribbean
ALBERT'S REAL JAMAICAN FOODS
558 Queen W, at Bathurst, 416-304-0767, www.albertsrealjamaicanfoods.com.
Lineups of taxi drivers and club kids snake out the front door late into the night for Albert's famous takeout jerk chicken dinners. Delicately spiced, the fowl comes bone-in, Island-style, and is ladled over a mess of rice and pigeon peas. Decor is minimal – the obligatory Bob Marley poster, natch – and the drink of choice is the JA soda dubbed Ting. Although there's a small stand-up counter that opens to the street, most do takeout. Bonus: roti skins for sale. Double bonus: rent Albert's condo at www.albertsrealjamaicanfoods.com. Best: slowly stewed bone-in

Urban Herbivore's all-organic menu will make you forget about meat.

Island-style jerk chicken with all-spiced rice 'n' peas and JA slaw; melt-in-your-mouth oxtail dinners; salt-cod fritters; in summer, fresh sugar cane juice and ginger beer; for the home cook, take-out containers of oxtail gravy. *Open for breakfast, lunch and dinner. Closed Monday. Unlicensed. Cash only. Access: barrier-free, no washrooms.* **$** ⊙

Contemporary

EPICURE
502 Queen W, at Ryerson, 416-504-8942.
Since its launch in 1981, this dimly lit bistro has quietly built itself into a downtown dining mainstay. It's now ensconced in identical digs five doors east, right down to the posters and paintings hung on exposed brick and deep burgundy walls, and the focus remains competently executed and value-minded mains. Bonus: backyard rooftop patio.
Best: to start, a massive mound of Provençal mussels in first-rate garlicky house tomato sauce; Old World lasagna ladled with meaty Bolognese and layered with creamy ricotta; plump pumpkin ravioli in Parmesan cream with button 'shrooms, spinach and roasted corn; 10-ounce black Angus sirloin with a rich peppercorn demi-glaze, sided with chimichurri, steamed veggies and skinny frites; thin-crusted Italiano pizza topped with shaved prosciutto, roasted garlic, sun-dried tomato and artichoke heart. *Open for breakfast, lunch and dinner. Licensed. Access: barrier-free.* **$$$** ⦂ ⊙

QUEEN MOTHER
208 Queen W, at Duncan, 416-598-4719, www.queenmothercafe.ca/.
The doyenne of Queen West perseveres after more than 25 years, dishing up savvy Thai specialties and vegetarian mains in definitive digs. High-backed booths, cool tunes and a private backyard deck make this the perfect spot for a cheap first date. Best: to begin, vegetarian Laotian spring rolls with crunchy peanut dip; legendary mains like the Cosmic veggie burger with high-protein grains, nuts, herbs and mushrooms in a whole-wheat pita with spiked mayo; ubiquitous pad thai (but, hey, they did it first!) with chicken, shrimp and coriander-peanut garnish; My Lunch In Provence of grilled Egyptian flatbread topped with grilled eggplant, zucchini and goat cheese, with chunky fries on a banana leaf; spinach and ricotta cannelloni in garlicky tomato sauce; at brunch, crepe du jour with home fries, salad and double-smoked bacon; St. Viateur bagels with cream cheese and lox. *Open for breakfast, lunch and dinner. Licensed. Access: barrier-free, washrooms in basement.* **$$$** ⦂ ⊙

RIVOLI
332 Queen W, at Spadina, 416-597-1908, www.rivoli.ca.
Celebrating its 25th anniversary, the Riv is the archetypal downtown boîte, complete with snazzy cocktail lounge (Toronto's first), upscale pool hall upstairs and performance space in the back. It also happens to be a respectable resto with a rockin' pan-Asian lineup – another local first – that beats the usual pub grub.
Best: to start, Siamese Wookie Balls, deep-fried sticky rice coated with black and white sesame seeds, sided with sweet chili dip; from the mains, teriyaki-glazed salmon over cool soba noodle salad with Thai-style stir-fried veggies in a sesame vinaigrette; vegan yellow curry with tofu topped with banana and toasted coconut, served with steamed jasmine rice; Mandalay mussels steamed in green curry with coconut splashed with lime served with taro frites and garlic toast; the legendary Rivoli burger topped with sweet caramelized onion; at the bar, lychee martinis and Singaporean Tiger beer. *Open for breakfast, lunch and dinner. Licensed. Access: barrier-free.* **$$** ⦂ ⊙

TARO GRILL
492 Queen W, at Portland, 416-504-1320.
A high tin ceiling and jazz playing at the right levels contribute to this welcoming bar's relaxed and comfortable bistro atmosphere. Taro's consistency, quality and charm should see it well into a third decade. Best: sandwiches of grilled calamari with mango chutney and wasabi drizzle, or marinated grilled steak topped with sautéed onions and mushrooms, tomatoes and lettuce, both on focaccia warm from the oven and served with house greens; at brunch, grilled Yummy Chicken with two poached eggs and hollandaise; smoked Arctic char on potato latke with sour cream and apple sauce. *Open for breakfast, lunch and dinner. Licensed. Access: barrier-free, washrooms in basement.* **$$$** ⦂ ⊙

Diner

SHANGHAI COWGIRL
538 Queen W, at Bathurst, 416-203-6623, http://bovineclub.com/shanghaicowgirl/scg.html.
Noisy day and night, this rockin' resto and Bovine Sex Club sibling delivers updated greasy-spoon grub with soul food twists in a room that recalls a sleek deco diner. Best: Sterling Silver Sirloin, a considerable 10-ounce steak sided with roasted potatoes, perfectly timed buttery green beans and pan jus; battered schnitzel-like Chicken-Fried Steak with dairy-rich country gravy and corn on the cob; Trailer Trash Sushi, grilled moist chicken breast on Portuguese pada with watercress and wasabi-spiked mayo; pecan pie or boozy Jägermeister chocolate mousse for dessert. *Open for breakfast, lunch and dinner. Licensed. Access: short step at door, washrooms in basement.* **$$$** ⦂ ⊙

French

CAFE CREPE
246 Queen West, at John, 416-260-1611.
Stylin' Vancouver chain comes to town with competent crepes, both savoury and sweet, but questionably executed sandwiches blow any credibility. *Open for breakfast, lunch and dinner. Licensed. Access: barrier-free.* **$$**

JULES
147 Spadina, at Queen W, 416-348-8886.
With its casual French comfort food card, is it any wonder this family-affair 30-seat café is a neighbourhood hit? Warning: show up early — especially at lunch — because the house doesn't take reservations. Best: traditional thin-crusted quiche – yes, quiche – thick with Swiss cheese, bacon 'n' broccoli, or eggplant ratatouille and chèvre as well as five other varieties; steamed mussels in cookbook-correct white wine alongside salt-dusted frites and lemony greens; steak frites, herb-dusted flank steak with mesclun, veggies and more first-rate fries; foot-long sandwiches on Portuguese pada like Le Parisien with Black Forest ham, Swiss cheese and tart cornichons, or creamy Brie with tomato and greens, all with puréed soup, mesclun or fries; oven-roasted chicken breast with the same sides; for dessert, house-baked tarte aux pommes. *Open Monday to Friday for breakfast and dinner. Monday to Saturday for lunch. Closed Sunday, holidays. Licensed. Access: one step at door, washrooms on same floor.* **$$** ⦂

Indian

GANDHI
554 Queen W, at Bathurst, 416-504-8155.
The winner of NOW's best roti roundup, a favourite of celebrity chef Greg Couillard and a sibling of the far pricier Babur and eclectic New York Subway (see page 63), this comfortable hole in the wall offers much fancier rotis than most of its nearby competition. Mind you, you pay extra for the added quality of the ingredients, but it's worth it. A few tables, but most

Casual comfort food at **Jules**. Page 64.

hit the street to eat. Bonus: Gandhi makes the wrappers in house on a pizza press. Best: boneless lamb roti with spicy potato and chickpea chana; tomato-sauced boneless chicken jalfoorezi with cauliflower and green peas; saag paneer (puréed spinach and tofu-like milk cheese) dalpoori roti. *Open for breakfast, lunch and dinner. Unlicensed. Cash only. Access: barrier-free, no washrooms.* $

TRIMURTI
265 Queen W, at Duncan, 416-645-0286, www.trimurti.ca.
Owned by long-time Nataraj server Danny Chin and his partners Sidney Leong and chef Pradeep Japdap, who also did time at the popular Annex institution, Trimurti duplicates – and substantially improves on – much of the Bloor eatery's menu. Bonus: attentive service and no mob scene. Best: Phool Gobi Tandoor, a flaming red head of cauliflower marinated in yogurt and spices, then fired whole in the tandoor, the results resembling electric brains; Chilly Paneer, mild Indian cheese with major chilies and onion; lamb vindaloo with potato and coriander; at the buffet, amazing made-to-order naan, blistered from the oven and cracker-thin; tandoori chicken, moist, pink and delicately charred around the edges; surprisingly tasty smashed potato salad laced with coriander leaf; hellishly hot coriander chutney with the head-rush of horseradish. *Open for lunch and dinner. Licensed. Delivery. Access: barrier-free.* $$$

Korean
HO SU
254 Queen W, at John, 416-322-6860, www.hosu.ca.
If you know nothing about Korea's language and culture, dining in a Korean restaurant can be intimidating. But this bright, spacious and informal spot

breaks through with modern takes on traditional Seoul food plus lots of Japanese options. Bonus: semi-private rooms as well as a window counter with a front-row view of Queen Street on parade. Best: thinly sliced charcoal-grilled bulgogi beef served with short-grain rice and steamed veggies; spicy kimchee and tofu soup over rice; Ho Su Roll, a half-dozen nori-wrapped maki loaded with salmon tempura, tobiko flying fish roe, avocado and English cucumber; Tikim Mon Doo, an egg crepe stuffed with wilted cole slaw in thin, sweet mayo; sizable Beef Bibim Bop, glutinous rice topped with stir-fried steak alongside pickled carrot, English cuke, hijiki and spinach, and sided with more slaw, slippery sesame Chap Chae noodles and steamed broccoli. *Open for breakfast, lunch and dinner. Licensed. Delivery. Access: barrier-free.* $$$

Pan-Asian
EAST!
240 Queen W, at John, 416-351-3278.
The former Beverley Tavern gets transformed into an elegant Asian-inspired supper club. Sharing most of the Southeast Asian lineup of its sibling, Spring Rolls, it also features a new all-day dim sum card as well as hawker-style street eats. Warning: since reservations are only accepted for dinner, come early or join the queue almost any time else. Bonus: twice the space now that they've opened up the second floor. Double bonus: front-row seat for MuchMusic. Best: from the dim sum lineup, buttery grilled baby squid in garlic-chili marinade, Malaysian-style eggplant with spinach in spicy sambal, and lemongrass-scented chicken wings over designer mesclun; palatable pad thai three ways – ketchup-pink Famous, yellow Curry and alarmingly red and accurately handled Unique; first-rate General Tao Chicken, elsewhere often a serving of deep-fried gristle, here tender tempura-like

chunks of chicken breast coupled with broccoli, sweet red pepper and whole chili pods; to finish, soothing mango crème brûlée. *Open for breakfast, lunch and dinner. Closed holidays. Licensed. Access: two steps at door, washrooms in basement.* **$$$**

Sandwiches

BLACK CAMEL
322 Adelaide W, at Peter, 416-260-4670.
Quick pit stop for the Rosedale set moves downtown and takes on the late-night post-clubbing crowd. Offering upscale takes on the Midwest U.S. phenom known as loose meat sandwiches: long-marinated and slow-cooked sloppy joes. With its distinctive decor – marble countertops, blond laminate flooring, white ceramic tile everywhere – and first-rate product, we smell franchise. Bonus: moist towelettes! Other locations: 4 Crescent, at Yonge, 416-929-7518. Best: super-tender Black Angus beef brisket and pork shoulder in sweet house barbecue sauce, topped with caramelized onions on a hefty leak-proof kaiser; Cumbrae free-range chicken breast with basil pesto and roasted red bell pepper; roasted veggies with hummus for the non-carnivorous; monthly specials like slow-roasted flank steak with chipotle mayo and grilled rocket. *Open for lunch. Monday to Saturday for breakfast and dinner. Closed holidays. Unlicensed. Access: five steps at door, washrooms in basement.* **$**

SANDWICH BOX
238 Queen W, at John, 416-204-9411, www.sandwichbox.ca.
Causing Soup Nazi-like scenes of mealtime mayhem, Sandwich Box is quite simply the most delicious budget dining find to hit the downtown core since Burrito Boyz. The brainchild of Abdi Ghotb, a former co-owner and chef of the Annex's upscale Serra and Goldfish, the concept's pure genius: inexpensive fast food with high-end attention to detail. Warning: count on a 15-minute wait in line during peak feeding frenzies. Best: for $5.48 (!), build a superb custom sandwich starting with a choice of nine different Ace Bakery breads, seven house-made spreads and another seven each of meats, veggies and cheeses, all assembled to order, drizzled with lemon juice and quality olive oil, then grilled to golden perfection on a sandwich press and served in a plain white paper container alongside garden-fresh mesclun lightly doused in a balsamic vinaigrette; ambrosial daily soups like vegan cream of tomato with fennel or cream-rich mushroom purée; DIY salad bar; to finish, Valrhona mousse and smooth crème brûlée. *Open for lunch and dinner. Closed Sunday. Unlicensed. Cash only. Access: barrier-free, no washrooms.* **$**

Midtown

Annex
Caribbean

ISLAND THYME
872 Bathurst, at London, 416-538-9729.
A laid-back Caribbean café, this bright compact space offers creative, reasonably priced takes on familiar island-style grub. No worries for those not in a hurry. What's the rush when affable owner/chef Marcia Carby executes some of the best island-style grub in town? Best: so tender it falls from the fork, slow-cooked young goat in subtle gravy with fabulous shoestring sweet-potato frites doused with house mango hot sauce; home-style oxtail with lima beans; for the vegetarian, escovitch of marinated tofu and onions in spicy sugar cane vinaigrette, sided with okra, chickpea and cho-cho chayote curry; dhalpoori roti with spinach, squash and chickpea channa; all mains served with nutty rice 'n' peas and tangy citrus slaw; for dessert, pineapple upside-down cake or bread 'n' butter pudding. *Open for dinner. Tuesday to Saturday for lunch. Closed Sunday. Unlicensed. Cash only. Access: four steps at door, another to washroom on same floor.* **$$**

Japanese
SUSHI ON BLOOR
515 Bloor W, at Brunswick, 416-516-3456, www.sushionbloor.com.
Often imitated and the winner of NOW's Readers Poll for best sushi four years running, this modish Annex spot rolls out bargain all-inclusive meal deals and

Live Organic, a casual setting for T.O.'s most adventurous veggie diner. Page 68.

comparatively inexpensive sushi and sashimi combos. Until recently, unless you'd made reservations – especially for a booth – you'd join the queue. But now that the all-white, very modern room upstairs has opened, peak feeding frenzy times are much more manageable. Best: fish fanatics will go gaga for Sushi Gold, a combo bento of nine pieces of nori-wrapped nigiri-zushi – tuna and fatty toro belly as well as shrimp, mackerel, octopus, salmon, yellowtail, tobiko flying fish roe and faux crab; delicately battered grease-free tempura dinners of shrimp, squash, sweet potato, broccoli and zucchini, with miso soup, sticky rice and miso-dressed iceberg lettuce salads; Nasu Dengaku, grilled Japanese eggplant slathered with sweet miso paste and tossed with sesame seeds; steak teriyaki on a bed of stir-fried onion with steamed strips of carrot, green bean and broccoli; to finish, green tea or red-bean ice cream topped with maraschino cherries. *Open for lunch and dinner. Licensed. Access: one step at door, washrooms in basement.* **$$$**

Lebanese

GHAZALE
504 Bloor W, at Bathurst, 416-537-4417.
For nearly a decade, the Ahmad family has been dishing up inexpensive Lebanese home-cooked comfort food from a small take-away located just under the marquee of the Annex's Bloor Cinema rep house. Despite its ongoing renovations (they still haven't gotten around to putting up a sign out front), business is as brisk as ever, especially once the bars close. Best: made-to-order falafel; chicken shawarma; yellow rice with potato and chicken; fava beans with green peas and spuds in sweet tomato sauce; minty vegetarian grape leaves stuffed with rice and chickpeas; massive veggie cabbage rolls in thin sauce; sour spinach purée studded with kidney beans; baklava by the box. *Open for breakfast, lunch and dinner. Unlicensed. Cash only. Access: barrier-free, no washrooms.* **$** ⊙

Mexican

DOS AMIGOS
1201 Bathurst, at Bridgman, 416-534-2528, www.dos-amigos.ca.
This former luncheonette by the TTC yards may seem to be situated in the middle of nowhere – blink and

you'll miss it – but the convenient location makes the cozy cantina popular with Annex denizens and patrons of nearby Tarragon Theatre. Some may find the Mexican card under-spiced unless they request that everything be cooked the way the kitchen staff would make it for themselves. Best: Pollo con Mole, boneless chicken breast in a deliciously rich sauce of unsweetened chocolate thickened with pulverized pumpkin seeds and garlic, sided like most mains with rice 'n' refried turtle beans; Pescado à la Veracruzana, pan-seared then roasted red snapper in a lemony sauce laced with garlic and green olives, with rice and salad; soft veggie burritos – sour-cream-squiggled flour tortillas stuffed with eggplant, broccoli, avocado and cactus; to finish, addictive custardy caramel flan. *Open for dinner. Bar till close. Closed Monday. Licensed. Access: two steps at door, washrooms in basement.* **$$$** ⋰

Nepalese

MOUNT EVEREST
469 Bloor W, at Brunswick, 416-964-8849, www.mteverestrestaurant.com.
Showing influences from neighbouring India and Tibet, Toronto's only Nepalese restaurant offers a short card of subtly spiced stir-fries and starters that combine the best of both cuisines. The remainder of the extensive menu features familiar northern Indian fare executed with equal skill. Best: to start, Poleko Pakheta, eight juicy tandoor-roasted chicken wings on a rough slaw of lightly pickled onion and lightly mustard-oiled purple cabbage; vegetarian curries (tarkari) like puréed yellow lentils sautéed with tomato and spiked with raw green chilies, colourful Bhuteko Cauli casserole, and Allo and Semee new potatoes mixed with Chinese long green beans; from the buffet, meaty tandoori chicken wings, pillowy naan, smoky dal makhani lentils and a terrific stir-fry of cabbage, tomato and kidney beans. *Open for lunch and dinner. Licensed. Access: barrier-free.* **$$$**

Patisserie

⬤ FRANGIPANE
215 Madison, at Dupont, 416-926-0303, www.frangipane.ca.
Seating all of four and prettified with purple orchids, the stylish bake shop features three display cases impressively packed with owner/chef Claudia Egger's spectacular cakes, pies and tarts. Bonus: daily lunchtime savoury quiche specials. Bonus: not only does Egger put up her own preserves, but she also picks the organic fruit they're made from herself! Best: as one would expect from a joint named for ground almond paste, frangipane tarts with either poached pear and slivered almonds, wild blueberries with hazelnuts, or bourbon-spiked pecans with chocolate; cakes – whole or by the slice – like three-layer lemon chiffon topped with meringue, and chunky apple walnut Bundt glazed with Calvados; bite-sized petit fours layered with frangipane, apricot 'n' red currant jelly and dipped in Kirsch fondant and bittersweet chocolate. *Open for breakfast and lunch. Closed Monday, Tuesday and holidays. Unlicensed. Access: short step at door, no washrooms.* **$** ⋰

Vegetarian

ANNAPURNA
1085 Bathurst, at Dupont, 416-537-8513, www.annapurna.ws.
Operated by the local followers of Hindu meditation guru Sri Chinmoy, Toronto's longest-running vegetarian restaurant (32 years and counting) features a time-warp lineup of 60s hippie-style health food like steamed veggies, tofu and organic brown rice. A recent renovation means the new tables in the large front window surrounded by plants are particularly appealing, but the best meal deals continue to be

found on the retro resto's South Indian card. Best: all-inclusive Indian Assortment comprises samosas stuffed with curried green peas and spuds, chickpea-battered potato bonda and fritter-like eggplant bhajia teamed with tart tamarind and coconut chutneys, two main courses like smashed potato with turmeric and mustard seeds or squash, spinach and carrot sabzi, and sides of sour anchaar pickle, puffed puri or flat pappadom and yogurty raita; to drink, rosewater-sweetened lassi or summer-only iced chai; for dessert, chocolate tofu mousse with vanilla hemp ice cream and ricotta whipped cream. *Open for lunch and dinner. Closed Sunday. Unlicensed. Access: one step at door, washrooms in basement.* **$$**

GOVINDA'S
243 Avenue Rd, at Roxborough, 416-922-5415.
Located in the Hare Krishna Temple, this vegan cafeteria offers a tasty ever-evolving lineup of South Indian curries, rice dishes and salads in the no-frills basement of an old Christian church. Although there's likely to be a celebration with singing and dancing going on in the main room, which everyone's welcome to observe — or join — there's no proselytizing. They do sing that same song over and over. Bonus: because the church is a registered charity, dinner's tax-deductible. Kid friendly, too. Best: no set menu, but expect things like hearty lentil dal studded with cinnamon bark and whole chilies; meatball-like chickpea kofta with yogurt sauce; puréed Brussels sprouts or tofuesque cabbage paneer sabzis; roti lashed with curry leaf; chapati; pappadom; cooling cabbage and carrot slaw; halwa semolina pudding with raisins and honey. *Open for lunch and dinner. Closed Sunday. Unlicensed. Cash only. Access: 10 steps at door, washrooms in basement.* **$**

KENSINGTON NATURAL BAKERY
460 Bloor W, at Brunswick, 416-534-1294, www.naturalbakery.redto.com.
Originally based in Kensington Market, owner/baker Quang Dieu's 99.8 per cent all-natural vegetarian

cafeteria — no dairy, egg, refined sugar, artificial colouring or preservatives — offers more than just a large selection of nutritious pastries and breads (42 at last count). Now located in humble Annex digs, this student-friendly eatery also dishes up more than 20 diet-conscious casseroles and prepared salads sold by weight. Best: genuinely hot 'n' spicy deep-fried tofu satay in tomato sauce with crunchy onion and garlic; sweet multi-bean and corn chili sided with nutty lentil brown rice; creamy potato, carrot and tofu curry; lasagna-like Rice Noodle or Tofu Banquet layered with veggie-full tomato sauce and — shudder — real mozzarella (the only dairy in the house), served with house roughage (lettuce, green pepper, red cabbage) in diled soy dressing; salads like cashew with diced bell pepper and corn; for dessert, old-school organic butter tarts and organic whole wheat blueberry croissants. *Open for breakfast, lunch and dinner. Unlicensed. Cash only. Access: one step at door, washrooms in basement.* **$**

LIVE ORGANIC FOOD BAR
264 Dupont, at Spadina, 416-515-2002, www.livefoodbar.com.
An offshoot of extremely tiny but widely acclaimed vegan, mostly organic, raw food eatery Live, owner/chef Jennifer Italiano's 30-seat bistro a few doors west is now stylishly done up in mod lime green and saturated orange. One of the best and certainly most adventurous vegetarian kitchens in town. Warning: loud juicers! Best: although Italiano changes the menu bimonthly, count on Live It Up Lasagna, uncooked zucchini noodles layered with cashew "ricotta," tomato marinara and basil pesto; vegan sushi rolled in un-toasted nori and stuffed with cooked brown rice (no purist, Italiano isn't afraid to bend the rules), sweetened with beet and mango and garnished with cashew wasabi; Hawaiian Pizza, sprouted buckwheat crust piled with red pepper hemp "cheese," pineapple, faux onion rings, cashew-coriander "cream"; for the newbie, the Raw Combo, a little bit of everything; daily cooked macrobiotic specials with hot miso soup. *Open for breakfast, lunch and dinner. Closed Monday. Licensed. Access: 11 steps at door, washrooms in basement.* **$$$** ⋮

Deli-style

MEL'S MONTREAL DELICATESSEN
440 Bloor W, at Howland, 416-966-8881.
The closest thing to authentic Montreal-style smoked meat you'll find in Toronto, at an extremely bright family-style deli that's open 24/7. Note: all smoked meat available in four grades: lean, medium, medium fat and downright fat. Best: massive half-pounder Montreal smoked meat sandwiches on rye with mustard plus a sizable side of crunchy coleslaw and a quartered dill pickle; house-made beef chopped liver with caramelized onion, hard-boiled egg and drippings of chicken fat; creamy homemade potato salad; smoked-meat poutine with gravy and melted cheddar curds; pickled garlic; blintzes stuffed with ricotta and cottage cheese topped with sour cream, blueberry sauce or rhubarb. *Open for breakfast, lunch and dinner. Closed Christmas Day. Licensed. Access: one step at door, washrooms on same floor.* **$$** ⋮

Church Street

Café

GARAGE SANDWICH COMPANY
497 Church, at Wellesley, 416-929-7575.
Located in the rear of Pusateri's Fruit Market, this down-home take-away decked out in auto erotica — hubcaps, license plates, fuzzy dice — offers substantial sandwiches, soups and stews for those in the Village with an appetite for more than a three-way. Best:

Frangipane is a dessert lover's dream and a weight watcher's nightmare. Page 67.

spicy vegetarian three-bean chili; corn-studded veggie pie; two-fisted "theme" sandwiches like meatloaf-stuffed Paradise By The Dashboard Light or smoked meat meets sauerkraut in the Kraftwerk-inspired Auto Reubahn; hearty vegan soups like broccoli with spinach, and fiery Thai sweet potato with peanuts; Greg's fabulous ice cream, too. *Open for breakfast and lunch. Closed Sunday. Unlicensed. Access: barrier-free, no washrooms.* **$**

Contemporary

BYZANTIUM
499 Church, at Wellesley, 416-922-3859.
Known for serving some of the best food in the nabe, the Village's favourite cocktail lounge sports a contemporary look, including a wall of floor-to-ceiling glass that opens to the passing parade. Out back, find a secluded Mykonos-style tented terrace for less public assignations. Bonus: Sunday to Wednesday $32 three-course prix fixe (steak frites $36). Double bonus: more than 100 martoonis! Best: from a market-seasonal roster, starters like crisp crab cakes with seedling salad 'n' jalapeño tartar or the house pizza topped with smoked chicken, artichoke hearts, caramelized onion and chèvre; follow with mains like roasted capon breast lacquered with honey mustard and sided with glazed veggies and herbed couscous; grilled ostrich medallions in black currant reduction sided with almond-crusted potato croquette; for those who eschew the flesh, marinated grilled tofu steaks glazed with mango chutney partnered with butternut squash fritters and snow pea ragout. *Open for dinner. Bar till close. Licensed. Access: barrier-free, washrooms in basement.* **$$$$** ☼ ⏱

SLACK'S
562 Church, at Wellesley, 416-928-2151,
www.slacks.ca.
The former Slack Alice's gets a truncated name, a much improved look and a far better menu than we've come to expect in this culinary wasteland. Late night, it's the typical cocktails 'n' cruising scene, but earlier in the evening Slack's is no gastro-slacker. Best: at dinner, sharable appetizers like mussels pan-

steamed in Gouda cream, and double-smoked pancetta paired with sweet potato frites à la poutine, with melted Brie and vegetarian cranberry jus; mains like pork tenderloin in Gorgonzola cream, sided with paprika-dusted roast potatoes; vegan strudel in olive oil phyllo pastry with mesclun and balsamic vinaigrette; at brunch, eggs Benny topped with prosciutto and house-made hollandaise; the DLT, a Texas toasted triple-decker of shredded duck confit, ripe tomato and designer lettuce with cranberry mayo; for dessert, gluten-free cheese cake. *Open for lunch and dinner. Bar till close. Licensed. Access: one step at door, washrooms in basement.* **$$$$** ☼ ⏱

Diner

CHURCH STREET DINER
555 Church, at Dundonald, 416-324-8724.
Since changing owners, what was formerly the Five Alarm Diner has been given a makeover, distancing it from its previous firehall image. The pseudo-retro resto's new decor has a fun urban feel. Breakfast, lunch and brunch items make the diner a worthy new addition to the village, but main courses are overpriced and under-executed. Avoid: the meat lover's mixed grill, a disappointment for carnivorous connoisseurs. Best: baked eggs saturated with garlic, herbs and Parmesan; toasty piled-high Reuben sandwich with a heap of fries, creamy coleslaw, Dijon and dill pickle slices; hearty vegetarian chili with fake ground round and lots of legumes; indulgent three-cheese spinach lasagna oozing alfredo sauce, with a crisp iceberg lettuce salad that could be improved with more acidity in its oily vinaigrette; to finish, super-sweet traditional Quebecois sugar pie, a.k.a. maple syrup with pastry. *Open for breakfast, lunch and dinner. Access: eight steps up to door, washrooms in basement.* **$$**

French

BUMPKINS
21 Gloucester, at Yonge, 416-922-8655,
www.bumpkins.ca.
A quick reno to update the 80s ambience would go a

lunch under $5

The spotless subterranean Chinese café **Mother's Dumplings** (79 Huron, 416-217-2008) specializes in delicious house-made Chinese dumpling and noodle dishes that are as much a treat for the pocketbook as for the taste buds, the most expensive priced at $4.95.

Ask the owner of any restaurant, regardless of price bracket, and they'll tell you Tuesday is the slowest day of the week. To compensate, Little India eatery **Narula's** (1438A Gerrard East, 416-466-0434) offers Toonie Toosday, when the damage on its already bargain-basement Subcontinent street eats – masala-scented bhel poori topped with cracker puffs, aloo tikki chickpea fritters stuffed with creamy lentils (all regularly $3.49) – get reduced to 2 bucks. As well, their fiery three-curry vegetarian thali with rice, griddled naan and papadam, an everyday steal at $3.99, goes for $2.99.

Also on Tuesdays, cheap 'n' cheerful **Flava** (606 Yonge, 416-967-0700) lowers the bill for its jerk chicken dinner – a moderately spiced leg, hot-sauce-splashed rice 'n' peas, lightly dressed slaw – from $4.99 to all of $2.50.

For the same price, **Kathy's Corner** (139 Dundas East, 416-367-0645) does a takeout order of Greek-style lima beans in dilled tomato sauce that makes a sensational supper coupled with a DIY salad and a good loaf of crusty bread.

Every day is Toonie Toosday at **Chinese Traditional Buns** (536 Dundas West, 416-299-9011), a modest Beijing-style café in Chinatown specializing in explosive pick-me-ups like jellied bean curd ($1.49) – hot silken tofu soup rich with slippery seaweed, swirled with salty shrimp, slivered scallions, chopped raw garlic, fresh coriander and a jolt of fiery chili oil – or similarly volatile shredded cured pork ($1.99) on grilled flatbread, like a Mongolian hamburger.

health-conscious fixin's, this early morning to late-night spot offers a unique take on Parisian pancakes. Best: the Monster, an eggy paper-thin flapjack stuffed with deli ham, cheddar and mozzarella as well as a veritable salad bowl of soft onion, baby spinach, raw 'shrooms, bell pepper strips and a last-minute runny egg; the Vegetable version, as above, hold the ham 'n' eggs; deconstructed tuna melts with creamy mayo and celery for crunch; the Nutty Fruit Salad, an open-faced crepe heaped with raw spinach, shredded cheese, pineapple chunks, strawberries, cranberries, blueberries, raisins, almonds, peanuts and pine nuts, all doused in a honeyed citrus vinaigrette; to finish, the Paris, chocolate syrup, hazelnuts and banana. *Open for breakfast, lunch and dinner. Closed Sunday, Monday. Unlicensed. Access: slight bump at door, small washroom on same floor.* **$** ⊙

Indian

 DEBU SAHA'S BIRYANI HOUSE
25 Wellesley E, at Yonge, 416-927-9340, www.biryanihouse.com.
Once a tiny take-away dishing up inexpensive lunchtime eats, this northern Indian spot now inhabits deluxe digs that match the richly sauced menu highlights. Yes, the previous joint's ridiculously low prices have nearly doubled (goodbye, $5 thali), but chef Saha's serious step up justifies the wallet damage. Bonus: a recent reno has considerably improved the room's dated decor. Best: no longer featuring an all-you-can-eat buffet, owner chef Saha now offers two prix fixe meal deals on his exquisite card – six courses for $45 ($40 vegetarian or vegan) and four for $30 ($25) by reservation; begin with the likes of avocado tomato salad with chili coriander vinaigrette, or salmon-laced samosas; continue with baby eggplant stuffed with blistered bell peppers, black-eyed beans in coconut sauce or chicken stuffed with apricot in ground lamb gravy; to conclude, cheesy rasgullah coated in white chocolate with raspberries, or mango mousse with cappuccino froth; rice pullao and tandoori-fired naan. *Open for dinner. Licensed. Access: 16 steps at door, washrooms on same floor.* **$$$**

Japanese

 OMI
451 Church, at Alexander, 416-920-8991.
More a casual local hangout than a severe Zen dining room, this Japanese joint is best when owner/chef John Lee – who learned the ropes under local sushi-meisters Hiro's Yoshida and Kaji – goes omakase with the day's fresh catch. Bonus: house-ground wild wasabi, pickled ginger and fermented soy sauce. Double bonus: obscure 50s and 60s on the sound system. Best: say omakase and get a daily changing improvised lineup of stellar seafood that could include briefly seared and ruby-centred tuna tenderloin; a mini-wok of steaming seafood soup; butterflied shrimp suspended in a frazzle of deep-fried sweet potato threads; flaky roasted whiting with buttery sake-soaked caramelized onion; steamed freshwater pickerel with delicious yellow-flecked skin; inside-out uramaki of crunchy soft shell crab lashed with lovely tamago-no-moto mayo and freshly shaved bonito flakes. *Open Monday to Friday for lunch. Tuesday to Saturday for dinner. Closed Sunday, holidays. Licensed. Access: eight steps at door, washrooms on same floor.* **$$$**

College
Café

AUNTIES AND UNCLES
74 Lippincott, at College, 416-324-1375.
Once a single-chair barbershop and now twice its original size, David Ginsberg and Russell Nichols's

long way in attracting patrons to this respectable, moderately priced French Continental restaurant. A wood-burning fireplace adds some warmth to the cavernous room, but not enough to redeem the stark oak furniture, fake ivy, grapes and disproportionate murals. A good place to bring the folks, if not the foodies. Best: French onion soup with plenty of sweet, slow-cooked onion, topped with melted Swiss on mini-toasts; beef tenderloin with portobello mushroom sauce, a giant serving of medium-rare beef covered in 'shrooms in velvety red wine sauce, sided with so-so steamed veg, roasted potatoes and crusty roll; spinach, mushroom and tinned crab crepe in béchamel. *Open for breakfast, lunch and dinner. Licensed. Access: two steps at door, 16 to washrooms on second floor.* **$$$** ⋮

CREPE IT UP
507-1/2 Church, at Wellesley, 416-916-3558.
There's more to this stylish takeaway than its name suggests. Replacing traditionally rich fillings with

neo-mod hole in the wall continues to attract a budget-conscious crowd that appreciates value as well as style. It's a jumble of cast-off kitchen furniture and diner kitsch set to a stomping soundtrack of 60s beat groups and 70s soul, so no wonder the joint's always jumping. Scooters optional. Warning: weekend brunch is so busy, benches on the sidewalk are provided for the queue. Best: fluffy omelettes du jour sided with challah toast or a classique croque monsieur of Black Forest ham and Swiss, both served with dill 'n' Dijon mashed-potato salad and cantaloupe wedges; signature classic club with grilled chicken, cheddar, bacon, lettuce and tomato on aïoli-smeared challah; Belgian waffles with fruit and maple syrup while they last; breakfast tacos stuffed with scrambled egg, house-made chorizo, pinto beans, cheddar, coriander and lettuce dolloped with sour cream; deliciously straightforward soups like leek and potato. *Open for breakfast, lunch and dinner. Closed Monday, holidays and long weekends. Unlicensed. Cash only. Access: barrier-free, washrooms in basement.* **$**

Chinese

PALS WT INTERNATIONAL
376 College, at Borden, 416-929-1212.
This minimally decorated storefront – tables layered in sheet polyethylene, stacking chairs, a poster or two – delivers northern Chinese specialties that make their Szechwan-fired selections seem tame in comparison. Best: the aptly named "Find chicken from a pile of chili peppers" the hottest dish in town? (tiny nuggets of bone-in deep-fried chicken blasted with more than 150 (!) Thai bird chilies); a counter-cooling salad of Tian Jin Green Beans Starch Sheet, rubbery lasagna-like bean noodles accented with cuke and smoky vinaigrette; fatty diced lamb scented with cumin; shredded chilies with bean-curd linguine. *Open for breakfast, lunch and dinner. Licensed. Access: one step at door, another to washrooms.* **$$**

Diner

BOOM BREAKFAST
808 College, at Ossington, 416-534-3447,
www.boombreakfast.com.
With its all-day breakfast lineup and modern diner decor, this busy storefront resto has the buzz of a frantic Fran's, equal parts animated conversation, steaming espresso machine and the clink of china and cutlery. Regulars know to show up early for assured variations on bacon 'n' eggs and comfort-food-style lunch classics. Best: remarkably grilled-to-order pink-centred 5-ounce patty of ground round topped with melted cheddar and raw red onion rings, sided with herbed chunky fries; Boom Benny topped with smoked salmon and lemony hollandaise; cookbook-correct salade niçoise with hard-boiled egg and crisp haricots verts; lassi-like smoothies with yogurt, honey, banana and blueberries. *Open for breakfast and lunch. Licensed. Access: one step at door, washrooms in basement.* **$$**

French

PONY
488 College, at Palmerston, 416-923-7665,
www.ponyrestaurant.com.
Back in the 80s, Jamie Kennedy and Michael Stadtlander operated this romantic francophone boîte as Palmerston. Since then, it's evolved into an unpretentious spot with what might be the best-kept foodie secret in town, its loss leader Monday to Thursday $22.95 three-course prix fixe ($25.95 Friday and Saturday). Bonus: septuagenarian server André Malibert's charming Old World service. Double bonus: come spring, the loveliest backyard rooftop deck on the strip. Best: to start, a salad of bitter greens and marinated veg in sage and sun-dried

tomato vinaigrette; orange and Stilton with walnut and pear in honeyed champagne emulsion; no-nonsense mains like deboned braised beef short ribs with garlic mash and demi glace; duck confit with cassoulet thick with beef brisket and pancetta, for the vegetarian, saffron-scented mushroom and asparagus risotto with snap peas; to finish, traditional cappuccino-kicked dark and white chocolate tiramisu with sliced strawberries. *Open for dinner. Closed Sunday. Licensed. Access: one step at door, washrooms in basement.* **$$$$**

Italian

CAFÉ DIPLOMATICO
594 College, at Clinton, 416-534-4637,
www.diplomatico.ca.
Long a magnet for sun-worshippers and moon-howlers as well as one of the first patios in Toronto, the Dip celebrates its 38th anniversary in 2006. With its old-school Italian menu – straightforward tomato-sauced pizzas, steamed mussels, leafy insalata – and rock-bottom prices, this family-run business prevails while neighbouring spots don't last 37 minutes. True, few are here strictly for the food. Best: veal sandwich – large breaded cutlet with tomato sauce, optional cheese, fried onions, hot peppers or mushrooms; panzerotto, deep-fried and stuffed with your choice of fillings like basic mozzarella, mushroom and pepperoni, topped with extra tomato sauce; medium pizza starting at $10; cheap daily pasta specials. *Open for breakfast, lunch and dinner. Licensed. Access: half step at door, washrooms in basement.* **$$**

VIVOLI
665 College, at Beatrice, 416-536-7575,
www.vivoli.ca.
Another pretty face on College Street. Food is not the main priority here at Vivoli. It's all about the drinking and laughing and smoking and looking good in the subdued lighting and watching, from the patio on high, the throng (or thong) below. If you've got time

Top five
places to avoid

360
Unfortunately, it's probably not the the revolving resto that will turn your stomach. It's the food *(at the CN Tower).*

CAPTAIN JOHN'S
An aging floating party boat offering for mutinous grub that deserves to be thrown overboard *(1 Queens Quay West).*

MANDARIN
An anomaly in a town full of great Chinese restos, the all-you-can-stomach cuisine is strictly food court calibre *(2200 Yonge).*

THE OLD SPAGHETTI FACTORY
The food is Chef Boyardee bad, made for tourists who won't return and children who won't remember *(54 The Esplanade).*

SASSAFRAZ
The only reason to go is for the primo celeb spotting, especially during TIFF *(100 Cumberland).*

restaurants

Café Diplomatico, the most lounge-worthy patio in all of Little Italy. Page 71.

to pay attention to what you're eating after all that, well, you're some kind of super-partier. But remember – nobody looks hot when they're chewing. Wood-fired pizzas could be good, but undercooking and clumsy prep bring them down. Pasta dishes are hit-and-miss. Service is friendly and informal. *Open for breakfast, lunch and dinner. Licensed. Access: two steps at door, limited front patio access, washrooms in basement.* **$$$$** ⦂⦂ ⓣ

Persian
POMEGRANATE
420 College, at Bathurst, 416-921-7557.
This invitingly unpretentious eatery delivers reasonably priced Persian specialties in a relaxed setting. Dishes range from sharable tapas to deluxe mains accessorized with sweet and fruity garnishes. Bonus: hookahs (sorry, folks, they're just for show). Best: Fesenjaan, a delicious stew available three ways – with portobello mushroom, chicken or lamb shank – rich with ground walnuts and pomegranate syrup, served over saffron-scented basmati rice; Adas Polo, a riot of rosewater-scented rice strewn with slivered almonds, al dente lentils, dates and sultanas, sided with barberries and subtly spiced slow-braised lamb shank topped with crispy onion threads; focaccia-style lavash flatbread spread with smoky Mirza Gasemi eggplant sweetened with garlicky tomato and onion; a near-tapenade of nippy Zeitoon Paravardeh, aged green olives laced with syrupy pomegranate molasses; summery specials like Aab doogh Khiar, an ice cube-chilled soup of fresh dill, cucumber, walnuts, raisins and red onion in yogurt; Khoresh-e rivaas, a green-herbed lamb stew redolent of tart rhubarb. *Open for dinner. Closed Monday. Licensed. Access: one step at door, washrooms on same floor.* **$$$**

Peruvian
EL BODEGON
537 College, at Euclid, 416-944-8297.
On the eastern edge of the College Street strip, traditional Peruvian fare is served in a relaxed atmosphere amidst upbeat Latin vibes and garden-like decor. Servers knowingly warn gringos about the house salsa: a hot-hot-hot lip-numbing blend of chilies and onion best used in moderation. Best: Camarones al Ajillo – five perfectly grilled shrimp awash in melted butter and white wine, with thin slices of garlic and fresh cilantro, ideal for dipping fresh bread; Pescado Frito – a mammoth fillet of mild white fish, slightly battered and pan fried, served on a bed of white rice

with three slices of fried plantain and a salad of leaf lettuce, diced tomatoes and sliced onion; Lomo Saltado – choice of tender chicken or beef strips sautéed with onions, piled on a fresh kaiser with fries or salad; a half-dozen Anticuchos kebabs, tender venison-like beef heart sided with Papa à la Huancaina, spuds smothered in rich mayo-like cheese dressing. *Open for dinner. Wednesday to Saturday for breakfast and lunch. Sunday for lunch. Closed Monday. Licensed. Access: one step at door, washrooms in basement.* **$$$** ⦂⦂

Pizza
BITONDO
11 Clinton, at Henderson, 416-533-4101.
Surrounded by row houses in Little Italy, Bitondo hasn't changed a bit since it opened in the mid-60s. A bare-bones operation, this tiny take-away is all mid-century ceramic tile and screaming-orange plastic furniture. Warning: nothing nouveau whatsoever. Best: the Bitondo family's authentic southern Italian medium-thick crusted pies come in four sizes piled with only four topping options: pepperoni, green pepper, mushroom and anchovies; massive and messy meatball sandwiches; tasty ravioli in house sauce; burp-inducing Brio. *Open for breakfast, lunch and dinner. Unlicensed. Cash only. Access: one step at door, washrooms in basement.* **$** ⓣ

Sandwiches
CALIFORNIA SANDWICHES
244 Claremont, at Treford, 416-603-3317.
The regular winner in NOW's Readers Poll best sandwich category, this venerable family-run business is famous for its substantially portioned southern-Italian-style panini. This location can be hard to find; keep an eye open for a slew of cabs, fire trucks and cop cars parked out front. Best: sizable old-school sandwiches ladled with sweet tomato sauce, caramelized onion and optional tongue-scorching hot peppers, cheese or fried mushrooms stuffed with grilled veal, chicken, meatballs or spicy Italian sausage. *Open for breakfast, lunch and dinner. Closed Sunday. Unlicensed. Cash only. Access: barrier-free, washrooms in basement.*

Southern US
⬤ PHIL'S ORIGINAL BBQ
838 College, at Ossington, 416-532-8161,
www.philsoriginalbbq.com.
This is as close as Hogtown gets to real Kansas City

barbecue. Despite a confusing name change a few years back, Phil Nyman's low-key beanery retains its nondescript digs; dig the grub – super slow-cooked, melt-in-the-mouth stuff with first-rate sides. After pigging out, follow the smoke, have a peek in the backyard and check out a smoker so large it cooks 250 pounds of meat at a time. Bonus: Phil's take-home merch line of hot sauces, T-shirts and baseball caps. Best: superb slow-cooked southern US-style barbecue unlike any found locally; gorgeous pulled pork, meaty moist spice-rubbed and/or sauced pork ribs, disintegrating beef brisket and grill-charred chicken served as combo platters or as substantial sandwiches sided with tremendous smoker-baked beans strewn with even more pork, cheesy Venezuelan cachapas pancakes, hush puppy corn-meal dumplings, classic slaw or potato salad kicked with horseradish. *Open for lunch and dinner. Closed Sunday, holidays. Licensed. Access: one step at door, washrooms in basement.* **$$$**

Tex Mex
RANCHO RELAXO
300 College, at Robert, 416-920-0366.
Best known as a rock 'n' roll venue, Rancho also offers solid Tex-Mex grub that's better than most this far north of two borders. With its eclectic digs and kitschy soundtrack (imagine Don Quixote on mushrooms), Relaxo is the perfect spot to kick back when you're in the mood for massive rice 'n' refried bean carb ingestion. Bonus: quite possibly the most authentic margaritas in town. Best: Pollo Borracho, tender chicken breast sautéed in tequila, salsa and Mexican herbs; Pescado Corona, pan-fried Atlantic grouper smothered in avocado salsa; Chile Relleno, poblano pepper stuffed with chicken, beef or bean picadillo; Mexican Mice, deep-fried jalapeño peppers stuffed with cheese, served with sour cream; for dessert, Sopa Pia, homemade banana ice cream swimming in Kahlua and honey, with deep-fried flour tortilla wedges. *Open for dinner. Bar till close. Licensed. Access: one step at door, washrooms on same floor.* **$$$** ⬦ ☉

UTOPIA
586 College, at Clinton, 416-534-7751.
This poser-free, casual café offers eclectic riffs on Tex-Mex standards lashed with flavoured mayos to sublime effect. À la carte burritos come optionally stuffed with grilled seafood, veggies and TVP. Bonus: bottled citrusy jalapeño hot sauce adds further kick and is available for purchase. Warning: though the secluded backyard patio provides much-needed additional seating, avoid its rear tables and potential dumpster odours. Best: multiple burgers – beef half-pounder, char-broiled chicken, and bison for the brave – with abundant toppings ranging from Asiago to zucchini; grilled salmon burrito, a toasted tortilla packed with fresh goat cheese, sweet bell peppers 'n' onions with garlic dill mayo, sided with sesame slaw, house salad or rice and black beans. *Open for breakfast, lunch and dinner. Licensed. Access: barrier-free, washrooms in basement.* **$$** ⬦ ☉

Harbord
Café
DESSERT TRENDS
154 Harbord, at Brunswick, 416-916-8155.
This south Annex patisserie has a lot going for it: a central location, a charming room and a casual card that includes classic French café fare and Asian-inspired specials, and, as its name suggests, some very impressive pastries. It's an instant hit, and a well-heeled crowd clamours for its 40-some seats, especially at weekend brunch. Best: the house

best pizza

Nothing can cause a culinary brouhaha quicker than arguing thick crust versus thin. In the former category, old-school pizza parlour **Pizza Gigi** (189 Harbord, 416-535-4444) kicks it old-school with more than 20 thick-crusted types of 'za loaded with pepperoni, mushrooms and unashamedly retro pineapple chunks.

Aficionados of thin swear by **Terroni's** (720 Queen West, 416-504-0320, other locations) artfully dressed 'za, though **Marcello's** (1163 St. Clair West, 416-656-6159) and **Gerrard Spaghetti & Pizza House** (1528 Danforth, at Rhodes, 416-463-7792) are certainly their equal.

Non-conformists dig **Live Organic Food Bar**'s (264 Dupont, 416-515-2002; see review, page 68) deliciously raw version made from sprouted buckwheat, topped with diced pineapple and faux cheese fabricated from sweet red pepper and hemp.

If all you want is a slice to go and not the whole damn pie, **Amato** (534 Queen West, at Ryerson, 416-703-8989, and others) has the largest selection, with some two-dozen varieties, notably the spicy model loaded with unseeded sliced jalapeños.

By comparison, **Pizzaiolo** (624 Queen West, at Markham, 416-507-9944, and others) only offers 16 varieties, including the Soprano (sopressata, sun-dried tomato and Gorgonzola), the deep-dish Godfather and sacrilegious low-carb, low-fat slices.

A bit farther north in the Young & Eligible area, **Madanto** (2311 Yonge, at Eglinton, 416-486-5529) offers an Amato-like range of tasty thin-crust slices.

DON'T SAY CHEESE
There's more to vegan pizza than telling your favourite 'za slinger to hold the mozzarella, Parmesan and pesto. In a blind taste test, you'd never know that **Magic Oven**'s (788 Broadview, at Danforth, 416-466-0111; 127 Jefferson, at King West, 416-539-0555) Vegan Magic (tomato sauce, dairy- and nut-free pesto, zucchini, artichoke, portobello mushroom, red pepper with organic spelt crust) wasn't a regular pizza.

Naturally Yours (First Canadian Place food court, 100 King West, at Bay, 416-368-0100) offers a gluten-free vegan pizza (tomato sauce, red onion, zucchini, eggplant, red pepper and mushroom) with a passable wheat-free soy flour crust and first-rate toppings. No doubt some will find the idea of Cher minus cheese unfathomable, but try the Cher Pizza (wild forest mushrooms, roasted red pepper, grilled zucchini, red onion and black olives on thin whole wheat crust, minus the mozzarella) at **Big Mamma's Boy** (554 Parliament, at Prospect, 416-927-7777).

restaurants

Read the sign. **Phil** wouldn't lie. Page 72.

quiche, a fabulously eggy custard thick with smoked chicken breast and tender asparagus with mesclun, dressed in raspberry balsamic; daily specials like beef stew in Italian-style gravy with tomato, miso and romano beans; at brunch, sweet potato and pumpkin fritters layered with house-cured salmon, capers, sour cream and raw red onion; mildly Thai-spiced pumpkin-seafood soup served in its gourd; to finish, tiramisu in a wine glass fashioned from chocolate; rustic apple strudel; chocolate croissant bread pudding; poached pear tarts. *Open for breakfast and lunch. Closed Monday, holidays. Unlicensed. Access: barrier-free, washrooms in basement.* **$$**

LINUXCAFFE
326 Harbord, at Grace, 415-534-2116.
Overlooking Bickford Park through huge windows crowded with plants, this cyber café popular with computer geeks – sorry, "open source enthusiasts" – offers free Wi-Fi access with every food purchase. Bonus: fair-trade roasts from i deal coffee. Best: served stuffed into Portuguese pada buns, pita pizza or tortilla wraps, build-your-own panini from three types of fillings: sliced meats or veggie pâté, cheese, from Brie to Swiss to chèvre, antipasto-style veggies like marinated mushrooms, roasted red pepper and sun-dried tomato; daily soups like rustic, chunky Tuscan white bean soup with cabbage, leek and potato; to drink, squeezed-to-order veggie juices and yogurt smoothies; join the interactive set at www.linuxcaffe.com and connect with techies to find out the time of the next computer workshop. *Open for breakfast and lunch. Friday and Saturday for dinner. Unlicensed. Access: one step st door, washrooms on same floor down narrow corridor.* **$**

Contemporary

◆ 93 HARBORD
93 Harbord, at Robert, 416-922-5914.
Launched by owner Charlotte Dowd and Palestinian chef Isam Kaisi, Toronto's first intentionally anonymous supper club continues to be very much of the moment: a stylish, comfortable room (warm brick walls hung with simply framed mirrors, warm lighting, long banquettes, kraft-paper-topped tables, tinkling cocktail jazz) coupled with a reasonably priced lineup of inventive North African and Middle Eastern dishes. Shame they can't come up with a name! Best: from a seasonally changing card, to commence, such

tapas-like mezes as eggplant baba ghannouj with pomegranate sauce; roasted red and yellow beets in minty bulgar salad; seared tiger shrimp over cumin-kissed apple rings with dilled sour grape coulis; mains like organic roasted chicken stuffed with preserved lemon, olives and saffron, plated with apricots, roasted almonds and raisins over Moroccan couscous; Tunisian tabil-marinated duck confit with pomegranate coulis and steamed dandelion; grilled halibut wrapped in vine leaves drizzled with citrusy cumin sauce. *Open for dinner. Bar till close. Closed Monday. Licensed. Access: no steps at door, washrooms on main floor.* **$$$$**

Fish & Chips

HARBORD FISH AND CHIPS
147 Harbord, at Borden, 416-925-2225.
As close to a true Brit take-away chippie – minus the mushy peas – as you're going to find downtown, this whitewashed vat o' fat close by Central Tech churns out ultra-crisp fish coupled with gargantuan sides of fresh-cut fries and prefab coleslaw so large we defy four adults to finish the prodigiously proportioned newspaper-wrapped supper described as "dinner for two." Lineups form at around 6 pm, but if the crush gets too much, you can always escape the intense heat from the fryers at one of the year-round sidewalk picnic tables. Best: delicately battered halibut, haddock and shrimp with fabulously hand-cut Yukon Gold fries; don't forget the tartar sauce, cider vinegar and generous lashings of salt. *Open for lunch and dinner. Unlicensed. Cash only. Access: one step at door, no washrooms.* **$**

Peruvian

BOULEVARD CAFÉ
161 Harbord, at Borden, 416-961-7676, www.boulevardcafe.sites.toronto.com.
Toronto's first Peruvian eatery, this lovely place with its awning-covered patio has been packing them in since 1979. The laid-back vibe contrasts with fiery fare fusing Latin tastes with contemporary techniques at prices higher than similar spots. Best: wine-marinated and coriander-kicked anticuchos (grilled skewers of chicken, beef, shrimp or sea bass) with rice and peppery mesclun greens in a lemony tarragon dressing; fish of the day like grilled tilapia fillets spiked with mango salsa alongside roasted new

potatoes, tomatoes and salad; starter or main-sized Creole salad – buttery Boston lettuce topped with chickpeas, red onion rings, avocado wedges, artichoke hearts, black olives and hard-boiled-egg garnish. *Open daily for lunch and dinner, brunch on Sunday Access: one step at door, washrooms on same floor.* **$$$** ⬤

Thai
FLIP, TOSS & THAI KITCHEN
141 Harbord, at Brunswick, 416-966-6955.
Former Salad King cook Sushen Sun offers first-rate takes on Thai standards that equal those of her ex-employer. Add uncommon attention to detail and this inexpensive Thai trat beats far fancier Bangkok-style boîtes. Dine-in if you must at a window-side lunch counter or at one of three formica-clad tables rung with folding chairs, but most do takeout or delivery. Warning: when this kitchen says spicy, it means thermonuclear! Best: green-shelled New Zealand mussels in chili-tastic sweet sauce strewn with matchstick carrots and bell peppers; spectacular Spicy Eggplant or Spicy Tofu in sweet basil-scented garlic chili; loosely wrapped Cold Rolls plump with carrot, Thai mint, coriander, rice noodles, scrambled egg and shredded chicken breast, with superbly textured peanut dip; glass noodle salad with chicken, shrimp, onion, lemony mint and coriander; vegetarian Sunshine Dumplings in sweet 'n' sour sauce with pineapple. *Open for lunch and dinner. Closed holidays. Unlicensed. Delivery. Access: one step at door, no washrooms.* **$$**

U of T
Contemporary
GALLERY GRILL
Hart House, 7 Hart House Circle, at Wellesley, 416-978-2445, www.gallerygrill.com.
A former private club room for U of T staff and faculty, the restaurant in Hart House's Great Hall still feels

Top five
for the ambience

SUSUR
One of the world's most creative chefs, Susur Lee's cool, comfortable all-white room makes his fabulous food the focus. *See page 104.*

GEORGE
NOW's 2005 resto of the year is a formally cool warehouse on the ground floor of an exclusive women's club with a gorgeous courtyard patio. *See page 56 and 129.*

RED TEA BOX
This chic bakeshop was featured in French fashion magazines before it had even opened. Quite possibly Toronto's ultimate al fresco dining experience. *See page 111 and 136.*

LAI WAH HEEN
Elegant five-star hotel dining with an internationally acclaimed dim sum menu. *See page 55.*

THUET
An open kitchen and sleek candlelit bar provide a warm backdrop to an understated Eurpopean-flavoured dining room at this top-notch second-floor space. *See page 115.*

exclusive, all Gothic revival stonework, severe wooden furniture and coat-of-arms china. However, the grub – from the highly capable kitchen of chef Mario Tucci – and welcoming professional service bring the former old boys club into the 21st century. Reservations recommended. Best: daily soups like a gingery purée of sweet potato sided with warm goat cheese and chive tea biscuits spread with sun-dried tomato butter; crispy braised duck ravioli with organic baby greens; souffléed Stilton and chèvre flan with thyme-poached pear; at brunch, spice-rubbed organic pork chop with spaetzle and cornmeal-dusted yellow tomato in sage-scented brown butter; to finish, lemon soufflé tart with fresh poached rhubarb or maple crème brûlée with orange pepita shortbread. *Open Monday to Friday for lunch. Sunday for brunch. Closed Saturday, holidays, all July and August. Licensed. Access: elevator access to second floor, then one step down to restaurant, washrooms on same floor.* **$$$**

Italian
L'ESPRESSO BAR MERCURIO
321 Bloor W, at St. George, 416-596-2233, www.barmercurio.com.
The streamlined sibling of Bar Mercurio kitty-corner across the street, this budget-minded bistro on the ground floor of U of T's Woodsworth College specializes in a short all-day card of panini, salads and traditional egg breakfasts. Swellegant digs, a great view of the passing street scene and friendly service make L'Espresso a hit straight outta the box. Best: on commendable house-baked baguette, panini piled with thinly shaved roast pork, house-smoked salmon with capers, or breaded veal dressed in herbed tomato sauce; at brunch, free-range egg omelettes such as the Calabrese with artichoke, sopressata and Asiago, or multiple mushrooms coupled with roasted red pepper and creamy mascarpone, both sided with salad, grilled baguette and fries; over flaky house-baked brioche, eggs Benedict, properly poached eggs with buttery hollandaise and Black Forest ham, served with fruit salad and house-baked scones and strawberry preserves. *Open for breakfast, lunch and dinner. Licensed. Access: barrier-free.* **$$$** ⬤

Yorkville
French
LE PARADIS
166 Bedford, at Davenport, 416-921-0995, www.leparadis.com.
Launched nearly 20 years ago, this atmospheric midtown bistro has never been flavour of the month, nor has it ever tried to be. As white-aproned servers careen about the series of three small rooms painted Gauloise yellow and hung with black-and-white photos, regulars relax on well-worn café chairs and somewhat lumpy banquettes that flank kraft paper-covered tables complete with carafes of iced tap water. Not cutting edge, but certainly one of the most consistent kitchens in town. Best: to start, grilled eggplant, zucchini and luscious red pepper splashed with olive oil and topped with broiled Morbier cheese; salt cod brandade, a garlicky seafood purée served with crisp toasts, grainy Dijon and cornichon; mains like the house bavette, surprisingly tender flank in demi-glace sided with occasionally crisp frites; superb Provimi calf's liver; duck confit with eggy Peking Duck-style scallion crepes; daily specials like Chicken Dijonaise, meaty legs in French mustard cream sided with sweet potato gratin; to finish, one of the best crème caramels in town. *Open for dinner. Tuesday to Friday for lunch. Licensed. Access: barrier-free.* **$$$$** ⬤

luxe restos

On the 54th floor of the TD Tower, **Canoe** (66 Wellington West, at Bay, 416-364-0054) looks south over the islands and the lake. After dark, the view stretches west toward glittering Etobicoke and beyond. The menu emphasizes Canadian themes – Maritime lobster, BC salmon and the beef comes courtesy of luxe local butcher **Cumbrae**'s (481 Church, at Maitland, 416-923-5600).

North 44 (2537 Yonge, 416-487-4897) is a Yabu Pushelburg-designed upper-Toronto spot where the upper crust dines and star chef Mark McEwan rules. Dim lighting and small print make the menu hard to read – don't worry, they supply reading glasses – but the highlights include roasted Quebec Artisan chicken, organic Irish salmon and slow-braised rabbit.

Set in swellegant Yorkville, **Opus** (37 Prince Arthur, 416-921-3105) serves up French continental cuisine suited to the surrounding nabe, from tantalizing pasta dishes to perfectly prepared meat, fish and fowl to desserts.

Tucked into a small courtyard beside an old church, the inviting covered patio at **Prego Della Piazza** (150 Bloor West, 416-920-9900) affords an ideal spot from which to spot Hollywood A-listers dining on an A-list card of Italian cuisine.

Drop your car keys with the valet and bring your pocketbook and a foodie's sense of adventure when you sit down at **Splendido** (88 Harbord, 416-929-7788), one of the city's top dining spots. Rarely conventional, Chef David Lee keeps gastros guessing with a six-course blind tasting menu (including a vegetarian version) that, at 110 bucks a pop, is the treat of the town.

Cabbagetown gets a touch classier at **Provence Delices** (12 Amelia, 416-924-9901). The long-running bastion of accessible French cuisine has a spiffy awning-draped terrace, while steak frites goes for $15 and on the weekend, tuck into the $16.95 brunch buffet.

Just a few steps from Yorkville is the upscale yet understated **Sotto Sotto** (116A Avenue Road, 416-962-0111). The menu of classic, simply prepared Italian fare presented in an intimate, romanesque dining room makes this a popular spot for celebrities and local media magnates.

Italian

CAFÉ NERVOSA
75 Yorkville, at Bellair, 416-961-4642, www.idesigngrafix.com/nervosa.
Forget Sassafrazz and MBCo. Come the film festival, is there a better seat in town than on one of Nervosa's two curbside patios for spotting Hollywood A-listers? Large portions and reasonably priced for the neighbourhood. Warning: $10 minimum, and unless you literally want to fade into the background, don't wear leopard print. Trivia: though the café takes its name from Frasier Crane's TV haunt, actor Kelsey Grammer has never visited, but he did walk by once. Best: diet-conscious barely there thin-crusted pizzas like the Classica with tomato, roasted peppers, mushrooms and Calabrese salami, or oyster 'shrooms with Gorgonzola, chèvre, onion and prosciutto; meal-size insalatas like spinach tossed with smoky shaved smoked provolone, hard-boiled egg and walnuts in white wine vinaigrette; straightforward linguine with pan-seared tuna, a mix of fresh and sun-dried tomato in nutty basil pesto. *Open for lunch and dinner. Licensed. Access: six steps at door, washrooms on second floor.* **$$$** ⁘

Mediterranean

AMBER
119 Yorkville, at Hazelton, 416-926-9037.
This chic tented A-list haunt located off touristy Old Yorkville Lane is very white – white fences, white awnings, white wicker furniture and even white light fixtures yet. But those lucky enough to gain entry to this inner sanctum of cool (Canadian Idol's Ben Mulroney – woohoo!) can add culinary colour with the likes of gazpacho with toasted pistachios, lobster ravioli and mussels four ways (steamed in sake, Corona, Pernod or Absolut Citron). *Open for dinner. Bar till close. Licensed.* **$$** ⁘

Pan-Asian

INDOCHINE
4 Collier, at Yonge, 416-922-5840, www.indochinethaicuisine.ca.
Its concept often appropriated (hello, Spring Rolls!), this sleekly elegant room was the first in town to offer a varied card of Southeast Asian dishes including those from Thailand, Vietnam, China, Malaysia and Japan. The decor immediately impresses – all chic blond wood moulded plywood chairs at linen-clad tables and elongated Noguchi-style paper lanterns – but friendly service and reasonably priced fare are reasons alone to return. Bonus: weekday lunch specials. Best: one of the better pad thai's around, wide ketchup-pink rice noodle countered with plump grilled shrimp, shredded chicken, scrambled egg, crunchy bean sprouts and crushed peanuts; Hanoi Chicken Salad over baby mesclun greens in sweet citrus vinaigrette; Thai basil beef, thinly sliced sirloin and scallion in a peppery sauce strewn with licorice-y basil leaf; tender, slow-cooked Yellow Beef Brisket Curry offering sweetness instead of fireworks, swimming in silky gravy over short-grain rice. *Open for lunch and dinner. Licensed. Delivery. Access: one step at door, washrooms in basement.* **$$$**

Pub Grub

PILOT
22 Cumberland, at Yonge, 416-923-5716, www.thepilot.ca.
Now that the venerable downtown institution (63 years and counting) has completed the long-term overhaul of its three floors, the Pilot's rooftop Flight Deck is one of the most impressive around. Fittingly, the Deck's been given a retro streamlined aeronautic look, all rivet-studded stainless steel and aluminum panels, that reflects the esteemed pub's heritage. Still in place, a pub-grub menu that ranges from trendy pad thai to something called Calgary Ginger Beef – a Pilot exclusive, apparently. Bonus: an automated awning makes patio partying possible year-round. *Open for lunch and dinner. Licensed.* **$$** ⁘ ◔

Vegetarian

SALAD HOUSE
24 Roy's Square, at Bloor E, 416-920-4964.
This tiny no-frills fluorescent-lit storefront on a pedestrian walkway just south off Bloor and Yonge is one of the busiest lunchtime destinations in the area. Warning: not strictly vegetarian (both tuna and salmon salad as well as roasted chicken show up on the short menu) and indoor seating is minimal. Best: specials like multi-layered roasted veggie terrine, a stacked lemony tier of firm carrot, eggplant, bell pepper and zucchini, sided with apple-juiced sweet pota-

Café Nervosa is more laid-back than its cerebral name suggests.

to purée and Chinese long bean salad; super-fresh baby arugula with shaved parmigiana in a citrusy balsamic vinaigrette, or summer-ripe tomato Caprese salad; deliciously smooth seasonal soups like lentil purée or cream of turnip; to finish, addictive crèmes brûlée and caramel, their sugary top crusts blackened by blowtorch. *Open for lunch. Closed on the weekend, holidays. Unlicensed. Cash only. Access: one step at door, no washrooms.* **$** ⁙

● WANDA'S PIE IN THE SKY
7 Yorkville, at Yonge, 416-925-7437, www.wandaspieinthesky.com.
For those who eat – rather than do – lunch, this little cubbyhole with a glass garage door that opens to the street has to be the best deal in Yorkville. Affordable, kookily quaint and especially quick service. Bonus: everything's trans fats-free. Double bonus: owner Wanda Beaver now has a second outlet in tandem with legendary caterer Dinah Koo called Wanda's in the Kitchen with Dinah (1057 Mt Pleasant, at

Sherwood, 416-483-0399). Best: rotating lineup of rustic seasonal tomato-sauced pizzas like roasted rapini with red onion and hot banana peppers; sells-out-immediately quiche with spinach, red pepper and old cheddar; sandwiches such as Brie on half a pumpernickel baguette piled with watercress, cucumber, lettuce and house lemon-garlic mayo, or sliced avocado on Doughheads' olive-potato focaccia with tomato, cheddar and coriander, sided with Mediterranean-style greens tossed with black olives and feta, doused in light balsamic; to finish, butter tarts. *Open for lunch. Monday to Saturday for breakfast. Unlicensed. Access: barrier-free.* **$$**

Yonge – Central
Café

7 WEST CAFÉ
7 Charles W, at Yonge, 416-928-9041.
Next time you need a little post-club grub, forget the slices and street dogs and check out this 24-hour

restaurants

haven. Three floors cater to varying moods, but only the second and least interesting is open all night. Ground level makes an ideal first-date locale, all red velvet drapes, intimate arched nooks and homey gas fireplace. The third is more modern – deep cranberry walls offset by a vaulted steel-blue ceiling, a pair of church windows and retro rock on the stereo. Best: Hot Bread, four thick slices of Italian loaf laden with a concassée of onion, mushrooms and sun-dried tomatoes, layered with melted cheddar and mozzarella; Fritte-Prosciutto sandwich, a salty pile of dried ham and sautéed onions on crusty baguette with tomato and optional buffalo mozzarella melt, sided with sweet red pepper, cucumber, chickpeas and greens; Rosie Ravioli, a large saucer of spinach- and ricotta-stuffed pasta in creamy rosé, paired with soft Italian bread. *Open for breakfast, lunch and dinner. Licensed. Access: five steps at door, washrooms in basement and second floor.* $$$

Ethiopian

ETHIOPIAN HOUSE
**4 Irwin, at Yonge, 416-923-5438,
www.ethiopianhouse.com.**
Think you can handle the heat? This two-storey Ethiopian resto bar just off the Yonge Street drag offers fiery steak dishes that get some cooling relief from milder veggie purées. Servers dressed in embroidered traditional garb present dinner under a domed wicker mosobe while porous East African injera and fingers replace forks. Best: gin-soaked steak seasoned with honey wine, clarified butter and aromatic spices; steak-tartar-like kitfo kicked with berbere pepper paste; relatively soothing chopped collard greens or sweet tomato atakelt wot – an almost Italian stew of potato, carrots and green beans; inexpensive vegetarian combination platters. *Open for lunch and dinner. Licensed. Access: four steps at door, washrooms on second floor.* $$$

French

LE PETIT GOURMET
1064 Yonge, at Roxborough, 416-966-3811.
Opened in the early 70s, Toronto's first Parisian patisserie and fancy takeaway continues to impress with its affordable luxury. Count on honest Gallic grub and low-key hospitality. Bonus wall decoration: an autographed photo of hockey great – and singer of Honky the Christmas Goose – Johnny Bower! Best: curried chicken salad – shredded chicken breast in alarmingly yellow mayo studded with ripe strawberry, apple and melon; whole, slow-roasted chickens dusted with thyme sold by the kilo; lovely coq au vin with diced carrot and button 'shrooms stewed in white wine rather than red; delicate filets of Atlantic salmon arrive sauced in dilled cream; salads and sides like green bean thick with cauliflower, broccoli and chunked avocado in a lemony egg dressing or scalloped-style potatoes in basic white bechamel sauce; to finish, Gateau Basque, a rustic vanilla-custard-filled crumbly crusted tart. *Open for breakfast and lunch. Closed Sunday. Unlicensed. Cash only. Access: two steps at door, washrooms in basement.* $$

MATIGNON
**51 Nicholas, at Inkerman, 416-921-9226,
www.matignon.ca.**
Off the beaten track, this down-to-earth neighbourhood bistro in a side-street row house has been serving hearty French fare that defies gastro trends since the late 80s. Attentive service, a working fireplace and a nightly three-course $29.95 prix fixe dinner deal. Best: to start, escargots in garlic butter or mussels steamed in white wine and shallots; at dinner, mustard-crusted roast rack of lamb with minty jus; bouillabaise with shrimp, clams, mussels, scallops and salmon, scented with saffron-tinged mayo, shaved Parmesan and garlic croutons; steak frites with crisply fried spuds; for dessert, triple-tier gateau layered with chestnut mousse; profiteroles with French vanilla ice cream, hot chocolate syrup and Grand Marnier. *Open for dinner. Monday to Friday for lunch. Closed Sunday, holidays. Licensed. Access: six steps at door, washrooms on second floor.* $$$$

Indian

KATHMANDU KATHMANDU
**517 Yonge, at Maitland, 416-924-5787,
www.kathmandurestaurant.ca.**
This unassuming spot on the strip is easy to miss. But once discovered, it's a true find. Non-greasy North Indian and Nepalese fare served seven days a week, including an all-you-can-eat lunchtime buffet every day but Sunday. Best: mixed veggie curry of cauliflower, eggplant, carrots and potato; eggplant bharta; cubes of lamb or goat in fiery tomato sauce; $3.99 bargain takeout-only shredded tandoori chicken wrapped in naan, coupled with a mango lassi. *Open for dinner. Monday to Saturday for lunch. Licensed. Access: one step at door, washrooms on same floor.* $$$

RUCHI
649 Yonge, at St. Mary, 416-926-0953.
Attention, hungry Blue Man fans! Located right next door to the Panasonic Theatre – and directly downstairs from the Duke of Gloucester pub – this inordinately narrow Indian eatery specializes in regional Andhran interpretations of northern Moghul favourites spiced with southern fire. Bonus: a daily $5.25 lunchtime vegetarian thali and quick takeout, too. Best: butter chicken in rich tomato cream amped up to 11; vinegary lamb vindaloo in fiery sauce studded with spuds; aloo korma, steamed potatoes 'n' onions in masala thickened with yogurt and poppyseed paste; first-rate samosas – potato, pea and carrot or minced chicken – as well as red pepper and tandoori chicken pakoras dunked in the house's super tamarind-ginger chutney; on the side, Chinese fried-style basmati rice strewn with cumin seeds and coriander leaf or garlic and raw green onion. *Open for lunch and dinner. Licensed. Access: one step at door, washrooms in basement.* $$

Italian

FOCACCIA ITALIAN SANDWICHES
13 Hayden, at Yonge, 416-922-8171.
From the folks at the upscale New World spot next door with the similar name, old-school southern Italian sandwiches, salads and pastas just like Mama used to make. The loyal followers of this long-running café don't want you to know about their tucked-away Bloor and Yonge find. Best: omigod veal 'n' pork meat loaf thick with veggies, topped by the ultimate sweet tomato sauce and sided with super-creamy potato/avocado/hardboiled-egg salad; no-nonsense lasagna; grilled olive-oil-brushed veggies (baby eggplant, zucchini, red peppers) layered with mozzarella and grilled a second time on a sandwich press. Prices include taxes. *Open for dinner. Monday to Friday for lunch. Closed Sunday, holidays. Licensed. Access: barrier-free, no washrooms.* $$

PASTA PERFECTION
462 Yonge, at College, 416-964-0929.
An anomaly amidst the fast food joints on Hogtown's main drag, this popular pasta-teria presents inexpensive noodle noshes from Italy and Southeast Asia with made-to-order stir-fixed fixings and sauces. Bonus: extra garlic! Best: grilled Cajun chicken breast on penne, fettuccine, linguini, fusilli or whole wheat spaghetti, with a chilied red pepper and onion tomato sauce; Mexi-meat lasagna – a slab of flat pasta,

ground beef, mozzarella and crunchy green pepper, or the veggie version where spinach noodles come layered with zucchini and mushroom; lemon-peanut chicken salad on a bed of romaine, tossed with garlic croutons and red pepper cubes, dressed in a sesame vinaigrette; pita pizzas topped with hot Italian sausage, green pepper and cayenne-kicked tomato sauce; simple primavera with veggies and olive oil. *Open for lunch and dinner. Licensed. Access: barrier-free, washrooms in basement.* **$$**

Japanese

MASA
15 Charles E, at Yonge, 416-920-3388, www.masanyc.com.
If you've ever enjoyed Katsu on the Danforth, you know the deal: flat price, better than average made-to-order all-you-can-eat sushi. This second location, an elegant 200-plus room on the first floor of the Comfort Hotel just off Toronto's main drag, also offers teppanyaki tables for group dining and an à la carte card for takeout and delivery. Best: from the buffet, tasty strips of beef in sweet teriyaki sauce; stir-fried teppanyaki chicken; superb Japanese fried rice flecked with scrambled egg, carrot and onion, with nary a frozen veggie in sight; crisp and grease-free vegetarian tempura; hand-formed nigiri topped with fatty striped salmon, or inside-out uramaki stuffed with crunchy salmon skin and tossed with tobiko; karaage-style deep-fried chicken wings; pan-fried udon mixed with chicken and scallions. *Open for lunch and dinner. Closed Christmas Day. Licensed. Delivery. Access: barrier-free.* **$$$**

OKONOMI HOUSE
23 Charles W, at St. Nicholas, 416-925-6176.
Thriving in an out-of-the-way location since the 70s, this long-popular Japanese fast food joint ("okonomi" translates as "favourite") specializes in Hiroshima-style street food. Part omelette, part pancake, it's a filling, quick meal for around six bucks. Bonus: count-

er seats offer an up-close view of the open kitchen where skilled chefs slice 'n' dice your dinner before your eyes. Best: from the nine varieties available – including chicken, pork, bacon, vegetable, squid and scallop – Okonomi Yaki, gingery tender slivers of crisply grilled chopped beef fried in a batter of flour, milk, egg, shredded cabbage, green onion and pickled ginger, spread with sweet barbecue-style sauce and topped with dollops of miso mayo; for the less adventurous, beef or salmon teriyaki combos with miso soup, fried veggies and plain ol' rice, or thick yaki soba noodles generously mixed with beef, chicken and shrimp. *Open for lunch and dinner. Closed holidays. Licensed. Access: barrier-free.* **$$**

Korean

YUMMY BAR-B-Q
522A Yonge, at Wellesley, 416-921-5158.
This food-court-style alterna noodle house specializes in inexpensive chili-tastic Korean combos. No frills, lots of thrills. Bonus: lots of traditional sides, but skip the god-awful macaroni salad. Best: char-grilled boneless Spicy Chicken marinated in red pepper paste and smoky sesame oil, sided with salty kimchee, delicately pickled daikon threads and rice; a barbecued pair of 8-inch mackerels in sweet soy with slivered scallions; deep-fried zucchini rings in omelette-like eggy batter; thickly sliced dense tofu in fiery chili-stoked veggie broth; Spicy Rice Cake – doughy rice noodles – with shredded Spicy Beef. Warning: Kimchee Fried Rice topped with a runny sunny-side-up egg reads better than the resultant mush tastes. *Open for lunch and dinner. Unlicensed. Access: one step at door, washrooms on same floor.* **$**

Lebanese

● PITA BREAK
565 Yonge, at Wellesley, 416-968-1032, www.pitabreak.com.
For anyone who finds falafel awful, the Middle Eastern sandwich sold at this busy fast food outlet is worthy of a second look. The reason? Double-thickness pitas in a mouth-watering range of flavours so delish these awesome flatbreads are sold in gourmet shops across town. Best: falafel chickpea nuggets topped with sesame-rich tahini, sliced iceberg lettuce, red cabbage, sprouts and coriander hot sauce in pita pouches, served in baskets; other fillings – grilled chicken breast, smoked turkey, tuna with melted cheddar or scrambled egg salad; baked-in-house super-pitas sold in bulk include non-disintegrating pesto, black olive, jalapeño, sun-dried tomato, tomato basil, organic spelt, pumpernickel and breakfast raisin-and-cinnamon. *Open for breakfast, lunch and dinner. Closed Sunday, holidays. Unlicensed. Access: barrier-free, washrooms in basement.* **$**

Pan-Asian

GINGER
695 Yonge, at Charles, 416-966-2424, 403 Yonge, at Gerrard, 416-263-9999, 546 Church, at Wellesley, 416-413-1053.
Although the original Yonge shop has some stiff competition nearby (Spring Rolls down the block, Green Mango across the street), this unpretentious Vietnamese pan-Asian self-serve cafeteria take-away has established itself as a foodie favourite and spawned two sister eateries since launching in 99. Bonus: windows that swing open to the passing parade when weather permits. Best: meal-in-one soups like hot 'n' sour seafood soup with shrimp, mussels, scallops, squid, enoki mushrooms and rice vermicelli; multiple meat and veg combos like skewered and grilled shrimp with flattened pork chops over sticky rice; chili beef with papaya, or chicken breast with mango salad; terrific Saigon subs on flaky

French rolls stuffed with grilled beef, lemongrass and onion; to spice things up, a plethora of condiments – Sriracha hot sauce, lime wedges, chili paste, hoisin and raw bird chillies; to finish, durian ice cream. *Open for lunch and dinner. Licensed. Access: barrier-free.* **$**

SPRING ROLLS
693 Yonge, at Charles, 416-972-7655, 40 Dundas West, 416-585-2929, 45 Eglinton East, 416-322-7655, 85 Front East, 416-365-3649, 120 Church, 416-815-7655, www.springrolls.ca.
Often imitated, this stylish pan-Asian chain mixes Thai, Chinese and Vietnamese dishes to create a kitchen, though not the most cutting-edge, that's certainly one of the most consistent around. Warning:

i scream
u scream
ice cream

The **Sicilian Sidewalk Café's** (712 College, at Montrose, 416-531-7755) Aurelio Galipo introduced Italian-style gelato to Toronto back in 1959. Almost 50 years later, the tradition lives on in the house's buttery spumone, stracciatella and ladyfinger tiramisu ice creams.

Up on the Corso Italia, **La Paloma Gelateria** (1357 St. Clair West, at Lansdowne, 416-656-2340) offers a spectacular array of ices – zabaglione, cassata and zuppa inglese, a fluorescent, frozen trifle of pink and yellow birthday cake studded with candied cherries, chocolate chunks and slivered almonds dribbled with strawberry.

Like something out of Willie Wonka, **Dutch Dreams** (78 Vaughan, at St. Clair, 416-656-6959) is famous for its unusual chilled creations, like Moose Droppings (Reese's Pieces mixed with fudge, chocolate and banana) and shocking-pink watermelon sherbet complete with chocolate-covered oats as seeds.

Greg's Ice Cream (750 Spadina, at Bloor, 416-962-4734) creates ices from all-natural ingredients for its Japanese green tea and legendary roasted marshmallow flavours.

In the Beach, **Ed's Real Scoop** (2224 Queen East, at Birch, 416-699-6100) relies on all-natural ingredients and 100 per cent real fruit for flavour rather than butter and cream when creating current faves Belgian-style Calebaut chocolate, Bordeaux cherry and Tahitian vanilla bean served in cups or cones (plain, sugared, chocolate-dipped, waffle and "fancy").

Kensington Market Organic Ice Cream (188 Augusta, at Denison Square, 416-835-7781, also at Dufferin Grove's Thursday farmers market) offers just that, especially its fruity Quebecois framboise and just-like-Christmas-cake ginger chai ices, while **Soma Chocolatemaker** (55 Mill, Distillery District, 416-815-7662) scoops up some fabulous gelato, churned daily, including dark Venezuelan chocolate and Madagascar vanilla.

insanely busy at peak feeding-frenzy periods. Best: to begin, smoked salmon and tiger shrimp cold rolls in raw rice paper; artfully presented and executed pho with rare beef, beef brisket, beef balls and rice noodles; communal mains like deep-fried tofu with wok-tossed asparagus and broccoli in garlicky Szechwan sauce; acceptable pad thai in several versions; carnivorous Cantonese chow mein; char-grilled Korean-style kalbi short ribs; to finish, deep-fried bananas with green-tea ice cream. *Open for lunch and dinner. Licensed. Delivery. Access: barrier-free.* **$$$**

Persian

TEMPUS
508 Yonge, at Maitland, 416-929-8893, www.tempus-bistro.com.
Formerly modish Retro Rotisserie, this surprisingly stylish eatery offers a mostly Persian lineup with unusual flare. Bonus: weekday lunch specials! Best: to start, skinny sweet potato frites, perfectly fried, lightly salted and perhaps the best in town, sided with thickened yogurt laced with toasted shallot; house greens crumbled with blue cheese and splashed with minty vinaigrette; from the mains, fesenjoon, chicken stewed with crushed walnuts and pomegranate upgraded with saffron 'n' barberry basmati; generously portioned lamb shank sided with basmati freckled with dill and green fava. *Open for lunch and dinner. Licensed. Access: barrier-free, washrooms in basement.* **$$$**

Pub Grub

BAR VOLO
587 Yonge, at Gloucester, 416-928-0008, www.barvolo.com.
Volo's been serving up the deluxe suds for almost 20 years now, and this is what you should focus on when you come here. Otherwise, you're looking at bar food with pretensions. Pizzas, sandwiches and pastas have fancy names and muddled preparations. This place just cries out for the simple approach, but instead you get unsuccessful variations on Euro-snacks. Even the burger fails to satisfy. Best: outstanding selection of beer and wine. At least 100 bottled beers, 12 local micros on tap and 13 Ontario wines by the glass. All reasonably priced. The room is cozy, the patio sunny and the service friendly. *Open for lunch and dinner. Licensed. Access: barrier-free, washrooms in basement.* **$$** ☼ ⓣ

Thai

GREEN MANGO
730 Yonge, at Bloor W, 416-928-0021, www.greenmango.ca.
Grab a tray and join the conga line! Ensconced in somewhat fancier digs across the street from its original location – which still operates as Green Mango Soup Kitchen, though, like its other outlets, with an expanded and pricier range of royal Thai classics – this cafeteria-style cantina has won NOW's Readers Poll for best fast food since the category was instigated. Well, maybe not that fast. At peak hours, a fast-moving lineup snaking out the 25-year-old spot's front door makes snagging a table nigh impossible. Best: for $6.25, combine pink peanut-garnished pad thai or mildly spiced cellophane noodles with lemongrass chicken, basil eggplant 'n' tofu, or vegetarian curry; on the side, regulation deep-fried spring rolls; the house salad – tart green mango tossed with onion, pepper and dried shallot in chili-dusted lemon dressing; to finish (what else?) mango mousse. *Open for lunch and dinner. Licensed. Access: barrier-free.* **$** ⓣ

Hope the cook-it-yourself Korean BBQ craze doesn't catch on at other restos. **Yummy Bar-B-Q**. Page 79.

North

North York

Japanese

SUSHI BONG
5 Northtown Way, at Yonge, 416-227-0022.
Named for its Korean owner/chef Tony Bong and not the popular recreational device, this infinitesimal eatery in the heart of North York can be found on the first floor of a high-rise condo development just off the main drag. Behind its anonymous facade, discover a small friendly sushi bar where staff sing along to the K-pop blasting over a boom box while slicing and dicing your dinner. Best: tempura of 10 large butterflied shrimp in grease-free batter; Zarusoba, firm bundles of slippery buckwheat noodles in deliciously sweet cold miso dressed with scallions, seaweed threads, minced white daikon and wasabi chef squeezes from a pastry bag; fluorescent green wakame salad, a Korean-style tangle of gingerly pickled nori; Moon River maki of avocado, crab, cucumber and salmon laced with Kewpie Japanese mayo. *Open for lunch and dinner. Cash only. Access: barrier-free, but no washrooms.* **$$**

St. Clair West

Cambodian

KHMER THAI
1018 St. Clair W, at Appleton, 416-654-0609.
Forget pad thai. This gaudy west-side storefront specializes in subtly spiced Cambodian dishes that combine influences from neighbouring Vietnam and Thailand as well as those further afield — India, Portugal, France. Best: substantial soups that verge on multi-portion stews, like hot and sour bamboo shoots, chicken and Asian eggplant in coral-hued coconut gravy, or Soup Delight, pineapple, tomato and Chinese celery in a clear aromatic broth detonated with whispers of salty prahok (fermented fish paste) and galangal; Khmer Pancake, a rice flour omelette stuffed with gently spiced ground chicken dunked into a complex sugary dip of chili, peanut and vinegar; tamarind-tanged Samlaw Khmer chicken with carrot, broccoli and bell pepper over jasmine rice; lassi-like green tea shakes. *Open for dinner. Wednesday to Saturday for lunch. Closed Christmas Day. Unlicensed. Access: one step at door, washrooms on same floor.* **$$**

Contemporary

RUSHTON
740 St. Clair W, at Rushton, 416-658-7874.
The Drake comes to St. Clair! Once a corner grocery, this 40-seat spin-off of Ferro has been recast as an art deco bistro complete with Frank Lloyd Wright-like flagstone accents and French doors that open to the street and a large summer patio. Sadly, all those hard surfaces make this one of the noisiest rooms in town. Warning: reserve or show up early unless you want to stand in line for a table. Best: to begin, daily soups like an ambrosial purée of sweet celeriac offset with poached pear and crumbled Roquefort; to continue, mains — most available in large or small portions — such as ale-battered halibut paired with first-rate chunky fries; the sizable house burger, a sirloin patty topped with red onion chiffonade sided

restaurants

with sweet potato frites; grilled bone-in pork chop in pan jus with roasted spuds and Swiss chard; à la carte sides like retro mac 'n' cheese; to finish, flourless chocolate cake with crème fraîche. *Open for dinner. Monday to Friday for lunch. Licensed. Access: one step at door, washrooms on same floor.* **$$$$**

Italian

BIG RAGU

1338 Lansdowne, at St. Clair W, 416-654-7248.
This smallish, old-school trat specializes in what owner/chef Carmine "The Big Ragu" Accogli refers to as grandma dishes, central and southern Italian favourites cooked with Old World skill. Bonus: every Thursday is house-made gnocchi night! Warning: ask the price of the nightly meat and fish specials, since they're often twice as expensive as the dishes on the printed card. Best: complimentary baskets of house-baked focaccia dunked in quality olive oil and balsamic; minimally appointed but maximum-flavoured pizzas like the Margherita with superb house tomato sauce, lotsa mozza and a fresh basil leaf or two; specials such as meaty pan-seared lamb chops in a red wine reduction accented with fresh rosemary and sage, sided with roasted russets; primi like ear-shaped orrechiette with bitter rapini, blackened almonds and the slightest suggestion of garlic and anchovy; at brunch, the Spaghetti Western, a clever frittata of pasta, peameal and grated Parmesan. *Open for dinner. Sunday for brunch. Closed Monday. Licensed. Access: two steps at narrow entrance, washrooms in basement.* **$$$$**

MARCELLO'S

1163 St. Clair W, at Dufferin, 416-656-6159.
Although it's not the trendiest place in town, how this outstanding old-school trat continues to fly under some foodies' radar mystifies. Substantial salads, simple yet satisfying grills, customized pasta and possibly the best wood-burning, thin-crust pizza in town, all at shockingly reasonable prices in a family-friendly room built for comfort, make this boisterous bistro a true find. Best: from the pizza lineup, the Mimmo, a 12-inch thin-crust beauty layered with roasted garlic, Asiago, Gorgonzola, mozzarella and strands of spinach; Fazzoletto, a pizza-crust turnover stuffed with goat cheese, ricotta, spinach and sun-dried tomatoes on a bed of bitter greens; Linguine con Gamberi, butterflied and grilled shrimp in a tomato cream over noodles, tossed with charred leeks and sun-dried tomatoes; rich chicken-broth-based Stracciatella Fiorentina strewn with tomato and spinach; balsamic-dressed house mesclun mixed with roasted red peppers, artichoke hearts and Asiago shavings. *Open for lunch and dinner. Licensed. Access: one step at door, washrooms in basement.* **$$$** ☼

Mediterranean

MEZZETTA

681 St. Clair W, at Christie, 416-658-5687.
Specializing in the Middle Eastern tapas known as mezzes, this once low-key take-away has evolved since it opened in the early 90s into a casual hacienda decked out with showbiz memorabilia. Bonus: live jazz Wednesdays from 9 pm. Double bonus: at Monday dinner, every second dish is a buck (with a limit of 15), and at Tuesday dinner they're a toonie; weekdays at lunchtime all vegetarian items are $2. Best: from the card of more than 40 mezzes, the house Evergreen Salad of romaine, spinach, coriander, parsley and walnuts in a light vinegary vinaigrette; somewhat sour Mezziki – cubed cuke in yogurt,

recalling Greek tzatziki and Indian raita; garlicky Egyptian Mush, an olive-oily purée of garlicky tomato, eggplant and green pepper suggesting Italy and Thailand; to finish, Crème Bavaria, vanilla custard laced with Triple Sec, topped with toasted almonds and chocolate syrup. *Open for dinner. Monday to Friday for lunch. Licensed. Access: four steps at door, washrooms in basement.* **$$$**

Patisserie
PATACHOU
835 St. Clair W, at Winona, 416-782-0122, other locations.
After decades of serving puff pastry to the upper crust at Summerhill and Yonge, Patachou's latest west-side location spreads the wealth. Located in a former automotive parts garage, the small dining area and patio are modern to the point of spartan. Bonus: almost everything is takeout-compatible and can go from microwave to table in minutes. Best: tart niçoise, a wedge of eggplant, zucchini and tomato topped with melted Gruyère; traditional onion soup full of slippery bulb and chewy cheese; a croque monsieur as minimalist as the decor; charismatic green bean salad with red onion in mustard vinaigrette; some of Toronto's best croissants; dessert pastries like the Supreme, a fluffy tennis ball of white chocolate, chocolate sponge cake and raspberry coulis, or the Karamanda layered with caramel cream and vanilla genoise; macaroons full of butter cream. *Open for breakfast and lunch. Unlicensed. Access: barrier-free.* **$$** ☼

Peruvian
EL FOGON
543 St. Clair W, at Vaughan, 416-850-8041.
With its minimal attempt at Latin American-inspired decor, this family-friendly cantina is the kind of place you might actually find in Peru. Though the focus is primarily seafood and rice, there are plenty of beef, chicken and pork choices. Bonus: impossibly polite service, no tacky Inca kitsch or pan flutes. Best: Lomo Saltado sandwich, perhaps the biggest lunchtime bargain in the GTA, a very fresh bun loaded with juicy strips of lean, char-broiled steak dripping with a wonderful barbecue-style sauce and sautéed Peruvian onions, served with salad or authentic chunky Peruvian fries; summery Ceviche Mixto (ample for two as an appetizer), rings of tender squid and octopus, a few clams, shrimp and white fish sided with sliced and chilled sweet potato, fresh coriander and a basket of fresh bread spread with a purée of garlic, clarified butter and hot chilies. *Open for lunch and dinner. Closed Monday, Tuesday. Licensed. Access: barrier-free.* **$$$**

Vietnamese
PHO RUA VANG
1776 St. Clair W, at Cloverdale, 416-656-1549.
No relation to the identically handled Ossington boîte, this bright and cheerful noodle house specializes in broken-rice plates and steamed savoury-stuffed banh cuon rice rolls. Impressive sweets, too. Best: breakfast-ready pho like lean shaved beef and slippery, slurpable rice stick in aromatic broth fragrant with lemongrass and garnished with crisp raw sprouts, slivered scallions and Vietnamese ram rau coriander; broken rice with skinny grilled pork and boneless chicken thigh sided with smoky bean-sprout slaw; lime-marinated house-made beef jerky threads over raw daikon julienne; for afters, frothy coconut cream over black-eyed peas in sticky rice. *Open for breakfast, lunch and dinner. Unlicensed. Access: bump at door, washrooms in basement.* **$$**

Uptown
Café
DAVID'S BY DAY/BUZZ BY NIGHT
413 Spadina Rd, at Lonsdale, 416-482-7871.
This Forest Hill Village café has two faces: by day a busy café populated by moneyed matrons and the help, by evening a somewhat pricier bistro bull of moneyed matrons and their husbands when it's the help's night off. Best: sunny curbside patio. *Open for breakfast, lunch and dinner. Licensed. Access: one step at door, tight tables, washrooms on same floor.* **$$$$** ☼

Chinese
CHA LIU
2352 Yonge, at Eglinton, 416-485-1725.
A bit of a hidden gem, atmosphere-wise, this dim sum spot rises above (literally, it's up a flight of stairs) the mundane strip of Yonge and Eglinton. While the food is Chinese – all dumplings and rolls – the decor and Zen tranquility are more Japanese. All items are competently executed, but flavours lack boldness. Best: octopus fingers with just a hint of curry and a side of sea salt, simple beef mushroom and green onion dumplings and house made chang fun. *Open for lunch and dinner. Licensed. Access: flight of stairs at entrance.* **$$$** ☼

Contemporary
SCARAMOUCHE: THE GRILL
1 Benvenuto, at Avenue Rd, 416-961-8011.
Stuck for a spot to take the 'rents? With its wonderful skyline view, Scaramouche has been one of Toronto's favourite – and priciest – dining destinations for over 20 years. This adjacent scenery-free lounge – once the Pasta Bar, now renamed The Grill to attract carbo-phobes and the Atkins-obsessed – offers co-owner/chef Keith Froggett's slightly less expensive noshes that take mainstream Cal Ital upscale. Bonus: complimentary valet parking (motorized vehicles only). Best: to start, cookbook-correct Caesar with anchovy dressing and shaved Parmigiana Reggiano; to continue, house-made ravioli stuffed with roasted chicken, escarole and ricotta over butternut squash in a toasted hazelnut broth; grilled Provimi calf's liver in lemon-parsley jus with Parmesan-whipped mash and buttermilk onion rings; house-made peppercorn fettuccine layered with sautéed beef tenderloin, oyster 'shrooms and braised tomato; red wine-braised lamb shank with Sardinian couscous, caramelized onion and wilted spinach; to finish, the legendary house-baked coconut cream pie topped with white chocolate shavings and dark chocolate sauce. *Open for dinner. Closed Sunday. Licensed. Access: barrier-free.* **$$$$** ☼

French
AUBERGE DU POMMIER
4150 Yonge, at York Mills, 416-222-2220.
Long a north Toronto dining destination for lovers, this faux stone cottage complex (think Disney does French country) surprises with its Gallic finesse, especially when chef Jason Bangerter gives old classics a contemporary spin. Best: intensely flavoured Auberge mushroom soup loaded with 'shrooms – enoki, cremini, shiitake – in rich vegetarian broth; chicken liver parfait with Bing cherry compote laced with port on teensy toasts; crisply seared tuna with peppered pineapple tartar, sided with a peti pois salade; deluxe lunch crepes du jour like pheasant confit mixed with caramelized Jerusalem artichoke over celeriac mash and Calvados-scented jus; veal tenderloin wrapped in bacon and sided with sweetbread vol-au-vent with green peppercorn cream.

burger kings

If you're hankering for a slab of beef on a bun, Toronto has a lot more to offer than just super-sizin' drive-throughs serving heat-lamped patties and stale frites.

Witness **Bymark**'s (66 Wellington, 416-777-1144) 40-buck whopper – $36.95 to be exact – made from beer-fed beef and topped with Brie de Meaux cheese, grilled porcini 'shrooms and shaved summer truffles.

Likewise check **Czehoski**'s (678 Queen West, 416-366-6787) quadruple quarter-pounder with heirloom tomatoes, double-smoked bacon, unpasteurized cheese and pure gold leaf (and for a penny less than Bymark's burger).

A bit too pricey? We understand. Try these easier-on-the-wallet burgers.

King of the quarter-pounders goes to the **Rivoli**'s (332 Queen West, 416-596-1501), served on challah and topped by sweetly sautéed onions. Sibling **Queen Mother Café** (206 Queen West, 416-598-4719) weighs in as crown prince with its 70s freakazoid vegetarian Cosmic Burger.

The rest of the royal court includes **Dangerous Dan's** (714 Queen East, 416-463-7310), where for less than five bucks you can order the 16-ounce Coronary Burger with bacon, cheddar and a fried egg, or the Quadruple C (Colossal Colon Clogger Combo), a 24-ounce burger layered with a quarter-pound of bacon, cheese and two fried eggs.

Meanwhile, the card at the **Yellow Griffin Pub** (2202 Bloor West, 416-763-3365) boasts 35 varieties of burger, including something called the Skippy Dipper that comes topped with peanut butter.

Utopia's (586 College, 416-534-7751) roster of burgers ain't too shabby either, from the basic half-pounder to the ground chicken and ground lamb patties.

If you can get past the faux 60s-diner style and cheesy a cappella singing by the counter staff, chain burger stand **Lick's** (654 Danforth, and others, 416-362-LICK) serves up a Nature Burger you'd swear contained beef. For an authentic 60s diner experience, head north to the **Golden Star** (7123 Yonge, 905-889-6891), where the burgers, fries and shakes are a definite step up from Harvey's. Or try Scarborough favourite **Johnny's Hamburgers** (2595 Victoria Park, 416-491-7222), where Mike Myers used to hang and the burgers are cheap and simple.

Finally, **Hero Certified Burgers** (650 1/2 Queen West, 416-368-9292, and others) serves up an Angus beef patty that tastes like it came from the backyard grill.

Open for dinner. Monday to Friday for lunch. Closed Sunday, holidays. Licensed. Access: barrier-free. $$$$$ ☼

Japanese

BLUE ZEN
2561 Yonge, at Sherwood, 416-481-3355.
Owner-chef Marco Tam has opened one of the most elegantly appointed restos in town, all white-on-white minimalism countered with a moving-wave lightbox built into the floor of his uptown Japanese eatery. The card's just as innovative, a contemporary lineup that honours tradition as well as experimentation. Bonus: 10 per cent cash discount. Best: Tuna Basil Wrap, a starter of scallop and tobiko smeared with mayo, wrapped in raw tuna and layered with Italian basil leaf; the Blue Zen Roll, maki rice spirals tangled with salmon, tuna, faux crab, avocado and cucumber, painted with pink wasabi mayo; mains like steamed asparagus stalk wrapped in a DNA helix of butterflied shrimp, or panko-crusted lobster tempura; hellaciously hot spicy miso soup with fresh spinach and smoky chili oil. Open for lunch and dinner. Licensed. Delivery. $$$

Patisserie

RAHIER
1586 Bayview, at Hillsdale, 416-482-0917.
Rapturously rich chocolate gateaux and fruit tarts from a Paris-perfect patisserie in nouveau-riche Bayview strip. Off hours, the café is a lovely respite from the day's chores, but on weekends the joint's a zoo. Best: single-serving cakes honouring famous French folks the likes of Napoleon (dark chocolate mousse with orange crème brûlée on rice-crisp sponge cake) or Hugo (fruity yellow mango mousse over a layer of red berry gelée on chocolate sponge); luscious seasonal fruit tartlets – raspberry, peach, apricot, kiwi, black and green grapes in custard on buttery pâte brisée; miniature chocolate explosions like florentins, tiny chocolate shells crammed with honeyed almonds and candied cherries; almond, apricot croissants, rustic walnut breads, savoury cheese palmiers. Takeout dessert for $5 per person, including all taxes. Closed Monday, Tuesday. Unlicensed. Access: barrier-free. $ ☼

East

The Beach

Italian

ANTOINETTE
2455 1/2 Queen E, at Silver Birch, 416-698-1300.
This petite eatery draws customers to the Beach from all over our Ital-mad city for homemade noodle noshes. Eschewing nouvelle cuisine, chef-owner Antoinette Sacco's menu features old-school fare last seen round these parts at Gio Rana's Nose circa 85. Bonus: checkerboard tablecloths and flickering candles in Chianti bottles. Warning: reservations not accepted for Friday or Saturday sittings. Best: tri-colour gnocchi with smoked chicken, sun-dried tomato, fresh tomato, green onion and sweet pepper; ricotta-stuffed ravioli in a red pepper, black olive and mushroom reduction; classic anchovy-laced Caesar plated fusion-style on a pappadom; oven-braised veal osso bucco with mushrooms, sided with risotto and veggies du jour; to finish, house-baked chocolate cake à la mode. Open for dinner. Closed Sunday, holidays. Licensed. Access: barrier-free. $$$$

Get your motor runnin' at old-school trat **Marcello's**. Page 82.

Cabbagetown

Café

PEARTREE
507 Parliament, at Carlton, 416-962-8190.
Amongst the dollar stores and donut dives, this cozy café is an oasis of taste. With adjoining spaces at the front and a bright solarium tucked in the back, patrons have the choice of three distinctive, homey dining environments. Flavours range from French to Creole, with a selection of pastas, quesadillas and all-day breakfast. Best: large saucer of hearty lentil and spinach soup flecked with pear and sweet potato, seasoned with a hint of curry; Sacramento Caesar Salad with serious chunks of moist roast turkey, cucumber, sweet peppers and feta, but go easy on the dressing; eggs Benjamin – two poached eggs on English muffins and smoked salmon with melted Swiss, covered with hollandaise and served with home fries, crispy fried onion and cubed melon. *Open for breakfast, lunch and dinner. Licensed. Access: barrier-free.* **$$$** ⬭

Contemporary

BIG MAMMA'S BOY
554 Parliament, at Amelia, 416-927-1593,
www.bigmammasboy.ca.
One-time Slack Alice and Looking Glass matriarch Heather McKenzie quits high-rent Church Street and moves east into a shabby-chic bistro in Cabbagetown. Bonus: much of Chef Michael Guenther's menu (comfort food meets pub grub with a sidetrack into pizza territory) is organic, locally sourced and often gluten-free. Double bonus: Cher liked the Boy's dairy-free veggie pizza so much, Mamma named it in her honour. Best: at dinner, slow-cooked Mennonite pork ribs in sugary barbecue sauce sweetened with maple syrup and peaches, sided with first-rate cabbage slaw and baked kidney beans with caramelized onion; gluten-free vegan spaghetti squash tossed with garlicky asparagus, snow peas and beets, sided with organic mesclun in Dijon vinaigrette; the house veggie burger, a large grilled portobello cap stuffed with lemony lentils and paired with salad and Kettle Creek; at brunch, $1.99 Morning Glorys; steak 'n' eggs with gluten-free almond toast. *Open for dinner. Sunday for brunch. Licensed. Delivery. Access: five steps at door, washrooms in basement.* **$$$$** ⬭ ⊙

Sri Lankan

RASHNAA
307 Wellesley E, at Parliament, 416-929-2099,
www.rashnaa.com.
Though its spicy menu boasts "authenticity is our word," this venerable South Indian and Sri Lankan cantina on the edge of St. James Town lives up to its hype. Combine huge portions, a casual atmosphere and delicate flavours and it's no wonder this out-of-the-way Cabbagetown cottage is one of downtown's favourite Subcontinental destinations. Best: to start, the mixed appetizer platter – crisp, house-made pappadom, unusually flaky vegetarian samosa filled with a highly charged mix of potato, carrot and garden peas and an unfortunately bland lentil fritter stuffed with tuna and potato, as well as fabulous pancake roll, breaded crepes wrapped around tender beef masala; fiery mains like Kottu Rotty – Sri Lankan specialty of chopped naan sautéed with onion, bell pepper and egg, plus a choice of chicken, beef, mutton or squid; Vegetable Delight, basmati rice lightly sautéed in ghee with three mild coconut-perfumed curries – eggplant/breadfruit, cashew/green pea, potato –

just desserts

The Queen of Cake, Dufflet Rosenberg of **Dufflet's Pastries** (787 Queen West, 416-504-2870; 2638 Yonge St, 416-484-9080, www.dufflet.com) has been whipping up dazzling desserts since 1975. Maker of more than 100 entirely natural products, from French apple raspberry flans and buttery Bundts to cappuccino dacquoise and chocolate banana cakes, Dufflet's is the city's premier purveyor of pastries. Mick Jagger even enjoyed one of her chocolate creations for a recent birthday.

Just Desserts (555 Yonge, 416-963-8089) might do exactly that, but Belgian-born François and Sonia Rahier's uptown patisserie, **Rahier** (1586 Bayview, 416-482-0917), makes some of the most impressive pastries this side of Paris. All made with pure butter and cream, their luscious fruit flans, pain au chocolat and single-serving cakes – named for famous French philosophers! – are the perfect finale for almost any occasion.

Patisserie **Pain Perdu** (736 St. Clair West, 416-656-7246) on St. Clair, makes a lemon tart that will make even the biggest sourpuss pucker up. Pain Perdu also battles it out with **Patachou** (835 St. Clair West, 416-782-0122; 1095 Yonge, 416-927-1105) for best croissant in the midtown area. Croissant freaks should definitely head downtown to **Clafouti** (915 Queen West, 416-603-1935), where the buttery bun, brioche and other French baked goods rule, and **Daniel et Daniel** (248 Carlton, 416-968-9275, ext 15) offers an exquisite selection of imported cheeses and pates along with its freshly baked pastries.

For a meal fit for a king – or at least a pontiff – then **Granowska's** (175 Roncesvalles, 416-533-7755) is definitely the place to go. This Roncesvalles Village shop had the distinction of baking the ceremonial bread for Pope John Paul II on his visit to Toronto and also provided pastries for his afternoon tea. Up the street, **Queen of Tarts** (283 Roncesvalles, 416-651-3009) is exactly that, with its variety of individual- and family-size tarts and cakes as well as witty hand-decorated cookies.

On the hipper part of Queen West, **Vienna Home Bakery** (626 Queen West, 416 703-7278) makes its signature pillar-shaped loaf, as well as bakery-style ginger muffins and maple-pecan tarts while cookie and cheesecake lovers might want to check out **Dessert Trends** (154 Harbord, 416-916-8155).

But if you're one of those who rejects the French sweets in favour of Jewish baking – the secret is in the salt, by the way – don't miss **Harbord Bakery** (115 Harbord, 416-922-5767), famous for its around-the-block challah line just before the High Holidays and for its legendary cheese danish all year round. Bagels are excellent here, too, though people in the know swear by **Gryfe's** (3421 Bathurst, 416-783-1552), farther north in the heart of the Jewish district.

sided with smoky carrot achar; hellishly hot Beef Devil – strips of boneless steak sautéed in onion, tomato and jalapeño in sweet chili sauce. *Open for lunch and dinner. Licensed. Access: barrier-free, washrooms upstairs.* **$$** ⁙

Chinatown East

Chinese
PEARL COURT
633 Gerrard E, at Broadview, 416-463-8778.
This busy east-side eatery calls itself the best Chinese restaurant in Toronto and has a wall plastered with rave reviews from the 80s to prove it. It may have been true back then, but today it's a solid mid-tier Cantonese cantina with a second, more intriguing Southeast Asian-influenced menu. Best: from the latter, house Special Noodle, Swatow-style wide rice noodles slippery with sesame oil, strewn with sweet red pepper strips and zucchini, garnished with raw bean sprouts; Spicy Vietnamese Beef, large pieces of pounded steak paired with carrot threads, bell pepper and button mushrooms, kicked with Thai basil and dried red chili in sweet, gloopy gravy; be warned that Paper Wrapped Chicken is not a plateful of egg rolls but eight parchment-encased bundles of juicy deboned thigh in five-spice with coriander leaf, so just eat the contents; deep-fried spring rolls stuffed with finely ground pork; deep-fried soft shell crab. *Open for breakfast, lunch and dinner. Licensed. Access: barrier-free, washrooms in basement.* **$$$**

French
BATIFOLE
744 Gerrard E, at Howland, 416-462-9965.
Former Sassafraz chef Jean-Jacques Texier reinvents this once-doomed 30-seat east-side boîte as a first-rate shrine to all things francophone. Casually chic (dig that Carla Bruni CD on the sound system), this welcoming spot has managed to succeed where previous tenants failed or bailed. Bonus: surprisingly deep wine cellar. Best: though the menu changes regularly, reckon on starters like velvety cream of watercress soup paired with frog leg fritters (escargots fricasse), or shredded duck terrine garnished with ground red Szechuan peppercorns and sided with a mound of contrasting sour cornichons; mains such as cassoulet with duck magret, lamb sausage and crispy pork belly; pan-fried Provimi veal liver with onions, deglazed with pricey Banyuls vinegar; Le Tartar de Cheval Bien Relevé

Order up a spicy dish at hot little Sri Lankan joint **Rashnaa**. Page 85.

– horse tartar; à la carte sides like spring asparagus in lemon butter, Basque-style veggie piperade, or the house frites with tarragon mayo. *Open for dinner. Closed Tuesday. Licensed. Access: one step at door, washrooms in basement.* **$$$$** ⟡

Vietnamese

HANOI 3 SEASONS
588 Gerrard E, at Broadview, 416-463-9940.
First-time restaurateur and chef Hai Luke beats the odds to create a charming North Vietnamese cantina straight out of the box. Unique flavours, attentive if leisurely service – hey, he's got his 80-year-old parents working for him – and stylish-on-a-budget decor make this a boîte to watch, especially if you go for tasty, aggressively spiced and inexpensively priced grub. Best: the starter known simply as Hen, minced baby clams stir-fried with wilted onion and fierce green chili in turmeric-flavoured oil, scooped with baked black sesame rice crackers; dill-scented Do Bien Sao Rau Cai, steamed green-shelled New Zealand mussels, grilled tail-on shrimp and shards of faux pink crab kicked with turmeric, black pepper, ginger and lemongrass stalk over skinny rice stick, garnished with fresh coriander, Thai basil, minty rau ram, crisp iceberg lettuce and crushed peanuts; Bun Bo Hue, the famous central Vietnam beef pho, a complex pairing of coriander, lemongrass, coconut, roasted chilies, fresh mint and sour tamarind. *Open for lunch. Tuesday to Saturday for dinner. Closed Monday. Licensed. Access: two steps at door, washrooms on same floor.* **$$**

MI MI
688 Gerrard E, at Degrassi, 416-778-5948.
No relation to Mimi's beanery on Bathurst, this spic-and-span spotless Vietnamese resto (not only are tables covered in plastic, they're glass-topped, as well) is an enduring family-run spot with a lengthy lineup of straightforward yet complex fare. Warning: a mid-sized room, it's often packed at peak dining hours. Best: to start, sizable rice paper-wrapped spring rolls dressed with lengths of green onion sticking out one end and stuffed with pork or shrimp; all-in-one rice vermicelli pho soups with the likes of barbecued chicken, beef or pork; lightly deep-fried minced shrimp on intensely sweet sugar cane with rice-paper roll-ups loaded with leaf lettuce, raw bean sprouts, shredded daikon and carrot dusted with crushed peanuts; boneless grilled chicken leg over steamed rice topped with salty shredded pork and a tasty wedge of Saigon-style quiche; to drink, durian milkshakes. *Open for lunch and dinner. Licensed. Cash only. Access: barrier-free, washrooms in basement.* **$$**

● ROSE CAFÉ
324 Broadview, at Gerrard E, 416-406-9906.
Located in the prettiest building in Riverdale's Chinatown East, this friendly east-side take-away with a few tables in the front window offers one of the best meal deals in town: super Saigon-style submarine sandwiches piled with veggies, Vietnamese cold cuts and incendiary chilies, all for a buck and a half, taxes included. Best: banh mi, lunch-sized sandwiches on flaky French roll stuffed with salty shredded chicken or pork, sweet lemongrass-scented Xiu Mai meatballs or slabs of dense tofu alongside sweetly pickled carrot and daikon strips, lengths of English cuke and the optional fire of minced Thai bird chilies; a large and extremely fresh selection of cellophane-wrapped prefab meals of spring rolls, shredded Asian-style deli meats and salads; to finish, crème caramel-style flan or black-eyed peas in coconut cream. *Open for breakfast and lunch. Unlicensed. Cash only. Access: one step at door, washrooms in basement.* **$**

Danforth

Café

MOCHA MOCHA
489 Danforth, at Logan, 416-778-7896.
After operating Lima Peru's only Dutch pancake house, Marijan and Mercedes Tripkovic opened this nutritious noshery in 1991. Count on a multiculti menu that incorporates Latin American, Italian and African influences. Bonus: spot the Barenaked Lady! Warning: chaotic on weekends. Best: spicy cacciatore-style East African chicken stew with brown rice and house salad – shredded carrot, red cabbage, cuke, tomato and leaf lettuce in a lemony honey Dijon dressing; spinach-rich vegetarian lasagna; workmanlike Tex Mex burritos stuffed with refried beans, topped with diced avocado, pickled jalapeño and sour cream; vegetarian club sandwiches, a triple-decker stacked with grilled eggplant, avocado and mozzarella on organic whole-wheat toast; made-to-order egg salad on Fred's multigrain; for dessert, Wanda's retro apple pie. *Open for lunch and dinner. Monday to Saturday for breakfast. Licensed. Delivery. Access: barrier-free, but very crowded room.* **$$** ⟡

restaurants

Cuban

MAMBO LOUNGE
120 Danforth, at Broadview, 416-778-7004.
Goodbye hoagie, hello mojito! Former sub shop morphs into Mambo Lounge, a sophisticated Latin-accented South Beach-style resto cum nightclub co-owned by first-time restaurateur Andres Gonzales. Bonus: live Latin musicians weekends. Best: to start, one of the tastiest salads in the city – designer greens in balsamic vinaigrette topped with fresh pineapple, ripe mango and explosively ripe tomato; daily soups like chicken breast in spicy tomato broth thick with corn kernels, baby carrot and roasted red pepper; mains like Cuban sandwiches on Ace baguette layered with Swiss cheese, Spanish ham, roasted pork and sweet pickle; picadillo quesadilla stuffed with ground beef, peppers, refried beans and cheddar; at brunch, Huevos Ranchero, scrambled eggs dolloped with sour cream and sided with creamy halved avocado and chunky salsa over a grilled tortilla; Mennonite grilled chorizo with eggs scrambled with cubed potato and sweet red pepper. *Open Monday to Saturday for dinner. Sunday for brunch. Closed Monday. Licensed.* **$$$$** ☼

Greek

MR. GREEK
568 Danforth, at Carlaw, 416-461-5470, other locations, www.mrgreek.com.
Though its been suggested that all of the Greek grub served at the boulevard's countless tavernas is mass-produced in a secret kitchen hidden under the Chester subway station, this long-running chain – 21 locations in southern Ontario alone – offers food that goes beyond mere souvlaki on a stick. Gruff old-school service and wallet-friendly prices guarantee a full house late into the night. Best: to start, saganaki flambé, a slice of Kefalotiri cheese doused in ouzo and set on fire at table; mezes starters like spanako-pita or taramasalata (red fish roe and new potatoes in lemony vinaigrette); considerable mains like mous-saka layered with eggplant, sliced spuds and lean ground beef baked in creamy béchamel, or marinated and grilled lamb chops, all sided with rice, double-roasted potatoes and grilled green beans. *Open for lunch and dinner. Licensed. Delivery. Access: barrier-free.* **$$$** ☼ ⏱

OUZERI
500A Danforth, at Logan, 416-778-0500, www.ouzeri.com.
Think Mediterranean resort meets urban Greek chic. Dazzling royal blue walls, artful ceramic tiles and mosaic-style mirrors offset an impressive wall of wine and olive oil behind the bar. A three-page seafood-dominated menu doesn't forget traditional moussaka, spanokopita and souvlaki. Best: sizzling Saganaki – a generous wedge of tangy, seared Kefalograviera cheese soaked in ouzo and flambéed and spread on fresh rolls like Greek fondue; Lamb Rosemary Pie, a dense phyllo roll bursting with ten-der lamb chunks and button mushrooms in a rich rosemary gravy laced with melted feta; lettuce-based Greek salad with plenty of mild feta, tomatoes, olives and cucumber in creamy garlic dressing. *Open for lunch and dinner. Licensed. Access: barrier-free, four steps to washrooms.* **$$$$** ☼

ZORBA'S
681 Danforth, at Pape, 416-406-1212.
Old-school taverna with home-style Greek grub on the boulevard of broken plates. Ignore the printed menu and point at whatever you fancy from the

steam table. Warning: scary offal-stuffed lamb heads. With teeth. Best: thick 'n' meaty grilled lamb ribs sided with fabulous baked lima beans and waxy oven-roasted spuds; super-moist 2-pound takeout chickens; lasagna-like pastitsio, penne over ground lamb topped with eggy béchamel-sauced mash; Arni Fricasse, slow-braised lamb shank with artichoke hearts in dilled avgolemono lemon sauce; traditional feta-strewn Greek village salad. *Open for breakfast, lunch and dinner. Licensed. Access: short step at door, washrooms on same floor.* **$$** ☺

Egyptian

PRINCE OF EGYPT
135 Danforth, at Broadview, 416-463-2228.
What this appealing Egyptian café lacks in decor it more than makes up for with a vegetarian-heavy card that's as tasty as it is inexpensive. Best: snacks like battered cauliflower pita wrap, cooked-to-order al dente veggies mixed with red onion, tomato and cuke in a light, creamy mayo; fresh mesclun salads topped with roasted Roma tomato and fennel; smooth soups like cream of red lentil; dinner specials like roasted chicken stuffed with veggie rice farci or veal shank with slow-cooked veg; to finish, rice pudding stuffed with sultanas. *Open for lunch and dinner. Unlicensed. Cash only. Access: barrier-free, washrooms in basement.* **$$**

Indian

SHER-E-PUNJAB
351 Danforth, 416-465-2125.
This casual and unassuming resto has been serving incendiary North Indian grub for more than 25 years. Dig into such standard mains as butter chicken, veal korma, chicken tikka masala and shrimp curry, or tempt your tastebuds with pork vindaloo, served in a thick, fiery curry, or the signature dish of sizzling chicken skewers with sliced onions, tomatoes and green peppers served smokin' to your table in the backyard grotto. *Open for lunch and dinner. Closed Sunday. Licensed.* **$$** ⁘

Japanese

KATSU
572 Danforth, at Carlaw, 416-466-3388.
Is there no greater culinary indignity than all-you-can-eat-sushi? But this skylit space with intimate booths offers just that – and, most surprisingly, the Japanese finger food is made to order, extremely edible and a mega-bargain to boot. Bonus: Katsu now has a sister restaurant, Masa, on Charles. Warning: the order form cautions not to order more than you can eat as you'll be charged extra for leftovers. Best: start with two orders of stellar teriyaki beef – quickly char-grilled slices of almost rare sirloin in sweet soy that will have you going coming back for seconds; deep-fried gyoza pork dumplings; golden cubes of addictive deep-fried tofu; sugary teppanyaki chicken nuggets; roughly chopped tempura vegetables; crunchy, spicy salmon-skin rolls; first-rate California mini-rolls equal to most Annex sushitoria; at dinner, simple salmon and red snapper sashimi. *Open for lunch and dinner. Licensed. Access: barrier-free, washrooms in basement.* **$$$** ⁘

SAKAWAYA
867 Danforth, at Jones, 416-778-6894.
The fact that a thoroughly modern room bills itself as a bistro will probably annoy francophones, but this surprisingly classy east-side Tokyo-centric cantina offers much more than the usual sushi, sashimi and tempura lineup found elsewhere. Bonus: front row seats for owner/chef Koki Oguchi's masterful knife display. Warning: lineups on weekends. Best: tapas-style zensai starters and mains such as kushiyaki, skewered and charcoal-grilled bite-size snacks like

great greek

Toronto's Boulevard of Broken Plates, Greektown on the Danforth (see **Sightseeing**, page 34), is the home of mostly mediocre dining combined with first-rate good times. While there are literally dozens of Greek – and a few non-Greek – restaurants on the five-block strip of Little Athens that runs from Broadview to just east of Pape, the menus offer almost identical fare of only mildly divergent quality.

But appropriate to the birthplace of democracy, diners vote with their feet – and their forks – to pack these fun-loving purveyors of grilled meats and seafood, deep-fried calamari, dips, iceberg lettuce-stuffed Greek salads and Opa-fuelled flaming cheese (saganaki).

Wide sidewalks make plenty of room for promenading couples and Greek families out for a stroll, and the packed patios always scream party. The most popular spots tend to be on the north side – the sunny side – and most places are full until well past midnight, as almost everybody stays open late, particularly during Toronto's long, hot summers.

Our favourites include the slightly more elegant **Avli** (401 Danforth, 416-461-9577) and **Pan** (516 Danforth, 416-466-8158), which have a more creative take on standard Greek fare. Avli adds traditional Greek savoury pies, rarely seen elsewhere on the strip, to their first-rate food.

Best of those with a less adventurous take on conventional Greek are **Pappas Grill** (440 Danforth, 416-469-9595) and **Mezes** (456 Danforth, 416-778-5150), although the biggest lineups are always in front of **Astoria** (390 Danforth, 416-463-2838), renowned for its chicken souvlaki.

But insiders swear the easily confused **Asteria** (292 Danforth, 416-466-5273), a decidedly down-market spot, actually has the best poultry on a pita.

For something with a touch more class – visiting celebs have been known to enjoy an intimate meal here – and a broader menu of Mediterranean fare, try **Lolita's Lust** (513 Danforth, 416-465-1751).

So come for the food, but stay for the party.

buttery scallops wrapped in bacon, tiny creamy quail eggs, fabulous chicken gizzards, and sweet gingko nuts; from the mains, Gomuko Hiyashi, cold chunky udon noodles in sweet broth strewn with thinly sliced chicken, faux crab, seaweed and shrimp tempura; fiery red Korean kimchi layered with marinated octopus and red pepper thread; sirloin sashimi with hot sesame sauce; marinated mackerel with wasabi; to finish, sugary grilled corn on the cob in sweet teriyaki glaze. *Open for dinner. Closed Monday, holidays. Licensed. Access: barrier-free, washrooms in basement.* **$$$**

Opa! For a taste of something Greece-y, try any of a dozen Danforth restos like **Ouzeri**. Page 88.

Mexican

EL SOL
1448 Danforth, at Monarch Park, 416-405-8074.
Part art gallery and performance space, this family-run cantina east of Greek Town is consistently the most authentic Mexican restaurant in town. Warm if slow service, a casual kid-friendly room and chef Yolanda Paez's (the former owner of once highly rated Gonzo's on O'Connor) northern Mexican grub push El Sol several notches above its competitors. Warning: there's a reason regulars refer to this laid-back spot as El Slo: since the kitchen cooks almost everything from scratch, dinner can be a long time coming. Management suggests those in a rush order two hours in advance from home. Best: to start, roughly textured made-to-order guacamole mixed with shredded mozzarella, sharp cheddar, fresh coriander, garlic and scallion with house-baked corn chips; 24-hour-notice-required Chiles Rellenos, a huge egg-battered sweet red pepper stuffed with ground beef or veggies along with green olives, cubed potato and raisins in a pulpy tomato-wine sauce; 65-spice Pollo En Mole, chicken breast in a fabulous hot chili and dark chocolate sauce sided with roasted tomato rice and flavour-packed, slow-cooked refried beans; to quaff, the Michelada, a Mexican lager served Margarita-style with salt-rimmed glass and lime juice. *Open for lunch and dinner. Closed Monday. Licensed. Access: barrier-free.* **$$$** ☺

Pizza

BONA PIZZA PASTA
431 Donlands, at O'Connor, 416-406-5000.
Reliable pies and amply portioned Italian noodle dishes make this a proven east-side favourite. Although it's recently relocated to roomier digs, other than a sticky lunch counter and a single small table for two, there's no reason to eat in, so call for delivery. Bonus: 72 pizza toppings including porcini mushroom, asparagus, steak and Drunken Goat Cheese! Best: thin, crisp-crusted 'zas like the Milan (garlic, basil, 'shrooms, diced tomato, leeks, kalamata olive and lotsa mozza) or the Suicide (hot sauce, jalapeños, spicy Italian sausage); vegetarian lasagna with broccoli, cauliflower and ricotta; spinach involtini – pasta layered with spinach and smothered in tomato sauce and cheese; deluxe pizza toppings like porcini mushrooms, asparagus, roasted garlic, grilled eggplant, prosciutto and provolone. Medium 14-inch pizzas with five toppings $20, including all taxes and tip. *Open for lunch and dinner. Unlicensed. Delivery. Access: bump at door, tight space, washrooms in basement.* **$$$**

East York

Pakistani

IQBAL KEBAB & SWEET CENTRE
2 Thorncliffe Park, unit 17, at Overlea, 416-425-7866.
Hard by hydro lines, this fast-food-style family restaurant in an industrial park offers Pakistan-by-way-of-East-Africa curries and stews heavy on halal meat, sided with tandoor-fired naan. Requested heat can run from milquetoast to meltdown. Best: Chili Chicken, chopped-up leg 'n' thigh in deliriously hot sauce of red and green chilies; slow-cooked beef Nihari stew garnished with fresh coriander; skewers of cubed yogurt-marinated Miskaki beef cooked in the tandoor; first-rate ground beef kheema samosas dunked in tart soupy tamarind or cardamom-dusted raita; turmeric-tinted vegetarian biryani rice with cassava and tomato; to drink, milkshake-like mango lassi. *Open for lunch and dinner. Weekend for breakfast. Unlicensed. Access: barrier-free.* **$$** ☺

Tanzanian

SIMBA GRILL
375 Donlands, at O'Connor, 416-429-6057.
Toronto's only Tanzanian restaurant might not be much to look at – blinding fluorescent lights, plastic plants, a big-screen TV blaring Bollywood music videos – but this East African eatery offers an adventurous hybrid of African and South Asian cuisine.

Bonus: buy two meals and get a free starter. Best: to start, deep-fried cassava mogo or chickpea-flour-battered potato slices dipped into one of four not-to-be-missed chutneys – sour tamarind, desiccated coconut, subtle coriander and salty Chinese-style red chili; continue with mains like tender char-grilled sekela chicken in sweet teriyaki-style glaze; garlicky barbecued very short ribs sided with cayenne-dusted fries; Sunday-only all-you-can-eat $7.95 vegetarian thali; to finish, Tanzanian ice cream, sugar-free Italian-style cassata topped with chocolate syrup and crushed pistachios. *Open for lunch and dinner. Closed Monday, Tuesday. Unlicensed. Cash only. Access: barrier-free, washrooms in basement.* **$$**

Leslieville

Café

 LE CAFÉ VERT
946 Queen E, at Morse, 416-778-1313.
This tiny Leslieville storefront luncheonette serves a tasty all-day card that's not only mostly organic, but cooked with heart as well as social conviction. Warning: start lining up now for weekend brunch. Best: Vert's massive gluten-free baked breakfast, a thick, eggy pseudo-quiche loaded with cheese and bacon in a crust made of home fries plated with baked sweet potato strips augmented with chipotle crème fraîche but completely free of wheat; spinach tortilla wraps stuffed with balsamic-roasted chicken breast plus avocado, carrot sticks and baby greens coupled with rustic vegan soups like Tuscan bean with kale; a surprisingly respectable take on pad thai, ketchup-free and cookbook correct; at brunch, chocolate croissant bread pudding splashed with organic maple syrup, sided with blackberry fruit salad; free-range eggs Benny with creamy organic hollandaise. *Open Tuesday to Friday for lunch. Wednesday to Friday for dinner. Weekend for brunch. Closed Monday, holidays. Unlicensed. Access: two steps at door, small room, washrooms on same floor.* **$$**

Contemporary

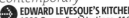 **EDWARD LEVESQUE'S KITCHEN**
1290 Queen E, at Hastings, 416-465-3600,
www.edwardlevesque.ca.
Leslieville's best-kept secret ain't so covert now that it's finally been discovered by the mainstream. Looking small from the street, this converted greasy spoon opens to a larger but equally low-key space that recalls a Sudbury church basement circa 1956. Warning: because he only take reservations for dinner Saturday, expect a queue at weekend brunch. Best: start with Levesque's signature "big" salad of organic greens topped with avocado and cherry tomato in blood orange tarragon vinaigrette or pesto-splashed calamari grilled with black olive; meaty mains – all naturally raised from Cumbrae Farms – like roasted pork rack stuffed with brandied cherries paired with braised cabbage and sweet potato frites; from the all-day lineup and especially at brunch, Montasio Frico, fried cheese pancake coupled with asparagus, poached egg and salad; latkes topped with Kristappson's smoked salmon; for dessert, pie à la mode. *Open Tuesday to Friday for lunch. Tuesday to Saturday for dinner. Weekend for brunch. Licensed. Access: four steps at door, washrooms in basement.* **$$$$**

JOY BISTRO
884 Queen E, at Booth, 416-465-8855.
This east-side brunch spot raises its profile with the introduction of big-name chef David Chrystian. The culinary trademarks that made him famous at Café Societa, Patriot and the original Drake are still there, if somewhat muted, but need focus in their delivery. Best: to begin, spring onion soup, an upside-down take on the French classic; Vertical Cobb Salad with cubed rare beef, blue cheese and deep-fried panko-crusted soft-boiled egg; meaty mains like the Flintstonian veal chop over baby asparagus and salsify; diminutive lamb tenderloin over lavender-scented green pea crepes; at brunch or lunch, Chrystian's signature burger with house frites; wrapped in a house-

restaurants

where's the beef?

After a tasting tour of global cuisine offered by the city's many ethnic restaurants, sometimes all you want is to Fred Flintstone your teeth into a thick slab of meat. Fortunately, T.O. has some grade A steak joints to satisfy your hunger.

Sidle up to **La Palette** (256 Augusta, 416-929-4900) for the city's top steak-frites experience. Chef and co-owner Michael Harrington makes his mark with a cookbook-correct interpretation of the bistro classic, a 10-ounce triple-A Black Angus sirloin daubed with herb butter, sided with ridiculously crisp skinny frites.

If you're looking for a place to impress Dad, try **Carman's Club** (26 Alexander, at Church, 416-924-8697), which once had an exclusive, even sophisticated, old-boy feel but approaches retro now, with dark wood panelling, oil paintings and kitschy celebrity photos (Lorne Greene, Nat King Cole). Dig into the Torontonian, a juicy, perfectly aged charcoal-broiled USDA Prime Certified Black Angus 14-ounce rib-eye served on a wooden platter with plain baked Idaho potato. Order a side of the garlic baguette — Carman's claims to have introduced garlic bread to North America.

The latest outlet of suburban steakhouse chain the **Keg** (165 York, at Richmond West, 416-703-1773, other locations) is located in stylish downtown digs and the deal's the same: too-damned-big red-meat specials sided with equally large-portioned sides. **Hy's** (120 Adelaide West, at York, 416-364-6600) delivers a British hunting club vibe and fine triple-A-aged Alberta beef, although the sold-separate sides are unimpressive and over-priced.

For a nice bottle of vino with your beef, try the venerable **Barberian's** (7 Elm, at Yonge, 416-597-0335), with its list of bottles up to $5,000. Southern US chain **Ruth's Chris's**(Hilton Toronto Hotel, 145 Richmond West, at University, 416-955-1455) basement beef bunker is popular with NBAers, while NHLers love **Harbour Sixty** (60 Harbour, 416-777-2111), a more attractive yet slightly full-of-itself meat manor.

Finally, **Morton's** (4 Avenue Rd, at Prince Arthur, 416-925-0648) wheels out a carnivore cart packed with steaks so you can preview your protein before the kitchen goes to work.

made flatbread, lamb and chickpea roti with seedlings 'n' greens in creamy coriander dressing; Eggs Teddy, hollandaised poached eggs on toasted English muffin layered with peameal bacon, spinach and roasted red onion; to finish, gelato-topped flourless cake over diced barbecued pineapple. *Open Monday to Friday for breakfast, lunch and dinner. Weekends for brunch. Licensed. Access: barrier-free.* $$$$ ☼

SAUVIGNON
1862 Queen E, at Rainsford, 416-686-1998.
An unpretentious bistro on the edge of the Beach (a neighbourhood, with a few exceptions, not known

for its food), this Gallic-flavoured spot offers straightforward fare with panache. Locals have already claimed it, but this stylish eatery deserves a larger audience. Lovely summer patio on the curb. Best: black Angus strip loin smeared with pommery mustard and smothered in onions, with Indo-spiced sweet potato frites; lemony asparagus risotto with porcini oil; Asian-grilled pork tenderloin with chickpea fritters and wilted dandelion; goat cheese, eggplant and pepper Napoleon; lemon tart; chocolate mousse. *Open Monday to Sunday for dinner. Licensed. Access: barrier-free.* $$$$ ☼

⬤ TOMI-KRO
1214 Queen E, at Jones, 416-463-6677.
Hailed as one of NOW's best new restos of 2004 — and 2005! — this intimately cool upscale boîte hidden behind bamboo curtains in an anonymous east-side storefront is even better now that acclaimed chef Laura Prentice (Lolita's Lust, Gus, Fancy Shoes) is in charge of its Mediterranean-inspired-by-way-of-the-Orient kitchen. Warning: those preferring a more sedate dining experience may want to do The Acadian Room instead. Best: to start, tapas-style kumquat-glazed pork belly over adzuki salad; foie gras over miniature strudel in a pool of tart apple puree; bulgogi-esque Miami Ribs glazed with soy, honey, slivered Thai chilies and coarsely ground black peppercorn; impressively plated mains like slow-cooked lamb shank in a white wine reduction of mushroom, leeks and Asiago; brazenly fatty slices of Muscovy duck breast in lingonberry jus coupled with vanilla-scented scalloped yams; à la carte sides like cauliflower in curried cream, asparagus in miso, and Brussels sprouts smoky with pancetta and Asiago; dessert calls for Prentice's legendary flourless chocolate cake, a closing salvo that's been on her card for nearly 30 years. *Open for dinner. Bar till close. Closed Sunday. Licensed. Access: one step at door, washrooms in basement.* $$$$

⬤ VERVEINE
1097 Queen E, at Pape, 416-405-9906.
Downtown comes to Leslieville in this mid-size bistro serving contemporary takes on classic European cuisine. A smart beige-on-beige room, smooth service and a proven kitchen make this local secret a deserved hit. Bonus: Sunday through Tuesday night $21 two-course and $25 three-course prix fixe. Dinner reservations recommended, brunch reservations not accepted for groups smaller than eight. Best: start with PEI mussels steamed in tomato concasse and roasted red pepper; follow with updated takes on comfort food like rare seared King Cole duck breast in maple glaze with roasted fingerling potato and Swiss chard; grilled 10-ounce Sterling Silver strip loin daubed with house steak sauce and plated with fabulous house frites and sautéed broccoli and caramelized onion; blanquette of rabbit with Yorkshire pudding and mushroom 'n' pearl onions ragout; for the inevitable vegetarian in the party, soy-marinated tofu with stir-fried veggies in hot 'n' sour broth; at brunch, Santa-Fe style toad-in-the-hole eggs in hollowed-out them grilled cornbread alongside sliced avocado and mild salsa. *Open for dinner. Weekend for brunch. Licensed. Access: barrier-free, washrooms in basement.* $$$$ ☼

Diner

OKAY OKAY
1128 Queen E, at Bertmount, 416-461-2988.
Once the lowest of low-rent dives, this lovingly restored east-side eatery captures the rock 'n' roll diner aesthetic to a T. Add cool 60s tunes on the radio, smooth professional staff and an upscale all-day breakfast card that includes weekday lunch as well as dinner specials and Okay Okay proves more

than okay, okay? Best: Eggs Brunhilde, two expertly poached eggs over deep-fried potato fritters layered with grilled asparagus and smoked Kristapson salmon in a somewhat wimpy horseradish hollandaise; Scrambles of the day – sloppy omelettes, more like – like caramelized leek with fancy French Brie; splendid blueberry or banana buttermilk pancakes; at lunch, classic Banquet Burgers and triple-decker grilled cheese sandwiches with fries 'n' gravy; at dinner, meatless meatloaf; grilled pork chops with five-spiced apple sauce; pan-seared chicken livers with caramelized onion, bacon and port. *Open Wednesday to Sunday for breakfast/brunch. Wednesday to Friday for lunch. Thursday to Saturday for dinner. Closed Monday,Tuesday. Licensed. Cash only. Access: short ramp at door, booth seating, washrooms in basement.* **$$$**

TULIP
1606 Queen E, at Coxwell, 416-469-5797.
Not a traditional steakhouse, this noisy family spot has offered straightforward steak dinners for less than half the price at downtown joints since the 50s. Now two doors west of its original location in much larger digs, its monstrous artery-clogging all-day breakfasts remain unchanged. Best: triple-A Canadian 10-ounce sirloin cooked greasy-spoon-style on a griddle instead of a grill, with butter and peppercorns, paired with two eggs, home fries, toast and coffee refill; a pair of terrific grilled pork chops with retro scoops of Mom-style mash and vinegary coleslaw; massive 20-ounce T-bones sided with greaselessly fried boiled potato home-fries, pale tomato no matter what the season, raw onion and

buttered French stick; house-made flashback pies like banana or coconut cream, the cafeteria classic complete with artificial aerosol-whipped topping. *Open for breakfast, lunch and dinner. Closed Christmas Day. Licensed. Access: barrier-free, washrooms in basement.* **$$$**

Italian
GIO RANA'S REALLY REALLY NICE RESTAURANT
1220 Queen E, at Leslie, 416-469-5225.
Old-school Italia served tapas-style in a gutted bank draws starving locals and hipsters alike. If you ever fancied Gio's and Five Doors on Yonge or Seven Numbers, you know the scene. Relatively quiet earlier in the week, by weekend the joint's the jumpingest party in the area. Warning: there's no sign, so look for the very large nose on the former Bank of Montreal. Best: since everything's ordered à la carte from a card divided into courses – antipasti, primi, secondi, contorni – start with the house meatballs in ragu; pan-seared scallops and cured pork belly in balsamic jus; grilled calamari with charred green-tomato relish and basil aïoli; continue with orecchiette alla Bolognese; crepe-like crespelle folded over sweet butternut squash and creamy mascarpone in sage butter; move on to mains like minty grilled lamb chops with cranberry couscous; osso buco finished with cremini 'shrooms and Asiago coupled with sweet potato mash with chestnut butter; to wind up, subtle house-made desserts like panna cotta custard blasted with smoky caramel. *Open for dinner. Bar till close. Closed Sunday, Monday and holidays. Licensed. Access: barrier-free.* **$$$**

Edward Levesque's Kitchen is one of the city's best-kept secrets. Page 91.

restaurants

Pizza

GHALI KITCHEN
4 Greenwood, at Queen E, 416-466-5140.
Toronto's only Jamaican pizzeria, this eclectically decorated east-side take-away fuses Italian technique with Caribbean ingredients and spicing. The result, a truly unique multiculti menu of pies with aggressive flavour. Warning: gentle stomachs may want to stock up on Bromo-Seltzer beforehand. Best: Shiraz jerk pork pizza, a thin-crusted pie piled with pink-centred tenderloin, wilted spinach, grilled caramelized onion, sweet red pepper, basil-scented olive oil and shaved Parmesan spritzed with fruity plonk; oxtail, saltfish and ackee pasta, a delicious collision of garlicky tomato sauce, fresh basil, cheddar cheese and rigatoni with tender-sweet 'tail on the bone, shredded salt cod and slippery ackee finished with more quality oil; vegetarian Rasta Pasta, grilled veggies and greens in curried olive oil; side them with the house salad of radicchio, arugula, iceberg and buttery Boston bibb tossed with grilled and lightly marinated Mediterranean-style veg in peppery pesto vinaigrette. *Open for dinner. Monday to Friday for lunch. Closed Sunday. Unlicensed. Cash only. Access: four steps at door, washroom on same floor.* **$$**

PIZZA PIDE
949 Gerrard E, at Pape, 416-462-9666.
This bare bones Turkish pizzeria specializes in pida, 20-inch long flatbread-based pies shaped like canoes. Bright fluorescent lighting and sticky tabletops won't make you want to hang around, but the more than 20 varieties of Middle Eastern 'za make terrific takeout. Best: thin, blistered cracker-crusted crepes like Lahmacun topped with spicy cumin-kicked ground beef and minced onion, sweet peppers and parsley or shawarma-style lean beef; flaky pide topped with spicy Turkish sausage and runny sunny-side up egg; Greek-style feta with wilted spinach; lamb stew flash-cooked in the pizza oven thick with mushroom, bell pepper and mozzarella; all of the above sided with a ton of curly leaf parsley, raw white onion, pale pink tomato, mild green chilies and lemon wedges. *Open for breakfast, lunch and dinner. Unlicensed. Cash only. Access: three steps at door, washrooms on same floor.* **$**

Southern US

CAJUN CORNER
920 Queen St E, at Logan, 416-703-4477.
Only open since April 2006 at its current location, Cajun Corner's most important addition in the new shop is a takeout counter. A small selection of Cajun and Creole food is available daily, from noon until it runs out. Best: the catfish dinner – spicy Louisiana slaw, catfish dredged in cornmeal and deep-fried, and a choice of hush puppies or corn on the cob; catfish or shrimp po'boys; the classic New Orleans Muffuletta, dripping with the juices of olive salad, provolone, salami and ham. Don't forget to buy some hot sauce or Cajun seasoning on the way out to try your hand at cooking the Big Easy's cuisine yourself. *Open Monday to Saturday for breakfast and lunch. Sunday for lunch. Unlicensed. Access: barrier-free, no washrooms.* **$**

Little India

Indian

LAHORE TIKKA HOUSE
1365 Gerrard E, at Highfield, 416-406-1668.
Yes, it looks like a construction site. But this hectic east-side Pakistani take-away takes it outdoors during summer months to a riotous 200-seat sari-tented patio set with family-style picnic tables. Warning: order any dish hot and be prepared for jet propulsion. Best: slashed red snapper tikka, smoky from the charcoal-fuelled tandoor, skewered with lightly charred turmeric-tanged onion, potato and tomato; aromatic minced lamb kebabs; lemon-scented aloo gobi rich with waxy spuds and al dente cauliflower; butter-brushed naan tossed with sesame seeds; house-made almond kulfi ice cream on a wooden chopstick. *Open for lunch and dinner. Unlicensed. Access: one step at door, washrooms in basement.* **$$** ☼

SIDHARTHA
1450 Gerrard E, at Craven, 416-465-4095,
647 King W, at Bathurst, 416-703-6684.
Considering Little India's low-rent standards, this charming North Indian eatery is easily the budget dining strip's classiest eatery. Most dig into the moderately spiced all-you-can-eat $8.99 lunch/$10.99 dinner buffet, but those who venture into the à la carte lineup will discover a few fiery gems. Best: Chicken Bolcha, large chunks of yogurt-marinated boneless tandoori chicken in an almost Italian tomato sauce spiked with chilies and slightly soured with vinegar; Mataar and Paneer Pulao, cubes of deep-fried paneer – yes, deep-fried cheese! – on a bed of white basmati studded with garden peas; Bhindi Do Piazza, al dente okra fingers in turmeric-tanged sauce; assertively spiced lamb vindaloo with potato in sweet curried gravy; lightly oiled and blistered naan straight from the tandoor. *Open for lunch and dinner. Licensed. Access: barrier-free, washrooms in basement.* **$$$**

Indian Vegetarian

KISSAN
1411 Gerrard E, at Hiawatha, 416-466-9777.
The latest offshoot of Sidhartha, quite possibly Little India's classiest curry house, this charming room in the former deplorable Bombay Bhel offers an all-vegetarian lineup that incorporates the rich sauces of the north and the fiery chilies of the

Too many meals at **Tomi-Kro** and this is how you'll feel. Page 92.

south. Warning: slim pickin's for vegans, since nearly everything comes dripping with clarified butter or substitutes meat with cheesy paneer. Best: from the all-you-can-eat buffet, fabulously fresh onion bhaja with both tamarind and mint sauce; buttery lentil dal makhani; tofu jalferezi with snow peas; al dente aloo gobi with potato and cauliflower; paneer in puréed spinach; deep-fried kofta "meatballs" in creamy turmeric gravy; from the bread basket, whole wheat parantha and aloo naan topped with curried potato; from the à la carte card, baked tandoori tofu; for dessert, cardamom-syrup-soaked gulab jamon and creamy kheer rice pudding; to kill the heat, a stomach-soothing lassi. *Open daily for lunch and dinner. Unlicensed. Delivery. Access: two steps at door, washrooms in basement.* **$$**

NARULA'S
1438A Gerrard E, at Ashdale, 416-466-0434.
Some may be put off by the way this spare Indian vegetarian kitchen looks, but the inexpensive spice-intensive — salty, sweet, fiery, sour — snacks dished up here cause the palate to detonate in myriad directions. And everything — except drinks — is 2 bucks on Tuesday! Best: Bhel Poori, spice-drenched basmati mined with chilies, firm boiled potatoes, crunchy chickpeas, lentils and coriander leaves; Sev Poori, milky yogurt dusted with cayenne, and shredded crispy rice noodles kicked with minty relish; Dahi Vada, lentil-flour doughnuts in cool yogurt or fiery sambar; daily thali with veggie subzi — say, eggplant, lentil dhal or cheesy matar paneer — and basmati, roti

and pappadom. *Open for lunch and dinner. Closed Monday. Unlicensed. Cash only. Access: one step at door, washrooms on same floor.* **$** ⋮

UDUPI PALACE
1460 Gerrard E, at Rhodes, 416-405-8189.
The first Canadian outlet of a US chain of South Indian-style vegetarian restaurants, this white-on-white room is so spotless one could eat right off the white ceramic floor. Or the white vinyl chairs. Or the sterile, unadorned walls if the food would stick to it. Through open doors, one notes a gleaming stainless steel kitchen where an all-male staff dressed in jeans and matching golf shirts polish things that are already lustrous. Warning: spicing is meek and the always busy space noisy, so bring the kids and grandparents. Best: dozen or so dosai, lacy crepe-like wraps made from fermented lentil flour that measure up to 24 inches in diameter and range from flapjack-thick to tissue-thin, like the vellum-esque Paper Dosa coupled with tame lentil, carrot and pepper sambal, pasty coconut relish and coriander-mint chutney, or Special Rava Masala Dosa, a green-chili-flecked pancake that's as hole-y as Swiss cheese; punch-packing chili pakoras, battered and deep-fried yellow banana peppers stuffed with curried potato and pea masala; smoky chickpea chana served with grilled chapati and basmati rice; tissue-thin crisp paper dosa with the usual sides; to sip, sugary mango lassi; to finish, sweet carrot halwa puréed pudding. *Open for lunch and dinner. Licensed. Access: six steps at door, washrooms on same floor.* **$$**

restaurants

Riverside

Café

FOOD SAVVY
782 Queen E, at Saulter, 416-466-0466.
Sophisticated Broadview Village bistro serving soups, salads and flatbread sandwiches called piadini. Interesting blends of fresh herbs and other ingredients in an "urban ethnic" style. Best: jerk chicken sandwich – excellent jerk flavour, with pickled red onions served on thick flatbread; lime chicken wrap – moist grilled chicken with cilantro and Jack cheese, jalapeños and choice of avocado cream or chipotle mayo; lemon dill couscous – in which dill successfully stands in for parsley, with chickpeas and minced onion. *Open for lunch. Unlicensed. Access: barrier-free, washrooms upstairs.* **$**

Caribbean

REAL JERK
709 Queen E, at Broadview, 416-463-6055.
An Island oasis in South Riverdale, this long-running cavernous tropical retreat offers groovy grub with groovesome dub. A former bank, the two-level space is decked out in corrugated tin, palm fronds and Christmas lights year round. Bonus: Jerk aficionados can recreate the experience at home with owner/chefs Ed and Lili Potingers' Real Jerk cookbook, hot sauce and seasoning mix. Best: moist, partially deboned fiery jerk chicken with nutty red beans 'n' rice and cooling coleslaw; smashed banana fritters; jerk shrimp over greens in tamarind vinaigrette; "Mannish Water" goat soup; vegetarian Rasta Pasta linguini with tropical veggies in coconut sauce; Red Stripe beer in stubby bottles; weekends-only Island Pizza; takeout jerk by weight. *Open for lunch and dinner. Closed some holidays. Licensed. Access: one step at door, washrooms in basement.* **$$$**

Contemporary

POP BISTRO
686 Queen E, at Broadview, 416-461-9663.
Goodbye jukeboxes, hello supper-club chic. This former greasy spoon gets recast as an intimate 24-seat Riverside resto complete with a card that combines French bistro fare with comfort food favourites. Bonus: nightly $30 three-course prix fixe. Warning: because of space limitations, reservations recommended. Best: at dinner, start with chunked chorizo with grapes in minty port syrup, or French onion soup topped with cheesy croissant; go on to mains like lamb meat loaf roulade of braised celery and blue cheese sided with buttery mashed yams; roasted pork tenderloin slathered in Pommery mustard; daily specials like braised veal shank or roasted rabbit in beurre blanc; to finish, chocolate bread pudding; at brunch, Eggs Norwegian, salmon gravlax topped with runny poached eggs over Ace Bakery brioche; Croque Legume, grilled zucchini, eggplant and bell pepper on baguette. *Open for dinner. Weekend for brunch. Closed Monday, holidays. Licensed. Access: one step at door, small room, washrooms on same floor.* **$$$$**

French

BONJOUR BRIOCHE
812 Queen E, at Degrassi, 416-406-1250.
Master baker Henri Feasson and partner Lori Feasson helm this long-running neighbourhood café famed for its all-day continental breakfasts and definitive Gallic charm. Bonus: every Saturday and Sunday Feasson bakes his signature giant brioche. Best: from the ever-changing chalkboard lineup, prosciutto, Gorgonzola and arugula pesto quiche; specials like Trailer Park Chili or Torta Rustica paired with designer greens in basil vinaigrette and a house-baked baguette; Pain Bagnat – tuna, cucumber, sliced hard-

boiled egg and mesclun on a milk bun, or barbecue turkey with tarragon mayo on multigrain; savoury flans like tomato, basil and chèvre or classic onion 'n' Gruyere; for the sweet tooth, blueberry custard Brioche Royale, tarte Tatin and collapsed flourless chocolate cake. *Open for breakfast and lunch. Closed Monday. Licensed. Cash only. Access: one step at door, washrooms in basement.* **$$$** ☼

Tex Mex

COYOTE WILLIE
689 Queen E, at Broadview, 416-778-4578.
Tiny Tex-Mex cantina churns out California-style gringo grub with an emphasis on beans. Makes great takeout. Best: whole oven-roasted chickens with spicy chorizo baked beans; huge veggie burritos sided with smooth guacamole, chunky tomato salsa and pickled jalapeños; fall-from-the-bone sloppy pork ribs in barbecue sauce; pre-fab pecan pie hits the sweet spot. *Open for lunch and dinner. Closed Sunday, holidays. Unlicensed. Access: one step at door, washrooms in basement.* **$$**

Scarborough

Chinese

DRAGON DYNASTY
2301 Brimley, at Huntingwood, 416-321-9000.
Located in a suburban Scarborough mall, Dragon Dynasty is an upwardly mobile Cantonese eatery – just check out all the late-model Mercedes, Lexii and Range Rovers in the parking lot. Dim sum is served daily until mid-afternoon, when the pricey seafood-heavy Cantonese menu takes over. Warning: the large room becomes almost as crowded as the nearby zoo by noon, so come early or fashionably late. Best: banana leaves stuffed with tender chunks of chicken and pork mixed with sticky rice; translucent made-to-order har gow shrimp and pea-stalk dumplings; golden tapioca with bean paste; fried rice noodle with kale and preserved olive leaf. *Open for breakfast, lunch and dinner. Licensed. Access: barrier-free.* **$$$$**

RUBY
1571 Sandhurst Circle, at Finch E, 416-298-1638.
One of Scarborough's famed cavernous Cantonese cafeterias, this upmarket banquet hall in an upscale suburban mall serves daily dim sum brunch. Trolleys trawl the aisles stacked with steamers full of pork shiu mei and shrimp har gow dumplings stuffed with the familiar and the unknown but usually delicious. Friendly, helpful servers assist the uninitiated: what may appear to be mandarin oranges with cashews is actually pig's intestines! Best: explosive potstickers overstuffed with pork and Chinese greens, dipped in hot mustard; tempura-battered eggplant wrapped around ground fish, coupled with a tartaresque mayo studded with white grapes and fresh pineapple chunks; oversized wontons in chicken stock swimming with pork, shrimp and black mushrooms; deep-fried tofu stuffed with whole shrimp and splashed with black bean sauce; to quell the fire, warmingly neutral hot tapioca pudding to finish. *Open for breakfast, lunch and dinner. Licensed. Access: barrier-free.* **$$$**

Japanese

LE CAFE MICHI
1802 Pharmacy, at Sheppard E, 416-490-9688.
Sushi-meister Mitsohiro Kaji – Kaji-san to his devoted followers – of the Queensway's pricey Sushi Kaji introduces high-end but budget-priced exotica to an extremely small suburban strip plaza café. Though the revered chef is only occasionally in the house (your best bet is weekday lunch), he leaves his able apprentice Mr. Lim in charge. Reservations recommended. Warning: Zamfir's pan flutes in permanent

Sari, sari night at **Lahore Tikka House**. Page 94.

rotation. Best: say "omakase" – whatever Kaji-san feels like – and begin with an ethereal bowl of rice lightly doused with mirin and topped with subtly nutty sea urchin and berry-sized salmon roe; exquisite nigiri like butterflied and briefly seared scallops, buttery yellowtail and terrific scored squid over shiso leaf; impossibly rich slices of kampachi – baby yellowtail – on raw spinach drizzled with walnut oil and minced garlic; green tea cheesecake to finish. *Open for lunch and dinner. Closed Monday. Licensed. Access: barrier-free, but cramped space.* $$$$

Sri Lankan
HOPPER HUT
880 Ellesmere, unit 217, at Kennedy, 416-299-4311.
As the name implies, this home-style Sri Lankan spot specializes in hoppers, the bowl-sized crepes served with both fiery and savoury curries. While there's a busy takeout counter, some dine in the family-friendly space out back. Best: lampries, the local take on Dutch Indonesian rijsttafel rice tables, here augmented with milky hodhi gravy, sweet eggplant curry, incendiary raw onion sambal and sensational legs-'n'-all crab curry in searing hot coconut sauce; Hopper Combo #2, a quartet of thin, cupped pancakes with the gentle heat of coconut Pol Sambal and mince-meat-like onion Seeni Sambal; fabulous three-for-a-dollar crisp and golden samosas straight from the fryer, stuffed with curried potato and peas; to finish, syrup-soaked Vatilappam sponge cake and smooth Pineapple Pluff custard. *Open for breakfast, lunch and dinner. Unlicensed. Access: barrier-free.* $$

Vietnamese
KRISPY ROLL
789 Warden, at Eglinton E, 416-759-5757.
Just off the Golden Mile and next door to the Scarborough water tower, the former Dai Nam thrives in the burbs. Devotees of the Spadina soup kitchen will make the pilgrimage if only for chef Khanh Nguyen's fabulous pho and partner Anh Mai's

genuine hospitality. Best: to begin, grilled rack of lamb, nine meaty on-the-bone chops with a sauce of red wine and purple basil; the house's signature Saigon-style hot 'n' sour soup brimming with green New Zealand mussels, faux crab and button 'shrooms; a French colonial pho with duck confit, Chinese mushrooms and chewy chow mein; "grilled beef wrapped in scented leaf" translates as beef kabobs draped with aromatic screw pine leaves rolled burrito-style in rice paper with raw veggies and herbs for dipping into sweet chili-fired nuac cham; a respectable if ketchup-heavy pad thai. *Open for lunch and dinner. Unlicensed. Cash only. Access: one step at door, washrooms in basement.* $$

West

Bloor West
Café
YASI'S PLACE
299 Wallace, at Symington, 416-536-9888, www.yasisplace.com.
Owner Yasemin Zorlutuna retains the luncheonette's original's fittings, including vintage mugs and salt 'n' pepper shakers and menu throwbacks like waffles topped with coconut whipped cream. Bonus: virtually everything's made in-house. Double bonus: a patio and community garden. Best: four kinds of grilled cheese sandwiches – from trad to rad (cheddar, avocado spread and red onion) – on Ace multigrain or open-faced over house-made cornbread paired with daily soups like vegan potato and spinach; black bean veggie burger; at weekend brunch, Turkish-style organic beef patties over feather-light couscous, sided with herb-dusted greens and feta; Eggs Florentinish, gently poached free-range eggs with homemade hollandaise, served with organic baby

Something for everyone at Japanese-Korean joint **Il Bun Ji.**

spinach, grilled polenta and Middle Easternized home fries; to finish, tofu chocolate mousse pie on caramelized crumb crust. *Open for breakfast and lunch. Unlicensed. Access: barrier-free, washrooms in basement.* **$$** ⁚⁚

Contemporary

UNIVERSAL GRILL
1071 Shaw, at Dupont, 416-588-5928.
Long-running luncheonette dishes out contemporary grub in nostalgic digs, a retrofitted soda fountain with swivel-able stools, comfy wooden booths, film noir venetian blinds. Best: to start, deluxe seasonal soups like creamy saffron-scented cauliflower purée or tomato with roasted garlic and tarragon; golden-crusted polenta with oyster mushrooms, roasted tomato, capers and chèvre; tortilla spring rolls with sweet and hot mango dip; to follow, vibrantly spiced comfort-food-style barbecued Spitfire baby back pork ribs or dry-rubbed Indo-style, both sided with magnificent yam frites; rosemary roast chicken with home-style gravy and seriously old-school scalloped potatoes; pan-seared calf's liver with Dijon-glazed onion; daily specials like grilled tandoori salmon with saag paneer, wild rice pancake and asparagus; at brunch, latkes with salmon gravlox, capers and designer greens; Tex Mex-esque Huevos Rancheros with a side of grilled chorizo. *Open for dinner. Weekend for brunch. Closed Monday. Licensed. Access: two steps at door, washrooms in basement.* **$$$$** ⁚⁚

Korean

BUK CHANG DONG TO FU
691 Bloor W, at Clinton, 416-537-0972.
One of many informal fast-food eateries along the Koreatown strip, this casual spot specializes in "soon," a fiery soup thick with tofu, seafood or meat served with kimchee, raw scallion and other incendiary condiments. Always busy, and service is indifferent at best. Best: to begin, a parade of banchan like vinegared wakame with onion and carrot; from the extremely short lineup, five varieties of soon — kimchee, New Zealand mussels, sliced pork or beef, or unshelled shrimp — all mixed with miso broth, red chili pepper, raw egg and scallions over oven-baked sticky rice; Bi Bim Bap, a meal-in-one crunchy rice casserole stirred with raw egg and layered with ground beef, slivered zucchini, carrot, marinated mushrooms and sprouts; to drink, bottles of Jinro Chamjinisulro, the potent 23-proof Korean grain spirit that goes down as smooth as homemade hooch and could probably be used to clean paint brushes. *Open for lunch and dinner. Licensed. Access: one step at door, washrooms in basement.* **$**

IL BUN JI
668 Bloor W, at Manning, 416-534-7223.
Hands down, this is Koreatown's most stylish eatery. While the menu is half Japanese — sushi, teriyaki, tempura — it's the Korean dishes that deserve attention. Warning: reservations are required to dine shoe-free and sitting on the floor in one of six gorgeous

semi-private rooms separated by shoji screens. Best: to start, Yaki Man Doo, golden-hued potstickers stuffed with shredded fish and Chinese leeks; Sunomo salad with raw octopus, scallops, nori and eggy tamago in rice wine vinaigrette; from the mains, Yuk Hwe, shredded sirloin tartar charged with garlic and pinenut brushed with egg yolk; Doo Boo Chigai, comfort-food-style casserole – pork, bok choy, tofu, enoki – in kimchee-kicked broth; brazier-grilled Kalbi marinated short ribs; soy-glazed broiled eel; vegetarian Chap Chae with 'shrooms and cellophane noodle; to finish, a sectioned orange; enormous daily lunch combos like bulgogi with soup, salad and steamed rice. *Open for lunch and dinner. Licensed. Access: one step at door, washrooms upstairs.* **$$$**

KOREA HOUSE
666 Bloor W, at Manning, 416-536-8666.
Formal as a tea house, this pleasant wood-trimmed room — think Swiss Chalet goes to Yokohama — offers nine (!) pickled starters, including incendiary kimchee, cooling cukes, marinated spinach 'n' seaweed salad and exceedingly salty hot chilies. Prices for surf 'n' turf mains skyrocket, but there are still bargains to be found on the leather-wrapped menu. Best: to start, marinated on-the-bone and butterflied Kol Bi beef ribs and cold Be Bim buckwheat soba noodle salad with sliced sirloin, hard-boiled egg and pear-like daikon with spicy red miso dressing; Yook Kae Jang, a hot-pot meal-in-one soup with egg drop, spinach sukiyaki steak and translucent rice vermicelli; Kan Cha Jang, an oversized tureen of thick soba mixed with pork, onion, sunny-side-up fried egg, tart black bean sauce and kimchee sided with a lidded stainless steel bowl of steamed rice. *Open for lunch and dinner. Licensed. Access: one step at door, washrooms in basement.* **$$**

OWL OF MINERVA
700 Bloor W, at Clinton, 416-538-3030.
With minimal signage, this second-storey spot is one of the more obscure fuelling stops in Korea Town. By day, this decidedly shabby spot attracts an older crowd bent on Old World comfort food, but as the night grows long and the volume of the booming Asian techno pop increases, the small room fills with animated club kids from nearby karaoke bars. Other locations: 5324 Yonge, at Churchill, 416-221-7275. Best: from quite possibly the shortest menu in town (four items), bulgogi, described as "some beef, some noodles, some vegetables," but actually stringy strips of quickly seared soy-marinated beef over sweet potato noodles stir-fried with carrot, scallions and button mushrooms in smoky sweet red pepper paste; Pork Bone Soup, the Seoul-food version of goulash, thick with delicious marrow-full shank slowly simmered in broth and thickened with potato, salty fermented miso paste and hellishly hot pepper powder. *Open for breakfast, lunch and dinner. Licensed. Access: eight stops at door, washrooms in basement.* **$$**

SE JONG
658 Bloor W, at Manning, 416-535-5918.
Smooth service and semi-private shoji-screened booths make for a great Seoul food experience. Don't fill up on the constantly replenished banchan starters – steamed egg custard swirled with coriander leaf, fiery cabbage kimchee, chewy seaweed, al dente adzuki in sweet molasses-like soy, mung bean sprouts drenched in garlic – and blond miso soup, because the mains are equally substantial. Bonus: upstairs party room! Best: combination dinners such as marinated bulgogi sirloin strips in mushroom and onion with shredded seafood mandu dumplings, retro iceberg salad and glutinous short-grain rice topped with black sesame seeds; Jap Chae Bap, a vegetarian stew of shiitakes, zucchini and Chinese cabbage over clear sweet-potato noodles; sporting a pink paper umbrella, grilled Salmon Gui with lemon, pickled ginger and wasabi; straightforward California-style sushi; set-price Korean combos grilled on braziers built into each table. *Open for lunch and dinner. Licensed. Access: barrier-free, washrooms upstairs.* **$$$**

Indian
SOUTH INDIAN DOSA MAHAL
1284 Bloor W, at St. Clarens, 416-516-7701.
This sketchy-looking neighbourhood takeout, eat-in spot is better than it looks. Bonus: always fresh, large veggie samosas are only $3 for 10 if you get them to go. Best: special vegetable meal thali, a hearty combo of basmati rice, roti, pappadom, yogurt, spicy pickled carrots, delicious citrusy split pea soup, a light tomato broth with mustard seeds, dal and three yummy veg curries: potato, crispy broccoli with scallion and anise seeds, and saucy eggplant with tomato; chicken biryani, or turmeric-stained fried rice that accompanies tender chicken pieces stewed in rich tomato broth; rustic fish poori, served with two deep-fried flatbreads; thin, crispy dosa enclosing a heap of thick potato curry, or the softer, more pancake-like uthappam, which is speckled with fresh chilies, tomato and onion. *Open Monday to Saturday. Closed Sunday. Unlicensed. Access: barrier-free.* **$**

Mexican
MEXITACO
828 Bloor W, at Shaw, 416-537-6693.
This cheap and cheerful taqueria delivers no-nonsense Mexican meals in a room of limited kitsch (sombrero count: three). Though it's quite small, the welcoming room is lined with mirrors and tall uncurtained windows that let light in on two sides while soft Mexican country rock plays on the stereo. Best: as the name would suggest, tacos – lime-scented tortillas layered with strips of grilled steak, pineapple-marinated shaved pork or spicy sausage garnished with raw red onion, fresh coriander leaf and house-made hot sauce; Gringa, a folded and fried flour tortilla stuffed with pork and lotsa mozza and, like most mains, sided with yellow achiote rice and textbook refried beans; to finish, chef Patricia Morales' deeply delicious flan that recalls Mexican bread pudding; to quaff, heat-cutting apple soda. *Open for lunch and dinner. Licensed. Access: one step at door, washrooms in basement.* **$$$** ⁖

Portuguese
● PIRI-PIRI GRILL HOUSE
1444 Dupont, at Symington, 416-536-5100.
Once a favourite on College, this authentic Portuguese grill house has found new casual and tastefully decorated digs at the edge of the Junction. Bonus: a year-round tented patio decked out with tables dressed with white tablecloths and cheerful yellow and blue napkins. Best: eponymous Piri-Piri Chicken, a crispy half-bird liberally sea-salted and slathered with a sauce of hot chili paste and oil, paired with excellent fries and rice; generously portioned grilled squid, flame-kissed and doused in white wine, melted butter and garlic, sided with boiled potato, broccoli, carrot and cauliflower; quality baguette for sopping duty. *Open for lunch and dinner. Licensed. Access: barrier-free.* **$$** ⁖

Salvadoran
TACOS EL ASADOR
690 Bloor W, at Clinton, 416-538-9747.
Funky taqueria serving down-home Latin American street eats. Eat in at slatted wood tables and benches or take away an inexpensive nosh. Best: humongous plate piled with thin pan-fried steak, mild tomato salsa, refried beans, rice studded with corn kernels and red pepper, and a salad of cucumber, multi-

coloured pepper and avocado; crisp tacos stuffed with lime-tenderized chicken, beef or pork; pupusas stuffed with cheese and bean-and-squash purée and topped with red and white cabbage slaw as well as sliced onion, jalapeño and chili salsa; house-made horchata, a creamy shake of sweet rice, pulverized peanuts, vanilla and milk. *Open for lunch and dinner. Licensed. Cash only. Access: one step at door, washrooms in basement.* **$$**

Dundas West & Ossington

Café

COFFEE SHOP @ IF LOUNGE
1212 Dundas W, at Lakeview, 416-588-4900.
All shiny chrome, exposed brick and curvy banquettes, this swanky west-side cocktail lounge might be a little too glam for a neighbourhood where the primary dining destinations are a KFC and a spoon that specializes in the appetizing hybrid that is Portuguese-Chinese cuisine. Against all odds, this remarkably welcoming boîte delivers a daily mid-morning breakfast and tapas menu with considerable skill. Best: to start, cinnamon and cardamom biscuits, spice-scented scones plated with ripe strawberry and mint; continue with the house's spectacular mini-burgers, a beefy trio of three-ounce medium-rare black Angus patties served on custom-baked miniature pada buns, the first topped with ripe Roma tomato, fresh buffalo bocconcini, garlicky mayo and a basil leaf, the second with crumbled feta and sliced English cucumber, the third dolloped with wasabi aïoli and crunchy tempura batter bits, sided with roasted baby red potatoes and/or sesame-dressed mesclun; for the sweet tooth, banana-stuffed 'n' toasted pecan-tossed French toast or vanilla-bean waffles sloshed with blueberry maple syrup. *Open for lunch. Bar till close. Closed Monday,*

Top five
kid friendly

FRAN'S
A 50s-style diner stablished in 1940, Toronto's longest-running resto, this 50s-style diner-cum-retro-chic lounge in the Pantages Hotel with a burger-n-fried menu supplemented with Asian and Tex-Mex. (*210 Victoria, and other locations*)

RAINFOREST CAFÉ
A jungle-themed resto – complete with elephants, apes and snakes – It's like the Hard Rock cafe for kids who watch too much Animal Planet. (*Yorkdale Mall, 3401 Dufferin*)

REGINA
Kids love spaghetti and meatballs, so check out this Little Italy pizza shop and trattoria. (*782 College*)

ROL SAN
The quintessential Chinatown dining experience, with good food served fast. *See review, page 50.*

TRE FONTAINE
Toronto's only Italian vegetarian all-you-can-eat buffet (don't worry, it's not all vegetarian), where children under 12 are half-price, those under five eat free. (*486 Bloor West*)

holidays. *Licensed. Access: one step at door, washrooms in basement.* **$$**

GAYLEY'S
1424 Dundas W, at Gladstone, 416-538-3443.
This brick-lined casual café fitted out with moulded plywood Eames-style chairs, a few pews and bare topped tables is a west-side secret. Rarely too crowded, the relaxed room – if it were any more laid-back, it'd be horizontal – always has stacks of newspapers to read, and its competent kitchen whips up a respectable all-day breakfast that goes for only $4.95. Just don't be in a hurry; everything's made to order. Very slowly. Bonus: kid-friendly. Warning: kid-friendly. Best: lineup of nearly 30 sandwiches built on super Calabrese ring, whole wheat or pita, including grilled zucchini, mild havarti, sweet sun-dried tomatoes and sprouts or triple-decker turkey club; basic eggs Benedict sided with perfunctory fries; porridge with toast 'n' and a good cup of coffee; to drink, yogurt-based fruit-juice smoothies. *Open for breakfast and lunch. Unlicensed. Cash only. Access: one step at door, washrooms on same floor.* **$**

SAVING GRACE
907 Dundas W, at Bellwoods, 416-703-7368.
When owner/chef Monica Miller's deceptively anonymous space – white-on-white walls, minimalist decor, 20 seats tops – opened six years ago, friends thought she was mad to open on this dreary inner-city strip. Now that Dundas West is the snazziest address around, they join the queue with the rest of us at her charming café for straightforward soups, salads and sandwiches priced to go easy on the pocketbook. Bonus: on the hi-fi, a brilliant mix tape featuring the likes of the Turtles, Go-Betweens and Bacharach-era Dionne Warwick. Double bonus: copies of hip UK music bible NME in the magazine rack (not for taking home). Best: devilishly textured corn cakes accompanied by chili-fired mango chutney and greens dressed with sun-dried tomato vinaigrette; weekday soups like Thai-style coconut cream thick with boneless chicken breast, green beans, garlic chives, lemongrass and bird chilies; such sizable sandwiches as grilled chicken, peameal, avocado, tomato and lettuce on raisin-bread toast spread with rosemary mayo; on the weekend, waffle du jour with real maple syrup, or very plain scrambled eggs with pumpernickel toast and oven-roasted home fries. *Open for breakfast and lunch. Closed Wednesday, first Tuesday of the month and holidays. Licensed. Access: one step at door, washrooms upstairs.* **$$**

Contemporary

EAT CAFÉ
1321 Dundas W, at Dovercourt, 416-537-3000, www.eatcatering.com.
Since it opened, owner/chef Anila Dhanji's fashionably but minimally appointed spot – 30 seats tops – has grown from a west-side secret into one of downtown's best-loved reliables. Count on a soft-priced card that runs from breakfast to late-night bistro delivered with adventurous pan-global style. Bonus: vegetarian substitutions. Best: to begin, peppery shrimp and lobster bisque with warm house-baked bread; mains like slow-braised veal shank with Asiago-laced garlic mash; Dhanji's exemplary thin-crust pizza – one of the best around – tastefully dressed with mozzarella, grilled chicken and sun-dried tomato; at lunch, cookbook-correct French onion soup topped with molten Gruyère; at brunch, eggs with Merguez sausage, rosemary-redolent home fries and challah toast; for dessert, chocolate brioche bread pudding with silken crème anglaise. *Open Tuesday to Friday for lunch. Tuesday to Saturday for dinner. Weekend for brunch. Closed Monday, holidays. Licensed. Access: one step at door, washrooms on same floor.* **$$$**

Cuban

JULIE'S

202 Dovercourt, at Argyle, 416-532-7397,
www.juliescuban.com.

Since the late 90s, this casually cool Cuban cantina on downtown's west side has been a well-kept secret among those looking for something a little different. A tree-shaded terrace sets the scene for late-night trysts, while inside, the room's former spell as a corner shop gives the vintage space a luncheonette feel. Bonus: a very private dining room out back. Best: grilled and then pressed marinated pork, ham and Swiss Cubano sandwiches; snacking tapas like three versions of the fried mashed-potato ball called Papa Rellena, one stuffed with lean ground beef, onion, tomato and green olives; purposefully bland Yuca con Mojo laced with lime and garlic; piquant tomato-sauced pork-sausage chorizos in red wine; subtly complex pork and beef hash (Picadillo de Mamita) with jalapeños, raisins, currants and almonds. *Open for dinner. Closed Monday. Licensed. Access: two steps at door, washrooms in basement.* **$$$**

Israeli

SIDE DOOR GRILL

771 Dundas W, at Markham, 416-603-6161,
www.sidedoorgrill.com.

A minimally appointed space, this unassuming resto offers first-rate takes on Israeli-style Middle Eastern fare. Sure, there's falafel. But more adventurous palates will appreciate the quality and value of nearly everything else on offer here. Best: to begin, puréed Green Eggplant laced with coriander and scallions or cumin-scented pickled beets; sizable mains like lamb chops, four thick cooked-to-order grilled chops dressed with squirts of lemon and slim-sliced raw onion; Kefta Kebob, three tasty cigar-sized skinless sausages; old-school pounded and pan-fried chicken schnitzel; all entrees sided with terrific twice-roasted baby red potatoes strewn with caramelized onion

and drizzled with olive oil, as well as the house's top-notch salad dressed in a lemony vinaigrette. *Open for breakfast. Tuesday to Saturday for lunch and dinner. Closed Monday. Licensed. Access: short step at door, washrooms on same floor.* **$$$**

Mediterranean

MUSA

847 Dundas W, at Euclid, 416-368-8484.

A low-key hipster haunt on the too-cool stretch of Dundas, this eastern Mediterranean-style resto offers contemporary takes on casual Greek and Turkish mezes and mains in a sunny, al fresco setting. Bonus: low-markup house plonk by the glass. Best: just-like-Mom's moussaka with béchamel sauce; Keftades — ground beef falafel patties zapped with cumin and onion, stuffed into a spectacular spelt pita piled with cucumber, tomato and romaine, sauced with creamy Dijon and sided with first-rate hand-cut fries; seared and sliced free-range chicken in the same pita with red chilies, jalapeño, piquant kefalotiri cheese, sautéed onions and arugula; lemony dandelion greens, navy beans and rapini sautéed in olive oil and garlic; at brunch, a rotating roster of omelette specials like asparagus with Swiss, or smoked salmon with arugula, coupled with roasted spuds and Cajun home fries. *Open Tuesday to Friday for breakfast and lunch. Monday to Friday for dinner. Weekend for brunch. Bar till close. Licensed. Access: one step at door, washrooms on same floor.* **$$$**

Portuguese

CAFFE BRASILIANO

849 Dundas W, at Euclid, 416-603-6607.

Since moving across the street into fancier digs, this west-side Portuguese cafeteria cum coffee house has become known by more than just cabbies and folks who happen to live close by. Around since the 60s, the place hosts a multiculti mix of grumpy old

men, coffee-swilling locals with toddlers in tow and early morning club kids still up from the night before, all starting the day substantially with Old World home cookin'. Bonus: exclusively roasted Brazilian house espresso and Colombian coffee so good that the owners supply several of downtown's most popular dining rooms. Best: the rotating list of weekday specials — veal chops on Monday, old-school veal 'n' veggie stew Tuesday, Wednesday-only lasagna, Thursday's pasta fagioli and Friday's well-done roast beef — all sided with roasted potato, lemony chickpea salad and mixed Portuguese veggies doused in olive oil; daily sweet tomato-sauced roasted chicken with creamy potato salad and tasty pizza squares. *Open for breakfast, lunch and dinner. Closed Sunday. Licensed. Cash only. Access: barrier-free.* **$**

Vegetarian
GET REAL
135 Ossington, at Argyle, 416-532-4564.
In a small converted row house in downtown's newest gentrified nabe, this veggie vittle venue encompasses a bright front room decked out with blond moulded chairs and glass-topped café tables and a private patio out back complete with acid-flashback mural and rocking horse. Bonus: where else can you hear the Velvet Underground's *Heroin* while munching sprouts? Best: from a short card of straightforward veggie dishes, plump samosas stuffed with curried tofu and spinach; Spicy Bean Burger on a whole wheat bun topped with dill pickle and cheddar, as close as a dedicated veg-head need ever get to Harvey's; house greens tossed with pump-

kin seeds and fresh basil and either crumbled tofu or creamy blue cheese; at brunch, hemp pancakes topped with maple-glazed plantain, grilled mango and kiwi salsa; organic granola with low-fat organic yogurt; a proper English breakfast of free-range eggs, tofu strips marinated in vegan Worcestershire and organic baked beans; vegan Belgian waffles made with unbleached spelt flour. *Open for dinner. Tuesday to Friday for breakfast, and lunch. Weekend for brunch. Closed Monday, holidays. Unlicensed. Access: barrier-free, small washroom on same floor.* **$$** ⛆

Etobicoke
Indian Vegetarian

⣿ BRAR SWEETS
2646 Islington, at Albion, 416-745-4449, other locations.
While its refrigerated display cases overflow with Indo sweets like gulab jameen, jalebis and toffee-like barfi, the all-vegetarian spread at the café's rear is where the real delights lie. Stick around the daily thali in a pistachio-painted, fluorescent-lit room with all the atmosphere of a donut shop, or opt, like most, for takeout. Warning: almost all dishes come heavy with ghee (clarified butter). Best: Mix Veg, a spice-mad stew of inordinately crunchy red 'n' green pepper, carrot, cauliflower and potato spiked with caraway and cumin in rich turmeric-laced coconut gravy; meatless chickpea kofta meatballs in satiny sauce; paneer with garden peas; sensational tomato curry studded with slivered almonds; to side, dark lentil dahl, minty over-

Julie's, a casually cool Cuban cantina with plenty of sizzle. Page 101.

sized chickpea chana, potato aloo, yogurty raita topped with yellow split peas, and a garden-variety salad bar; to finish, halva and milk-cooked shredded carrot with almonds, pistachios and sultanas layered with edible silver leaf. *Open for lunch and dinner. Unlicensed. Cash only. Access: one step at door, washrooms in basement.* **$**

Mexican

🔵 EL JACALITO
1500 Royal York, at Lawrence, 416-244-4447.
Transposed Mexican taqueria moves into a Sopranos-style banquet hall without losing the spectacular grub that made its name. But it's Saturday night's $35 all-you-can-eat buffet, complete with riveting after-dinner performances by folkloric dance troupe Tonatiuh and wise-guy mariachi quartet Viva Mexico that make this modest cantina in a strip mall next to a bowling alley a deserved foodie destination. Reservations essential for ringside seats. Best: superb banana-leaf-wrapped pork or chicken Cochinita Pibil, tender slow-cooked shredded meat doused in tangy achiote paste and sour orange; deeply rich refried turtle beans crumbled with queso fresco; Pico de Gallo, a salad of shredded iceberg, ripe tomato, red onion and coriander in a lime vinaigrette sided with a slow-burn condiment called Tomorrow Sauce (you'll know why then); Sunday-only Barbacoa de Borrego, party-style barbecued lamb to go; to drink, the Chelada, a beer margarita. *Open Monday to Saturday for dinner. Wednesday to Sunday for lunch. Closed Tuesday. Licensed. Cash only. Access: 17 steps at door, washrooms on same floor.* **$$$$**

Turkish

ANATOLIA
5112 Dundas W, at Kipling, 416-207-0596.
Consider Turkish cuisine true crossroads cooking. Combining familiar elements from Greek, Persian and Arabic dishes, this friendly eatery in an Etobicoke strip mall offers classic stews and starters that are not only tasty but health-conscious, too. Best: amazing just-baked pide bread (think thick pita) drizzled with oil; phyllo-wrapped Beyti stuffed with ground beef and lamb, served with garlicky pressed Haydari yogurt dusted with dried mint and a trio of lightly olive-oiled salads — sweet carrot julienne, purple beet-and-cabbage slaw and ripped iceberg with English cuke; baked Manti dumplings filled with ground beef and sauced with yogurt and hot clarified butter; meze for sharing like smoky Patlican Ezme eggplant purée, Yaprak Sarmasi (grape leaves wrapped around long-grain rice studded with currants and pine nuts) and delicious slices of fried eggplant Platican Kizartmasi swimming in buttery yogurt; salty lassi-like Ayran and dark, sweet Turkish coffee to quaff. *Open for lunch and dinner. Closed Monday. Licensed. Access: one step at door, washrooms on same floor.* **$$$**

King West

Chinese

BAMBOO BUDDHA
752 King W, at Tecumseth, 416-504-9311.
A mere block away from chichi Susur, Thuet and Amuse-Bouche, this modest storefront buffet offers great value and tasty MSG-free rewards if you dig a little deeper into its lengthy (but sadly predominantly deep-fried) card. Friendly, attentive service and several blends of specially imported green tea. Bonus: delivery downtown and to the west side. Best: the dish that will put BB on the foodie map, Coca Cola Chicken — pounded, boneless thigh and leg marinated in soda pop, lightly breaded and quickly deep-fried, stir-fried with scallion, chewy Chinese 'shrooms and sculpted carrot; eat-in-only bamboo steamers reveal aromatic lotus leaf packets of sticky rice, Chinese broccoli and several meaty toppings; stir-fried asparagus or wilted watercress with chopped garlic; steamed New Zealand mussels on the shell with scallion and sweet red pepper in spicy satay-style black bean sauce. *Open for lunch and dinner. Closed holidays. Licensed. Delivery. Access: barrier-free though small room, washrooms in basement.* **$$$**

Contemporary

◆ AMUSE-BOUCHE
**96 Tecumseth, at Whitaker, 416-913-5830,
www.amusebboucherestaurant.com.**
Take two talented young chefs — Jason Inniss and Bertrand Alépée, former sous and pastry chef respectively at the Fifth under Marc Thuet — and a gorgeously overhauled space that once housed Susur Lee's legendary Lotus and watch downtown's demi-monde descend en masse. Though many of the plates overextend themselves with too many elements, when the kitchen keeps them simple, the results impress even more. Warning: reservations essential. Best: seasonal contemporary French card with Caribbean and Southeast Asian inspiration starts with oxtail consommé strewn with black trumpet mushrooms and ravioli; seared foie gras in pomegranate jus with Jerusalem artichoke rosti; follow with mains like sliced pink duck breast on a dark reduction of cardamom and coffee paired with soursop purée; Australian lamb loin stuffed with apricot 'n' pinenut sided with polenta du ratatouille; to finish, passion fruit panna cotta with pineapple sorbet; chocolate and banana bread pudding with rum raisin

ice cream. *Open for dinner. Closed Monday. Licensed. Access: one step at door, washrooms through kitchen.* **$$$$$** ⟡

LEE
603 King W, at Portland, 416-504-7867.
Gorgeous room. Shame about the food. Susur Lee attempts to pull a Jamie Kennedy by offering smaller and supposedly inexpensive tapas-like plates meant for sharing. Instead, an uneven kitchen and haphazard delivery fail to live up to the stellar chef's otherwise deserved reputation. *Open for lunch and dinner. Closed Sunday. Licensed. Access: two steps at door, washrooms on same floor.* **$$$$**

NIAGARA STREET CAFÉ
169 Niagara, at Wellington, 416-703-4222, www.niagarastreetcafe.com.
With the arrival of chef Michael Caballo, this casually cozy west-side eatery continues its evolution from funky home cooking to bistro-style basics. Bonus: all meats naturally raised or certified organic. Warning: although they're taken at dinner, reservations are only accepted at brunch for the 10:30 am first sitting. Best: to start, lemony house-made papardelle with roasted mushroom, sage and Grana Padano; terrine of duck confit and pork over lentils in vinaigrette; dinner mains such as slow-cooked veal tongue pot-au-feu with marrow ravioli; roasted duck breast in creamy mushroom pasta; at brunch, begin with irresistible potato rosti dolloped with sour cream and roasted-apple compote, and follow with Huevos à la Mancha, a pair of poached eggs coupled with pork belly, Manchego pistou and home fries. *Open for dinner. Sunday for brunch. Closed Monday, Tuesday. Licensed. Access: two short steps at door, small washrooms on same floor.* **$$$$** ⟡

● SUSUR
601 King W, at Portland, 416-603-2205, www.susur.com.
Recognized as one of the most creative chefs in the world today, Susur Lee traded the shabby chic of Lotus for this austere, all-white room that makes his fabulous food the focus. Occasionally, his gorgeous grub borders on overkill, but what a spectacular way to go! Reservations essential. Best: place yourself in

b.y.o.b.

Did you know that there are approximately 100 restaurants in and around Toronto that allow you to bring your own bottle(s) of wine? At most restaurants there's going to be a charge for this called "corkage." This is usually in-line with the restaurant's overall pricing and $20 isn't unusual, but it can still work out to be a savings. Let's do the math. You buy a wine for $30 at the LCBO, pay $20 corkage + 6% GST = $53.50. You order the same wine at the restaurant which will cost at least $60 + 10% Liquor Tax + 6% GST = $70.20. There are a few exceptions like PAESE and Mammina's which charge little or no corkage and both, incidentally, have great wine lists. At the opposite end of the spectrum you're looking at $40 plus to brown bag it into some place like Splendido or North 44. Try it at a restaurant like the Pearl Court, which has a limited wine list. Take in a nice Riesling to complement the fiery fare, pay $10 corkage and you've got a feast for the least.

the hands of a culinary wunderkind and order the $120-per-person seven-course tasting menu (the five-course vegetarian version is a steal at a mere $65): served backwards, start with mains like rack of lamb sauced with black olive and artichoke 'n' Stilton and sided with eggplant caviar and cheesy wild rice gnocchi; seared foie gras accompanied by a spicy shortbread tart filled with duck confit, roasted Ontario apple and Japanese pickled plum; increasingly smaller plates such as mahi-mahi satay paired with spinach-lemon confit and yellow Scotch bonnet tomato sauce; go à la carte with the likes of garlic-roasted lobster with pink Szechuan peppercorn lobster bisque, or caramelized black cod with carrot, ginger and dill sauces; to finish, pear brioche bread pudding with warm walnut brittle, wine-poached pear and apricot ice. *Open for dinner. Closed Sunday, holidays. Licensed. Access: one step at door, washrooms on same floor.* **$$$$$**

French

LE SELECT
432 Wellington W, at Spadina, 416-596-6405, www.leselect.ca.
After nearly three decades on Queen West, long-running French bistro re-locates to more spacious digs. Every detail from the original's art nouveau facade to the welcoming zinc bar and the posters plastered to its pale faux-nicotine-stained walls have been duplicated. New chef Jean-Paul Challet — the Fifth, Bouchon — fits the room like a glove, but where are those legendary hanging bread baskets? Best: to commence, coral-hued fish purée paired with garlic crisps spread with sweet pepper rouille; frisée salad with scalloped potato dolloped with whipped chèvre; al dente house-made ravioli stuffed with puréed pumpkin further sweetened with maple syrup; to continue, poached salmon quenelles teamed with tiger shrimp dusted with cocoa butter and sauced with cream bisque; the house bavette — aged flat-iron — topped with shallot and sided with fabulously skinny frites. *Open for breakfast, lunch and dinner. Licensed. Access: one step at door, washrooms in basement.* **$$$$** ⟡ ⏲

Indian

● DHABA
309 King W, at John, 416-740-6622, www.dhaba.ca.
Spice fiends have been dancing in the streets ever since Toronto's best Indian eatery relocated from the wilds of Etobicoke to King West's restaurant row. The decor may have gone upmarket, but the hosts are as charming and their fiery fare as breathtaking as ever. Don't wimp out — make sure to order everything the way the chef would make it for himself. Bonus: chef P.K.'s six-course $50 tasting menu and four-course $30 prix fixe. Best: French rack of lamb marinated in papaya and garlic splashed with rum and roasted in the tandoor; volcanic lamb vindaloo in coconut-scented curry; from the considerable veggie options, potatoes stuffed with raisins, pinenuts and paneer in ambrosial cream sauce; incendiary Bhurven Baingan — stuffed baby eggplants; tandoor-fired tofu; heavenly naan studded with garlic; to conclude, house-made pistachio-encrusted kulfi; unparalleled $10.95 ayce lunch buffet. *Open for lunch and dinner. Licensed. Access: 20 steps at door, washrooms on same floor.* **$$$$**

Roncesvalles
Contemporary

● SILVER SPOON
390 Roncesvalles, at Howard Pk, 416-516-8112, www.silverspoon.ca.

Reservations are a must at **Amuse-Bouche**.. Page 103.

This elegant flower-filled boîte is a calming oasis of sophistication on rough 'n' tumble Roncey. Owner/chef Rocco Agostino's – of Ferro back in the day – confident contemporary card combines with unobtrusive but informed service to deliver dazzle with detail. Reservations recommended. Bonus: linen napkins come rung Uri Geller-style with bent spoons. Best: from a seasonal card, begin with a sharable bowl of PEI mussels steamed in lemongrass and chive cream sauce; sensational soups like Jerusalem artichoke finished with truffle oil; mains like a massive rack of Dijon-glazed, pink-centred New Zealand lamb plated with butter-sautéed veggies and grilled-then-roasted red-jacketed potatoes; roasted free-range chicken in apricot jus with squash risotto and market veg; for the herbivore, daily specials like a truffle-oiled terrine of baby beets, carrots and asparagus; to finish, clichéd but delicious molten flourless chocolate gateau with crème Anglaise and warm ganache. *Open for dinner. Closed Sunday, Monday and some holidays. Licensed. Access: one step at door, washrooms in basement.* **$$$$**

Diner

FRESHWOOD GRILL

293 Roncesvalles, at Westminster, 416-537-1882, www.freshwoodgrill.com.
Fresh wood grill, more like, as this diner cooks nearly all of its comfort-food card on a Canadian-hardwood-burning stove. Sometimes it's a bit overpowering – smoky grilled salad? – but when it's under control there's no question why locals have made this retro resto a hit straight out of the box. Bonus: a large, tree-lined enclosed patio out back away from the avenue. Best: terrific Martha Stewart-style shepherd's pie with quality ground sirloin, fresh garden peas and cubed carrot layered with old-school smashed spuds; a baseball-sized burger of the same sirloin dressed with grilled yellow onion and charred tomato, sided with chunky skin-on fries dunked in roasted garlic mayo; on house-made flatbread, thin-crust pizza with designer toppings, or substantial sandwiches like pulled pork in smoky barbecue sauce; rotating daily all-day specials like grilled lamb chops paired with roasted beets and an ambrosial purée of white navy beans in Gorgonzola. *Open for breakfast, lunch and dinner. Licensed. Delivery. Access: ramp at door, washrooms in basement.* **$$$** ☼ ⊙

Mauritian

BLUE BAY CAFÉ

2243 Dundas W, at Roncesvalles, 416-533-8838.
An anonymous west-side storefront, this Mauritian restaurant serves spice-powered dishes that combine elements of Indian, Thai, French, Cajun and African cooking. Call it crossroads cuisine. Figure in a low-fat, low-carb lineup and extremely reasonable prices and it's easy to understand Blue Bay's long-running success. Warning: call ahead to make sure it's open. Best: dense pan-sautéed hake (a cod cousin) in garlicky ginger sauce; tender baby octopus tendrils in fiery curry; daube of chicken, a boozy spice-rich tomato stew thick with dark chicken meat and potato; Touffe Legume, mixed Asian veggies spiked with tiny red Thai chilies; Mine Frire, a hot and cold collision of spaghetti-like noodles and crunchy napa cabbage. *Open for dinner. Closed Monday. Licensed. Access: barrier-free.* **$$$**

restaurants

Patisserie

QUEEN OF TARTS
283 Roncesvalles, at Westminster,
416-651-3009.
After her modest start on Bathurst a few years back, Stephanie Pick's relocation of her patisserie to expanded premises on Roncesvalles has also resulted in an extended line of sensational sweet and savoury tarts. Strictly take-away, but unparalleled. Best: treats fit for royals like dark Mexican chocolate tarts kicked with chipotle chili or Calebaut chocolate tart with Chinese five-spice and candied orange zest; tart cranberry tart with baked apple and caramel-coated almonds; grandmotherly mincemeat and butter tarts; intensely flavoured family-sized quiches like ham, Gruyère and caramelized onion, or spinach with chèvre; topical gingerbread figures of George Bush, Martha Stewart in prison drag, Michael Jackson attended by Bubbles the chimp and baby Blanket, and the Trailer Park Boys. *Closed Monday, holidays. Unlicensed. Access: one step at door, no washrooms.* **$**

Polish

CAFÉ POLONEZ
195 Roncesvalles, at Fern, 416-532-8432.
Those yearning for some Old World big food won't be disappointed by this Roncesvalles gem. Impeccably clean and minimally adorned, this family-friendly spot specializes in extremely hearty Polish fare. Outgoing staff make first-timers feel like long-lost relatives, helping with translations and pronunciations, sincerely interested in customer satisfaction without being the least bit fawning. Best: sold by the dozen, perogies (meat, cheese with apple, or cabbage 'n' mushroom) come boiled and never fried, sided with sour cream, fried onion and bacon, all drizzled in oil; potato pancakes folded over stewed-pork goulash served with sour cream, delicious shredded-beet-and-horseradish salad, coleslaw and boiled carrot; bowls of thick tripe soup alongside baskets of fresh rye bread; the minimally breaded house schnitzel heaped with lightly sautéed mushrooms and pillow-like potato dumplings in rich beef and tomato gravy. *Open for breakfast, lunch and dinner. Licensed. Access: barrier-free, washrooms in basement.* **$$**

Thai

VICKY'S FISH & CHIPS/SUE'S THAI FOOD
414 Roncesvalles, at Howard Park, 416-531-8822.
At this plain-Jane Parkdale diner with a split personality, ignore Vicky (good fish, terrible chips) and concentrate on Sue. A former Salad King cook, she may not dish up the best Thai in town, but she's certainly owner of the cheapest card. Despite the low prices, shrimp dishes come with butterflied jumbo shrimp — not a lot of them but better than the tiny frozen ones offered most elsewhere. And the vegetarian versions are even more inexpensive! Bonus: everything's MSG-free. Best: better-than-most pad thai laced with coconut milk garnished with deep-fried tofu, spring onion and crushed peanuts; green curry with sweet pepper, onion and Thai basil over jasmine rice; tom yum soup — lemongrass-scented broth brimming with seeded plum tomato, button 'shrooms and coriander leaf; cashew shrimp with red peppers, tart green apple and onions; Icelandic cod with industrial coleslaw (hold the fries). *Open for lunch and dinner. Unlicensed. Cash only. Access: barrier-free, washrooms in basement.* **$$** ⋮

Bloor West Village

Contemporary

BLOOM
2315 Bloor W, at Windermere, 416-767-1315.

Now that Lemon Meringue has drifted off into the ether, here's the best resto west of Roncesvalles. Bringing a touch of downtown chic to a decidedly conservative neck of the woods, this Focaccia offshoot features chef Sam Gassira's post-post-fusion comfort food card in a cool, understated contemporary space. Best: to start, savoury chèvre tart with frisée in honeyed poppyseed dressing, or pan-seared foie gras glazed with brandy sided with apple compote and toasts; mains like wild boar strip loin wrapped in pancetta coupled with baby French beans and chipotle-lime yams, or pulled lake trout over saffron risotto and Cajun shrimp; at lunch, baby back ribs in chipotle glaze, or roasted duck leg over cassoulet, both sided with fab house frites; for dessert, avocado and white chocolate marquise with lime 'n' coriander crisps and coconut foam, or dark chocolate crème brûlée with orange blossom syrup. *Open for lunch and dinner. Closed Sunday, Monday and holidays. Licensed. Access: barrier-free.* **$$**

The Junction

Café

COOL HAND OF A GIRL
2804 Dundas West, at Keele, 647-892-0271.
An eclectic, sans-attitude, low-budget addition to the Junction that would be at home anywhere along the Queen West strip. Best: tarragon chicken sandwich (all sandwiches served on Sasha bread, most with lettuce and tomato) — juicy chicken breast in a light tarragon sauce; avocado and Parmesan 'wich topped with basil leaves and a lemon-pepper sauce that, like most of Cool Hand's sandwiches, has a vegan mayo base; meaty slabs of tofu deliciously marinated in tamari and balsamic vinegar in a stellar vegan sandwich; sharp aged cheddar and homemade chunky apple-tomato chutney 'wich; house salad with greens, abundant cucumber pieces, grape tomatoes and loads of shredded cabbage with a sweet apple-cider vinaigrette warmed by the pungent essence of toasted cumin

Playing with the **Queen Of Tarts**, where the devil comes cheap and the gingerbread men dress cheap.

seed. To finish, spelt flour chocolate chip espresso cookies or Cool Hand's own walnut-date coffee cake, moist and reminiscent of Grandma's warm hand. *Open Tuesday to Friday 8 am to 4 pm, Saturday and Sunday 9 am to 4 pm. Unlicensed. Cash only.* **$$**

Diner

PURPLE ONION
603 Keele, at St. Clair W, 416-760-8208.
Funky 40s diner complete with soda-fountain bar, wooden booths and Venetian blinds rustles up huge meat 'n' potato platters at equally retro prices. Sound like the Tulip? It should, because co-owners Steve Lai and Sunny Sun are former employees of the long-time Queen East institution. Warning: except for coleslaw, there's little here for herbivores. Best: like the Tulip, flat-griddled rather than grilled New York strip loin – 10-, 12- or 14-ouncers – served with lumpily perfect new-potato mash and minced garlic gravy; Kresge cafeteria-style tender pink-centred veal liver piled with caramelized onion and meatier-than-most bacon rashers; thickly sliced roast beef with creamy spuds and crunchy coleslaw; weekend brunch only poached Eggs Florentine over spinach and halved English muffins, with home fries and Texas toast; and unless you're trapped in the 50s, rubbery retro coconut cream pie topped with aerosol whipped cream is best left to memory. *Open for breakfast, lunch and dinner. Closed Monday. Licensed. Access: one step at door, washrooms in basement.* **$$$**

Indian

CURRY TWIST
3034 Dundas W, at High Park, 416-769-5460.
First-time restaurateurs score right out of the box with this charming Indian gem in the Junction. Soothing music, attentive service and startlingly tasty food make this the perfect dining equation. Warning: though insanely popular, Twist takes no reservations. Good luck! Best: tomato-rich butter chicken in assertive gravy; saag paneer made with puréed mustard greens and spinach; minced lamb kebabs skew-

ered with both sweet bell and fiery jalapeño peppers; bread rolls – deep-fried sandwich loaf stuffed with coriander, potatoes 'n' peas. *Open for dinner. Closed Monday, holidays. Licensed. Access: barrier-free.* **$$$**

West Queen West

Café

EASY
1645 Queen W, at Roncesvalles, 416-537-4893, www.easybreakfast.ca.
Surrounded by junk shoppes, Peter Morrison's funky luncheonette at the far end of Queen has been a hit with Parkdale artsy types since it launched. The reason: a crowded, cacophonous storefront offering a reasonably priced card of all-day brunch/breakfast alongside substantial soup 'n' sandwich combos. Warning: weekend lineups! Best: Huevos Divorciados – two eggs topped with both red and green salsas, with cool refried black beans, chunky tomato-spiked guacamole, rosemary-tossed home fries and a toasted baguette with homemade ancho chili jam; a pair of soft-boiled eggs sided with toast soldiers 'n' salad or fries; signature sandwiches like grilled chicken breast, avocado, lettuce and tomato on organic, yeast-free spelt toast spread with chipotle mayo; retro Cobb salad with smoked turkey, hard-boiled egg, avocado, bacon and tomato in blue cheese dressing; to quaff, banana latte smoothies, cheap pints, plonk by the tumbler and jumbo Bloody Caesars. *Open for breakfast and lunch. Licensed. Cash only. Access: barrier-free.* **$$**

MITZI'S
100 Sorauren, at Pearson, 416-588-1234.
So popular it's opened a sibling spot – Mitzi's Sister on west Queen West – this quirky kid-friendly storefront luncheonette on a tree-lined street in Parkdale has been serving formidable weekday lunches and weekend brunches for over a decade. Warning: lineups Saturday and Sunday. Best: at brunch, a constantly rotating card of eggy things like thick challah

French toast dolloped with ripe strawberries and whipping cream, sided with herbed home fries and brunch garnish; perfectly poached eggs over wilted spinach chiffonade; maple syruped lemon poppyseed pancakes tossed with pecans; plain scrambled eggs for the rug rats; from the lunch card, apricot, date and pork meat loaf paired with warm potato salad and mesclun; pan-fried Newfoundland cod cakes splashed with red-pepper aïoli; lemon-basil-infused tuna salad sandwich on sourdough. *Open for breakfast and lunch. Closed some holidays. Licensed. Cash only. Access: one step at door, two steps to washroom on same floor.* **$$$** ⬝⬝⬝

POOR JOHN'S CAFÉ
1610 Queen W, at Callender, 647-435-2688.
Cool and casual lunch 'n' brunch spot decked out in retro castaways – 30s velvet settees, 40s formica dinette sets and 50s Danish modern coffee tables. The lineup's limited, not more than a few sandwiches with soup and salad combos, but the flavours are big. Best: terrific sandwiches like buttery ripe avocado, smooth creamy Brie and thick slices of super-sweet mango spread with basil pesto on Micalense marbled rye, sided with mesclun tossed with toasted walnut and dried cranberry in marketable balsamic mango vinaigrette; seasonal soups like beef with barley or cream of tomato; at brunch, superbly poached eggs over toasted Sapucaia cornbread topped with sweet tomato sauce and sharp Pico cheese, a grilled rasher of spicy chorizo on the side; to finish, dense carrot cake topped with whipped cream cheese frosting or double-fudge brownies. *Open Monday to Saturday for breakfast and lunch. Sunday for breakfast. Unlicensed. Access: barrier-free, washrooms in basement.* **$** ⬝⬝⬝

⬤ VIENNA HOME BAKERY
626 Queen W, at Markham, 416-703-7278.
Though not as well known as her superstar-chef sibling Greg, Gay Couillard has an equally stellar pedigree. A consummate baker and true Queen Street original, she's been turning out posh breakfasts and super south-of-France quiche-and-salad lunch combos from this retro spot for 20 years. But it's her fruit-tastic pies and cassis-soaked cakes that cause the most fuss. Most mornings, and especially for weekend brunch, you'll find a group out front waiting for the authentic 40s luncheonette to open. Best: Liptauer cheese sandwich on house-baked whole wheat toast; seasonal egg dishes like smooth ricotta and caramelized onion quiche with beet 'n' feta salad; vegan black bean burritos; for dessert, old-fashioned sky-high apple pie, sticky date pudding and cranberry apple crumble; weekend-only poached Eggs Bombay on house toast with curried coconut-milk hollandaise and home fries. *Open for breakfast and lunch. Closed Monday and Tuesday. Unlicensed. Cash only. Access: barrier-free, but narrow room, washrooms in basement.* **$** ⬝⬝⬝

Caribbean

BACCHUS ROTI
1376 Queen W, at Brock, 416-532-8191.
In trendy California, foodies call them wraps, but here in multicultural Toronto they're better known as rotis. What makes this Parkdale institution unique is its baked-when-ordered whole-wheat shells and Guyanese-flavoured fillings, many of them vegetarian. Food court seating, friendly servers and long worth-it waits at lunch and dinner. Bonus: Bacchus's atomic hot sauce sold by the jar. Double bonus: $3.25 domestic beer. Best: trademark rotis like curried shrimp, spinach, squash and cheddar cheese; more trad curried chicken, beef or goat rotis topped with submarine-style lettuce, onion, tomato and X-rated hot sauce; vegan mix 'n' match fillings like sweet squash, green beans, cabbage, okra, chana, potato, eggplant or meat-loaf-like tofu; on the side, crisp deep-fried plantain and sweet potato fries; to snack, doubles and veggie samosas; for the sweet tooth, Key West lime pie, old-school apple pie and Caribbean-correct peanut butter cake. *Open for breakfast, lunch and dinner. Closed Sunday, Monday, holidays. Licensed. Access: barrier-free.* **$**

Contemporary

CAJÚ
922 Queen W, at Shaw, 416-532-2550. www.caju.ca.
Taking its name from the Portuguese word for "cashew," this sleek, chic spot dishes up authentic Brazilian cuisine with an upmarket bent – imagine Latin fusion where African, Caribbean and Portuguese influences meld. First-time restaurateurs Mario Cassini and Tina Giontsis succeed where many fail, creating an elegant yet casual eatery with a line-up of interesting, well-executed and reasonably priced dishes. Best: to awake the appetite, Pao de Queijo, delicate cheese popovers offered gratis; from the lineup of tapas-inspired aps, grilled sardines over lemon salsa vinaigrette; grilled polenta topped with roasted peppers, leek and melted Gorgonzola; Sopa de Feijo, subtle garlicky black bean purée garnished with leek chiffonade; Madeira-braised Lombo, seared pork tenderloin dressed with oyster mushrooms in a port reduction over garlicky puréed beans and cassava chips; every Friday and Saturday, Feijoada, the traditional Bahian stew of pork, beef and chorizo braised in black beans with rice, greens and smoky farofa. *Open for dinner. Closed Sunday, Monday. Licensed. Access: barrier-free, washrooms in basement.* **$$$$**

⬤⬤⬤ ROSEBUD
669 Queen W, at Bathurst, 416-703-8810, www.therosebud.ca.
Formerly Mr. Pong's, the home of the jumbo egg roll, this one-time greasy spoon is now a sophisticated, candlelit supper club seating 30 or so and serving upscale grub. Owner/chef Rodney Bowers's card offers slow-cooked dishes that take their cue from classical French filtered through old-school comfort-food cooking. Bonus: warm and informed service. Warning: massive portions! Best: to start, ambrosial soups like sweet pea soup dressed with lightly curried shrimp salad; grilled quail with dried cherry and sour verjus reduction; from the mains, beef short ribs braised in Shiraz with glazed shallot; Kobe flatiron steak paired with garlicky crushed potatoes; orrechiette with rapini and sweet sausage in pomodoro sauce; slow-cooked navarin of spring lamb neck with baby peas 'n' carrots, fingerlings and puff pastry puffs; à la carte sides like roasted asparagus, or snap peas in mint; for dessert, cookbook-basic crème brûlée or praline semifreddo with mocha ganache. *Open for dinner. Closed Sunday and some holidays. Licensed. Access: barrier-free, washrooms in basement.* **$$$$**

Czech

PRAGUE FINE FOOD EMPORIUM
638 Queen W, at Palmerston, 416-504-5787, www.theprague.ca.
Don't let the sophisticated new look and fancy name confuse. Other than fancy window dressing, nothing else has changed at this Old World Czech deli in nearly 40 years. Though the Kral family now serves it at trendy banquettes, the menu of rib-sticking grub stays true to its Eastern European roots. Best: slow-roasted duck freckled with caraway seeds and sided with doughy dumplings doused in gravy and sweet shredded cabbage; Hungarian Letcho, house-smoked sausage in a sauce of sweet peppers, tomato and swirled egg; chicken or veal schnitzel paired with smoky puréed spinach; tubs of frozen meaty Serbian

 This **Swan** is no dive.

goulash, beet borscht and tripe soup sided with pota-to dumplings; addictive chocolate honey cake with crushed walnuts and macerated raisins. *Open for breakfast and lunch. Closed holidays. Unlicensed. Access: one step at door, washrooms in basement.* **$$**

Diner

MIMI'S
218 Bathurst, at Queen, 416-703-6464.
For the past 20 years, vivacious owner/chef Mimi, "just a cowgirl cookin' with love," as her menu explains, has been dishing up grub for musicians, arty types and the occasional cowboy from this tiny diner located on the ground floor of the Oak Leaf Steam Baths. Warning: flexible hours – if she's open, she's open. Best: named for the Mexican Elvis imperson-ator, the El Vez omelette stuffed with Texas-style chili and maple-syrup-infused cheddar cheese, sided with herbed Yukon Gold hash browns fit for the King; the house BLT on fresh 10-grain toast layered with quality bacon, ripe tomato and designer lettuce; corned beef hash topped with two fried eggs; cheese blintzes, three light crepes stuffed with mild farmer's cheese in a pool of homemade berry compote, served with sour cream and honeydew melon; for the hung-over, fresh-ly squeezed pink grapefruit juice. *Open for brunch. Closed Monday to Wednesday. Unlicensed. Cash only. Access: one step at door, washrooms in basement.* **$**

SWAN
892 Queen W, at Crawford, 416-532-0452.
This ugly duckling luncheonette has shed its greasy-spoon past and emerged as a swanky joint du jour. Warm service and cool tunes — Louis Prima, 60s Hammond organ jazz — match the low-key restora-tion of the diner's original furnishings, right down to the period vinyl booths, mother-in-law's tongue and venetian blinds. Warning: plan on lengthy lineups unless you've got a reservation, especially for week-end brunch. Best: to commence, freshly shucked Oyster Boy's own on the half-shell with fresh grated horseradish; crisp, cold spinach salad with dried cran-berries and toasted pumpkin seeds in house vinai-grette; comfort-food-style mains like oatmeal-crust-ed free-range capon breast with vanilla bourbon peppercorn gravy over buttermilk mash; marmalade-and-beer-marinated then braised beef short ribs with more marvellous mash; seared Black Angus sir-loin with red-wine shallot reduction, roasted spuds and Yorkshire pudding; at lunch, Oyster Boy po'boys with Spanish onion and house-made mayo; at brunch, Hangtown Fry, scrambled eggs with pancetta and even more oysters (smoked this time). *Open for lunch and dinner. Weekend for brunch. Licensed. Access: barrier-free, washrooms in basement.* **$$$**

Fish & Chips

CHIPPY'S
893 Queen W, at Gore Vale, 416-866-7474, www.chippys.ca.
Former Susur general manager John Lee brings upscale fish and chips to Hogtown. Daily fresh fish delivery and hand-cut fries guaranteed this tiny take-away's instant success. After recently opening an out-post in the Annex, Lee plans to expand as far afield as Collingwood and Whistler. Best: crisply deep-fried cod, haddock, Atlantic salmon, prawns, cod cakes or scallops battered with Guinness-spiked Japanese panko breadcrumbs and sided with fabulous skin-on Yukon Gold frites double-fried in vegetable shorten-ing, sprinkled with sea salt and malt vinegar, then dipped in Brit-authentic curried gravy, mushy mar-rowfat peas or smooth garlicky mayo; sides of cor-rectly crunchy red cabbage slaw; to drink, Coke in retro glass bottles. *Open for breakfast, lunch and din-ner. Unlicensed. Cash only. Access: barrier-free, no washrooms.* **$$** ⊘

French

CLAFOUTI
915 Queen W, at Strachan, 416-603-1935, www.clafouti.ca.
Before sun-up each morning, ex-Parisian patissiers Boris Dosne and his brother Olivier Jensen-Reynaud start a fresh batch of what are arguably Toronto's best croissants. No wonder there's a lineup out front before the too-chic café has even opened. Cramped quarters and a few tiny tables guarantee a near-per-petual mob scene when there's a total of three peo-ple in the joint. Best: the now-legendary house crois-sant, oversized and warm from the oven, available plain, almond-crusted or filled with chocolate or figs as well as stuffed and baked with asparagus and Swiss cheese or mushrooms and Asiago; superb crois-sant-wiches like mango 'n' curried chicken, spectacu-lar chicken breast salad in creamy house-made mayo, or smooth duck pistachio pâté with red currant jelly;

fish & chips

Since it opened, the queue for **Chippy's** (893 Queen West, at Gore Vale, 416-866-7474) extraordinary fish 'n' chips has been deservedly long. Using fresh fish – tail-on prawns, a 4-ounce slab of salmon and Guinness-battered scallops dusted with panko bread crumbs – and deep-frying hand-cut Yukon Gold double-cooked frites in vegetable shortening, this west-side take-away raises the bar on after-the-pub grub. Across town, dreadlocked chef Marc White of the east side's **White Bros Fish Co.** (2248 Queen East, at Beech, 416-694-3474) delivers a stellar fry-up of crisply battered halibut or had-dock sided with superb house-made tartar sauce and creamy coleslaw. Wrapped in news-paper, the fish suppers at **Harbord Fish and Chips** (147 Harbord, at Borden, 416-925-2225) are as UK-trad as they come in the colonies, while 80-year-old **Reliable Fish & Chips** (954 Queen East, at Verral, 416-465-4111) has been knocking off knockout noshes since George V was on the throne.

namesake Clafouti tarts such as wild berry, lychee in caramel, or sour cherry; a rotating roster of seasonal gourmet take-away like quartered roast chicken with curried sour cream; red-jacketed potato slaw with capers and slivered celery; comfort-food-style mac 'n' cheese. *Open for breakfast and lunch. Closed Monday. Unlicensed. Cash only. Access: three steps at door, washrooms on same floor.* **$**

Italian

BAR ONE
924 Queen W, at Shaw, 416-535-1655, www.bar-one.com.
With its stylish Ralph Giannone design and a family connection to two of College Street's most fabled haunts (Bar Italia and Ellipsis), this streamlined satel-lite brings cachet to Queen West's condo frontier. Hip decor and mid-range prices make the long, narrow room dominated by a long, communal table one of the strip's most happening spot. Best: to start, bagna cauda salad, meaty porcini and cremini mushrooms coated with bread crumbs and Parmesan on spinach leaves doused with anchovy dressing; to follow, superb thin-crust pizza with potato, hot Italian sausage, sweet onion and Danish blue cheese; grilled chicken salad on arugula with toasted pinenuts, shaved Asiago and fennel julienne with lemon-rose-mary dressing; bison ravioli in brandied basil cream; at brunch, perfect Ovo Buco – baked egg in focaccia with wilted spinach and smoked salmon in chipotle hollandaise. *Open for dinner. Weekend for brunch. Closed Monday, holidays. Licensed. Access: two steps at door, washrooms in basement.* **$$$$** ⊙ ⊘

ONE OF A KIND
746 Queen W, at Niagara, 416-203-2229, www.oneofakindpasta.com.
When owner/chef Raymond To launched his northern Italian bargain-basement noodle noshery back in 2001, it was dolled up so much froufrou – doilies! chintz! – that it resembled some seaside tea room. Now it's a near-elegant space dominated by freshly cut flowers and polished mahogany tables. Only the oversized dripping candle in the front win-dow remains. And while spicing is still generally mild-mannered, portions are plentiful. Bonus: 10 per cent discount on takeout pasta. Best: squid-ink Indigo lin-guine with grilled calamari, ham, mushrooms and snow peas in white-wine cream; tricolour meat ravio-li with peppers and onions in mild curry; sautéed shrimps Newberg with buttery broccoli over basil lin-guine in a sherry-scented sauce; grilled New Zealand rack of lamb with asparagus, peppers and somewhat salty garlic mash; butterflied, then barbecued eel fil-let over mesclun; Pernod-spiked scallops over fresh spinach and grilled portobello with balsamic. *Open for breakfast, lunch and dinner. Closed holidays. Licensed. Delivery. Access: one step at door, washrooms in basement.* **$$$** ⊘

Korean

SAN
676 Queen W, at Euclid, 416-214-9429.
Despite its retro 90s Wallpaper look, Monica Chang's San offers a serene setting for an introduc-tion to Korean cuisine. Couple that with approach-able and welcoming service and get something you won't find on Bloor – a friendly and inexpensive Korean restaurant. Bonus: most mains come with mushroom-garnished miso soup, sticky rice, smoky sweet potato Chap Chae salad and mandu dumplings. Best: Dolsut Bi Bim Bap, a meal-in-one hot pot of rice, veggies, steak and eggs sided with homemade kimchee; marinated and barbecued Kalbi beef short ribs; good-as-most Japorean-style sushi and shrimp or vegetarian tempura; to sip, sinus-clearing hot ginger tea; to finish, wasabi ice

Sometimes you crave the simpler things. **Chippy's.**

Chippy's
FISH & CHIPS
893 Queen Street West

cream and a palate-cleansing shot of ginger-and-cinnamon-infused tea sprinkled with toasted pine nuts. *Open for dinner. Tuesday to Saturday for lunch. Closed Monday. Licensed. Access: one step at door, washrooms in basement.* **$$$**

Mexican
JOHNY BANANA
181 Bathurst, at Queen W, 416-304-0101.
This cute west-side cantina combines vivid graphics and a creative card that make it much more than just another beanery dishing up trendy burritos. Bonus: an extensive lineup of licuados, the Mexican milkshake/smoothie hybrid. Best: to start, cream of cilantro soup garnished with coriander leaf, slivered almonds, sour cream and a depth charge of grapes, paired with crusty sourdough spread with chili-spiked pesto; chunky Sopa de Hongas thick with button mushrooms, delivered in three levels of heat; no-fault mains like Lasagna Maya made with shredded tortillas, nippy tomatillo sauce, grilled chicken 'n' cheese; Chillanga burger, a medium-rare beef patty on a sesame-seed bun, topped with grilled pineapple, mozzarella, red onion, lettuce, tomato and jalapeño-avocado salsa; whole-wheat burritos stuffed with chunk chicken, cheddar, salad, sour cream, rice and refried beans, coupled with mesclun in a tart hibiscus vinaigrette; to finish, house-made flourless corn cake; to drink, spicy hot Chocolate Azteca. *Open for breakfast, lunch and dinner. Closed Monday. Unlicensed. Access: one step at door, washrooms on same floor.* **$$$** ☼

Pan-Asian
🔴 RED TEA BOX
696 Queen W, at Euclid, 416-203-8882.
Featured in French fashion magazines before it had even opened, this chic bakeshop's tiny rear terrace and coach house are quite possibly Toronto's ultimate al fresco dining experience. Luxuriate under a picture-perfect pear tree while supping sensational pan-Asian bento boxes and spectacular Pacific Rim sandwich 'n' salad combos. Breathtaking desserts as well as pricey cups of estate teas help make this downtown's most romantic rendezvous. Warning: reservations are not taken, so if you manage to snag one of the three or so mismatched French-country tables in the coach house, consider yourselves very lucky indeed. Best: lacquered bento boxes laden with exotica like honey-roasted chicken with rhubarb and spinach, or seared Swiss chard with pumpkin and red lentil stew, sided with citrusy shrimp on soba noodles, enoki salad dressed with yuzu and kumquat, and roasted baby Yukon, fingerling and Peruvian blue potatoes tossed with lavender, rosemary and thyme; superb sandwiches such as Indo-spiced grilled chicken breast with onion marmalade on raisin-studded sourdough, or gingery Asian pulled pork on ciabatta, paired with lime-laced green papaya-carrot slaw; seasonable soups like white bean with olive pistou; for the sweet tooth, awesome house-baked organic sour cherry chocolate brownies or orange maple pumpkin tarts tossed with pepito brittle; to drink, 30 biodynamic and organic teas. *Open for lunch. Closed Tuesday. Access: small step at door, washrooms on same floor. Unlicensed.* **$$** ☺

Top five late night nosheries

7 WEST
Spread over three floors (and a rooftop patio) in a midtown Victorian and serving the basics(tuna melts, pita pizzas). Open 24/7. *See page 77.*

ALBERT'S REAL JAMAICAN
Popular with club kids, this irie-inspired spot is famous for its jerk chicken dinners. Open till 1 am Sun-Wed, till 2 am Thu, till 4 am Fri-Sat. *See page 63.*

MEL'S
An authentic Montreal delicatessen known for great omelets, matza ball soup, smoked meats and all-day breakfasts. Open 24/7. *See page 68.*

SWATOW
A Chinatown standard at any time of the day or night. *See page 51.*

ZORBA'S
An Old-school taverna with home-style Greek grub on the Danforth. Open till 4 am Tue-Sun, till midnight Mon. *See page 88.*

SWEET LULU
859 Queen W, at Niagara, 416-203-2228, www.sweetlulu.com.
Launched by a former flight attendant inspired by his travels to Asia, Lulu offers a unique menu that allows diners to create their own dishes. Though similar in quality to other pan-Asian eateries, the ingredients here are fresh, the service attentive, and the room's sleek, minimalist decor references Hello Kitty. Bonus: sexy bathrooms! Best: fragrant jasmine rice with crisp fresh veggies stir-fried in oyster sauce, served on a square white plate; hot 'n' sour Tom Yum Soup, a bowl of thermal-powered goodness; rice stick noodles with tender shrimp and bright veggies in Malaysian peanut sauce, presented on an elegant wooden tray complete with a side dish for discarded tails. *Open for breakfast, lunch and dinner. Licensed. Access: tiny step at the door, washrooms in basement.* **$$**

Persian
BANU
777 Queen W, at Euclid, 416-777-2268. www.banu.ca.
Subtitled Iranian Kabob Vodka Bar, this chic, modish lounge offers upscale takes on Persian classics in a room decked out with low, boxy banquettes and turquoise-tiled tables. Bonus: all certified organic meat from pricey Healthy Butcher. Warning: "alno" means an awful lot of offal. Best: mains like grilled vodka-marinated lamb's testicles, literally mildly flavoured meatballs; a meaty quartet of shish lik lamb chops; juicy cut-against-the grain beef tenderloin; chewy chunks of heart, all served swathed in sheets of soft lavash flatbread that also includes fresh mint, tarragon and basil as well as scallion and red radish; to start, braised cow's tongue in meek curried cream; on the side, yogurt thickened with shallot; to drink, sour cherry or pomegranate juice; perfunctory pastries for dessert. *Open for lunch and dinner. Closed Monday. Licensed. Access: barrier-free, washrooms in basement.* **$$$** ⓟ

Pizza
TERRONI
720 Queen W, at Claremont, 416-504-0320, www.terroni.ca.
Although Toronto's favourite nu-skool pizzeria slash Italian grocery store has recently doubled in size since it annexed the storefront next door, this upscale 'za 'n' panini joint still dishes out what might be Toronto's best pizza. The famed Queen West pies are also available at two additional outlets – one deep downtown, the other way uptown. Warning: Terroni doesn't do slices. Best: ultra-thin-crust pizzas artfully decorated with minimal yet full-strength sauce and cheese and maximum flavour from quality toppings like fresh basil, spicy Calabrese sausage, grilled peppers and arugula; the Ciccio, a summery folded pizza stuffed with both sun-dried and fresh tomato, bocconcini and arugula; old-school pastas like orecchiette with anchovy and extra-virgin olive oil or housemade potato gnocchi in tomato sauce and fresh ricotta. Other locations: 106 Victoria, at Queen East, 416-955-0258; 1 Balmoral, at Yonge, 416-925-4020. *Open for breakfast, lunch and dinner. Closed Sunday. Licensed. Access: barrier-free.* **$$** ⁛

Seafood
OYSTER BOY
872 Queen W, at Massey, 416-534-3432.
Casually chic shellfish shack from the folks responsible for nearby Swan. Warning: gets crowded early and reservations are not accepted. Best: raw on-the-shell oysters – Malpeque, Belon, Wallace Bay, Bras d'Or Lake – served with myriad condiments but best simply drizzled with lemon; milky butter-rich Boston-style chowder; crisp apple, daikon and cabbage slaw in tart citrus vinaigrette; fresh berries with whipped cream. *Open for dinner. Closed holidays. Licensed. Access: one step at door, washrooms on same floor.* **$$$**

Tex Mex
LA HACIENDA
640 Queen W, at Palmerston, 416-703-3377, www.lahacienda.ca.
The hardcore crowd may be gone, but little else has changed since this Tex-Mex hole in the wall opened two decades ago. Against a backdrop of mosaic tiles, vintage melamine kitchen tables and discarded vinyl chairs, wait staff move to their own special beat – so what's it to ya? Bonus: house-baked cornbread. Best: chorizo burrito, a 10-inch flour tortilla crammed with loose chili-flecked sausage, sautéed onions, lettuce and melted Jack, plated with with corn chips, house jalapeño salsa and mucho cilantro; arteries be damned: Hacienda shrimp, eight plump shrimp sautéed with mango and lime, then flambéed in tequila and submerged in cheddar over rice; open-faced quesadilla with goat cheese, zucchini, peppers and onion coupled with rice 'n' beans; at brunch, chorizo hash with baked eggs, salsa and whole-wheat toast; to drink, margaritas by the litre! *Open for breakfast, lunch and dinner. Licensed. Access: one step at door, washrooms in basement.* **$$$** ⁛ ⓣ

Red Tea Box is a magazine spread from every angle. Page 111.

Tibetan

LITTLE TIBET
712 Queen W, at Manning, 416-306-1896.
This former Yorkville favourite is now a calm oasis amidst the crowds of local hipsters. The decor, inspired by the Tibetan flag, employs a palette of yellows, blues and reds. Soft, meditative chants complete the soothing ambience. Warning: Tibetan food isn't spicy as a rule, so add your own chili paste or fresh tomato salsa for extra heat. Best: Shogo Khatsa – Lhasa-style spicy potato salad with fresh coriander and onion; Tse-Momo Takpa – six hearty pan-fried dumplings stuffed with finely shredded cabbage, carrots, dried mushrooms and ginger, served with seasonal salad greens; Potse – gently sautéed fresh spinach and tofu loaded with minced ginger. *Open for dinner. Tuesday to Saturday for lunch. Closed Monday. Licensed. Access: barrier-free, washrooms upstairs.* **$$**

Vegetarian

FRESH BY JUICE FOR LIFE
894 Queen W, at Crawford, 416-913-2720, www.juiceforlife.com.
Ruth Tal Brown's string of health-conscious cafes are an undisputed favourite amongst the recently pierced set. However, ineptly prepared hippie casseroles, though no doubt karmic, do little for discerning tastebuds. Lovely rooms, shame about the rest, dude. Peace! *Open for breakfast, lunch and dinner. Licensed. Access: barrier-free.* **$$** ⬡

let's do brunch

BELLA'S BISTRO AT FREE TIMES CAFE
320 College, at Major, 416-967-1078,
www.freetimescafe.com
Despite its hippie digs, this cozy, casual eatery offers
a first-rate Jewish-grandmother-style
all-you-can-eat Sunday brunch that will make
you feel like a mensch no matter what your
ethnic identity.

BONJOUR BRIOCHE
812 Queen East, 416-406-1250.
This long-running nabe café is famous for its
all-day continental breakfasts and definitive Gallic
charm.

CLAFOUTI
915 Queen West, 416-603-1935.
Before sun-up each morning, ex-Parisian patissier
Olivier Jensen-Reynaud starts a fresh batch of what
are arguably Toronto's best croissants. No wonder
there's a lineup out front before the too-chic café
has even opened.

COFFEE SHOP @ IF LOUNGE
1212 Dundas West, 416-588-4900.
All shiny chrome, exposed brick and curvy banquettes, this remarkably welcoming boîte delivers a
considerably skilled early-morning menu – think
pecan-tossed French toast or vanilla-bean waffles –
to a neighbourhood where the primary dining destination up till now has been the local KFC.

CZEHOSKI
678 Queen W, at Tecumseth, 416-366-6787,
www.czehoski.com.
This swellegant hipster haunt offers assured if
pricey takes on contemporary classics with an
accessible weekend brunch.

EDWARD LEVESQUE'S KITCHEN
1290 Queen East, 416-465-3600.
Leslieville's best-kept secret ain't so secret now that
it's been discovered by the mainstream. This converted greasy spoon opens to a large but equally
low-key space that recalls a Sudbury church basement circa 1956.

GALLERY GRILL
Hart House, 7 Hart House Circle, 416-978-2445.
This former old boys' club for U of T staff and faculty
still feels exclusive (and Gothic), but the grub and
welcoming professional service bring it into the
21st century.

L'ESPRESSO BAR MERCURIO
321 Bloor West, 416-596-2233.
The streamlined sibling of Bar Mercurio kitty-corner
across the street, this budget-minded bistro on the
ground floor of U of T's Woodsworth College specializes in a short all-day card of panini, salads and traditional egg breakfasts.

MILDRED PIERCE
99 Sudbury, at Dovercourt, 416-588-5695,
www.mildredpierce.com.
In the heart of hipster condo land and consequently a
zoo on Sundays, Mildred offers a theatrical setting –
think Medieval Times minus the horses – and a
brunch card of retro comfort food make this the
perfect joint to take your mom.

PLANET KENSINGTON
197 1/2 Baldwin, at Augusta, 416-341-0310.
First you have to get past the gang of 20 or so
punks in studded, ripped leather and DIY hairdos who
crowd the front patio. And unless you consider
Florida death metal ideal dinner music, ear plugs
might be a good idea. The Black Metal Brunch is still
one of the best around.

POP BISTRO
686 Queen East, 416-461-9663.
An intimate 24-seat Riverside resto complete with a
card that combines French bistro fare with comfort
food favourites.

PULP KITCHEN
898 Queen East, 416-461-4612.
This loungy, diner-style stop with organic fair-trade
goods and a rack of browsable books is further proof
Queen East is the new Queen West, and healthy the
new hip.

SAVING GRACE
907 Dundas West, 416-703-7368.
A charming café for straightforward brekkies priced to
go easy on the pocketbook. Warning: from the menu,
"There are no substitutions, be pleasant to your server,
Saving Grace girls are always right; and you may be
asked to change seats."

SWAN
892 Queen West, 416-532-0452.
Warm service and cool tunes – Louis Prima, 60s
Hammond organ jazz – match the low-key restoration of the diner's original furnishings, right down
to the period vinyl booths.

THUET
609 King W, at Portland, 416-603-2777,
www.thuet.ca.
This upscale brasserie moves slightly down-market
with an accessible card of classic comfort food that
often dazzles. Warning: since this is one of the
hottest brunches around and they don't take
reservations, show up early or stand in line. For what
seems like days.

VIENNA HOME BAKERY
626 Queen West, 416-703-7278.
A consummate baker and true Queen West original,
chef Gay Couillard has been turning out posh breakfasts from this authentic 40s luncheonette for more
than 20 years. Most weekends, you'll find a group
out front waiting for him to open.

Cameron House, an 1880s watering hole where art and music collide. Page 118.

bars

Admittedly, we're a beer-loving people. But there's more to Toronto's bar scene than suds and stale pretzels. Whatever your taste, from biker bars to Ol' English taverns to swanky cocktail lounges, you're sure to find a hip watering hole to wet your whistle.

For the latest bar reviews, pick up NOW Magazine every week or visit www.nowtoronto.com.

Downtown

Clubland

CHARLOTTE ROOM
19 Charlotte, at Adelaide W, 416-598-2882.
Named one of the top 10 pool rooms in North America by Billiards Digest, the Room resembles an olde English gentleman's club. With nine tournament-quality tables and an upscale pub-grub menu, this inviting, carpeted space is a favourite with the media gang.

FOOTWORK
425 Adelaide W, 416-913-3488.
The last two attempts at running a bar in this space floundered after short runs, but the third time seems to be the charm for this boutique club, which has helped fill a void of decent small clubs. It feels like a scaled-down version of a large underground dance club and generally focuses on variations of house and techno.

MONSOON
100 Simcoe, at King, 416-979-7172,
www.monsoonrestaurant.ca.
Winner of the prestigious James Beard Award for best bar/restaurant design in North America, this Yabu Pushelberg creation evokes gasps. The tiki shtick's so thick, you almost expect Dorothy Lamour to jump into an erupting volcano. Even if you don't have to go, the washrooms alone make a visit to Monsoon worthwhile. They're bigger than most condos! *Closed Sunday.*

SMOKELESS JOE'S
125 John, at Richmond W, 416-591-2221.
This cozy subterranean rock-lined room has a constantly changing roster of more than 275 beers from around the world.

WAYNE GRETZKY'S
99 Blue Jays Way, at Mercer, 416-348-0099,
www.gretzkys.com.
Despite its fancy Broadway decor, this shrine to hockey's Great One is as Canadian as a Tim Hortons donut. Plasma TVs above an underlit stand-up bar play Wayne's greatest moments on the ice while the loyal check out the souvenir shop selling Gretzky gear.

WIDE OPEN
139 Spadina, at Richmond W, 416-727-5411.
Vaguely reminiscent of the old Spadina Hotel's Cabana Room, this low-key lounge features cool alterna-tunes on the CD player, the game on the tiny TV over the bar and a couple of pleather Brick couches at the back.

Central

BEERBISTRO
18 King E, at Yonge, 416-861-9872,
www.beerbistro.com.
Upscale resto bar celebrates everything beer.

BETTY'S
240 King E, at Princess, 416-368-1300.
When this east-side watering hole opened several years ago, it was amusingly called the Betty Ford Clinic, after the famous celebrity rehab facility. Betty Ford's lawyers failed to see the humour and slapped a cease-and-desist order on the bar. You can see an enlargement of the paperwork hanging in the stairwell that leads to the second floor, where the pool tables and foosball are located.

BYMARK
66 Wellington W, at York, 416-777-1144,
www.bymark.ca.
Enter this power-broker hot spot from the Wellington side of the TD Centre and find a gorgeous modern lounge separate from the restaurant below: warm slatted wood on the walls, slate on the floor, chunks of hewn logs as sculpture, with the towers rocketing high all around through floor-to-floor tinted glass. TD architect Mies van der Rohe would approve of the sympathetic Yabu Pushelberg design.

C'EST WHAT
67 Front E, at Church, 416-867-9499,
www.cestwhat.com.
Home of hemp beer and coffee porter, this cozy Old York basement with walls of exposed foundation stone houses a friendly neighbourhood pub in the heart of the downtown core. Under a very low ceiling, the bar side serves better than average pub grub alongside microbrews, single malts and Irish whiskeys.

CANOE
66 Wellington W, at Bay, 416-364-0054,
www.oliverbonacini.com.
On the 54th floor of the TD Tower, Canoe looks south over the islands and the lake during the day. After dark, the view stretches west toward glittering Etobicoke and beyond, all for the price of a sidecar or a measure of single malt.

COURTHOUSE
57 Adelaide E, at Church, 416-214-9379,
www.libertygroup.com.
Located in Toronto's first judicial building circa 1850, this multilevel space features several working fireplaces and a spectacular two-storey ballroom. Make sure you visit the washrooms in the basement in the original courthouse's jail cells. *Closed Sunday.*

FOUNDATION ROOM
19 Church, at Front E, 416-364-8368.
Downtown's latest hot haute spot, the former base-

ment room that once housed the performance space of next door's C'est What has been transformed into a luxurious lounge that recalls the Moroccan casbah, thankfully minus the touristy belly dancer shtick of nearby Sultan's Tent. Buddha Bar muzak, a short North African-influenced tapas card and industry night with drink deals Sundays.

HARD ROCK CAFE
279 Yonge, at Dundas Sq, 416-362-3636, www.hardrock.com/toronto.
The first Hard Rock anywhere, this rock 'n' roll landmark comes plastered with plasma TVs and crammed with music memorabilia like Jim Morrison's boots, Tina Turner's purple sequined outfit worn at the Apollo, and one of Prince's fun-fur numbers. ☼ ⓘ

IMPERIAL PUBLIC LIBRARY
58 Dundas E, at Victoria, 416-977-4667.
A popular after-class hangout for students of the nearby Ryerson University and construction workers, the Library features one of Toronto's best jukeboxes and a number of tropical fish tanks. Pool tables and foosball, too. ☼

LAIDE
138 Adelaide E, at Jarvis, 416-850-2726, www.laide.ca.
This touchy-feely sex-themed lounge provides a space where clandestine lovers can canoodle on low-slung sofas while sipping a Deep Throat (Frangelico, vanilla vodka and cream). The after-work crowd bangs back a pint of Stella at the horseshoe-shaped bar while grainy girl-on-girl porn gets projected on a wall overhead. Sexy tapas from chef Sam Gassira. *Closed Sunday and Monday.*

LIBRARY BAR @ ROYAL YORK HOTEL
100 Front W, at Bay, 416-368-2511.
Wingback chairs to sink into and plush carpeting underfoot give the bar the feel of a private club. Bonus: $45 sidecars.

MCVEIGH'S NEW WINDSOR TAVERN
124 Church, at Richmond E, 416-364-9698.
A popular spot with downtown office drudges, McVeigh's is a working-class pub proud of its Irish heritage. It's a small carpeted room with a stage where Celtic combos play most nights in one corner and dart boards in the opposite corner.

NOW LOUNGE
189 Church, at Shuter, 416-364-1301, www.nowtoronto.com/lounge.
Knock back boilermakers with grizzled socialist journos in this spare but stylish space hung with rotating photography shows. A cool spot for private parties.

P.J. O'BRIEN'S
39 Colbourne, at Church, 416-815-7562, pjobrien.com.
Hidden behind the King Eddie, this upscale Irish pub comes equipped with Windsor chairs, a snug and a bar loaded with more than a dozen whiskeys.

PRAVDA VODKA BAR
36 Wellington E, at Church, 416-306-2433, www.pravdavodkabar.ca.
This downtown lounge not only appropriates the name of the old Soviet newspaper, it lifts its name and concept from über-restaurateur Keith McNally's similarly named bar on New York City's Lafayette Street. Like the Big Apple saloon, it's painted winter white-out white and decked out with revolutionary-chic tchotchkes: portraits of Lenin, Gorbachev and Chairman Mao over the marble-topped bar and enough Soviet-era flags to sink

a decommissioned Cold War battleship. Bonus: 36 different vodkas, and caviar sold by weight. *Closed Sunday.* ⓘ

REMINGTON'S
379 Yonge, at Gerrard, 416-977-2160.
Remington's is a seven-days-a-week male strip club in the middle of Yonge Street's decidedly hetero sleaze zone. No cover Mondays, ladies' night Sunday.

RESERVOIR LOUNGE
52 Wellington E, at Church, 416-955-0887, www.reservoirlounge.com.
Below street level and reminiscent of a New York City 50s-era jazz joint, the Reservoir presents a rotating roster of live jazz performers six nights a week. Reservations for this small 100-seat venue are mandatory on weekends. *Closed Sunday.* ⓘ

TURF LOUNGE
330 Bay, at Adelaide, 416-367-2111, turflounge.com.
Other than the track, where else can you bet on the ponies while belting back a Cosmojito? One of downtown's most dramatic spaces, this swanky Bay Street off-track betting boite has some of the best visuals in town: vaulted ceilings hung with ornate chandeliers and walls plastered with plasma TVs turned to the 3:30 out of Santa Anita. Bonus: separately ventilated cigar lounge.

Queen West

BLACK BULL
298 Queen W, at Soho, 416-593-2766.
Despite its reputation as a weekend-biker spot – and padded vinyl booths that wouldn't look out of place at some family-style Ponderosa – this ever-popular spot has large windows that look out to one of Toronto's trendiest streetscapes. Pool tables and decent pub grub, too. ☼

BOVINE SEX CLUB
542 Queen W, at Bathurst, 416-504-4239.
From the outside, the Bovine looks like the aftermath of an accident in an ironworks. Bits of scrap steel, bicycle wheels and wrought iron railings have been welded to form a heavy metal facade that protects the equally heavy-drinking clientele from the real world outside. Inside, where it's dark, dank and down-and-dirty, DJs spin vintage AC/DC, glam or whatever's loud and happening. And if you're buying, its a Jägermeister.

CAMERON HOUSE
408 Queen W, at Cameron, 416-703-0811.
The sign on the bar sums up the Grand Ol' Cameron perfectly: this is paradise. Once a no-go tavern, the Cameron has been the epicenter of Queen West's most creative music-and-art collision. In fact, this 1880s watering hole is a work of art in itself, a constantly evolving mix of installation art and Salvation Army sofas. The small back room hosts music and theatre events, while tasteful tunes act as backdrop to intellectual repartee in the bordello-like living room up front. Bonus: day prices till 8:30 pm. ☼

CHICAGO'S
335 Queen W, at Beverley, 416-977-2904.
A sports bar slash pub with raucous blues and R&B acts upstairs nightly and a split-level first-floor bar that boogies over all-day breakfasts to Melissa Etheridge and Van Morrison on CD. ☼

HORSESHOE
368 Queen W, at Spadina, 416-598-4753.
Once Stompin' Tom's stompin' grounds, the 'Shoe has undergone several overhauls, but its upfront cocktail bar remains minimally changed since the 50s. Except

for the Triumph over the pool table, of course. During the day, it's quiet enough for afternoon boozers to overhear sound-checking headliners like Neko Case, the Tragically Hip, El Vez and those damned Rolling Stones doing yet another of their secret gigs. Celebrity bartender: rockin' Teddy Fury. ☼

REX
194 Queen W, at St. Patrick, 416-598-2475.
Known for its all-day jazz sessions, when the music's off – early afternoons – the Rex makes a great spot for a quiet drink. Although the old hotel tavern has been gussied up over the years, it still retains elements of its original style: terracotta floors, draught by the glass and Victorian men's room urinals.

RIVOLI
332 Queen W, at Spadina, 416-597-1908, www.rivoli.ca.
The home of the Tidy Bowl – Blue Curaçao and Alka Seltzer. ☼ Ⓨ

 ### ULTRA
314 Queen W, at Peter, 416-263-0330, www.ultrasupperclub.com.
When this swanky South Beach-style lounge turns into a disco later in the evening, those who show up for an after-work drink run for the exits. But early tipplers get the best of both sides of Toronto's coolest supper club. Through the gauzy floor-to-ceiling curtain that divides the former Bamboo in two, they watch celebrities swoon in the club's highly rated resto. Don't miss the luxe lounge's glowing-pink backroom bar and over-the-top chandelier-hung washrooms. Bottle service, too. *Closed Sunday.* ☼ Ⓨ

VELVET UNDERGROUND
510 Queen W, at Ryerson, 416-504-6688.
Behind its rusted steel facade, VU is decorated with spiky angel statuary by Antonella Sigismondi, the sister of Floria Sigismondi, the multidisciplinary Toronto artist famous for the gothic-inspired videos she directed for David Bowie and Marilyn Manson. Dance on the bar to loud top-40 alterna-rock.

Midtown

Annex

DANCE CAVE
529 Bloor W (2nd floor), at Albany, 416-532-1598.
Long-time student alternative rock hangout features dancing to DJs four nights a week.

GREEN ROOM
296 Brunswick, at Bloor, 416-929-3253.
First-timers have a hard time finding this obscure boozer hidden down the alleyway behind the Poor Alex Theatre. Eventually, they discover a two-storey warehouse full of Goodwill furniture and shelves of books that provide distraction when conversation dies amongst the literary set. Cheap all-day breakfasts, too. ☼ Ⓨ

LABYRINTH LOUNGE
298 Brunswick, at Bloor W, 416-925-7775.
This cozy, quiet, out-of-the-way spot tucked behind Future Bakery makes a great stage to while away the afternoon over a book or secretly meet an art student for a late-night snog. Cheap drink specials. ☼

LEE'S PALACE
529 Bloor West, at Croft, 416-532-1598, www.leespalace.com.
Famed for its appearance as the archetypal rawk 'n' roll club in countless shot-in-Toronto movies, Lee's is one of the city's best venues for catching a live show, especially after 2005's series of renovations that resulted in a raised stage, cleaned-up floors and walls, and – most importantly – moving the bar from its original sightline-compromising location to a spot hugging the back walls of the club. The overall vibe is totally rock 'n' roll, but not in the way that makes you try to avoid touching anything for fear of contracting a disease.

MADISON
14 Madison, at Bloor, 416-927-1722, www.madisonavenuepub.com.
A maze of interconnected rooms spread over three Victorian row houses, this popular boozer has a Brit pub look, all red-velvet banquettes and some 150 brass draft pumps with 20 beers on tap. Pool tables, gas fireplaces and four heated winter patios. ☼ Ⓨ

PAUPERS
539 Bloor W, at Albany, 416-530-1331, www.pauperspub.com.
Once the local branch of the CIBC, this converted three-storey bank is now one of the most popular pubs on the strip. Great rooftop patio with a skyline view, too. ☼

RED GUITAR
603 Markham, at Bloor W, 416-913-4586, www.theredguitar.com.
Run by Toronto jazz singer Corry Sobol, the cozy Red Guitar Art House Café has quickly become one of T.O.'s top nightspots for exciting jazz and improvised music. A warm, homey atmosphere, partly due to the living-room size of the dining venue, makes for an intimate night out. ☼

Laide has a sex theme? How can you tell?

ROXTON
379 Harbord, at Roxton, 416-535-8181.
Looking like it's been here forever instead of less than two years, the intimate space recalls a 40s saloon, complete with a painting of a reclining female nude over the bar. Open kitchen, venetian blinds and intimate naugahyde booths, too. ☼

VICTORY CAFÉ
581 Markham, at Lennox, 416-516-5787,
www.victorycafe.ca.
This rambling student-friendly Victorian attracts the literary crowd for Tuesday's poetry slams and those with a more boho bent Wednesdays for the Hot Jazz String Quartet. ☼

YE OLDE BRUNSWICK HOUSE
481 Bloor W, at Brunswick, 416-964-2242.
Long an Animal House of collegiate hijinks, the new Brunswick has been restored to its former Victorian splendour. On the weekends, the rear party space where Rockin' Irene once rocked on is now a dance space spinning top 40 hits.

Chinatown/ Kensington Market

BOAT
158 Augusta, at Dundas W, 416-593-9218.
The latest oddball venue to be appropriated by the indie kids, this restaurant and karaoke bar has been made to look like the inside of a ship's hull, with curved wooden walls and fake windows. It's cheap and a bit grimy, but the eclectic programming has been drawing capacity crowds surprisingly often for 50s rock 'n' roll parties, electro nights, grime showcases and many an indie rock night.

EL MOCAMBO
464 Spadina, at College, 416-777-1777,
www.elmocambo.ca.
The infamous El Mo has undergone tons of transformations since its legendary days when rock icons like the Rolling Stones shook the walls of the then crusty, sticky-floored dive. The cleaned-up club occupies two floors where on any given night you can catch live acts ranging from gentle indie pop to reggae to underground hiphop to metal. On ground level you'll find a nicely laid out space with exposed brick, tasteful Moroccan-inspired decor, a decent-sized stage at the front and a long bar that can be accessed from both the entranceway and the general show-watching area. Head up a twisty flight of stairs and there's a slightly less polished room with a stage at the front and a small bar at the back.

GRAFFITI'S
170 Baldwin, at Kensington, 416-506-6699,
www.graffitisbarandgrill.co.
Chock full of Elvis Presley memorabilia, this cozy room offers live music, mainly roots rock-slash-acoustic, seven nights a week. When weather permits, the front garage door is opened to the street and the band and fans spill outside. ☼

GROSSMAN'S TAVERN
379 Spadina, at Cecil, 416-977-7000.
Since the 60s, when it was draft dodger central, this extremely low-rent watering hole has appealed to both musicians and artists alike. The old girl's had something of a makeover – her infamous basement washrooms are now panelled in galvanized sheet metal. So much easier to hose down. ☼

LAST TEMPTATION
12 Kensington, at Dundas W, 416-599-2551.
One of Toronto's first island-style getaways, this relaxed JA joint hasn't changed since it opened 20 years ago as the legendary Spider's: cheap Asian Caribbean bar food and imported beer quaffed to alterna reggae rhythms. ☼

PLANET KENSINGTON
197-1/2 Baldwin, at Augusta, 416-341-0310.
Once the Market's raunchiest dive, a lovable drunk tank known by all as the Greek's, this tiny diner now sports a coat of black paint and fancy new faux leopard barstools. The menu offers the expected burgers and all-day breakfasts but improves greatly with surprisingly tasty Black Metal Brunch on Sunday. Monday is $3 pasta and movie night, Tuesday $2.50 taco 'n' tequila night, and Friday from 6 to 9 pm all domestic beer goes for $2.50. Bonus: dog- and vegetarian-friendly. ☼

SILVER DOLLAR ROOM
486 Spadina, at College, 416-975-0909.
Now that T.O.'s premier blues club has widened its musical palate – thanks to promoter Dan Burke – and refurbished its menu, it's increased its appeal as an entertainment hot spot.

SUPERMARKET
268 Augusta, at College, 416-840-0501,
www.supermarkettoronto.com.
Part restaurant, part club, Supermarket has become one of the more consistently busy nightspots in the area. The front half is dominated by booths and a long bar but opens up into a dance floor and stage in the back, where you can hear underground hiphop, funk, soul, house and broken beat as well as live bands, depending on the night. *Closed Sunday.* ☼

THYMELESS
355 College, at Augusta, 416-928-0556.
A place that could only make sense in Kensington Market, it's a rough-around-the-edges Greek/Jamaican bar and grill that functions primarily as a roots reggae spot but also hosts queer-friendly punk funk nights, 60s soul parties and even a few electro- and techno-themed events. The main attractions are the massive stack of speakers flooding the bar with bass and the passionate foosball games on the back patio. Licensed. ☼

Church Street

BABYLON
553 Church, at Gloucester, 416-923-2626.
A three-storey Victorian with a casual room on the first floor, a martini lounge where bartenders mix up over 200 different cocktail concoctions on the second, and weekend DJs on the third.

BAR 501
501 Church, at Wellesley, 416-944-3272.
The 501's long-running Sunday-evening drag shows literally stop traffic – tour buses from out of town have been known to make a detour and park out front. The action attracts crowds that spill off the sidewalk while inside regulars play pool and pinball.

BLACK EAGLE
457 Church, at Maitland, 416-413-1219.
Even in the middle of the day, this leather bar is dark as fuck. As tough guys gaze blankly at the hard-core porn videos broadcast on several TVs on the first floor, muscle-bound daddies stand and pose upstairs under camouflage netting. Don't miss the dungeon fixtures and cages installed by Master R. Free pool Mondays 6 to 11 pm. Bonus: year-round barbecues on the rooftop every Sunday. Double bonus: Sunday is also Underwear Night. ☼

BYZANTIUM
499 Church, at Wellesley, 416-922-3859.
The upscale lounge and dining room has been brought into the 21st century complete with sleek

Enjoy the view from **Paupers'** fab rooftop deck. Page 119.

beige banquettes, bare blond tables and mirrored accents everywhere that allow for cultured cruising. Big glass doors that open to the street mean you can just grab someone you fancy as they're strolling past. Still known for serving some of the best food in the nabe (faint praise), and the lengthy martini lineup remains timeless. ☼ ⏱

CREWS/TANGO
508 Church, at Maitland, 416-972-1662, www.crews-tango.com.
Drag shows happen nightly at Crews on the first floor, while upstairs at Tango dykes get down to DJs. ☼

LUB
487 Church, at Wellesley, 416-323-1489.
Church Street's most stylish space attracts Prada preeners who sip martinis and tap their Guccis to house muzak played at a discreet volume. Upstairs, a rooftop patio overlooks the street scene below. ☼

SNEAKERS
502A Yonge, at Alexander, 416-961-5808.
The specialty of the house at this darkly lit emerald-green saloon is chicken – and we aren't talking about the Colonel or Buffalo wings. ☼

STATLER'S
471 Church, at Maitland, 416-925-0341, www.statlers.ca.
More of a College-style lounge than the usual booze 'n' cruise joints found in Boystown, this small elegant boîte hosts regular sessions with warbling jazz thrushes who broadcast to the street.

WISH
3 Charles E, at Yonge, 416-935-0240, www.wishrestaurant.ca.
Divided into two diminutive halves – one an upscale cantina, the other an haute lounge – Wish has a high wow factor. Whitewashed walls, ceiling and floors provide a neutral backdrop for low-slung over-stuffed sofas piled with pillows and cashmere throws. A heated terrace, too. ☼ ⏱

WOODY'S
467 Church, at Maitland, 416-972-0887.
If you ever watched Queer As Folk, you know what Woody's looks like from the street. It's exterior appears as the facade of the fictional Pittsburgh bar. Unfortunately – or fortunately – the real thing is nothing like the TV version. Instead, this rambling room has several stand-up bars, areas for reposing, pool tables and stuffed faux rhinoceros heads. ⏱

ZELDA'S
542 Church, at Maitland, 416-922-2526, www.zeldas.ca.
You don't go to campy Zelda's to hide in the corner when you can sip potent potables in a series of madly decorated rooms to the soundtrack of 70s disco instead. ☼

College

ANDY POOLHALL
489 College, at Markham, 416-923-5300.
This ain't your parents' snooker hall. Replace aging pool sharks with an eclectic College Street crowd, and replace televised sports with a packed dance floor and hip DJs and you're getting closer. Weekends find the lounge packed to the gills with hipsters, students and lots of random suburban types looking for a good party.

BIRD
503 College (2nd floor), 416-323-3957.
If you don't know what you're looking for, it's easy to walk by Bird, the stylish intimate lounge above Xacutti. Making your way up the stairs, you're immediately struck by the extremely high ceilings and sexy minimalist decor. DJs play funky mellow tunes most nights, and you may find people dancing toward the end of some of their busier nights.

BISTRO 422
422 College, at Bathurst, 416-963-9416.
The 422 gets the considerable overflow of cheap

drunks from Sneaky Dee's across the street. A narrow basement space lined with wooden benches and wainscotting, Bistro furnishes would-be punks with cheap pitchers and Schnapps schnooters.

CIAO EDIE ROXX
489 College, at Markham, 416-922-7774.
Named in homage to Warhol superstar Edie Sedgwick, this intimate below-street-level space attracts a Church-meets-College crowd. Though it's recently been re-branded as a showcase for local indie combos — hence the addition of Roxx to its handle — much of owner Michael Sweeney's campy kitsch decor remains. Sundays, the subterranean room continues to host its long-running womyn's night Here Kitty Kitty. ☼

CLOAK & DAGGER
394 College, at Borden, 416-921-8308.
A tiny little traditional-style pub with a good selection of beers on tap. Recent renovations by new owners made more functional than aesthetic changes, opening up some space by moving the bar back. Live acts and DJs play in the front window, and you can hear everything from classic reggae to punk to gospel, depending on the night. ☼

COBALT
426 College, at Bathurst, 416-923-4456.
A swanky downbeat cocktail bar with walls painted cobalt blue and a perfect-for-dancing wooden floor, Cobalt shakes up some unusual martinis. Try the Beef Jerky!

EAT MY MARTINI
648 College, at Grace, 416-516-2549.
As the evening progresses and as its name suggests, intimate Eat shifts from a 90s-style dining room to a martini bar serving nearly 100 lethal 2-ounce cocktails. ☼

EIN STEIN
229 College, at Beverley, 416-597-8346.
This boisterous student pub across from U of T offers a slew of drink specials – $4.75 martinis Monday, $8.50 pitchers before 9 pm Thursday and bargain-priced pints of Guinness Friday. Bonus: free pool Sunday and Canadian Tire money accepted at par all weekend. ☼

Cobalt, home of the beef jerky martini.

ÉL CONVENTO RICO
750 College, at Crawford, 416-588-7800.
A subterranean cha-cha-teria that's as popular with cross-dressers as it is with straights ready to rumba, the Rico is a scene that has to be experienced to be believed. Even those with two left feet will find themselves on the end of a conga line.

IL GATTO NERO
720 College, at Crawford, 416-536-3132.
Firmly ensconced in its snazzy new digs down the street from its old coffee-house days, the Nero has cast off its low-rent sports drag to become a semi-upscale bar with hipper than expected patrons glued to the big-screen TV. Bonus: open every day of the year. ☼

LA CERVEJARIA
842 College, at Ossington, 416-588-0162.
A refurbished 80s-style saloon with occasional Latin music, this Portuguese cantina goes into overdrive whenever Benfica plays on the satellite TV screens.

LOUNGE 88
14 Clinton, at Henderson, 416-531-5833.
The brushed steel bar, animal-print chaises and grand piano centre stage in this jazzy piano bar will come as a shock to those who remember this student hang from its former incarnation as the divey Monarch Tavern.

MATADOR
466 Dovercourt, at College, 416-533-9311.
After the bars close, for nearly 40 years this west-side honky-tonk rocks till dawn Friday and Saturday nights, even though the party's officially alcohol-free. *Unlicensed.*

MIDTOWN
552 College, at Euclid, 416-920-4533.
Don't bother looking for the sign, because there isn't one. Only a blue-and-white striped awning over its sidewalk patio identifies this watering hole for media types. Bonus: three pool tables. ☼

MOD CLUB THEATRE
722 College, at Crawford, 416-588-4663.
Founded by the promoters behind the long-running Mod Club parties, the Mod Club Theatre – with an upper balcony excellent for checking out the dance floor below – is a popular concert venue and dance club. ☼

NEU+RAL
349a College, at Augusta, 416-926-2112.
An unpretentious basement bar at the top of Kensington Market, Neu+ral hosts alternative DJs most nights, as well as live bands. It's dark and a bit grimy, the opposite of the generic chi-chi bottle-service lounge that has flooded Toronto in recent years.

OCTOPUS LOUNGE
293 Palmerston, at College, 416-929-7214.
This split-level converted garage gets busy early on the weekends with well-dressed crowds looking to socialize and dance to soulful house, funk and soul. For those who remember the original Octopus from the 90s, this is like a more grown-up version of it.

ORBIT ROOM
580A College, at Clinton, 416-535-0613.
The easy going Orbit is partially owned by Rush guitarist Alex Leifson but you won't hear prog rock or metal from the live bands that play here. Look for a big phat Booker T and Memphis soul vibe from the retro-rockers who take the stage most nights, while patrons pig out on better-than-average pub grub. ☼

SNEAKY DEE'S
431 College, at Bathurst, 416-603-3090.
Known by habitués as Sneaky Disease, this Tex-Mex tornado comes fronted with a psychedelic Fiona Smyth mural. Inside the cluttered space, graffiti-scrawled booths encourage late-night lounging. After the bar

Fine al fresco dining at **Il Gatto Nero**.

Aisles filled with hiphop, funk, soul, house and break at **Supermarket.** Page 120.

closes on Friday and Saturday nights, it still slings hangover helpers like cheesy nachos till 4:30 am.

SOUZ DAL
636 College, at Grace, 416-537-1883.
Open only after dark, Souz Dal suggests a romantic rendezvous at the casbah, complete with tented ochre-patterned walls and ceiling fans churning the sheltering air overhead.

WILD INDIGO
607 College, at Clinton, 416-536-8797.
A chic Indochine vibe makes this one of the strip's hipper spots and one of the most relaxed. Though you won't find the backwards-baseball-cap brigade in the house, tasteful fashionistas and just plain folks sip smart drinks to a soulful soundtrack that rarely breaks a sweat.

Yorkville

DUKE OF GLOUCESTER
649 Yonge, at Charles, 416-961-9704, www.thedukeofgloucester.com.
At one end of this second-storey space hidden away over an Indian restaurant – all leaded glass, mahogany panelling and red-velvet-lined booths – sports fans gather every Saturday afternoon for UK footie matches piped in by satellite TV. Great UK-themed jukebox, too.

PANORAMA
55 Bloor W, at Bay, 416-967-0000, www.eatertainment.com.
Take a short ride in a tiny elevator up to the penthouse bar on the 51st floor of the Manulife Centre and find an elegant nightclub in the clouds with two outdoor terraces offering spectacular views looking south and north.

PILOT
22 Cumberland, at Yonge, 416-923-5716, www.thepilot.ca.
Established in 1944, this Yorkville watering hole is one of Toronto's longest-running bars. The Pilot's deserved reputation comes from its days as a 1950s version of the Cameron. And though artists and beatniks have given way to decidedly non-scene lit-

erary types and jazz heads since it moved around the corner in 1972, its heritage continues. A long silver-trimmed stand-up bar overlooks a performance area and a wall of clocks all telling the wrong time. When one of them accurately hits 3:30 on Saturday and Sunday afternoons, it's time for a jazz matinee.

ROOF LOUNGE
4 Avenue Rd, at Bloor W, 416-924-5471.
The rooftop bar at the Park Hyatt – formerly the Park Plaza – has been a literary landmark for more than 50 years. Writers like Mordecai Richler, Graeme Gibson and Margaret Atwood, whose novel Cat's Eye has a scene that takes place in the bar, have been known to frequent this elegant saloon. Even Gourmet magazine called it one of North America's 10 best gin joints. From the patio, check out the great skyline view looking south over U of T and the ROM.

North

Uptown

ABBOT ON THE HILL
1276 Yonge, at Woodlawn, 416-920-9074.
A two-level pub decked out in molded plywood, the Abbot attracts a less genteel cross-section of the Rosedale/Summerhill set who scarf Scotch eggs, fish 'n' chips and shepherd's pie while getting the next round of pints in.

CENTRO
2472 Yonge, at Castlefield, 416-483-2211, www.centro.ca.
Located in the lower level of one of Toronto's most exclusive restaurants, this swank piano bar features selections from its extensive wine cellar. Dim sum and tapas, too. *Closed Sunday.*

GRANITE BREWERY
245 Eglinton E, at Mt Pleasant, 416-322-0723, www.granitebrewery.ca.
Cavernous brewpub near Yonge and Eligible makes its own suds.

YAMMY THE CAT
1108 Yonge, at Roxborough, 416-515-1729.
This minuscule bar serves all-day brekkies in a room decked out with funky 50s couches while appropriately programmed tunes rock the CD player. House martini: the Furball – gin or vodka, Lemoncello and Chartreuse.

East

The Beach

FEATHERS
962 Kingston Rd, at Scarborough, 416-694-0443.
Brit-style pub à la Coronation Street's Rovers Return in the north Beach.

Cabbagetown

LAURENTIAN ROOM
51A Winchester, at Parliament, 416-925-8680,
www.geocities.com/salonnoir.
This stylish restaurant and lounge feels like an oasis of nightlife fun hidden in an otherwise quiet neighbourhood above the former Winchester Tavern. It's retained many aspects from its original heyday in the 30s that give it a different kind of class than the average lounge. DJs and live acts, from house to jazz to Latin, are featured, and dancing does go on wherever people can find space. *Closed Sunday and Monday.*

Danforth

ALLEN'S
143 Danforth, at Broadview, 416-463-3086,
http://allens.to.
Huge draught beer selection and plenty of Scotches served in a room that looks straight out of the 50s New York City bar scene owner John Maxwell grew up around – his Dad owned a joint there. There's a friendly Irish subtext – think Jimmy Breslin – great food and a killer patio.

AULD SPOT
347 Danforth, at Hampton, 416-406-4688,
www.auldspot.ca.
Guinness flows from the taps as regulars fill the small room with animated chatter. Despite the pub's decor, the grub's surprisingly pan-global. Bonus: oyster-shucking every other Monday night.

DORA KEOGH
141 Danforth, at Broadview, 416-778-1804.
Next door to Allen's, this no-frills Irish cousin features Celtic musicians, semi-private snugs and an Olde World kitchen that can be booked for dinner parties.

ETON TAVERN
710 Danforth, at Pape, 416-466-6161.
The marquee describes this spotless Danforth tavern as "3,200 km to Newfoundland, five steps to Newfoundland on the Danforth." An unchanged men's taproom from the 50s, the Eton sports cafeteria furniture, shiny terrazzo floors and wood panelling everywhere. Belt screech while catching the club's Saturday-afternoon Newfie country matinee.

ONLY CAFÉ
972 Danforth, at Donlands, 416-463-7843,
www.theonlycafe.com.
Regulars will be mad we even mention it but with special guests like nearby resident Ron Sexsmith trying out new tunes on the joint's tiny stage we've got to tell you about this funky, slightly dowdy gem with a massive bottle beer selection.

SARAH'S CAFÉ
1426 Danforth, at Monarch Park, 416-406-3121.
Part Celtic pub, part Greek taverna, Sarah's stocks a large range of Belgian, German and UK marques and has more than a dozen Euro-brews on tap.

Leslieville

DUKE OF YORK
1225 Queen E, at Leslie, 416-463-5302.
Hipsters and wrestling fans pack out this east-side tavern for Saturday afternoon's country karaoke with iconic Canuck wrestler-slash-crooner Sweet Daddy Siki.

KUBO RADIO
894 Queen E, at Logan, 416-406-5826,
www.kubo.com.
Paris meets Saigon at this east-side brasserie with a number of libation options: Kubo lager on tap as well as several Japanese, Singaporean, Vietnamese and Thai brews, lychee martinis, sake flights and el cheapo wine by the box.

West

Bloor West

CLINTON'S
693 Bloor W, at Clinton, 416-535-9541.
One of Toronto's oldest alternative venues – Cowboy Junkies got their start here back in the 1980s – this log-lined multi-storey tavern also features stand-up on Mondays, wing night Tuesdays, karaoke upstairs every night and brunch seven days a week from 11 am to 5 pm.

GEM
1159 Davenport, at Ossington, 416-654-1182.
Casual, funky and fun (vintage jukebox, eclectic bric-a-brac and lunch counter complete with stools), think of the Gem as a diner where, instead of malted milks, regulars chug single malts and microbrews. Licensed.

MR. SEVEN DRAFT BEER TOWN & SOJU
686 Bloor W, at Clinton, 416-537-0062.
Behind its scary boarded-up front window and unusual signage, this dimly lit dive in Little Seoul offers cheap suds and shots of soju, the deadly high-roof Korean rotgut.

Dundas West & Ossington

COCKTAIL MOLOTOV
928 Dundas W, 416-603-6691.
Once a trendy knick-knack boutique of the same name, this Cocktail is as sleekly fashionable as the former tenant, from its tall Eames-style bar stools to its chic blond-on-blond back space. The soundtrack: classic rock, real loud.

THE COMMUNIST'S DAUGHTER
1149 Dundas W, at Ossington, 647-435-0103.
Although there's a tiny, smudged chalkboard hanging in the front window of the diminutive Dundas dive, most people can't find this local named for a Neutral Milk Hotel tune. Hint: look for a sign that reads "Nazarre" one door west of Ossington on the south side. With only half a dozen seats at the bar and a few tables, and one of the best CD jukeboxes in the city, no wonder the joint's always packed. Bonus: pickled eggs!

CROOKED STAR
202 Ossington, 416-536-7271.
Decked out with folksy wooden booths and lit by regu-

lation candles, this cozy neighbourhood spot has been a hit with regulars since it opened 18 months ago. Watch for alterna-DJs and the odd acoustic act.

MAGPIE
831 Dundas W, at Palmerston, 416-916-6499.
When it first launched last summer, the former Benifica soccer supporters' club was briefly a vegetarian restaurant. The gang from nearby Musa have taken over since and turned it into a low-key local-slash-lounge with an impressive beer lineup.

PRESS CLUB
850 Dundas W, at Euclid, 416-364-7183.
The former Caffe Brasiliano storefront has morphed into a low-profile jazzy joint that's more geared to local artsy types than to any media interlopers. Think Irish pub minus the blarney and annoying music. Bonus: a typewriter!

SWEATY BETTY'S
13 Ossington, at Queen W, 416-535-6861.
A tiny two-room dive decked out in chandeliers and fugly sofas that seat about 12 max, this extremely popular storefront bar also happens to be conveniently located steps from the Queen West Centre for Addiction and Mental Health. Sunday afternoons, Betty unspools free Asian chop-socky flicks to discounted sake accompaniment. And any boozer that offers Cheez Whiz on toast in its lineup and has Motörhead on the CD jukebox is all right by us. Bonus: absinthe!

King West

CRUSH
455 King W, at Spadina, 416-977-1234, www.crushwinebar.com.
A pretty, if pricey, New York loft-style French bistro in a warehouse conversion with sandblasted limestone brick and bare hardwood floors, Crush also contains an attractive wine bar up front that features a rotating roster of regional plonk. Serious oenophiles can sign up for courses and tastings organized by the Centre for Vine Affairs located on its lower level. *Closed Sunday.*

LUX
720 King W, at Bathurst, 416-203-2883.
Toronto club czar Charles Khabouth turns the moribund Loft around with a sophisticated Munge/Leung design that merges the best of downtown dining with the late-night lounge scene. With an eclectic card from chef Jonathon Lucas — prawn chop suey, anyone? — and signature cocktails like the French Martini (vodka, Chambord, pineapple juice and ice-balls), it's no wonder everyone wants to get in. Secret: the swellegant joint's virtually empty at lunch.

606
606 King W, at Portland, 416-504-8740.
Past its alleyway entrance, encounter a sunken restaurant area fronted by a large glass garage door that opens to the street. A long stainless steel bar leads past an open kitchen to a larger DJ-driven dance and romance space.

2 CATS
569 King W, at Portland, 416-204-6261.
Feeling feline? Though we're still not sure just who these two cats might be, we do know a good-looking club when we see one — a cozy lounge-like front room leading to a rear stand-up bar lined with mirrors and a few stray couches.

UNDERGROUND GARAGE URBAN SALOON
365 King W, at Peter, 416-340-0365, www.undergroundgarage.ca.
Bucking the ultra-lounge trend, this no-nonsense

subterranean headbangers' ballroom rocks to the classics — Zeppelin, Ozzy-period Sabbath, Soundgarden and Alice in Chains, if you didn't know.

WHEAT SHEAF
667 King W, at Bathurst, 416-504-9912.
Opened in 1849, the Wheat Sheaf is Toronto's oldest bar. Somewhat tarted up, it still remains a classic watering hole. Urban legend has it there's a secret underground tunnel to nearby Fort York.

Roncesvalles

GATE 403
403 Roncesvalles, at Howard Park, 416-588-2930.
Right across the street from the old Revue rep cinema, this retro jazz lounge recalls the 52nd Street of 1950s New York — polished wooden floors, an old-school stand-up bar — right down to a grand piano in the corner where jazzy crooners sing the blues.

HUGH'S ROOM
2261 Dundas W, 416-531-6604.
If you'd like to hear some classy folk, blues or gospel by a marquee act to go with your three-course meal and imported brew, Hugh's Room is your one-stop food and roots music nourishment centre in Roncesvalles Village. The stuffy, banquet-hall ambience is a drawback, but where else in town can you see the Campbell Brothers?

LOONS
416 Roncesvalles, at Howard Park, 416-535-8561.
This Brit-style pub wouldn't be out of place in a far tonier area — Summerhill, say — but punters swear by its draft selection.

The Communist's Daughter is a diminutive Dundas dive named for a Neutral Milk Hotel tune. Page 125.

West Queen West

ACADEMY OF SPHERICAL ARTS
38 Hanna, at Atlantic, 416-532-2782,
www.sphericalarts.com.
Once the home of billiard manufacturer Brunswick, this former 5,000-square-foot warehouse space has been converted into an elegant Victorian-style club. *Closed Sunday.*

BEACONSFIELD
1154 Queen W, at Beaconsfield, 416-516-2550,
www.thebeaconsfield.com.
Unlike the slew of bars in this quickly gentrified nabe that launched following the success of the Drake, this relaxed space isn't simply a holding pen for those less fortunate fashionistas who can't make it past the velvet rope. With its art deco decor and stainless steel bar, red leather banquettes and period light fixtures turned way down low, first-timers can't help but be reminded of the Paddock. Expect a crowd of neighbourhood regulars who would rather belly up to the bar with a pint than swan about swigging from a bottle of champagne.

CADILLAC LOUNGE
1296 Queen W, at Grove, 416-536-7717,
www.cadillaclounge.com.
You can't miss the Cadillac – there's half of a 1962 Caddy stuck to the storefront. This narrow, dimly lit local is a shrine to all things Elvis and Cadillac: automotive memorabilia and pictures everywhere of a pompadoured King shaking his blue suede shoes.

DONE RIGHT INN
861 Queen W, at Manning, 416-703-0405.

What other bar in Toronto would know when to celebrate John Lydon's birthday? With its wrecked rec-room ambience and long wooden stand-up bar, if this joint were any more laid-back it'd be horizontal. In the rear, find vintage arcade video games and ratty couches that give way to a secluded backyard patio.

DRAKE HOTEL
1150 Queen W, at Beaconsfield, 416-531-5042,
www.thedrakehotel.ca.
Its dramatic facelift changed the landscape of this edge of Parkdale, bringing glitz, money and tourists into the area. Founded by dot.com dandy Jeff Stober, this artsy and hip-as-hell spot offers eclectic and adventurous programming in the Underground, where you can catch anything from noise rock to techno, balancing the busy 905er-dominated weekends in the lounge and patio.

GLADSTONE HOTEL
1214 Queen W, at Dufferin, 416-531-4635,
www.gladstonehotel.com.
Well, it took long enough! After what seemed like a decade, the restoration of this Parkdale landmark – a massive Edwardian hotel-bar complex – is finally complete. The once dumpy 'Stone is now giving the nearby Drake a run for its money as downtown's trendiest destination. The Melody Bar continues to host its notorious and insanely popular karaoke extravaganzas Thursday through Saturday evenings, but a second much larger performance area, the Ballroom, handles the spillover crowd.

GYPSY CO-OP
815 Queen W, at Claremont, 416-703-5069.
A fixture on Queen West for a decade (before that it was Marcus O'Hara's legendary Squeeze Club). Its

most recent owners have been slowly renovating and updating the restaurant and lounge over the past year, moving away from the sloppy 90s boho feel while retaining the original laid-back charm. DJs play assorted soulful and funky sounds in the back lounge area, as well as the upstairs room, known as the Hooch. *Closed Monday.*

HEALEY'S
178 Bathurst, at Queen W, 416-703-5882, www.jeffhealeys.com/abouthealeys.html.
Owned by blues guitar legend (and Roadhouse star) Jeff Healey, this sprawling basement pub underneath the Paddock features blues artists, retro rockers and a weekly Battle of the Bands. And yes, Healey often jams.

KEI'S
936 Queen W, at Shaw, 416-534-7449.
A tiki-tastic cocktail lounge cum pricey Malaysian resto located in a converted greasy spoon, Kei's best when you keep it liquid. ☼

LOT 16
1136 Queen W, at Beaconsfield, 416-531-6556.
This minimally appointed, very brown space was once the Elvis Restaurant, the greasiest of spoons. And though the current clientele has moved slightly upmarket – slightly – the no-frills Parkdale attitude remains the same.

MITZI'S SISTER
1554 Queen W, at Fuller, 416-532-2570.
Sibling offshoot of popular Parkdale brunch spot Mitzi's, this rootin'-tootin' saloon – formerly the Tennessee Tavern – attracts more rough-around-the-edges types from the local alt-art and music scene.

NOT MY DOG
1510 Queen W, at Fuller, 416-532-2397, www.notmydog.ca.
Parkdale's latest art bar, this small exposed-brick storefront features a weekly Johnny Cash tribute Fridays, cheap cocktails Wednesdays and movies on its heated patio year round. ☼

PADDOCK
178 Bathurst, 416-595-9997, www.thepaddock.ca.
Queen and Bathurst may be one of the grubbiest corners in town, but the Paddock's remarkably

swank. Built circa 1947, the saloon's been faithfully refurbished, restoring its original charm. Padded burgundy booths, dark wooden wainscotting and a leather-tufted wraparound bar with a Bakelite counter make the perfect backdrop for cocktail swilling or sampling single malts. Expect an animated mix of literary and theatre types. Urban legend has it Old Blue Eyes stopped by here back in the Rat Pack years. Bonus: weekend brunch! ☼

QUEEN'S HEAD PUB
659 Queen W, at Bathurst, 416-368-9405.
The Queenshead Pub has quickly become a hot spot for students and indie rock fans, and features DJs most nights playing punk, indie, ska, hiphop and death disco, depending on the night. Cheap drinks and low cover charges are two reasons for its success, but the music and atmosphere keep them coming back.

SOCIAL
1100 Queen W, at Dovercourt, 416-532-4474, www.thesocial.ca.
Just look for the giant red flashing sign shaped like an arrow to find a cavernous room that's quickly become one of the hottest spots in towns. Scenesters and hip suburbanites – who knew? – schmooze on shocking-pink vinyl couches while DJs spin an eclectic mix of rock and electronica. Bonus: a fireplace, hors d'oeuvres and $3 drink specials every night from 5 to 10 pm.

SQUIRLY'S
807A Queen W, at Manning, 416-703-0574.
A shrine to west-side grunge, this laid-back watering hole is all leopard skin, skull Christmas lights and blood-red walls. Regulars knock back killer cocktails like the Zeppelin while grooving to tunes that range from relaxed alterna-folk to rockabilly. ☼

STONES PLACE
1255 Queen W, 416-536-4242.
If you love the Rolling Stones, you'll dig this long stand-up bar decked out with comfy sofas and curtain-covered walls hung with Stones' memorabilia: hundreds of autographed portraits, gold records galore and a sizable collection of original Ronnie Wood paintings. The Stones occasionally come here to hang but, surprise, never to play.

Check out the scenesters and hip urbanites getting **Social**.

patios

Our summers are short so we have to make the most of the time we've got. Which explains why Toronto has so many delicious decks and patios, whether just for a cool afternoon bevvie or a full-blown five-course dinner.

For the latest reviews, pick up NOW Magazine every week or visit www.nowtoronto.com.

Downtown

Clubland

BRASSERIE
**133 John, at Nelson, 416-595-8201,
www.thebrasserie.ca.**
Recently rebranded to suggest a sophisticated Parisian boîte, the former Frisco's may have changed its name, but the scene remains the same. Sprawling over several levels, the busy streetside terrace of the original Amsterdam brew pub is a favourite of the after-work crowd who like to blow off steam over Buffalo-style chicken wings and any of several of the house's absinthe-based cocktails, including the Van Gogh's Ear. Bonus: half-price aps Monday to Friday 5 till 7 pm.

C LOUNGE
456 Wellington W, 416-260-9393.
Launched with much media hoopla – the opening party honoured Late Night's Conan O'Brien – C has so far managed to fly below most local clubgoers' radar. Regulars wouldn't have it any other way. Deeply padded chaises make the fenced-in backyard patio – complete with VIP cabanas that attract fabulosi like Prince and Duran Duran – a cool comfort zone. *Closed Sunday, Tuesday and Wednesday.*

Central

BETTY'S
240 King E, at Princess, 416-368-1300.
Surrounded by very tall walls, Betty's sequestered patio (once the "Betty Ford Clinic" until a certain ex-president's wife took exception) is the local of choice for students from nearby George Brown and members of the gutter press. Bonus: nearly 20 microbrews on tap, as well as pub grub like suicide wings and Deep Six nachos. ⓟ

BIAGIO
155 King E, at Jarvis, 416-366-4040.
This pricey Italian trat located on a water-featured terrace behind the historic St. Lawrence Hall is one of the core's most romantic destinations. While fountains tinkle, regulars tuck into starters like cookbook-correct Caesar salad and Atlantic salmon tossed with fresh fennel and tart mandarin orange, delivered to table on a slab of ice, followed by Flintstonian secondi of Costoletta Milanese, the classic northern Italian Provimi veal cutlet. Bonus: thoroughly professional old-school servers. *Closed Sunday, holidays.*

BYMARK
**66 Wellington W, at York, 416-777-1144,
www.bymark.ca.**
Dwarfed by the four black Modernist monoliths of the Mies van der Rohe-designed Toronto Dominion Centre, the terrace at Bymark sits at the centre of downtown's liveliest midday dining scene. While most of the white-collar crowd brown-bag it next to a grazing herd of cast-bronze cows on one of the few green spaces in the core, here on the elegant Yabu Pushelburg-appointed patio, the captains of industry knock back sea salt margaritas and chow down on expense-account meals of butter-braised lobster poutine, prime USDA steaks and the notorious $36.95 Bymark burger topped with shaved truffles.

GEORGE
**111 Queen E, at Mutual, 416-863-6006,
www.georgeonqueen.com.**
NOW's resto of the year for 2005, this luxe supper club in a converted east-side warehouse cum spa takes it al fresco once the weather permits on a terrific terrace in the complex's four-storey atrium. Against a backdrop of shade trees glowing with fairy lights and a water wall, foodies nosh on chef Lorenzo Loseto's genre-busting five-course tasting menu while the rest of us make do with his slightly more accessible lunchtime card. *Closed Sunday and Monday.*

Harbourfront & Islands

RECTORY
**102 Lakeshore, Ward's Island, 416-203-2152,
www.rectorycafe.com.**
Nestled in a grove of tall pines, this idyllic island café off the south-shore boardwalk is open 7 days a week for the summer starting in mid-June. While its front-yard beer garden makes the perfect pit stop for those who want to grab a quick pint while blading, the main attraction's the former community centre's patio on its south lawn, complete with shuffleboard court and weekend brunch. Bonus: dog- and bicycle-friendly! *Closed Monday and holidays.*

WATERSIDE BISTRO
**255 Queens Quay E, at Sherbourne, 416-203-0470,
www.watersidesports.com.**
Don't tell anyone, but there's a fabulous spot right on the lake that nobody knows about even though it's been there for years hidden behind an inflatable tennis club. Throw in free parking and three decks on the water's edge and those who fondly remember the similar but long-gone Sgana Café will make this their new summer hideout. Situated in the middle of a bleak parking lot, the Muskoka-style deck takes in a panoramic view of skyscrapers, idyllic Ward's Island and passing sailboats. Although the reliable resto's kitchen rarely falters, everyone's here for the dazzling scenery.

King West

AMUSE-BOUCHE
**96 Tecumseth, at Whitaker, 416-913-5830,
www.amusebboucherestaurant.com.**
Since its launch, owners/chefs Jason Inniss and Bertrand Alépée's beautiful bistro in Susur Lee's old Lotus has been hailed as one of the finest dining

Join the A-list at **Ultra**.

experiences in Toronto. Come summer, it's even more so, especially when you're tucking into Forbidden black rice cake and tomato confit in jasmine emulsion in the exclusive street-side grotto next to a burbling water feature. Warning: reservations mandatory. *Closed Monday.*

BAR WELLINGTON
520 Wellington W, at Portland, 416-341-8880.
From the owners of Bloor's Bedford Ballroom and Academy comes this newly opened three-storey downtown adjunct located kitty-korner from historic Victoria Memorial Park. Expect a slightly more upscale version of the Bedford's student-friendly card – including a massive 16-ounce house burger – as well as pizza, panini 'n' pitchers.

BRASSAII
461 King W, at Spadina, 416-598-4730,
www.brassaii.com.
Located in the same gorgeous cobblestoned courtyard as Crush Wine Bar's sequestered patio, this South Beach-style terrace offers a late-night al fresco alternative to noisier neighbouring clubs. Bonus: live jazz combos during dinner Thursday through Saturday, and daily cocktail specials.

Queen West

BLACK BULL
298 Queen W, at Soho, 416-593-2766.
The hip strip's busiest patio is a zoo from noon until late in the night. Partially covered and with 200-plus seats right on the curb, it's the perfect perch for watching the non-stop parade of alterna-types marching past. Warning: the badass dude in head-to-toe leather who just pulled up on a Harley may look like an outlaw biker, but he's likely a newly single dental supply salesman from Uxbridge.

QUEEN MOTHER
208 Queen W, at Duncan, 416-598-4719,
http://queenmother.sites.toronto.com.
With its overgrown trellis overhead and cobblestones underfoot, the Queen Mum's backyard terrace has been one of downtown's definitive outdoor

destinations for more than 20 years. While soft 80s rock plays at a comfortable level, kick back with an eclectic card that includes pad thai, wasabi guacamole and the notorious Cosmic Burger, a ground nut patty topped with flakes and sprouts slathered in Thousand Island dressing on a sesame-seed bun. Warning: to reach the rear deck you must navigate two steep stairways and a trek through the very low-ceilinged basement. ⏱

ULTRA
314 Queen W, at Peter, 416-263-0330,
http://ultrasupperclub.com.
As tasteful as a centre-spread layout in a design mag, the swanky white-on-white rooftop deck at downtown's hottest A-list joint is a complete contrast from its former incarnation as the Bamboo's funky treetop lounge. Instead of roots reggae and Red Stripe, expect a South Beach-style spa complete with former YYZ chef Chris Zielinski's sharable seafood platters and Monday night's $20 whole lobster specials. Those looking for a somewhat more sedate scene can fashionably lounge in the boîte's shady inner courtyard. Warning: elitist dress code. *Closed Sunday.* ⏱

Midtown

Annex

GREEN ROOM
296 Brunswick, at Bloor W, 416-929-3253.
First-timers have a hard time finding this obscure inner courtyard, complete with burbling water, hidden in the alley behind the Poor Alex Theatre. Eventually, they find a grotty grotto decked out in rickety Goodwill castoffs serving cheap all-day breakfasts to the local slacker crowd.

KENSINGTON KITCHEN
124 Harbord, at Spadina, 416-961-3404.
For years, KK won NOW's Readers Poll in the best patio category. It's not hard to see why: moderately

priced Mediterranean mezes – baba ghanouj, lamb burgers, vegetarian couscous with hand-cut frites – all served on a romantic rooftop under a spreading chestnut and evening stars.

LATITUDE WINE BAR & GRILL
89 Harbord, at Spadina, 416-928-0926.
Taking its well-chosen name from "Latin with attitude," Latitude has two outdoor eating areas. Those who prefer truck exhaust with their pan-seared tilapia over potato pavé in Tequila saffron cream will prefer the curbside tables out front, but most head for the Miami Modernist rear garden, especially for its acclaimed nuevo Latino brunch and a couple of Caipirinhas. Extensive New World wine list, too.

MADISON
14 Madison, at Bloor, 416-927-1722,
www.madisonavenuepub.com.
Taking up two three-storey Victorian homes in the south Annex, the Madison is party central for the nearby University of Toronto. A maze of interconnected rooms, all red-velvet banquettes and brass draught pumps, leads to four separate covered and heated decks that face into the evening sunset. The spot's so popular, lineups snake down the alleyway and out front to the street. The management insists that customers wear shoes, but remember that rollerblades are unacceptable footwear. Bonus: 20 beers on tap! ⓘ

PAUPERS
539 Bloor W, at Albany, 416-530-1331,
www.pauperspub.com.
Once the local branch of the CIBC, this converted three-storey bank is now one of the most popular pubs on the Bloor student strip. There's a roadside patio on the ground floor, but up a series of stairways to the roof is one of Toronto's best-kept secrets. Reminiscent of the old Bamboo, this Caribbean-themed deck has a panoramic skyline view as long as you're standing. Bonus: daily half-price food specials.

Top five
wine cellars

OPUS
A power-packed 90-page list of 2,500 wines goes deep into burgundies, Bordeaux, Super Tuscans, Californians and Australians. (*37 Prince Arthur, 416-921-3105*)

VIA ALLEGRO
Offering 5,500 different wines, 50,000 bottles, the world's largest list of Amarones and 49 wines by the glass. (*1750 The Queensway, 416-622-6677*)

BARBERIAN'S
This downtown steakhouse staple has a deep list, especially Californians. (*7 Elm, 416-597-0335*)

JAMIE KENNEDY WINE BAR
When it comes to pairing a fine wine with a fine meal, look no further. *See page 56.*

IL MULINO
Serves up some of the best selections of Ontario VQAs, for when you want a taste of the local grape. (*1060 Eglinton W, 416-780-1173*)

Cabbagetown

PROVENCE DELICES
12 Amelia, at Parliament, 416-924-9901,
www.provencerestaurant.com.
First as Le Canard, then Provence and now Provence Delices, this long-running bastion of accessible French cuisine has proved one of the most popular bistros in town. On an awning-draped terrace, regulars tuck into $15 steak frites while swilling glasses of sparkling Café De Paris. Bonus: $16.95 weekend brunch buffet.

Chinatown/ Kensington Market

BELLEVUE DINER
61 Bellevue, at Nassau, 416-597-6912.
The north market stretch of Nassau between Bellevue and Augusta has to be one of downtown's most happening blocks. But outlaw coffee houses, knitting boutiques and Rent-A-Wreck all take a back seat to the Bellevue's bucolic all-day-sun patio action. Figure in first-rate Mediterranean mains and weekend brunch and its no contest of cool.

BODEGA
30 Baldwin, at Henry, 416-977-1287,
www.bodegarestaurant.com.
The stretch of Baldwin between Beverley and McCaul is probably home to more patios than any two blocks in the city. Though John's Italian and Margarita's are always packed to the gills, our favourite on the strip is the vine-wrapped curbside terrace of this classy French bistro owned by former Le Select chef Paul Biggs.

HOT BOX CAFE
191A Baldwin, at Augusta, 416-203-6990,
www.roachorama.com.
Hidden discreetly away from prying eyes in a walled-in backyard behind a head shop, this hippy-dippy café happens to be the only patio in town that allows its customers to smoke marijuana in the open. To the inevitable Bob Marley soundtrack (with occasional breaks for Dave Matthews or new Pink Floyd Coldplay), tie-dyed stoners and their grandchildren share tokes with suits or knock back smoothies while killing the munchies with hemp cookies and veggie-friendly sandwiches. Bonus: a makeshift rock-lined pond, complete with snapping turtles. *Unlicensed.*

LAST TEMPTATION
12 Kensington, at Dundas W, 416-599-2551.
Despite the name change about 20 years ago, not much else has been altered since this JA-inspired joint was known as the legendary Tiger's: cheap Asian Caribbean grub and budget-minded booze on a tree-lined terrace in the heart of Toronto's vintage fashion district.

Church & Wellesley

BYZANTIUM
499 Church, at Wellesley, 416-922-3859.
This secluded deck at the rear of this crazy popular cocktail cantina is also known for serving some of the best food in the nabe.

FIRE ON THE EAST SIDE
6 Gloucester, at Yonge, 416-960-3473.
Formerly Fenton's, Toronto's most-glamorous restaurant circa 1977, this laid-back lounge off the Village's main drag offers a Cajun card with soul food and Tex-Mex accents, and seats on the pretty curbside terrace are particularly desirable for weekend brunch.

patios

NOW reader fave **Kensington Kitchen**. Page 130.

LE PETIT LIBAN
580 Church, at Dundonald, 416-963-2222.
Liban's two terraces – one street-side, the other more formal around the back – take the crown as the street's coolest. While the backyard deck suggests a night at some Indonesian resort, the antebellum patio out front would make the perfect stage for a drag king/queen reading of Gone with the Wind.

ZELDA'S
542 Church, at Maitland, 416-922-2526.
Griping about the not-so-great grub chez Zelda is as fruitless as whining about the Leafs. Instead, join the queue for a hard-to-get curbside table on the street's cruisiest patio.

College
CAFÉ DIPLOMATICO
594 College, at Clinton, 416-534-4637.
Long a magnet for sun-worshippers and moon-howlers, as well as one of the first patios in Toronto, the Dip offers an old-school Italian menu and rock-bottom prices. True, few are here strictly for the food. Most come to soak up the view on the sunny-all-afternoon terrace that by nightfall morphs into front row seating for College Street in all its glory.

CHURRASQUEIRA BAIRRADA
**1000 College, at Havelock, 416-539-8239,
www.bairrada.ca.**
While its front space is a noisy Portuguese barbecue take-away, its huge, grassy family-style backyard, complete with rows of picnic tables and a water feature, makes a great spot to pig out in the great outdoors. Besides suckling pig, count on succulent grilled-over-steam chickens doused with house piri-piri, sided with roasted potato balls, gargantuan carnivorous platters of egg-topped steaks sided with smashed spud 'n' olive, grilled sardines and barbecue salt cod. Roast pig on the patio all day Wednesday! *Closed Monday.*

OLIVIA'S
53 Clinton, at College, 416-533-3989.
Steps from the epicenter of Toronto cool, this Cal-Ital resto in a converted row house (owner Olivia Mizzi still lives upstairs) occupies two levels, one a small roadside affair out front, the other a breathtakingly beautiful backyard garden complete with trellises and creeping vines. If only the welcome were this inviting.

PONY
**488 College, at Palmerston, 416-923-7665,
www.ponyrestaurant.com.**
Down a narrow alley and up a flight of dark wooden stairs wait two of downtown's loveliest outdoor dinner theatres: an intimate shady deck rung with flowerpots, and a second flagstoned grotto below, complete with smoker and garden shed. It's a rooftop with history, too. Back in the 80s, Jamie Kennedy and Michael Stadtlander operated it as Palmerston. Since then, the gastrodome has evolved into a cozy neighbourhood bistro with a wallet- and palate-pleasing three-course prix fixe francophone menu ($22.95 Monday to Thursday, $25.95 Friday and Saturday). Bonus: charming septuagenarian server André Malibert. *Closed Sunday.*

SOUZ DAL
636 College, at Grace, 416-537-1883.
Named for the smoky Russian city whose ornate domes inspired the decor of this casbah-like lounge, Souz Dal is appropriately open only after dark. A true College original since 1992, its candlelit enclosed rear patio's a cross between some futuristic sci-fi flick and the set of West Side Story, complete with fire escapes to the sky. Bonus: $3.95 martini specials Sunday to Tuesday.

The back deck at the **Queen Mother** is downtown's definitive outdoor dining destination.
Page 130.

TRATTORIA GIANCARLO
41 Clinton, at College, 416-533-9619.
If this romantic tree-shrouded Italian trat just off the College drag is good enough for visiting celebs like Sophia Loren and Gina Lolabrigida, who are we to argue? Though you won't find the quirky crowd that inexplicably flocks to nearby Kalendar, you can count on a well-heeled clientele tastefully dining out on a classic lineup like grilled Cumbrae lamb chops and garlicky tiger shrimp. *Closed Sunday.*

XACUTTI
503 College, at Palmerston, 416-323-3957, www.xacutti.com.
Though the fashionistas who made this Toronto's hottest spot to see and be scene circa 02 have thankfully moved on to trendier trats (hello, Doku 15), owner chef Brad Moore's Indo-inspired card remains intact. But the best thing about the former Ellipsis continues to be its minuscule secret courtyard where a select few can dine on the likes of Bengali-style chicken curry served with cashew-studded basmati under a starry nighttime sky.

Yonge – Central

REBEL HOUSE
1068 Yonge, at Roxborough, 416-927-0704.
Customers who know their suds fill this boozer's back garden to sip microbrews (Wellington, Neustadt, Trafalgar and a slew of others) and pig out on an upscale pub grub menu that includes buffalo burgers under an impressive parachute roof.

Yorkville

AMBER
119 Yorkville, at Hazelton, 416-926-9037.
Though this intimate subterranean boîte has attracted the likes of Justin Trudeau, Ben Mulroney and Sean "Puffy" Combs long into the night, by afternoon its shady backyard deck just off Old York Lane is one of the least pretentious spots in the nabe. Bonus: chef Signe Langford (ex Riverside Café and East Meets West) has just introduced her first patio menu. Salmon tartar with wasabi mayo, or pan-fried halloumi splashed with Pernod on grilled Ace baguette, anyone?

BOBA
90 Avenue Rd, at Cumberland, 416-961-2622, www.boba.ca.
A favourite of Elvis Costello and Diana Krall when they're in town, owner/chef Bob Berman's and Barbara Gordon's upscale uptown kitchen has been one of Toronto's most innovative for more than 25 years. Come May, the cutting-edge culinary action spills to its curbside terrace, where, under a large striped awning, Elvis and Diana dig into slow-cooked barbecued ribs and miniature grilled cheese sandwiches paired with salads of locally sourced heirloom tomatoes. *Closed Sunday.*

PANORAMA
55 Bloor W, at Bay, 416-967-0000.
If you suffer from claustrophobia or acrophobia – or both – this penthouse bar on the 51st floor of the Manulife Centre won't be your idea of a good time. Two terraces, one facing north toward tree-shrouded Rosedale, the other south to the downtown core and islands beyond, are lined with patio furniture and a sure-grip rubber carpet. No one's been blown away by anything other than the view.

PILOT
22 Cumberland, at Bay, 416-923-5716.
The venerable downtown institution – 61 years and going strong – has undergone a major overhaul of its three floors, including its rooftop Flight Deck.

Gone are the high wooden fences that shielded the sunny deck from the street below, so patrons can now look down on Yorkville. Fitting with the name, the Deck features a retro streamlined aeronautical look – all rivets and stainless steel – although the pub grub is more grounded, ranging from trendy pad thai to something called Calgary Ginger Beef.

ROOF LOUNGE
4 Avenue Road, at Bloor W, 416-924-5471.
Gourmet magazine called it one of North America's 10 best saloons, so who are we to argue? The rooftop bar has been an historic landmark for more than 50 years. Not only was it one of the first patios in town, it was also a major hangout for local artists and writers like Harold Town, Graeme Gibson and Margaret Atwood (whose novel Cat's Eye has a scene set in the bar). And while the current rooftop terrace is a 10th the size it was in its 70s heyday, it's still a great perch to monitor architect Daniel Libeskind's crazy quilt reconstruction of the ROM directly below.

SKYLOUNGE
220 Bloor W, at Avenue Rd, 416-324-5893, www.toronto.intercontinental.com.
Hidden away behind the chi-chi Intercontinental Hotel (hint: turn right at Harvey's), this serene Ultralike lounge is miles away from the noisy street scene mere steps away. Decked out with pillow-tossed sofas made for, well, lounging, this sequestered gem features not only a Cecconi Simone design but a tapas-style grazing menu as well.

North

Uptown

AUBERGE DU POMMIER
4150 Yonge, at York Mills, 416-222-2220, www.aubergedupommier.com.
Snuggled between two recreated 19th-century crofters' cottages (think Disney does French country), this out-of-the-way Hogs Hollow garden has been a dining destination for lovers since 1987. Next to a fountain ambiently burbling centre court and a wall of pruned apple trees that fill with fruit come late summer, chef Jason Bangerter offers a card of classic Gallic grub with contemporary spin. Don't miss the house's signature dairy-free multiple mushroom soup. *Closed Sunday, holidays.*

MILLER TAVERN
3885 Yonge, at Mill, 416-322-5544.
In a heritage building at the top of Hogg's Hollow that once housed the notorious Jolly Miller roadhouse (establish 1860), this new-look supper club supplies a pricey surf 'n' turf menu for local gentry who like to roost on its three-tiered terrace while keeping an eye on their multimillion-dollar piles and the golf course below.

East

The Beach

BOARDWALK PUB
1681 Lakeshore E, at Northern Dancer Blvd, 416-694-8844, www.boardwalkpub.com.
The only patio in the Beach anywhere remotely near the water, this family-style roadhouse on Ashbridge's Bay offers a spectacular view of the park's volleyball court and the dappled waters of Lake Ontario beyond. Bonus: much of the pub-grub menu of burgers, pizza and pastas comes accompanied by the

Chalk one up for the **Black Bull**'s picture- and pitcher-perfect patio. Page 130.

house heat rating: "one glass of beer," "two beers," and "how 'bout a pitcher?"

MURPHY'S LAW
1702 Queen E, at Kingston Road, 416-690-5516.
Those looking for a respite from the smoggy summer din can take to the fourth-floor rooftop deck of this regulation pub and rise above the hubbub. Bonus: a view that looks south over Ashbridges Bay Park and dappling lake Ontario beyond.

Distillery District

BALZAC'S
55 Mill, at Trinity, 416-207-1709.
Specializing in organic fair-trade beans, this Stratford-based coffeehouse also brings in sandwiches from Clafouti and Daniel et Daniel as well as pastries from dessert diva Dufflet. Bonus: grab a table on the cobblestoned patio and watch the historic 19th-century warehouse complex turn into a location for Hollywood flicks like X-Men, Chicago and Cinderella Man. *Unlicensed.*

BOILER HOUSE
55 Mill, at Trinity, 416-203-2121.
The prettiest patio on the 13 Victorian cobblestoned acres of the Distillery belongs to this former boiler house. Under a towering black chimney, adventurous day-trippers dig into braised ribs and veggie burgers.

Danforth

ALLEN'S
143 Danforth, at Broadview, 416-463-3086.
Once through this New York-style saloon complete with a Wurlitzer jukebox programmed with really golden oldies, find this celebrated fenced-in hideaway. Waiters in white aprons serve credible burgers from the tree-lined terrace's barbecue while regulars guzzle a large cross-section of microbrews, an all QVA Canadian wine list — many available by the glass — and over 200 single-malt scotches. Bonus: check out the winner of NOW's Readers Poll category Best Tree six years running!

patios, few offer more than souvlaki served up with a side order of car exhaust. One of the rare exceptions is this Italian pizza chain's east-side outlet located in a stylish art deco storefront that once housed a gun shop. Here, a good-looking crowd wolf down thin-crusted pies topped with the likes of warm prosciutto, mascarpone and honeyed figs.

OUZERI
500A Danforth, at Logan, 416-778-0500, www.ouzeri.com.
The stylish front patio of this urban Greek chic spot offers an ideal people-watching venue right on the Danforth strip.

ONLY CAFÉ
972 Danforth, at Donlands, 416-463-7843, www.theonlycafe.com.
You and three friends can slug back any of close to 100 brews on the tiny front patio of this Danforth local, where regulars have perfected the art of maintaining the all-day buzz.

SARAH'S CAFÉ
1426 Danforth, at Monarch Park, 416-406-3121.
Part Celtic pub, part Greek taverna, Sarah's stocks a large range of Belgian, German and UK marques and has more than a dozen Euro-brews on tap.

Leslieville

VERVEINE
1097 Queen E, at Pape, 416-405-9906.
The stretch of Queen east of the DVP is quickly becoming a nabe of retro furniture shops, hipster bars and fashionable restaurants in unmarked storefronts. But other than the small fenced-in garden draped with boxwood and climbing clematis at the rear of this busy bistro, few have patios worth visiting.

Little India

LAHORE TIKKA HOUSE
1365 Gerrard E, at Highfield, 416-406-1668.
This inexpensive Indo-Pakistani resto/take-away has always been the east side's busiest summer patio scene, but now that its two-year renovation is nearly complete, House is destined to become even more hectic. Under billowing tents made from sari silk, more than 400 diners feast al fresco on a fiery card of tandoor-baked entrees while sipping plastic tumblers of frothy sugar cane juice at family-style picnic tables lit by twinkling Christmas lights. Bonus: horse 'n' carriage rides up and down Gerrard every Friday, Saturday and Sunday. *Unlicensed.*

AULD SPOT
347 Danforth, at Hampton, 416-406-4688, www.auldspot.ca.
Guinness flows from the taps as regulars fill the small room with animated chatter. Despite the pub's decor, the grub's surprisingly pan-global. Bonus: oyster-shucking every other Monday night.

COCO BANANA
1690 Danforth, at Coxwell, 416-406-0534, www.cocobananato.com.
This funky east-side Caribbean roti shop might look like something straight out of Shaft, with its luridly hued fuzzy 70s sofas and potted palms, but its secluded garden grotto out back — though still painted in seriously psychedelic colours — is one of the avenue's most serene spaces. Overstuffed couches, pots of geraniums and the chef's own special herb garden, too. *Closed Sunday and Monday.*

IL FORNELLO
576 Danforth, at Carlaw, 416-466-2931.
Although the Danforth is clogged with curbside

West

Bloor West

CIRO'S HOUSE OF IMPORTED BIER
1316 Bloor W, at Lansdowne, 416-533-4914.
As its name suggests, this west-side pub is home to more than 100 different imported suds, with a strong emphasis on Belgian marques. Out back, find a heated deck shaded by an overhanging canopy of trees where regulars devour better-than-average pub grub in between shots of absinthe and $3.75 tax-inclusive domestic lager chasers.

YELLOW GRIFFIN
2202 Bloor W, at Runnymede, 416-763-3365.
Typical of Swansea, that affluent semi-retired burg that runs west from High Park to Bloor West Village, the Grif is a small Guinness-slinging pub with a six-table curbside veranda where the biggest attractions are Thursday's poker night and Friday's 80s disco.

Dundas West & Ossington

IF LOUNGE
1212 Dundas W, at Lakeview, 416-588-4900.
On leafy Lakeview Avenue Parkette and directly across from the Beer Store and KFC, this Little Portugal lounge has a distinctly split personality. By day it's home to Coffee Shop, a remarkably assured lunch 'n' brunch spot. Then, after dark, it morphs into If, a swanky (considering the nabe) cocktail joint. Check out the new Mediterranean late-night lineup.

JULIE'S
202 Dovercourt, at Argyle, 416-532-7397, www.juliescuban.com.
For a decade now, Jesus's and Sylvia's relaxed Cuban grotto on a west-side residential street has been everybody's secret rendezvous. Sure, the people-watching amounts to occasional neighbours strolling past on their way to the laundromat, but the romantic resto's seductive ambience, all whispering trees overhead and the sparkle of candle-light on wine glasses, is a scene all its own. Add a pre-Castro Havana tapas card – grilled and then pressed marinated pork, ham and Swiss cheese sandwiches with sweet pickle, fried mashed potato Papa Rellena stuffed with spicy ground beef and green olives, powerful pork Picadillo de Marnita hash with jalapeños and raisins on saffron-scented rice – and understand why reservations are essential. *Closed Monday.*

Roncesvalles

FAT CAT TAPAS
331 Roncesvalles, at Westminster, 416-535-4064.
Formerly the short-lived Idoru and now an offshoot of chef Matthew Sutherland's Eglinton eatery, this sleek supper club has one of the loveliest patios on the avenue. Hidden from prying eyes, its chic walled-in courtyard is the perfect spot to nibble abbreviated takes on surf 'n' turf while sipping low-mark-up consignment wines by the glass.

FRESHWOOD GRILL
293 Roncesvalles, at Westminster, 416-537-1882, www.freshwoodgrill.com.
Once the greasiest of spoons, this overhauled west-side diner appeals to both daytime moms with stroller-bound toddlers and late-night hipsters who linger over all-day breakfasts on the sizable shady backyard deck. Bonus: nearly everything on the luncheonette's lineup is made on the premises and additive-free. ⏱

VICKY'S FISH & CHIPS/SUE'S THAI FOOD
414 Roncesvalles, at Howard Park, 416-531-8822.
No other resto in town has such a disparate card at war with itself – so-so fish and chips versus terrific Southeast Asian eats. The difference between this grungy diner and its downright luxurious backyard deck is just as jarring. Who knew this lovely oasis of calm lurked behind its fading facade? Bonus: still one of the most inexpensive good Thai spots in town. *Unlicensed. Cash only.*

St. Clair West

RUSHTON
740 St. Clair W, at Rushton, 416-658-7874.
Since it opened last winter, this boisterous bistro sibling to the equally raucous Ferro has been north Toronto's hottest cantina, the uptown Drake, as it were. With the launch of the just-completed patio that doubles its capacity, you now have twice the chance to snag a table. Bonus: now serving lunch and weekend brunch.

West Queen West

BEAVER CAFÉ
1192 Queen W, at Dufferin, 416-537-2768.
Situated between the Drake and the Gladstone, this funky luncheonette couldn't be any more laid-back if it tried. Though its sheltered backyard terrace attracts few slumming celebs, its reasonably priced comfort-food card.

CADILLAC LOUNGE
1296 Queen W, at Grove, 416-536-7717, www.cadillaclounge.com.
Behind this storefront marquee of a slightly obvious sawn-in-half Cadillac, Parkdale's leopard-printed self-described "home of roots, rock and country music" is also home to the biggest backyard hideaway in the area. Partially covered and now twice as large as when it first opened, this grungy grotto is a favourite with local music buffs, who stop by to knock back five bottles of Amsterdam Blonde for 18 bucks while chowing down on 35-cent chicken wings on Mondays. ⏱

NOT MY DOG
1510 Queen W, at Fuller, 416-532-2397, www.notmydog.ca.
In the short time that it's been open, this modest neighbourhood watering hole has become Parkdale's boho central. Watch it become even more so once word of its heated, semi-covered backyard grotto hits the blogs. There, trucker-hatted denizens catch vintage B-movies on Tuesdays, gargle $4.50 cocktails Wednesdays and take in comedians performing stand-up while perched on a wooden crate once a month. *Closed Monday.*

RED TEA BOX
696 Queen W, at Euclid, 416-203-8882.
This luxe bake shop with a tiny rear terrace and coach house was featured in French fashion magazine spreads long before it even opened its doors. Kick back and relax under a picture-perfect pear tree while supping on sensational pan-Asian bento boxes and spectacular Pacific Rim sandwich 'n' salad combinations. Breathtaking desserts, as well as pricey cups of estate teas help make Red Tea Box downtown's ultimate al fresco dining experience. Warning: they don't take reservations, so if you manage to snag one of the three or so mismatched country-chic tables in the coach house, consider yourselves very lucky indeed. *Unlicensed.*

SKY YARD @ DRAKE HOTEL
1150 Queen W, at Beaconsfield, 416-531-0429.
Since it launched two seasons back, the hipster haunt's Sky Yard rooftop deck has proven so popular you expect a wristband policy to be in effect to gain exclusive entry. The attraction? A breezy island-style hideout complete with overstuffed day beds, a contemporary lineup of pan-global grub served at communal tables and Bob Marley in permanent rotation on the sound system. Lineup too long? Check out the less frenzied wraparound curbside patio off Beaconsfield for weekend brunch.

TERRONI
720 Queen W, at Claremont, 416-504-0320, www.terroni.ca.
Now that the city's favourite nu-skool pizzeria has doubled in size since it annexed the storefront next door, its neoclassical backyard grotto has grown as well. One thing that has been left unchanged: the minimally appointed but beautifully rendered thin-crust pies topped with garden-fresh basil, spicy Calabrese sausage and grilled red peppers. Side your slice with a summer Mediterranean-style salad and Italian cold cut panini. Now, that's Italian! *Closed Sunday.*

entertainment

music

Sure, we're homebase for Canadian Idol and MuchMoreMusic. But there's a helluva lot more to Toronto's music scene than pop-diva wannabes and cranky old folkies. From underground hiphop and basement punk to roots reggae and alt rock – oh yeah, and opera and jazz, too! – we've got what you're listening for.
For the latest music listings and features, pick up NOW Magazine or visit www.nowtoronto.com.

DUSTIN RABIN

k-os reigns over Toronto's hiphop parade.

Montreal may have dominated recent pop music media hype, but when it comes to sheer volume, activity, international credibility and, most importantly, quality, Toronto's served as Canada's de facto music capital for over half a century.

Not convinced? Back in the 60s, when American psych fiends were freeing their minds in Haight-Ashbury, Toronto nurtured its own paisley-spattered hippie enclave in current chi-chi shopping destination **Yorkville** (see **Sightseeing**, page 25). The narrow townhomes near Bay and Bloor that today hold upscale boutiques served as head shops and incense-clouded coffee houses like the Riverboat, the Mynah Bird, the Mouse Hole and the Purple Onion, where scruffy upstarts Neil Young (fresh from Winnipeg), Joni Mitchell and Gordon Lightfoot got their start strumming prettily indignant folk songs.

The Beatles quickly clued into the city as a crucial Canuck pop hot spot. Besides holding a mega press conference here in August 1965, they tantalized T.O. teenyboppers on all three North American tours, playing shows at former hockey arena **Maple Leaf Gardens** (see **Sightseeing**, page 26). And on September 13, 1969, as the Fab Four were falling apart, John Lennon played his first ever gig with the Plastic Ono Band as part of the Toronto Rock 'N' Roll Revival Festival at the now-demol-

ished **Varsity Stadium** (Bloor and Bedford), the same concert during which shock rock pioneer Alice Cooper bit the head off a live chicken. A fresh-faced Eric Clapton helped out on lead guitar, as captured on the Plastic Ono Band's only official album, on which they sang Give Peace a Chance with the crowd of 15,000 providing backup.

Not to be outdone, Beatles nemeses Mick and Keef showed their love for the T-dot by recording a seminal live album – The Rolling Stones: Love You Live – at grotty rock hot spot the **El Mocambo** (College and Spadina, see page 140) in 1977, laying the groundwork for Brit nerd-king Elvis Costello to follow suit a decade and a half later. The Stones still warm up for every world tour by rehearsing in T.O. for months followed by a "secret" club gig guaranteed before they leave town.

In the 80s, downtown strip **Queen West** was ground zero for crusty punks and new wave freaks – rock scenesters like Martha & the Muffins and the Dishes drank pints at the late, lamented Beverley Tavern (now a swank restaurant) at Queen and Beverley, and dyke pioneer Carole Pope romanced blue-eyed soul siren Dusty Springfield while they holed up in a **Cabbagetown** pad – when Pope wasn't busy breaking queercore ground with her subversive band

More recently, Toronto the Good experienced an indie renaissance in the early 90s, when college rock stalwarts like Lowest of the Low, Treble Charger, the Pursuit of Happiness, By Divine Right, rock god Ian Blurton's Change of Heart and Weeping Tile (which helped introduce rootsy sweetheart Sarah Harmer) scored hits on then-edgy alt-rock radio outlet 102.1.

Today the city's literally overflowing with internationally acclaimed artists of all stripes, from Cuban jazz innovator Jane Bunnett to alt-country mainstay Blue Rodeo to indie rock's pre-eminent dysfunctional family Broken Social Scene to alt-rock angsties Billy Talent to rock-meets-hiphop heavy k-os to His Royal Purpleness, Prince, who happily shelled out millions for a mansion on the chi-chi Bridle Path in north Toronto. (He sometimes drinks and even jams at **Panorama**, the lounge on the top floor of the Manulife Centre.) Dude, when Prince gives the thumbs-up to a city, you know there's got to be something going on.

Weekly Attractions

The beauty of Toronto's diverse music community is that, on any given day of the week, you're bound to find at least one kickass music event that won't set you back much (if any) cash. From offbeat noise to homespun bluegrass, here's a sampling of some of the city's most-reliable weekly destinations. Check **NOW Magazine**, available free every Thursday or **www.nowtoronto.com** for up-to-the-minute live music listings.

WAVELENGTH
Sunday nights at Sneaky Dee's, 431 College Street, 416-603-3090, pwyc, www.wavelengthtoronto.com.
For all the petty griping about cliquey scenesters in this city, this amazing uber-indie Sunday night concert series-slash-rock throwdown officially counts as a Toronto institution. Sure, you might feel a little weird at first cuz all the shoulder-bag-and-leg-warmer regulars know each other, but there's no better place on Sunday nights than the grotty Sneaky Dee's (cheap beer and nachos!) to see art school fashions, cool zine-ish art and some of the most-interesting under-the-radar bands that come through the city, from experimental noise to haligonian hiphop. Or you might catch tuneless collage-rock performed entirely on dollar-store instruments, ferocious drum-pounding math-rock, whimsical harmony-drenched orch-pop or nouveau klezmer – the lineup depends on the volunteer organizers' twisted minds. Awesome T.O. bands like Broken Social Scene, Do Make Say Think, the Constantines and Republic of Safety are past Wavelength alums, so you might even see the next local candidates for international superstardom.

ELVIS MONDAYS
Mondays at the Drake Hotel, 1150 Queen West, 416-531-5042, no cover.
Started by Groovy Religion dude William New back in 1981 to help struggling bands like his own find a regular place to play, this free showcase for indie artists now at the super-swank Drake Hotel attracts something other than the hipster hang's usual 905-skewed tan-and-blond pod people who come to see folks like Ron Sexsmith and By Divine Right. While the slate of arty oddballs and up-and-comers can be hit-or-miss, it's rarely less than interesting. Check out their reduced-rate grub at the the Starving Artist Buffet while catching the latest upstart indie bands in town.

NU MUSIC TUESDAYS
Tuesdays at the Horseshoe, 370 Queen West, 416-598-4753, no cover.
Radio personality and local stalwart Dave "Bookie" Bookman hand-picks wide-ranging indie talent for his longstanding Tuesday night showcase at the Legendary Horseshoe. It's free to get in, the bartenders are rock 'n' roll awesome, and though many of the acts are relative unknowns just passing through town, it's not unlikely to catch a more established band taking advantage of the cover-free evening to test out new material or launch a new album (as East Coast faves the Trews did a couple summers ago).

HIGH LONESOME WEDNESDAYS
Wednesdays at the Silver Dollar, 486 Spadina, 416-763-9139, no cover.
Before T-Bone Burnett and his O Brother buds made bluegrass cool again, a group of Toronto's finest fingerpickers were teaming up every week at the blues-centric Silver Dollar to deliver a stellar hootenanny that attracts an incredibly eclectic crowd. With past and present members including Dan and Jenny Whiteley (members of Canada's most respected roots dynasties), banjo bosses Chris Coole and Chris Quinn, mandolin master Andrew Collins (also of fab local countrified acts the Foggy Hogtown Boys and the Creaking Tree String Quartet) and guitar ace Mark Roy, the Dollar's Crazy Strings ensemble is a sure bet for a consistently killer Wednesday night twangfest.

CAMERON FAMILY SINGERS
Saturday evenings at Cameron House, 408 Queen West, 416-703-0811, pwyc.
If classic country's your thing, you might want to check out honky-tonk heavyweights the Cameron Family Singers, who start off Saturday nights with a 6 pm hoedown in the cozy front room of Queen West staple the Cameron House. Build up your all-night buzz with bargain beer and kick back on the cozy couches to the strains of familiar standards and timeless-sounding originals.

Bars & Clubs

THE BIG BOP
651 Queen West, 416-504-0711.
Three unique clubs are located in the Big Bop complex at the southeast corner of Queen and Bathurst. On the main floor, the ominous dungeon-like **Kathedral** frequently hosts goth, punk and metal shows. Upstairs, the 420-capacity **Reverb**, a lovely, twinkling-lighted space with a large stage in front of a good-sized dance floor, attracts bands ranging from funk-punk crew the Salads to conscious hiphop femcee Ursula Rucker. Wee **Holy Joe's** (up another small flight of stairs) is best suited to singer/song-writers trying to get their sea legs.

THE BOAT
158 Augusta, 416-593-9218.
In the heart of boho enclave Kensington Market, the Boat's decor follows a decidedly nautical theme, portholes and all, and the small floor-level stage is squeezed in between heavy round tables and captain-style chairs. In the past few years, it's been taken over by enterprising grassroots types who've succeeded in establishing it as a hotspot for weird local indie talent. Events have included the Ace of Spades-athon for charity (DJs spin Motörhead's Ace of Spades ad infinitum), regular gigs by bands from great local underground labels like the Blocks Recording Club and Permafrost, and the filming of T.O. scene star Final Fantasy's This Is The Dream Of Win & Regine video.

entertainment

BOVINE SEX CLUB
542 Queen West, 416-504-4239.
A Queen West institution and official hangout for several generations of the black leather-and-rock 'n' roll crowd, the scrap-metal-strewn decor hasn't changed much since the early days and still evokes some post-apocalyptic bar from Mad Max. You can hear live bands, and most nights DJs focus on glam, hard rock, metal and retro 80s tunes.

CADILLAC LOUNGE
1296 Queen West, 416-536-7717.
If low-key country, pub grub, patio lounging and serious drinking are your bag, this Parkdale fave is a safe bet for a good night out. Occasional comedy shows and big-screen TV hockey nights compete with local honky-tonkers (check out Scotty Campbell and the Wardenairs) and travelling icons like Wanda Jackson and Janis Martin for neighbourhood regulars' attention on the smallish stage beside the entrance. Bonus: the vegetarian Guinness pie sounds repulsive but tastes divine.

THE CAMERON HOUSE
408 Queen West, 416-703-0811.
Though its cachet has dropped since Queen West's 80s heyday, the good ol' Cameron is still a reliable spot to catch cheap performances by resident bands (the Cameron Family Singers serve up classic country on Saturday evenings, Kevin Quain concocts jazzy cabaret noir on Sundays) and promising upstarts in both the front and back rooms. The former space features cushy couches and minimal cover, the latter reveals graduated seating facing a small stage where singer/songwriters, avant-garde thespians and literary types do their thing.

CHICAGO'S DINER
335 Queen West, 416-977-2904.
This basic hole-in-the-wall jazz and blues club features bar circuit-quality live acts who happily improvise while drop-ins indulge in a long menu that sneaks surprises like escargot and plate-filling steaks in amongst the expected jalapeño poppers and onion rings. Not necessarily notable as the place to catch rising stars, but a good compromise for decent live music, no attitude and substantial grub.

EL MOCAMBO
464 Spadina, 416-777-1777.
A vital part of Toronto's music history, the once-grungy El Mo used to be a sticky-floored dive bar where the likes of the Rolling Stones and Elvis Costello recorded live albums back in the day. Today, it's under new ownership and boasts a posh Moroccan-themed interior, but the neon palm tree out front and two floors of rock-, rap-, pop- and metal-ready stages remain. Downstairs, where Howe Gelb, Polysics, Martha Wainwright, Ben Lee and Har Mar Superstar have played, there's space for 250 eager concertgoers. Great for seeing bands on the verge and awesome local hiphop.

GROSSMAN'S TAVERN
379 Spadina, 416-977-7000.
This WWII-era grotty blues joint sits inconspicuously alongside the dim sum spots and plastic-tablecloth seafood restaurants of Chinatown. Some regulars have taken in the loud-and-dirty blues and N'Awlins jazz at Grossman's pretty much since the club opened in 1949, though it's just as likely you'll end up sitting beside a pack of anarchists or arts students from nearby U of T who've dropped by for cheap pints.

HEALEY'S
178 Bathurst, 416-703-5882.
A pet project of Juno-winning Canadian blues guitar star Jeff Healey – the sightless ace known for his role in Patrick Swayze's Roadhouse often shows up for regular Saturday guitar jams – this downstairs rec-room-style venue tends toward the bluesier end of the spectrum, though rock and pop acts perform here on occasion. A bit cramped, with obstructed sightlines, but there's a nice cozy vibe that makes you feel like you're watching classic rock obsessives from high school jamming in their mom's basement.

HUGH'S ROOM
2261 Dundas West, 416-531-6604.
Those who've graduated from Molson Canadian to Chardonnay and are in search of a more "civilized" musical experience will delight in the dinner-theatre-meets-folk-club atmosphere here. Perched on the edge of High Park, the tastefully decorated, sit-down-table-appointed spot books high-profile folkies like the McGarrigle Sisters and Murray McLauchlan, country ball-busters like Mary Gauthier and Gurf Morlix, globally conscious acts like Jason Wilson & Tabarruk and mature pop purveyors like Jane Siberry. The sophisticated concert destination is the realization of the dream of late folk fan Hugh Carson, who'd likely be proud of the solid roster and delectable dishes.

Blues and cheap beer at the **Silver Dollar**. Page 143.

486 SPADINA AVE.

KOOL HAUS/THE GUVERNMENT
132 Queens Quay East, 416-869-0045.
Back in the day, the faux-Germanic Kool Haus was known as the Warehouse – a totally apt name for the then-cavernous, stark space frequented by suburban ravers and alt-rock fans (and where the Stones and Prince have played). These days, a total redesign has spruced up the 27,000-square-foot joint, which now resembles a silver and black-light bunker and hosts major rock, pop and hiphop shows (Yeah Yeah Yeahs, the Roots). The attached Guvernment has also been given a cartoonish nightclub makeover. Though best known as a venue for international superstar DJs and weekly club nights, the space is also one of the few in town equipped to accommodate all-ages shows, which attracts bands like Le Tigre and Scissor Sisters to its stage.

LEE'S PALACE/THE DANCE CAVE
529 Bloor West, 416-532-1598.
A perennial favourite for catching the trendiest, hottest shows, Lee's has undergone a number of improvements in recent years that make the joint a failsafe destination for superlative rock 'n' roll action. A raised stage (sightlines in pretty much any part of the downstairs 600-capacity room are great), high benches along one wall and a relocated bar mean that the erstwhile movie theatre provides an even better show-going experience than when Kurt Cobain smashed beer bottles during Nirvana's inaugural swing through T.O. Bands like the Go! Team have shot DVDs in the joint, and Neko Case recorded parts of her excellent The Tigers Have Spoken live disc here. Upstairs in the Fiona Smyth-decorated Dance Cave (black-light murals!), you can get your drink 'n' dance on with up to 250 sloshed students from nearby U of T while DJs crank retro hits and nouveau wave bangers.

THE LEGENDARY HORSESHOE TAVERN
370 Queen West, 416-598-4753.
Yet another venue synonymous with Toronto's music scene, the 'Shoe comes by its legendary title honestly, with over half a century under its belt. Franz Ferdinand played here before they blew up, No Depression icons like Wilco, Son Volt and Uncle Tupelo found it a home away from home, and the Rolling Stones (yep, them again) blew the roof off by beginning 1997's No Security tour here. The oddly shaped back room inadvertently lends itself to good sightlines, and the sound is great (if a bit bass-heavy). Shows range from killer alt-country and roots to vicious rock and twee pop. It's a testament to the Horseshoe's cred that a real-life rockabilly icon, the Royal Crowns' pint-sized Teddy Fury, serves pints behind the bar.

LULA LOUNGE
1585 Dundas West, 416-588-0307.
Filling a niche in T.O.'s all-too-often whitebread club bookings, which frequently fall on the side of straightforward rock and pop, Lula Lounge provides a locale for Latin-leaning acts, featuring salsa (bands and lessons), Latin jazz (Amanda Martinez is a fave), fado, samba and more alongside South and Central American-inspired culinary fare. Things get mixed up with occasional alternative shows (courtesy of satellite promoter Gary Topp and others), ranging from the Sun Ra Arkestra and Shivaree to local curiosity Friendly Rich's vaudevillian weirdness. But in general, Lula's a great bet for those whose tastes veer away from typical radio-friendly fare.

MOD CLUB THEATRE
722 College, 416-588-4663.
Originally conceived, at least in part, to house T.O.'s longstanding Brit-tastic retro Mod Club dance night, this medium-sized venue features a raised stage,

essential T.O. tracks

Oscar Peterson – Hogtown Blues (1964)
The Mynah Birds – I'll Wait Forever (1966)
Neil Young – After The Gold Rush (1970)
Joni Mitchell – Little Green (1971)
Gordon Lightfoot – Sun Down (1974)
Martha & the Muffins – Echo Beach (1980)
Rush – Spirit Of Radio (1980)
Jane Siberry – Mimi On The Beach (1983)
Parachute Club – Rise Up (1984)
Bruce Cockburn – Lovers In A Dangerous Time (1984)
Blue Rodeo – Try (1987)
Maestro Fresh Wes – Let Your Backbone Slide (1990)
Lowest of the Low – Just About "The Only" Blues (1991)
Jane Bunnett – Spirits Of Havana (1991)
Fifth Column – All Women Are Bitches (1992)
Barenaked Ladies – If I Had A Million Dollars (1992)
Snow – Informer (1993)
Treble Charger – Red (1994)
Ron Sexsmith – Secret Heart (1995)
Choclair, Kardinal Offishall, Checkmate, Thrust & Rascalz – Northern Touch (1997)
Hawksley Workman – Baby This Night (2001)
Broken Social Scene – Almost Crimes (2002)
k-os – Heaven Only Knows (2002)
Billy Talent – Try Honesty (2003)
Metric – Combat Baby (2003)
The Hidden Cameras – Ban Marriage (2003)
The Constantines – Nighttime Anytime (It's Alright) (2003)
Death from Above 1979 – Little Girl (2004)
Final Fantasy – This Is The Dream Of Win & Regine (2005)
FemBots – The City (2005)
Republic of Safety – Vacation (2006)

extended dance floor, elevated table area and generally good sound. Look beyond the Vespa and Mary Quant-ified target murals adorning the walls (unless you're up for the weekly Anglo-crazy DJ night) and focus on efficient shows by touring acts like Lady Sovereign, OK GO and Wilco. If all that music gives you the munchies, give thanks for nearby College Street businesses – from a 24-hour mega-grocer to a slew of late-night pizza spots.

NOW LOUNGE
189 Church, at Shuter, 416-364-1301.
Located on the first floor of the NOW Magazine building, in the evening this laid-back lunch space hosts a variety of live music – folk, pop and jazz mostly, with the occasional big name (INXS, Tori Amos, Sarah Harmer) stopping by – as well as regular exhibitions by local artists. The lounge is also a free wireless hot spot.

OPERA HOUSE
735 Queen East, 416-466-0313.
Back in 1997, arena rockers Radiohead previewed their groundbreaking OK Computer album to a packed house of rapt fans at this double-decker, relatively intimate club on Queen East. It may be at the opposite end of the city from the regular club drag in a once sketchy (sneak a peek at nearby strip joint Jilly's) but rapidly gentrifying area, but the good-sized venue is beautifully designed and attracts bands ranging from Sleater-Kinney and Cat Power to AFI and Dillinger Escape Plan.

NORTH BY NORTHEAST

the best new music

Sarah Harmer, Bran Van 3000, Feist, Death from Above 1979, Sufjan Stever
Black Rebel Motorcycle Club, The Constantines, Tift Merritt, Milton Mapes,
Kathleen Edwards, Sam Roberts, Ambulance Ltd., Drive-by Truckers, Sum
Mooney Suzuki, The Duke Spirit, Burning Brides, John Kastner and King Kh
all had major breakthroughs at NXNE. Who will be next

NXNE Music & Film Festival & Conference
Toronto • 7/8/9 June 2007

nxne.com

THE ORBIT ROOM
580A College Street, upstairs, 416-535-0613.
Co-founded by Rush's Alex Lifeson, this R&B-centric club is one of those spots that attracts devoted regulars but sits just under the radar (and up a flight of stairs) for the typical College Street crowd. Bands like guitarist Kevin Breit's Sisters Euclid fusion ensemble and funk crew LMT Connection hold residencies, and recent addition Stifler's Mom (made up of more youthful members of Canuck alt-rock bands) adds a Top-40 jolt.

PHOENIX CONCERT THEATRE
410 Sherbourne, 416-323-1251.
In terms of size and scope, the Phoenix is a perfect stepping-stone for bands who've outgrown Lee's Palace and the Horseshoe but aren't quite ready for stadium-sized success. Along with regular weekly DJ club nights (T.O. kids who came of age in the 90s fondly remember 102.1's Live To Air From The Phoenix broadcasts), the concert venue usually features a number of all-ages and 19-plus rock shows (past acts have included everyone from Elliott Smith to Ladytron and the Flaming Lips). An elevated back tier and a sweet balcony ensure great sightlines, and multiple bars around the club mean it's always easy to nab a drink.

RESERVOIR LOUNGE
52 Wellington East, 416-955-0887.
Well-heeled 20- and 30-somethings who work in the nearby banks and office buildings bring their dates for scotch and swing bands at this upscale spot. Though the buzz has died down along with the swing revival of the mid-to-late-90s, jazzy crooners like Tori Cassis and the slick cats in Big Rude Jake keep it hopping for stylish couples willing to shell out while they paint the town red. The babes wear bias-cut dresses; the fellas well-fitted suits — it's so money, baby!

REVIVAL
783 College, 416-535-7888.
Once upon a time, this peculiar but posh venue had ecclesiastical roots, and despite a lot of gussying up, the dinner-club-style space retains remnants of a church basement vibe. Better suited to dance parties than to live shows, Revival offers decent sound but crappy sightlines — unless you score one of the tables along the right-hand wall, you'll wind up with an aching back before the show's over. Mandatory coat check and jacked-up drink prices don't help to sweeten the deal, though good bands — everyone from violindie star Andrew Bird to neo-soul crooner Vivian Green and ex-New Kid Jordan Knight — still draw crowds.

THE REX
194 Queen West, 416-598-2475.
Founded in the 80s on the main floor of a sketchy (yet still operational) hotel, the club is all about jazz with a side of fries. Low-key, slightly grimy and completely unpretentious, the jazz joint (which features several cheap or cover-free shows every night of the week) is one of those places where you're likely to be drinking discount draft beside a crusty regular with stories to spill about the seedy side of Toronto's musical history. Lots of live jams, which attract more than a few visiting famous bebop aficionados.

THE RIVOLI
332 Queen West, 416-596-1908.
Despite its humble appearance, the back room, which can accommodate a crowd of 200, has had a special place in the hearts of Toronto music and comedy fans for almost three decades. Thanks to the **Alt.COMedy Lounge**, many a local comic started out by testing material on the Riv's Queen West crowd, and musicians like Iggy Pop, Lenny Kravitz, Sarah Slean, Sarah Harmer and the Barenaked Ladies all did turns on the cramped stage. The upside: for such an unassuming venue, the Riv is actually one of the best-sounding rooms in the city and it's air conditioned.

THE SILVER DOLLAR
486 Spadina, 416-763-9139.
Gloriously sketchy — it's located above the notorious Comfort Zone, which has hosted after-parties for the amphetamine set for years, and beside a men's shelter — the Silver Dollar is the ideal place to weep into your dirt-cheap beer while international blues grandfathers belt out the trouble they've seen. Frequent appearances by stateside stars from Mississippi to Chicago compete with the always-raucous garage rockstravaganzas booked by notorious local wacko promoter Dan Burke. Wednesday night's no-cover bluegrass hootenannies — dubbed the High Lonesome Hoedown — featuring Toronto bluegrass stars Crazy Strings are a regular, popular highlight. Besides, the crowd's eclectic and the beer's super-cheap.

Concert Venues

AIR CANADA CENTRE
40 Bay, 416-815-5500.
Better known as a sports arena (Go Leafs! Go Raptors!) than a destination for seeing live music, the sleekly designed ACC has nevertheless stolen the neighbouring Rogers Centre's fire as the indoor venue most likely to host over-the-top spectacles by visiting international pop idols. Everyone from U2 to Madonna to Coldplay has strutted their stuff on the 21,000-seater's stage, and though the tin-can acoustics can leave something to be desired, the ACC has been able to create cozier concert-going experiences by curtaining off a segment as the Sears Theatre, where the likes of Alicia Keys, Radiohead and Maxwell have crooned to a crowd of 5,200.

DANFORTH MUSIC HALL
147 Danforth, 416-978-7989.
A bat-infested old-school concert venue that hosts rock shows — Arcade Fire played three sold-out concerts here in 05 — and Hollywood movie shoots, like Chicago and 54.

GEORGE WESTON RECITAL HALL
5040 Yonge, 416-733-9388.
Though it's a bit of a schlep to access the George Weston — located in the **Toronto Centre for the Arts** — from downtown, the 1,036-seat concert hall is still a mere hop, skip and jump away from the North York Centre subway stop (Yonge-University-Spadina line). Classical ensembles from here and elsewhere are drawn to the spectacular acoustics and posh Old-World design of this recent addition to Toronto's musical culture.

GLENN GOULD STUDIO
205 Front West, 416-205-5555,
www.glenngouldstudio.cbc.ca.
Snugly tucked into a corner of the **CBC** headquarters (see **Sightseeing**, page 14) on Front Street, this lovely, sonically sophisticated concert hall named in honour of Canada's eccentric piano genius is used for both live ticketed performances — more frequently by quiet, experimental and classical groups than by amped-up rockers — and live studio recordings. The Ceeb's innovative programming and commitment to Canadian music means that it books both highbrow virtuosos of the jazz and baroque varieties and clever pop performances (one memorable show featured roots sweetheart Sarah Harmer and prairie folk-rockers the Weakerthans paying tribute to each other), and you might find your applause recorded for posterity.

HARBOURFRONT CENTRE
235 Queens Quay West, 416-973-4000,
www.harbourfrontcentre.com.
The publicly funded Harbourfront Centre (see **Sightseeing**, page 12) is a local, if not national treas-

ure. Though the complex consistently features free (or budget-conscious) cultural activities throughout the year, summertime is when your astounding musical events take off. Themed festivals – almost all free – run through pretty much every weekend. Performances include left-field electronic acts and incredible DJs (the perennially stellar **Beats, Breaks & Culture** fest) and local and international indie rock (Broken Social Scene once played to a crowd of thousands). Ethnocultural celebrations provide new perspectives on First Nations artists, new Latin culture or African diaspora talents. The beauty of Harbourfront's outdoor concert stage is that it sits directly beside the water, which means you can enjoy awesome music while soaking up Lake Ontario's balmy breeze. Of course, the round open-air theatre also has its drawbacks – along with the fact that performances by pop, folk, roots, soul and electronic groups are frequently interrupted by the echoing bellow of passing ships and the irritating putter of motors, the seats are literally a pain in the ass. Small sacrifices for a venue mostly used for seriously great free events. Harbourfront also contains a smaller stage in a grassy expanse just north of the main concert theatre, the clubby Lakeside Terrace (which often features late-night DJ events) and the indoor Brigantine Room. Seriously not to be missed.

MASSEY HALL
178 Victoria, 416-593-4822.
Established over a century ago by industrial heavy-hitter Hart Massey as an arts-centric auditorium in memory of his late son, the gorgeous, multilevel Massey Hall once hosted The Greatest Concert Ever – a one-time-only performance by bebop legends Dizzy Gillespie, Charlie Parker, Max Roach, Bud Powell and Charles Mingus in 1959. Today, it remains a positively lovely place to take in highbrow classical events, hard-bopping jazz performances and more pedestrian rock and pop shows. With stunning acoustics, divine decor (though the balcony seats have less than ideal sightlines and butt comfort), you can't beat the experience of catching a living legend like Loretta Lynn in such an intimate (2,765-seat), well-designed locale.

MOLSON AMPHITHEATRE
909 Lakeshore West, 416-260-5600.
In Toronto, the summer concert season is synonymous with two major lakeside locales: the fab free entertainment down at **Harbourfront Centre** (see above) and the outdoor lawn bowl that is the Molson Amphitheatre, which is operated by Live Nation-House of Blues. Picking up where the infamous (and now gone) rotating stage at Ontario Place left off, the Amphitheatre is a Jumbotron-equipped, sheltered clamshell with pretty rad sound that seats 9,000, with an additional fenced-off grassy knoll that can accommodate 7,000 additional lawn seats (perfect for sparking a joint during those Dave Matthews Band extenda-jams). Lilith Fair lived here back in the day and the current incarnation of alt-rock bonanza Edgefest sets up here as well. In typical corporate style, everything at the Amphitheatre is expensive enough to require a second mortgage on your house, but it's still an iconic mega-concert landing spot where you can build up a store of nostalgic lighter-hoisting memories.

ROGERS CENTRE
1 Blue Jays Way, 416-341-3663.
When the erstwhile SkyDome first opened its doors in June 1989, the novelty of the stadium's retractable roof drew flocks of folks who weren't even baseball fans (it's the Blue Jays' home when they're in town). Almost two decades later, the geeky-cool factor's worn off, though the outdoor-indoor factor is still a neat trick, and the venue still

Funk-soulster **King Khan** at NXNE.

SVEN FRENZEL – www.zttstills.com

seats twice as many people for massive rock shows than its younger, prettier cousin down the road (up to 55,000 versus the Air Canada Centre's 21,000). Like the ACC, the Rogers Centre is able to mimic both a 5,000-seat "intimate theatre" and a pseudo-concert hall that seats twice that amount of people. The centre itself may be more suited to WWE-style exploitainment events and larger-scale initiatives like the Canadian Aboriginal Festival, but if you like your music big and loud and your beer in plastic cups, it'll suffice.

ROY THOMSON HALL
51 Simcoe, www.roythomson.com.
When the industrial-feeling muffin of Roy Thomson Hall opened its doors in 1982, it held the promise of impeccable acoustics and space-age chic design in contrast to Massey Hall's vintage charm. The anticipated high-quality sound makes it easy to understand why the Toronto Symphony Orchestra selected it as its home base, and why the nearly 3,000-seat theatre is a destination of choice for catching larger classical ensembles. Happily, recent renovations have improved the aesthetics, sound and overall vibe of the venue (it's less of a Kubrickian fantasy, more of a classy night-out-at-the-theatre), and visiting pop, roots and blues acts who cater to a larger, more sophisticated crowd often perform there as well.

Events & Festivals

CANADIAN MUSIC WEEK
www.cmw.net.
Canadian Music Week is an off shoot of a radio based industry conference. Held in March, the three-day event focuses on the business side of making music, with a conference that addresses everything from new developments in recording technology to the future of radio to how major labels can use online blogs to their advantage.

CELEBRATE TORONTO
www.toronto.ca/special_events/streetfest/index.htm.
Designed as an annual tourist destination, the Celebrate Toronto streetfest takes the novelty of main north-south drag Yonge Street and slaps a mind-boggling amount of Canadian talent at a num-

things jazz, the Downtown Jazz Fest has been celebrating local ensembles and bringing legends to town for over two decades. In addition to free public events, many of which take place in open-air venues like parks and centrally located **Nathan Phillips Square** (see Sightseeing, page 20), Downtown Jazz puts on tons of ticketed shows by artists ranging from hiphop (De La Soul) to soul (Amp Fiddler) to pure jazz heroes (Pharoah Sanders). It may make you ask the question "What is jazz?" but the performances are definitely worth it. Look for Downtown Jazz in late June and early July.

WINTERFOLK
www.winterfolk.com.
Touching down at a half-dozen clubs in downtown Toronto in the gruesome days of early February, Winterfolk serves as a lower-key, cold-weather counterpart to the cherished folk-fest circuit that provides strummers with a clear-cut tour path every summer. Founded in 2002, Winterfolk has a homey community-centric vibe (most attendees and musicians tend to know each other from the city's open mic and coffee house scene) and attracts the likes of Jenny Whiteley and Josh White Jr. among its 100-plus roots, folk and blues-oriented artists.

Going Classical
Though Toronto's rep on the international pop/rock stage has recently started to overshadow the city's accomplishments in more traditional – i.e. highbrow – arenas, we more than hold our own in the realm of classical and opera performances.

CANADIAN OPERA COMPANY
416-363-8231, www.coc.ca.
With the opening of the much-discussed **Four Seasons Centre for the Performing Arts** (145 Queen West, 416-363-6671, www.fourseasonscentre.ca, see Sightseeing, page 23) in 2006, Toronto's heralded Canadian Opera Company finally has a proper home to call its own. The country's most prestigious organization for creating and producing opera performances, the COC has started catering to more unconventional audiences. Folks who might not be inclined to dress up in monkey suits and ball gowns and shell out hundreds of bucks for a night at the opera are drawn to free and cheap open-air performances at **Harbourfront Centre** (235 Queens Quay West, 416-973-4000, www.harbourfrontcentre.com), while film and lit geeks unfamiliar with Wagner or Puccini might be chuffed about the COC's choice of unorthodox directors (filmmaker Atom Egoyan), and their production of new, somewhat more populist works, like Margaret Atwood's The Handmaid's Tale: The Opera!

TAPESTRY NEW OPERA WORKS
55 Mill, Distillery District, 416-537-6066.
A leading company dedicated solely to the development and production of original works of Canadian opera and music theatre.

TORONTO SYMPHONY ORCHESTRA
416-598-3375, www.tso.on.ca.
Another high-profile (and internationally recognized) favourite among Toronto's various performing arts groups, the TSO calls the acoustically endowed **Roy Thomson Hall** (60 Simcoe, 416-872-4255, www.roythomson.com) home. While it's true that, like most North American philharmonic ensembles, the TSO is currently struggling with the age-old battle between pleasing loyal (older) patrons and attempting to attract new, young audiences, public funding and a steady stream of star-calibre special guests – from Canadian soprano Measha Brueggergosman and Yo-Yo Ma to Yehudi Menuhin

ber of major intersections. Taking place over a weekend in early July, all performances are free (and run throughout the day), and local vendors often take advantage of the higher pedestrian traffic to set up dirt-cheap sidewalk sales and outdoor food kiosks. Stages are programmed by theme, with an eye to representing neighbourhood demographics, so you get rising indie rock and pop acts busting out guitar riffs at teen- and young-adult-friendly Yonge and Eglinton (a.k.a. Young and Eligible) and gentle jazz and blues at Yonge and St. Clair, generally populated by boomers and their blue-haired parents.

NORTH BY NORTHEAST (NXNE)
416-863-6963, www.nxne.com.
One of your best bets to catch tons of killer indie rising stars waiting to be discovered, Canada's best new music festival quite literally takes over the downtown core in early June. Inspired by and partnered with Austin's revered South By Southwest club crawl when it began in 1994, NXNE has evolved into three gloriously sweaty, drunken days of showcases by underground artists from North America and beyond in over 30 different clubs, plus high-profile bonus events by the likes of Television, the Dears and the MC5, a music-centric film fest and a conference that caters to both suits and bands trying to get a break.

TORONTO BEACHES INTERNATIONAL JAZZ FESTIVAL
www.beachesjazz.com.
A Toronto institution for almost as long as the higher-profile **Downtown Jazz** extravaganza, the Beaches Jazz fest is a totally free outdoor event that dominates the slightly crunchy but still classy Beach southeast neighbourhood for more than a week each July. Geared toward supporting the local community, Beaches Jazz features Toronto talents spanning the spectrum from Cuban innovators to classic swing on formal stages (the **Kew Gardens** mainstage is always a great bet; see **Sightseeing**, page 33) and a number of more casual streetside set-ups along Queen East.

TORONTO DOWNTOWN JAZZ FEST
www.tojazz.com.
Toronto's most prestigious multi-day event for all

and Ben Heppner – have upped the ante. With repertoires ranging from breezy Gershwin standards to sophisticated Stravinsky works, the TSO's also started livening things up with pre-show talks that allow even the most non-musical Philistine to gain an understanding of the many nuances of classical music.

TAFELMUSIK BAROQUE ORCHESTRA & CHAMBER CHOIR
416-964-6337, www.tafelmusik.org.
Putting a surprisingly sassy spin on dusty old baroque music, Tafelmusik is based in cozy **Trinity-St. Paul's Centre** (427 Bloor West), in an Annex church well-known for its beautifully warm acoustics and that often hosts pop and rock shows by more laid-back performers. Tafelmusik has drawn many fans for its usually sold-out annual singalong Messiah shows in the winter holiday season. Specializing in period instruments and compositions, it's won a number of Juno Awards (two apiece in 2005 and 2006) and received tons of acclaim here and abroad. Recently, the choir-orchestra combo started their new Face The Musik initiative, a discount subscription series, in the hopes of attracting 18- to 30-year-old music fans.

MUSIC GALLERY
416-204-1080, www.musicgallery.org.
If new music is more your bag, make sure to check out what's going on at the Music Gallery, the city's go-to destination for experimental and unusual works. The not-for-profit organization has been around since 1976, when it was founded by members of Toronto musical innovators CCMC including acclaimed visual artist Michael Snow of Eaton Centre geese fame. After weathering a number of geographical moves (it's been based everywhere from a YMCA basement to a multi-purpose space in what's now the club district), it has happily settled in the cathedral at **St. George the Martyr Church** (197 John, north of Queen). Performances range from free-jazz improv freak-outs to contemporary off-beat indie folk and avant-pop outfits, attracting an extremely diverse spectrum of music aficionados.

NATHANIEL DETT CHORALE
416-340-7000, www.nathanieldettchorale.org.
This nearly decade-old pro choral group founded by African-Canadian artistic director and conductor Brainerd Blyden-Taylor focuses on Afro-centric music ranging from gospel to jazz to blues. The Chorale is dedicated to educating the public about and raising the profile of composers of African descent, and follows a stereotype-smashing mandate that's made them a perfect choice to perform at events honouring the likes of Nelson Mandela, Desmond Tutu and Muhammad Ali.

THE ROYAL CONSERVATORY OF MUSIC
416-408-2824, www.rcmusic.ca.
Skedded to settle into its new digs in the swank new **TELUS Centre for Performance & Learning** (273 Bloor West), which has been designed by famed Canuck architects Kuwabara Payne McKenna, in 2007, the RCM is noted for teaching wee prodigies how to saw away on their quarter-sized violins. It hosts classical recitals and performances of music from global cultures.

TORONTO MENDELSSOHN CHOIR
416-598-0422, www.tmchoir.org.
Tafelmusik's main competitor for the snowy season's singalong Messiah dollar, the TMC has developed a strong reputation for being one of the city's finest

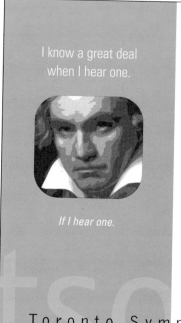

dance clubs

From jungle to Euro to techno to trance, Toronto's club scene dances to the beat of many drums. So ditch the iPod and let the city's top selectors be your guide.

For dance club listings and features, pick up NOW Magazine weekly or visit www.nowtoronto.com.

Toronto has an extraordinarily diverse and healthy dance music scene. No matter what your preferred beat, you can find some local club playing it. In recent years, though, many of the dark dens of debauchery have gone the upscale VIP booth-and-bottle-service route, and many of the old standbys have undergone name changes and makeovers to keep au courant.

As a result, the hipper underground events have gone back to the warehouses, lofts and art galleries from which the scene first gyrated. Your best bets for tracking down these kinds of off-the-radar parties is to open **NOW Magazine**'s Vibes section for up-to-date listings, check **www.nowtoronto.com**, or look for the flyers plastered on every lamppost and bare wall in the downtown or ask around.

The vast majority of Toronto's dance clubs are crammed into the area bounded by King, Queen, University and Bathurst. Most of these joints favour top-40 and mainstream dance and tend to attract a more suburban than urban crowd.

Due to the sheer density of nightlife, you're bound to find something going on any night of the week, but don't expect anything particularly cutting-edge. Check out **Republik** (261 Richmond West, 416-598-1632) or **Level** (102 Peter, 416-599-2224) if you're looking for some big shiny club fun.

For more club listings, see **Queer**, page 220.

Little Italy

All along College from Spadina to Ossington, you'll find dozens of lounges and restaurants, many featuring DJs after dinner, and at some spots live entertainment. Not the best nabe to find a bumping dance floor, but it's a popular area to tart out the night. **Paaeez** (569 College, 416-537-0767) is a cute hookah bar and lounge that sometimes sees some ass-shaking on busier nights, or check out the **Octopus Lounge** (293 Palmerston, 416-929-7214) for a slightly more clubby atmosphere.

Queen West

Over the past couple of decades, the cool section of Queen has crawled westward. The ongoing gentrification has pushed out the artists who used to take advantage of cheap rents in favour of condos targeting those who'd like to purchase a stake in cool. But there are still lots of interesting things going on regularly in the neighbourhood.

Closer to Bathurst you'll find a few alt-rock and goth venues. For goth, try the **Savage Garden** (550 Queen West, 416-504-2178), while rock fans will want to visit the **Bovine Sex Club** (542 Queen West, 416-504-4239). Stroll past Ossington and you'll find numerous art galleries and a handful of bars, with a curious balance between upscale lounges like the **Drake Hotel** (1150 Queen West, 416-531-5042) and down-market oddities like the Rolling Stones-themed bar **Stones Place** (1255 Queen West, 416-536-4242).

Church Street

Church Street south of Bloor has long been home to Toronto's gay community, and features plenty of watering holes. In recent years the number of nightclubs has shrunk, partly the result of younger queers taking more interest in – and feeling more comfortable at – mixed events outside of the Village. While neither **5ive** (5 St. Joseph, 416-964-8685) nor **Fly** (8 Gloucester, 416-410-5426) are on Church, they're two of the bigger gay clubs in the area, with plenty of go-go boys and girls to keep the joint jumping.

Clubs

CIRCA
126 John.
Nightclub impresario Peter Gatien – best known for The Limelight in NYC – has taken over the 53,000-sq-ft space formerly called Lucid, turning it into a live music and DJ space that mixes art, film, fashion and a high-tech interactive design. And if there weren't already enough drinks the colour of piss – a washroom bar.

DANCE CAVE
529 Bloor West, 416-532-1598.
This second-floor space above venerable rock club Lee's Palace in the Annex is a university friendly alternative dance club with plenty of retro, soul, garage and alt-rock on the playlist.

THE GUVERNMENT
132 Queens Quay East, 416-869-0045.
If you're looking for the sensory overload of a big mega-club, you're looking for the Guvernment, winner of NOW Magazine's best big club. It's easy to get lost in the sea of sweaty bodies in this maze of clubs-within-a-club, which also provides a variety of moods and music. The sound is great, the light show crazy, the crowds are huge, the guest DJs superstars and the overall production values higher than everywhere else. Granted, being the biggest means you'll never be the coolest. You don't go to the Guvernment looking for the underground, but to get lost among thousands of people and for complete sensory overload.

FOOTWORK
425 Adelaide West, 416-913-3488.
A relative newcomer to the scene, Footwork has already built a strong identity as an intimate boutique club focusing mainly on house and techno. It feels like a scaled-down big club but with more cutting-edge music and a more down-to-earth atmosphere. Good place to see your favourite underground artists playing to a receptive crowd.

Euro DJ **Steve Bug** spins at a local club.

spin that wheel

Whatever your favourite rhythm, someone in Toronto is throwing a party catering to it. Of course, like everything else in dance music, the scene changes at an extraordinary pace. But there are a handful of promoters in Toronto who have been around long enough that you can always count on them to have something exciting up their sleeves.

If you're digging that electro-house and indie-rock crossover vibe, **AD/D** (www.addevents.com) has emerged as the central player in town, presenting all the big international names, like Tiga, LCD Soundsystem, and Mylo, alongside such up-and-coming local acts as MSTRKRFT and Kids On TV.

On the urban side, your hiphop and R&B needs are usually taken care of by **REMG** (www.ramosent.com), who have hosted events all around the city since 1993, concentrating mainly on the conscious and soulful side of the genre (think De La Soul, the Roots, Common). If you're not into underground hiphop, there's easily dozens of clubs in the downtown core that cater to the bling-and-rims set.

For your tech-house thump, **Fukhouse** (www.fukhouse.ca) is easily the frontrunner, throwing dirty late night parties with a good mix of cutting-edge electronic artists and crowd-pleasing DJs, like Matthew Dear, Steve Bug and Akufen.

Soulful house, broken beat, rare groove, and organic left-field beats are mainly handled these days by **Milk** (www.milkaudio.com) and **Hot Stepper** (www.hotstepper.com), who both have long histories bringing in top-notch talent, including Joe Claussell, Little Louie Vega and Dimitri From Paris, and who occasionally collaborate on events.

On the drum 'n' bass side, **Theory** has been holding things down for some time. Most of their events are affiliated with the **Government Nightclub** (www.theguvernment.com, see Clubs, page 147), but they also host events in other clubs and venues around town. Past guest DJs have included Roni Size, Kenny Ken, and Goldie.

SONIC
270 Spadina, 416-599-5550.
A former theatre, this space is now onto its second incarnation as a nightclub. NYC house legend David Morales has put his name and money behind the venture, which gives you some idea of what to expect musically. There's no liquor license, meaning no booze, so it doesn't tend to get busy until the bars close. But it should still be bumping late into Sunday morning most weeks. The crowd is mixed, with a strong gay presence.

COMFORT ZONE
480 Spadina, 416-975-0909.
For truly hardcore partiers, the Comfort Zone puts on a long-running Sunday party that will shock even the most jaded. The doors open at sunrise – you read that right, sunrise – and the party keeps going until late at night. Some patrons wake up early to party and others look like they haven't slept for days. The tunes tend to be hard, banging and twisted. This is definitely NOT a party for the faint of heart.

THIS IS LONDON
364 Richmond West, 416-351-1100.
The inexplicably named This Is London is an upscale dance club in the middle of the club district. A second floor overlooks the action on the dance floor, and plenty of exposed wood gives the room a warm feel. Some nights the music and crowd are mainstream, while on others you might find acclaimed underground DJs throwing down.

MOD CLUB THEATRE
722 College, 416-588-4663.
The Mod Club is part anglophile dance club and part concert venue. Despite the name, it's not exclusively Brit-pop-oriented, but expect mod anthems to dominate their long-running Saturdays. The upper balcony makes for great people watching, not to mention a great view of the action onstage.

ULTRA SUPPER CLUB
314 Queen West, 416-263-0330.
Little remains of the reggae joint that used to occupy this space since it was dramatically transformed into a high-end restaurant and lounge. The large rooftop patio is already notorious for celebrity sightings and the DJ booth has also seen some big names pass through for the occasional special event.

SUPERMARKET
268 Augusta, 416-840-0501.
A new addition to the colourful Kensington Market area, it's a restaurant by day and a small club by night. The entertainment programming is as eclectic as the neighbourhood – DJs playing underground hiphop one night, live bands the next.

EL CONVENTO RICO
750 College, 416-588-7800.
Purists may complain that the Latin gay institution El Convento Rico has been overrun by straight couples, but that's part of the charm of this lovably eccentric club. Expect drag queens, salsa, wide-eyed tourists and plenty of ass-shaking.

film

A film shoot on every street corner, a film festival on every weekend, it's hard to argue with Toronto's rep as North America's most cinematic city.
For film listings and reviews, pick up NOW Magazine each week or visit www.nowtoronto.com.

Hollywood North

If you love film, you're in the right city. Most days of the year, you can see movies from noon till last call. Where you see them, however, is another story, especially since the closings of many downtown movie houses and the advent of the monsterplex-style theatre.

In addition, there's a staggering number of film festivals, some lasting merely a day or two, where you can gorge on films before they open commercially (if they ever do) and impress your friends with your knowledge of world cinema. You can also count on seeing a film crew or three, recognizable by the line of white trailers lining the curbs along many downtown side streets, diverting local traffic or lighting up the streets at 1 in the morning. And finally, we know you're above it all, but you can indulge in celebrity-spotting. Yes, when the cameras aren't rolling, movie stars like to eat, shop and party, too.

What and where

Toronto's a key market for North American film distribution. Most films open here before they roll out across the country (if they do at all), usually simultaneously with releases in New York and Los Angeles.

Sadly, the days of the grand old movie palaces are over. The University Theatre is now a Pottery Barn, the Uptown has gone condo, and the York (a few blocks east of Yonge on Eglinton) is some sort of party rental. Don't get us wrong, we like the generic multiplexes, or at least their stadium seating, film variety and souped-up sound systems, but for more arty fare check out the **Cumberland** or **Carlton**. Many indie, queer or small Canadian films go directly to the latter.

The **Rainbow Cinemas** chain charges roughly half what you'd pay elsewhere. Conversely, check out the **Varsity**'s cozy VIP theatres, where for a few extra bucks you can kick back, enjoy unlimited leg room, have your snacks brought to you and pretend you're one of the Weinstein brothers. See theatre listings, page 152.

Toronto on film

If you live in Toronto, going to the movies isn't much of an escape. The city crops up so often onscreen (usually subbing for New York, Boston or Chicago) that spotting the cleverly camouflaged landmarks can be downright distracting.

The Oscar-winning film Chicago was shot in and around Toronto, with the music sequences filmed in the **Elgin & Winter Garden Theatre** (189 Yonge) and **Danforth Music Hall** (147 Danforth). Set roughly during the same era, Cinderella Man occupied a pre-Loblaws **Maple Leaf Gardens** (see **Sightseeing**, page 26) for its fight scenes, and the south exterior of the downtown Hudson's Bay building (corner of Yonge and Wellington) stood in

The only yellow cabs in T.O. are starring in Hollywood movies.

Hungry?

Dig in.

Search over 900 restaurants on the NOW Magazine website. Search by cuisine, price and location. Discover the best patios, the best pubs, the trendy hot spots and the places to avoid.

www.nowtoronto.com/food

for New York's Madison Square Garden.

One of the futuristic-looking staircases in **Roy Thomson Hall** (60 Simcoe, see page 144) played a part in the first X-Men film, while the interior of **Casa Loma** (see **Sightseeing**, page 28), one of the most frequently lensed local buildings of all, provided the inside of Professor Xavier's mutant school. On the subject of schools, **U of T**'s downtown campus (see Sightseeing, page 22) has formed a film backdrop for movies as varied as The Paper Chase, Black Christmas and Good Will Hunting.

Of course, local director David Cronenberg prefers to shoot his flicks in the city, having utilized the **Flatiron** building (see Sightseeing, page 23) prominently in The Fly, the Bell building near the Eaton Centre for Dead Ringers and various real Toronto-area highways in his auto-erotic thriller Crash. Winner of the worst film featuring Toronto is debatable, but it probably goes to Resident Evil: Apocalypse, which put the goings-on at the new **City Hall** (see **Sightseeing**, page 19) in a new perspective.

Coolest appearance by T.O. in a film is probably the closed-off lower platform at Bay subway station for the sci-fi horror flick Mimic.

Festival frenzy

It's hard to keep track of all the city's film festivals. Some years it feels like there are 100, all of them happening in the spring. In fact, there are a few dozen, some lasting a mere day or two. Many are organized around language or culture (Reel Asian, ImagineNATIVE, Hispano American), others around genre (NXNE Film Fest for music-related films, Images for experimental works). Here, in terms of size, influence and attendance, are five you don't want to miss.

TORONTO INTERNATIONAL FILM FESTIVAL

TIFF is the biggie, 10 days of glitz, glamour and, oh yeah, movie-gorging. The 300-plus-film blowout was originally labelled the Festival of Festivals because it screened the best of the world's other film festivals. It's since expanded to include lots of high-profile premieres. Its post-Labour Day slot makes it a key time to launch prestige films (Ray, Capote) before they're rolled out during the lead-up to awards season. It's also a bustling market for studios to bid for films (Paul Haggis's Crash, Jason Reitman's Thank You For Smoking).

What keeps it fresh is the diversity of the product. You've got Oscar bait, highbrow foreign films and spotlights on obscure directors, but you've also got blood-splattered B movies in the fest's cult Midnight Madness program (Hostel, Saw). TIFF maintains a commitment to its own, traditionally opening with a big Canuck movie.

But what really sets it apart from other big fests is the public screening component. Regular folks can't get into Cannes, the only fest that's got a bigger international profile than TIFF's. This is what has people lining up around the block for 10 days each September at many of the city's downtown cinemas.

The TIFF Group also runs the year-long **Cinematheque** art house series as well as **Sprockets** (www.bell.ca/sprockets), a world-class film fest for kids held each April.

And finally, there's nothing like the gala red carpets (or, take note, groupies, the lobbies and bars of the big hotels) for star-sightings. For tickets, contact the box office (416-968-3456, www.bell.ca/filmfest). September.

HOT DOCS CANADIAN INTERNATIONAL DOCUMENTARY FESTIVAL

Chalk it up to the public's dissatisfaction with Hollywood pap or a more discerning aging baby boomer population. The documentary rules, and no more so than at Hot Docs (www.hotdocs.ca), a massive feast of facts (and a bit o' fiction) on film. Commercially released movies like Murderball and Wordplay have upped the fest's public profile a lot. There may not be many starlets to ogle during these 10 days in spring, but remember that this is a fest where Errol Morris, Werner Herzog and our own Allan King get oohs and ahhs at post-screening Q&As. April.

WORLDWIDE SHORT FILM FESTIVAL

A few years ago, all most of us knew about short films came from those two difficult categories in the annual office Oscar pool. Suddenly there's a huge interest, perhaps sparked by local boy Chris Landreth's own Oscar-win for Ryan, and the fact that many shorts are easily downloadable (and watchable on everything from your cellphone to your iPod) or available on DVD compilations. Introducing more than 300 of the best in the world is the Worldwide Short Film Festival (www.worldwideshortfilmfest.com), which in addition to screenings, hosts seminars and lectures for veteran and neophyte filmmakers alike, proving that style and substance is more important than size. June.

INSIDE OUT GAY AND LESBIAN FILM AND VIDEO FESTIVAL

In a town with one of the world's biggest gay and lesbian communities, it's no wonder Inside Out (www.insideout.on.ca) attracts big numbers to its screenings and parties. It's here that you'll find sneak peeks at films by queer indie champs like John Greyson, Gregg Araki and Monika Treut. There's an inclusionary, experimental feel to many of its shorts programs, often grouped according to irreverent themes. If you question the fest's relevance after the success of films like Brokeback Mountain, viewing a film made from a country where homosexuality is outlawed will quickly set you, er, straight. May.

TORONTO JEWISH FILM FESTIVAL

Oy. It's hard to say that a festival devoted to one culture or language is more important than another. Cinéfranco (www.cinefranco.com, see page 249) is popular with francophones, and Reel Asian (www.reelasian.com) screens lots of Asian movies you just won't find anywhere else (except maybe on bootleg DVDs in Chinatown). But for breadth of programming and organization, the Toronto Jewish Film Festival (www.tjff.com) is one of the best of its kind in the world. Its recent roundup of films exploring the connection between black and Jewish music was revelatory. May.

And here's five more worth your screen time:

FEMALE EYE FILM FESTIVAL Eclectic short films and features by debut, emerging and established female directors. www.femaleeyefilmfestival.com. June.

NORTH BY NORTHEAST FILM FESTIVAL Film component to indie rock showcase NXNE (see page 145), screens films where music is star of the show, including shorts, docs and features such as Stewart Copeland's Police rockumentary. www.nxne.com. June.

RENDEZVOUS WITH MADNESS FILM FESTIVAL Annual film festival that presents features and shorts touching upon the facts and mythology surrounding mental health and addiction. 416-583-4339, www.rendezvouswithmadness.com. November.

SPROCKETS INTERNATIONAL FILM FESTIVAL Feature-length, animated and short films for children and families. 416-967-7371, www.bell.ca/sprockets. April.

mediatheque: a must for movie lovers

One of the coolest and most frequently overlooked places to watch movies in Toronto is the National Film Board of Canada's Mediatheque. At its bland little building just around the corner from MuchMusic and across the street from the Famous Players Paramount multiplex (259 Richmond West), the $1.5-million **NFB Mediatheque** offers close to 2,600 movies, from one-minute shorts to feature-length documentaries and dramas representing almost 70 years of Canadian filmmaking. Just sign up at the front desk for one of the 14 Star Trek-style "personal viewing stations" with wide-screen TV and speakers that wrap around your head. Films include the Oscar-winning computer-animated short Ryan, the Oscar-nominated documentary short Hardwood and the acclaimed feature doc Shake Hands with the Devil about the failed UN peacekeeping mission in Rwanda. The NFB Mediatheque also features the newly renovated NFB Cinema, an intimate 79-seat theatre that hosts festivals, com-

Thousands of movies on demand at the **Mediatheque**.

munity events, conferences, workshops, lectures and private screenings, and the Atelier, a multi-functional space used for animation workshops, cocktail receptions and events.

150 John (416-973-3012, www.nfb.ca)
Open Mon-Tue 1-7 pm, Wed 10 am-7 pm, Thu-Sat 10 am-10 pm, Sun noon-5 pm.

TORONTO REEL ASIAN INTERNATIONAL FILM FESTIVAL
A showcase of contemporary Asian films and videos from the East and Southeast Asian diaspora. 416-703-9333, www.reelasian.com. November.

Movie theatres

Downtown

CARLTON
20 Carlton, 416-598-2309.

CUMBERLAND 4
159 Cumberland, 416-646-0444.

DOCKS LAKEVIEW DRIVE-IN
176 Cherry, 416-461-3625.

PARAMOUNT
259 Richmond West, 416-368-5600.

RAINBOW MARKET SQUARE
Market Square, 80 Front East, 416-494-9371.

VARSITY & VARSITY V.I.P.
55 Bloor West, 416-961-6303.

Midtown

CANADA SQUARE
2200 Yonge, 416-646-0444.

MT. PLEASANT
675 Mt. Pleasant Rd, 416-489-8484.

REGENT
551 Mt. Pleasant Rd, 416-480-9884.

SILVERCITY YONGE & EGLINTON
2300 Yonge, 416-544-1236.

West end

QUEENSWAY
1025 The Queensway, at Islington off the QEW, 416-503-0424.

RAINBOW WOODBINE
Woodbine Centre, 500 Rexdale Blvd, 416-494-9371.

East end

BEACH CINEMAS
1651 Queen East, 416-646-0444.

North

BAYVIEW
Bayview Village Plaza, 416-646-0444.

GRANDE - YONGE & SHEPPARD
4961 Yonge, 416-590-9974.

EMPIRE THEATRES AT EMPRESS WALK
5095 Yonge, 416-223-9550.

RAINBOW FAIRVIEW
Fairview Mall, 1800 Sheppard East, 416-494-9371.

SILVERCITY YORKDALE
3401 Dufferin, 416-787-2052.

Scarborough

401 & MORNINGSIDE
785 Milner Ave, 416-281-2226.

COLISEUM SCARBOROUGH
Scarborough Town Centre, 416-366-8437.

EGLINTON TOWN CENTRE
1901 Eglinton East, 416-752-4494.

KENNEDY COMMONS 20
Kennedy Rd & 401, 416-335-5323.

Rep cinemas

BLOOR
506 Bloor West, 416-516-2330,
www.bloorcinema.com.

CINEMATHEQUE
Jackman Hall, Art Gallery of Ontario, 317 Dundas West, 416-968-FILM, www.Bell.ca/cinematheque.

FOX
2236 Queen East, 416-691-7330, Festival Cinemas Film Hotline 416-690-2600.

NATIONAL FILM BOARD
NFB Mediatheque, 150 John, 416-973-3012,
www.nfb.ca/mediatheque.com.

ONTARIO PLACE CINESPHERE
955 Lakeshore West, 416-314-9900,
www.ontarioplace.com.

SCIENCE CENTRE OMNIMAX
770 Don Mills, 416-696-3127,
www.ontariosciencecentre.ca.

stage

If all the world's a stage, then Toronto's theatre scene must have a starring role, thanks to big-budget world premieres and an edgy and exciting indie scene.
For stage listings and features, pick up NOW Magazine each week or visit www.nowtoronto.com.

Check out the latest in Canadian alt theatre at **Theatre Passe Muraille.**

Theatre

Toronto is the world's third-largest centre for English theatre (after New York and London), although not so long ago most productions were American or English imports. The local renaissance, which sparked a similar growth across the country, began in the 70s thanks to a nationalistic group of artists who gave the city its theatrical voice.

Tarragon Theatre, **Theatre Passe Muraille**, **Factory Theatre** and the Toronto Free Theatre (which teamed with CentreStage in the late 80s to form **CanStage**, the city's largest regional theatre) were among the newly formed companies, and they're still vital contributors to the growing body of new Canadian plays. Each company puts on six to eight shows a seasons.

A typical Toronto theatre season includes hundreds of productions by dozens of theatre companies, with performances all year long. During the summer months you can catch outdoor park productions by CanStage, **Shakespeare Works** (416-463-4869, www.shakespeareworks.com) and **Shakespeare in the Rough** (647-438-6742, www.sitr.ca). **Harbourfront Centre** (235 Queens Quay West, 416-973-4000, www.harbourfront.on.ca) offers lots of theatre, much of it alternative, throughout the year and in its performance series **New World Stage**.

If you want mainstream work, Mirvish Productions provides it at the **Royal Alexandra Theatre** (260 King West, 416-872-1212, www.onstagenow.com) and the nearby **Princess of Wales Theatre** (300 King West, 416-872-1212, www.onstagenow.com); recent fare has included Mamma Mia!, The Lion King and the world premiere of The Lord of the Rings.

The local theatre scene also reflects the diversity of Toronto itself. There's gay and lesbian theatre (**Buddies in Bad Times**), black theatre (**Obsidian**, **b current**, **Theatre Archipelago**), theatre for kids (**Lorraine Kimsa Theatre for Young People**), Asian theatre (**fu-GEN**), feminist theatre (**Nightwood**), aboriginal theatre (**Native Earth**) and French theatre (**Théâtre Français de Toronto**).

And always worth a look are shows by **Theatre Columbus**, **Cahoots**, **Crow's**, **Modern Times**, **Necessary Angel**, **Theatre Smith-Gilmour**, **Video-Cabaret**, **Pea Green**, **Planet 88**, **Theatrefront**, **UnSpun**, **Volcano**, **Shadowland**, **The Company**, **Pleiades**, **Theatre Gargantua**, **Theatre Rusticle**, **Independent Aunties** and anything at the **Theatre Centre**.

entertainment

Companies

B CURRENT
416-525-2994, www.bcurrent.ca.
Home of the innovative **rock.paper.sistahz festival**, which concentrates on performance work by black women artists, b current popped onto the Toronto theatrescape in 1991. Since then, the company has been carving out a unique identity, with unconventional approaches to developing alternative and obscure performance material and artists.

BUDDIES IN BAD TIMES
12 Alexander, 416-975-8555, www.buddiesinbadtimestheatre.com.
Established in 1979 and located in the heart of the Gay Village, this theatre company is the essence of queer culture. It produces edgy and provocative new Canadian works, some of which are definitely NOT for the faint of heart. Buddies also stages Canadian adaptations of well-known works like Ibsen's Hedda Gabler. In addition to splashy mainstage theatrical productions, the theatre also hosts outrageous special events, youth initiatives, play development programs and late-night weekend cabarets.

CANSTAGE
416-369-3110, www.canstage.com.
This venerable company is the city's "big daddy" not-for-profit theatre. Productions are mounted at various theatres in the city, notably the 875-seat **Bluma Appel Theatre** (St. Lawrence Centre, 27 Front East, 416-368-3110) and the **Berkeley Street Theatre** (26 Berkeley, 416-368-3110).

FACTORY THEATRE
125 Bathurst, at Adelaide, 416-505-9971, www.factorytheatre.ca.
The first company to devote itself exclusively to producing Canadian plays (and currently one of the country's largest producers of homegrown works), Factory's recent successes have included Adam Pettle's Zadie's Shoes (remounted by Mirvish Productions at the Winter Garden), Florence Gibson's Chalmers Award-winning Belle (remounted in association with the National Arts Centre in Ottawa) and Jason Sherman's The League of Nathans.

FU-GEN THEATRE COMPANY
www.fu-gen.org.
Founded in 2002, fu-GEN (short for "Future Generation") is dedicated to providing a voice for Asian-Canadian artists.

LORRAINE KIMSA THEATRE FOR YOUNG PEOPLE
165 Front East, 416-862-2222, www.lktyp.ca.
Now comfortably in its 40s, the LKTYP is still very much a child at heart, dedicated to professional productions of classic and contemporary works from around the world written especially for children and their families.

NATIVE EARTH PERFORMING ARTS
Distillery District, 55 Mill, bldg 74, 416-531-1402, www.nativeearth.ca.
Founded in 1982, Native Earth is Canada's oldest professional aboriginal theatre company and is dedicated to the expression of the native experience.

NIGHTWOOD THEATRE
Distillery District, 55 Mill, bldg 74, 416-944-1740, www.nightwoodtheatre.net.
Devoted to producing plays by and about outspoken Canadian women, Nightwood is also the driving force behind the **Groundswell Festival**, Canada's national play development program for new works by women, and **FemCab**, the company's notorious annual celebration of International Women's Day.

OBSIDIAN THEATRE COMPANY
943 Queen East, 416-463-8444,
www.obsidian-theatre.com.
The OTC produces international and Canadian plays that focus primarily but not exclusively on the works of acclaimed playwrights of African descent. Performances are held at various theatres in the city.

SOULPEPPER THEATRE
Young Centre, Distillery District 55 Mill,
416-866-8666, www.soulpepper.ca.
A fine cast of actors perform in the artist-founded Soulpepper, Toronto's pre-eminent classical repertory theatre company.

TARRAGON THEATRE
30 Bridgman, at Howland, 416-531-1827,
www.tarragontheatre.com.
Its mandate to develop and produce new work, with a particular emphasis on Canadian scripts, has made Tarragon one of the most lauded companies in the country. The theatre houses two playing spaces, the 205-seat Mainspace and the 100-seat Extra Space. Major playwrights who have premiered their work here include David French, Joan MacLeod, John Murrell, Morris Panych, James Reaney, Jason Sherman and Judith Thompson.

THÉÂTRE FRANÇAIS DE TORONTO
2333 Dundas West, 416-534-7303,
www.theatrefrancais.com.
Dedicated to francophone theatre works, the Théâtre Français mounts its productions at the Berkeley Street Theatre (26 Berkeley).

THEATRE PASSE MURAILLE
16 Ryerson, 416-504-7529,
www.passemuraille.on.ca
One of the country's first alternative companies, Passe Muraille makes it a point to produce innovative and provocative Canadian theatre. Writers such as Rick Salutin, Linda Griffiths, Maria Campbell and Michael Ondaatje have all created original works for Passe Muraille. Canadian classics such as Timothy Findley's The Stillborn Lover, the stage adaptation of Margaret Laurence's The Stone Angel and Michael Healey's The Drawer Boy are among the theatre's productions.

Stratford & Shaw
If your taste runs to the classics, Toronto's only a two-hour drive to two of the largest classical companies in North America, the highly revered **Stratford Festival of Canada** (1-800-567-1600, www.stratfordfestival.ca) and **Shaw Festival** (1-800-511-7429, www.shawfest.com). Both are summer fests, with performances from May through October.

Stratford, founded in 1953 in the swan-laked city of the same name, highlights the works of William Shakespeare on its four stages, though in recent seasons it's also produced at least one Broadway musical staple and begun mounting Canadian works.

The mandate at Niagara-on-the-Lake's Shaw Festival, founded in 1962, focuses on the works of George Bernard Shaw and plays written both during and about his lifetime (1856-1950). The three-stage festival regularly presents unknown or rarely staged plays.

playing for cheaps
There's an idiotic notion that live theatre's way pricier than film. Don't believe it. Great deals are available at Dundas Square's **T.O. Tix** (at the northwest end of the platz at the corner of Yonge and Dundas), which sells same-day discount, week-of discount and full-price advance tickets to pretty much every play, dance show and opera in town, as well as some stand-up comedy shows. Keep in mind that the hottest shows might not be available, and lineups can start well before the noon opening Tuesday through Saturday (Sunday and Monday tickets go on sale on Saturday). T.O. Tix is also an official outlet for TicketKing, ShopDineTour Toronto, Gray Line Sightseeing and the Ontario Science Centre. T.O. Tix accepts payment by Visa, Mastercard, cash and Interac in person and Visa, MasterCard and American Express online (at www.totix.ca). T.O.TIX is open Tuesday through Saturday from Noon to 6:30 pm. Because many shows have pay-what-you-can performances on Sundays and no performances on Mondays, T.O. Tix is closed on these two days. Go online or call the Infoline (416-536-6468) to hear a recorded message listing the shows that are on sale.

Sunday's the bargain day for pwyc performances at theatres like **Buddies in Bad Times** (12 Alexander, 416-975-8555), **Factory** (125 Bathurst, 416-504-9971), **Tarragon** (30 Bridgman, 416-531-1827) and **Theatre Passe Muraille** (16 Ryerson, 416-504-7529), where matinee performances (usually at 2 or 2:30 pm) go pwyc. No one will turn up their nose if you throw in $5 or $10. CanStage's **Bluma Appel** (27 Front East) and **Berkeley Street Theatres** (26 Berkeley, 416-368-3110) are pwyc on Monday nights and offer limited same-day rush tickets Tuesday to Saturday. Get there early and be prepared to share theatre stories with your neighbours. Pwyc/rush lines are a great place to see and be seen.

Festivals
COOKING FIRE THEATRE FESTIVAL Outdoor performances ranging from ancient Japanese folk tales to cowboy musicals and puppets. Dufferin Grove Park, Dufferin, S of Bloor, www.cookingfire.ca. June.

FRINGE OF TORONTO THEATRE FESTIVAL Unjuried theatre performances happen at dozens of venues in and around the Annex and beyond. 416-966-1062, www.fringetoronto.com. July.

NEW IDEAS FESTIVAL Festival of new short plays. Alumnae Theatre, 70 Berkeley, 416-364-4170, www.alumnaetheatre.com. March.

SUMMERWORKS THEATRE FESTIVAL Juried festival of plays, most of them premieres. www.summerworks.ca. August.

Dance

Dance in this city isn't as popular – or well-attended – as in Montreal, but we come a respectable second. Apart from the **National Ballet of Canada**, now in its brand new home (see **Sightseeing**, page 23), most of the dance scene consists of contemporary works, and many companies are outgrowths of the cultural boom of the 1970s. A funny thing, though. Attend a contemporary dance show any given night (runs are generally two to four days) and up to half the audience could be in the biz, students or friends of the performers.

Perhaps looking to build an audience, some adventurous souls are joining forces (and combining grant monies) with writers, musicians, filmmakers and theatre types to create exciting multidisciplinary works. Still, with **Harbourfront**'s well-programmed international dance series, a handful of solid local companies and some edgy experimenters, you can count on at least two or three must-see dance shows a month, ranging from hauntingly imagistic spectacles to esoteric head-scratchers.

Not surprising for a city with a diverse ethnic mix, artists from India, South America, Africa and Asia have spiced up the formerly WASP-centric scene with their traditions, usually with a contemporary twist. The presence of strong dance schools (**Toronto Children's Dance Theatre**, the **National Ballet School**, **School of Toronto Dance Theatre** and York University's dance department) means there's lots of fresh talent each year.

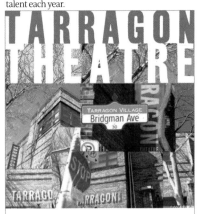

Seven Wonders of the World:
Theatre – **TARRAGON THEATRE**

"as close as Canada has ever come to having an English-language national theatre"

– The Globe and Mail

call for tickets | 416.531.1827
www.tarragontheatre.com

Companies

NATIONAL BALLET OF CANADA
Four Seasons Centre, 145 Queen West, 416-345-9595, www.national.ballet.ca.
Under the artistic directorship of former prima ballerina Karen Kain, the National Ballet is executing the delicate balancing act of maintaining their classical repertoire while building new ballets for the future. Nurturing star-quality dancers (like Kain herself) remains a challenge, however.

TORONTO DANCE THEATRE
416-967-1365, www.tdt.org.
Since the scene is so small and everyone sees everyone else's works, most contemporary companies suffer from an identity problem. The TDT has marked out its territory with playful, sexy works that draw heavily on design and music. A recent show included a collaboration with indie rockers the Hidden Cameras.

DANCEMAKERS
Distillery District, 55 Mill, bldg 74, 416-367-1800, www.dancemakers.org.
Dancemakers recently changed artistic directorship and is moving away from intellectual-based works to merge with other artistic disciplines.

DANNY GROSSMAN DANCE COMPANY
157 Carlton, 416-408-4543, www.dannygrossman.com.
As a recent retrospective of choreography master Grossman's works showed there's still an appetite for good physical storytelling.

KAEJA D'DANCE
734 Euclid, 416-516-6030, www.kaeja.org.
Kaeja frequently draws on the lives of its two founders, the husband-and-wife team of Karen and Allen Kaeja. Many of their works are now available on film.

PEGGY BAKER DANCE
www.peggybakerdance.com.
Once a part of Lar Lubovitch Dance Company and Mikhail Baryshnikov's White Oak Dance Projects, Peggy Baker is in a class all her own. She performs solos (hers and others), often to live music or with storytelling.

Venues

If you're a dance lover, you'll probably spend a lot of time down at the lakeside **Premiere Dance Theatre** (207 Queens Quay West, 416-973-4000) and **Harbourfront Centre Theatre** (231 Queens Quay West, 416-973-4000), the city's major modern dance venues that play host to international and local hoofers.

THE BETTY OLIPHANT THEATRE
404 Jarvis, 416-964-3780.
Offers a nice wide stage area and surprisingly intimate feel, but beware the lousy leg room (perhaps because it was designed for students at the National Ballet School).

THE WINCHESTER STREET THEATRE
80 Winchester, 416-967-1365.
Home to the rehearsal hall of Toronto Dance Theatre and its school, it's pretty informal. It's frequently rented by low-budget indie outfits.

Festivals

CANASIAN DANCE FESTIVAL Harbourfront Centre, 235 Queens Quay W. 416-973-4000. June.

DUSK DANCES Outdoor festival of dance. Dufferin Grove Park, Dufferin S of Bloor. www.dufferinpark.ca. July.

TORONTO INTERNATIONAL DANCE FESTIVAL
The renamed Fringe dance event that features dozens of dance artists and choreographers, with performances ranging from ballet to belly dancing to breaking. 416-410-4291, www.tidf.org. August.

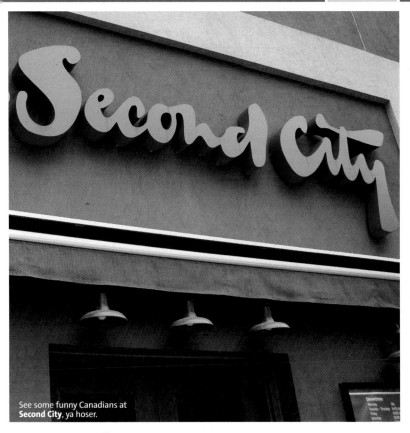

See some funny Canadians at **Second City**, ya hoser.

Comedy

Canadians congratulate themselves on being funny, and Torontonians smugly admit to being the funniest of all. Forget theories about why. We're geographically the country's comedy hub, which is a mixed blessing. Most aspiring comics hone their acts here, and if they're young, hungry and hooked up with the right agent, they bolt for the US faster than you can say "green card," which is NOT a pun on Tom Green. What's good about this is that at many comedy clubs you can see world-class acts on the same bill as amateurs. What's bad is that there are an awful lot of unfunny people who think they're the next Jim Carrey or Mike Myers. The exodus of talent continues to this day, but recently, many funny folk (Colin Mochrie, Elvira Kurt, Jessica Holmes and Gavin Crawford, to name a few) have decided to stay, partly due to increased opportunities on Canadian TV.

There's comedy going on every night of the week. An obvious spot to hit is **Yuk Yuk**'s (224 Richmond West, 416-967-6425), the legendary club created by Mark Breslin and former stomping ground for some of the best in the biz, like Jim Car-

rey, Howie Mandel, Mike MacDonald, Harland Williams and Russell Peters. And two bucks gets you into Toonie Tuesdays Amateur Night.

The Laugh Resort (370 King West, 416-364-5233), a few blocks away, is a more intimate and laid-back venue that has featured the likes of Adam Sandler and Ellen Degeneres.

If sketch comedy is your thing, you can't go wrong with the **Second City** (51 Mercer, 416-343-0011), which spawned the careers of future SCTV and Saturday Night Live stars like Dan Aykroyd, John Candy, Mike Myers, Catherine O'Hara and Martin Short. Stick around for the free improv sets after most Saturday shows (around 12:15 am), which often draw cool guests who want to flex their improv muscles. Second City has also housed comedy-based shows. A few years ago, a little piece called My Big Fat Greek Wedding played under its roof.

Some of the most exciting comedy happens in the smaller rooms, weekly nights or one-offs. The **Rivoli** (332 Queen West, 416-596-1908) back room is where the legendary Kids in the Hall got their start, and it's also where the Broadway comedy hit The Drowsy Chaperone appeared in its first incarnation. Mike Myers's SNL German club character Dieter was inspired by a Riv waiter. Don't miss the

it's always something

Canadians have a reputation for being funny. Like Jim Carrey funny. Mike Myers funny. In fact, funny is one of our most popular exports. And our humorous roots can be traced back to the Old Firehall Theatre, which opened as the Second City sketch comedy club in 1973 and helped launch the careers of Dan Aykroyd, John Candy, Eugene Levy, Martin Short and Gilda Radner, among others. Today the Firehall is one of 20 Canadian and US Gilda's Clubs, which provide support for people touched by cancer. (Radner died of ovarian cancer at age 42.) The annual It's Always Something gala variety show, attended by many of her old Second City chums, raises funds for the programs. 110 Lombard, 416-214-9898, www.gildasclubtoronto.org.

Riv's **Monday Alt.COMedy Lounge** (332 Queen West, 416-596-1908) a pay-what-you-can night featuring short sets by many pros and amateurs. Folks like Janeane Garofalo, Will Ferrell, Robin Williams and Tom Green have all showed up. (Tom's puke-fest with stand-up Jason Rouse is legendary.) Tuesday night sees the Rivoli's **Sketch-COMedy Lounge**, a good place to check out the city's emerging sketch troupes.

Also on Tuesday nights, **Jo-Anna Downey's Standing On The Danforth** night at the Eton House (710 Danforth, 416-466-6161) draws an eclectic lineup, as does the same host's long-running Wednesday-night **Spirits Open Mic Night** (Spirits Bar & Grill, 642 Church, 416-967-0001). Thursdays have got a whole lot funnier since Dawn Whitwell and Richard Ryder began running the **Upstairs Show at Big Mamma's Boy** (554 Parliament) in Cabbagetown.

Bad Dog Theatre (138 Danforth, 416-491-3115) is the unofficial home of improv comedy in the city. It hosts a number of improv-related shows like the Saturday-night Bad Dog Sessions and the latest trend, several improv shows based on movies or TV shows. Also look for comedy at places like the **Drake Hotel** (1150 Queen West), the **Gladstone** (1214 Queen West, 416-531-4635), the **Savannah Room** (294 College, 416-238-7337) and **Timothy's World News Café** (320 Danforth, 416-461-2668). You can get into most of these shows for nothing – or at most the price of a beer.

Festivals

TORONTO INTERNATIONAL IMPROV FESTIVAL
Showcasing top improv talent from Canada and the US, including the occasional Saturday Night Live alum, plus panel discussions and workshops. www. torontoimprovfest.com. August.

art

No matter the medium – painting, photography, installation, sculpture, mixed media, melted bits of junk from the recycle bin – Toronto has a vibrant art scene.
For art listings and reviews, pick up NOW Magazine each week or visit www.nowtoronto.com.

While Manola Blaniks and Jimmy Choos are de rigeur in ritzy Yorkville today, back in the 60s and 70s, barefoot and Birkenstocks were commonplace in the then-thriving beatnik enclave.

A regular hang for the city's most celebrated artists, on any given day you might've found Joyce Wieland, Gordon Rayner or Michael Snow lolling around Av Isaac's gallery on Yonge Street or tipping back a pint over at the **Pilot Tavern** (22 Cumberland).

Just up the road, rival gallerist Carmen Lamanna claimed his stake in the still-young art scene with, among others, Felix Partz, Jorge Zontal and AA Bronson of General Idea, who garnered international acclaim as publishers of FILE Magazine, a send up of LIFE Magazine rife with post-modern mockery of the status quo.

The wave of American draft-dodgers brought to town artists like Lisa Steele, who soon formed an integral part of the local artistic community. Artist-run centres like **A-Space** (#110 - 401 Richmond West; 416-979-9633) sprang up, balancing commercial art with the government-sponsored avant-garde.

As Yorkville devolved into a chic shopping mecca in the 80s, the art scene shifted. While the area retained a few notable spaces – the **Drabinsky Gallery** (122 Scollard; 416-324-5766) is still going strong with artists like Sky Glabush – Yorkville's relevancy to art in Toronto faded significantly as a patch of galleries festooned on and around Queen West.

Queen West has long had its share of galleries, including the original digs of Toronto art mavens **Olga Korper**, **Ydessa Hendeles** and **Leo Kamen**, who still makes the gallery complex at 80 Spadina Avenue home.

In the last few years, the hip strip's importance has increased exponentially as the art scene stretches west from Spadina Avenue, bleeding beyond Trinity-Bellwoods Park towards Parkdale, where it's pooled into a plethora of galleries and a new hive of artistic activity.

The first gallery to venture west of the park was **Angell** (890 Queen West; 416-530-0444), which is still going strong. **Paul Petro Contemporary Art** (980 Queen West; 416-979-7874) reps Stephen Andrews and Allyson Mitchell, and **Katharine Mulherin Fine Art Projects** (1086 Queen West; 416-537-8827) has immensely talented painters like Dana Holst and Margaux Williamson. **Spin Gallery** (1100 Queen West; 416-530-7656) shows Balint Zsako and Fiona Smyth in its huge lofty space.

Recently, more established commercial spaces like **Edward Day** (952 Queen West; 416-921-6540) and the photo-centric **Stephen Bulger Gallery** (1026 Queen West; 416-504-0575) have moved in and the **Museum of Contemporary Canadian Art** (MOCCA, 952 Queen West; 416-395-7430) even made its new home in an old fabric warehouse in the heart of the strip.

Suddenly lousy with artists, West Queen West needed a social hub or two, and the **Gladstone** (1214 Queen West, 416-531-4635) and **Drake** (1150 Queen West, 416-531-5042) hotels obliged. Once a dive and a derelict, respectively, both hotels have been revived and revamped, and make visual arts and culture the focus of their considerable attraction.

The expanding galaxy that is art on Queen West also holds in orbit a few notable satellites.

Check out galleries like **YYZ** and **Wynick/Tuck** at **401 Richmond West** (one block north of Queen, at Richmond and Spadina). The **Olga Korper Gallery**, which represents the likes of Susanna Heller and John McEwen, has settled into a stylish complex near the junction of Dundas West and Roncesvalles (17 Morrow; 416-532-8220) along with the **Christopher Cutts Gallery** (21 Morrow; 416-532-5566), which handles artists Janieta Eyre, Carlos and Jason Sanchez and Michael Snow, and the **Peak Gallery** (23 Morrow; 416-537-8108), which reps Cheryl Sourkes and Raffael Iglesias, among others.

Way out east, the **Distillery District** (Parliament and Mill; see Sightseeing page 36) makes for a fancy but soulless home for the **Monte Clarke** and **Corkin Shopland** galleries, among others.

Finally, if you've got the time, and a car, the **McMichael Canadian Art Collection** (10365 Islington, Kleinburg, 905-893-1121), just north of the city is worth a visit to see their quintessentially Canadian Group of Seven paintings (see Sightseeing, page 42).

Public galleries

ART GALLERY OF ONTARIO
317 Dundas West, 416-979-6601.
Big and full of art – it's the eighth-largest art museum in North America. The gallery is partially closed during its Frank Gehry sneezeguard makeover but in general it is a great place to see well-established Canadian and European artists and the occasional (and occasionally) fascinating contemporary show. While visiting, tour the historic **Grange** house (see **Sightseeing**, page 23) nearby.

West Queen West is home to hip galleries like **Clint Roenisch**.

ART GALLERY OF YORK UNIVERSITY
4700 Keele West, 416-736-5169.
In its brand new digs, you can rely on the AGYU for consistently excellent contemporary shows from internationally renowned artists like Stan Douglas. Be warned though: it takes forever to get there and the landscape is, to say the least, alienating. If you're around for an opening, head to the Art Gallery of Ontario and board the Performance Bus, a packed yellow school bus that turns the journey into a raucous destination of its own.

MUSEUM OF CONTEMPORARY CANADIAN ART
952 Queen West, 416-395-7430.
Since its relocation to Queen West, MOCCA has proven itself to be indispensable, as a museum with vision and a gracious host to various art-related events. Curator David Liss's ongoing Future Species series is bound to fascinate if not freak you right out.

POWER PLANT
231 Queens Quay West, 416-973-4949.
Once, literally, a powerhouse, the large space brings in big name installation and conceptual artists. Shows have been a little cold and minimal in the past but their opening parties should not be missed.

401 Richmond
An historic warehouse in downtown Toronto, 401 Richmond (www.401Richmond.net) has been dubbed a "village in a box" as it is home to 138 cultural producers and microenterprises, from magazine publishers and music studios to film co-op Trinity Square Video and, of course, several galleries.

YYZ
401 Richmond, #140, 416-255-1958.
One of the city's best artist-run centres, YYZ shows wholly unpredictable installation and video art.

PREFIX ICA
401 Richmond, #124, 416-591-0357.
Prefix shows contemporary video, photography and installation, and publishes a gorgeous photography magazine.

WYNICK/TUCK GALLERY
401 Richmond, #128, 416-504-8716.
One of the few commercial galleries in the building, Wynick/Tuck represents among others, the likes of collage-master Paul Butler, Kim Adams and Kelly Mark.

Private galleries
LEO KAMEN GALLERY
80 Spadina, #406, 416-504-9515.
After 20 years, Leo Kamen has become an institution himself, an art Godfather to artists on Queen West, showing a mix of emerging and established artists.

GALLERY TPW
560 Ossington, 416-504-7242.
Artist-run centre TPW explores the limits of photog-

raphy and new media for surprising, sometimes racy results.

ART METROPOLE
788 King West, 416-703-4400.
Founded three decades ago by General Idea, this museum/store of artist multiples by everyone from Yoko Ono to local art celeb Luis Jacob is a must-see.

YDESSA HENDELES ART FOUNDATION
778 King West, 416-603-2227.
Probably the most famous and celebrated Toronto dealer, collector and curator, Hendeles puts together much talked about shows connecting the dots between works in her private collection.

PAUL PETRO CONTEMPORARY ART
980 Queen West, 416-978-7874.
It's hard to imagine the West Queen West gallery strip without Paul Petro. Also check out his second shop with affordable artists' multiples. Beats buying a Toronto sweatshirt or keychain.

CLINT ROENISCH GALLERY
944 Queen West, 416-516-8593.
Roenisch looks a little like Michel Foucault, is almost as smart and has fabulous, eclectic taste. From painting to sculpture to installation to photography, anything can appear here, from the creepy to the sweet.

STEPHEN BULGER
1026 Queen West, 416-504-0575.
A late transplant to West Queen West with a solid reputation for showing documentary works, the name Stephen Bulger is synonymous with photography in Toronto.

KATHERINE MULHERIN CONTEMPORARY ART PROJECTS
1086 Queen West, 416-537-8827.
A pioneer in the current wave of storefront galleries, Mulherin has earned a glowing reputation in the city with her incredible eye for painting. Representing artists like Seth Scriver and Margaux Williamson, Muherin is a maven-in-training.

SPIN GALLERY
1100 Queen West, 416-530-7656.
SPIN has it all: a huge space, great roster of painters and photographers, and a reputation for throwing parties so spectacular that you can go all night without once noticing the art.

LE GALLERY
1183 Dundas West, 416-532-8767.
Le is a relative newbie storefront space, but young proprietor Wil Kucey has tapped into a mainline of solid artists flowing out of the Ontario College of Art and Design.

MERCER UNION
37 Lisgar, 416-536-1519.
One of our favourite spaces in the city, Mercer curates some of the city's most innovative and beguiling shows, like the one in which Quebec collective BGL built a whole new interior for the space and trashed it.

DIAZ CONTEMPORARY
100 Niagara, 416-361-2972.
Ben Diaz came all the way from Mexico to attract some of the city's best contemporary talent, like Tony Romano and rising star Kristan Horton.

Art Fests

ALLEYJAUNT
For one August weekend, the back-alley garages surrounding **Trinity-Bellwoods Park** (see **Sightseeing**, page 40) are transformed into art exhibits, installations and performance, film and video venues. A modest but fun urban art experiment, AlleyJaunt involves more than 40 artists and invites the public to explore their work by following the path of chalk drawings and flags set out to guide you to the participating garages-turned-galleries. www.alleyjaunt.com

ARTSWEEK
Painting, music, dance, visual arts, craft, theatre, film, video, literature – there are more arts events in Toronto during September's ArtsWeek than any other time of year. 416-392-6800, www.artsweek.ca.

CONTACT: TORONTO PHOTOGRAPHY FESTIVAL
One of the world's largest photography festivals, the month-long May event features the work of more than 500 local, national and international artists. Contact fills not only the city's galleries but spills out into a huge number of coffee shops, cafés and restaurants across the city, encompassing more than 170 venues in all. Contact also presents public art installations, a lecture series, workshops and many other exciting programs. Admission is free to most of the exhibitions. 416-539-9595, www.contactphoto.com.

IMAGES FESTIVAL
Now in its third decade, Images has grown into the largest event of its kind in Canada, dedicated to showcasing and supporting independent works in video, film, new media and installation from across Canada and around the world. Held in April. 416-971-8405, www.imagesfestival.com.

JUNCTION ARTS FESTIVAL
The largest of its kind in North America, this street-cum-arts festival weekend in September in the historic Junction neighbourhood (Keele and Dundas) offers everything from acrobats to art exhibits, puppet shows to poetry readings. 416-767-5036, www.junctionartsfest.com.

QUEEN WEST ART CRAWL
Drawing the public onto the trendy strip's many galleries, the Art Crawl (like a pub crawl with significantly less alcohol consumption) is a multidisciplinary, community-based festival. Held each September. 416-392-1038, www.torontoartscape.on.ca.

TORONTO ALTERNATIVE ART FAIR INTERNATIONAL
Created by local artists and gallerists in response to the more-mainstream **TIAF** (see below) in 2004, TAAFI is an adventurous counterpunch co-hosted by the Drake and Gladstone Hotels), along with several galleries. The hotels set up rooms to exhibit artwork and hold numerous parties and concert performances. Takes place in November. 416-537-3814, www.taafi.com.

TORONTO INTERNATIONAL ART FAIR
TIAF has been running every fall at the Metro Toronto Convention Centre for several years now, featuring booths from Canadian and international galleries. It does showcase some remarkable contemporary work, but generally caters to pricey, established artists making market-ready (read: boring) art. Held in November. 604-925-0330, www.tiafair.com.

TORONTO OUTDOOR ART EXHIBITION
For three days each July, **Nathan Phillips Square** (see **Sightseeing**, page 20) becomes the largest outdoor art exhibition in Canada. Hundreds of artists show and sell, and tens of thousands of art aficionados, art snobs, art collectors, art fans and the just plain curious attend. It's probably one of the best places to pick up work by hot, new artists if you have sharp eyes. 416-408-2754, www.torontooutdoorart.org.

festivals

No matter when you visit Toronto there's always something to celebrate.
For the latest festival listings and features, pick up NOW Magazine or visit www.nowtoronto.com.

Spring

CANADA BLOOMS Celebrate your green thumb with acres of gardens, flower shows, gardening gadgets and designer innovations at Canada's largest annual indoor flower and garden show. 416-447-8655, 1-800-730-1020, www.canadablooms.com. March.

CANADIAN WOMEN'S EXPO A three-day expo featuring celebrity guests, fashion shows, makeovers, cooking demonstrations, home decor advice and business networking events. 1-800-787-9328, www.canadianwomensexpo.com. March.

CANNABIS WEEK This peaceful celebration of pot culture features live music, lectures, comedy, poetry and more. The highlight is the Global Marijuana March to urge the goverment to decriminalize marijuana. 416-367-4679, www.cannabisweek.ca. May.

INTERNATIONAL CHILDREN'S FESTIVAL Arts festival for children and families featuring theatre, dance, storytelling, visual art, activities and more. School programs during the week and family programs on the weekends. Harbourfront Centre. 416-973-4000, www.harbourfrontcentre.com/milk. May.

MAYWORKS A multi-disciplinary arts festival that celebrates working class culture. www.mayworks.ca. April-May.

MILK INTERNATIONAL CHILDREN'S FESTIVAL OF THE ARTS Harbourfront Centre's prestigious annual festival showcases the world's finest theatre and music for young audiences. 416-973-4000, www.harbourfrontcentre.com/milk. May.

NATIONAL HOME SHOW The largest home show in North America — more than 800 exhibitors — with the latest trends, product innovations and services. 416-385-1880, www.nationalhomeshow.com. April.

TORONTO FESTIVAL OF STORYTELLING http://festival.storytellingtoronto.org. April.

Summer

AFROFEST African music with a roster of international artists, plus a children's village, workshops, crafts, drumming and more. Free. Queen's Park. 416-469-5336, www.musicafrica.org. July.

ASHKENAZ Festival of new Yiddish culture, with klezmer and Middle Eastern-inspired music, theatre performances and comedy. Free. Harbourfront Centre, 416-973-4000, www.harbourfrontcentre.com. Aug-Sep.

BEACHES INTERNATIONAL JAZZ FESTIVAL Stage, street and rooftop performances, workshops, lectures and more. 416-410-8809, www.beachesjazz.com. July.

BEATS, BREAKS & CULTURE Electronic music festival with cutting-edge artists. Free. Harbourfront Centre, 416-973-4000, www.harbourfrontcentre.com. July.

BUSKERFEST A four-day celebration of PWYC street theatre, acrobats, dancers, musicians, comics, jugglers and anyone else earning a buck from curbside entertainment. Held in the St. Lawrence Market (see Sightseeing, page 17) and neighbourhood. 416-964-9095, www.torontobuskerfest.com. August.

CANADIAN NATIONAL EXHIBITION Ferris wheels, merry-go-rounds, midway games, agricultural displays, an air show and more. Exhibition Place (Lakeshore West). August.

CELEBRATE TORONTO STREET FESTIVAL Multiple stages on Yonge featuring roots, jazz, world, pop and children's music plus stilt-walkers, theatre, dance and more. Free. 416-338-0338, www.toronto.ca. July.

CITY ROOTS Acoustic music festival featuring folk, world, blues, gospel, roots, children's, storytelling and more. Distillery District, 55 Mill, www.torontocityroots.com. June.

CORSO ITALIA Italian fiesta with food, entertainment, kids activities, sales and more. Free. Earlscourt Park (St Clair and Caledonia) and on St. Clair, between Westmount and Lansdowne, www.torontocorsoitalia.com. July.

DRAGON BOAT FESTIVAL Dragon boat racing and multicultural family entertainment. Free. Centre Island, www.torontodragonboat.com. June.

FESTIVAL OF BEER Beer lovers' celebration with live entertainment, grilling demos and suds. Free admission. Fort York, Garrison off Fleet, www.beerfestival.ca. August.

FESTIVAL OF SOUTH ASIA South Asian music and dancing, food tasting tables and more. 416-698-9053, www.gerrardindiabazaar.com. August.

FOLSOM FAIR NORTH Leather and fetish celebration with fashions, entertainment and more. www.ffnto.com/ffn4. July.

HUMANITAS FESTIVAL Forums, exhibitions, stories, performances, interactive media installations and debate illustrating how Toronto's creative energy is rooted in its history and diversity. www.livewithculture.ca/humanitas. June.

HOT & SPICY FOOD FESTIVAL Celebrity chefs, sampling, a chef cook-off, live music and a marketplace. Free. Harbourfront Centre, 416-973-4000, www.harbourfrontcentre.com. August.

IRIE MUSIC FESTIVAL Celebration of music, art, dance and culture with reggae and global music performers, Caribbean food, a marketplace and more. Free. 905-799-1630, www.iriemusicfestival.com. August.

ISLAND SOUL Caribbean cultural festival with live reggae, soca, calypso, fire dancers, jerk cooking classes and more. Free. Harbourfront Centre, 416-973-4000, www.harbourfrontcentre.com. August.

MASALA! MEHNDI! MASTI! Festival of South Asian arts and culture with music, dance, film, theatre, food, spoken word and more. Free. Exhibition Place. 416-910-5057, www.masalamehndimasti.com. July.

NORTH BY NORTHEAST MUSIC AND FILM FESTIVAL A killer indie festival where you can catch plenty of rockers on the rise and cool movies waiting to be dis-

CONTINUED ON PAGE 164

Groove to the island rhythms at **Caribana**.

Caribana

This massive celebration of island life attracts more than 1 million partiers.

Get ready to wine yuh waist, but leave that hip-hop head-nodding for some other, lesser party. Because even as it approaches 40 and becomes saddled with the mouth-marbling moniker Toronto Caribbean Carnival Caribana – or the slightly less cumbersome but even more ridiculous Carnivalibana – the event still has "mas" appeal. Held over the Simcoe Day long weekend (the first weekend in August), the city blazes to the bacchanal beat of calypso, dancehall and roots reggae, soca, steel pan and straight-up hiphop. Based on Trinidad Carnival and now also including the music, dance, food and costumes of Jamaica, Guyana, the Bahamas, Brazil and other cultures, Caribana attracts more than one million visitors, including hundreds of thousands from south of the border – just scan the license plates while you're watching the rims spin during the Friday night woofer-thumping parade of Lexuses and lowriders down Yonge Street. There's no shortage of events at this jump up, from the thousands of vibrantly – and scantily – costumed masqueraders jamming the Lake-shore parade route to the King and Queen of the Bands Competition to the Olympic Island throwdown and Caribbean Arts Festival. Outdoor concerts of Caribbean music, calypso harbour cruise parties and glamourous dances round out the entertainment roster. Meanwhile, old-school Caribana fans now prefer the vibe at **Afrofest** (see page 162), which is happily settled in Queen's Park, where Caribana vendors once sold beef patties and Trini flags. www.caribana.ca.

covered. Inspired by and partnered with Austin's revered South By Southwest club crawl, Canada's best new music festival quite literally takes over the downtown core in early June for three gloriously sweaty, drunken days of showcases by underground artists from across canada, the US and around the world. Hundreds of bands, over 30 different clubs, plus high-profile bonus events by the likes of Television and the Dears, MC5 and a revived-and-kickin' New York Dolls, coupled with a music-centric film fest and conference that caters to both record label suits and bands trying to catch a break.
416-863-6963, www.nxne.com

PARTI GRAS Celebration of music and culture in conjunction with the Beaches International Jazz Festival, featuring live music, dance, food, prizes and more. Outdoor shows free. Distillery District, 55 Mill, www.torontopartigras.com. July.

RITMO Y COLOR Latin American cultural festival. Free. Harbourfront Centre, 416-973-4000, www.harbourfrontcentre.com. Held every other year in July.

ROOTS:REMIX Roots music and culture festival. Free. Harbourfront Centre, 416-973-4000, www.harbourfrontcentre.com. July.

SALSA ON ST. CLAIR Street festival celebrating Toronto's Latin cultures with music, dancing, art, food and more. Free. St. Clair, between Winona and Christie. July.

SCREAM LITERARY FESTIVAL Spoken word, poetry, dub and more leading up to the grand finale, The Scream In High Park. www.thescream.ca. July.

SOUNDAXIS City-wide festival of acoustic and architectural exploration with music, film, visual art and lectures. 416-925-3457, www.soundaxis.ca. June.

SUMMERLICIOUS Participating restaurants celebrate Toronto's diverse cuisine with special prix fixe menus. www.toronto.ca. July.

TAIWANESE CULTURAL FESTIVAL Food, music, dance and traditional crafts of Taiwan. Free. Harbourfront Centre, 416-973-4000, www.harbourfrontcentre.com. August.

TASTE OF THE DANFORTH Food samplings, live music, dancing, family activities and other events happen on the streets of Greektown. Free admission. www.tasteofthedanforth.com. August.

TASTE OF LAWRENCE FESTIVAL Food, live entertainment, rides, kids activities, artisans and more. Free. Lawrence East, from Crockford to Warden, 416-288-1718, www.tasteoflawrence.com. July.

TORONTO FESTIVAL OF CLOWNS Clowns, mimes, bouffons and physical performers for adults and children. Distillery District, 55 Mill, www.torontoclown.com. July.

TORONTO INTERNATIONAL CIRCUS FESTIVAL Acrobatics, daredevil stunts, fire-eaters, mimes, live music and more on three outdoor stages. Distillery District, 55 Mill, 416-872-1212, www.tocircusfestival.com. July.

TORONTO JAZZ FESTIVAL Euro-jazz, a cabaret series and performances by major artists happen around the downtown. www.torontojazz.com. June.

WAKESTOCK ACTION SPORTS & MUSIC FESTIVAL Wakeboarding, skateboarding, youth stages, live music, films, parties and more than 30 bands. Centre Island. www.wakestock.com. August.

WOOFSTOCK Festival for dogs with doggie fashions, experts, fundraising walks for Canadian Chihuahua Rescue and more. www.woofstock.ca. June.

Get bent at the **Circus Festival**.

Making his own b

R. JEANETTE MARTIN

JOSHUA MELES

Fall

CABBAGETOWN FESTIVAL Festival includes pub crawl, film festival, street festival and more. www.oldcabbagetown.com. September.

Winter

CANADIAN INTERNATIONAL AUTO SHOW Part of the international auto show circuit that includes Paris, Detroit and Tokyo, displaying the latest cars, prototypes, concepts and classics. www.autoshow.ca February.

CAVALCADE OF LIGHTS Month-long festival of events including sparkling lighting displays and one-of-a-kind tour of Toronto's picturesque neighborhoods. www.toronto.ca/special_events. Nov-Dec.

ROYAL AGRICULTURAL WINTER FAIR The largest indoor agricultural, horticultural, canine and equestrian event in the world. 416-263-3400, www.royalfair.org. November.

SANTA CLAUS PARADE Tons of brightly decorated floats, marching bands and costumed paraders lead the way for St. Nick's arrival in the longest-running children's parade in North America. www.thesantaclausparade.com. Late November.

TORONTO INTERNATIONAL CHAMBER MUSIC FESTIVAL Celebration of vocal and instrumental music. 416-763-5066, www.torontochambermusic.com. January.

WINTERCITY FESTIVAL A 14-day outdoor festival featuring concerts, circus performances, buskers, kids' entertainment and fireworks. 416-338-0338, www.toronto.ca/special_events. Jan-Feb.

Celebrate Toronto Street Festival. Page 162.

Literary Festivals

DUB POETRY FESTIVAL
Readings, panels, performances and improv aimed at giving voice to the black experience. Various locations. Held in late July. 416-598-4932, www.dubpoetscollective.com.

INTERNATIONAL FESTIVAL OF AUTHORS
If you like rubbing shoulders with heavyweight literary stars, you'll love this annual end-of-October fest at **Harbourfront Centre** (235 Queens Quay West). An offshoot of Harbourfront's International Readings Series (a year-round slate with its own always impressive roster), the festival was launched in 1980 with a mandate to bring Canadian audiences face to face with the world's best writers. The program goes beyond readings to include interviews with authors, sometimes pairing writers onstage for what turn into intense discussions, and festival director Geoffrey Taylor has widened the mandate to include graphic novelists and writers for children. Over 4,500 authors have participated in the fest's 25-year history. Another big bonus – they really know how to party. www.readings.org.

SCREAM LITERARY FESTIVAL
This annual poetry-centric festival runs at venues across the city, culminating in the Scream In High Park outdoor poetry reading on the Dream in High Park's Shakespearean stage among the trees of **High Park** (see **Sightseeing**, page 38). Held in early July. 416-466-8862, www.thescream.ca.

THIS IS NOT A READING SERIES
Yes, it isn't. This innovative literary series sponsored by the hip book depot **Pages** (see Shopping, page 185) encourages authors to go beyond the standard reading. Sometimes you'll get a Q&A, sometimes an interview, always handled by a local scribe of note. Gene Wilder, for example, is not the kind of person you'd want to hear read from his memoir. But his onstage interview with TV personality Ralph Benmergui rocked. Panels, performances, demonstrations, whatever This Is Not A Reading Series has on its slate, it spells the end of anyone's assumptions that literary events are inevitably snoozeworthy. Held throughout the year at the **Gladstone Hotel** (1214 Queen West). www.pagesbooks.ca.

THE WORD ON THE STREET
Readings by just about every local author with a pulse, 250 exhibitors, big deals on books and mags – no wonder over 190,000 lit fans pack this hugely popular free event celebrating the writing and publishing community. Word On The Street exploded onto the scene in 1989, and what began as a street festival taking over the Queen West strip soon grew out of its three-block site and now blankets all of **Queen's Park** (see **Sightseeing**, page 23). One of T.O.'s top family-friendly events has one more claim to fame – since day one this fall festival has been blessed with freakishly good weather. Held in late September at Queen's Park (at Wellesley). 416-504-7241, www.thewordon-thestreet.ca.

don't know what they're into?

give...
the HMV
gift card

shopping
& services

shopping

Crave a fashion fix? Need a decorative addition for your humble abode? Don't bother jetting to Paris or London or New York. There are plenty of indie boutiques full of wares and wears to keep the style-conscious buzzing right here in Toronto.
For the latest shopping and style coverage, pick up NOW Magazine or visit www.nowtoronto.com.

Shopping by neighbourhood

Downtown

The best way to tackle shopping downtown is by putting one foot in front of the other. The smartest jump-off is the corner of Yonge and College. The walk south guarantees you a wander by electronics superstores, a sex shop or 10, chain outlets galore and the **Eaton Centre** mega-mall. When you hit Lake Ontario, turn west and wander through **Queens Quay Terminal** (207 Queens Quay West; see **Sightseeing**, page 13) for a dose of touristy trinkets and sit by the water to plan your retail route into one of the city's far-flung strips.

Kensington Market

Kensington Market and neighbouring Chinatown are where Toronto's tribe of vintage vixens and style-on-a-budget shoppers score one-of-a-kind finds. Sheri Decaro's **Iki** (19 Kensington, 416-598-0790) features her own line of cutesy hand-stitched bags and local indie designer wears. **Tap Phong** (360 Spadina, 416-977-6364) is stocked with bamboo steamers, kitschy cat coin banks and other Chinese housewares. **Bungalow** (273 Augusta, 416-598-0204) outfits the most swinging mid-century mod pad with smoked-glass tumblers and teak furniture displayed next to racks of second-hand duds.

Midtown

The centre of the city is where Toronto's big shopping bucks come out to pay. Nabes like Summerhill and Bloor Street's **Mink Mile** (see **Sightseeing**, page 26) provide ample options for bottomless budgets. The trick to avoiding a high-end hangover is tracking down expensive stuff that's worth every penny.

Yorkville

Yorkville's hippie past is long gone and the toking set would knot their bell bottoms into a noose if they scoped the 'hood's current fancy-pants shoppers cruising cobblestone streets in their mega-buck SUVs. Luxe shoppers leave their wheels in the block's overpriced parking lots to swan through its alleyways and lanes and stores like **M0851** (23 St. Thomas, 416-920-4001, www.mo851.com), where supple leather gets cut into subtly stylish coats and bags. **Uncle Otis** (26 Bellair, 416-920-2281, www.uncleotis.com) does streetwear of the high-end Stussy variety, and next-door neighbour **Rolo** (24 Bellair, 416-920-0100, www.rolostore.com) hawks cutesy gadgets, trendoid accessories and a timely watch collection featuring pieces by Acme and Cross.

North

Picking out shopping destinations in the wilds of North Toronto is a tricky task. The area is as big as the gas bill you'll rack up cruising from purchase to purchase. So keep an eye out for landmark stores on stroll-friendly strips. If you pick **Bark & Fitz** (see page 187), you can walk the strip of Yonge between Eglinton and Lawrence, where furniture stores and flowery women's clothing boutiques line up. A morning spent at **Elte Carpets & Home** (see page 180) can lead to an afternoon planning an impromptu reno at its neighbouring lighting and home improvement warehouses. And if you make it all the way up to **Pacific Mall** (see page 188), the expansive Asian market extravaganza will have you camping in the parking lot for a week. For the factory outlet experience, check out **Orfus Road**, a city block in the centre of Dufferin and Lawrence's most bustling industrial park where you'll find **Roots** (120 Orfus, 416-781-8729), **Fairweather** (95 Orfus, 416-784-0355) and **Nine West** (53 Orfus, 416-256-3988). And if you get a little peckish from all your spending, stop in to **Grande Cheese** (22 Orfus, 416-787-7670) for some Italian antipasto goodies.

East

Until recently, anyone who lived west of Yonge would wince at the idea of crossing the Don Valley to shop. The Danforth, where the old Greek community collides with yuppie-oriented shops, Leslieville's strip of cafés and collectibles stores and the Beach's restos and indie-owned shops fill up during summer weekends but quickly revert to local hangouts on Monday morning. Now, as more Torontonians move into the area's warehouses and semi-detached fixer-uppers, shopkeepers have swung open their doors to welcome the new design-savvy neighbours. Even if you haven't made the exodus yourself, their shops are definitely worth a short Rocket ride to the east side.

Distillery District

The Distillery District's (55 Mill) contemporary retail options are hidden inside the vintage Victorian stone blocks lining its narrow cobblestone lanes. The hardest find is **Lileo** (building #35, 416-413-1410), just inside the main Mill Street gates. Sportswear and sneaker-pimp-coveted kicks fill the lofty space dedicated to the casual cool lifestyle. Across the square at **distill** (building #56, 416-304-0033), Alison Skinner shows off ceramics and other handmade goodies crafted by emerging art school talents and expert do-it-yourselfers. The **Case Goods Warehouse** (building #74) is where you'll find artist studio spaces like **Wildhagen Hats** and their collection of bold-coloured chapeaus. (For more on the Distillery District, see page 36.)

The vintage shops of **Kensington Market** are a retrosexual nirvana.

West

Go west for the city's wealth of indie retailers. The King, Queen, Dundas and College strips have always been pocked with boutiques, but a recent gentrification boom means attention-deficit shoppers can find great stuff at every step. Visit King West for high-end decor, Dundas for locally designed fashion and College for a combo of the two. Queen West is a store sample platter with a tasty mix of anything your wallet desires.

Roncesvalles

Just before Queen West explodes into a six-lane parkway to suburbia, it crosses over one of the city's most delightful neighbourhood retail routes. Roncesvalles still shows off its Polish immigrant roots, but sprinkled among kielbasa butchers and strolling babcias are great shopping discoveries. **Frock** (97 Roncesvalles, 416-516-1333, www.frock.ca) is where west-side fashion folks spend post-brunch Saturdays surveying a collection of colourful clothing and accessories. **Jackdaw Antiques** (1710 Queen West, 416-538-0846) is one of the area's many retro furniture shops. Across the street, **Stella Luna** (1627 Queen West, 416-536-7300) is the city's most loved vintage clothing boutique. Smart shoppers can usually assemble a throwback dress/shoes/handbag look for under $100.

Fashion
Accessories

AUGUSTINA
138 Cumberland, 416-922-4248.
A handbag heaven hidden on Old York Lane.

BIG IT UP
58 Spadina, 416-591-0864; Eaton Centre.
Big It Up's faux fur trapper hats, fabric collage trucker styles and po' boys and fedoras keep downtown heads toasty and stylish.

BUTTERFIELD 8
235 Danforth, 416-406-5664.
Frieda Kalho totes, Madonna belt buckles by Barbie's Basement Jewellery and other gifty finds fill this Greektown spot.

CHOCKY'S
352 Queen West, 416-977-1831, 2584 Yonge, 416-483-8227.
Chocky's has been the hookup for cheap PJs, onesies and undies for more than 50 years. Look for brands like CK and Elita.

DECIBEL
200 Queen West, 416-506-9648.
There's no sign out front, so just keep an eye out for the cool Kangols on display in the window of this scen-

ester-wear shop, the big bro' to more streetwise **Noise** (275 Queen West, 416-971-6479) across the street.

ENDS
1930 Queen East, 416-699-2271, 140 Avenue Road, 416-968-7272, 3376 Yonge, 416-486-0591.
Just like it says in the name. You never know what retail remains you'll find at this end-of-the-line emporium, from wool overcoats to cargo shorts and all the cheapie tube socks in between.

LILLIPUT
462 College, 416-536-5933, www.lilliputhats.com.
Milliner Karyn Gingras fills her hat shop and studio with frothy headwear confections and smart everyday hats. Old-school silhouettes, including classic cloches and felty fedoras, perch on stands next to more modern Fidel caps and fisherman styles.

LINEA INTIMA LINGERIE
1925 Avenue Road, 416-780-1726, 2901 Bayview, 416-245-3633, 250 Wincott, 416-245-3633, other locations, www.lineaintima.com.
At this bra boutique, one look from expert owner Liliana Mann can change your life (including posture and perk factor). The boutique is also known for its skilled prosthesis fittings and wide range of lingerie styles.

McGREGOR SOCKS OUTLET
70 The East Mall, 416-252-3716; 1260 Birchmount, 416-751-5511 ext. 3, other locations.
You can have too many socks, but when they're practically giving them away, consider disposable a concept.

MELMIRA SWIMSUITS
3212 Yonge, 416-485-0576, www.melmiraswim.com.
Book an appointment, discuss what you're looking for with your sales associate, then wait in the change room while they navigate the warehouse-like back room and return with several versions of your dream-suit-to-be. Best part: sizes range from AA to H cup and from 4 to 26.

PROPAGANDA
686 Yonge, 416-961-0555, www.propaganda.bz.
Lined with floor-to-ceiling cases, this Yonge Street must-shop is a retail museum of Canada's cutest on-trend merch. If you're looking for the perfect girly-yet-cool present for a persnickety fashionista, Propaganda won't disappoint.

ROTMAN'S HAT SHOP
345 Spadina, no phone.
Top-notch men's toppers – if you can catch it open.

SECRETS FROM YOUR SISTER
476 Bloor West, 416-538-1234, www.secretsfromyoursister.com.
Custom bra fittings for finicky busts.

SHANTI
2 Kensington, 416-593-0318.
Amazing selection straight from India. Look for scarves and Indian-inspired jewellery in a multitude of colours, handmade sweaters and mittens and incense and oils.

SUPER SELLERS
474 Yonge, 416 925-5031.
Pit stop dollar-store-esque beauty products and a large selection of discounted women's designer bras, underwear, hose and athletic wear.

TROVE
793 Bathurst, 416-516-1258, www.trove.ca.
Tons of top-it-off goodies make Trove and its across-the-road sister shoe store **Shoon** (760 Bathurst, 416-531-4211) a double accessory hit.

Beauty

AVEDA
95 Bloor West, 413-1333 other locations, www.aveda.com.
Aveda offers an eco-friendly bath, body, hair and beauty line.

B. SKIN
766 King West, 647-222-9054, www.becleansmellgood.com.
Soy candles that combine spice, sugar, floral and herb notes light up bath time while candy-coloured soap bars scrub you clean and scented.

KIEHL'S
407 Queen West, 416-977-3588, other locations, www.kiehls.com.
Kiehl's claims it invented the musk scent, and its line of luxuriously textured lotions, creams and body washes often come with a hint of the smoky note.

LUSH
312 Queen West, 416-599-5874, other locations, www.lush.com.
LUSH lovers dig the intense scents contained in the handmade cosmetics company's jelly-coloured bars and bath bombs.

M.A.C
363 Queen West, 416-979-2171, other locations, www.maccosmetics.com.
Professional-quality blushes and shadows and hyper-pigmented lip glosses deliver M.A.C's signature glam look.

PIR COSMETICS
77 Front East, 416-703-2480; 25 Bellair, 416-513-1603, www.pircosmetics.com.
When makeup from the drugstore rack gives you a metaphorical rash and department store cosmetics counters leave your eyes rolling, Pir comes to the rescue as the urban shopper's oasis. Pricey, but you're worth it, right?

SEPHORA
220 Yonge, 416-595-7227, other locations, www.sephora.com.
Sephora's endless aisles are cosmetic crack for make-up addicts.

Children's wear

BUBBLE FACE
926 College, 416-535-8506.
"It's just cute" is the criteria Bubble Face kids' boutique owner Sylvie Monge uses to pick the wooden toys, felt puppets and miniature biplane mobiles that hang next to embroidered Ts, organic cotton jumpers and cutie booties imported from France, Vancouver and Toronto's own creative kids wear labels.

KINGLY
1078 Queen West, 416-536-2601.
When you're looking for a zany alternative to traditional children's clothes, Kingly comes to the rescue with off-the-wall designs, bold colours and wild prints.

Eyewear

JOSEPHSON
60 Bloor West, 416-964-7070, other locations.
This spot may be over 70 years old, but they keep up, for sure. One of the newest lines is the Oliver Goldsmith collection from London featuring bespoke, vintage-inspired and oversized specs.

MINH CHAU OPTICAL
305 Spadina, 416-979-1828.
Fashion know-it-alls hit Minh Chau for smartly priced, big-name designer frames.

RAPP OPTICAL
788 College, 416-537-6590, www.rapplimited.com.
A pair of peepers purchased at Little Italy's Rapp is guaranteed to help you create a signature look.

SPECTACLE EYEWEAR
752 Queen West, 416-603-0123, other locations, www.spectacle-eyewear.com.
A clear focus on fashion and more than 1,300 designer frames (as well as contacts) make this the place to score those trademark shades.

Jewellery

BIRKS
Manulife Centre, 55 Bloor West, 416-922-2266, other locations, www.birks.com.
Start saving two month's salary to score a well-set ring from the city's swankiest jewel joint.

THE DEVIL'S WORKSHOP
955 Queen West, 416-855-4321, www.thedevilsworkshop.ca.
Jewellery designer Sarah Wan shares her beading, silversmithing and casting skills at her Trinity-Bellwoods studio and gallery.

MADE YOU LOOK
1338 Queen West, 416-463-2136, www.madeyoulook.ca.
In-house designers focus on metalwork, but the 50 jewellers who show their bracelets, rings, necklaces and earrings in individual storefront curio cabinets incorporate glass, stone, fabric, resin and wood into their designs.

NANOPOD
322a Harbord, 647-219-0585, www.nanopod.tv.
Technology-inspired jewellery displayed under clear mini-biosphere domes, plus eight-week classes on working with silver, gold and enamel.

NATHALIE ROZE & CO
1015 Queen East, 416-792-1699, www.nathalie-roze.com.
Local indie designer champion Nathalie-Roze Fischer is a huge favourite among lovers of handcrafted jewellery, fashion and accessories.

Local designers

BOUTIQUE LE TROU
940 Queen West, 416-516-7122.
Le Trou proudly champions the gutsy kids of Toronto's couture scene. Zoran Dobric's gothorific, hand-painted collection easily hangs next to more modern pieces by Juma and Vawk. The common thread is owner Marlene Shiff's lust for fresh, off-the-fashion-map finds.

COMRAGS
654 Queen West, 416-360-7249, www.comrags.com.
Since 1983, local ladies have gone ga-ga over Joyce Gunhouse and Judy Cornish's Comrags line. Favourite pieces get reinvented each season in new fabrics for loyal clients who love their staple silhouettes.

MODEL CITIZEN
913 Dundas West, 416-553-6632.
Girls visit Georgie Bolesworth's Canadian-chic mecca for staple lines like Mercy and Lydia K, while boys dress themselves up in Julian Finkel's reworked silkscreened blazers as well as tailor-made jeans by Sydney's Custom.

PEACH BERSERK
507 Queen West, 416-504-1711, www.peachberserk.com.
Silkscreen queen Kingi Carpenter blazed the Toronto design trail and continues to ink perfect prints. Go for colourful camis, made-to-measure prom wear and workshops for budding fashion entrepreneurs.

PRELOVED
613 Queen West, 416-504-8704, www.preloved.ca.
Before every novice sewer started ripping apart childhood Superman Ts to stitch up sassy summer halters, Julia Grieve had already perfected well-tailored, re-worked vintage with her Preloved label.

SKIRT
903 Dundas West, 647-436-3357.
This little store curates an extensive collection of locally stitched clothing and accessories. Easy (in style and price) pieces by Soos jewellery and Nathalie-Roze are long-term loves of the shop's Cancon-loving costumers.

Ready to wear

ANNE HUNG
829 Queen West, 416-364-7251.
Home to Toronto's mistress of the cheeky party frock.

ANTI-HERO
113 Yorkville Ave, 416-924-6121.
Pleated khakis need not apply for hanger space on racks full of sleek menswear labels.

BODY BLUE
201 Danforth, 416-778-7601; 724 Queen West, 416-703-7601.
Body Blue helps denim-frustrated shoppers into the perfect bod-flattering pair of designer jeans. All the biggie brands, including Diesel and Gas, get mixed and matched with Fly London brand boots and racks of casual-to-dressy T-shirts and jumpers.

EWANIKA
490 College, 416-927-9699.
Owner Trish Ewanika's simple silhouettes and earthy fabric palette have developed a loyal following of shoppers. Frye boots and sculptural handbags mix up the look but maintain the smart, serene vibe.

FREEDOM CLOTHING
939 Bloor West, 416-824-7807.
Ryerson University fashion grads brewed up Freedom Clothing as a boutique home for local design.

FRESH COLLECTIVE
692 Queen West, 416-594-1313.
Stop in to support designers selling it for themselves.

GIRL FRIDAY
776 College, 416-531-1036; 740 Queen West, 416-364-2511, www.girlfridayclothing.com.
Since opening on College in 2002, Girl Friday has staked its claim on it-girl shopping central and opened an equally cute sister location on Queen West in 2004. Each shop carries different lines, including owner Rebecca Nixon's house label. Both locations focus on strong day-into-night pieces, ideal for the city's mix of career-and party-minded shoppers who don't mind a realistic price tag.

GOTSTYLE
489 King West, 416-260-9696, www.gsmen.com.
This menswear loft's mannequins, dressed in dashing, mid-pricey labels like Ben Sherman and Junk deLuxe, stare down from their second-storey windows at the ad agencies and swanky nightclubs where the GotStyle guy works and plays.

GRREAT STUFF
870 Queen West, 416-536-6770.
An awesome little shop filled with sophisticated and way inexpensive menswear.

H&M (HENNES & MAURITZ)
1 Dundas West, 416-593-0064, 15 Bloor West, 416-920-4029, other locations, www.hm.com.
Better watch your back, Le Chateau. With three floors of impossibly low-priced goods and of-the-second stylings, there's clearly no competing with this international 57-year-old mega-brand.

Prepare to prelike **Preloved**'s re-tailored retro styles.

HOLT RENFREW
50 Bloor West, 416-922-2333, other locations, www.holtrenfrew.com.
Don't let the staff's snooty attitude deter you from browsing through Holt's four floors of ritzy buys. Men's stuff in the basement, kids' wear and shoes on the third floor and luxe women's fashion and accessories everywhere in between.

HOLT RENFREW LAST CALL
Vaughan Mills Shopping Centre, Globe 1 Bass Pro Mills, Vaughan, 905-886-7444.
This ultimate ends source provides the price point of a lifetime – up to 70 per cent off – on Armani and the like.

KITSCH BOUTIQUE
325 Lonsdale, 416-481-6712.
Labels like BCBG and Laundry by Shelli Segal cut gowns from bold-coloured cloths and embellish their fishtail and princess silhouettes with rhinestones and sparkly crystals. Make sure to check the basement level for huge discounts.

KORRY'S
596 Danforth, 416-463-1115.
Men's designer suits with smart price tags and thoughtful service.

LILEO
55 Mill, building 35, 416-413-1410, www.lileo.ca.
Nestled in one of the choicest spots in the Distillery District, Lileo is a shopper's dream, featuring the coolest clothes, hottest skin care lines and an abundance of faint-worthy accessories. There's even the Livia juice bar for refuelling.

MAXI BOUTIQUE
575 Danforth, 416-461-6686.
Womenswear from local star labels like Lida Baday and Thien Le.

NORTHBOUND LEATHER
586 Yonge, 416-972-1037, www.northboundleather.com.
Strap yourself into Northbound's collection of leather, pleather and glossy vinyl gear, toys and clothing.

OVER THE RAINBOW
101 Yorkville, 416-967-7448,
www.rainbowjeans.com.
High-priced labels like Citizens of Humanity, 7 for All Mankind and Vancouver's Fidelity fly off the shelves here. Weekends bring hordes of 'tweens, so it's best to shop midweek for maximum salesperson attention.

PHO PA
698 Queen West, 416-979-9444.
Fashionistas eat up Alexia Lewis's hot clothing and accessory picks, especially Toronto-designed goodies, including patchwork-perfect Las Valentias blazers, Dagg and Stacey's textile-collage separates and Pho Pa's own line of chic'd-up staples.

SENSE OF INDEPENDENCE
511 Eglinton West, 416-481-8242.
Twenty-something shopkeep Naomi Shamash caters to North Toronto fashionistas.

STUDIO LABIRI
548 Danforth, 416-778-6820.
Whether it's for a gala, graduation, garden party or just going out with the gals, you can count on Mary Labiri's designer darling to have a stunerrific dress to impress.

SYDNEY'S
795 Queen West, 416-603-3369.
Custom cut jeans and men's- and womenswear from Ted Baker and Alessandrini.

TOM'S PLACE
190 Baldwin, 416-596-0297.
Seriously cram-packed with bargain-priced menswear, it even offers on-site alterations. Bargain with Tom to sweeten the deal on one of his three-for-one suit offerings.

TRIXIE
2313 Bloor West, 416-762-0084.
Foreign entries from Dex, Gentle Fawn and Guess hang happily with Canadian designers Jessie May, House of Spy and Chulo Pony.

TUXEDO ROYALE
Yorkdale Shopping Centre, 3401 Dufferin, 416-785-7940, other locations.
Need a monkey suit for your special occasion? Whether you rent or buy, the wide selection of styles, colours and sizes – plus super service (they even do house calls) – make this chain the first name on the lips of budget-conscious gents across the nation.

URBAN OUTFITTERS
235 Yonge, 416-214-1466.
Trendy clothing for lads and ladies. Funky houseware buys, too.

VOLUPTUOUS
Dufferin Mall, 900 Dufferin, 416-533-3298, other locations.
The name says it all, as this shop provides fab fashions for fuller figures.

WINNERS
57 Spadina, 416-585-2052, other locations.
This chain store carries a bevy of discount designer clothing, handbags and shoes, not to mention household goods.

Shoes

BROWNS
Eaton Centre, 220 Yonge, 416-929-9270 other locations, www.brownsshoes.com.
Both big spenders and budget shoppers mingle over Browns' rack of high-fashion boots, brogues, sandals and stilettos. Decadent designer lines include Prada, Boss, Burberry and Laboutin but smaller, mid-priced collections such as Brava, ID, and B2 are there, too.

DIVINITAS DESIGNS
156 Avenue, 416-944-9491.
Calling Alecia Guevara the city's best cobbler doesn't begin to convey the fabulousness of her footwear.

FLUEVOG
242 Queen West, 416-581-1420, www.fluevog.com.
John Fluevog draws on vintage car design and ultra-modern shapes for his hip, gutsy and sometimes surrealist styles. Favourites get recycled seasonally in bold new colours with smart price tags.

GET OUTSIDE
437 Queen West, 416-593-5598.
Get Outside is Queen West's go-to spot for teens and 'tweens taking their first steps into the post-mall shopping universe. Walls of Puma and Adidas sneaks, granola Birkenstocks and 80s-inspired fluorescent club pumps keep them coming back long into adulthood.

GOODFOOT
431 Richmond West, 416-364-0734, www.getonthegoodfoot.ca.
HQ for the sneakerphile community, Matt George's specialty sneaker store features a selection of exclusive kicks, including rare limited editions, one-off samples and unusual colour combinations.

HEEL BOY
682 Queen West, 416 362 4335, www.heelboy.com.
Women's options including crafty sandals and Mary Janes by Fairyl Robin and Steve Madden's take on runway fresh styles mirror a wall of men's finds, including chunky city loafers and sandals by Kenneth Cole and Diesel.

JOE SINGER SHOES
903 Bloor West, 416-533-3559; 2852 Danforth, 416-693-6045.
Cruise the bountiful racks crammed full of women's (sorry, fellas) leather shoes. Great for both work and club styles, and prices are often as low as $9.99!

LINDSAY PERRY
55 Avenue Road, 416-924-6000, www.lindsayperry.com.
Worn by celebrities and produced in Italy – as all quality shoes inevitably are – Lindsay Perry's design is all Canadian. So go on, click those heels. There's no place like home.

OLLY
2600 Yonge, 416-487-3100, other locations, www.ollyfit.com.
Everyone gets in on the act with Olly's cute kicks for kids.

ROTERING SHOES
545 King West, #408, 416-596-9854, www.roteringshoes.com.
For approximately $400, Sarah Rotering will sculpt you a pair of awesome leather leg covers that will rekindle your love affair with winter. She also gives shoemaking classes.

TOWN SHOES
131 Bloor West, 416-928-5062, other locations, www.townshoes.com
A selection of big-name designer labels (Lacoste, Geox, BCBG to name a few) share space with the store's own stylish line. Town is the exclusive shoe sponsor for every Toronto Fashion Week fashion show, but its footwear looks just as fab on the street as on the runway.

ZOLA SHOES
1726 Avenue Road, 416-783-8688; 45 Avenue Road, 416-922-8688, www.zolashoes.com.
London's Patrick Cox and Paul Smith, Milan's Sergio Rossi and New York bling brand Sigerson Morrison line the shoebox-sized shops with lux footwear. Browse the haute handbags and fashion collections by Toronto labels Izzy Camilieri, Joeffer Caoc and RU.

Vintage

69 VINTAGE
1100 Queen West, 415-516-0669.
More art gallery than vintage store, 69 Vintage stocks the crème de la crème in used clothing, with a neat presentation of the store's wares in a trendy atmosphere and a cool selection of 70s track jackets.

ACT TWO
596 Mount Pleasant, 416-487-2486.
Drastically reduced high-end designer castoffs from the nabe's well-heeled make the trip uptown worth risking the nosebleed.

AMBER DELICIOUS
388 College, 416-913-5248.
If you've got an eye for fab fashion flashbacks or a limited budget, you'll find what you're looking for among Amber's well-priced dresses, shirts and short shorts.

ASTRO
24 Kensington, 416-593-9860.
Make your own T-shirt (and statement) with Astro's collection of heat-transfer designs. Great vintage movie posters and ball gowns, too.

BLACK MARKET
38 Kensington, 416-596-6461, other locations.
The definitive place for cool T-shirts, whether you like 'em with punk rock band names, 80s pop culture staples or slogans about how you love your grandma. Plus awesome silkscreens and a signature brand of reworked vintage.

BRAVA
553 Queen West, 416-504-8742.
A cute, laid-back vintage store for serious finds. Look for 50s beaded cardigans and 60s wool suits. Retro cheerleading uniforms – woo-hoo!

BUNGALOW
273 Augusta, 416-598-0204.
Trendy houseware and clothing outlet with 70s tea sets and silkscreened blazers. Dress and live like a member of the Strokes.

CABARET
672 Queen West, 504-7126.
Wardrobes needing a sprinkle of yesteryear can boost their back-in-the-day look with Cabaret's racks of frothy gowns and stingy brimmed fedoras.

COURAGE MY LOVE
14 Kensington, 416-979-1992.
This Toronto shopping legend is the one-stop shop for neo-hippies and fashionista trendsters searching for killer one-of-a kind vintage threads and accessories.

DANCING DAYS
17 Kensington, 416-599-9827.
Get grooving in this store's collection of vintage wares and tie-dyed tutus.

EXILE
20 Kensington, 416-596-0827.
Organized by item – leopard print coats, Lacoste polo shirts and kilts all have their own racks – Exile also has a great selection of clever shirts and belts.

FLASH BACK
33 Kensington, 416-598-2981.
The 70s are alive again in this Market fave. A great selection of sneakers, flared jeans and sunglasses.

GADABOUT
1300 Queen East, 416-463-1254.
Guys dig Gadabout's Manly Man corner stocked with vintage card decks and fishing gear, while ladies go gaga for way-back-when stylish wears.

GOODWILL
365 Bloor East, 416-362-4711, other locations, www.goodwill.org.
The godfather of thrift stores works two ways: super second-hand deals for you (scavenging required) while providing job placement/training for the disadvantaged and disabled.

HOUSE OF VINTAGE
571 Queen West, 416-363-8343.
Traditional wares in the front, hipster-oriented selection in the back room. All the basics: track jackets, cords and T-shirts. Coolest change rooms on the Queen West circuit.

MARMALADE
44 Kensington, 416-979-8097.
Good thing for you mods that Marmalade's shift dresses and striped T-shirts are there while you wait to get your Vespa out of the shop.

MELANIE'S CLOSET
146 Brock, unit 302, 416-532-4238.
Years of collecting have built Melanie Janisse's clothing cache into a shopper's fantasy. Not only does she offer up a to-die-for selection, if you come at the right time she'll even make you waffles. Call before you drop in.

OFF THE CUFF
5 Broadway, 416-498-4248.
Pair an undercover uptown location with incredible gently used designer duds (from Prada kicks to Jill Sander suits) for a perfect example of shopping heaven. Menswear only.

Don't turn your back on **Bungalow**.

PAPER BAG PRINCESS
287 Davenport, 416-925-2603.
A satellite location of Hollywood's favourite vintage boutique, PBP boasts fabulously pristine designer garments and an A-list clientele. Prices, though, are not exactly thrift shop.

PRINT FINE VINTAGE
834A College, 416-975-8597.
This teensy shop has a killer selection of on-trend vintage picks. Always a good starting point if you're looking to recreate runway-worthy ensembles.

SECOND THOUGHTS CLOTHING
503 Parliament, 416-963-9426.
This Cabbagetown must-shop is the place to go for 50 per cent off on men's and women's retail goods (mostly seconds and factory samples), from jeans to evening wear.

SECOND TIME AROUND,
113 Yorkville, Unit 7, 416-916-7669.
A Yorkville attic full of vintage designer labels.

SPA_CE VINTAGE CLOTHING GALLERY
608Ā Markham, 416-916-6219.
Spa_ce is a mini vintage mecca in Mirvish Village that rarely creeps the prices of its 50s dresses above $50.

STELLA LUNA
1627 Queen West, 416-536-7300.
Everybody's favourite for high-heeled shoes, 40s housedresses and pearl necklaces. Look like a lady and still look hot.

STICKS & STONES
1854 Queen East, 416-699-9611.
Display cases of vintage jewellery (both faux and whoa) line the room and represent the best styles, from the Victorian era to the 80s.

SUNSHINE DELI
895 Dundas West, 416-364-8832.
If you're looking for sassy 80s pumps or any other fashionista must-haves (not to mention fashion inspiration from the staff), this sweet boutique is your ultimate hookup.

TRIBAL RHYTHM
248 Queen West, 416-595-5817, other locations.
It takes time to dig through this vintage lover's dream for supreme clothing, but it's worth a look. Cute accessories and sweaters are found alongside retro dresses and jackets.

VALUE VILLAGE
1319 Bloor West, 416-539-0585.
A second-hand department store featuring a treasure trove of housewares, clothing, accessories and books. Get down early – good stuff goes fast.

Flowers

DUFFLET AND QUINCE FLOWERS
2638 Yonge, 416-484-4343, www.dufflet.com.
If only the two human needs were pastry and flowers, we'd never shop anywhere else. Dufflet represents with fruity tarts and chocolate glazed Bundt cakes, while Quince fills vases with shapely, colourful blooms.

GARDEN'S PATH
327 Queen East, 416-466-0116, www.gardenspath.com.
Like the rest of us, most florists have hit-or-miss days. Not so at Garden's Path. Arrangements here straddle the fine line between tasteful and designed without ever looking too out there or contrived. No worries about offensively lame bouquets; these bunches only evoke joy, which is kinda the point, isn't it?

JONG YOUNG
128 Avenue Road, 416-922-4421.

KAY AND YOUNG
136 Avenue Road, 416-922-5651.
We've searched everywhere for a way to get more bloom for your buck, but nothing beats these perennial flora faves at Av and Dav.

LADYBUG FLORIST
513 Church, 416-922-9971.
Blooms, sprays and sprigs get artfully assembled into stylish arrangements, while potted plants spruce up concrete patios and apartment balconies.

POPPIES
1094 Queen West, 416-538-2497.
Barb Goode and Laura Tarbat's flower boutique overflows with bold-coloured blooms and lush greens. They accent bouquets with frothy marabou feathers and juicy berries for the chicest homes, hotels and VIP green rooms. You can test out your own green thumb with their collection of garden-ready buds and balcony-boosting potted plants.

Food
Bakeries

ACE BAKERY
1 Hafis, at Sheffield, 416-241-3600.
Preservative-free European-style rustic breads. Multigrains, focaccias and sour doughs are superb, and the owners donate a percentage of its pre-tax profits to local charitable organizations.

HARBORD BAKERY
115 Harbord, at Major, 416-922-5767.
Sure, you'll find the expected bagels, breads and blintzes – the cheese danish is famous – at this hallowed bakeshop , but it also has Salvadoran empanadas, Greek spanakopita and Pita Break's amazingly thick, flavoured flatbread.

HODO KWAJA
656 Bloor West, at Manning, 416-538-1208.
To produce his Korean cakes that look like walnuts filled with sweet red bean, almond or walnut paste, Jong Sik Lee uses a hydraulically powered assembly-line-like machine (see it in action in the shop) that steams rather than bakes his golden nuggets to a Timbit crisp. Also available – Proustian madeleines and winter-warming griddle cakes stuffed with stir-fried veggies that reference pupusas.

ST. JOHN'S BAKERY
155 Broadview, at Queen East, 416-850-7413.
Although it's only open to the public on Fridays, this totally organic and very reasonably priced bake shop located in an east-side mission not only makes some of the best loaves around (note the whole wheat sourdough and walnut-studded raisin bread), it has a social conscience, offering a six-month apprentice program to people at risk.

Butchers

COPERNICUS MEAT PRODUCTS AND DELICATESSEN
79 Roncesvalles, 416-536-4054.
The Pakulskis have been in the business for 60 years. Oven-roasted meats like bacon, hams and pork loins are popular as are the sausages. For less meaty fare, check out the freezer full of perogies made by Beata's mother and some of the other women in the neighbourhood.

CUMBRAE
481 Church, at Maitland, 416-923-5600.
Those who care about the provenance of their Provimi veal flock to what many consider Toronto's choicest butcher. Along with such unusual meats as

its naturally raised ostrich, venison and buffalo, find an extensive line of prepared foods – house-made quiches, lasagna, garlic mashed potatoes and pre-fab appetizers like pesto-topped bruschetta and Bombay chicken salad.

FRESH FROM THE FARM
350 Donlands, at O'Connor, 416-422-3276.
Only open Thursday to Saturday, this low-key operation acts as a go-between for the province's Amish and Mennonite farmers and those looking for locally raised and preservative-free meat. Best to order in advance at www.freshfromthefarm.ca from a lengthy lineup of naturally raised products.

HEALTHY BUTCHER
565 Queen West, at Denison, 416-703-2164.
Located in a beautifully restored 19th century storefront, this recent addition to Toronto's gourmet scene only sells meat that is certified organic, grown humanely and free of chemicals.

KARL'S BUTCHER
105 Roncesvalles, 416-531-1622.
You can smell the smoke that defines Karl's meat specialities when you step into this Polish time machine. Karl Jarzabek's been in the house for 44 years. Side bacon, kielbasa, hunters sausage and knobbly, smoke-tinted pork shoulders glow behind the counter. Hundreds of jars of pickles, sauces and mustards complete the Polish picture.

MEAT ON THE BEACH
1860 Queen East, at Rainsford, 416-690-1228.
This quirkily named east-side butcher shop specializes in meat that's hormone-free and environmentally sound if somewhat pricey. Come summer, this old-fashioned grocery expands curbside with a lineup of locally grown veg and flowers. Don't miss the house-baked butter tarts!

Cheese
ALEX FARMS
St. Lawrence Market, 93 Front East, 416-368-2415, 377 Danforth, 416-465-9500, other locations.
Like all other Alexes, the St. Lawrence branch is, as their slogan says, "an adventure in cheese," and it posts very helpful little signs that tell you all about the cheese you're looking at. Colston and Bassett Stilton, Alex's own cheddar, Brie de Meaux and Papillon Noir Roquefort are just some of the odiferous aristocrats that await you.

CHEESE DAIRY
454 Bloor West, 416-533-3007.
Imagine trying to run a fine cheese shop when the majority of the population you serve are 19-year-olds working on their BA in gym history. Well, that doesn't stop Zemfira Shevelenko from stocking a fine bunch of fromage in her homey Annex shop. Over 300 cheeses with big action in raw milk cheeses from Quebec. Lots of other jars and packaged goodies line the uncheesed walls.

CHEESE MAGIC
182 Baldwin, 416-593-9531.
Blended and flavoured cheeses are popular here: English smoked applewood cheddar, garlic Havarti and horseradish cheddar just give a hint of the flavouring possibilities.

LA FROMAGERIE
868 College, 416-516-4278.
Hazel Eccelstone and Robert Burns focus on hard-to-find farmhouse, French and Quebec raw milk cheeses. To accompany such delights as Barbiche de St-Roche or Crottin de Chavignol, they sell breads supplied by Pain Perdu or Thuet. Great bread and cheese.

The cheese stands alone at **La Fromagerie**.

Chinese markets
HAU LONG SUPERMARKET
253-259 Spadina, 416-977-8597.
The most chaotic of the big Chinese stores, this one is a sensory fun house. Conforming to type, it's produce up front, flesh in the back and row upon row of dried goods in the middle. The fish zone is especially engaging with tall crowded tanks, choppers chopping and dead things on ice all over the place.

HAU SHENG SUPERMARKET
293-299 Spadina, 416-263-9883.
The second part of Chinatown's "Hau's-on-first" supermarket comedy routine, this one is just a little more placid. But not much. If you want to try some of China's great cuisine at home, comb the aisles for anything and everything you might need. Deals await, especially in the seafood and produce departments. All signs in Chinese and English.

TRINITY SUPERMARKET
587 Gerrard East, 416-462-1211.
The east end's mirror image of Spadina's Chinese supermarkets. Especially good for those unfamiliar with Asian specialities. Oh yes, that is a big tub of pig uteri you're staring at.

Dry goods
STRICTLY BULK
924 Bloor West, 416-533-3242; 638 Danforth, 416-466-6849; 1898 Eglinton West, 416-686-8666, other locations.
Strictly speaking, it's not just strictly bulk, which is a good thing. But they do have lots of bins full of healthy stuff for seed munchers and bean cookers everywhere. Also excellent coffee for cheap.

LOUIE'S COFFEE
235 Augusta, 416-593-9717.
Fronted by a corner coffee bar, this market veteran never ceases to please with row-upon-row of glass candy jars. In addition to the confectionery, there's a great selection of spices and bulk. Louie's real claim to fame, though, is the wall of teas, with exotics like white monkey paw and jasmine dragon. If it's good enough for Brenda Vaccaro, it's good enough for you.

Fish
BILL'S LOBSTER AND FISH MARKET
599 Gerrard East, 416-778-0943.
It's ironic that so much of Bill's stock is alive in tanks,

Hau Long can they stare without blinking? Wait, are they checking out the cheese?

because seafood lovers will think they've died and gone to heaven. Lobsters, one-clawed lobsters, Dungeness crab and turbot imported live from France get in the swim. Choice fillets recline on ice. Bill Cheng's enthusiasm is unequalled.

PISCES GOURMET
1103 Yonge, 416-921-8888.
It's full steam ahead at this acclaimed long-standing shop, recently taken over by the mother and daughter team of Silvia and Melissa Blackwood. Big chunky kabobs of halibut and salmon scream barbecue. The carriage trade is attracted by sushi-grade tuna, billiard-ball-sized crab cakes, trolled wild spring salmon and Russian caviar. Regular folks could try the less expensive herring avruga.

SEA KINGS FISH MARKET
189 Baldwin, 416-593-9949.
This is one of several unglamorous, pungent, blood-soaked fish mongers that defy the onset of Kensington Market's vintage Danish furniture stores. Beautifully Kensington in its politics, Sea King is Portuguese-owned and -operated for a clientele that's almost completely Caribbean. Here they shop for whole snappers, porgies, grunts and kingfish.

Indian grocers

BJ SUPERMARKET
1449 Gerrard East, 416-469-3712.
When somebody decides to write the story of how Little India built itself into a prosperous retail strip in a hard nabe southeast of Riverdale, BJ, which opened almost 30 years ago, will be the starting point. Since then it's remained in the same location with an effective mix of Eastern and Western staples.

AHMAD GROCERS
1616 Gerrard East, 416-461-3104.
This humble shop tells another part of Little India history in that Ahmad was the first to sell meat. And that's still their main gig. Lamb, beef and fresh yellow chicken are the mainstays. Father-and-son team Anwar and Vick Ahmad are behind the counter.

KIHINOOR FOODS
1438 Gerrard East, 416-461-4432.
There was a time when those who were attempting to cook the cuisine of India and Pakistan would have to make a pilgrimage to this spice and rice centre. Now that you can get garam masala at Loblaws, it's still worth the trip to Kihinoor. Although it's small, it's got it all.

Produce

HARVEST WAGON
1103 Yonge, 416-923-7542; 546 Eglinton, 416-487-0388.
Here's a place to make the vegetarian swoon. Donut peaches, pluots, gooseberries, white asparagus and zucchini blossoms tell you this place knows its produce. Rosedale presentation and Rosedale prices are to be expected, but the staff, headed up by owner Tony Di Marco, are fine folks who know their glorious fruit.

K&K SPECIALTY
298A Spadina, 416-979-3435.
"Mango, mango, mango, mang-O•O-O-O," hawks the lean, mohawked fruit seller at the front stalls. Bring your appetite and your guide to Asian produce, because unless you speak, I'm guessing, Cantonese, consultations will be brief. Luckily, signs are also in English. Incredible array of exotics like pomelos, mangosteens, sugar-apples and that showoff, the dragon fruit.

MAGNOLIA
548 College, 416-920-9926.
If ever there was a place that could be called a fruitique, Julio Ferrante and Roberto Vicenzo's Magnolia is it. Nature's finest bask in pools of incandescent light. Meander the hardwood floor not only for the sweet array of sweet fruit, but for a large selection of other gourmet items.

OXFORD FRUIT
255 Augusta, 416-979-1796.
K.T. and Ah Tee Ng own this well-stocked, reasonably price fruitatoreum in the heart of the market, with rock-bottom prices on staples like bananas. Melons are a real favourite here, including lesser-knowns like Santa Claus and Sharlyn varieties, and watermelon is the big seller. Presentation is a cut above Market standards.

RONCESVALLES FRUIT VILLAGE
147 Roncesvalles, 416-538-3470.
While Roncie is definitely meat street, there are other food attractions, and Fruit Village represents the greens as well as anyone. Like any good fruit-and-veg shop, its goods spill out onto the sidewalk, but specialty items such as quince and granadilla reside within. Nice little garden centre on the side.

Specialty

ALL THE BEST
1099 Yonge, 416-928-3330, other locations.
A lot of what's stocked here, like sauces, condiments and dressings, are made in the store's own kitchens. Especially tempting is the frozen cookie dough.

THE BIG CARROT
348 Danforth, 416-466-2129, www.thebigcarrot.ca.
Good living with eco-friendly groceries (and beauty products).

DINAH'S CUPBOARD
50 Cumberland, 416-921-8112.
Teas, coffees and spices are attractively displayed, but the takeout counter really brings in the swells. Mother's meat loaf, grilled ratatouille and an attractive salad counter sustain those on the go.

JS BON BONS
163 Dupont, 416-920-0274; 811 Queen West, 416-703-7731, www.jsbonbons.com.
Chocolate cooking classes and a hot cocoa bar at the Queen Street location cover every chocoholic base.

PUSATERI'S
57 Yorkville; 1539 Avenue Road, 416-785-9100.
Never mind about a looney for the shopping cart; this place has valet parking. Ridiculously plump pickled peppers, 2-inch-thick AAA T-bones and champagne-marinated lamb chops get the juices flowing. Something to go? How about a little miso-and-mirin-coated Brome Lake duck breast?

ST. LAWRENCE MARKET
92-95 Front E, 416-392-7120.
A one-stop food shopping experience with dozens of stalls offering everything from fresh meats at Scheffler's Deli (415-364-2806) and Brown Brothers (416-364-7469) to sushi-grade seafood at Domenic's Fishmarket (416-368-1397) and organic fruits and vegetables at Golden Orchard Fine Foods (416-860-0288). See **Sightseeing**, page 17.

SPRINGCREEK FARM PRODUCE
291 Roncesvalles, 416-534-9703.
Anna Lipiec looks after this tidy meat and fish emporium that emphasizes non-factory, organic, locally raised products. AAA steaks tempt, as does lamb. Especially worth checking out is the freezer full of fresh-frozen pickerel, whitefish, rainbow trout and splake, all caught in Georgian Bay.

SUN VALLEY FINE FOODS
583 Danforth, 416-469-5227.
While it functions perfectly well as an attractive neighbourhood grocery, you can drop a lot of green in the Valley. The deluxe butcher and deli counter will give you the AAA treatment. Stock up on the milk and eggs and then head over to the caviar display. Or just have a good long look at the 30 or so cakes on display. Putting the "super" back in supermarket.

TASTE: THE 4TH SENSE
375 Danforth, 416-649-0024.
Hardcore chili heads who hit this condiment emporium can numb tongues with sauces spiced up to 7.1-million Scoville units, a measure of a pepper's potency (jalapeño is 8,000 units, while a blast of pepper spray tears you up with 2 million). Take home bottles labelled Acid Rain, Alberta Crude or Liquid Stoopid.

24-hour

Toronto has plenty of chain mega-markets – **Sobeys, Loblaws, Real Canadian Superstore** – but when you need groceries at 2 am, here's where you go.

BLOOR SUPER SAVE
384 Bloor West, 416-964-8318.
Toronto's first 24-hour store, opened in 1976, has changed hands after 30 years of hands-on ownership by the Taddeo family. In that time they've seen it all: fight, thefts, movie stars, the Golden Girls. Produce is the big item here, but the generously equipped chip stand speaks to the 3 am crowd.

RABBA
256 Jarvis, 416-595-9679, other locations.
These brightly lit, inviting shops in locations across the city provide a solid range of produce, groceries, deli and junk food to early risers, nightlifers and everybody in between.

DOMINION
735 College, 416-533-2515, other locations.
Dominion's slogan, "We're fresh obsessed," may seem pretty ironic when you drag your all-night-long self through their automatic doors for that lifesaving jug of Tropicana, but you know you love this full-service supermarket chain for being there when you need it the most.

Gifts

KOL KID
670 Queen West, 416-681-0368.
Kiddies dig Kol's plush stuffed animals and young reader books.

MAGIC PONY
**694 Queen West, 416-861-1684,
www.magic-pony.com.**
This trendy gallery shops offer artsy goodies with a pop-culture slant at newbie-collector prices. Japanese and Western figurines of wonky characters hang out next to racks of graphic T-shirts and collectable retro toy sets. The slick white backroom gallery welcomes a rotation of local artists and international finds.

MOTORETTA IN THE BEACH
1971 Queen East, 416-694-4800.
Vespas and preppy, colourful clothing.

ONTARIO SPECIALTY CO.
133 Church, 416-366-9327.
Loot bag stuffers and club kids hunting for plastic Elvis shades and wooden gum-ball necklaces mingle in this gift store in Church Street's pawn shop alley. Their collection of colourful kazoos and retro tin toys offers an alternative to the usual beeping, buzzing, hyperactive kids' toys.

OUTER LAYER
430 Bloor West, 416-324-8333, www.outerlayer.ca.
Find your local postcard fix among Outer Layer's great gifts.

RED PEGASUS
628 College, 416-536-3872.
Cute gifts and everything you need to wrap them up.

ROLO
24 Bellair, 416-920-0100, www.rolostore.com.
If you're a gift certificate away from being labelled a generic-gift bore, hit this Yorkville shop, jam-packed with everything from designer jewellery to cutesy knick-knacks, colour-morphing lighting, chocolate-covered cherries, computer bags and scented body care. No matter what the situation, occasion, relation or motivation, the perfect prezzie's here.

TOKEN
888 Queen West, 416-516-9586.
This neighbourhood gift shop, a mandatory pit stop before hitting any style-savvy housewarming or dinner party, has shelves stocked with cool greeting cards, journals and other frilly houseware and stationary finds.

ZIGGY'S AT HOME
794 College, 416-535-8728.
Furniture and bath products create complete nesting nirvana.

Green

See Green Toronto, page 211.

Home decor
Fabric

BB BARGOONS
**2784 Yonge, 416-481-5273, other locations,
www.bbbargoons.com.**
Upholstery fabric to jazz up your home's drapeless windows, worse-for-wear sofas and bare basic pillows. Swatches available.

DESIGNER FABRIC OUTLET
1360 Queen West, 416-531-2810.
The ground floor of this two-storey king of Toronto fabric shops is full of upholstery swatches, and every rod, finial and ribbon needed to swank up your home. Upstairs, rolls of weighty pinstriped suiting wools and raver-pant-era fun furs are marked down for the budget-conscious.

FABRICLAND
**2450 Bloor West, 416-769-2835, other locations,
www.fabricland.ca.**
Fabricland might not cut you the cheapest yard, but the clean, well-organized, one-stop shops for cloth, thread and notions are a good starting point for stitching beginners.

KING TEXTILES
445 Richmond West, 416-504-6000.
A lot of Queen and Spadina's original fabric shops have bolted for cheaper rents in north Toronto, but King is holding strong in the city's original shmata district.

Furniture & fixtures

ADDISON'S
41 Wabash, 416-539-0612.
Here's a rescue mission for vintage plumbing and other fixtures. Whether you're looking for a claw-foot tub or just a claw foot, this is the place to score both.

ART METROPOLE
**788 King West, 416-703-4400,
www.artmetropole.com.**
If you're not a do-it-yourselfer but still want great art cheap, this is the place to go. An archive for work by artists exploring the use of alt-media, the 30-year-old org specializes in book works, audio-visuals and artist-made multiples. Feel free to browse through the vast collection in this reference art-brary.

ARTEMIDE
20 Camden, 416-628-6718, www.artemide.ca.
If you've got the dough and you're ready to trick out your pad in designer home gear, Artemide – part high-brow designer lighting store, part homewares gallery featuring gorgeous stainless steel kitchen necessities by Alessi – should be your first stop.

CASA LIFE
**170-171 East Liberty, 416-922-2785,
www.casalife.com.**
This Liberty Village decor store specializes in small furnishings with big style. Microsuede ottomans that

open to reveal ample magazine-stashing space and comfy sofas that break down to fit through the tightest front doors are must-haves for tiny flats where every square foot counts.

DOLLAR JOINT
1499 Gerrard East, 416-465-0915, other locations.
Dollar stores are a neighbourhood thing, but with two storeys of $1 goodies – from barware to underwear to hardware – Dollar Joint is the classic old-school dollar store.

THE ELEGANT GARAGE SALE
1588 Bayview, 416-322-9744.
If mishmash rocks your world, this retail and consignment store is the place for you. From junk to treasure and every variable in between, it's worth the scavenge.

ELTE
80 Ronald, 416-785-7885, www.elte.com.
Carpet king Elte fills its floors with cushy area rugs and contemporary sisal mats. Large-scaled furniture fits mansion-sized floor plans, while Summerhill Hardware's door pulls help gussy up ragged kitchens in a weekend mini-reno.

EQ3
222 King East, 416-815-2002, www.eq3.com.
EQ3 delivers style-on-a-budget furniture and housewares. Crayola crayon-coloured glassware and storage boxes mix and match with choose-your-own-fabric living room sets.

ETHEL
1091 Queen East, 416-778-6608.
This shop and its second-hand furniture neighbours make Leslieville the city's primo vintage decor 'hood.

EYE SPY
1100 Queen East, 416-461-4061.
Kitschy home accessory stock is always changing, so weekly visits are a must. Finds have included Andy Warhol banana split bowls, Freida Kahlo dolls and pillows patchworked from the store's secret vintage fabric stash.

FLUID LIVING
55 Mill, building #8, 416-850-4266.
Distillery District shoppers scoop up mid-priced, modern sofa sets for their chic loft lifestyles here.

GINGER'S BATH
95 Ronald, 416-787-1787.
Across from Elte, this lavatory heaven has every faucet, tub and rain shower head to build your dream home spa.

HABITAT FOR HUMANITY RESTORE
29 Bermondsey, 416-755-8023; 1120 Caledonia, 416-783-0686.
They say "recycled," you say "retro." Call it what you will, Restore sells salvaged home components – think fireplaces, sinks, lighting – at thrift-store prices. Plus, the proceeds go directly toward helping the community.

INABSTRACTO
1160 Queen West, 416-533-6362.
Owner Kate Eisen fills her shop windows with Freitag's recycled-truck-tarp bags and its floor with coveted retro desks and lamps.

ITAL INTERIORS
359 King East, 416-366-9540, www.italinteriors.com.
Outfitting the city's decorator elite with the best designer furniture from Italy – everything from sofas to dining sets, beds to wall units, plus kitchen and bath by Boffi – for more than 25 years, this family-owned business is the place to be if you're looking to add high-end names like Cassina, Flexform, Moroso, Molteni & C, Cristian and Matteo Grassi to your collection of contemporary modern.

Eye Spy something that is orange and purple and red

KOMA DESIGNS
1239 Queen West, 416-532-5662, www.komadesigns.com.
With Ikea styling our homes with its patented affordable minimalism, the need for decor individuality couldn't be greater. Enter this West Queen West shop and its eclectic (meaning a stylie mix of old and new, modern and rustic, locally made and imported) grouping of items that will remedy that blank-slate look.

MA ZONE
63 Jarvis, 416-868-0330, www.ma-zone.com.
Armin Martiros's home decor boutique stocks gummy-candy-coloured housewares by worldly design-savvy outfits like Koziol, Ritzenhoff and Leonardo that find their way into chic homes, lounges and restaurants.

MONTAUK SOFA
280 King East, 416-361-0331, www.montauksofa.com.
If your pockets are deep, check out this selection of massive white-cotton-slip-covered chaises and sofas.

MORBA
665-667 Queen West, 416-364-5144, www.morba.ca.
An endless selection of vintage globes, starburst clocks, film equipment and fly pad-perfect furniture fills the shop's double Queen West storefront.

ONI ONE
1335 Dundas West, 416-850-8111, www.oni-one.com.
This sleek 4,000-square-foot showroom sandwiched between Little Portugal's churrasqueiras and sports bars specializes in big style for small spaces.

PAUL WOLF ELECTRIC
775 King West, 416-504-8194, www.paulwolf.com.
DIY electrical can be a dangerous oxymoron, which is why the pros at Paul Wolf don't let you finger the quality-on-a-budget merch. Custom service prevents any MacGyvered home jobs.

UP TO YOU
1483 Queen East, 416-778-6487.
This is one voyeuristic retail experience. It's set up as a stylishly decorated apartment where everything from the shower curtain to the clothes on the hangers are for sale. The boutique boasts an amazing selection of gifty items from New York, London, Paris, Athens and Helsinki.

rowed and creepy and lampy.

UPCOUNTRY
310 King East, 416-777-1700, www.upcountry.com.
A contemporary furniture fan's wet dream, with multiple levels of luxe lounger couches and awesome accessories.

Kitchenware

CALPHALON CULINARY CENTRE
425 King West, 416-847-2212,
www.calphalonculinarycenter.com.
Outfit your expert kitchen or take a cooking class.

INNER LUXE
2358 Bloor West, 416-915-3982, www.innerluxe.ca.
This Bloor West Village store sells clever serving gadgets like cheese platters made from flattened Jack Daniel's bottles and refined rosewood chopsticks.

IQ LIVING
542 Danforth, 416-466-2727.
Chrome wire kitchen racks get loaded with espresso cups, pots and pans, bottle openers and every culinary accoutrement.

KITCHEN STUFF PLUS
703 Yonge, 416-944-2718; 2887 Yonge,
416-504-0515, other locations.
From flan pans to frying pans, blenders to BBQ utensils, glassware to silverware, great stuff at reasonable prices. The "plus" part includes bathroom items, curtains and picture frames.

WILLIAMS-SONOMA
100 Bloor West, 416-962-9455, other locations,
www.williams-sonoma.ca.
This high-end source for baterie de cuisine provides your kitchen tool case with apple corers, egg slicers, hand juicers and other gadget-lust-inducing cooking gear.

Home electronics

ACTIVE SURPLUS ELECTRONICS
347 Queen West, 416-593-0909,
www.activesurplus.com.
The iconic gorilla at the front door leads to two madly jumbled floors of DIY paradise. Find refurbished phones, disco mirror balls and just about any cable you could possibly ever need: phone extension cords, gold RCA jacked audio lines, computer and coaxial cables and splitters you need to hook up cable TV, plus a gazillion boxes of random junk perfect for the basement engineer in you.

BAY BLOOR RADIO
55 Bloor West, 416-967-1122,
www.baybloorradio.com.
Dreams of shopping for electronics and gadgets minus the big-box setting and stalker sales tactics are answered here. Hidden away on the basement level of the Manulife Centre is an oasis of flat-screens TVs, well-tuned stereo sets and personal entertainment devices.

CARBON COMPUTING
772 Queen East, 416-535-1999,
www.carbonation.com.
The friendliest place in the city to blow your student loan on a new Mac. Nice service and cheap prices to boot.

CPUSED
488 Dupont, 416-533-2001, www.cpused.com.
A good place to pick up a used or refurbished Mac. Check the Web site for the price list, updated daily.

FACTORY DIRECT
290 College, 416-962-7788, other locations.
For great deals, culture pirates head for this discount computer store in the old Cinema Lumiere movie house near U of T. Warning: because the deals are sweet, the lineups at the cash register are often long and slow-moving. Bring some required reading.

FUTURE SHOP
355 Yonge, other locations, 416-971-5377,
www.futureshop.ca.
You can buy cellphones and iPods in corner stores, strip malls and from curious-looking sidewalk dealers these days, but for sheer variety and the lowest possible price, no one beats big-box stores like Future Shop.

VISTEK
496 Queen East, 416-365-1777, www.vistek.ca.
A one-stop shop for pro-level gear, with a full rental service on the first floor, a huge array of digital cameras, printers, scanners and video equipment on the second, and pro hardware in the third-floor Pro Centre. Vistek also offers a hands-on demo lab and deals on new and used equipment. Check the huge inventory online.

Deals

PC users looking to put together a box on a budget have to take the walk down College Street's silicone alley. Shops like **Alpha Plus Computer** (287 College, 416-323-0898), **Canada Computer** (343 College, 416-926-0107) and **Inmax Computer** (322 College, 416-975-8886) sell gear cheap cheap cheap.

D.I.Y.
Art

ABOVEGROUND ART SUPPLIES
74 McCaul, 416-591-1601.
In the shadow of OCAD's big box on stilts, this is a great cheap place to find tools and materials.

CURRY'S
573 Queen West, 416-260-2633, 490 Yonge, 416-967-6666, 283 Dundas West, 416-585-9292, other locations, www.currys.com.
Hemingway bought pens here, and it's where artists, art school kids and part-time painters stock up on canvases, acrylics and craft sets. Painting pupils score extra discounts by showing their student cards.

GWARTZMAN'S CANVAS & ART SUPPLIES
448 Spadina, 416-922-5429.
For huge stretched canvases on an artist's budget this is the place to go. It also offers a great selection of art materials like sable brushes, leather notebooks, paints, etc.

TERN ART
847 Queen West, 416-537-7338.
The lesser-known Tern Art is an hidden treasure, with a good selection despite its small size.

WOOLFITT'S
1153 Queen West, 416-536-7878, www.woolfitts.com.
A blobby Will Alsop-designed condo sales centre that will eventually become the art supply store's own gallery recently went up in the Woolfitt's parking lot. Artists gunning for a show in the new space should stock up on painting gear in the warehouse-sized shop until units sell out.

Clothes

LETTUCE KNIT
66½ Nassau, 416-203-9970, www.lettuceknit.com.
Blame it on techno backlash, but knitting is a growing trend. Headquarters for yarn junkies is Lettuce Knit. Pick up this valuable skill now and maybe in, like, 50 years you'll have something to teach your grandkids. Bamboo yarns for vegan knits and purls. Workshops, too.

SEW BE IT STUDIO
2156 Yonge, 416-481-7784, www.sewbeitstudio.com.
Stitching and crafting classes here take do-it-yourself-ing beyond the basics. Beading appliqué, bra making, millinery and pattern drafting are some of the skills creative folks pick up during weekend workshops and month-long weekly classes.

WINKEL
1107 Queen East, 416-465-4247.
This shop won over our retail hearts by stocking bolts of vintage patterns like fruitful Tuscany Red and graphic Paradise Lace, suitable for hearty summer totes or patio-friendly placemats. Recycled ad-sign bags and Mexican-wrestling-themed cross-stitch sets round out the crafty stock.

Music

CAPSULE MUSIC
921 Queen West, 416-203-0202, www.capsulemusic.com.
A jaw-dropping selection of previously loved instruments – Fender, Nash, Gibson, Gretsch – priced from affordable to oh-my-god-how-much?

LONG & McQUADE
925 Bloor West, 416-588-7886, other locations, www.long-mcquade.com.
Whether you're looking for a flugelhorn or the latest special edition Gibson guitar, L&McQ have a large selection of new, used and rental instruments to choose from.

RING MUSIC
90 Harbord, 416-924-3571, www.ringmusic.com.
As clichéd as it sounds, this is the place for all your guitar needs. Gordon Lightfoot, Bruce Cockburn and the Barenaked Ladies are all customers. Ring also offers a full on-site repair shop.

SONGBIRD
801 Queen West, 416-504-7664, www.songbirdmusic.com.
Since 1988, the store has offered new but mostly used instruments and accessory gadgets. A must-stop shop for the popular models of the moment, with wide selection.

ST. JOHN'S MUSIC
109 Vanderhoof, 416-785-5000, www.stjohnsmusic.com.
When it comes to saxamaphones and other reed or brass instruments, this shop – 80-plus years and still blowing strong – is among the best in the biz. Rentals and repairs also available.

STEVE'S MUSIC STORE
415 Queen West, 416-593-8888, www.stevesmusic.com.
Amazing selection – stringed intruments, drums, keyboards, DJ and recording equipment – across the whole range of prices. The little glass cabinet in the back corner is always worth drooling over.

TWELFTH FRET
2132 Danforth, 416-423-2132, www.12fret.com.
Guitars and banjos, new, used and vintage – this is the place for 'em, as many as 40 new instruments each week.

Photography

BLACK'S PHOTOGRAPHY
50 Bloor West, 416-922-8475; Eaton Centre, 416-598-1596; other locations, www.blackphoto.com.
A full line of digital and SLR cameras and equipment for the newbie and experienced amateur photographer alike.

FUJI 1-HOUR PHOTO
604 Bloor West, 416-530-1104, other locations.
Cameras, film, accessories and one-hour developing.

HENRY'S
119 Church, 416-868-0872, www.henrys.com.
One of the city's top stops for shutterbugs, with a full line of cameras and equipment for the amateur and professional shooter and a very knowledgeable staff.

JAPAN CAMERA CENTRE
48 Front, 416-363-7476; 1456 Yonge, 416-920-3756, other locations.
Need to see that pic of yourself standing in front of the CN Tower while you're still standing in the tower's shadow? Perhaps you've run out of film. It's that kind of camera shop.

Records/DVDs/Books
Records

AROUND AGAIN
18 Baldwin, 416-979-2822.
Tucked away at Baldwin and McCaul, this quaint little shop is worth investigating for rare vintage jazz, blues, psych, R&B and classical music at well-below-collectors' prices. They also stock cool reissue Latin, Brazilian, psych vinyl LPs.

COSMOS RECORDS
607 Queen West, 416-603-0254.
Known as a high-end shop primarily serving the esoteric vinyl requirements of jet-setting European DJs with loads of cash to blow on rare funk, Brazilian, Latin jazz, hiphop and indie disco 12-inch singles, Cosmos also has piles of hard-to-find jazz and R&B records from the 70s and 80s, reasonably priced between $5 and $15. A second shop, Cosmos West (663 Queen West, 416-861-9228), has a solid selection of classic Blue Note and Prestige label jazz and rare funk.

DISCOVERY USED & COLLECTORS RECORDS
1140 Queen East, 416-778-6394.
The prices here are reasonable enough that there's really no need for a dollar bin. You'll be amazed by the quality 60s rock, blues, country, jazz and soca records.

HARMONY
711 Mount Pleasant, 416-440-1386.
A bit off the beaten path, but well worth the trip for its unparalleled selection of vintage rock, R&B, blues and jazz vinyl, top-notch used jazz and world CDs, music and film books and an impressively large stock of used DVDs.

HMV
333 Yonge, 416-586-9668; Eaton Centre, 416-340-9801, 50 Bloor West, 416-324-9979 other locations.
The international chain stocks all the latest goods, from top 40 hits to jazz and classical recordings.

SLINKY MUSIC
442 Queen West, 416-603-2600.
Kops Kollectibles (229 Queen west, 416-593-8523) used to be the Queen West mecca for roots reggae, soul and rock reissues, but that's all changed since some ex-Kops employees opened up Slinky down the street and took the DJ equipment store Moog Audio with them. A lot to choose from and with a choice assortment of hiphop, funk, Brazilian, jazz and reggae reissues.

Don't fret about the price on second-hand axes at **Songbird**.

LOST N FOUND
974 Bathurst, 416-538-2788.
Top-notch 60s and 70s psych, prog, jazz and soul collectibles and reissues rarely stocked by other Toronto stores.

NEUROTICA
642 Queen West, 416-603-7796.
Home to a huge stockpile of easy listening, lounge and exotica records in addition to some strange spoken word stuff and an oddball mix of alt-rock, blues and jazz.

PLAY DE RECORD
357A Yonge, 416-586-0380.
Chock-a-block with old-school hiphop, house, trance, R&B, disco, Euro club, jazz and funk.

ROTATE THIS
620 Queen West, 416-504-8447.
A fab selection of cool indie rock, roots reggae, soul, avant jazz, hiphop and electronic music that people working at the big chain stores never knew existed.

SAM THE RECORD MAN
347 Yonge, 416-646-2775,
www.samtherecordman.com.
A local landmark, Sam's is the only big-box music store in the city that retains the grimy, labyrinthine feel of an old-timey record shop. Famous for its frequent sales and often deeply discounted product.

SECOND VINYL
2 McCaul, 416-977-3737.
Boldly proclaims to specialize in "classical and jazz," so most beat junkies give it a pass. Too bad, since a really incredible gospel album or weird Japanese anime soundtrack will sometimes find its way into the dollar bins under the racks.

SIX SHOOTER RECORDS
1118 Queen East, 416-465-2459,
www.sixshooterrecords.com.
This retail and gallery space features music by the label's stable of artists along with posters, jewellery and books.

SONIC BOOM
512 Bloor West, 416-532-0334.
Since Sonic Boom seems to buy used CDs by weight, there are often some real gems among the castoffs. At the back are a few racks of vinyl, mostly stuff even your grandmother wouldn't want, but for every Esthero or Haywire disc you might encounter a dope German fusion record.

SOUNDSCAPES
572 College, 416-537-1620.
This unassuming space outfitted entirely in Ikea shelves is Toronto's hottest record store thanks to excellent selection and knowledgeable staff who are happy to place special orders.

DVDs

QUEEN VIDEO
480 Bloor West, 416-588-5767, 412 Queen West, 416-504-3030, 688 College, 416-532-0555.
The archenemy of Suspect Video (see below) boasts thousands of new, old and obscure titles in every genre, from documentary to French New Wave, and has been visited by the likes of world-class DVD geek Quentin Tarantino.

REVUE VIDEO
207 Danforth, 416-778-5776.
For 20 years, this has been a prime source for vintage, classics and contemporary film, boasting a catalogue of over 5,000 movies. Bonus: a whack of film books and one of the best documentary and Canadian film sections in the city.

SUSPECT VIDEO
605 Markham, 416-588-6674; 619 Queen West, 416-504-7135.
If you're looking for impossible-to-find oldies, obscure Asian imports or old eps of Sho Kosugi Ninja Theatre, this is the place, with more than 32,000 video and DVD titles in the vault.

Books – new

ANOTHER STORY
315 Roncesvalles, 416-462-1104,
www.anotherstory.ca.
Terrific store with a very knowledgeable staff focuses on social justice, equity and diversity and has an excellent kids' collection and educational materials. Educators get 10 per cent off.

BALLENFORD BOOKS ON ARCHITECTURE
600 Markham, 416-588-0800.
This Mirvish Village bookshop is a must-visit for interior designers, both amateur or pro. Books cover everything from architectural theory to urban design.

BOOK CITY
501 Bloor West, 416-961-4496, 2350 Bloor West 416-766-9412, 663 Yonge, 416-964-1167, 348 Danforth, 416-469-9997, 1950 Queen East, 416-698-1444.
Over 25 years old, Book City is a bookstore with history. The store's membership card ($20 a year) gives you 20 per cent off hardcovers and 10 per cent off everything else except mags, cards and newspapers.

THE COOKBOOK STORE
850 Yonge, 416-920-2665, www.cook-book.com.
The name says it all: from recipe books to health and nutrition guides and books on entertaining.

DAVID MIRVISH BOOKS
596 Markham, 416-531-9975, www.dmbooks.com.
A great spot to browse for deep discounts on art, architecture, design and photography books.

Screw Canadian Idol. For the latest local artists flip thr

FLYING DRAGON BOOKSHOP
1721 Bayview, 416-481-7721,
www.theflyingdragon.ca.
A bookstore that will make you yearn to be five again (or eight or 11 or 14) as you discover there's a world of great reading beyond Harry Potter.

GLAD DAY BOOKS
598A Yonge, 416-961-4161,
www.gladddaybookshop.com.
Toronto's widest selection of lesbian and gay titles and provides a queer-positive space for book browsers and a strong voice against censorship (see **Queer**, page 220).

INDIGO
55 Bloor West, 416-925-3536, Eaton Centre (Yonge and Dundas), 2300 Yonge, 416-544-0049, other locations, www.chapters.indigo.ca.
This Canadian mega-chain (it also includes Chapters, Coles Books and the World's Biggest Bookstore) is big and it's always a threat to indie bookstores, but the commitment to Canadian content is impressive. You can suck back lattes at its in-store Starbucks and with its couches and chairs you just want to sit down and crack a spine.

MABEL'S FABLES
662 Mt. Pleasant, 416-322-0438,
www.mabelsfables.com.
Specialty store offers a better-than-average selection, but the key here is owner Eleanor LeFave's insistence on hiring staff who are encyclopedic on the subject of kids' books.

NICHOLAS HOARE BOOKS
45 Front East, 416-777-2665,
www.nicholashoare.com.
Wooden cases full of food-porn-filled cookbooks and hardcover fiction with a British bent stretch deep into the space.

iscs at music hot spot **Soundscapes**.

Graphically speaking

If you're into comics and graphic novels – the biggest growth industry in lit land after DaVinci rip-offs, it seems – you're dealing with duelling bookshops, the **Beguiling** (601 Markham, 416-533-9168, www.beguiling.com) and **Silver Snail** (367 Queen West, 416-593-0889, www.silversnail.com). The Beguiling definitely has more buzz these days and a wider selection, and Peter Birkemoe, who runs it, is an indie comix visionary. If your tastes run more toward X-Men and Superman, then Silver Snail is the fortress of solitude for hardcore fanatics and Marvel/DC nerds, and there's a huge selection of action figures, playing cards and other collectibles on display over its two floors.

OPEN AIR BOOKS & MAPS
25 Toronto, 416-363-0719.
This downtown shop caters to nature lovers, tree huggers and travel buffs in equal measure.

PAGES
256 Queen West, 416-598-1447,
www.pagesbooks.ca.
Cultural criticism, the best in small-press fiction, extremely knowledgeable staff and an ultra-hip location make Pages a prized spot for browsing. And the newsstand is superb.

PARENTBOOKS
201 Harbord, 416-537-8332.
This unique specialty store offers all the info you need on planning a family, everyday parenting, special needs and, of course, an excellent selection of books for children.

SLEUTH OF BAKER STREET
1600 Bayview, 416-483-3111,
www.sleuthofbakerstreet.com.
Any mystery lover worth his or her salt will tell you Baker Street is where Sherlock Holmes lived (221B, to be precise). Well, 1600 Bayview is home to one of the widest selections of crime novels, detective fiction, Sherlockiana, spy novels and thrillers, new, used and out of print.

SWIPE BOOKS
477 Richmond West, 416-363-1332, www.swipe.com.
Swipe Books on Advertising and Design shares its Design District digs with FontShop Canada and, as its website promises, stocks every damn graphic design and advertising book and magazine worthy of shelf space.

THEATREBOOKS
11 St Thomas, 416-922-7175,
www.theatrebooks.com.
A mecca for theatre professionals, students and ardent fans, this shop stocks a broad range of stage plays as well as books about the theatre, film and television, from play- and screenwriting and acting to directing and cinematography.

THIS AIN'T THE ROSEDALE LIBRARY
483 Church, 416-929-9912.
Located in the heart of the gay village for some 26 years, This Ain't the Rosedale Library has some of the savviest purchasers in the city. The community-minded store specializes in small-press releases, the mag rack is excellent, and deals abound. Biannual overstock sales offer 30 to 80 per cent off.

TORONTO WOMEN'S BOOKSTORE
73 Harbord, 416-922-8744,
www.womensbookstore.com.
One of the best of its kind on the continent, stocking an extensive collection of women authors, women's issues, children's and parenting books, cultural diversity and queer issues, small-press works, obscure poets, graphic novels and cutting-edge fiction. Not for women only: sections on global, environmental and race issues are superb.

TYPE
883 Queen West, 416-366-8973, www.typebooks.ca.
Type combines a neighbourhood newsstand stocked with international papers and glossies, a library of hardcover coffee table volumes, a great architecture and design section and a kids' nook in the back where the Queen West neighbourhood's hive of moms and dads finds books and gifts for junior.

U OF T BOOKSTORE
Koffler Centre, 214 College, 416-640-7900,
www.uoftbookstore.com.
The largest bookstore on the downtown campus of the country's largest university, this emporium carries a full compliment of new and used textbooks, stationary, computer equipment and U of T clothing.

WORLD'S BIGGEST BOOKSTORE
20 Edward, 416-977-7009.
While the moniker is debatable, there's no denying that this former bowling alley is at least Toronto's largest bookstore, with an extensive fiction and non-fiction catalogue.

Books – new & used

BALFOUR BOOKS
601 College, 416-531-9911.
Old-school library feel with dark wood shelves and over 20,000 general interest titles. Lots of relatively new stock, too, especially in the art, architecture and design categories. Browsing strictly encouraged.

ELIOT'S BOOKSHOP
584 Yonge, 416-925-0268.
Huge, we mean really huge, like three floors, with a big fat fantasy/science fiction selection.

THE MONKEY'S PAW
1229 Dundas West, 416-531-2123,
www.monkeyspaw.com.
A pulp fiction collection and retro typewriter displays lure vintage book buyers.

THE RECYCLED BOOKSHOP
162 McCaul, 416-351-0802.
Dig into piles of old industrial design books and lots of cheap soft-cover fiction. Membership is free: buy five books and get a book credit for the average price of those five purchases. Warning: don't expect the staff to tell you what's buried in the bins.

TEN EDITIONS
698 Spadina, 416-964-3803.
An excellent source of literature, Canadian history, children's classics and hard-to-find childhood faves. No discounts, but prices include GST, and the staff know their stuff.

more – new & used

ABC BOOKS
662 Yonge, 416-967-7654 Pulp, lit.

ABELARD BOOKS
519 Queen West, 416-504-2665 Theology, classics.

ANNEX BOOKS **1083 Bathurst, 416-537-1852** Lit, especially Canlit.

ATTICUS BOOKS
84 Harbord, 416-922-6045 Scholarly.

BABEL BOOKS & MUSIC
123 Ossington, 416-533-9138 Poetry a plus.

BAKKA-PHOENIX BOOKS
697 Queen West, 416-963-9993,
www.bakkaphoenixbooks.com Science fiction.

BMV BOOKS
10 Edward, 416-977-3087; 2289 Yonge, 416-482-6002 Quality remainders, art books.

JAMIE FRASER BOOKS
427A Queen West, 2nd Floor, 416-598-7718 Mysteries, pulp.

ORION BOOKS
544 Yonge, 416-923-5537 Supernatural.

SEEKERS BOOKS
509 Bloor West, 416-925-1982 As it sounds, New Age.

SHE SAID BOOM!
72 College, 416-944-3224; 393 Roncesvalles, 416-531-6843 Philosophy, literature.

TRISKELION
1081 Bathurst, 416-588-3727 Psychology, sci-fi, occult.

Sports & recreation
Bikes

CURBSIDE CYCLE
412 Bloor West, 416-920-4933.
The Curbside folks pride themselves on hunting down two-wheeled trends before the city's other bike shops catch up. Their stock of sturdy city bikes is complemented by fancy Brompton folders and elegant Pashley cruisers.

DUKE'S CYCLE
625 Queen West, 416-504-6138.
This family-owned store is a one-stop shop for riders looking for mountain bikes (XC, all mountain, downhill), road bikes (race, triathlon, comfort/performance) and street and commuter bikes.

McBRIDE CYCLE
2923 Dundas West, 416-763-5651.
In the bike biz 95 years, and it shows in the shop's friendly and knowledgeable service.

URBANE CYCLIST
180 John, 416-979-9733.
Two-wheel newbies and professional pedal pushers check out the UC to pick up, trick out and maintain rugged mountain bikes, dandy cruisers and streamlined racers.

Bike repair

BISEAGAL
388 Carlaw, 416-466-2212, www.biseagal.ca.
From fixing flats to hand-brazing frames, Biseagal (Scottish-Gaelic for "bicycle") offers a range of services rarely found in neighbourhood bike shops. If they can't fix it, no one can.

Skateboards

ADRIFT
299 Augusta, 416-515-0550,
www.adriftskateshop.com.
A solid selection in Kensington Market of decks, hardware, clothing and accessories from all the credible brands. It moves ahead of the pack by offering private and group lessons, as well as summer camp programs and private parties in their behind-shop skate park. Awesome.

HAMMER SKATEBOARD
2225 Queen East, 416-698-0005,
www.hammertoronto.com.
Basement-level shop provides skaters young and old with high-quality decks and service. The owners have been skating themselves for decades and go out of their way to create a family-friendly vibe. Lessons can be arranged with local pros.

HOGTOWN EXTREME SPORTS
401 King West, 416-598-4192,
www.hogtownextreme.com.
Around since 1984, this shop has more in the way of hard goods for skating, snowboarding, BMX and wakeboarding than anywhere else in the city. One of the few retailers to carry cult fave Skull Skates, the country's oldest skate company. Super-friendly and helpful staff.

SHRED CENTRAL (INDOOR SKATE PARK & SHOP)
19 St. Nicholas, 416-923-9842,
www.shredcentral.com.
Skaters have year-round access to a wide variety of ramps, half-pipes, a vert wall and a flat freestyle area with smaller jumps and rails, not to mention an on-site skate shop. Girls skate free.

SO HIP IT HURTS
323 Queen West, 416-971-6901.
If you can get past that whole too-cool-for-the-customer thing, you'll find a varied selection of quality skate and snowboards in this second-floor shop. The store also has a decent selection of clothes ranging from hip street brands like independent to mod labels like Fred Perry.

Sporting goods

LULULEMON
130 Bloor West, 416-964-9544, other locations.
Outfits for workouters whose tastes run more toward downward dogging than workout-room pumping. Be warned, everyone else in your Bikram class will be wearing the same black lycra capris.

MOUNTAIN EQUIPMENT CO-OP
400 King West, 416-340-2667, www.mec.ca.
Rock climbers, cyclists, backpackers and outdoor lifestylers of every stripe trick themselves out in MEC's collection of knapsacks and assorted active gear.

RUNNING ROOM
309 Wellington, 416-867-7575, other locations.
Take a workshop to prep for your first half-marathon or buy shoes, clothing and gear to help you make it to the finish line.

THE SIGN OF THE SKIER
2794 Yonge, at Lawrence, 416-488-2118,
www.thesignoftheskier.com.
An all-in-one ski shop with a personal, hands-on approach to customer service, the Sign carries a full range of mid- to high-end cross-country and downhill skis, snowboards, boots, bindings and equipment, as well as sportswear. During the summer months, it also handles a wide variety of quality patio, deck and lawn furnishings.

SPORTING LIFE
2665 Yonge, at Lawrence, 416-485-1611; Sporting Life Bikes and Boards, 2454 Yonge, 416-485-4440; other locations.
Catering to the sporty set who want one-stop shopping for all their outdoor activity needs, like bikes, boards, ski stuff and running sneaks from all the major brands, along with mid-to-high-end sportswear to outfit clothes-conscious athletes.

Miscellaneous
Cigars

CHEZ TABAC
1724 Avenue Road, 416-424-4277.
In this North Toronto cigar shop's lounge, you can sip an espresso and savour a fine Cuban cigar from Cohiba, Monte Cristo, Partagas or Romeo y Julieta.

LA CASA DEL HABANO
141 Yorkville, 416-926-9066.
A walk-in humidor, smoking lounge and large selection of Habanos, all in a 20s art deco setting.

THOMAS HINDS
8 Cumberland, 416-927-7703.
Supplying fine smokes for over 30 years, this Yorkville tobacconist is where stars like Bill Cosby, Matt Dillon and Alec Baldwin buy their cigars.

Costume

MALABAR
14 McCaul, 416-598-2581.
Toronto's best costume shop. Book early for Halloween.

Pets

BARK & FITZ
2570 Yonge, 416-483-4431; 2116 Queen East, 416-699-1313, www.barkandfitz.com.
Plush dog beds, fashion-forward collars and other canine accessories will please the most pampered

pooches. An in-store bakery dishes out treats that look so delicious that owners have been known to drool. Downstairs, a doggy spa keeps Fido's coat shiny and paws well-clipped.

LITTLE CHLOE'S CHIC BOUTIQUE
128 Harbord, 416-923-7297.
This store near Spadina stocks doggy and kitty gear at lower prices than pet stores in hoitier hoods.

Sex
See Sex, page 229.

Spirits
See Drugs, page 235.

Stationery & gift wrap

MIDOCO
555 Bloor West, 415-588-9253, other locations.
University of Toronto kids and Annex-area shoppers on the hunt for bargain bristol board, manila envelopes and other stationary supplies stop by this Bloor and Bathurst outlet.

MOKUBA
575 Queen West, 416-504-5358.
Ribbon-tying experts raid Mokuba's racks of rainbow coloured satin, silk and grosgrain rolls.

OUT ON THE STREET
551 Church, 416-967-2759.
This shop fills up during Pride Week with partiers hunting for cheeky favours and reach-for-the-rainbow gifts.

OUTER LAYER
577 Queen West, 416-869-9889, other locations.
Pick up a postcard from Outer Layer's smart selection to let them know you wish they were here.

THE PAPER PLACE
887 Queen West, 416-703-0089,
www.thepaperplace.ca.
Renowned for its chiyogami collection of Japanese, bold-coloured and nature-inspired stock, plus Asian-style notebooks and art supplies.

THE PAPERY
124 Cumberland, 416-962-3916; 1425 Yonge,
416-968-0706.
Screen-printed cards, luxe organza ribbon and paisley foil wrapping to posh up your presents.

Toys

SCIENCE CITY
50 Bloor West, 416-968-2627, www.sciencecity.ca.
Young Einsteins and junior astronomy clubbers fill their shopping bags with telescopes, chem sets and other tech toys at this shop underneath Holt Renfrew.

SPOTTED ZEBRA
1062 Yonge, 416-944-0251.
Books, games and kitschy wind-up toys lure in the young ones while moms and dads pick up spa stuff, gourmet condiments and baby shower gifts.

THE TOY SHOP
62 Cumberland, 416-961-4870.
The first floor only hints at the Lego sets, antique tin toys and Dungeons and Dragons figurines filling its tickle-trunk basement.

TOY SPACE INC.
106 Bathurst, 416-203-0792.
Educational toys and frivolous playthings like a zoo-themed croquet set with animal-shaped gates guarantees kiddo is smart and sporty.

TREASURE ISLAND TOYS
581 Danforth, 416-778-4913.
Toys, games, art supplies, chemistry and science sets, dolls, doll accessories, dollhouses, and more for kids of all ages.

malls

Shop till you drop with just one stop at these city shoplexes.

EATON CENTRE
220 Yonge, 416-598-8560,
www.torontoeatoncentre.com.
The trick to navigating the city's largest downtown mall is knowing your floors. The lower levels are lined with teen hot spots (**Urban Planet**) and electronic shops (the **Sony Store**), while big-name and bigger-price-tag chains (**Sephora**, **Club Monaco**, **Indigo** and **Harry Rosen**) start popping up more frequently as you climb the escalators.

HAZELTON LANES
87 Avenue Road, 416-968-8680,
www.hazeltonlanes.com.
The one mall where the city's fancy boutique clique dare plant their sky-high stilettos. The Yorkville spot is anchored by organic grocer **Whole Foods** and littered with pricey shops, including **TNT**, **Browns Shoes** and **Andrew's**. Finds like the **T.h.e. Total Home Environment**, which sells earth-friendly housewares, and garden shop **Teatro Verde** are worth braving the snoots.

PACIFIC MALL
4300 Steeles East, 905-470-8785,
www.pacificmalltoronto.com.
Getting to Pacific Mall on the edge of suburban Toronto where Scarborough morphs into Markham is the easy part (cruise up Highway 404 and head east on Steeles or ride the 43 bus north from Kennedy station or the 53 bus east from Finch Station). It's navigating through its 400 stores to track down a mix of traditional and modern Asian goodies that can bruise your brain. Embroidered Chinese jackets with faux fur cuffs are modern takes on a traditional silhouette at **Styleasian.com** (905-480-9624), while **Notebook Outlet** (905-415-1182) stacks computers to its ceiling. Carb up for the big haul with a handmade noodle dish from **Sun's Kitchen** (905-947-8463) in the Pacific Heritage Town Food Court.

OUTLET HEAVEN
No matter where you're located in the T-dot, factory outlet shopping is only a 20-minute drive away – so skip Niagara Falls, New York, and keep your bucks on Canadian soil. Those on the east side can head up to **Markville Mall** (5000 Hwy 7, at McCowan, in Markham). It has a huge **Winners** and a great **Jacob** outlet. Living central? The infamous **Orfus Road** (west off Dufferin, south of Lawrence; see page 168) is a heavenly stretch where bargains abound. On the west side, **Dixie Mall** (1250 South Service) in 'Sauga is a deal haven, with outlets including **Footlocker** and, for jeans and such, **Jean Machine**, **Levi's** and **Urban Planet**.

THE PATH
Toronto's subterranean city holds the Guinness world record for biggest underground shopping complex with 27 kilometres (16 miles) of pedestrian walkways linking hotels, shopping arcades, restaurants, theatres, sports complexes, attractions and the TTC. More than 50 buildings and office towers, 20 parking garages, five subway stations, two major department stores, six major hotels, a railway terminal and roughly 1,200 shops and services are connected through PATH, as are such tourist and entertainment attractions the **Hockey Hall of Fame**, **Roy Thomson Hall**, **Air Canada Centre**, **Rogers Centre** and the **CN Tower**. **City Hall** and **Metro Hall** are also connected through PATH. The building farthest north on the PATH network is the

Endulge your flights of fancy at downtown mega-mall the **Eaton Centre**.

Toronto Coach Terminal at Dundas and Bay; the building farthest south is the Toronto Convention Centre's Convention South Building.

Mall Rats

Toronto's one-stop shopping destinations.

BAYVIEW VILLAGE
2901 Bayview, 416-226-0404,
www.bayviewvillageshops.com.
Highlights: Teatro Verde, Sandro, Super Loblaws, Dolce Boutique, Guess, Roots, Simon Chang.

DUFFERIN MALL
900 Dufferin, 416-532-1152, www.dufferinmall.ca.
Highlights: Wal-Mart, Winners, Toys R Us, Le Chateau, La Senza.

FIRST CANADIAN PLACE
100 King West, 416-862-8138,
www.firstcanadianplace.com.
Highlights: HMV, Gap, Harry Rosen, Nine West.

GERRARD SQUARE
1000 Gerard East, 416-461-0964,
www.gerrardsquare.com.
Highlights: Home Depot, Zellers, Winners.

HONEST ED'S
581 Bloor West, 416-537-1574.
In 1948, theatre impresario Ed Mirvish cashed in his wife's insurance policy – all $214 of it – and opened this discount superstore: 160,00 square feet of cheap furniture, cheap clothes, cheap groceries, cheap utensils and appliances, cheap anything you can imagine. There's even a dental clinic, optical shop and pharmacy on site. The outside of the building is lit up like a carnival ride, while the inside is like a theatrical museum, the walls covered with photos of celebrities who have appeared in Mirvish productions. Next door is Mirvish Village, a unique Annex community of craft and antique shops, book vendors, record stores and restaurants.

MANULIFE CENTRE
55 Bloor West, 416-923-9525,
www.manulifecentre.com.
Highlights: William Ashley, Birks, Bay Bloor Radio, Indigo, Cineplex Odeon Varsity Theatre.

SCARBOROUGH TOWN CENTRE
300 Borough, 416-296-0296,
www.scarboroughtowncentre.com.
Highlights: Sears, the Bay, Wal-Mart, M.A.C Cosmetics, Sony Store.

SHERWAY GARDENS
25 The West Mall, 416-621-1070,
www.sherwaygardens.ca.
Highlights: Abercrombie & Fitch, French Connection, Hollister.

YONGE-EGLINTON CENTRE
20 Eglinton West, 416-489-2300,
www.yongeeglintoncentre.com.
Highlights: Famous Players SilverCity Cinema, LCBO, HMV.

YORKDALE SHOPPING CENTRE
1 Yorkdale, 416-789-3261, www.yorkdale.com.
Highlights: Holt Renfrew, Sears, the Bay, Davids, Capezio, Sephora, Williams-Sonoma, H&M, Mexx, Jacob, Aritzia, Harry Rosen, Club Monaco.

services

You've got the clothes, the shoes, the jewellery, the sunglasses. Now, it's time to get some body work done, to pump your pecs, highlight your hair, ink up your skin and soothe your senses starting at these spas who love you.

For the latest shopping and style coverage, pick up NOW Magazine or visit www.nowtoronto.com.

Spas

BODY BLITZ
471 Adelaide West, 416-364-0400,
www.bodyblitz.ca.
Women only steep in Body Blitz's circuit of therapeutic water baths to prep for their menu of bod-relieving mud and massage treatments.

CLINIC INEED
128½ Cumberland, 416-944-8055,
www.clinicineed.com.
Seven different kinds of massage, from reflexology to shiatsu, and several guys-only treatments, including manis, pedis, waxing and the exotic-sounding Les Soins Au Masculin facial and peel.

CONCEPTS DAY SPA
Holt Renfrew Centre, 60 Bloor West, 416-922-2823, Hudson's Bay Centre, 20 Bloor East, 416-928-6845, www.conceptstoronto.com.
The Bloor West spot offers services for men, including the four-hour Executive package (haircut, facial, massage, mani/pedi), while Bloor East has the couples-oriented Aphrodite package.

CRU
164 Davenport, 416-966-4636.
Lose the stubble with a classic hot lather shave at this men-only barber shop and spa.

ELIZABETH MILAN SPA
Fairmont Royal York Hotel, 100 Front West,
416-350-7500, www.elizabethmilanspa.com.
Dip yourself in dark chocolate with the Chocolate Body Indulgence or tickle your fancy with a Balinese Beauty Ritual that includes something called a "vagina smoke cleansing."

THE ELMWOOD SPA
18 Elm, 416-977-6751, www.elmwoodspa.com.
Offers the Li'Tya treatment inspired by Australia's Aboriginal peoples.

GUERLAIN
110 Bloor West, 416-929-6114.
Customized facial treatments are offered at the back of the Parisian company's perfume and makeup boutique.

JEANET SPA & SALON
140 Yorkville, second floor, 416-921-2996,
www.jeanetspa.com.
A great post-shopping pit stop – try the Pressotherapy foot treatment – for guys and gals on the go.

LUX
25 Bellair, 416-921-1680, www.lux-spa.com.
Get your nails buffed and feet rubbed in this celeb-popular spa.

OLD MILL INN SPA
21 Old Mill, 416-232-3700, www.oldmilltoronto.com.
A weekend escape from the city in the city, specializing in couples' services.

PANTAGES ANTI-AGING & LONGEVITY SPA
200 Victoria, fifth floor, 416-367-1888,
www.pantagesspa.com.
The Fountain of Youth of spas, where treatments involve a variety of specialty waters.

PURE + SIMPLE
2375 Yonge, 416-481-2081; 27 Bellair,
416-924-6555; www.pureandsimple.ca.
Skin in crisis mode? Book an appointment at Pure + Simple ASAP. Pairing Ayurvedic skin care principles (enabling the holistically trained estheticians to read your skin condition from the inside out) with Western esthetics techniques (and all-natural botanical products), the services here give you the best of both worlds. An extensive selection of all-natural skin care and mineral cosmetics help you boost your chemical-free home beauty regime.

SHIZEN SPA
Cosmopolitan Hotel, 8 Colborne, 416-350-2424,
www.shizen.ca.
Mellow out to the max with a massage at the Cosmo's über-luxe spa.

STILLWATER SPA
Park Hyatt Hotel, 4 Avenue Road, 416-926-2389,
www.hyatt.com/gallery/stillwater/toronto.
Stop in for a massage or stay for the day – work up a sweat in the gym, relax in the salon or watch a movie in the personal DVD viewing areas.

SUMMERHILL SPA
154 Cumberland, 416-924-0531,
www.summerhillspa.com.
This intimate spa uses only organic products.

VICTORIA SPA
Intercontinental Hotel, 225 Front West,
416-413-9100, www.victoriaspa.com.
Aromatherapy is a key part of the services.

VILLAGE SPA
2901 Bayview, 416-224-1101,
www.thevillagespa.sites.toronto.com.
Put on a happy face with one of the 14 facials – along with micro-dermabrasion, Botox and collagen injections – available.

WINDSOR ARMS SPA AND BARBERSHOP
Windsor Arms Hotel, 18 St. Thomas, 416-971-9666,
www.windsorarmshotel.com.
Get an old-school straight-razor shave in the manly man barber shop downstairs, then head upstairs to the unisex spa for the facials, mani, pedis and massages.

Hair salons

BARBERELLA
891 Dundas West, 416-703-4398.
Hipster residents don't have to stray far for a snip now that Dundas West is filling up with fab salons.

Coupe Bizzarre. Need we say more.

CIVELLO
887 Yonge, 416-924-9244, other locations, www.civello.com.
Master stylist Ray Civello has every coif-conscious nabe covered with his four Toronto-area salons. (Hot tip: hairdressing students being trained in Civello's laid-back cutting style snip for cheap at downtown's Aveda Institute, 125 King East, 416-443-7847). The Yonge Street flagship offers quality cuts and colours minus the stuffiness and scene of salons in neighbouring Yorkville and Rosedale.

COUPE BIZZARRE
704 & 710 Queen West, 416-504-0783, www.coupebizzarre.com.
The Coupe Bizzarre cut's asymmetrical line and punky texture is easily spotted in west-end hipster hangouts where clients party with the rock stars who slice their shag.

IODINE + ARSENIC
809 Queen West, 416-681-0577, www.iodineandarsenic.com.
A move east brings Iodine into the epicentre of Queen West cool. The hair salon dominates the new location, but there's still a corner of beauty babe-friendly bath and body products.

TAZ
11 Yorkville, 416-922-6060, www.tazhair.com.
Yorkville's Taz creates a breezy, laid-back space for chilled-out cuts, colours and esthetic goodies.

TONI & GUY
102 Bloor West, 416-920-7775.
Salon-perfect cuts and colours.

Gyms

GOOD LIFE FITNESS
12 St. Clair East, 416-927-8042, other locations, www.goodlifefitness.com.
While this national chain of 122 gyms doesn't allow drop-ins, if you're a member at one, you're a member at 'em all. So let your body flow, spin and pump itself up in this national chain of thoroughly outfitted workout temples.

YMCA
20 Grosvenor, 416-975-9168, other locations, www.YMCA.ca.
Member of the YMCA somewhere in the world? Then drop in to a local Y and sample well-priced aqua-fit, yoga and other do-your-body-good classes.

Laundromats
The laundromat lane on Harbord (a two-kilometre stretch between Spadina and Ossington) is loaded with wash/dry spots. For environmentally friendly laundries, see **Green Toronto**, page 212.

HOLLYWOOD COIN LAUNDRY
180 Ossington, 416-537-6002.
Separate your whites and colours under vintage movie heartthrob photos of Leo DiCaprio and Elvis Presley.

SPLISH SPLASH
590 College, 416-532-6499.
It must be the up-front convenience store full of junk food and tabloid mags to help pass the wash cycle that keeps Splish Splash winning NOW's Best of Toronto prize.

ST. LAWRENCE SUPER COIN LAUNDRY
222 The Esplanade, 416-363-1223.
Regulars sip complimentary cups of coffee and cheer for their favourite American Idol contestant while their loads tumble dry at this market-area 'mat.

Shoe repair

MARKET SQUARE SHOE SERVICE
80 Front East, 416-763-6137.
A hero to the fashionista set, killer cobbler Peter George of Market Square will make you believe in miracles when he fixes the impossible, but will also advise you of a lost cause when your shoes just aren't worth saving.

NICK'S CUSTOM BOOTS & SHOE REPAIR
169 Dupont, 416-924-5930, www.nickscustomboots.com.
In business for more than 40 years, Nick's will keep you well-heeled, whether it's a simple resoling or crafting an entirely new pair of boots.

MONEYSWORTH & BEST QUALITY SHOE REPAIR
Eaton Centre, 220 Yonge, 416-593-8745, other locations.
Prompt, friendly service – increasingly rare in the retail world – is a hallmark of this downtown fix-it shop.

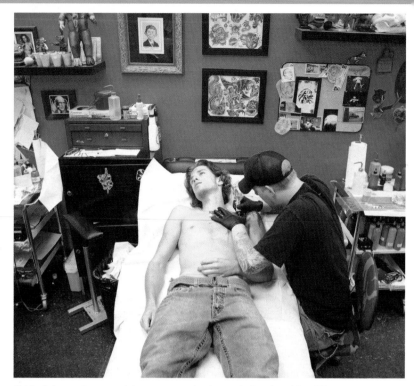

Think of a happy place as you ink your arms, maybe pierce a nipple or two at **New Tribe**.

Tattoos, piercings and scarification

BLACK LINE STUDIO
577 King West, 416-850-8227,
www.blacklinestudio.ca.
The new kid on the block, located on the ultra-cool King West strip, Black Line was opened as an alternative from the traditional flash-on-the-wall tattoo shop. With its upscale-jewellery-store-meets-private-medical-clinic decor, the shop should be a welcome change for anyone – especially nervous tattoo newbies – looking for that extra bit of comfort. The staff are friendly and knowledgeable and there's a regular cast of respected guest artists, all more than willing to sit down for a no-pressure chat about what you're looking for.

BOBBY FIVE
1239 Queen West, 416-538-6528,
www.bobbyfive.com.
Opened in 2004 by artist and art school graduate Rob Coutts, a veteran of the New York and Toronto tattoo scene, and joined by fellow skin-jabber and visual artist Dave Glantz, Bobby Five specializes in custom work, especially traditional Japanese and American designs mixed with classical influences and art nouveau. And with 10 years of tattooing experience between them, expect exceedingly high-quality, long-lasting work and a comfortable professionalism. Not exactly a typical tattoo parlour in appearance, the sleek-looking shop also doubles as an art gallery with rotating monthly shows.

NEW TRIBE TATTOOING & PIERCING
232 Queen West, 416-977-2786, www.newtribe.ca.
New Tribe's 4,000-square-foot studio may be the biggest of its kind in the city. It serves both the casual walk-in and specialized customer. Although the volume of clientele, first-come, first-served policy and occasional abruptness of the artists gives it the feel of a fast-food chain, New Tribe's reputation for tattoos and piercing has kept it in business since 1994.

PASSAGE TATTOO & BODY PIERCING
473 Church, suite 2, 416-929-7330, www.passage.ws.
Known for its wide range of piercing and body-mod techniques, Passage is also a prime destination for scarification and branding done by resident artist Blair, who boasts a wide portfolio of somewhat painful, if highly decorative and beautiful work. As for tattooing, the shop's artists employ both old- and new-school techniques and styles suitable for both first-timers and old hands.

TCB TATTOO PARLOUR
618 Queen West, 416-203-1615,
www.scottmcewantattoos.com.
About as traditional as you're gonna get, TCB has a cool and classic tattoo shop vibe without any fancy bells and whistles. Opened by long-time artist Scott McEwan, TCB has bragging rights for some of the best and most classic flash art around hanging on the walls – perfect for walk-in appointments. Not to mention plenty of cool original tattoo-themed paintings, regular guest artists from all over the place and a friendly, lighthearted atmosphere.

sports &
recreation

sports

Admittedly, more of us play soccer than shinny and the winningest pro team in the city is the Toronto Rock of the National Lacrosse League. So even though we're hockey hungry pretty much year-round, there's more to pro sports than our beloved Leafs.
For the latest sports listings, pick up NOW Magazine or visit www.nowtoronto.com.

Auto Racing

Each July, the Toronto lakeshore is filled with the sounds of roaring engines and screeching tires and the smell of burnt rubber as the **Grand Prix of Toronto** (www.grandprixtoronto.com) races into town. The three-day event takes over several streets around **Exhibition Place** (see Sightseeing, page 12) and draws top Champ Car drivers and race aficionados from around the world, including Paul Newman and David Letterman.

Baseball

Toronto Blue Jays
The American League-contending Blue Jays, back-to-back World Series champs in 92 and 93, play out of the former **SkyDome** (now **Rogers Centre**; see Sightseeing, page 15). 416-341-1234 or 1-888-OK-GO-JAY, www.bluejays.mlb.com.

Toronto Maple Leafs
The best spectator sports bargain in the city has to be the Toronto Maple Leafs. No, not the sell-your-kidney-for-a-season-ticket Leafs of the NHL. The diamond-in-the-rough Leafs of the Intercounty Baseball League, a quasi-amateur southern Ontario men's circuit. While not affiliated with the Blue Jays, several former major leaguers have suited up for the Leafs, including Rob Butler and Paul Spoljaric, and it's common for IBL teams to round out their rosters with pro ballers from Mexico, the Caribbean and South America. Home games are played out of west end park **Christie Pits** (750 Bloor West, at Christie), which has three baseball diamonds, basketball courts, a bocce field, a soccer/rugby/football pitch, ice rink, splash pad and pool. Admission to Maple Leafs games is absolutely free. Visit www.leafsbaseball.com for the schedule.

Basketball

Toronto Raptors
While two-time MVP Steve Nash might be the most famous Canadian basketball player of all time, Toronto has produced a couple of hot NBA hoopsters in Jamaal Magloire and Rick Fox. The Raptors franchise – mercifully Vince-less, sadly championshipless – routinely sells out the **Air Canada Centre** (see Sightseeing, page 14). 416-366-3865, www.nba.com/raptors.

Football

Toronto Argonauts
Canadian football is different from football played south of the border – our field is slightly longer and wider, there are three downs instead of four – but not that different. If anything, it's faster than Yankee ball, even if it doesn't get the same kind of respect in some quarters. Still not convinced? Consider that reefer-mad running back Ricky Williams served out an NFL suspension by playing the 2006 season in toke-friendly Toronto for the hometown Argonauts. At the Rogers Centre (see **Sightseeing**, page 15). 416-872-5000, www.argonauts.ca.

Hockey

Toronto Maple Leafs
Tickets are next-to-impossible to come by, so you're probably better off finding a good sports bar to watch the game. The beer's cheaper, too, which makes drowning your playoff disappointment that much easier. At the Air Canada Centre (see **Sightseeing**, page 15). 416-872-5000, www.torontomapleleafs.com.

Toronto Marlies
Can't score tix to see the big boys? Try the Leafs' AHL farm team (formerly the St. John's Maple Leafs), where you'll see tomorrow's – and yesterday's – NHL stars slugging it out for only 10 bucks a ticket. At Ricoh Coliseum. 416-597-7825, www.torontomarlies.com.

St. Michael's Majors
A top-flight junior squad in the Ontario Hockey League, the storied St. Mike's Majors have been vying for the league's Memorial Cup since 1934. Among the Majors who have gone on to NHL careers and spots in the Hockey Hall of Fame are Frank Mahovlich, Bobby Bauer, Turk Broda, Gerry Cheevers, Dave Keon, Andy Chiodo and Tim Horton (of donut shop fame). At St. Michael's College School Arena (1515 Bathurst, at St. Clair West). (For the 2007-08 season the Majors will move to Mississauga's Hershey Centre, 5500 Rose Cherry Place, 416-872-5000, www.stmichaelsmajors.com.)

Horse Racing

They're at the post and they're off and running at **Woodbine Race Track**, the most famous name in Canadian race track history. The suburban track for thoroughbred and standardbred horse racing – and betting, of course – Woodbine is home to the $1-million Queen's Plate, North America's oldest continuously run stakes race; the $1 million ATTO Mile; the $1.5 million Canadian Interna-

You've never seen lacrosse like this **Toronto Rock** net-cam action.

tional and the $1 million North America Cup for Standardbreds. 555 Rexdale. 416-675-7223, www.woodbineentertainment.com.

Lacrosse

Toronto Rock

Easily – and literally – the best bang for your buck when it comes to pro sports in the city are the hacking, slashing, body-checking blue-collar bad boys of the Toronto Rock. Don't know lacrosse? High scores and heavy hits are the name of the game in this sport that was invented by Native Canadians hundreds of years ago and, contrary to hockey nuts' assumptions, is Canada's official national sport. At the ACC. 416-596-3075, www.torontorock.com.

Soccer

Toronto Lynx & Toronto FC

Anyone who's been in Toronto during the World Cup knows that the city is silly for soccer. Too bad the local pro teams don't get the same kind of attention. The little-heralded Toronto Lynx (www.lynxsoccer.com; 416-251-4625 ext 31) men's team plays in the North American USL First Division. Their counterpart on the women's side are the Lady Lynx. Both teams play out of the 3,500-seat **Centennial Park Stadium** (Renforth and Eglinton West in Etobicoke) until the completion of the brand-new 20,000-seat stadium on the grounds of **Exhibition Place** (see **Sightseeing**, page 12). Joining the Lynx squads in the new stadium will be the newly formed Toronto FC (www.mlsnet.com) of the Major League Soccer circuit, who hit the pitch for the first time in 2007.

Tennis

The hard courts at the $45-million, 11,500-seat **Rexall Centre** on the campus of York University (1 Shoreham) may not be Wimbledon or Roland Garros, but every August these courts play host to the top tennis players on the ATP tour for the **Toronto Masters Series** championship (www.tenniscanada.com). Sharing the tournament with Montreal, even-numbered years see the top men's players in Toronto, while women make a racket in odd-numbered years.

recreation

Not only do we like to watch sports, we also like to lace up our skates, cleats, sneakers, snowshoes, whatever, and get out there and enjoy what the city has to offer.

Summer

Cycling resources

Though we lag behind other cities, like Amsterdam or Portland, Oregon, Toronto is becoming more bike friendly. Here's who's doing what to improve the scene.

BICYCLE SAFETY HOTLINE
City of Toronto program. 416-392-1311, www.toronto.ca/cycling.

BIKESHARE
Bike-lending project of the CBN. Hubs offer yellow bikes for daily use. $30 season pass. 416-504-2918, www.communitybicyclenetwork.org.

BIKETORONTO
Website devoted to cycling issues in Toronto. www.biketoronto.ca.

BUG (BICYCLE USER GROUP)
Encourages workplaces, neighbourhoods, communities and schools to work together towards improving conditions for cyclists. Organizes group rides. 416-338-5091, www.toronto.ca/cycling.

CAN-BIKE
Cycling Committee-sponsored low-cost cycling training and safety program. Courses for all levels across the GTA: Adult Learn To Ride, Teens Can-Bike, children's courses and instructor workshops. 416-338-4386, www.toronto.ca/parks/torontofun.

CITY OF TORONTO BIKE PLAN
Objectives and recommendations for cycling in Toronto and making a more bicycle-friendly city. www.city.toronto.on.ca/cycling/bikeplan.htm.

CLUB MTB
Mountain bike website provides a list of Ontario clubs and local bike shops. www.clubmtb.com.

CBN – COMMUNITY BICYCLE NETWORK
Non-profit organization supports and links community-based sustainable transport initiatives. (See BikeShare, Wenches With Wrenches, West Toronto RailPath Project and Intersection.) 761 Queen West, 416-504-2918, www.communitybicyclenetwork.org.

CRITICAL MASS CYCLING EVENTS
Hundreds of cyclists take over the streets the last Friday of each month year round. Meet at Bloor and Spadina at 6 pm. www.cmtoronto.ca.

DON VALLEY TRAIL USERS CLUB
Mountain bikers who appreciate the Don Valley trail system and advocate sustainable trail use. Rules of the trail, events, links, forums and photos. www.dvtuc.com.

MISSISSAUGA BMX CHALLENGE PARKS
Clarkson BMX park has beginner to intermediate rhythm sections with rolling tabletop features. BMX park for dirt jumping hosts its annual competition July 22. Syntex Park, Mississauga and Meadowvale. 416-578-DIRT.

ONTARIO CYCLING ASSOCIATION
Organizing body for 100 affiliated clubs promoting competitive cycling. Oversees and issues racing licences and memberships for road, track, cyclocross, BMX and mountain biking. 416-426-7416, www.ontariocycling.org.

OUTING CLUB OF EAST YORK
Non-profit volunteer-run club organizes cycling outings for weekend day trips, evenings and weekends. Trips usually 60K with shorter evening trips offered. 416-724-3316, www.ocey.org.

TOOLWORKS
A do-it-yourself bike repair workshop that provides tools, equipment and mechanical advice. Base fee $5/hr, Sat 1-3 pm. www.communitybicyclenetwork.org/toolworks.

TORONTO BICYCLING MEETUP GROUP
Get together with other cycling enthusiasts for weekend ride planning, gear talk, training tips and fun. www.bike.meetup.com.

TORONTO BICYCLING NETWORK
Largest recreational cycling club in Canada organizes riding events evenings and weekends. Workshops on cycling skills, safety and maintenance. 416-760-4191, www.tbn.ca.

WENCHES WITH WRENCHES
CBN-hosted free bike repair workshops run by and for women in a friendly learning environment. Tools provided, four-week courses begin in early April. Intersection, 761 Queen West, www.communitybicyclenetwork.org/wrench.

WEST END BIKE CLUB
Volunteer-run drop-in bicycle repair and recycling club. Thu 6:30 to 8:30 pm. Lower-level parking garage (P2) at Dufferin Mall, 900 Dufferin, chittar99@yahoo.com.

Bike rentals

CYCLEPATH
1510 Danforth, 416-463-5346, 2106 Yonge, 416-487-1717, www.twowheeltravel.ca.

TORONTO ISLAND BIKE RENTAL
1 Island Airport, Centre Island, 416-203-0009.

WHEEL EXCITEMENT
249 Queens Quay W, unit 110, 416-260-9000. www.wheelexcitement.ca.

One of Toronto's long and winding bike paths.

Mountain bike trails

For a map of official bike trails that snake through the city's ravines and parks, check out www.toronto.ca/cycling/map/map.html.

DON VALLEY TRAILS
Access from Mt. Pleasant Cemetery, Bayview and Pottery Road.
Beginner to expert trails in the ravine from the Brick Works (see page 204) in the south to Thornhill Park in the north run approx 10K.

DUNDAS VALLEY CONSERVATION CENTRE
Trail Centre 905-627-1233,
www.conservationhamilton.ca.
40K of trails along the Niagara Escarpment open from 8 am to sunset daily.

DURHAM FOREST
Brock Rd (Pickering) to Durham Rd 21, to Sideline 7,
www.canadatrails.ca/mtb/on/durhamforest.html.
Huge forest with 85K of trails and double tracks, good hill climbs and variety for all levels. Free.

ETOBICOKE CREEK
18K of trails run south from airport along Centennial Park Ravine and Markland Woods. Burnhamthorpe to Ponytrail, north to Rathburn, follow to the end.

GLEN MAJOR FOREST AND WALKER WOODS
www.trca.on.ca.
Forest located on the Oak Ridges Moraine in the Duffins Creek watershed offers 19K of Trans Canada trail.

HUMBER VALLEY
Can be accessed from Kipling at Steeles.
20K-plus trails for beginners to experts run through from Thackery Park at Steeles.

TAYLOR CREEK
Enter at Don Mills, Haldon or Dawes.
Similar to the Don Valley trail system, but some variations on this 10K beginner-expert set of trails.

Golf courses

Sure, you could truck out to Oakville's Jack Nicklaus-designed Glen Abbey GC, where Tiger Woods captured the 2000 Canadian Open title. But at $235 a round, you might be better off saving yourself the time, money (and 18 holes of frustration) by hitting one of these local courses. (For information, greens fees and to reserve tee times, call individual courses. www.toronto.ca/parks/golf.)

DENTONIA PARK GOLF COURSE
781 Victoria Park, 416-392-2558.
18 hole, par 54.

DON VALLEY GOLF COURSE
4200 Yonge, 416-392-2465.
18 hole, par 71.

HUMBER VALLEY GOLF COURSE
40 Beattie, 416-392-2488.
18 hole, par 70.

SCARLETT WOODS GOLF COURSE
1000 Jane, 416-392-2484.
18 hole, par 62.

TAM O'SHANTER GOLF COURSE
2481 Birchmount, 416-392-2547.
18 hole, par 72.

Outdoor pools

All pools feature adult and recreational swims at various times. For hours, call pool hotline, **416-338-POOL (7665)**. Toronto Parks and Recreation, **416-392-1111.**

East of Yonge

DONALD D SUMMERVILLE OLYMPIC POOL
Woodbine and Lakeshore East, 416-392-0740.

GREENWOOD POOL
SW corner of Gerrard and Greenwood, 416-392-7060.

MONARCH PARK POOL
Three blocks W of Coxwell, S of Danforth, 416-392-7060.

REGENT PARK POOL
S of Gerrard, E of Sackville, 416-392-5490.

RIVERDALE POOL
W of Broadview, south of Danforth, 416-392-0751.

West of Yonge

ALEX DUFF POOL
In Christie Pits, N of Bloor at Christie, 416-392-0745.

ALEXANDRA PARK POOL
SE corner of Bathurst and Dundas West,
416-392-0335.

GIOVANNI CABOTO POOL
SW corner of Lansdowne and St. Clair West,
416-338-POOL.

GUS RYDER/SUNNYSIDE POOL
Lakeshore W of Parkside, 416-338-POOL.

HIGH PARK POOL
In the middle of High Park, off High Park Ave, S of
Bloor West, 416-392-7807.

NORTH TORONTO POOL
Eglinton W between Avenue and Yonge,
416-392-6591.

STANLEY PARK POOL
S of King, three blocks W of Bathurst, 416-392-0743.

Indoor pools

East of Yonge

BEACHES RECREATION CENTRE
6 Williamson, 416-392-0740.
Distance and rec swims weekday evenings and
weekend afternoons.

BEDFORD PARK COMMUNITY RECREATION CENTRE
81 Ranleigh, 416-392-0618.
Recreational swim Sun, adult swim Mon-Thu.

EARL BEATTY COMMUNITY CENTRE
455 Glebeholme, 416-392-0752.
Distance and rec swims Tue-Thu and Sat.

FRANKLAND COMMUNITY CENTRE
816 Logan, 416-392-0749.
Adult and rec swims Fri eve and Sat-Sun aft.

JIMMIE SIMPSON RECREATION CENTRE
870 Queen E, 416-392-0751.
Distance and rec swims daily.

JOHN INNES COMMUNITY RECREATION CENTRE
150 Sherbourne, 416-392-6779.
Distance and rec swims Mon-Sat.

MATTY ECKLER COMMUNITY RECREATION CENTRE
953 Gerrard East, 416-392-0750.
Distance and rec swims Mon-Sun. Times vary.

ST. LAWRENCE COMMUNITY RECREATION CENTRE
230 The Esplanade, 416-392-1347.
Distance and rec swims Mon-Sun.

West of Yonge

ANNETTE RECREATION CENTRE
333 Annette, 416-392-0736.
Family swim Wed, adult swim Mon-Thu and
Sat-Sun, rec swims Fri-Sun.

BROWN COMMUNITY CENTRE
454 Avenue Rd, 416-392-6826.
Distance swims Mon-Thu and Sat-Sun, leisure swims
Sat-Sun.

HILLCREST COMMUNITY CENTRE
1339 Bathurst, 416-392-0746.
Distance swims Mon-Thu and Sat-Sun, rec swim
Sat-Sun.

**JOSEPH J PICCININNI COMMUNITY RECREATION
CENTRE**
1369 St. Clair W, 416-392-0036.
Adult distance swims daily, rec swim Fri-Sun, Muslim
women rec swim Sat-Sun

KEELE COMMUNITY CENTRE
181 Glenlake, 416-392-0695.
Distance swims Tue and Thu, rec swims Mon, Wed,
Fri and Sun, adult daily.

MARY MCCORMICK RECREATION CENTRE
66 Sheridan, 416-392-0742.
Parent and tot swims Mon and Wed, length swims
Mon-Fri. Rec swims Mon, Wed and Fri eve.

TORONTO MEMORIAL COMMUNITY CENTRE
200 Eglinton W, 416-392-6591.
Daily distance and leisure swims daily.

PARKDALE COMMUNITY RECREATION CENTRE
75 Lansdowne, 416-392-6696.
Distance and rec swims Mon-Thu and Sat-Sun.

SCADDING COURT COMMUNITY CENTRE
707 Dundas W, 416-392-0335.
Distance and rec swims daily.

SWANSEA COMMUNITY RECREATION CENTRE
15 Waller, 416-392-6796.
Distance swims daily and rec swim Sun.

TRINITY RECREATION CENTRE
155 Crawford (in Trinity-Bellwoods Park),
416-392-0743.
Distance and rec swims daily.

WALLACE-EMERSON COMMUNITY CENTRE
1260 Dufferin, 416-392-0039.
Distance swims Mon-Fri, recreational swims Tue,
Thu-Sun.

WINONA DRIVE SCHOOL
101 Winona, 416-392-0036.
Distance and recreational swims Wed-Thu.

Toronto loves tennis, with dozens of free public courts throughout the city.

Tennis courts

East of Yonge

COLEMAN PARK
Barrington, one block N of Danforth.
Two courts.

DAVISVILLE PARK
Davisville and Mt. Pleasant.
Six floodlit courts.

FAIRMOUNT PARK
Gerrard, E of Coxwell.
Four courts.

HODGSON PUBLIC SCHOOL
Davisville, E of Mt. Pleasant.
Four floodlit courts.

JIMMIE SIMPSON PARK
Queen and Booth.
Two floodlit courts.

JOEL WEEKS PARKETTE
Queen, three blocks W of Broadview.
Two courts.

JONATHAN ASHBRIDGE PARK
Queen, four blocks W of Coxwell.
Two courts.

KEW GARDENS
Kew Beach and Waverley.
10 floodlit courts.

LAWRENCE PARK
Yonge and Glengrove.
Three floodlit courts.

MOOREVALE PARK
Mt. Pleasant and Moorevale.
Five floodlit courts.

MOSS PARK
Queen and Sherbourne.
Two courts.

NORWOOD PARK
Norwood, S of Gerrard.
Five courts.

RENNIE PARK
Morningside and Rennie Terrace.
Four floodlit courts.

RIVERDALE PARK
Broadview, S of Montcrest.
Seven courts.

ROSEDALE PARK
Schofield, N of Roxborough.
Eight floodlit courts.

WANLESS PARK
Wanless and Kappele.
Five floodlit courts.

WITHROW PARK
McConnell, between Logan and Carlaw.
Two courts.

West of Yonge

DOVERCOURT PARK
Dovercourt, between Bartlett and Westmoreland.
Two courts.

FOREST HILL COLLEGIATE
Eglinton and Mayfair.
Four floodlit courts.

GIOVANNI CABOTO
Lansdowne, at St. Clair W.
Four floodlit courts.

HIGH PARK
S of Bloor, W of Parkside.
14 courts, some floodlit, seven near the swimming pool at the north end of the park

HILLCREST PARK
Davenport and Christie.
Four floodlit courts.

HUMBERSIDE COLLEGIATE INSTITUTE
Quebec, at Clendenan, two blocks N of Bloor.
Four courts.

HURON STREET PUBLIC SCHOOL
Huron, N of Lowther.
Two courts.

LYTTON PARK
Avenue Rd and Lytton.
Three floodlit courts.

NORTH TORONTO MEMORIAL CC
Oriole Pkwy and Edith.
Four floodlit courts.

ORIOLE PARK
Oriole Pkwy and Chaplin.
Two courts.

RAMSDEN PARK
Yonge, N of Pears.
Twelve courts.

RUNNYMEDE PARK
Ryding and Ethel, S of St. Clair.
Two courts.

SIR WINSTON CHURCHILL
St. Clair and Spadina Rd.
10 floodlit courts.

SORAUREN PARK
Sorauren, S of Dundas.
Two courts.

STANLEY PARK
King West, three blocks W of Bathurst.
Two courts.

SYMINGTON AVENUE PLAYGROUND
Perth, N of Dupont.
Two courts.

TRINITY-BELLWOODS PARK
Queen and Crawford.
Eight courts.

Winter

Outdoor ice rinks

All rinks are free and are usually open by November (if not before) and close at the end of February, give or take a week or two. Call the **Rink Hotline** at **416-338-RINK (7465)** for more information; www.toronto.ca.

BARBARA ANN SCOTT
Single surface, pleasure skating Mon-Sat 10 am-10 pm, Sun 10 am-6 pm. Yonge and College, 416-392-1111.

CAMPBELL
Single surface, pleasure skating and shinny hockey. 255 Campbell, at Antler, 416-392-0039.

CHRISTIE PITS
Single surface, pleasure skating, shinny, permit, girls' and women's hockey, learn-to-skate and hockey lessons. 779 Crawford, at Bloor and Christie, 416-392-0745.

DIEPPE PARK
Twin surface, pleasure skating, shinny, girls' and women's, learn to skate and permit hockey. Cosburn, east of Greenwood, 416-396-2862.

DUFFERIN GROVE
Twin surface, pleasure skating and shinny hockey. Dufferin, south of Bloor, 416-392-0039.

GIOVANNI CABOTO
Twin surface, pleasure skating, shinny, house-league hockey, adult and children's skating lessons. 1369 St. Clair West, 416-338-7465.

GREENWOOD
Twin surface, pleasure skating daily, learn to skate lessons, shinny and women's hockey. 870 Queen East, 416-392-0750.

HARBOURFRONT CENTRE
Single surface, pleasure skating Sun-Thu 10 am-10 pm, Fri-Sat to 11 pm. Special DJ skating nights. Skate rentals. Lessons for beginners to advanced. York Quay Centre, 235 Queens Quay West, 416-973-4866, lessons 416-973-4093.

HARRY GAIREY
Twin surface, pleasure skating and shinny hockey. Bathurst and Dundas, 416-392-0335.

HIGH PARK
Twin surface, pleasure skating, shinny and permit hockey. Colborne Lodge, south of Bloor, 416-338-7465.

HODGSON
Twin surface, pleasure skating and shinny hockey. Davisville, east of Mt. Pleasant, 416-392-0747.

JIMMIE SIMPSON
Single surface, pleasure skating, skating lessons and shinny hockey. 870 Queen East, west of Logan, 416-392-0751.

KEW GARDENS
Single surface, pleasure skating, shinny, permit, learn to skate, hockey skills, women's and girls' hockey. Lee, south of Queen, 416-392-0740.

MEL LASTMAN SQUARE
Single surface, pleasure skating daily 10 am-10 pm. North York Civic Centre, 5100 Yonge, 416-392-1111, 416-395-7584.

MONARCH
Single surface, pleasure skating, shinny and permit hockey, hockey school and skating lessons. Felstead, southwest of Danforth and Coxwell, 416-392-0752.

NATHAN PHILLIPS SQUARE
Single surface, pleasure skating daily 9 am-10 pm. Skate rentals. City Hall, 100 Queen West, 416-392-1111.

NORTH TORONTO MEMORIAL CC
Twin surface, pleasure skating, shinny and women's hockey. 200 Eglinton West, 416-392-6591.

OTTER CREEK
Twin surface, pleasure skating, and shinny hockey. Chatsworth, south of Lawrence West, 416-392-0618.

RAMSDEN
Twin surface, pleasure skating daily and shinny hockey. Yonge, opposite Rosedale subway, 416-392-6826.

REGENT PARK NORTH
Single surface, pleasure skating and shinny hockey. Northwest of Dundas and River, 416-392-0753.

REGENT PARK SOUTH
Single surface, pleasure skating and shinny hockey. Shuter and Sumach, 416-392-5490.

RENNIE
Twin surface, pleasure skating, shinny and permit hockey. 1 Rennie Terrace, Morningside at Runnymede, 416-338-7465.

RIVERDALE
Single surface, pleasure skating, shinny and permit hockey, skating lessons. Broadview and Montcrest, 416-392-0749.

ROBERT STREET
Single surface, pleasure skating, and shinny hockey. Robert and Sussex, 416-392-1111.

ROSEDALE
Single surface, pleasure skating, shinny and permit hockey. Schofield and Roxborough, 416-392-6826.

RYERSON
Single surface, pleasure skating daily 9 am-10 pm. Dundas and Victoria, 416-338-7465.

TRINITY-BELLWOODS
Single surface, pleasure skating, shinny, permit, women's hockey, parent and child hockey and skating lessons. 155 Crawford, 416-392-0743.

WALLACE EMERSON
Twin surface, pleasure skating, shinny and skating and hockey lessons. 1260 Dufferin, south of Dupont, 416-392-0039.

WITHROW
Single surface, pleasure skating, shinny and permit hockey and skating lessons. 725 Logan, 416-392-0749.

Tobogganing

Take your super slider to Christie Pits or a cardboard box to Trinity-Bellwoods Park, or, for something a little more scenic, try hurtling down Riverdale Hill, with the view of downtown in the distance.

the skinny on shinny

This is the Canuck version of what Americans do on inner city hoops courts and Europeans do on soccer pitches. It's totally democratic. Whoever comes plays – at the same time. There are no goalies, no raises, no checking and no whistles. And you can skate in all-ages and all-women games, depending on the sked.
(see www.toronto.ca/parks)

ADAMS PARK
N of Lawson, W of Port Union, 416-338-3278.

CEDARBROOK PARK
Markham, S of Lawrence, 416-338-3278.

CEDARVALE PARK
S of Eglinton, W of Bathurst.

CENTENNIAL PARK
Rathburn and Centennial Park.

CHRISTIE PITS
Bloor and Christie, 416-392-1111.

HIGH PARK
Bloor and High Park, 416-392-7251.

MILLIKIN PARK
McCowan and Steeles, 416-338-3278.

RIVERDALE PARK
Broadview, S of Montcrest, 416-392-1111.

THOMSON MEMORIAL PARK
Brimley and Lawrence, 416-338-3278.

TRINITY-BELLWOODS PARK
Gorevale, S of Dundas, 416-392-1111.

WINSTON CHURCHILL PARK
Spadina Rd and St. Clair West.

WITHROW PARK
Carlaw, S of Danforth, 416-392-1111.

Skiing & snowboarding

Shred the freshest powder, pimp the perfect pipe, carve a new trail on these hills and valleys around the GTA.

CENTENNIAL PARK SNOW CENTRE
256 Centennial Pk, Rathburn and Centennial Park, 416-394-8754, snow phone 416-338-6754.
Etobicoke's main park features a ski hill, T-bar and Poma lifts, night skiing/boarding, alpine and snowboard lessons and equipment rentals.

HIGH PARK
Toronto's largest park offers cross-country skiing every day on its trails. Parkside, between Bloor and the Queensway, 416-392-1111.

NORTH YORK SKI CENTRE
This North York site offers downhill with one beginner and three intermediate slopes (all patrolled), one double chair lift and a rope tow. Ski and snowboarding lessons available. Equipment rentals. Earl Bales Park, Bathurst and Sheppard, 416-395-7931, snow phone 416-338-6754.

ALBION HILLS CONSERVATION AREA
1,200 acres with 26K of groomed and track-set trails for all cross-country skiing levels; equipment rentals. 16500 Hwy 50, 8K north of Bolton. Snow conditions/info 905-880-4855, 1-800-838-9921.

ALGONQUIN PARK
Cross-country, classic, skate-ski and dogsledding trails on over 100K of trails, with loops from 5 to 24K. Permits at the east and west gates. 705-633-5572, info@algonquinpark.on.ca for event details. www.algonquinpark.on.ca.

BLUE MOUNTAIN
Ontario's highest and largest mountain resort, two hours north of Toronto, has skiing/snowboarding on 34 trails, three half-pipes including two super-pipes, three terrain parks with 12 lifts, a snow-tubing park and offers night skiing. Special events throughout the winter. 11K west of Collingwood, 705-445-0231, www.bluemountain.ca.

KATHRYN GAITENS

Lace 'em up at one of Toronto's two dozen outdoor skating rinks.

HOCKLEY VALLEY
Near Orangeville, this resort offers alpine and cross-country skiing and night skiing on 11 trails, a ski school and full equipment rentals. 793522 Third Line East, 416-363-5490, 519-942-0754, www.hockley.com.

KORTRIGHT CENTRE
This year-round conservation area offers 10K of ungroomed trails for beginner and intermediate cross-country skiers. No equipment rentals. 9550 Pine Valley, south of Major Mackenzie, Kleinburg, 905-832-2289, www.trca.on.ca.

LAKERIDGE SKI RESORT
Thirty minutes northeast of T.O., offering a half-pipe, alpine skiing, snowboarding and tubing. 790 Chalk Lake Road, north of Whitby, 905-686-3607, snow phone 905-686-SNOW, www.ski-lakeridge.com.

Icy index

Check the following websites for more outdoor winter activity info:
www.brucetrail.org
www.ontarioguide.com
www.orta.on.ca
www.skiontario.ca
www.canadatrails.ca
www.OntarioParks.com
www.ontariotravel.net/winter
www.ontariooutdoor.com
www.skicentral.com
www.skiontario.ca
Snow and Road Reports: 1-800-668-2746

Fitness & Exercise

Martial arts

AIKIDO YOSHINKAI CANADA
Offers daily beginner, advanced and children's classes under 8th-degree blackbelt Kimeda Sensei. 399 Yonge, at Gerrard, 416-585-9602, www.aikido-yoshinkai.org.

HONG LUCK KUNG FU
Offering traditional kung fu training for more than 40 years, including lion dance training and women's self-defence. 548 Dundas W, 416-596-8581, www.hongluck.org.

KALI DELEON
Teaches Filipino stick fighting that progresses to bladed and empty-hand techniques. www.kalideleon.com.

KIMONOGIRL
Fight like a girl with Brazilian Jiu-jitsu. Self-defence and strengthening class. Drop-in group/private classes. Yoga Studio, 40 Eglinton E, 8th floor, 416-710-8271, www.kimonogirl.ca.

MASTER TOMMY CHANG'S BLACK BELT WORLD
Classes for children and adults in judo, karate, tae kwon do, hap ki do, sparring, self defence, leadership and Olympic training. 885 Bloor W, 416-533-1221, www.taekwondo.ca.

TAI CHI & MEDITATION CENTRE
Health and healing through Tai Chi, Qi Gong and insight meditation. 745 Danforth, 416-465-6122, www.powerofbalance.com.

TORONTO KICKBOXING & MUAY THAI ACADEMY
This fully air-conditioned facility is the largest kickboxing gym in downtown T.O., offering classes for all skill levels from beginners to advanced, as well as Brazilian Jiu-jitsu/submission wrestling classes. Drop-ins welcome. 610 Queen W, third floor, 416-998-3674, www.tkmt.ca.

TRINITY SAVATE & JKD
Classes in boxe francais (French kickboxing) and Jeet Kune Do, a mixed martial art created by Bruce Lee for street defence. 243 Queen W (inside Kamal Yoga Studio), www.trinitymartialarts.com.

Yoga & pilates

ACTIVE YOGA
Bikram yoga drop-in classes for adults and children. 2281 Dundas W, 416-538-1628, activeyoga.ca.

ASHTANGA YOGA SHALA
Mysore, hatha, power flow, prenatal and more. Twist Yoga Studio, 321½ Bloor W, 416-819-9642, www.aystoronto.ca.

BIKRAM YOGA
Yoga practised in a hot room is offered in studios throughout the city. 1911 Queen E, 416-686-2584, 720 Spadina Ave, 416-961-9530, 25 Merton, 416-769-9076, 372A Danforth, 416-778-7744, 500 Sheppard E, 416-250-0076 and others, www.bikramtoronto.com.

BODY HARMONICS
Pilates, Swiss ball classes and rehabilitative exercise. 672 Dupont, 416-537-0714, www.bodyharmonics.com.

CATFISH YOGA SHALA
Ashtanga yoga for beginners to advanced, partner yoga, yoga improv classes and workshops. 20 Leslie, ste 215, 416-876-7169, www.catfishyoga.com.

CENTRE FOR WELL BEING
Hatha yoga, Chi-kung, yoga, meditation, reiki and more. 480 Roncesvalles, 416-653-2335.

DOWNWARD DOG YOGA CENTRE
Group classes at all levels and teacher training in Ashtanga. 735 Queen W and 1977 Queen E, 416-703-8805, www.downwarddog.com.

IYENGAR YOGA STUDIO
Classes for students of all levels including special needs. 3300 Yonge, ste 205, 416-483-5800, www.iyengaryoga.ca.

JIVAMUKTI YOGA AND MEDITATION CENTRE
Downtown studio offering classes in Jivamukti hatha yoga, Ashtanga, workshops, moksha events and more. 5 Shuter, 3rd floor, 416-530-0039, www.jivamuktiyoga.ca.

MOKSHA YOGA
Hot yoga, traditional yoga practised in a heated environment. 372A Danforth, 416-778-7744, 25 Merton, 416-769-9076 and 860 Richmond W, 416-361-3033, www.mokshayoga.ca.

PURE INTENT
Wellness centre offering yoga, capoeira, Pilates, nia, meditation, dance, health and nutrition seminars, naturopathic medicine. 64 Oxford, 2nd floor, at Augusta, 416-466-3237, www.pureintent.ca.

RIVERDALE PILATES
Stott Pilates instruction in the heart of Greektown. 456 Danforth, 416-466-7733, riverdalepilates.com.

SIVANANDA YOGA VEDANTA CENTRE
Daily yoga asana, pranayama and meditation classes, courses and workshops at all levels. 77 Harbord, 416-966-9642, www.sivananda.org/toronto.

TURNING POINT FITNESS
Pilates, dance and yoga. 29 Bloor E, 416-920-6532, www.eclipsedance.com.

VENICE FITNESS
Yoga, pilates, spinning and free weights. 750 Warden, 416-752-8364, and 393 King W, 416-341-0606, www.venicefitness.com.

THE YOGA LOUNGE
Hatha, ashtanga, stretch, restorative and prenatal yoga. 103 Church, 3rd floor, 416-864-1973, www.theyogalounge.net.

THE YOGA STUDIO
Ashtanga, Ansura, hatha and Pilates for all levels. 40 Eglinton E, 416-322-9936, and 87 Avenue, 416-961-8400, www.yogastudio.net.

THE YOGA SANCTUARY
Post-natal yoga, ashtanga, hatha, mysore, Pilates and more. 2 College, ste 306, 416-928-3236, 95 Danforth, 416-461-6161, theyogasanctuary.net.

Rock climbing

JOE ROCKHEAD'S
Climbing gym with 21,000 square feet of climbing terrain and courses for all levels. 29 Fraser, 416-538-7670, www.joerockheads.com.

ROCK OASIS
Indoor climbing facility for all levels, with two 60-foot climbing towers, two bouldering caves and steep roof routes. 27 Bathurst, 416-703-3434, www.rockoasis.com.

TORONTO CLIMBING ACADEMY
Offers 16,000 square feet of climbing terrain, with lessons at all levels. 100A Broadview, 416-406-5900, www.climbingacademy.com.

green toronto

green toronto

We're the biggest city in the country and we've got a lot of country in the city. There are acres of parks, miles of rivers, fields of rich farmland, even whole forests. And while it isn't easy being green, we work damn hard to protect our environment. For current eco-friendly listings, pick up NOW Magazine every week or visit www.nowtoronto.com.

When postcard makers try to epitomize Toronto, they snap photos of the CN Tower jutting above the skyline and call it a day. But come on, doesn't every major North American city have a tangle of skyscrapers? Ours just happens to have a funny-looking concrete needle sticking out of it.

What really brings T.O. to life is the life – the 8,000 hectares of parks, meadows, ravines, valleys, wood lots and, yes, even a few farms, altogether covering nearly one-fifth of the city. Or the more than 300 kilometres of rivers, brooks and creeks that trickle through it. That doesn't even factor in our sprawling shoreline along a freshwater lake so vast you'd think you were sunbathing seaside. It is one of the Great Lakes, after all.

Toronto's not only blanketed in green – it bleeds the damn colour. Scratch the surface of the pretty places for hiking, biking and weekend picnics and you'll find a municipality committed to hugging the earth. It's a city that's banned pesticides and plants some 8,000 trees a year (you can't cut one down in your own yard if it's over 30 centimetres thick). It collects compostable scraps door-to-door more often than it picks up regular trash.

It was the first town in North America to take on a comprehensive green roof policy that will see energy-conserving eco-friendly lids slapped on most city-owned buildings – NOW Magazine is leading the way with its own green roof. Toronto was the first in Canada to be recognized by the international Blue Flag program for cleaning up its beaches and the first to say it would retire any carbon credit it may earn from its many green programs rather than just swapping it with polluters.

Toronto was also voted Low Carbon Leader in 2005 by British org the Climate Group, in part for cutting corporate greenhouse gas emissions by 42 per cent in eight years. Our eco status even got Mayor David Miller into the pages of Vanity Fair's 2006 Green Issue.

So while Toronto may market itself as a concrete city, maybe it's time to yank the CN Tower off our postcards and make our lakefront wind turbine Toronto's proudest symbol instead.

Great outdoors

CLOUD FOREST CONSERVATORY
South of Richmond, between Yonge and Bay, 416-392-1111.
A walk-through greenhouse with lush tropical foliage and a five-storey waterfall nestled in the heart of the Financial District, offering a welcome respite from the surrounding concrete canyons.

DON VALLEY (DON RIVER TRAIL)
Yes, the city slapped an expressway through this gorgeous stretch of terrain, but there's still plenty of hike life far from the sound of cars in the Don. Meander along 20 kilometres of riverside trails and explore restoration efforts along the way, including Chester Springs Marsh, **Todmorden Mills** wildflower preserve and the **Brick Works**.

DON VALLEY BRICK WORKS PARK
550 Bayview, 416-596-1495, www.evergreen.ca.
Not just an old brick factory, the building is surrounded by dynamic restored wetlands, meadows and forests. The old excavated quarry offers a good geology lesson in ice age glacial and fossil deposits, and eco org **Evergreen** (see page 214) is planning a cultural centre that will showcase the best in green design. The planned organic farmers market, restaurant run by star organic chef Jamie Kennedy and nursery of native plants are just the tip of the iceberg. Until then, the park makes for an enchanting walk back to Dickens' day in the Don Valley.

ELEVATED WETLANDS
www.elevatedwetlands.com.
These giant white sculptures in Taylor Creek Park may look like enormous polar bears without heads, but they're actually living, breathing creations of artist Noel Harding (funded by the Canadian Plastics Industry Association). Waste plastic inside the forms filters polluted water from the Don River just as non-plastic wetlands do. Definitely a must when hiking the Don Valley.

EDWARDS GARDENS/TORONTO BOTANICAL GARDENS
777 Lawrence East, 416-397-1340, www.torontobotanicalgarden.ca.
North of the core sits some of the prettiest parks in town. The former estate garden is favoured by wedding photographers. The horticulture centre's glass pavilion, complete with green roof and rainwater collection system, is one of the city's most environmentally friendly buildings.

ERNEST THOMPSON SETON PARK
Don Mills, behind the Ontario Science Centre.
Named for the eccentric naturalist who wrote Wild Animals I Have Known, reputedly the inspiration for Rudyard Kipling's Jungle Book, this park offers picnic areas, an archery range and equestrian trails.

HIGH PARK
Toronto's version of Central Park, only a little smaller. Over a third of the 399 acres are in their natural state, including hilly woodlands, wetlands and oak savannahs. It has an animal paddock, playgrounds, sports fields, and tree-lined Grenadier Pond turns into an ice rink in winter. The park is home to **Dream in High Park**, an open-air Shakespeare stage. (See **Sightseeing**, page 38.)

We take our eco-activism seriously. It's not a hybrid, but it makes a statement.

HUMBER ARBORETUM
205 Humber College, 416-675-5009, www.humber-arboretum.on.ca.
Urban ecology centre on the West Humber River in northwest Toronto offers garden tours, pond and insect studies, nature walks, camps and a biodiversity and climate change research program.

HUMBER BAY BUTTERFLY HABITAT
Humber Bay Park East, Park Lawn south of Lakeshore, 416-392-1339, www.toronto.ca/parks/hbbh.htm. Open daily dawn to dusk.
An ecological restoration project providing critical habitat for native butterfly species.

HUMBER RIVER TRAIL
West of the core lies this river system loved by joggers, cyclists and weekend strollers alike. But with 32 kilometres of scenic trails, how do you know where to start? Lampton Woods is a favourite spot, but South Humber Park, Humber Marshes, Scarlett Mills Park, Étienne Brulé Park as well as **Humber Bay Park** and the **Butterfly Habitat** are some of the trail's other entry points.

RIVERDALE FARM
201 Winchester, www.friendsofriverdalefarm.com.
Nestled amongst historic Cabbagetown's Victorian townhouses sits a barnful of farm life – if it barks, bleats, quacks or moos, they've got it. Surrounding Riverdale Park has about 7.5 acres of pathways, ponds, gardens and dog-walking space just perched over the valley (making it a prime tobogganing point come winter). (See **Sightseeing**, page 26.)

ROUGE PARK, GEORGE PEARSE HOUSE
2262 Meadowvale.
Avid hikers will tell you you haven't hiked in T.O. until you've roamed Rouge Park. This is, after all, the world's largest natural park in an urban area. Okay, so it's not smack downtown, but it's worth the small trek to the city's edge for breathtaking trails that wind through 12,000 acres of forests, meadows, wetlands, beach and the rolling glacial **Oak Ridges Moraine** hills. Perhaps the most scenic hike is accessible by jumping on the Scarborough 86 bus to the **Zoo** (see page 44), then setting out from historic Pearse House, near the entrance, through wooded brush that yields to gorgeous clifftop views of the Rouge River, followed by a riverbank stroll among noshing beavers hard at work. Too far? Our runner-up follows Highland Creek from Colonel Danforth Park at Kingston Road north of Lawrence all the way to the Scarborough Bluffs. For details on both these urban escapes, check out www.torontohiking.com.

Wander back to Dickens' day at the **Don Valley Brick Works**, page 204.

SCARBOROUGH BLUFFS (BLUFFERS PARK)
Brimley Road, south end.
Stretching about 14 kilometres along the lakeshore, these sweeping packed-clay cliffs jut out up to 65 metres above the water. Bluffers Park is a great launching point for nearby trails, or just park your butt at a picnic table, peek out from scenic lookouts or make a sandcastle on the beach. (See **Sightseeing**, page 36.)

TORONTO FIELD NATURALISTS
2 Carlton, #1519, 416-593-2656, www.sources.com/tfn.
Dispenses maps and info on nature walks throughout T.O.'s network of parklands. Open Fri 9 am to noon.

TORONTO ISLANDS
No need to hop on a jumbo jet south to vibe on island life. Just catch a ferry from the terminal at the foot of Bay. This string of long, stabilized sandbars now houses a quietly bucolic and bohemian cottage community (Ward's Island), kids' amusement park (Centre Island), clothing-optional beach (Hanlan's Point) and lots of strolling room. Renting a bicycle built for one or two is probably the best way to get around the largest car-free community in North America. (See **Sightseeing**, page 15.)

YORK UNIVERSITY ASTRONOMICAL OBSERVATORY
4700 Keele, NW corner of the campus, 416-736-2100 ext 77773, www.yorku.ca/observe.
Other than the Toronto International Film Festival, this is the best way to see some stars. Open for public viewings Wed from 9 pm. Free.

For the birds
With a long shoreline and network of ravines, the city is prime birding real estate. And Tommy Thompson Park (a.k.a. the **Leslie Street Spit**), a dump site-turned-inadvertent sanctuary that pokes out into Lake Ontario, is a feathered wonderland. Every year, thousands of waterfowl congregate from late fall to early spring, and songbirds, shorebirds and waders splash through during spring and fall migration. In winter, look for black and white long-tailed ducks, common goldeneyes and small buffleheads that swoop down from Arctic and boreal regions. Honourable mention to **High Park** (see page 204), where in autumn, north of the restaurant, birders meet for the Hawk Watch, the best migrant raptor viewing in any urban location in the world.

Eco-tourism

ADVENTURE SEEKER TOURS
416-898-3573, www.adventureseekertours.com.
This eco-friendly company will take you kayaking, horseback riding, hot-air ballooning, hang-gliding, rock climbing, snowshoeing – you name it.

DISCOVERY WALKS
www.toronto.ca/parks.
Nine self-guided walks set up by the city through parks, ravines, beaches and cool 'hoods get you exploring natural and social history and beauty. Signs mark the way. Download routes from the city's website.

LOST RIVER WALKS
416-781-7663, www.lostrivers.ca.
A joint project of the Toronto Green Community, Toronto Field Naturalists and Hike Ontario, this walking group is all about discovering the city's watersheds. Explore creeks, streams and rivers, with a special focus on historical and environmental issues that bubble to the surface along the way.

TORONTO BAY INITIATIVE
30 Duncan, 416-598-2277, www.torontobay.net.
This non-profit fights to improve Toronto's watershed and offers boat, canoe and bike tours to educate people about the city's delicate natural habitat.

TORONTO BICYCLE NETWORK
416-760-4191, http://tbn.ca.
Canada's largest recreational cycling club. But this isn't just a two-wheeled fair-weather operation offering a litany of weekend and weekday rides. They also set out on fall hikes, city walks and, once the snow falls, cross-country skiing and ice skating outings, making them a full-on all-season club.

TORONTO KAYAK AND CANOE ADVENTURES
1854 Bloor West, 416-536-2067, www.torontoadventures.ca.
Paddle your way through the green side of Toronto on guided river and beachside tours. They also offer paddle-and-pedal combo trips or just plain cycling, as well as kayaking birthday parties and races.

URBAN EXPEDITIONS
30 Concord, ste 3, 416-606-7227, www.urbanexpeditions.com.
This tour group generally offers more metropolitan adventures – their concrete jungle walking tour, for instance, involves stops at a yoga class and live music venue. They also have a two-day, two-night Green Is Gold bike tour that pedals through Toronto before participants are shuttled to **Niagara-on-the-Lake** (see **Sightseeing**, page 44) for some vineyard exploration and wine tasting.

VOYAGEUR QUEST
22 Belcourt, 416-486-3605, www.voyageurquest.com.
Canoe around the **Toronto Islands** on one of three Native Canadian-inspired trips, including one that involves pipe breaks, an indigenous feast and traditional singing.

Where to stay
Feeling guilty about all those little plastic bottles and sheet changes you go through at a typical hotel? You need a place to hang your hat without racking yourself with green guilt. Luckily, Toronto has several earth-conscious hotels and B&Bs that will help you sleep with a clear conscience.

FAIRMONT ROYAL YORK HOTEL
100 Front West, 416-368-2511, www.fairmont.com.
These guys wrote the book on how to green the industry. Besides making sure every piece of paper, coat hanger and bar of soap from every swanky room is reused or recycled, it's long had water-conserving shower heads, toilets and tap aerators and now ensures that all organic waste is composted.

HOLIDAY INN ON KING
370 King West, 416-599-4000.
Winner of the 2003 Environmental Award for the InterContinental Hotel Group, the hotel has a green purchasing policy as well as an environmental committee, and low-flow shower heads and toilets conserve 8,000 gallons of water and 50 gallons of detergent every month.

LES AMIS VEGETARIAN BED AND BREAKFAST
31 Granby, 416-591-0635, www.bbtoronto.com.
This downtown B&B serves up gourmet vegetarian and vegan breakfasts using organic ingredients (from $79/$85 for single occupancy).

TERRACE HOUSE BED AND BREAKFAST
52 Austin Terrace, 416-923-1171, www.terracehouse.com.
This early 20th-century heritage home not only uses green cleaning products, it's a member of the Vegetarian Association and is known for its mouthwatering breakfasts.

Events

Every April, Earth Day is celebrated by millions of environmentally conscious people around the globe. And while we're not taking to the streets to protest the planet's abuse the way we used to back in Earth Day's heyday, the annual event still does a planet good while bringing Toronto's eco-community together in the name of Mother Nature. In fact, Toronto takes this 24-hour enviro marker and turns it into a week of consciousness-raising fun. Whether you want to roll up your sleeves and sweep up the city alongside the mayor, help plant thousands of native trees at Downsview Park or hit the annual Spring Fling cleanup, BBQ and wildflower walk at **Todmorden Mills** (see **Sightseeing**, page 34), there's always lots to do to get the city squeaky green.

BIKE WEEK
http://biketoronto.ca.
This annual event should really be renamed Bike Fortnight, seeing as it involves 14 days of action-packed two-wheeled mania each spring. Expect plenty of bike rallies, group commutes, evening rides, workshops, fairs, free tune-ups and, yes, free food (check out the all-important post-commute breakfasts). Held in late May-early June.

FAIR TRADE WEEK
www.fairtradetoronto.com.
Early May is National Fair Trade Week, which means that it's the perfect time to discover what makes justly grown and traded goods so important — and tasty. A Fair Trade Fair displays some of the best socially and ecologically sound chocolate, coffee and crafts from around the world, as well as booths by fair-trade-minded orgs. There are even movie screenings on the topic.

FEAST OF FIELDS
www.feastoffields.org.
Just as summer is winding down, the good people behind Feast of Fields give you something to get excited about. The "feast" part comes courtesy of Ontario's top chefs, who come out to showcase just what can be done with local organic ingredients. The "field" part arises from the picturesque natural setting. Expect lots of good local wine and beer, as well as dozens of organic farmers' displays. All of the funds raised from event — admission runs approximately $100 — goes to support organic agriculture. Held in September.

PLANET IN FOCUS
www.planetinfocus.org.
If the glitz and glamour of the Toronto International Film Festival leaves you feeling you can't handle the sight of another Starbucks-swilling, SUV-driving, photog-ducking celeb, this international environmental film and video fest is certain to provide you with a breath of fresh air, and some good clean green fun. Documentaries, short films, dramatic features and animation from filmmakers around the planet on subjects about the planet are the focus. Plus workshops, panels and networking events give you the chance to rub elbows with the city's keenest and greenest. Held in early November.

VEGETARIAN FOOD FAIR
www.veg.ca/foodfair.
In its second decade and going strong, this annual taste-testing festival of all things deliciously meat-free is a must for anyone with taste buds. Follow sumptuous smells into the vegetarian food tent, nibble and nosh at over 100 vendor stalls, steal culinary ideas from cooking demonstrations and more. Held in September.

Food

Health food stores

BIG CARROT NATURAL FOOD MARKET
348 Danforth, 416-466-2129, www.thebigcarrot.ca.
Besides having a massive organic fresh- and packaged-food mart and holistic dispensary, this eco-conscious cooperative offers workshops, small eco appliances, as well as the city's largest alt-cosmetic and personal care selection.

ESSENCE OF LIFE
50 Kensington, 416-506-0345.
This Kensington Market health shop has more selection than your average neighbourhood store and rock-bottom prices to boot.

KARMA COOP
739 Palmerston, 416-534-1470, www.karmacoop.org.
Tucked away up a quiet Annex laneway, this non-profit member-owned and operated co-op is all about organic and locally grown food. Just pitch in for a two-hour shift once a month or show up for a one-time trial round of shopping.

NOAH'S NATURAL FOODS
2401 Yonge, 416-488-0904, 667 Yonge, 416-969-0220, 322 Bloor West, 416-968-7930, 7117 Bathurst 905-731-2098.
If Noah built an ark filled with natural supplies, this place would be it. Good all-round source for healthy food, natural cosmetics, vitamins and chem-free cleaning supplies.

WHOLE FOODS
Hazelton Lanes, 87 Avenue Road, 416-944-0500, www.wholefoodsmarket.com.
Okay, so it's a little "Hollywood goes organic," but Whole Foods does have a hell of a selection of pretty much everything healthy.

Organic food delivery

FRONT DOOR ORGANICS
415 Horner, #9, 416-201-3000, www.frontdoororganics.com.
Boxes include 10 to 15 organic fruits and veggies; up to two substitutions allowed. Organic groceries like milk, bread and coffee can be added.

GOOD FOOD BOX (FOODSHARE)
416-363-6441 ext 221, www.foodshare.net.
For a decade now, FoodShare has been delivering boxes full of affordable seasonal fruits and veggies to church basements, social housing centres and 200 neighbourhood drop-offs. Choose between small or large boxes filled with organic or non-organic, largely locally grown produce and feel good about supporting a charity that helps people get back on their feet and fosters holistic community living. Weekly, biweekly or monthly delivery. Come January you can join their Cooking Out of the Box club and learn two dozen tasty, easy and healthy recipes.

GREEN EARTH ORGANICS
70 Wade, #3, 416-285-5300, www.greenearthorganics.com.
Choose between regular or family-size boxes; up to four substitutions allowed. Ten per cent of profits goes to charities like Oxfam and the Breast Cancer Foundation.

ONTARIO NATURAL FOOD CO-OP
416-503-3663, www.onfc.ca.
Pool your purchasing power and gather up five or more adults (friends, family or a community group) to start your own buying club. This not-for-profit distributor will let you in on the great discounts they offer to health food stores and co-ops across the province on natural and organic dry goods as well as dairy, fridge and freezer foods. Some of the surplus funds the ONFC makes go back into educational work and community development projects.

ORGANICS DELIVERED
416-556-7833, www.organicsdelivered.com.
Get a bushel of 100 per cent organic assorted fruits and veggies delivered anywhere in the GTA (and Peterborough). Every customer can give the company a list of favourites. Don't like cauliflower? Just tell 'em. They also donate food to women's shelters.

WEEKLY ORGANIC WONDER (WOW)
1-877-926-4426, www.torontoorganics.com.
Create your own box by choosing from a wide selection of fruits, vegetables, meats and grocery items, but prepackaged boxes of seasonal produce are cheaper. No time to cook? No problem. WOW can drop off organic frozen entrees.

Farmers markets
Hardcore veg-heads believe a direct relationship with the person who grows the food they eat is as important as the veggies themselves. Here's where to find both.

DISTILLERY DISTRICT FARMERS MARKET
This weekly market held just inside the complex's main gate presents produce from Holland Marsh's Spring Farms (salad greens, herbs and potted plants), Prince Edward County's Haystrom Farms (chemical-free heritage veg) and Georgetown's Alison Farms (fresh corn, green beans and blueberries). (See **Sightseeing**, page 36.)
55 Mill, at Trinity, Jun-Sep, Sun 10 am-5 pm, 416-561-8340, www.distilleryfarmersmarket.com.

DUFFERIN GROVE FARMERS MARKET
Year round, rain or shine, this community-minded park features seasonal veggies from Sosnicki Farms, Plan B Organics and Greenfields Farms, as well as fruit from Feast of Fields Farms. Other veggie-minded vendors include Country Meadows Garden for organic goat cheese and olive oil, Fun Guy Farms for mushrooms and forager Jonathan Forbes's Wild Food for preserved fiddleheads and huckleberries. (See **Sightseeing**, page 38.)
875 Dufferin, south of Bloor, Thu 3-7 pm, 416-392-0913, www.dufferinpark.ca/market/market.html.

FARMERS ORGANIC MARKET
Toronto's longest-running organic market, it's also our smallest. Expect a limited but esoteric range of veggies – green tomatillos, hot peppers, gigantic puffball mushrooms, say – and farm-preserved pickles and kimchee. Veggie-stuffed jalapeños and grape leaves, too.
St. George the Martyr Church, 197 John, at Stephanie, Sat 8:30 am-2:30 pm, 647-226-2418.

NATHAN PHILLIPS SQUARE FARMERS MARKET
Located right outside the mayor's office window, this weekly gathering features a number of merchants who don't appear at any other local market. They include Andrew's Scenic Acres, offering rhubarb, raspberries and sweet corn, Sahota Farms, specialists in Asian veggies and dill pickles, and Caledon Spring Farm, selling strawberries, asparagus and Ontario-grown peanuts. (See **Sightseeing**, page 20.)
100 Queen West, at Bay, Jun-Oct, Wed 8 am to 2 pm, 416-392-7341, www.toronto.ca/special_events/wednesdays/index. htm.

RIVERDALE FARMERS MARKET
Some of the Dufferin market's suppliers participate in this weekly meet on the lawn next to Riverdale Farm, among them Sosnicki's, Plan B, Country Meadows, Feast of Fields and Forbes – but some are exclusive to this gathering, like greengrocers Grenville Farms for field tomatoes, Hosswood Farms for organic herbs and the Quinte Organic Farmers Co-operative for heirloom tomatoes, sweet corn and fresh garlic. (See **Sightseeing**, page 26.)
Riverdale Park, Winchester at Sumach, May-Oct, Tue 3-7 pm, 416-961-8787, www.friendsofriverdalefarm.com.

ST. LAWRENCE FARMERS MARKET
Toronto's largest farmers market stocks organic veggies and cut flowers from Marvin Gardens, apples and homemade pies at Boychyn Orchards and 100 per cent vegetarian soaps and beauty products at Sasha's.
North Hall, 92 Front East, at Jarvis, Sat 5 am-5 pm, 416-392-7120, www.stlawrencemarket.com.

Other planet-friendly purveyors

AMBROSIA NATURAL FOODS
55 Doncaster, at Yonge, 905-881-7811.

APPLETREE NATURAL FOODS
845 Queen West, at Niagara, 416-504-9677.

BALDWIN NATURALS
16 Baldwin, at McCaul, 416-979-1777.

BULK BARN
17 Leslie, at Eastern, 416-466-4512, and others.

BULK MINE
655 Yonge, at Charles, 416-513-0783.

THE BUTCHERS
2636 Yonge, at Eglinton, 416-483-5777.

CUMBRAE BUTCHERS
481 Church, at Maitland, 416-923-5600.

ETHEREA NATURAL FOODS
1151 Davenport, at Ossington, 416-916-1894.

EVERGREEN NATURAL FOODS
161 Roncesvalles, at Garden, 416-534-2684.

FLYING MONKEY
314 College, at Borden, 416-968-1515.

FRESH FROM THE FARM
350 Donlands, at O'Connor, 416-422-3276.

HEALTHY BUTCHER
565 Queen West, at Denison, 416-703-2164.

HEALTH SHOPPE
41A Charles West, at St. Nicholas, 416-923-5071, and others.

KENSINGTON MARKET ORGANIC ICE CREAM
188 Augusta, at Denison Square, 416-835-7781.

LENNY'S
489 Parliament, at Carlton, 416-920-3777.

LIVING SEED HEALTH CENTRE
179 Avenue Road, 416-921-7486.

MEAT ON THE BEACH
1860 Queen East, at Woodbine, 416-690-1228.

OLIVE TREE ORGANICS
366 Bloor East, at Sherbourne, 416-920-5003.

ORGANIC ABUNDANCE
3066 Bloor West, at Royal York, 416-234-5258.

ORGANIC BOUTIQUE
970 Queen West, at Shaw, 416-536-3851.

ORGANICS ON BLOOR
468 Bloor West, at Brunswick, 416-538-1333

STONEMILL BAKEHOUSE
92 Front East, at Jarvis, 416-601-1853; factory outlet 426 Nugget, at Markham Rd, 416-757-5767.

STRICTLY BULK
638 Danforth, at Pape, 416-466-6849, and others.

SUGAR & SPICE
265 Augusta, at Nassau, 416-593-1664, and others.

TASTE OF NATURE
380 Bloor West, at Spadina, 416-925-8102.

TUTTI FRUTTI
64 Kensington, at St. Andrew, 416-593-9281.

WHOLESOME MARKET
2234 Queen East, at Beech, 416-690-9500.

Organic restaurants

BIG CARROT
348 Danforth, at Jackman, 416-466-2129.
The takeout counter, complete with a few tables and chairs for those who want to hang around, situated in the centre of Toronto's largest one-stop alternative supermarket, offers a health-conscious card that's 100 per cent vegetarian and at least 60 per cent organic. Bonus: all ingredients clearly marked. Double bonus: organic ketchup!

CAMROS ORGANIC FOODS
25 Hayden, 416-960-0723.
Serving up a full card of Persian cuisine, including several nutritious Middle Eastern rice-and-bean casserole combos.

GUERRILLA GOURMET
647-831-3377, www.guerrilla-gourmet.com.
Up for a spontaneous meal at a top-secret location with an intriguing mix of strangers? Guerrilla Gourmet will take you on a culinary adventure with organic, locally grown ingredients, be it for lunch, brunch or dinner. Just leave all the planning to them.

JAMIE KENNEDY WINE BAR
9 Church, 416-362-1957 ext 354,
www.jkkitchens.com.
Organic guru and chef extraordinaire Jamie Kennedy serves up fine naturally raised meats, organic produce and organic and biodynamic wines at both his wine bar and his restaurant on Church.

LE CAFÉ VERT
946 Queen East, 416-778-1313.
The archetype for eco-conscious eateries, not only is most of its mainly vegetarian menu organic, but it's also prepared with heart and social conviction.

LIVE ORGANIC FOOD BAR
264 Dupont, 416-515-2002.
Crisp and colourful eatery uses virtually all organic ingredients in its deliciously innovative half-raw, half-not-so-raw vegan menu.

RADICAL ROOTS
International Student Centre, 33 St. George, at College,
www.radicalroots.ca.
Though ostensibly a U of T self-serve organic vegan cafeteria, this worker-run non-profit café that promotes "equitable access to good food" is open to the general public as well as student radicals of every bent. Place your order from the small kitchen's menu and soon receive a helping of earnest nourishment. And since these eco-minded folks don't do disposables, if you want takeout, it's strictly BYOB (bring your own bowl).

SUNNY CAFÉ
322 Bloor West, 416-963-8624.
Haven't a clue what to feed a vegan dinner guest? Tucked away in a corner of Annex health food store **Noah's** (see page 208), Toronto's first organic dairy-free take-away also offers downtown's most extensive health-conscious salad bar. It features old standbys like macrobiotic brown rice with steamed broccoli and beets as well as garlicky tomato tofu salad and Asian greens in sunflower oil vinaigrette, all sold by the kilo.

TINTO
89 Roncesvalles, at Marion, 416-530-5885,
www.tinto.ca.
This airy two-story café is part neighbourhood hang, part activist art gallery. Dawdle over fair trade lattes while browsing a selection of leftist zines or connect the laptop to the interweb with free Wi-Fi. Bonus: though not entirely vegetarian, nearly everything's organic and/or planet friendly, even the takeout containers.

Organic veggies of every shape and colour are a really

Organic coffee shops

ALTERNATIVE GROUNDS
333 Roncesvalles, 416-534-6335,
www.alternativegrounds.com.
West-end café serves up a rotating array of fresh-roasted fair trade beans and blends.

BIRDS AND BEANS ROASTERY CAFÉ
2415 Lakeshore West, 416-913-9221.
Organic, bird-friendly, fair trade coffee beans, chocolate, syrups and teas, plus home grinders and a storefront café.

MERCHANTS OF GREEN COFFEE
2 Matilda, 416-741-5369,
www.merchantsofgreencoffee.com.
Green coffee and all the gear including coffee roasters, grinders and accessories.

MERCURY ORGANIC ESPRESSO BAR
915 Queen East, 647-435-4779.
Riverside neighbourhood spot serves 100 per cent organic fair trade coffee in biodegradable cups.

MOONBEAN COFFEE COMPANY
30 St. Andrew, 416-595-0327,
www.moonbeancoffee.com.
About 80 per cent of this boho Kensington café's selection is organic fair trade. Plus their patio is tops for people watching in the heart of the market.

NOW LOUNGE
189 Church, 416-364-1301,
www.nowtoronto.com/lounge.
Serving organic fair trade coffee and light lunches in a laidback space.

al at alt-supermarkets like **Big Carrot**, page 208.

TINTO
89 Roncesvalles, 416-530-5885, www.tinto.ca.
Colombian slang for coffee, this hip west-side fair trade java shop also hosts the occasional art exhibition.

Shopping

COME AS YOU ARE
701 Queen West, 416-504-7934, www.comeasy-ouare.com.
Stock up on organic lube, petroleum-free massage oils and even a solar-powered vibrator at this classy west-end sex supply shop. Good selection of PVC-free vibrators and dildos.

FERTILE GROUND ENVIRONMENTAL BOOKSTORE
11 Irwin, 416-964-0161, www.fgbooks.com.
This independent bookstore is dedicated to all things earth-bound, from books on eco activism and animal rights to urban planning and the water crisis. It's also a business bookstore – go figure.

FRIENDLY STRANGER
241 Queen West, 416-591-1570, www.friendlystranger.com.
This (relatively) swank head shop has a line of natural-clay-dyed dress shirts, tanks and pants made from hemp, as well as the usual stoner supplies.

GOOD FOR HER
175 Harbord, 416-588-0900 www.goodforher.com.
Homeopathic organic lube and vegan fun fur restraints help make your sex life eco- and animal-friendly at this intimate sex store. Ask about women- and trans-only hours.

GRASSROOTS
372 Danforth, 416-466-2841; 408 Bloor West, 416-944-1993, www.grassrootsstore.com.
Until this store opened its doors in 1994, Torontonians had trouble getting their hands on earth-friendly wares. The one-stop shop offers everything from organic clothing, bedding (including natural rubber mattresses) and creams to solar-powered radios and air and water filters, as well as gifts like salvaged wood picture frames and earth-conscious games and toys.

HABITAT FOR HUMANITY RESTORE
29 Bermondsey, 416-755-8023 ext 33; 1120 Caledonia, 416-783-0686, www.torontohabitat.on.ca.
Picture a thrift shop for reusable building materials like second-hand lumber, sinks, doors and windows. And all the money goes to the kick-ass charity that builds affordable housing for families in need.

LEFT FEET
88 Nassau, 416-360-5338, www.leftfeet.ca.
Okay, so we don't like the fact that this vegan shoe store uses off-gassing PVC as a leather-alternative, but they do offer fair trade shoes and sandals, and we like that.

PRELOVED
613 Queen West, 416-504-8704, www.preloved.ca.
This Toronto original takes old sweaters, sheets and raincoats and reworks them into funky, unique dresses, pants and tops. (For more recycled threads, see **Shopping**, page 174.)

SILKROAD FLOORING
300 Esna Park Drive, unit 26, Markham, 905-947-1688, www.silkroadtoronto.com.
Eco-Logo-certified bamboo flooring, plywood and veneers made from a type of bamboo that doesn't steal food (and homes) from the mouths of panda bears.

TEN THOUSAND VILLAGES
362 Danforth, 416-462-9779; 2599 Yonge, 416-932-1673, www.tenthousandvillages.ca.
Everything in this fair trade gift and home furnishings shop has not only been purchased at a fair price, often from developing-world cooperatives, but it also tries to use ecologically sustainable materials (like Peruvian earrings with recycled glass).

T.H.E. STORE
Hazelton Lanes, 87 Avenue Road, 416-921-7317, www.t-h-e-store.com.
Green goes upscale at this tony Yorkville home shop. Total Home Environment offers hard-to-find items like organic wool pillows, natural rubber mattresses and organic cotton crib blankets, as well as clothing, candles and more. Plus they have a catalogue full of reclaimed Baltic pine vanities, dinner tables, armoires, etc.

TORONTO HEMP COMPANY
637 Yonge, 416-920-1980, www.torontohemp.com.
Besides eco weed paraphernalia like tree-free rolling papers, this store has all sorts of clothing and footware made with earth-friendly, low-pesticide hemp. They even have bolts of hemp cloth, canvas, silk and denim, as well as hemp yarn for crafty stoners.

URBAN TREE SALVAGE
91 Hymus, Scarborough, 647-438-7516, www.urbantreesalvage.com.
Old city trees that have been struck by lightning, disease or old age get a second life here, where they're turned into hardwood lumber, flooring, even funky coffee tables and stools.

Services

Laundromat

BEACH SOLAR LAUNDROMAT
2240 Queen East, 416-712-1488.
Solar panels heat the building and the hot water used in the machines. Offers wash-and-fold services for the chronically lazy or busy ($1/pound). It's partnered up with Eco Cleaners, which will pick up and deliver all your laundry. Beach Solar handles the wash-and-fold while Eco Cleaners (see below) will do the dry cleaning.

CAREFUL HAND LAUNDRY AND DRY CLEANERS
206 Dupont, 416-923-1200, and others, www.carefulhandlaundry.com.
Careful has been in the laundry biz since 1929 and now operates four Toronto locations that offer eco-friendlier wet cleaning.

Dry cleaner

ECO CLEANERS
719 Mount Pleasant, 416-425-9474, www.ecocleaners.ca.
Many cleaners call themselves green but use toxins like petroleum hydrocarbon (considered a hazardous air pollutant). Eco Cleaners insists it's Toronto's first truly non-toxic cleaner using a silicone-based process called GreenEarth.

Florists

ECO FLORA
416-254-2674, www.ecoflora.ca.
Delivers wildcrafted, organically grown or fairly trad-ed bouquets anywhere in the Toronto area. Eco Flora also does weddings.

HATCHER FLORIST
5455 Yonge, 416-221-5557, www.hatcherflorist.com.
This florist isn't all organic, but it does have a selection of Sierra eco-certified flowers grown with fewer pesticides, at farms where workers are treated according to international labour standards for a change.

Professional cleaning

EARTH CONCERNS CLEANING SERVICE
294 Symington, 416-535-9397, www.earthconcerns.com.
This eco-friendly, health-conscious company will make your home or office sparkle without resorting to chems.

LIVELIFE GREEN CLEANING
416-402-6177, www.livelife.ca.
Earth-conscious scrubbing and dusting of your home or office using natural products. They'll even run errands for you and watch your pets while you're away.

Car rental

AUTOSHARE
24 Mercer, 416-340-7888, www.autoshare.com.
Perfect for people who don't own a car but still need wheels. Just join and pick up a car whenever you like from over 50 fleet locations. They even have hybrids!

DISCOUNT CAR AND TRUCK RENTALS
13 locations across Toronto, including 134 Jarvis, 416-864-0696.
This rental chain is the first of its kind to offer hybrid cars. The Toyota Prius is available for $39.95 a day plus taxes.

ZIPCAR
www.zipcar.com.
This American operation runs just like AutoShare and hit the city in spring 2006, with a 50-car fleet. Check their site for rates and locations.

Bike rental

BIKESHARE
416-504-2918, www.bikeshare.org.
Get a season pass and you can pick up a retro yellow bike from any conveniently located hub and drop it off at any other hub. Can't afford the fee? Just volunteer anywhere, for anyone, a minimum of four hours and they'll just give you a pass. Isn't that nice?

TORONTO ISLAND BIKE RENTALS
Centre Island, 416-203-0009.
Pick up a cruiser or quad to get you around the Islands in comfort. You can even form a family biker gang on tandems.

WHEEL EXCITEMENT
249 Queens Quay West, 416-260-9000, www.wheelexcitement.ca.
Rollerblade and bike rentals right along the waterfront trail.

Diaper service

ABC DIAPER SERVICE
205 Gamble, 416-429-8459.
Folded cloth diapers delivered to your door via pedal power.

DIAPER-EEZ
2309 Bloor West, 416-604-0916, www.diaper-eez.com.
Don't burden your baby with an ecological footprint the size of a diaper-filled soccer stadium. This one-stop mommy shop has all the fixings for DIY reusable bum wrappers, as well as the usual mommy and baby devices.

Like New York cabs, only they don't smell funny. **BikeShare**, page 212.

Resources

COMMUNITY BICYCLE NETWORK
761 Queen West, #101, 416-504-2918,
www.communitybicyclenetwork.org.
An amazing resource for every cyclist. Not only do
they run the **BikeShare** program (see above), they also
put on **Wenches With Wrenches** repair workshops for
girls by girls, **ToolWorks** (supervised bike repair space)
and the **Green Fleet** program, all of which give cyclists
the skills and confidence they need to get moving. For
more cycling resources, see page 196.

GREEN MAP OF TORONTO
www.greentourism.ca
Put out by the Green Tourism Association of Toronto,
this veggie-ink map illustrates just how much greenery (and eco-friendliness) blankets the city even in the
core. One side of the fold-out guide pinpoints vegetarian restaurants, markets, hotels, plus the usual tourist
attractions and landmarks. The other spreads out
beyond the city's borders to show you just how many
conservation areas, parks, campgrounds, watersheds
and trails are in arm's (or bike's) reach.

PLANET FRIENDLY
www.planetfriendly.net
Online portal to all things eco, including a listing of
"eco experience centres" and eco villages throughout
Ontario as well as an invaluable calendar highlighting every workshop, summit and movie night related
to the planet.

TORONTO COMMUNITY GARDEN NETWORK
238 Queen West, 416-392-1668,
http://dir.gardenweb.com/directory/tcgn.
This outcrop (pardon the pun) of Foodshare fosters
the vibrant community gardening network and will
connect you to one of the city's 100-plus community
gardens. It also puts on monthly workshops and
publishes a monthly newsletter.

TORONTOHIKING.COM
Online resource centre will help you plan your hike in
Toronto and southern Ontario. Find detailed descrip-
tions of trails, tutorials and info on ruby throated
hummingbirds and the like to get you primed for a
nature walk.

TORONTO AND REGION CONSERVATION AUTHORITY
416-661-6600, www.trca.on.ca.
Get info on conservation efforts and ideas on how
to get involved in community stewardship programs. TRCA also manages wonderful conservation
centres (including Tommy Thompson and Rouge
Parks) and offers countless programs for everything
from bird studies and nature photography to
canoeing and compass mapping. Its events calendar is a must for finding out about quirky happen-
ings like fiddling contests and fishing derbies, as
well as ecology sessions like Tree Talk and Fungus
Among Us.

TORONTO VEGETARIAN ASSOCIATION
www.veg.ca.
Besides listing veg-head-friendly events (including
the org's vegetarian food fair, see page 208) and linking you to animal-loving podcasts, this group puts
out a directory of all things — you guessed it — vegetarian. Download it online or order a hard copy to
get listings of vegetarian- and vegan-positive restaurants, bakeries, caterers, cooking classes, even day-
cares.

Green orgs

ACT FOR THE EARTH
238 Queen W, lower level, 647-438-6398, www.actfortheearth.org.
Specialty: peace, ecology and human rights.

ANIMAL ALLIANCE OF CANADA
221 Broadview, #101, 416-462-9541, www.animalalliance.ca.
Specialty: animal rights.

ANIMAL LIBERATION FRONT
www.animalliberationfront.com.
Specialty: saving animals through direct action.

CANADIAN ASSOCIATION OF PHYSICIANS FOR THE ENVIRONMENT (CAPE)
130 Spadina, #301, 416-306-2273, www.cape.ca.
Specialty: eco-protection for human health.

CANADIAN INSTITUTE FOR ENVIRONMENTAL LAW AND POLICY (CIELAP)
130 Spadina, #302, 416-923-3529, www.cielap.org.
Specialty: research in enviro laws and policy.

EARTHROOTS
401 Richmond West, #410, 416-599-0152, www.earthroots.org.
Specialty: wildlife, wilderness and watersheds.

ENVIRONMENTAL DEFENCE
17 Adelaide West, #705, 416-323-9521, www.environmentaldefence.ca.
Specialty: greening cities and saving species.

EVERGREEN FOUNDATION
355 Adelaide West, 416-596-1495, www.evergreen.ca.
Works toward creating healthy outdoor spaces (see **Don Valley Brick Works**, page 204).

FATAL LIGHT AWARENESS PROGRAM (FLAP)
416-366-3527, www.flap.org
Specialty: protecting migratory birds.

FOODSHARE
200 Eastern, 416-363-6441, www.foodshare.net.
Specialty: improving community access to healthy and affordable food.

FRIENDS OF THE SPIT
P.O. Box 51518, 2060 Queen East, 416-699-3143, www.interlog.com/~fos/.
Specialty: preserving the Leslie Street Spit.

GREENPEACE
250 Dundas West, #605, 416-597-8408, www.greenpeace.ca.
Specialty: climate change, ancient forests, GE, nuclear power and oceans.

LOCAL ENHANCEMENT AND APPRECIATION OF FORESTS
73 Bathurst, #305, 416-413-9244, www.leaftoronto.org.
Specialty: protecting urban forests.

NATURE CONSERVANCY OF CANADA (NCC)
110 Eglinton West, #400, 416-932-3202, www.natureconservancy.ca.
Specialty: preserving ecologically significant areas.

NORTH TORONTO GREEN COMMUNITY
40 Orchard View, #252, 416-781-7663, www.ntgc.ca.
Specialty: improving local environment.

ONTARIO CLEAN AIR ALLIANCE (OCAA)
625 Church, #402, 416-926-1907, www.cleanair.web.net.
Works toward eliminating coal-burning plants and promoting sustainable energy.

ONTARIO NATURE
355 Lesmill, 416-444-8419, www.ontarionature.org.
Specialty: protecting and restoring habitats.

POLLUTION PROBE
625 Church, #402, 416-926-1907, www.pollutionprobe.org.
Specialty: environmental research.

PROBE INTERNATIONAL
225 Brunswick, 416-964-9223, www.probeinternational.org.
Specialty: exposes enviro and economic effects of Canada's aid and trade abroad.

RIVERSIDES
511 Richmond West, 416-868-1983, www.riversides.org.
Specialty: restoration of local watersheds.

SAVE THE OAK RIDGES MORAINE (STORM) COALITION
401 Richmond West, #380, 647-258-3281, www.stormcoalition.org.
Specialty: protecting the Moraine.

SIERRA CLUB OF CANADA ONTARIO CHAPTER – GTA GROUP
24 Mercer, 416-960-9606, www.Ontario.sierraclub.ca/toronto.
Specialty: creating sustainable communities.

TASK FORCE TO BRING BACK THE DON
55 John, 23rd floor, 416-392-0401, www.toronto.ca/don.
Specialty: revitalizing the Don River.

TORONTO ATMOSPHERIC FUND
75 Elizabeth, 416-392-0271, www.toronto.ca/taf.
Specialty: reducing greenhouse gas emissions and energy conservation.

TORONTO BAY INITIATIVE
30 Duncan, #201, 416-598-2277, www.torontobay.net.
Specialty: improving water quality and regenerating habitat.

TORONTO CYCLING COMMITTEE
Meets at City Hall, 100 Queen West, 416-392-7592, www.toronto.ca/cycling/committee.
Specialty: promoting cycling.

TORONTO ENVIRONMENTAL ALLIANCE (TEA)
30 Duncan, #201 416-596-0660, www.torontoenvironment.org.
Specialty: greening Toronto.

TORONTO PUBLIC SPACE COMMITTEE
www.publicspace.ca
In a city of mega money and marauding development, these frenetic grassrootsers are to be found wherever there's a chance to redo the landscape in ways that promote human connection. Spacers head out into the night to plant seeds and seedlings in our commons, paint abandoned bikes, protect the rights of the people's press (posterers) and campaign against neuron-blitzing billboards. In their downtime, they try to sell residents on de-fencing, the better to hang with our neighbours. Pick up their Spacing magazine and give your besieged inner citizen an inspiring jolt.

WILDLANDS LEAGUE
401 Richmond West, #380, 416-971-9453, www.wildlandsleague.org.
Specialty: protection of waterways, forests and ecosystems.

WINDSHARE
401 Richmond West, #401, 416-977-5093, www.windshare.ca.
Specialty: urban renewable energy.

WORLD WILDLIFE FUND CANADA
245 Eglinton East, #410, 416-489-8800, www.wwf.ca.
Specialty: habitat and endangered species protection.

queer

queer

Toronto is a seriously gay-positive town. New York had Stonewall, San Francisco has the Barbra Streisand Museum, but Toronto has the best-organized queer community on the planet.

Gays and lesbians live just about everywhere in the city – the Annex is one hub and the artist enclaves, no matter where they move to, are always home to queers. Right now, the burgeoning **West Queen West** (see sidebar, page 221) area between Ossington and Dufferin has seen a major spike in its queer population.

But the centre of T.O.'s gay universe continues to be what's casually referred to as the Gay Village, centring on the Church and Wellesley intersection. Year round it has a thriving club and dining scene, a raft of queer-owned businesses and dozens of queer-based organizations committed to serving their community (see page 222). For over 20 years, **Buddies in Bad Times** (see **Entertainment**, page 154), Toronto's queer theatre company, has been delivering original plays and cabarets and is thriving in its permanent home on Alexander.

And of course, there's the Pride Week celebrations each summer, climaxing with the spectacular Pride Parade. The crowd of nearly 1 million who watch the more than 90 floats go by are as much a part of the party as any of the drag queen divas and bondage boys marching through the city's downtown.

But not so long ago, Toronto's Pride was not nearly so visible. Prior to the 1970s, the gay scene was mostly underground. **Allan Gardens** was cruise central (and now hosts the annual FFN fetish fair), and the most notable bar was the St. Charles Tavern on Yonge near the **Glad Day Bookshop** (see page 220), Canada's first gay-oriented bookstore, which opened in 1970.

As for the city's **Pride** festivities – we love that moment every year when the mayor raises the rainbow flag at City Hall – that culminate in the world's largest Pride Parade on the last Sunday in June, it began when 236 demonstrators marched through the streets over 25 years ago. The Dyke March, which hits the streets the day before, has grown steadily over its 10-year history to the point that nearly 10,000 women dominate Church Street for the event.

At this stage in T.O.'s queer history, Pride Day is obsolete – it's all about Pride Week now.

So whatever you call yourself – gay, lesbian, queer, transgendered, bisexual, fluid pansexual – you can find a home in Toronto.

Landmarks

ALLAN GARDENS
Carlton and Sherbourne, 416-392-7288, http://collections.ic.gc.ca/gardens/opening.html.
Founded in 1858 as the Horticultural Gardens, this 13-acre downtown plot is laid out with flower beds, paths, a fountain and various trees and shrubbery. Indoors is a 16,000-square-foot conservatory with seasonal plants, including the rare and exotic. Open wkdays 9 am-4 pm, Sat-Sun and holidays 10 am-5 pm. Free.

CAWTHRA PARK
This park behind the 519 Church Street Community Centre is home to the first-of-its-kind AIDS Memorial. Erected in 1993, it bears the names of members of the community who've been lost to AIDS etched into bronze plaques. A memorial candlelight vigil is held here each year during Pride Week.

GEORGE HISLOP PARK
This tiny park east of Yonge between Charles and Isabella is dedicated to the late Toronto businessman, long-time gay activist and unofficial mayor of Toronto's gay community. Hislop co-owned the Barracks gay bathhouse, one of the four that were raided by Toronto's finest back in 1981, galvanizing the gay and lesbian community and firmly establishing once and for all the Church and Wellesley area as the Gay Village.

Entertainment
Restaurants

BYZANTIUM
499 Church, at Wellesley, 416-922-3859.
A restaurant of two halves – one a copper-hued cocktail lounge, the other a Prada-green swanky boîte where, if planned carefully, the action on diners' plates beats the non-stop cruise-a-rama parading past the spot's seasonally open French doors. And make sure to check out the secluded deck at the rear of this crazy-popular cocktail cantina.

FIRE ON THE EAST SIDE
6 Gloucester, at Yonge, 416-960-3473.
Featured in Queer As Folk, this laid-back lounge off the Village's main drag offers a Cajun card with soul food and Tex-Mex accents. Seats on the pretty curbside terrace are particularly desirable for weekend brunch. Bonus: $6 martini Tuesdays!

CHURCH STREET DINER
555 Church, at Dundonald, 416-324-8724.
Since changing owners, what was formerly the Five Alarm Diner has been given a makeover, distancing it from its previous firehall image. The pseudo-retro resto's new decor has a fun urban feel. Breakfast,

Best Ass Contest, every Saturday at **Zelda's**.

lunch and brunch items make the diner a worthy addition to the village, but main courses are over-priced and under-executed.

LE PETIT LIBAN
580 Church, at Dundonald, 416-963-2222.
This Middle Eastern boîte's two terraces – one street-side, the other more formal 'round the back – take the crown as the street's most glamorous. While the backyard deck suggests a night at an Indonesian resort, the antebellum patio up front (complete with portico) would make the perfect stage for a drag king/queen reading of Gone with the Wind come Pride weekend. Warning: iffy food, great firewater.

MATIGNON
51 St. Nicholas, at Inkerman, 416-921-9226.
A down-to-earth neighbourhood boîte, this bistro serves hearty French fare that defies gastro trends. Check out the three-course $26.95 prix fixe dinner deal.

ZELDA'S
542 Church, at Maitland, 416-922-2526.
Staff in gender-fuck drag and the sunniest patio on the Village strip make this a very hot spot. And grip-ing about the not-so-great grub is as fruitless as whining about the Leafs – get over it, girlfriend! Instead, join the queue for a hard-to-get curbside table at the street's cruisiest patio. Tank up on Zeldatinis, like the Bitch Slap (sour apple, raspberry and melon liqueur with cranberry juice) and tune in to non-stop 70s disco while taking in Saturday night's Cheap Show – with its notorious Best Ass Contest – hosted by drag queens Lena Over and Justine Touch. Bonus: the first Sunday of the month, Zelda throws her trailer trashy all-you-can-eat Leather Brunch.

Bars & patios

BABYLON
553 Church, at Gloucester, 416-923-2626.
A three-tiered space with as many personalities. The first floor is a comfortable room serving Mediterranean snacks and dinners. Up a flight is a martini lounge where bartenders mix up over 200 different cocktail concoctions for the swizzle-stick set. DJs take over the third floor room on weekends.

BAR 501
501 Church, at Wellesley, 416-944-3272.
The 501's Sunday-evening drag shows literally stop traffic. The action in the club's large front window at 6 pm attracts crowds that spill off the sidewalk and often block the neighbourhood's main drag. Inside is a saloon complete with pinball machines and pool tables.

BAR VOLO
587 Yonge, at Gloucester, 416-928-0008.
Quaff till you can quaff no more courtesy of BV's slew of microbrews on tap.

THE BLACK EAGLE
457 Church, at Maitland, 416-413-1219.
Even in the middle of the day this leather bar is dark as fuck. As tough guys gaze blankly at the hard-core porn videos broadcast on several TVs on the first floor, stogie-smoking daddies stand and pose upstairs under camouflage netting. Remember: no girlish laughing.

CELLBLOCK
72 Carlton, at Church, 416-921-0066.
A jail-themed party space in the Zipperz complex.

R. JEANETTE MARTIN

1 million people celebrated Pride in 2006.

pride week

For one week each summer Toronto wears its rainbow colours louder and prouder than any other city. Take that, San Francisco!

You could say Pride started with the first Gay Day picnic at Hanlan's Point in 1971. Or maybe it was the Gay Days event in Cawthra Park in 1978. But why don't we just credit the cops? Pride – both the feeling and the event – really kicked off in February 1981 when Toronto police raided four gay bathhouses in Toronto, rounded up more than 300 people and carted them off to jail. The raids sparked a huge, high-profile demonstration. It was the first in-your-face declaration of outrage by gay Toronto.

That summer, a small group of activists decided they couldn't allow the energy to dissipate. Let it out again, they said, but this time more in celebration than demonstration. The plan was to have a small parade that would pass 52 Division police station on Dundas and culminate in a party at the Grange just south of the art gallery. Two hundred people attended, though the numbers of partiers multiplied as the sun went down and the city went dark.

By 2006 there were over 1 million people celebrating Pride Day on Toronto streets and the event has turned into one of the city's prime free celebrations.

How does an event grow to such gigantic proportions? A strong queer press helps. The Body Politic was publishing in full force in 1981 and galvanized queer energy. It later morphed into the

alt-weekly Xtra!, still going strong. The lesbian-feminist magazine Broadside was also active during Pride's early days, and all of these acted as promo for the brave political activism.

By 1987, sexual orientation was included in the Human Rights Code. Openly gay Kyle Rae won a seat on city council in 1991 and convinced the city to officially proclaim Pride Day that year. Getting the city's approval for Pride eased the way for gays and lesbians to participate openly in the event.

But let's be honest. The real reason Pride burst out the way it did was because it turned into such a terrific party, a visually spectacular celebration of sexuality in all its forms. By the time police Chief David Boothby agreed to allow all four lanes of traffic on Yonge to close for the parade, the celebration had taken over both Church and Yonge from Bloor to Wellesley and the straight contingent observing the scene had burgeoned, cramming the sidewalks throughout the entire parade route. Pride organizers welcomed them – they knew it meant that Pride had grown into a city celebration.

At this point in world queer history, no other city's Pride festivities – including San Francisco's and New York's – come close to the energy Toronto's generates every year on the last weekend in June.

CREWS
508 Church, at Maitland, 416-972-1662.
The main attraction of this straightforward barroom, complete with neon beer signs, is the regularly scheduled drag shows. See local drag legends get messy on Sunday afternoons.

HAIR OF THE DOG
425 Church, 416-962-2708.
A loungy neighbourhood bar with good bar food and popular with couples of any persuasion.

INSPIRE
491 Church, at Maitland, 416-963-0044.
Though this stylishly minimal and candlelit space's menu rarely inspires, its small lounge and bar area makes a great spot for a champagne cocktail or three. Bring a flashlight – you'll need it to find your drink.

LOCAL 4
4 Dundonald, at Yonge, 416-915-0113.
Local 4 comes into its own thanks to the raised sightlines afforded by the trellised 20-seat deck out front. And the lineup of globally inspired pub grub makes this prime Pride real estate.

THE LOUNGE
1820 Dundas E, Mississauga (between Dixie/427), 416-760-3470.
Okay, it's a hell of a long way from the Village, but it features shemale and T-girl strippers on Tuesdays and Wednesdays and "nude boys" on Saturdays.

LÜB
487 Church, at Wellesley, 416-323-1489.
Pronounced "loob." A casual after-work hang, with a retro blue bar area and wood-and-fireplace upstairs lounge where DJs spin a mix of Eurobeat and house. The cozy second-storey deck is a great spot to take in all of the rainbow-flavoured life below.

MANHATTAN CLUB
19 Balmuto, at Charles, 416-920-9119.
Weekend DJs throw down hiphop and R&B tracks for an upscale but laid-back clientele.

O'GRADY'S
518 Church, at Maitland, 416-323-2822.
Formerly Wilde Oscar's, this boîte's huge two-tiered patio offers lounging at its best. The BBQ-ed card ain't bad either.

THE RED SPOT
459 Church, at Maitland, 416-967-7768.
A second-floor room with a Latin twist and occasional comedy nights.

REMINGTON'S
379 Yonge, at Gerrard, 416-977-2160.
A seven-days-a-week male strip club in the middle of Yonge Street's decidedly hetero sleaze zone. With almost as many celebrities offstage as on, Remington's and its Men of Steel dancers create an atmosphere that's a lot less uptight than the surrounding straight burlesque clubs. No cover, and day prices till 8 pm. Stud Muffin Thursdays, Dirrrty Saturdays and Ladies' Night Sundays.

SAILOR
467 Church, at Wellesley, 416-972-0887.
Part of the Woody's empire, it offers nautical digs for getting hammered with the hammerhead shark over the bar.

SLACK'S
562 Church, at Wellesley, 416-969-8742.
Holder of more NOW Readers Poll awards than any other establishment: best bartender, best gay bar and restaurant, best place to drink alone, best place to pick up a lesbian, best cocktail napkin and best pickled egg.

SNEAKERS
502A Yonge, at Alexander, 416-961-5808.
The specialty of the house at this darkly lit emerald-green saloon is chicken, and we aren't talking about Buffalo wings. The main thing that attracts the middle-aged clientele is that supposedly teenaged hustlers from the nearby Breadalbane and Grosvenor track hang out here – despite the sign on the door saying that anyone under 19 will not be admitted. It's all somewhat desperate, tawdry and delicious. Day prices till 8 pm.

STATLER'S
471 Church, at Maitland, 416-925-0341.
More of a College-style lounge than most of the booze 'n' cruise joints found in Boystown, this small, elegant boîte hosts regular sessions with warbling jazz thrushes who broadcast to the street.

TANGO
508 Church, at Maitland, 416-972-1662.
Part of the Crews complex, this minimally decorated upstairs room is primarily a women's bar. Expect a cozy conversation pit on one side and a small, busy dance floor on the other.

TRADE
76 Wellesley E, at Church, no phone.
This mirror-lined cruise bar was once home to Zelda and her trashy kin. Today, it's a sleek, mirrored cruising space complete with bleachers, bubbly light fountains, a pool table and a disco jukebox.

TRAX V
529 Yonge, at Maitland, 416-963-5196.
Toronto's top-selling suds-swilling gin mill and one of Toronto's oldest and most popular gay bars, Trax is located behind a signless purple Victorian storefront. It looks its age; floors are rough timber and the exposed brick walls appear about to collapse. Wall-to-wall mirrors guarantee you'll be checked out even if you're not interested. Day prices till 9 pm and bingo every afternoon from 2 to 6 pm.

VILLAGE RAINBOW
477 Church, at Maitland, 416-961-0616.
Check in for a streamlined nouveau-Danforth lineup, and make sure to ask for table 26 – the Village's peak people-watching perch.

WETT BAR
7 Maitland, at Yonge, 416-966-9388.
With no sign and whited-out windows obstructing the view in and out – a good thing considering its just-off-Yonge location – Wett is the nabe's most stylish and smallest lounge. Recline on knockoff Mies van der Rohe day beds under Calderesque mobiles swilling swelegant 'tinis to the latest house hits.

WISH
3 Charles E, at Yonge, 416-935-0240.
Wish's decor has a high wow-factor. Whitewashed walls, ceiling and floors provide a neutral backdrop to low-slung overstuffed sofas piled with pillows and pashminas. How 1998! Trendy fashion mags hang on racks while media types gather at the walnut bar. This swanky lounge goes all South Beach under its tented curbside terrace. And come summer, it's a hot spot thanks to fine brunches and a bevy of fancy frozen blender concoctions.

WOODY'S
467 Church, at Maitland, 416-972-0887.
If you watched Queer As Folk, you know what Woody's looks like from the street. Its exterior is the facade of the fictional Pittsburgh bar. Unfortunately (or fortunately) the real thing is nothing like the TV version. Instead, this rambling room has several standup bars, areas for reposing, pool tables and stuffed faux rhinoceros heads.

ZIPPERZ
72 Carlton, at Church, 416-921-0066.
Since the Leafs left the Gardens, things haven't been the same round here. Cocktail-hour piano player, late-night cruising to house DJs.

Dance clubs

EL CONVENTO RICO
750 College, 416-588-7800.
A bit outside Boystown but worth the trek, this subterranean cha-cha-teria's as popular with cross-dressers as it is with straights ready to rumba. The Rico is definitely a scene that has to be experienced to be believed. Not at all decadent, it's actually charming in a down-at-the-heels-drag-queen kinda way. Early evening dance lessons Sunday ensure that neophytes will be able to mambo when the night hits full swing after midnight. Drag shows start at 1 am.

5IVE
5 St. Joseph, at Yonge, 416-964-8685.
Mainstream house DJs seven nights a week. Warning: Thursday is straight night.

FLY
6 Gloucester, at Yonge, 416-925-6222.
Circuit Party every Friday and Saturday night, with occasional big-name NYC DJs.

TALLULAH'S CABARET
12 Alexander, at Church, 416-975-8555.
Alternative types of unspecific gender writhe to the latest hip sounds (a.k.a. anything but house).

CANADA'S HOME FOR QUEER CULTURE

CUTTING EDGE THEATRE, RAUCOUS SPECIAL EVENTS, LARGE-SCALE FESTIVALS AND MORE...

BUDDIES IN BAD TIMES THEATRE

for event listings, check us out at
buddiesinbadtimestheatre.com
box office 416-975-8555
12 Alexander Street Toronto

buddies
IN BAD TIMES THEATRE

Theatre

BUDDIES IN BAD TIMES
11 Alexander, 416-975-8555, www.buddiesinbadtimestheatre.com.
Established in 1979 and located in the heart of the Gay Village, this theatre company is the essence of queer culture. It produces edgy and provocative new Canadian works, some of which are definitely NOT for the faint of heart. Buddies also stages Canadian adaptations of well-known works like Ibsen's Hedda Gabler. In addition to splashy mainstage theatrical productions, the theatre also hosts outrageous special events, youth initiatives, play development programs and late-night weekend cabarets.

Shopping

ASLAN LEATHER Durable, custom bondage gear made to fit. By appt only. 416-306-0462, 1-877-467-1526, www.aslanleather.com.

BODY BODY WEAR Basement clearance shop for the menswear line that's sold tees, tanks, slacks and unders to the likes of Jason Priestley, the Queer as Folk folk, Christina Aguilera and Christ himself, Jim Caviezel. 471 Church.

DOC'S LEATHERS Leather and latex including gay-orientated, biker and BDSM gear. 726 Queen W. 416-504-8888, www.docsleathers.com.

FLATIRONS Gifts for the gay and gay friendly. 95 Maitland, 416-968-9274.

GLAD DAY BOOKSHOP T.O.'s widest selection of lesbian and gay literature, videos, periodicals, music and novelties. Also provides a queer-positive space for book browsers and a strong voice against censorship. 598A Yonge. 416-961-4161, www.gladdaybookshop.com.

NORTHBOUND LEATHER Fetish shop, leather, rubber, PVC, corsets, restraints, BDSM books, magazines and more. Custom work. 586 Yonge and 7 St. Nicholas. 416-972-1037.

OUT ON THE STREET Across from **Cawthra Park** (see page 216) and decked out in rainbow flags and rainbow steps and and a rainbow fence, this Village boutique features T-shirts, tchotchkes and campy cards with hot naked folks on the front. 551 Church, 416-967-2759.

PRIAPE Gay videos, books, clothing, leather, toys, lube, erotica, etc. 465 Church. 416-586-9914, www.priape.com.

TAKE A WALK ON THE WILD SIDE Where the stars go to be women, includes a boutique, guest rooms, makeover, transformations and Paddy's Playhouse Theatre. 161 Gerrard E. 416-921-6112, www.wildside.org.

THIS AIN'T THE ROSEDALE LIBRARY The literary hub of the gay village for more than 25 years, it's more than just a bookstore, with art shows, classes and special events. 483 Church, 416-929-9912.

Where to stay

BENT INN
107 Gloucester, 416-925-4499, www.bentinn.com.
As an erotic-themed B&B, the Bent offers the BDSM enthusiast everything under the sun, including complimentary lube and condoms in every soundproof room, vinyl sheets, rubber floors, an 800-square-foot dungeon, medical examination and bondage tables, cages and plenty of restraints, clamps, chains, whips and other themed services.
Rooms from $100, porn library, kitchen facilities.

DUNDONALD HOUSE
35 Dundonald, 416-961-9888, 1-800-260-7227, www.dundonaldhouse.com.
Recently married hosts Warren and Dave serve up a ton of comfort and class in this mansion that preserves its classic Scottish charm. Always accommodating to special requests, the Dundonald offers romantic packages and a gourmet breakfast.
Rooms from $100, fitness room.

LAVENDER ROSE B&B
15 Rose, 416-962-8591.
Small and gorgeous, the Lavender is a restored Victorian house in Cabbagetown designed to make visitors feel right at home with hosts Jenny and Fran and their cat Emma, who lounges in the public areas.
Rooms from $80.

CAWTHRA SQUARE BED & BREAKFAST
10 Cawthra Square, 416-966-3074, 1-800-259-5474, www.cawthrasquare.com.
This Edwardian-style home with six classically and uniquely decorated rooms caters to the queer community. It offers afternoon tea tastings, spa packages and a library with DSL broadband connection.
Rooms from $99, spa, Internet.

WILDSIDE HOTEL
161 Gerrard East, 416-921-6112, 1-800-260-0102, www.wildside.org.
Overlooking Allan Gardens and just around the corner from the Sherbourne Transgender Health Centre in Cabbagetown, Paddy Aldridge's Wildside is geared to cross-dressers, transvestites, drag queens, transsexuals and the transgendered. Located above the discreet Walk on the Wildside boutique and lounge, a cross-dresser transformation service where you'll find everything you need to transform into the woman of your dreams, the hotel's four rooms are small but comfortably furnished.
Rooms from $71.96, kitchen, Internet.

Bathhouses

THE CELLAR A dark facility offering showers, a sauna, stall/glory-hole area. 24 hrs daily. 78 Wellesley E (black door), 416-975-1799.

CENTRAL SPA Wet steam rooms and sauna. Mon-Thu 11 am-2 am, weekends to 3 am. 1610 Dundas W, 2nd floor, 416-588-6191.

CLUB TORONTO Health-club atmosphere, with whirlpool, sauna, steam room and outdoor swimming pool. 24 hrs daily. 231 Mutual, 416-977-4629, www.clubtoronto.com.

G.I. JOE Dry and wet steam rooms, whirlpool, hot tub, porn video in every room. 24 hrs daily. 543 Yonge, 416-927-0210.

OAK LEAF STEAM BATHS European wood-fired dry and wet steam rooms, oak leaf brooms, massage. 24 hrs daily (closed Tue 8 am-4 pm). 216 Bathurst, 416-603-3434.

PUSSY PALACE Women's Bathhouse Committee, a volunteer-run collective, organizes women's bathhouse nights. For information or to join a subcommittee, 416-925-9872 ext 2115, www.pussypalacetoronto.com.

ST. MARC SPA Dry and wet steam rooms, whirlpool, hot tub, porn video in every room. 24 hrs daily. 543 Yonge, 416-927-0210.

SPA EXCESS TV lounge, licensed bar, steam bath, booths, public sling and dungeon. 24 hrs daily. 105 Carlton, 416-260-2363, www.spa-excess.com.

STEAMWORKS Bodybuilders' gym, hot tub, steam room and sauna, showers, lockers, video lounge, cruise and play space. 540 Church, 416-925-1571, www.steamworksonline.com.

queer west village

While Boystown is popular with the old guard of muscle twinks and bull dykes, Toronto's younger gay community is turning its queer eye westward to the nabes around Dupont, High Park, Trinity Bellwoods and Parkdale. Here's the lowdown on where the party's at.

BEAVER CAFÉ
1192 Queen W, 416-537-2768.
Various queer events almost daily, including queer DJ Will Munro.

CIAO EDIE ROXX
489 College, 416-927-7774.
Women's Night (every Saturday); Here Kitty Kitty girls' night with dirty, grimy, nasty rock, metal, funk and anything white trash – boys welcome if accompanied by a girl (every Sunday).

DANCE CAVE (LEE'S PALACE)
529 Bloor W, 416-532-1598.
Rockers, drag queens and bad girls start the week with DJ Shannon's mix of disco, old school, punk, ska and new wave (every Monday); sinful queer rock (Sundays).

DRAKE HOTEL
1150 Queen W, 416-531-5042.
Hosts a queer dance night, Calling All Dandies (third Thursday/month).

HACIENDA LOUNGE
794 Bathurst, 416-536-0346.
Gay, queer, gender-bender events, with DJs spinning reggae, R&B, hiphop and house on Saturday nights.

GLADSTONE HOTEL
1214 Queen W, 416-531-4635.
Dust off your dancing shoes for a night of two-steppin' at the Country & Western Hoedown (last Saturday/month), a fave of East Coast queers. Foxhole (second Friday/month) is a Big Gay Mixer (with drag show). Java Knights Schmooze Fest (last Tuesday/month) is a social event for gay, bisexual and queer men, while Paul Petro and the Saints spin dance music at Hump Day Bump (every Wednesday).

LULA LOUNGE
1585 Dundas W, 416-588-0307.
Trans-Girl Tuesdays with shemale entertainer Amanda Taylor (second Tuesday/month). Offers a night of live cabaret performances (third Wednesday/month).

SMILING BUDDHA BAR
961 College, at Dovercourt, 416-516-2531.
A queer college student hangout that hosts a regular alt dance party.

STONES PLACE
1255 Queen W, 416-536-4242.
It's queer party central at this homage to Mick and Keef, with the DJ-driven Big Primpin' (first Saturday night/month) for hiphop homos and curious heteros and the Shake A Tail 60s queer dance party (second and fourth Saturday/month).

SWEATY BETTY'S
13 Ossington, 416-535-6861.
Rotating DJs play rock, punk, alt country, pop on Queer Night (every Tuesday).

Resources

Community & activism

AIDS ACTION NOW Political advocacy group for research and treatment of HIV/AIDS. Provincial, steering, treatment access and research committees. 416-925-9872 ext 2820.

COALITION FOR LESBIAN AND GAY RIGHTS IN ONTARIO CLGRO is dedicated to eliminating homophobia and dealing with issues of homosexuality in schools, health care and social welfare. 416-405-8253, 416-925-9872 ext 2037, www.web.net/clgro.

COMING OUT/BEING OUT Non-judgmental discussion and support group for lesbian, gay, bisexual, transgendered, two-spirited, questioning and queer individuals at all stages of the coming-out process between 20 and 40. Meet every Wed 6 pm at 519 Church Community Centre, 416-925-9872 ext 2120, www.geocities.com/comingout-beingout/index.html.

EQUALITY FOR GAYS AND LESBIANS EVERYWHERE EGALE works to advance equality and justice for gays, lesbians, bisexual and transgendered persons and their families across Canada. 1-888-204-7777, 416-925-9872 ext 2078, www.egale.ca.

519 CHURCH COMMUNITY CENTRE This meeting place for the queer community also houses Cawthra Square Café. 519 Church, 416-392-6874, www.the519.org.

FOUNDATION FOR EQUAL FAMILIES Organization acts as intervenor in precedent-setting cases for recognition of queer relationships. 552 Church, 416-925-9872 ext 2199, www.ffef.ca.

GAY AND LESBIAN BASHING HOTLINE AND VICTIM ASSISTANCE Support and info for assault victims, and assistance with police and court appearances. Mon-Fri 9 am-10 pm, Sat-Sun noon-5 pm. 519 Church Community Centre, 416-392-6877, 416-925-9872 ext 2034.

GAY MENTOR BUSINESS SERVICE Business mentoring and role-modelling for professionals and students. 416-488-0651, www.gaymentor.com.

HIV/AIDS LEGAL CLINIC Community-based legal clinic serving low-income people with HIV and AIDS. Government-funded legal aid. 65 Wellesley E, ste 400, 416-340-7790, 1-888-705-8889, www.halco.org.

LESBIAN AND GAY IMMIGRATION TASK FORCE Grassroots organization LEGIT provides immigration info and support for lesbians and gays. Meets third Thu of month, 7 pm. 519 Church, 416-925-9872 ext 2211, www3.sympatico.ca/arbutus/legit.html.

LEGAL CLINIC U of T law students give legal advice (free to those who meet financial guidelines) to gays, lesbians and bisexuals on criminal charges, housing, immigration and refugee claims, university affairs and the homeless project. Downtown Legal Services, 655 Spadina, 416-934-4535.

LESBIAN AND GAY COMMUNITY APPEAL Fundraising body supports advancement of lesbian and gay projects. To volunteer, call 416-920-5422, 416-925-9872 ext 2099.

Arts & media

COUNTERPOINT COMMUNITY ORCHESTRA Fine classical music concerts by this predominantly gay musical group. Mon evg practices. 416-925-9872 ext 2066.

FAB MAGAZINE Ontario's bi-weekly gay paper, full of diva drama and gossip. 511 Church, 2nd floor, 416-925-5221, www.fabmagazine.com.

FORTE – TORONTO MEN'S CHORUS Auditioned group highlighting the talents of the gay community through music and theatrical presentations. 416-961-5708, 416-925-9872 ext 2221, www.forte-chorus.com.

INSIDE OUT FILM AND VIDEO FESTIVAL The yearly spring queer film fest welcomes volunteers. 401 Richmond W, 416-977-6847, 416-925-9872 ext 2229, www.insideout.ca.

NATIONAL LESBIAN AND GAY JOURNALISTS Regular meetings and salons featuring speakers, at various locations. 416-925-9872 ext 2029, nlgja-canada@hotmail.com.

OASIS VOCAL JAZZ ENSEMBLE Amateur 12-member jazz group performs several times a year. Rehearsals Wed 7:45-9:45 pm at Church of the Redeemer (Bloor/Avenue). 416-925-9872 ext 2208, auditions@oasisvocaljazz.com, www.oasisvocaljazz.com.

Q-PRESS Small press focusing on LGBT literature. Inquiries to clake@sympatico.ca.

QUEER WRITING GROUP Writers of all levels get together for communal editing workshops, timed writing exercises and constructive feedback at supportive meetings. 519 Church Community Centre, 416-925-9872 ext 2095, www.outwrites.org.

RAINBOW VOICES OF TORONTO Non-auditioned community chorus of straight, lesbian and gay singers. 416-925-9872 ext 2166, www.rainbowvoicesoftoronto.com.

TORONTO PUBLIC LIBRARY'S GAY AND LESBIAN COLLECTION Large collection of fiction, biography, health, art, social sciences and books for children of gay and lesbian parents at Yorkville Library, 22 Yorkville, 416-393-7660, 416-925-9872 ext 2206, www.torontopubliclibrary.ca.

XTRA! A gay and lesbian biweekly. 491 Church, 2nd floor, 416-925-6665, www.xtra.ca

Well-being

ACROSS BOUNDARIES Provides services and programs for adults (16 and older) from ethnoracial communities who are suffering from severe mental illness. 51 Clarkson, 416-787-3007, www.acrossboundaries.ca.

ADULT CHILDREN OF ADDICTIVE AND DYSFUNCTIONAL FAMILIES ACA's lesbian and gay 12-step program meets regularly Fri 6:30-8 pm. 519 Church, 416-631-3614, 416-925-9872 ext 2032.

AIDS COMMITTEE OF TORONTO ACT provides info, referrals and counselling for people with HIV/AIDS. Mon-Thu 10 am-9 pm, Fri to 5 pm. 399 Church, 4th floor, 416-340-2437, 416-925-9872 ext 2019. www.actoronto.org.

AIDS HOTLINE Referrals and counselling in various languages, Mon-Sat 10 am-10 pm, Sun noon-7 pm. 416-392-AIDS, 416-925-9872 ext 2035, 1-800-686-7544, 1-800-668-2437.

ALLIANCE FOR SOUTH ASIAN AIDS PREVENTION Counselling, referrals and volunteer opportunities for South Asian people who are HIV positive. 20 Carlton, ste 126. 416-599-2727, 416-925-9872 ext 2183, www.asaap.ca.

BASHING REPORT LINE 416-392-6878 ext 337.

BISEXUAL NETWORK Bisexual men and women meet for support, info and referrals the third Thu of every month and social events. Trans friendly. 416-925-9872 ext 2810.

BLACK COALITION FOR AIDS PREVENTION Black CAP's goals are to reduce the spread of HIV and enhance life for those affected. 110 Spadina, ste 207, 416-977-9955, 416-925-9872 ext 2104, www.black-cap.com.

KAREN CHAPELLE

Village people

CANADIAN AIDS SOCIETY Coalition of 115 community-based organizations focusing on care, education and research. Based in Ottawa. 613-230-3580, www.cdnaids.ca.

CASEY HOUSE Hospice support and palliative care facility for 12 residents with AIDS. 9 Huntley, 416-962-7600, 416-925-9872 ext 2025, www.caseyhouse.com.

COMMUNITY AIDS TREATMENT INFO EXCHANGE CATIE is a non-profit organization committed to improving the health and quality of life of people living with HIV/AIDS. 555 Richmond W, ste 505, 1-800-263-1638, www.catie.ca.

CENTRE FOR ADDICTION AND MENTAL HEALTH Lesbian/bi/gay services include reducing or quitting drug and alcohol use, couples counselling, assessment and referrals. Covered by OHIP. Various locations. 416-535-8501 ext 7001 or 6781.

DAVID KELLEY LGBT AND HIV/AIDS COUNSELLING SERVICES Individual, group and family counselling with lesbian and gay therapists. 355 Church, 416-595-9618 www.fsatoronto.com.

FIFE HOUSE Supportive housing and services for people with HIV/AIDS. Operates three houses, an 82-unit apartment building, a homeless outreach program and the Ont HIV and substance use training program. 571 Jarvis, 416-205-9888, www.fifehouse.org.

519 ANTI-VIOLENCE PROGRAM Support and advocacy group for individuals who have experienced violence, harassment or abuse in same-sex relationships. Self-defense classes for gay men and lesbians (416-392-6878 ext 117), TS/TG self-defense classes (416-392-6878 ext 104). www.the519.org.

FRONTRUNNERS GAY AND LESBIAN AA Alcoholics Anonymous group meets Sat 7:30 pm. St. Luke's Church, Carlton and Sherbourne, 416-924-9619, 416-925-9872 ext 2055.

GAY FATHERS OF TORONTO Social functions, meetings and support for gay dads and partners. Support line 416-410-0438 (Mon-Thu 7-10 pm), 416-925-9872 ext 2124, www.gayfathers-toronto.com.

GAY PARTNER ABUSE PROJECT Support for men in violent relationships. 416-876-1803, www.gaypartner-abuseproject.org.

HASSLE FREE CLINIC Anonymous HIV testing, STD care, women's health, needle exchange. 66 Gerrard E, 2nd floor. Women's clinic (416-922-0566); men's clinic (416-922-0603), www.hasslefreeclinic.org.

HEALTH EDUCATION AIDS LIAISON HEAL is a non-profit education network providing information on non-toxic and holistic approaches to recovering from AIDS-defining illnesses. www.healtoronto.com.

McEWAN HOUSE Supportive housing for men and women with HIV/mental health/addiction issues in a shared setting with 24-hour staff. 416-929-6228.

NARCOTICS ANONYMOUS TRUE COLOURS A 12-step program for recovering gay, lesbian, bisexual, transgendered and transsexual addicts. Fri 6 pm, 519 Church, 416-236-8956, www.torontona.org.

PARENTS, FRIENDS AND FAMILIES OF LESBIANS AND GAYS (PFLAG) TORONTO Educational and support meetings at various locations. 416-406-1727, toronto@pflag.ca.

SAMESEXMARRIAGE.CA Info on the fight for equal marriage for same sex couples. www.samesexmarriage.ca, www.equal-marriage.ca.

SEX AND LOVE ADDICTS ANONYMOUS A 12-step program for dealing with addictive sexual and emotional patterns. 416-486-8201, 416-925-9872 ext 2087.

X marks the spot at Pride.

R. JEANETTE MARTIN

SHERBOURNE HEALTH CENTRE This primary health-care facility serves the lesbian, gay, bisexual, trans-gendered and transsexual communities. 333 Sherbourne, 416-324-4180, www.sherbourne.on.ca.

SOUL SURVIVORS This support group is for anyone who has been hurt in any way in the name of a religion, spiritual belief or doctrine. 416-925-9872 ext 2058, www.soulsurvivors.biz.

SOUTHERN ONTARIO GAY AND LESBIAN ASSOCIATION OF DOCTORS SOGLAD publishes a public referral directory for patients seeking gay and gay-positive physicians. 416-357-6839, 416-925-9872 ext 2158.

SURVIVORS OF INCEST ANONYMOUS Self-help group for survivors of childhood sexual abuse meets Wed, 6 pm, 519 Church, 416-925-9872 ext 2062.

TAGL Queer support, information and peer counselling phone line operated Mon-Fri 7-10 pm by volunteers. 416-964-6600, tagl.org@sympatico.ca.

TORONTO PEOPLE WITH AIDS FOUNDATION Info and support services to help people with HIV/AIDS. 399 Church, 416-506-1400.

TORONTOVIBE.COM Information about safer drug use for gay and bisexual men in the Toronto club scene. www.torontovibe.com.

TRANSSEXUAL TRANSITION SUPPORT GROUP Meets second and fourth Fri of every month at 7 pm. 519 Church, 416-925-9872 ext 2121.

TWO-SPIRITED PEOPLES OF THE FIRST NATIONS Support for lesbian and gay aboriginal people and those with HIV/AIDS. 43 Elm, 2nd floor, 416-944-9300.

U OF T SEXUAL EDUCATION AND PEER COUNSELLING CENTRE Gay, lesbian, bisexual and transgendered-positive counselling and referrals. 416-978-8732.

WOMEN'S COUNSELLING REFERRAL AND EDUCATION CENTRE Referrals for women and trans people to self-help groups and screened private therapists. 525 Bloor W, 416-534-7501.

Recreation & social groups

ARC-EN-CIEL GROUPE FRANCOPHONE French-speaking gays and lesbians meet monthly. 416-925-9872 ext 2245.

BISEXUAL NETWORK OF TORONTO Social and discussion meeting monthly. 416-925-9872 ext 2810.

CENTRE FOR SPANISH SPEAKING PEOPLE Gay-positive Spanish classes and Latin dance lessons. 2141 Jane, 416-533-8545.

DOWNTOWN SOCCER Gay and lesbian co-ed recreational soccer league plays at Jimmie Simpson Rec Centre, 870 Queen E, 416-925-9872 ext 2249, www.downtownsoccertoronto.org.

DOWNTOWN SWIM CLUB Recreational and competitive swimmers train at Jimmie Simpson Rec Centre, 870 Queen E, and U of T Athletic Centre. 416-925-9872 ext 2064, call for schedule 416-694-8062, www.dsc.toronto.ca.

THE FRATERNITY Gay men's social and professional club for networking. 416-925-9872 ext 2930, 416-652-2212, www.thefraternity.ca.

FRONTRUNNERS TORONTO All genders, orientations and ability levels are welcome for 5 to 15-km runs Sat 9 am, Cawthra Square behind 519 Church; faster runs happen Thu 6:15 pm. Trail running and walking also. 416-925-9872 ext 2042.

GALLEY Gays and lesbians living in East York, Riverdale and the Beaches hold monthly meetings and social events. 416-925-9872 ext 2145.

GAY WEST BICYCLE CLUB Gay and lesbians bicycle club, with weekly rides and social events. 416-533-6428, http://gaywest.905host.net.

NOT SO AMAZON SOFTBALL LEAGUE Lesbian-positive women of all athletic levels play softball weekly and hold social sporting events. 416-925-9872 ext 2260, www.notsoamazon.com.

OUT AND OUT CLUB Outdoor sports club for gays and lesbians offers hiking, cycling, scuba, skiing, canoe trips, rock climbing, horse riding, volleyball and more. Car pools for out-of-town events. Yearly membership $30, couples $50. 416-925-9872 ext 2800, www.outandout.on.ca.

PINK TURF SOCCER LEAGUE Lesbian-positive women of all athletic levels play soccer weekly. Games at Withrow Park. Applications and registration at 519 Church, 416-925-9872 ext 2096, www.lfbntoronto.com/pinkturf.

RAINBOW HOOPS WOMEN'S BASKETBALL LEAGUE Register in Sep for Oct-April season. $135 registration fee. 416-925-9872 ext 2252, www.rainbowhoops.com.

RAINBOW TAI CHI Yang-style tai chi practice for queer-positive people. No experience necessary. Sun 10 am-noon at 519 Church, 416-925-9872 ext 2136, 416-516-0135.

SPEARHEAD LEATHER DENIM SOCIAL CLUB All-male club runs social and charity events, including the winter Fantasy Ball. www.spearheadtoronto.com.

SWINGIN' OUT Swing classes, dances and performances. Beginner drop-in classes offered, no experience or partner needed. 416-925-9872 ext 2068, www.swinginout.ca.

TNT!MEN/TOTALLY NAKED TORONTO MEN ENJOYING NUDITY Social nudist club for men who like to get naked with other men. 416-925-9872 ext 3010, www.tntmen.org.

TORONTO GAY HOCKEY ASSOC A league for gay and bisexual men over 18. Oct-Apr. 416-925-9872 ext 2110, www.gayhockey.com.

TORONTO SPARTAN VOLLEYBALL LEAGUE Gay, lesbian and homo-friendly volleyball league with more than 180 members plays at various locations. Registration in Aug and Sep. 416-925-9872 ext 2152, www.tsvl.org.

TORONTO TRIGGERFISH Gay, lesbian and transgendered water polo club practice twice weekly starting in Sep at U of T Athletic Centre and Jimmy Simpson Rec Ctr, 870 Queen E, 416-925-9872 ext 2010, www.dsc.to/triggerfish.

TRIANGLE SQUARES Gay, lesbian, bi and trans square dance club. Classes, monthly dances and special events. Activities begin in Sep. 416-925-9872 ext 2014.

WRIB – WOMEN FOR RECREATION, INFORMATION AND BUSINESS This social, recreational and business network for LBTT women holds lunches, sports, workshops, arts and entertainment events and dances. 416-925-9872 ext 2083, www.wrib.ca.

WOMEN'S HOCKEY CLUB OF TORONTO An adult recreational non-body-checking ice hockey league open to gay or gay-positive women. Season runs Sep-Apr at Moss Park Arena. Register in June. www.whct.ca.

WOMEN'S SM DISCUSSION GROUP Meets for discussion first Tue of month, 8 pm, plus social events and brunches. 416-925-9872 ext 2007.

queer timeline

1969 Parliament decriminalizes homosexual acts as Prime Minister Pierre Trudeau famously announces, "The state has no place in the bedrooms of the nation."

1970 Community Homophile Association of Toronto forms. **Glad Day Books** (see **Shopping**, page 185), devoted to queer content, opens its doors

1971 Toronto's first Gay Day Picnic is held at Hanlan's Point.

1973 Canadian Gay and Lesbian Archives founded in Toronto. YWCA holds first ever Canadian lesbian conference in Toronto.

1977 The Lesbian Organization of Toronto (LOOT) is founded. Anita Bryant declares war on homosexuality, sparking demonstrations during a Toronto visit.

1978 Pride-precursor Gay Days is organized in **Cawthra Park**.

1979 **Buddies in Bad Times** theatre company (see **Theatre**, page 154), devoted to queer theatre, opens.

1981 Bathhouse raids trigger a new wave of consciousness. First **Pride Parade** culminates in a party at Grange Park.

1984 **Xtra!** bi-weekly launches and continues to publish. Pride moves to Cawthra Park; Church Street closes for the day.

1987 Sexual orientation is included in the Ontario Human Rights Code.

1989 Pride participation grows to 25,000 people.

1991 First annual **Inside Out** festival of gay and lesbian film and video (see **Festivals**, page 151). City Council proclaims **Pride Day** for the first time. Openly gay candidate Kyle Rae wins a seat as city councillor for Ward 6.

1992 Pride participation breaks the 100,000 mark.

1995 Police chief David Boothby allows four lanes on Yonge to close for Canada's second largest parade; over 500,00 people participate.

1996 First **Dyke March** unfolds the Saturday before Pride Day.

1997 Pride celebrations become **Pride Week**.

2001 City officials declare Pride Week.

2005 Courts decide in favour of same-sex marriage.

2006 Pride celebrates its 25th anniversary.

Youth resources

BLACK QUEER YOUTH (BQY) Safe space for black, multiracial, African/Caribbean youth under 29 who identify as lesbian, gay, bisexual, transgender, transsexual and questioning and their allies, Wed 6:30 pm. 365 Bloor E, ste 301, 416-324-5083, soyprojects@sherbourne.on.ca.

CENTRAL TORONTO YOUTH SERVICES Counselling and support groups for people 18 and under. 65 Wellesley E, ste 300, 416-924-2100.

COLAGE: CHILDREN OF LESBIANS AND GAYS EVERYWHERE A social support group for students with lesbian, gay, bisexual and trans parents meets second and fourth Tue of every month, 6:30 pm at 519 Church, 416-994-8936, steven.solomon@utoronto.ca.

ESSENCE A group where queer, trans and questioning youth gather. 365 Bloor E, ste 301. 416-324-5083, soyprojects@sherbourne.on.ca.

FRUIT LOOPZ This group organizes cool events for queer/trans youth, such as the Pride Prom. Volunteer hours can be used towards OSSD. 365 Bloor E, ste 301, 416-324-5077, soy@sherbourne.on.ca.

HUMAN SEXUALITY PROGRAM Counselling and support for LGBT students, teachers, parents and families. Anti-homophobia group work for kindergarten to grade 12. Contact Toronto District School Board. 416-985-3749, adrienne.magidsohn@tdsb.on.ca.

LESBIAN GAY BI YOUTH LINE Peer support phone line by and for queer youth province-wide. Volunteer opportunities for those under 27. Phone line operates Sun-Fri 4-9:30 pm. 416-962-9688, 1-800-268-9688, www.youthline.ca.

LESBIAN GAY BI YOUTH HOTLINE Support group for youth under 26. Peer discussion meetings, Alternatives, an informal social gathering, various times, 519 Church, 416-925-9872 ext 2880, 416-962-9688.

LGBT HUMBER Queer students at Humber College north campus meet regularly during the academic year. 416-675-6622 ext 3382.

POSITIVE YOUTH OUTREACH Peer support, referrals for housing, treatment and counselling for people under 29 with HIV/AIDS. 399 Church, 4th floor, 416-340-8484 ext 281, www.positiveyouth.com.

Q2 (QUEER AND QUESTIONING YOUTH GROUP) East Metro drop-in for gay, lesbian, bisexual and trans teens. Wed 4-8 pm during the school year. 416-438-9419 ext 255, www.emys.on.ca.

QUEER NOISE Group for LGBT youth up to age 26 who love to sing. No musical background necessary. Fri 7 pm. Trinity-St. Paul Centre, 427 Bloor W, queernoise@hotmail.com.

QUEER PEERS Queer youth 13-20 meet during the school year, for a variety of programs including expressive arts. Deslisle Youth Services, 40 Orchard View, 416-482-0081, www.delisleyouth.org.

RYEPRIDE Queer students at Ryerson. 416-979-5255 ext 7527.

SOY/SUPPORTING OUR YOUTH A community development project designed to improve the lives of lesbian, gay, bisexual, transsexual and transgendered youth. Various programs and meetings available. 365 Bloor E, ste 301, 416-324-5077, www.soy-toronto.org.

TBLG ALLIANCE AT YORK Support, referral, social and educational programs providing a safe space for the queer community. Call for summer hours. 416-736-2100 ext 20494. www.yorku.ca/tblgay.

TRANS_FUSION_CREW Transgender, transsexual, inter-sex, two-spirit and gender-questioning youth chill, share info and work on amazing activist projects. Thur 6-9 pm. 365 Bloor E, ste 301, 416-324-5078, tfc@sherbourne.on.ca.

TRIANGLE PROGRAM Canada's only high school classroom for lesbian/gay/bi/trans students of the Toronto school board at the Oasis Alternative Secondary School. 416-406-6228 ext 169, http://schools.tdsb.on.ca/triangle.

WORD OUT! Queer and trans youth meet every month to discuss books, films and more. Starbucks, 485 Church, 416-324-5077, soy@sherbourne.on.ca.

Spirituality

AWARE Christian Reformed lesbians and gays meet in members' homes. Meetings Oct-May. 416-925-9872 ext 2098.

BRETHREN AND MENNONITE COUNCIL CANADA FOR LESBIAN, GAY, BISEXUAL AND TRANSGENDER INTERESTS Queer Mennonites of faith or cultural upbringing meet periodically for social events and meetings, and the council runs a group for parents of lesbian and gay Mennonites. 519-880-9780.

CHRISTOS MCC Gay, lesbian, bisexual and transgendered Christian group committed to loving and healing meets regularly. Trinity-St. Paul's Centre, 427 Bloor W, 416-435-1211.

DHARMA FRIENDS Gay and lesbian Buddhist meditation group meets Wed 7:30 pm for sitting/walking meditation. 416-935-1759.

DIGNITY TORONTO Support group for reconciliation for gay/lesbian Roman Catholics. Meets monthly. 416-925-9872 ext 2011.

GAYS AND LESBIANS AND FRIENDS AT ST. JAMES CATHEDRAL Meets regularly in St. James Parish House, 65 Church, 416-364-7865 ext 221.

METROPOLITAN COMMUNITY CHURCH Large gay-lesbian Christian congregation, Sunday worship at 8:55 and 10:55 am, plus many other programs. 115 Simpson, 416-406-6228, www.mcctoronto.com.

METROPOLITAN UNITED Affirming congregation runs Sun services at 11 am, and a Pride float. 56 Queen E, 416-363-0331.

PEOPLE WITH AIDS YOGA Yoga class and meditation for people with HIV/AIDS and their supporters. Wed 4:30 pm. 519 Church Community Centre, 416-506-1400, www.pwatoronto.org.

PROPITIATION Gay and lesbian Anglican fellowship uses traditional wording of the Book Of Common Prayer, holds services in members' homes. 416-925-9872 ext 2149, 416-977-4359, propitiation@hotmail.com.

RUAH An eco-centered community of faith, emphasizing spiritual growth, liberation and eco-theology has Sunday gatherings at 10:30 am at Ralph Thornton Ctr, 765 Queen E, 416-459-0912, 416-925-9872 ext 226, www.ruahtoronto.org.

SAGA Fellowship for gay and lesbian Presbyterians, both lay and clergy, fourth Fri of month at 7:30 pm. St. Andrew's Ctr, 75 Simcoe, 416-269-7828.

SALAAM TORONTO Supportive community for gay, lesbian and bisexual Muslims with peer support, social events, referrals, advocacy and volunteer opportunities. 416-925-9872 ext 2209, www.salaamcanada.com.

sex & drugs

sex

Toronto may have had a puritanical upbringing, but it's certainly not afraid to endulge its inner perv. From S&M to swingers clubs, bath houses to bawdy shops, this city's just as kinky as the rest of them.

Shops

AREN'T WE NAUGHTY Adult products and lingerie. 1300 Finch West, 416-733-9878, www.arentwenaughty.com.

ASLAN LEATHER Durable, custom bondage gear made to fit. 416-306-0462, 1-877-467-1526. By appt only. www.aslanleather.com.

COME AS YOU ARE See sidebar, page 231.

CONDOM SHACK Protection, safety first, etc. 231 Queen W, 416-596-7515, www.condomshack.com.

DOC'S LEATHERS Leather and latex including gay-orientated, biker and BDSM gear. 726 Queen W, 416-504-8888, www.docsleathers.com.

ETERNAL MOMENT BOOKSTORE Videos and books on tantric techniques and sexuality. 497 Bloor W, 416-924-3780, 3300 Yonge, 416-486-9887, www.eternalmoment.ca.

GLAD DAY BOOKSHOP Large collection of gay and lesbian literature, videos, periodicals, music and novelties. 598A Yonge, 416-961-4161, www.gladdaybookshop.com.

GOOD FOR HER See sidebar, page 231.

KISSES & ECSTASY Adult products, lingerie, movies, costumes and more. 2081 Yonge, 416-322-9999, www.kissesandecstasy.com.

LOVECRAFT Sex-positive shop offers sex toys, lubricants, books, videos and more. 27 Yorkville, 416-923-7331, 2200 Dundas E, Mississauga, 905-276-5772, www.lovecraftsexshop.com.

METALEATHER Leather garments with metal insets, including corsets, bustiers and armour. By appointment. 445 King E, 416-868-0002, www.metaleather.com.

MISSBEHAV'N Lingerie, fetish wear and toys, including plus sizes. Live window models Sat. 650 Queen W, 416-866-7979, www.missbehavn.com.

NORTHBOUND LEATHER Fetish shop, leather, rubber, PVC, corsets, restraints, BDSM books, magazines and more. Custom work. 586 Yonge and 7 St. Nicholas, 416-972-1037.

PRIAPE Gay videos, books, clothing, leather, toys, lube, erotica, etc. 465 Church, 416-586-9914, www.priape.com.

SEDUCTION Downtown adult department store selling toys, books, fantasy and SM stuff, videos and more. 577 Yonge, 416-966-6969, www.seduction.ca.

STAG SHOP BOUTIQUE Adult toys for naked play. 449 Church, 416-323-0772, 239 Yonge, 416-368-3507, www.stagshop.com.

TAKE A WALK ON THE WILD SIDE Where the stars go to be women, includes a boutique, guest rooms, makeover, transformations and Paddy's Playhouse Theatre. 161 Gerrard E, 416-921-6112, www.wildside.org.

Strip Clubs

THE BRASS RAIL TAVERN
701 Yonge, 416-924-1241.
The most popular peeler bar in town, decked out with enough tacky Vegas-type brass and mirrors to make Liberace hard. Private areas for parties, as well as an exclusive second level where celebrities – Gene Simmons and Colin Farrell, for example – have been known to enjoy the, ahem, view.

CEASAR'S EXOTIC SPORTS BAR
3313 Danforth, 416-694-3256.
Sure, a lot of guys would love to take their girlfriends to a strip club (nudge, nudge, wink, wink), but this one is truly for couples, with one floor for men and one for the ladies.

CLUB PARADISE
1313 Bloor W, 416-535-0723.
Possibly the most non-strip club-looking strip club in town, it resembles something more along the lines of a sports bar with a dancing stage.

FOR YOUR EYES ONLY
563 King W, 416-585-9200.
Boasting an enormous 5,000-square-foot main dinning/bar/entertainment area and a cigar bar.

REMINGTON'S
379 Yonge, at Gerrard, 416-977-2160.
A seven-days-a-week male strip club in the middle of Yonge Street's decidedly hetero sleaze zone. With almost as many celebrities offstage as on, Remington's and its Men of Steel dancers create an atmosphere that's a lot less uptight than the surrounding straight burlesque clubs.

Bathhouses

women
PUSSY PALACE Women's Bathhouse Committee, a volunteer-run collective, organizes women's bathhouse nights. For information or to join a subcommittee, 416-925-9872 ext 2115, www.pussypalacetoronto.com.

men
THE CELLAR A dark facility offering showers, a sauna, stall/glory-hole area. 24 hrs daily. 78 Wellesley E (black door), 416-975-1799.

CENTRAL SPA Wet steam rooms and sauna. Mon-Thu 11 am-2 am, weekends to 3 am. 1610 Dundas W, 2nd floor, 416-588-6191.

CLUB TORONTO Health-club atmosphere, with whirlpool, sauna, steam room and outdoor swimming pool. 24 hrs daily. 231 Mutual, 416-977-4629, www.clubtoronto.com.

G.I. JOE Dry and wet steam rooms, whirlpool, hot tub, porn video in every room. 24 hrs daily. 543 Yonge, 416-927-0210.

OAK LEAF STEAM BATHS European wood-fired dry and wet steam rooms, oak leaf brooms, massage. 24 hrs daily (closed Tue 8 am-4 pm). 216 Bathurst, 416-603-3434.

ST. MARC SPA Dry and wet steam rooms, whirlpool, hot tub, porn video in every room. 24 hrs daily. 543 Yonge, 416-927-0210.

SPA EXCESS TV lounge, licensed bar, steam bath, booths, public sling and dungeon. 24 hrs daily. 105 Carlton, 416-260-2363, www.spa-excess.com.

STEAMWORKS Bodybuilders' gym, hot tub, steam room and sauna, showers, lockers, video lounge, cruise and play space. 540 Church, 416-925-1571, www.steamworksonline.com.

Fetish groups

ASHLEY MADISON When monogamy becomes a drag, this agency helps people in committed relationships find romantic affairs. www.ashleymadison.com.

BOUNDANDGAGGED.CA Domain for safe and consensual domination, submission and role-play fantasies. 416-462-1521, www.boundandgagged.ca.

CLOSE ENCOUNTERS The group holds dances and theme nights every weekend for couples and single women at a west-end hotel. Membership 905-458-2229.

CLUB ABSTRACT Club for couples meeting at west-end locations and clubs. www.clubabstract.ca.

CLUB EROS Private-members, off-premise (no on-site sexual activity) club for couples. Bisexual and bi-curious event nights and seminars for couples new to the lifestyle. 416-410-2582, www.cluberos.ca.

CLUB PRIVÉ Private club for couples who want to connect with others for sex. Happy Hedonist parties, travel adventures and invitations to monthly events. 416-944-9221, www.club-prive.com.

DSSG TORONTO Group offers support, educational and social gatherings for pansexual women and men, singles or couples involved in or interested in learning about BDSM. www.dssg.org.

HAPPY HEDONIST Social and leisure entertainment for people who like meeting people with fun and pleasure in mind. Private on-premise parties at hotel and condos in T.O. www.happyhedonist.com.

PATRICIA MARSH HOUSE OF DOMINATION AND FANTASY Mild to advanced BDSM, fetish and role play. Consultations, telephone training, dungeon rentals. Individuals of all genders, couples. 416-963-9871, www.patriciamarsh.com.

MR. LEATHERMAN An annual competition is part of a weekend of events including SM seminars, a leather ball and dungeon dance. 416-925-9872 ext 2051.

PARTIES WITHOUT BORDERS Group involved in organizing festivities in unpredictable forms at hot, stylish locations. www.partieswithoutborders.com.

STRIP-O-GRAM Experienced male or female exotic dancers come to your party in costume and entertain the guest of honour. 1-800-730-7824, www.stagmasters.com.

SM WOMEN'S DISCUSSION GROUP Meets first Tue of month, 7 pm at Zelda's, 542 Church, 416-925-9872 ext 2007.

SOCIETY OF SPANKERS Fraternity of men who meet for spanking parties and discussion. 416-925-9872 ext 2102.

SPEARHEAD Leather and denim social club for gay men. 416-925-9872 ext 2054, www.spearheadtoronto.com.

TRYSTMAG.COM Website for swingers run by swingers. Publishers of Tryst magazine, e-mail ads, chat and

more than condoms

When it comes to helping Torontonians get off in the coolest, safest, healthiest ways possible, two sex shops stand above the rest by offering more than just condoms, vibrators and smut tapes. **Come As You Are** (701 Queen W, 416-504-7934, 1-877-858-3160, www.comeasyouare.com) is unique in that it's the only co-operatively run sex store in the country. In addition to a full compliment of books, videos and toys for the bedroom, Come As You Are offers a variety of workshops on subjects ranging from erotic photography to female ejaculation. And as the name suggests, **Good For Her** (175 Harbord, 416-588-0900, www.good-forher.com) is the only specifically woman-friendly sex shop in the city, offering special women and trans-only shopping hours. The store features high-quality sex toys, vibrators, women- and couples-friendly porn, educational and erotic books, zines and sensual art. Good For Her also hosts a wide variety of sexuality seminars where customers can learn about everything from oral and anal sex to G spots, body image to tantra for couples and queers. In 2006, Good For Her also made history by hosting the world's first-ever Feminist Porn Awards.

events. 905-847-5351, www.trystmag.com.

WICKED CLUB Club offering erotic parties for selective women and their partners. Events held at 67 Richmond E, 416-669-5582, www.wickedclub.com.

Free clinics

HASSLE FREE CLINIC Community-based medical and counselling services in all areas of sexual health. The clinic operates at different hours for men and women. The women's clinic has birth control, pregnancy tests, abortion referrals, STD and HIV testing and counselling, while the men's clinic does STD and HIV testing and counselling. Each clinic is staffed by a medical director and nurse. Treatments for most STDs are free. No OHIP card is required in the women's clinic. Men's clinic doctors are paid through OHIP but no one will be refused service without a health card, and no health card number is taken for anonymous HIV testing. 66 Gerrard East, 2nd floor. Men 416-922-0603; women 416-922-0566, www.hasslefreeclinic.com.

PLANNED PARENTHOOD OF TORONTO Community-based sexual and reproductive health programs for women and youth (ages 13-25) promoting healthy sexuality and informed decision making. Woman to Woman program offered in conjunction with the Bay Centre for Birth Control (see **Sex**, page 232). PPT practises a cooperative approach to health care, and services include physical examinations, anonymous HIV testing, sexually transmitted infection testing and treatment, birth control information and prescriptions, pregnancy testing and options, social work services and health promotion activities, workshops on birth control, healthy relationships, teen sex and confronting homophobia. Patients without an OHIP card will not be refused. 36B Prince Arthur, 416-961-0113, www.ppt.on.ca.

Sex info

ACT (AIDS COMMITTEE OF TORONTO) Community-based AIDS organization offering counselling and support services for those living with and at-risk for HIV/AIDS or those touched by the epidemic. 399 Church, 4th floor, 416-340-2437, www.actoronto.org.

AIDS AND SEXUAL HEALTH INFO LINE Province-wide free, anonymous referral service offered in various languages. 416-392-2437, 1-800-668-2437.

ANNE JOHNSTON HEALTH STATION The Barrier Free Health Zone provides family medicine and related services to people with disabilities involving the spine. Advocacy, workshops and a resource collection also available. Personal attendants are on site and the facility is fully wheelchair accessible. 2398 Yonge, 416-486-8666.

BAY CENTRE FOR BIRTH CONTROL Cooperative approach to health care, sexual and reproductive health services of Planned Parenthood. Counselling on healthy sexuality, STDs, pregnancy tests and options, reproductive health and emergency contraception. 790 Bay, 416-351-3700.

BLACK CAP The Black Coalition for AIDS Prevention is a volunteer not-for-profit organization working to reduce the spread of HIV within black communities. 110 Spadina, ste 207, 416-977-9955, www.black-cap.com.

BOARD OF EXAMINERS IN SEX THERAPY AND COUNSELLING Provides referrals to accredited sex therapists. 118 Eglinton West, ste 210, www.bestco.info.

CANADIAN HEALTH NETWORK Website sponsored by Health Canada has information on sexuality, relationships, birth control, HIV/AIDS and more. Links to a variety of resources on sexuality. www.canadian-health-network.ca.

CANADIAN MEN'S CLINIC Medical doctors focus on the treatment of impotence, premature ejaculation and low sex drive. Helpline 1-888-636-7377.

DAWN Disabled Women's Network advocacy group publishes a pamphlet on sexuality and women with disabilities. Box 1138, North Bay, P1B 8K4.

THE HOUSE COMMUNITY HEALTH CENTRE Offers medical, mental health and sexual and reproductive health counselling services to young women and men 13-25. Planned Parenthood project. 36B Prince Arthur, 416-927-7171.

IMMIGRANT WOMEN'S HEALTH CENTRE Family planning clinic offers information, counselling and referral on birth control, sexually transmitted diseases, pregnancy and AIDS. Chinese (Cantonese and Mandarin), Italian, Portuguese, Spanish, Tamil and Vietnamese spoken. 489 College, ste 200, 416-323-9986, iwhc@canada.com.

SAFER SM EDUCATION PROJECT Project of AIDS Committee of Toronto (ACT), offers monthly workshops on SM play. 399 Church, www.SaferSM.org.

SIECCAN Sex Information and Education Council of Canada, a non-profit organization, provides contacts for educators, researchers, journalists and students. Publishes the Canadian Journal of Human Sexuality. 416-466-5304, www.sieccan.org.

SEXABILITY Health care and peer counselling services for youth and young adults with mobility disabilities. Deals with issues related to sex and sexual health through peer counselling, workshops and resources. Anne Johnston Health Station, 2398 Yonge, 416-486-8666 ext 267.

SEXAHOLICS ANONYMOUS 12-step fellowship program for sexual sobriety. 416-410-7622.

SEX AND LOVE ADDICTS ANONYMOUS Volunteer-operated 12-step program combating love addiction. 416-486-8201.

SEXUALHEALTH.COM Comprehensive online source for disability and sexuality information. ww.sexualhealth.com.

SEXUALITYANDU.CA Website devoted to sexuality education and information. Covers topics such as sexually transmitted infections, contraceptives, and sex advice for teens, adults, parents, teachers and health professionals. www.sexualityandu.ca.

SHE'S GOT LABE Zine about sex, gender, the body and loving it. Submissions range from stories, photos, advice columns, interviews and more from sex-positive girls, guys, trans and intersex people with a dash of queer. $2. shegotlab@hotmail.com.

SHOUT Health services for people under 25 who are or have been street-involved. 467 Jarvis, 416-927-8553.

SHERBOURNE HEALTH CENTRE This primary health care facility serves the lesbian, gay, bisexual, transgender and transsexual communities. 333 Sherbourne, 416-324-4180, www.sherbourne.on.ca.

U OF T SEXUAL EDUCATION & PEER COUNSELLING CENTRE Drop-in centre provides information, referrals, one-to-one counselling, free condoms and lubricant, literature and pamphlets, reference books and videos (lending for U of T students). Phone lines are operated by trained volunteer peer counsellors. 91 St. George, 416-946-3100, http://sec.sa.utoronto.ca.

YORKVILLE LIBRARY Gay and lesbian special collection of fiction, health, parenting, magazines and books for children of gay and lesbian parents. 22 Yorkville, 416-393-7660, www.tpl.toronto.on.ca.

Relationships

ABANDONMENT SUPPORT GROUP If you are going through a recent breakup, if your partner left you, if you feel rejected and wonder if you will ever be loved again, this support group for gay men and women age 20-35 can help. mike_will_survive@yahoo.ca.

E-CLOSURE Breakup letters for the bitter, jaded and broken hearted, documenting breakups anonymously. 416-554-5263, www.e-closure.com.

1981

2006

Toronto experts
for over 25 years

Available free everywhere – a new issue every Thursday
Everything Toronto. Every Week.

A FIFTH COLUMN SOWING DESTRUCTION
IN THE YOUTH OF AMERICA · · ·

DEVIL'S HARVEST

A
GOOD GIRL
UNTIL
THE LIGHTS
A
"REEFER"

THE TRUTH ABOUT
MARIJUANA

drugs

Ok, ok. So our country may not be nearly as liberal as say, the Netherlands when it comes to recreational cannabis use. But when it comes to the long, strong, straight-laced arm of the law cracking down on dope smokers, Toronto sure beats the pants off places like Alabama or Singapore any day of the week.

Pot Luck

While becoming more understanding towards the recreational and medicinal usage of marijuana in all its wonderful forms, Canada's laws concerning the drug are ambiguous and often misunderstood. Although marijuana hasn't been decriminalized, several changes to the law have been made since 2003, most notably making it (slightly) easier to acquire pot for medicinal purposes.

And things seem to be getting better for the recreational user. The annual **Global Marijuana March** attracts thousands who head to Queen's Park (home of the provincial legislature) to spark up in protest, and the city has plenty of discreet locals where you can toke up – think Kensington Market, the Toronto Islands or any one of our fabulous parks. So basically, if you're gonna get high, don't be stupid about it. Be discreet.

Head Shops

THE FRIENDLY STRANGER
241 Queen W, 416-591-1570.
Touting itself as a "cannabis culture shop," the Stranger has paid its dues by actively promoting a Cheechier way of life for the last 12 years. Inside the sleek and hip Queen West store you'll discover items demonstrating just how fetishized pot and its smoking accessories have become, from flavoured bong water to the dizzying selection of cartoonish pipes and hookahs.

JUPITER CANNABIS SHOP
611 Queen W, 1-780-433-1967.
One of the new kids on the block, Jupiter offers a cool, comfortable interior that's rammed with product and paraphernalia, from bongs to possibly the largest selection of Bob Marley shirts this side of Jamaica.

SHANTI BABA TRADING CO. LTD.
546 Queen W, 416-504-5034.
Among the burning incense, the hand drums, masks and other wooden statues taking up a good chunk of the floor space, the Baba boasts a fine selection of everything you'll need to start feeling nice and toasty. So hey, why not kill two birds with one stone and buy something you can actually take back home with you, like a hand drum to remind you of that time you got really baked at that afternoon drum circle?

THC (TORONTO HEMP COMPANY)
637 Yonge, 416-920-1980.
Right at the edge of prime downtown shopping territory, this shop champions hemp as a complete lifestyle, as opposed to a recreational, uhh, drug thingy. Browse the wide assortment of hemp clothing, bags and accessories and the more predictable, but no less impressive selection of pipes, bongs, papers, vaporizers and even literature on the subject at hand. Spending time inside THC's friendly walls will lead you to question those silly little hippy, burnout, pothead stereotypes.

Smoke 'em if you got 'em

Looks like the Big Smoke is living up to the nickname – and finally catching up to herb-friendly Vancouver – with its growing list of marijuana cafés.

HOT BOX CAFE
191A Baldwin, at Augusta, 416-203-6990, www.roachorama.com.
Hidden discreetly away from prying eyes in a walled-in backyard behind the Kensington Market head shop the Roach-O-Rama, this hippy-dippy café has been serving local tokers since we forgot when. But it's more than just a place for potheads to feed their munchies on vegan, vegetarian and meateater meals, like the Ganja Lovers Grilled Cheese, Couchlock Cordon Blue, Oy vay Toked Salmon, Hemp Nut Caesar, washed down with a Citrus Skunk smoothie. As Toronto's first self-style marijuana café the Hot Box allows customers – from tie-dyed stoners and their grandkids to suit-smart biznobs – to partake of the herb on its leafy backyard "patio" to the inevitable Bob Marley soundtrack. But heads up – this place is strictly BYOP, so no dealing, asking, fishing or mooching. Warning: one hour maximum seating and $2 minimum.

KINDRED CAFE
7 Breadalbane, at Yonge, 416-920-0404, www.kindredcafe.com.
It may have been the first, but the Hot Box Café isn't the only joint in town that allows ganja to be consumed on the premises. Conveniently located next to Queen's Park, Kindred advertises itself with a nudge and a wink as a spot "for those interested in a higher level of café enjoyment." And they're not talking sky-high pie. The first-floor, side street resto looks innocent enough – a chicly appointed coffeehouse equipped with the latest high-tech espresso machines and presses serving up organic fair-trade brew. Upstairs, it's a different story. Those who've purchased a membership ($5/day, $20/month, $100/year, half-price for Toronto Compassion Centre members) have access to Kindred's exclusive rooftop patio where patrons are permitted to smoke whatever they like regardless of city bylaws. For $10 an hour, members can also rent one of three "meeting rooms" on the second floor decked out with leather couches, LCD TVs, sound systems and Xboxes.

CLANDESTINY
768 Queen E, at Bolton, 416-732-7761.
This, Toronto's third marijuana café, is set to open in December 2006. Currently a clothing shop specializing in hemp wear, the east-side storefront will launch a lounge in its back room that will feature an all-hemp menu of sprouted salads and special baked goods as well as regular comedy, music and spoken word nights.

Alcohol

Unlike our neighbour to the south or our provincial partner to the north (that's Quebec, folks), you can't pick up a six-pack or a bottle of vino at the corner grocer. Even sadder is the fact that most liquor stores in Toronto close by 10 pm, meaning a little planning is required if you're heading to a house party and don't want to go empty handed.

Liquor stores here are known as the **LCBO** (that's what the "L" stands for; www.lcbo.com). There are easily a couple of dozen of them scattered throughout the city and they have excellent selections of foreign and domestic wines, spirits and, of course, beer. They also happen to have the worst hours and are often closed on holidays.

This being Canada, there's also a chain of stores that only sells beer, called, appropriately, **The Beer Store** (www.thebeerstore.ca), offering 300 brands from around the world and slightly better hours than the LCBO.

For a glass or three of the grape, try the **Wine Rack** (a.k.a. the Shmeckie), the largest indie retailer of wine in the province, although they only sell Ontario vino and soft liquor products like hard cider and wine coolers. For something a bit more upscale, try **Vineyard Estates**, with a handful of downtown locations.

There are also a handful of independent micro-breweries that run retail outlets at their brewery locations, including **Amsterdam Brewing Company**, **Steam Whistle Brewing Company**, **Mill Street Brewery** and **The Granite Brewery & Restaurant**.

Finally, The Beer Store more than a block away? Too lazy to make the trek to the LCBO? Can't find the Shmeckie? Fear not. A 2-4 is only a mouse click away when you order from **The Beer Guy** (www.thebeerguy.ca), delivering to your door (Mon-Thu 10 am-9 pm, Fri-Sat 10 am-9:30 pm, Sun 12-5 pm).

Visit **www.beerhunter.ca** for a map of beer, wine and liquor store locations with real-time updates on which ones are open.

Before you get your buzz on: the legal drinking age in Ontario is 19. Expect to be carded (show I.D.) if you're under 25 or even look like you might be under 25. Same goes at bars and nightclubs. It's also illegal to supply liquor to someone who's under age, and the fine is upwards of $200,000 and a year in jail. Just so ya know.

LCBO

2 COOPER STREET, Queen's Quay, 416-864-6777. Open Mon-Sat 9 am-10 pm, Sun noon-5 pm.

UNION STATION, Lower Concourse, Front and Bay, 416-368-9644. Open Mon-Wed 10 am-8 pm, Thu-Sat 10 am-9 pm, Sun noon-5 pm.

FIRST CANADIAN PLACE, Lower Concourse, Bay and King, 416-594-9040. Open Mon-Fri 10 am-6 pm, Sat-Sun closed.

87 FRONT EAST, St. Lawrence Market, 416-368-0521. Open Mon-Wed 10 am-8 pm, Thu-Sat 10 am-9 pm, Sun noon-5 pm.

595 BAY STREET, at Yonge, Lower Concourse, Atrium On Bay, 416-979-9978. Open Mon-Sat 10 am-9 pm, Sun noon-5 pm.

337 SPADINA, at Dundas, Chinatown, 416-597-0145. Open Mon-Sat 10 am-9 pm, Sun noon-5 pm.

545 YONGE, at Wellesley, 416-923-8498. Open Mon-Sat 10 am-9 pm, Sun noon-5 pm.

10 SCRIVENER SQUARE, Summerhill Subway, 416-922-0403. Open Mon-Fri 10 am-10 pm, Sat 9 am-10 pm, Sun 11 am-6 pm.

The Beer Store

350 QUEENS QUAY WEST, 416-581-1677. Open Mon-Wed 10 am-8 pm, Thu-Fri 10 am-9 pm, Sat 9:30 am-9 pm, Sun noon-5 pm.

614 QUEEN WEST, at Bathurst, 416-504-4665. Open Mon-Wed 10 am-8 pm, Thu-Fri 10 am-9 pm, Sat 9:30 am-9 pm, Sun noon-5 pm.

452 BATHURST, between College and Dundas, 416-923-4535. Open Mon-Fri 10 am-9 pm, Sat 9:30 am-9 pm, Sun noon-5 pm.

227 GERRARD EAST, between Parliament and Jarvis, 416-923-2122. Open Mon-Thu 10 am-9 pm, Fri 10 am-10 pm, Sat 9:30 am-10 pm, Sun noon-5 pm.

720 SPADINA, between Bloor and Harbord, 416-323-0566. Open Mon-Wed 10 am-8 pm, Thu-Fri 10 am-9 pm, Sat 9:30 am -9 pm, Sun noon-5 pm.

10 PRICE, at Yonge, 416-925-0366. Open Mon-Fri 10 am-10 pm, Sat 9:30 am-10 pm, Sun noon-5 pm.

Wine Rack

731 QUEEN EAST, at Broadview 416-465-5454. Open Mon-Sat 9:30 am-10 pm, Sun 11 am-6 pm.

560 QUEEN WEST, at Bathurst, 416-504-3647. Open Mon-Sat 9:30 am-10 pm, Sun 11 am-6 pm.

77 WELLESLEY EAST, at Church, 416-923-9393. Open Mon-Sat 9:30 am-11 pm, Sun 11 am-6 pm.

2447 YONGE, at Eglinton, 416-481-5226. Open Mon-Sat 10 am-10 p.m, Sun 11 am- 6 pm.

746 KING WEST, at Bathurst, 416-504-5926. Open Mon-Sat 10 am-9 pm, Sun 11 am-6 pm.

581 BLOOR WEST, at Bathurst (Honest Ed's), 416-588-3510. Open Mon-Fri 11 am-9 pm, Sat 10 am-6 pm, Sun 11 am-6 pm.

81 ST. CLAIR EAST, at Yonge (inside Sobey's), 416-929-9633. Open Mon-Sat 10 am-9 pm, Sun 11 am-6 pm.

Vineyard Estates

228 QUEENS QUAY WEST, 416-598-8880. Open Mon-Sat 10 am-9 pm, Sun 11 am-6 pm.

HAZELTON LANES, 87 AVENUE, 416-923-6336. Open Mon-Sat 9:30 am-9 pm, Sun 11 am-6 pm.

3143 YONGE, at Lawrence, 416-488-7114. Open Mon-Fri 10 am-9 pm, Sat 9 am-7 pm, Sun 11 am-6 pm.

Micro-Breweries

AMSTERDAM BREWING COMPANY
21 Bathurst, between Lakeshore and Front, 416-504-6882. Open Mon-Sat 11 am-11 pm, Sun 11 am-6 pm.

STEAM WHISTLE BREWING COMPANY
255 Bremner, The Roundhouse, 416-362-2337. Open Mon-Sat noon-6 pm, Sun noon-5 pm.

MILL STREET BREWERY
55 Mill, Building 63, 416-681-0338 (see **Distillery District**, page 36). Open Sun-Fri 11 am-6 pm, Sat 11 am-8 pm.

GRANITE BREWERY & RESTAURANT
245 Eglinton East, at Mt. Pleasant, 416-322-0723. Open Mon-Sat 11:30 am-11 pm, Sun 11 am-6 pm.

where to stay

hotels

Toronto has always been a hot town for sleeping around. But with more than 35,000 guest rooms it can be difficult to decide which hotel, motel, inn, B&B or hostel is worth your dime. Here are 72 of our best bets, give or take a dive or two.

Budget

PRIMROSE BEST WESTERN HOTEL
111 Carlton, 416-977-8000, 1-800-268-8082, www.torontoprimrosehotel.com.
While the upper floors offer a fairly decent view of the city, the Primrose is pretty much what you'd expect from a downtown hotel: acceptable, if slightly sterile and devoid of character. On the upside, there's a pool and fitness area, and let's not forget that view.
Rooms from $160.25, bar, restaurant, gym, pool, Internet, meeting facilities.

BOND PLACE HOTEL
65 Dundas E, 416-362-6061, www.bondplacehoteltoronto.com.
Undeniably one hell of a middle-of-the-road tourist hotel close to the eyesore known as the Eaton Centre, the Bond Place actually just looks like an apartment building standing tall, dull and brown. The rooms are what they are – basically, a bed, bathroom and colour TV – and the café serves food all day.
Rooms from $96.20, Internet.

CASA LOMA INN
21 Walmer, 416-924-4540, www.casalomainn.com.
Built in 1894 as a private home just a few blocks south of the **Casa Loma** castle (see **Sightseeing**, page 28), the Casa Loma is a heritage building that offers turn-of-the-century ambience and elegance. There are 23 finely appointed rooms, all with private four-piece baths, some equipped with Jacuzzis, fireplaces and wireless Internet service.
Rooms from $80, wireless Internet.

COMFORT HOTEL DOWNTOWN
15 Charles E, 416-924-1222, www.comfortinn.com.
Conveniently near everything, from the Elgin and Winter Garden Theatre to the Air Canada Centre, the Comfort Hotel offers a limited but reasonable list of amenities, with decent-sized rooms as well as several convenient travel packages, from tickets to see Blue Man Group to shopping excursions.
Rooms from $119, restaurant, meeting facilities.

CLARION HOTEL & SUITES SELBY
592 Sherbourne, 416-921-3142, www.hotelselby.com.
Located in a splendid historic mansion, the Clarion has been around in one form or another since 1882. Ernest Hemingway stayed here when he was a star reporter for the Toronto Star in 1923, and his namesake suite boasts a fireplace.
Rooms from $107.99, gym, meeting facilities.

DUNDAS SQUARE HOTEL
223 Church, 416-703-3939, www.dundashotel.com.
The inconspicuous-looking Dundas Square is a budget-style complex sandwiched between local businesses. Even though the outside (or some of the people standing there) tends to look a bit sketchy, the hotel has newly renovated rooms and a super location just south of the Village and a couple of blocks east of Yonge.
Rooms from $70.

WAVERLEY HOTEL
484 Spadina, 416-921-2141.
Ever wonder what it'd be like to rent a room in Satan's asshole? Look no further than the Waverley, a prime destination for sex workers and their johns, junkies and their dealers. Even taking into account the fact that the hotel's right beside the infamous Silver Dollar blues club – made more infamous by its appearance in the pulp fiction of Elmore Leonard – there's no reason for trying to live in a Charles Bukowski novel for a night.
Rooms from $50.

Family

COMFORT SUITES CITY CENTRE
200 Dundas E, 416-362-7700, www.comfortsuites.sites.toronto.com.
After a long day of shopping at the nearby retail hot spot that is Yonge, soak your bones in the penthouse Jacuzzi, pop the cork on a bottle of bubbly and stoke the embers in the in-room fireplace. That's comfort.
Rooms from $88, bar, pool, gym, wireless Internet.

DAYS INN TORONTO BEACHES
1684 Queen E, 416-694-1177, www.daysinn.ca.
Those visitors uninterested in the perpetual beat of downtown should look east to the Beaches, a picturesque and family-friendly nabe near the lake, where the Days Inn offers a modest but perfectly snug atmosphere. Besides, it's all about the beautiful sandy beaches just a 10-minute walk away.
Rooms from $57.93, Internet.

DELTA CHELSEA HOTEL DOWNTOWN TORONTO
33 Gerrard W, 416-595-1975, 1-877-243-5732, www.deltahotels.com.
This may be Canada's largest hotel, boasting some 1,590 guest rooms, but it's hardly impersonal. In addition to an indoor swimming pool, billiards room, 24-hour room service, arcade and game room and supervised childcare for parents who need a little alone time, the Delta is also highly conscious of accessibility issues for the disabled. So it's no surprise it also frequently hosts conferences relating to disability issues.
Rooms from $149, bar, restaurant, gym, pool, arcade, Internet, meeting facilities.

HOLIDAY INN EXPRESS TORONTO DOWNTOWN
111 Lombard, 416-367-5555, 1-877-508-1763, www.hiexpress.com.
A family-oriented hotel conveniently located within walking distance of the Eaton Centre and St.

The artsy-fartsy **Drake** is a boutique hotel and a hipster Queen West hang. See page 241.

Lawrence Market. Complimentary continental breakfast, children 18 years and under stay free and pets are allowed.
Rooms from $131.47, bar, gym, wireless Internet.

HOLIDAY INN ON KING
370 King W, 416-599-4000, 1-800-263-6364, www.hiok.com.
The exterior may look like some kind of futuristic robot overlord, but the Inn on King's got the market cornered on accessibility to Toronto's famous and lively Theatre District, and it's got a great rooftop pool.
Rooms from $219, restaurant, pool, comedy club, Internet.

HOLIDAY INN TORONTO-MIDTOWN
280 Bloor W, 416-968-0010, 1-877-508-1763, www.hiinn.com.
Sandwiched between the hip Annex and chic Yorkville near U of T, the Midtown is all about being cozy and efficient for the visitor on the go. Hit the adjoining pub for a pre-party bevvie before a night on the town.
Rooms from $116.99, restaurant, Internet.

INTERCONTINENTAL TORONTO CENTRE
220 Bloor W, 416-960-5200, www.toronto.intercontinental.com.
A sleek, upscale hotel for playboys and primadonnas yet a perfectly comfortable and relaxing middle-of-the-road destination, the InterContinental covers the basics with a variety of room styles, a tennis court, indoor swimming pool and rooftop patio.
Rooms from $239, bar, restaurant, gym, pool, Internet, meeting facilities.

RADISSON PLAZA HOTEL ADMIRAL-TORONTO HARBOURFRONT
229 Queens Quay W, 416-203-3333, 1-800-333-3333, www.radisson.com.
Sick of the sea... uh, lake? Tired of berthing below deck? Then tie up at the Radisson's on-site marina and step ashore for some top-notch landlubbing accommodations. (Did someone say "spa"?) And in case you miss the water, there's a stunning view of Lake Ontario from the south-facing outdoor pool.
Rooms from $189, bar, restaurant, gym, pool, spa, Internet, meeting facilities.

RENAISSANCE TORONTO HOTEL DOWNTOWN
1 Blue Jays Way, 416-341-7100, 1-800-237-1512, www.marriott.com.
Take in a Blue Jays game without ever getting out of bed. Located inside the Rogers Centre (formerly SkyDome), the Renaissance offers upscale service and quality for the business and leisure classes. Recently renovated, the hotel boasts friendly and delightfully knowledgeable staff, while 75 of their two-floored suites overlook the baseball field. When it's time for the seventh-inning stretch, just kick back and crack open the mini-bar.
Rooms from $149, bar, restaurant, gym, pool, wireless Internet, meeting facilities.

TORONTO MARRIOTT DOWNTOWN EATON CENTRE
525 Bay, 416-597-9200, 1-800-905-0667, www.marriott.com.
The weird dark-salmon interior shouldn't cause anyone to shy away from this hotel catering to the business and leisure class with style and comfort in mind. Look out for the mini outdoor oasis at the south exit complete with a soothing fountain.
Rooms from $189, bar, restaurant, gym, pool, wireless Internet.

TOWN INN HOTEL SUITES
620 Church, 416-964-3311, 1-800-398-2755, www.towninn.com.
Travelling with the family? This apartment hotel offers suites with full kitchens. Here on business? Book a room on the executive floor and take advantage of a full range of business services. Looking to shop? Spend some serious dough in Yorkville, just a few blocks away. Want to relax? Try the the indoor pool or tennis courts.
Rooms from $119, gym, pool, tennis court, wireless Internet.

Business

ALEXANDRA HOTEL
77 Ryerson, 416-504-2121, 1-800-567-1893, www.alexandrahotel.com.
While definitely not a big fancy-pants luxe-fest, the Alexandra has small rooms made for the visitor on the go – i.e., clean but nothing special – and with ensuite kitchenettes, laundry services and Internet access.
Rooms from $80, kitchenette, Internet.

COURTYARD BY MARRIOTT DOWNTOWN TORONTO
475 Yonge, 416-924-0611, 1-800-847-5075, www.marriott.com.
If staying on the main street through downtown Toronto isn't enough for you, this cosmopolitan hotel will be happy to help you arrange a round of golf at GTA courses or sightseeing excursions to the CN Tower or the Toronto Islands. If you're done with all the "business" on your business trip, that is.
Rooms from $169, bar, restaurant, gym, pool, Internet, meeting facilities.

THE CROMWELL FURNISHED SUITES
55 Isabella, 416-962-5670, http://cromwell.sites.toronto.com.
The namesake of the famous Brit offers a comfortable and appealing alternative to your average prefab hotel options, especially if you're in town for more than a few days – the Cromwell offers daily, weekly and monthly rates. Located near the bustling Yonge and Bloor intersection, the suites give off an attractive lived-in feel.
Rooms from $90/nt, $560/wk, $1,650/mth, kitchen, wireless Internet.

DAYS HOTEL & CONFERENCE CENTRE TORONTO DOWNTOWN
30 Carlton, 416-977-6655, 1-800-DAYS-INN, www.dayshoteltoronto.ca.
The uninspired exterior may lead you to believe this is your typical downtown biz-traveller trap. Inside you'll find a swimming pool, typically comfortable rooms and best of all, a pub called the Beer Cellar, which means the drunken walk home at the end of the night only takes about two minutes.
Rooms from $99, bar, restaurant, gym, pool, Internet, meeting facilities.

GRANGE HOTEL
165 Grange, 416-603-7700, 1-888-232-0002, www.grangehotel.com.
Somewhere between the convenience of a hotel and autonomous hostel life is the Grange, a six-storey apartment-style building that, aside from being affordable and close to you-name-it, offers cozy, modest rooms complete with kitchenettes and private bathrooms.
Rooms from $94.95, kitchenette, Internet.

NOVOTEL TORONTO CENTRE HOTEL
45 The Esplanade, 416-367-8900, www.novotel.com.
Located on one of the purdiest little stretches of road in the city's core not more than a five-minute walk to the historic St. Lawrence Market (see **Sightseeing**, page 17), the Novotel combines a little Old European style with the feel and convenience of the modern hotel with spacious rooms and charming downstairs bistro.
Rooms from $145, restaurant, gym, pool, Internet, meeting facilities.

RAMADA HOTEL & SUITES DOWNTOWN TORONTO
300 Jarvis, 416-977-4823, 1-800-567-2233, www.ramadahotelandsuites.com.
This hotel across from the beautiful Allan Gardens (see **Queer**, page 216), a 10-minute walk to the Eaton Centre, is where businessmen on a budget and garage bands tired of sleeping in their van spend the night. The rooms are big and bright, and the on-site health club boasts an indoor pool, exercise room and squash courts. The nabe can be a bit dodgy after dark, however.
Rooms from $169. bar, restaurant, gym, pool, wireless Internet, meeting facilities.

SHERATON CENTRE TORONTO
123 Queen W, 416-361-1000, 1-866-716-8101, www.sheratontoronto.com.
With a newly refurbished lobby filled with plenty of plaid and leather (in shades of reds and blues, no less), this mega-sized hotel features a classic English-style pub and a stunning patio garden with babbling brook and waterfalls, ideal for an evening stroll or a grand moonlit reception.
Rooms from $242.75, bar, restaurant, gym, pool, wireless Internet.

STRATHCONA HOTEL
60 York, 416-363-3321, 1-800-268-8304, www.thestrathconahotel.com.
Since 1945, the Strathcona has been all about offering the quality and service one might expect from an upscale metropolitan locale at a very decent rate. With 194 rooms, the European-inspired hotel is ideal for the business traveller.
Rooms from $125, bar, restaurant, meeting facilities.

TRAVELODGE TORONTO
621 King W, 416-504-7441, 1-800-578-7878, www.travelodgetorontodowntown.com.
Sticking out like a relic from the 70s among the trendy shops and restos of the King West strip, the Travelodge is one of the downtown's only motels. You remember motels, don't you, where you park your car at your front door? The three-storey, 88-room go-tel boasts plenty of room and wireless high-speed Internet access, not to mention a good location and helpful employees.
Rooms from $129.95, wireless Internet.

Boutique

COSMOPOLITAN TORONTO HOTEL
8 Colborne, 416-350-2000, 1-800-958-3488, www.cosmotoronto.com.
The Cosmo is a tranquil boutique hotel that offers a wide array of amenities, while the suites are straight out of an Ikea catalogue. Anyone in need of stress relief should check out the Shizen Spa.
Rooms from $179, bar, restaurant, gym, spa, Internet.

THE DRAKE HOTEL
1150 Queen W, 416-531-5042,
www.thedrakehotel.ca.

A $6-million facelift has transformed this former railway hostel into one of the two key hipster hangs on the trendy West Queen West strip (the other is the Gladstone Hotel, see below). Tucked in among galleries, boutiques and bistros, the Drake offers 19 cool crash pads, a European-influenced lounge, sushi bar and restaurant, a café, rooftop patio, yoga studio and the über-hip Underground performance space.
Rooms from $179, bar, restaurant, wireless Internet.

GLADSTONE HOTEL
1214 Queen W, 416-531-4635,
www.gladstonehotel.com.

The most unique hotel experience in the city, perhaps the entire country. Built in 1889 and recently redesigned to reflect the surrounding artsy-hippie West Queen West community, the Gladstone (see photo, page 237) is a vital part of the local arts scene, hosting cabaret performances, film screenings, book launches and art exhibits. Indeed, 37 of its 51 rooms and suites have been individually designed by local artists, including the red-and-black-accented Biker Room, an homage to 70s biker culture; woodsy retreat the Faux Naturelle Room, described as a room where a "lesbian separatist commune meets Storybook Gardens"; and the pink Tiger Beat explosion of the Teen Queen Room. There are also six super-large Gimme More rooms with full four-piece baths and kitchenettes, as well as two special suites: the justifiably dubbed Best Room and the two-level honeymoon/rock-star Tower Suite, with a turret bedroom overlooking the city and lakefront.
Rooms from $165, bar, wireless Internet.

ISABELLA HOTEL & SUITES
556 Sherbourne, 416-922-2203,
www.isabellahotel.com.

Visitors wanting to take a trip back in time should look to the Isabella. Built in 1891, the hotel is an historical landmark, with 31 rooms that offer plenty of comfort to those with a taste for the traditional.
Rooms from $79, bar.

MADISON MANOR BOUTIQUE HOTEL
20 Madison, 416-922-5579, 1-877-561-7048,
www.madisonavenuepub.com.

There's really only one drawback to staying at this English-country-style inn in the Annex – it happens to be adjacent to the **Madison Pub** (see **Bars**, page 119), with its six patios, one of the coolest bars in town. Not that rowdy neighbours are the problem; it's just that you'll likely join the party and never leave. Of course, it does make the drunken stumble to bed a little easier to bear. As for the hotel itself, it has 23 quaint and quiet rooms, five with balconies, fireplaces and alcove windows.
Rooms from $89, bar, restaurant, Internet, meeting facilities.

HOTEL VICTORIA
56 Yonge, 416-363-1666, 1-800-363-8228,
www.hotelvictoria-toronto.com.

It may be small, but the Victoria holds the bragging rights for being the second-oldest hotel in town. You can bet on friendly and personal service before hitting the Theatre District.
Rooms from $105, Internet.

Luxury

FOUR SEASONS HOTEL TORONTO
21 Avenue Road, 416-964-0411,
www.fourseasons.com/toronto.

This Yorkville luxury spot is prime celeb-spotting territory, especially the ground-floor Avenue Lounge

---

Rolling stoned

In 1977, Keith Richards was busted for heroin and cocaine possession at the **Westin Harbour Castle** (see page 242) after the Stones playing a concert at the **El Mocambo** (see **Music**, page 140). As part of the plea bargain that saw Richards avoid serious jail time, he played two charity shows in support of the Canadian National Institute for the Blind.

---

during the Toronto International Film Festival. The rest is as you'd expect from a Four Seasons. Have cocktails or afternoon tea in the Lobby Bar or dinner at Truffles Restaurant. There are also fitness facilities, swimming pool and spa services.
Rooms from $315, bar, restaurant, gym, pool, spa, wireless Internet, meeting facilities.

GRAND HOTEL & SUITES TORONTO
225 Jarvis, 416-863-9000, 1-877-32-GRAND,
www.grandhoteltoronto.com.

Check out the cityscape from the rooftop patio garden (with whirlpools), or perhaps take in a twilight movie on the giant movie screen. Work up a sweat in the fitness centre, then cool off in the indoor pool. There's more to the Grand than just a bed to sleep in. Ideal for families and business travellers alike.
Rooms from $169 (incl full breakfast for two), bar, restaurant, gym, pool, spa services, wireless Internet, meeting facilities.

HILTON TORONTO
145 Richmond W, 416-869-3456, www.hilton.com.

Yeah sure, nowadays mention the name Hilton and you think of the annoying heiress Paris, but her undeserved fortune wasn't amassed through shoddy service. Located near hip Queen West, the Hilton offers sleek, sexy rooms, a salon and helpful, multilingual staff. Hey, they even allow pets, so bring the Chihuahua along for the trip.
Rooms from $150, bar, restaurant, gym, pool, salon.

HOTEL LE GERMAIN
30 Mercer, 416-345-9500, 1-866-345-9501,
www.germaintoronto.com.

A spinoff of its Montreal counterpart, this is a cool rendezvous in the heart of the **Entertainment District** (see **Sightseeing**, page 14). The rooms are smart and sophisticated, and the luxe resto Luce is one of the city's top rated.
Rooms from $245, bar, restaurant, gym, wireless Internet.

LE ROYAL MERIDIEN KING EDWARD HOTEL
37 King E, 416-863-3131,
www.toronto.lemeridien.com.

More than a century old, the King Eddy has had many famous guests, including Rudyard Kipling, Mark Twain and the Beatles. Though a bit austere and imposing – the terracotta trimmings on the exterior, stern-faced doorman, massive marble columns in the lobby – the hotel does know how to take care of its guests in Old World style. The Café Victoria, with its baroque decor and floor-to-ceiling windows, is typical of its Edwardian charm, while the plush chairs of the Consort Bar, looking onto busy King Street, offer great people watching.
Rooms from $244, bar, restaurant, gym, spa services, wireless Internet, meeting facilities.

OLD MILL INN & SPA
21 Old Mill Road, 416-236-2641, 1-866-653-6455,
www.oldmilltoronto.com.
The original mill was built in 1793 on the banks of the Humber River to process lumber for the then town of York. Rebuilt several times since, the Old Mill still offers the flavour of Old Toronto (by way of Victorian England), with its Tudor-style architecture, scenic gardens and a live orchestra in the dining room. No wonder it's booked solid with wedding banquets every weekend from May till September.
Rooms from $202, bar, restaurant, chapel, flower shop, spa, Internet.

PANTAGES SUITES HOTEL & SPA
200 Victoria, 416-362-1777, 1-866-852-1777,
www.pantageshotel.com.
In this 400-thread-count downtown lifestyle hotel a block east of the Eaton Centre, the 111 luxe suites still sparkle with newness. There's a slick, cool martini bar near the lobby and a first-rate spa. If all that shiny sophistication makes you wish for something just a bit simpler, grab a burger and shake at Fran's, the ground-level 50s-style diner.
Rooms from $209, bar, restaurant, gym, spa services, wireless Internet, meeting facilities.

PARK HYATT TORONTO HOTEL
4 Avenue Road, 416-925-1234,
http://parktoronto.hyatt.com.
Situated along Toronto's famed Mink Mile (see **Sightseeing**, page 26) a stone's throw from fashionable Yorkville and just across the street from the Royal Ontario Museum, the Park Hyatt (formerly the Park Plaza) offers quiet comfort and tasteful luxury. Enjoy a meal in one of two restos, Annona and Morton's Steakhouse, cocktails in one of two lounges or on the famed rooftop patio, a fine Cuban in the ground-floor La Casa del Habano Cigar Shop, or just spend the day being pampered in the hotel's Stillwater Spa.
Rooms from $285, bar, restaurant, gym, pool, spa services, wireless Internet, meeting facilities.

SOHO METROPOLITAN HOTEL
318 Wellington W, 416-599-8800, 1-866-SOHO-MET,
www.metropolitan.com/soho/.
If you really want to Trump yourself, book a night in the SoHo Met's 4,000-square-foot, three-storey penthouse with floor-to-ceiling windows, multiple fireplaces, two bedrooms, two kitchens, five washrooms, library, dining room, two living rooms, private rooftop terrace with hot tub and an in-suite glass elevator. The other 88 or so rooms in the hotel are great, too (Frette linens, heated marble floors in the bathrooms, big windows). Salon Daniel & Spa and Senses Bakery and Restaurant help make your stay even more pleasant.
Rooms from $300, bar, restaurant, gym, pool, spa, wireless Internet, meeting facilities.

SUTTON PLACE HOTEL
955 Bay, 416-924-9221, 1-866-3SUTTON,
www.suttonplace.com.
If elegance takes top priority, then the Sutton's classic marble and brass decor will have you feeling like you're rubbing elbows with high-society types in Monte Carlo. And at film festival time, you actually do rub elbows with Hollywood glitterati. The posh experience continues in the hotel's specialty suites that feature original works of art and antiques.
Rooms from $143.65, bar, restaurant, gym, pool, wireless Internet, meeting facilities.

TORONTO MARRIOTT BLOOR YORKVILLE
90 Bloor E, 416-961-8000, 1-800-859-7180,
www.marriott.com.
Appropriately located in the upscale and occasionally stuffy Yorkville nabe, the Marriott offers everything you'd expect from a four-star hotel at a reasonable

Hotel Le Germain offers guests a certain swanky *je ne*

price. And with expensive shopping and the Royal Ontario Museum at its doorstep, why not?
Rooms from $139, bar, restaurant, gym, Internet.

WESTIN HARBOUR CASTLE
1 Harbour Square, 416-869-1600, 1-800-228-3000,
www.westin.com.
Right on the picturesque waterfront, the Westin is ideal for the upscale traveller who wants to stay downtown without being surrounded by the downtown. No wonder it hosts more than its share of rock stars. The Toronto Islands ferry and Harbourfront Centre (see **Sightseeing**, page 12) are both within walking distance. Everything else will require a quick streetcar or cab ride.
Rooms from $199, bar, restaurant, gym, pool wireless Internet, meeting facilities.

WINDSOR ARMS HOTEL
18 St. Thomas, 416-971-9666, 1-877-999-2767,
www.windsorarmshotel.com.
Tucked into a quiet side street mere steps from über-chic Yorkville, the Windsor Arms is where Hollywood stays when the stars come here to play. The 26 newly appointed luxury suites have 24-hour butler service. Enjoy fine French cuisine dining in the Courtyard Café, traditional high tea in the Tea Room, cocktails and casual dining in Club 22 and a cigar lounge. The Windsor Arms also offers old-school straight razor shaves in the Barber Shop as well as a full spa.
Rooms from $275, bar, restaurant, gym, pool, spa, wireless Internet.

i. Or maybe it's just this cool lobby-library combo. See page 241.

Queer-Friendly Hotels

For LGBT-positive accommodation listings, see Queer, page 220.

Airport

BELAIRE HOTEL TORONTO AIRPORT
240 Belfield, 416-241-8513, www.belairehotel.ca.
Rooms from $87, bar, restaurant.

COMFORT HOTEL AIRPORT NORTH
445 Rexdale, 416-740-9500,
www.comforthotelairport.com.
Rooms from $87, bar, restaurant, gym, pool, wireless Internet.

COURTYARD BY MARRIOTT MISSISSAUGA AIRPORT CORPORATE CENTRE WEST
5050 Creekbank, Mississauga, 905-625-3555,
www.marriott.com.
Rooms from $99, restaurant, gym, pool, Internet, meeting facilities.

DAYS HOTEL & CONFERENCE CENTRE TORONTO AIRPORT EAST
1677 Wilson, 416-249-8171, 1-800-267-0997,
www.daysto.com.
Rooms from $119, bar, restaurant, gym, pool, Internet, meeting facilities.

DOUBLETREE INTERNATIONAL PLAZA TORONTO AIRPORT
655 Dixon, 416-244-1711, 1-800-668-3656,
www.hilton.com.
Rooms from $139, bar, restaurants, gym, pool, Internet, meeting facilities.

FOUR POINTS BY SHERATON MISSISSAUGA
6090 Dixie, Mississauga, 905-670-0050,
www.fourpointsmississauga.com.
Rooms from $135, bar, restaurant, gym pool, Internet, meeting facilities.

HILTON TORONTO AIRPORT
5875 Airport, Mississauga, 905-677-9900,
www.hilton.com.
Rooms from $210, bar, restaurant, gym, pool, squash courts, postage facilities, wireless Internet, meeting facilities.

HOLIDAY INN TORONTO AIRPORT EAST
600 Dixon, 416-240-7511, 1-800-491-4656,
www.holiday-inn.com.
Rooms from $118, restaurant, gym, pool, games room, Internet, meeting facilities, National Car Rental kiosk.

QUALITY HOTEL & SUITES TORONTO AIRPORT EAST
2180 Islington, 416-240-9090, 1-866-220-6916,
http://qualityairport.sites.toronto.com.
Rooms from $69, bar, restaurant, gym, wireless Internet, meeting facilities.

RADISSON SUITE HOTEL TORONTO AIRPORT
640 Dixon, 416-242-7400, 1-800-333-3333,
http://www.radisson.com.
Rooms from $119, restaurant, gym, wireless Internet, meeting facilities.

where to stay

RAMADA HOTEL TORONTO AIRPORT
2 Holiday, 416-621-2121.
Rooms from $109, bar (w/ live music), restaurant, gym, pool, wireless Internet, meeting facilities.

RENAISSANCE TORONTO AIRPORT HOTEL AND CONFERENCE CENTRE
801 Dixon, 416-675-6100, 1-800-668-1444, www.marriott.com.
Rooms from $224, bar, restaurant, gym, pool, golf, Internet, meeting facilities.

RESIDENCE INN MISSISSAUGA AIRPORT WEST
17 Reading, 416-798-2900, www.marriott.com.
Rooms from $109, restaurant, gym, pool, kitchenette, Internet, meeting facilities.

TRAVELODGE HOTEL TORONTO AIRPORT
925 Dixon, 416-674-2222, 1-888-483-6887, www.travelodgedixon.com.
Rooms from $92, bar, restaurant, gym, pool, wireless Internet, meeting facilities.

WYNDHAM BRISTOL PLACE TORONTO AIRPORT
950 Dixon, 416-675-9444, www.wyndham.com.
Rooms from $89, restaurant, gym, pool, wireless Internet.

Bed & Breakfast

AMBASSADOR INN DOWNTOWN TORONTO BED & BREAKFAST
280 Jarvis, 416-260-2608, www.ambassadorinntoronto.com.
Anyone tired of big, impersonal hotels should feel more at home at the Ambassador, a classic 20-room Victorian mansion that offers home-cooked brecky and private Jacuzzis, saunas and fireplaces. Make sure to call ahead 'cause they don't take too kindly to walk-ins.
Rooms from $129, Internet.

ASHLEIGH HERITAGE HOME BED & BREAKFAST
42 Delaware, 416-535-4000, www.ashleighheritage.com.
As a large, beautifully restored Victorian house, the Ashleigh and its owners enthusiastically offer all the homey appeal you'd expect from a B&B, with large, friendly rooms, a garden, kitchen facilities and even wireless Internet.
Rooms from $111.38, wireless Internet, kitchen facilities.

BONNEVUE MANOR BED AND BREAKFAST
33 Beaty, 416-536-1455, www.bonnevuemanor.com.
Just because you're away from home, you don't have to feel like it. The Bonnevue Mansion offers plenty of familiar charm, with unique and individually decorated rooms and warm service. Besides, any mansion that has an on-site barbecue should make you feel right at home.
Rooms starting at $95, pool.

JARVIS HOUSE BED & BREAKFAST
344 Jarvis, 416-975-3838, www.jarvishouse.com.
Reminiscent of the home of the Golden Girls in decor and comfort, Jarvis House offers a variety of different-sized rooms and a yummy bacon-and-egg breakfast to lure you out of bed.
Rooms from $85, Internet.

GLOBAL GUEST HOUSE
9 Spadina Road, 416-923-4004.
A supremely cheap destination with the added bonus of being smack dab in the heart of the Annex, Global Guest House is a quaint semi-detached Victorian house offering simple-yet-comfy rooms adorned with paintings done by the hotel manager's wife.
Rooms from $49.

TORONTO B&B RESERVATION SERVICE
253 College, 1-877-922-6522, www.torontobandb.com.
This reservation service will recommend a B&B at one of 20 homes in the central part of the city and in the Beaches.

VICTORIA'S MANSION GUEST HOUSE
68 Gloucester, 416-921-4625, www.victoriasmansion.com.
Just minutes away from downtown, the Mansion has been around since the 1880s and maintains a traditional Victorian garden and several uniquely decorated rooms. Perfect for the cosmopolitan traditionalist on the cheap.
Rooms from $82.22, Internet.

Hostels

COLLEGE HOSTEL & GUEST HOUSE
280 Augusta, 416-929-4777.
It may not be the Ritz-Carlton, but the College Hostel is ideal for budget-conscious visitors in need of a safe place to hang their hats. The 48-room hotel in reach of trendy College West offers the necessities, including shared dorm rooms that give solo travellers a great chance to connect with others.
Rooms from $22, sushi bar.

GLOBAL VILLAGE BACKPACKERS HOSTEL
460 King W, 416-703-8540, 1-888-844-7875, www.globalbackpackers.com.
In its previous life as the Spadina Hotel, this hostel hosted the likes of Jack Nicholson and the Rolling Stones. And at least one thing hasn't changed: it still knows how to show guests a good time. Shoot some pool with backpacking blokes from the UK, share a blunt with some babes from Barcelona on the patio, pound back a few with travellers from Taiwan in the pub. Nightly events include BBQs, beer Olympics and karaoke. GV offers single, quad and dorm (6-10 guests) rooms, shared washrooms on every floor and self-serve kitchen and laundry.
Beds from $23, bar, wireless Internet.

NEILL-WYCIK COLLEGE-HOTEL
96 Gerrard E, 416-977-2320, www.neill-wycik.com.
A student residence during the school year, it's a hotel open to visitors in the summer, offering very studentesque lodgings, a common area and a café. The dealmaker, though, is the building's rooftop patio, barbecues and sauna.
Rooms from $42.41, bar, restaurant.

ST. LAWRENCE RESIDENCES & SUITES
137 Jarvis, 416-361-0053.
More like a hostel or boarding house than a traditional hotel, the rooms at the St. Lawrence are small and sparsely decorated but perfectly clean and well kept, although many require you to share the washrooms. But you can't beat the price.
Rooms from $38, kitchenette, Internet.

Camping

GLEN ROUGE CAMPGROUND
Located off Highway 2 (Kingston Road) just north of Hwy 401 and east of the Sheppard/Port Union interchange, 416-338-CAMP (2267).
If you're one of those roughin'-it types, pitch your tent or park your camper in the only campground in the city. Not that it will feel like the city – it's nestled in 12,000 acres of forests and fields in Rouge Park, Canada's largest urban park, with plenty of wildlife outside your tent flap. The park offers 27 unserviced campsites, 11 sites designed specifically for backpackers and cyclists and 87 fully serviced RV sites. The grounds has washrooms, change rooms, showers, coin laundry, vending machines, fire pits and barbecues.
Rates (daily/weekly/monthly) $30/$189/$718 serviced, $22/$138/$526 unserviced; $14/night backpacker.

resources

A NOW survival guide of important numbers for visitors and residents alike.

GETTING HERE

BY AIR T.O.'s main airport is **Lester B. Pearson International**, one of the busiest in North America. It's located 45 minutes – about a $40 cab ride – from downtown. In addition to taxi and limo services, there's an airport bus that picks up and drops off at several hotels in the city centre (at about one-third the cost of cabbing it). Even cheaper – $2.75 – take the TTC city bus that runs between the airport and Kipling subway station in the city's west end. There's also the much smaller – and much hated by local residents – Toronto City Centre Airport located on the Toronto Islands, which is used primarily by private planes.

BY TRAIN Union Station, on Front (at Bay), is next door to the Air Canada Centre and just a few minutes walk to the Entertainment District, the Rogers Centre (formerly Skydome), the CN Tower and the Metro Toronto Convention Centre. VIA Rail trains to destinations in Canada and the U.S. operate out of Union, which is also directly linked to the subway and the **GO Train** system of trains and buses to the burbs.

BY BUS Toronto's bus station is conveniently located a few blocks north of City Hall and the Financial District (610 Bay, at Edward).

BY CAR Driving into Toronto can be a bit complicated (although not compared to Montreal). **Highway 401** (the 401) runs east-west into the city, north of the downtown core. **Highway 400** (the 400) connects to the 401 from the north. Approaching from the south, the **Queen Elizabeth Way (QEW)** sweeps up from Niagara Falls and along Lake Ontario into the city, where it becomes the **Gardiner Expressway**, an elevated highway that cuts along the city's waterfront.

LET ME IN Though this could change soon, American visitors to Canada DO NOT need a passport to cross the border in either direction (although we recommend having one in our paranoid, post-9/11, George Dubya-is-watching world). All visitors may be asked to verify citizenship (birth certificate, naturalization certificate, green card or passport) and show a photo ID (e.g. driver's license). If you're under 16 and travelling parent-free – and good for you! – you should have a letter of authorization from a parent or guardian to travel to Canada. Anyone with a criminal record (including a drunk-driving charge) should contact the Canadian Embassy or nearest Consulate General before travel. U.S. citizens entering Canada from a third country must have a valid passport. In general, non-Americans will require a passport. For more information, call 1-800-992-7037 (from outside Canada), 1-888-242-2100 (from within Canada).

TOURIST INFO

ONTARIO TRAVEL INFORMATION CENTRE (Mon-Fri 10 am-9 pm, Sat 9:30 am-7 pm, Sun noon-5 pm, 1-800-668-2746) is located inside the Atrium on Bay. 20 Dundas W, at Yonge. 1-800-668-2746.

TOURISM TORONTO Keeps track of the city's events and places of recreational interest. Also provides hotel information. 207 Queens Quay W, 5th floor. Maps, brochures available. 416-203-2600, www.torontotourism.com.

TORONTO ON TOUR

Toronto's not hard to navigate on foot – the CN Tower makes a pretty nifty compass needle and the downtown core is fairly compact. And public transportation is clean, safe and straightforward. But if you'd rather someone show you around, here are a few options:
Gray Line Bus Tour, a two-hour narrated bus tour on a double-decker bus offers a hop-on/hop-off option of the Toronto area departing from downtown hotels at various times and from the Bay Street bus terminal (610 Bay) twice daily. Year round except Dec 25. $34, srs $30, child $19. 416-594-3310, www.grayline.ca.
Hippo Bus Tours This colourful vehicle, made up of a school bus chassis, flotation devices and a glass-roofed body, offers 90-minute narrated (Japanese, Mandarin, Spanish, French and German) urban safari tours of downtown and then enters the lake for a ride around Ontario Place. May-Oct daily, hourly 11 am-6 pm. $38, srs/stu $33, child $25. 151 Front W, 416-703-4476, www.torontohippotours.com.
Tall Ship Tours A three-masted schooner sails the Toronto harbour and Lake Ontario. Various times. All tours depart from Queens Quay Terminal. 207 Queens Quay W. $10.95-$19.95. Reservations 416-203-2322, www.tallshipcruisestoronto.com.
Toronto Helicopter Company For the ultimate Toronto sightseeing experience, take in the whole city from 2,000 feet. The flights are short (choose between a 9- and 14-minute flight) and they aren't cheap (close to 100 bucks for the shorter tour), but the view – and the experience – is hard to top. Departs from Toronto City Centre Airport (Bathurst ferry). Reservations 416-203-3280, www.HeliTours.ca.

SUBWAYS, BUSES & STREET CARS (TTC)

TORONTO TRANSIT COMMISSION
Route information:
416-393-INFO (4636)
www.city.toronto.ca/ttc
Lost & Found: 416-393-4100
(Bay Station).
The Toronto Transit Commission (**TTC**) is an integrated network of subways, buses and streetcars that serves all areas of the city 24/7. Daily, weekly and monthly individual and family passes and single-ride tokens and tickets are available at all TTC booths as well as some convenience stores, newsstands and pharmacies. If you are paying cash on a bus or streetcar, you'll need exact change since drivers don't make change. A paper transfer obtained at your point of entry (from the driver on streetcars and buses or from the red machines in subway stations) allows you to board any connecting TTC vehicle without paying another fare. Free TTC maps are available at subway stations, the Toronto Convention and Visitors Association (207 Queens Quay W, Queens Quay Terminal) or the Ontario Travel Information Centre in the the Atrium on Bay (20 Dundas W,

at Yonge, 1-800-668-2746).
The **subway** – a.k.a. the Rocket – is about as uncomplicated as it gets. A horseshoe-shaped north-south line (the Yonge-University-Spadina line) loops up from Union Station and is bisected by the east-west Bloor-Danforth line that runs through the city centre. A third line (the Sheppard line) runs east-west in the north of the city and connects to the Yonge line. Most subway stops connect to a bus or streetcar line and require a token, ticket or transfer obtained within the subway stations. The TTC offers a Request Stop program that allows female passengers who are travelling alone at night (9 pm-5 am) to exit buses between regular TTC stops.

OTHER TRANSIT

AIRPORT BUS SERVICE Times and locations for direct bus service to the airport. 905-564-6333.

BUS TERMINAL Schedule and ticket information. Greyhound and other bus lines. 610 Bay, 416-367-8747.

FERRY SCHEDULES Ferry rides to the Toronto Islands. $6, stu/srs $3.50, child $2.50. 416-392-8193.

GO TRANSIT Schedule and ticket info for greater Toronto region commuter trains and buses. 416-869-3200, www.gotransit.com.

UNION STATION Schedule and ticket information for VIA Rail and other interurban train services. Corner of Bay and Front. 416-366-8411.

WHEEL-TRANS Public city-transit service for handicapped persons. For information and reservations, call 416-393-4111, trip reservation 416-393-4222.

TAXIS

Taxis are everywhere in Toronto and can be hailed from any street corner. And while many of the cabs are painted like an ugly bruise, the only ones that are New York yellow are ones being filmed for a movie. The standard fare starts at $2.75 and increases 25 cents for every 0.19 km driven or 31 seconds of waiting. Drivers are required to take whatever route you request or the most direct route to your destination, and they are not allowed to make restaurant or hotel recommendations unless you request them. Should you encounter a problem, the 24-hour cab complaint line is 1-877-868-2947.
Beck 416-751-5555
Co-op 416-504-2667
Crown 416-750-7878
Diamond 416-366-6868

DRIVING

If you've got your own wheels, Toronto is laid out on a grid system of easy-to-follow north-south, east-west streets. Parking, however, can be a bit of a pain. Curbside spaces are highly prized and offer only a couple of hours of meter time, so try one of the many city-run lots that offer the cheapest rates (just look for the green P sign). One more thing: you can make a right turn on a red light in Toronto (after stopping and yielding to other traffic and pedestrians, of course). Failing to do so will earn you honking horns and angry looks from drivers stuck behind you.

CAR RENTAL
Advantage Car & Truck Rentals
20 Eglinton W, other locations, 416-487-4994, www.advantage-carrentals.com.
Alamo Car Rental
930 Yonge, other locations, 416-935-1533, www.alamo.com.
AutoShare
24 Mercer, 416-340-7888, www.autoshare.com
Avis Car Rental
80 Bloor E, other locations, 416-964-2051, www.avis.ca.
Budget Car and Truck Rental
141 Bay, other locations, 416-364-7104, www.budget.ca.
Discount Car and Truck Rentals
416-251-3759, www.discountcars.ca.
Dollar Rent-A-Car
370 King W, other locations, 416-977-6749, www.dollar.com.
National Car and Truck Rental
128 Richmond E, other locations, 416-364-4558, www.national-car.com.
Thrifty Car Rental
65 Front, Union Station, other locations, 416-947-1385, www.thrifty.com.
Zipcar
416-432-3114, www.zipcar.com.

ROADSIDE SERVICE
Canadian Automobile Association
461 Yonge, and other locations, 416-221-4300, 416-222-5222, www.caa.ca.

WALKING, BLADING & BIKING

The Toronto core is neatly organized and fairly compact, making it easy to explore on foot. Blading and biking are common during the warmer months. A network of bike paths runs through ravines and parks, and some streets have designated bike lanes. For a list of bike rental shops, see **Recreation**, page 196.

MONEY, TAX, DUTY & TIPPING

CURRENCY Canada's currency is the dollar. For denominations under $5 we use coins, including the loonie ($1 coin) and toonie ($2 coin). Paper money comes in different colours and designs: $5 bills (blue), $10 bills (purple), $20 bills (green), $50 bills (red) and $100 bills (brown). DO NOT accept $100 bills. Many businesses won't take them because of counterfeiting. American money is widely accepted, although exchange rates can vary and change will be returned in Canadian currency. Currency exchange is available at banks and kiosks (look for the Thomas Cook sign) throughout the city, as well as in the airport. Cash machines/ATMs (Plus/Cirrus/Interac) are numerous and easy to find, and even the pay-and-display parking machines accept credit cards (Visa, MasterCard, American Express).

SALES TAX The Goods and Services Tax (GST) is a 6 per cent tax charged on most goods and services sold or provided in Canada. Purchases are also subject to the 8 per cent Provincial Sales Tax (PST). Foreign visitors can apply for a GST rebate (similar to the European VAT rebate) on accommodation (up to 30 nights per visit) and on goods exported within 60 days of purchase, so keep your receipts. For more info, visit www.cra.gc.ca/visitors or call 1-800-668-4748 (within Canada) or 1-902-432-5608 (from outside Canada).

DUTY FREE BOOTY Visitors should check the customs regulations in their home country regarding what items they may bring back. American citizens, for example, are allowed to bring back $400 (retail value) in merchandise duty-free from Canada, provided they have been out of the U.S. for 48 hours. This amount may include:
- 1 carton of cigarettes
- 100 cigars (not Cubans)
- 2 kilograms of smoking tobacco
- 1 litre of alcohol

If the stay is less than 48 hours, $200 in merch may be taken back, including 5 ounces of alcohol and 50 cigs.
The following items are not permitted:
- Cuban or Iranian products
- fruits and vegetables
- uncooked grains

Goods bought in Canada but manufactured in the U.S. are duty free, as are handmade crafts and works of art (although make sure to keep your receipts handy). For more info on U.S. customs regulations, visit www.customs.ustreas.gov or call 905-676-2606.

TIPPING If the food was good and the service friendly, a 15 to 20 per cent tip on the pre-tax bill is standard. (Note: some restaurants automatically add the gratuity, so check your bill.) The same goes for services such as haircuts and taxi rides.

METRIC SYSTEM
Distance is measured by kilometres (km); speed signs are in kilometres per hour (km/h). Miles x 1.6 = kilometres; kilometres x 0.6 = miles (50 mph = 80 km/h; 100 km/h = 62 mph).

PUBLIC HOLIDAYS
New Year's Day:
January 1
Good Friday:
Friday before Easter
Easter Monday:
Monday following Easter
Victoria Day:
Monday before May 24
Canada Day:
July 1
Civic Holiday:
first Monday in August
Labour Day:
first Monday in September
Thanksgiving:
second Monday in October
Remembrance Day:
November 11
Christmas Day:
December 25
Boxing Day:
December 26

LANGUAGE
Canada has two official languages, English and French. In addition, the top five languages spoken in Toronto are Cantonese, Italian, Tamil, Portuguese and Spanish.

TELEPHONE
AREA CODES
The GTA has three area codes: **416**, **905** and **647**, with 416 being the most central.

INFO LINES
ACCESS TORONTO Public info, general inquiry service and referrals for the City of Toronto. Call centre Mon-Fri 8 am-5 pm, access in person at City Hall and civic centres Mon-Fri 8:30 am-4:30 pm. 416-338-0338, www.toronto.ca.

ARTS, CULTURE & HERITAGE Responsible for operating and administering many museums, historic sites and performing and visual arts centres. 416-338-3888.

BEACH HOTLINE AND SUN REPORT Starting in June, a recorded message on the hotline indicates which T.O. beaches are safe for swimming. 416-392-7161.

CHILDREN'S SERVICES Provides info and referrals to families seeking licensed childcare in group or private home settings, before- and after-school care, summer camps, family support services and special needs resources. 416-392-KIDS (5437).

COMMUNITY INFO TORONTO This free, multilingual community, social, health and government information and referral service runs 24 hours a day. Dial 2-1-1, www.211toronto.ca.

GOVERNMENT OF CANADA Dial 1-800-O-Canada (622-6232).

HERITAGE TORONTO Gatekeeper of the old amid the new, Heritage historical sites are maintained by the City of Toronto. St. Lawrence Hall, 157 King E, 416-338-0684, www.heritagetoronto.org.

MARRIAGE LICENCES Issued for gay, lesbian and straight marriages at City Hall and civic centres. Ceremonies can also be held at City Hall. 416-338-0338.

PARKS AND RECREATION INFO Information on T.O. recreation programs such as tree planting, nature-trail hiking, swimming and tennis. 416-338-4FUN (4386), 416-392-1111.

POOL HOTLINE Information on locations and opening hours of Toronto's outdoor pools. 416-338-POOL (7665).

PROVINCE OF ONTARIO Dial 416-326-1234.

SHELTER, HOUSING & SUPPORT Provides emergency shelter to single people and families. 416-397-5637.

TENANCY ISSUES Referral service for tenants and landlords. 416-397-4502.

TORONTO ANIMAL SERVICES Licenses and registers pets, picks up stray and injured animals, gives advice and info on city wildlife. 416-338-PAWS (7297).

TORONTO COMMUNITY HOUSING Provides affordable housing for seniors, families and individuals with low to moderate incomes. 416-981-6111.

TORONTO PARKING AUTHORITY Dial 416-393-7275.

TORONTO PUBLIC HEALTH Provides programs for new mothers, dental care, drug and substance abuse treatment, immunizations and restaurant inspections. 416-338-7600.

TORONTO SOCIAL SERVICES Provides employment assistance programs and support services. 416-392-2956.

WASTE MANAGEMENT SERVICES Collects and disposes of garbage and recyclable materials. 416-338-2010.

WEATHER
Weather info line
416-661-0123.
A 24-hour, regularly updated, recorded weather report from Environment Canada. See also www.theweathernetwork.com.

Contrary to some perceptions, Canada is not an Arctic wasteland (at least not all of it). While conditions vary from season to season (and sometimes hour to hour), Toronto's climate is among the mildest in Canada, and the city experiences weather similar to New York and Detroit. Toronto is also on the same geographic latitude as the French Riviera, although that's where the similarities – geographic and otherwise – end. Toronto summers are warm and sunny and often pretty damn humid. Shorts, T-shirts and a good antiperspirant are definitely needed. The respiratorily challenged might want to pack inhalers and oxygen masks due to Toronto's frequent smog alerts. Other than the occasional need to chew your air before swallowing, it's perfect weather for seeing the sights. Yeah, but what about the winters? Sure, there's snow – Canada isn't called the Great White North because of a cocaine habit – and Toronto routinely gets a few inches of powder here and there. There's the occasional freezing-rain shower, but for every bitter cold snap there's a mild period that triggers a midwinter afternoon of premature patio sitting. Really, though, it's the wind chill that most locals complain about. For the uninitiated, wind chill is the "feels like" temperature created by that little breeze off the lake that in summer is pleasantly cooling and in winter is just plain ass-numbing, as in "If it wasn't for the wind chill I could still feel my ass." Fortunately, such bitter cold days are becoming fewer and fewer (thank you, global warming!) and besides, much of the downtown area is linked by enclosed walkways and underground tunnels (see **PATH**, page 188). If you do have to venture out on one of these cold days and you don't want to risk frostbite, dress in layers, lots and lots of layers. And gloves. And hats. And scarves. And boots. (As you can tell, fashion takes a back seat to a Toronto winter.) The rest of the year – that's spring and fall – the temps are moderate (and occasionally quite balmy).

24-HOUR PLACES

Bloor Super Save All-night grocery store with a good – and crunchy – selection of fresh vegetables and fruits.
384 Bloor W, 416-964-8318.
Dominion Large supermarket open daily around the clock. 425 Bloor W, and others, 416-923-9099.
Kinko's Copies For late-night workaholics. Well equipped with assisted and self-serve photocopying equipment.
459 Bloor W, 416-928-0110.
Rabba's Fine Foods For the best ingredients in trendy cuisine for late-night noshing. 252 Queens Quay W, and others, 416-260-8869.

EMERGENCY SERVICES

Emergency Dial 911.
Ambulance Dial 911 or 416-392-2000.
Fire Dial 911 or 416-338-9050.
Police Dial 911 or 416-808-2222.

CRISIS LINES

24-HOUR ASSAULTED WOMEN'S HELPLINE Counselling, plus information on legal assistance and shelter for women experiencing emotional, mental, physical, sexual or verbal abuse.
416-863-0511.

24-HOUR FIRE, MEDICAL, POLICE EMERGENCY LINE Immediate service from ambulance, fire department and police services. Dial 911.

24-HOUR KIDS HELP PHONE Toll-free number for children experiencing any sort of distress, abuse, sex, health problems, suicide, pregnancy. Phone staff provide counselling and crisis intervention. 1-800-668-6868.

24-HOUR POISON HOTLINE Provides advice and assistance for getting to the emergency poison specialist at Sick Kids hospital, 555 University, 416-813-5900.

24-HOUR RAPE CRISIS LINE Crisis intervention and counselling for women who have been sexually assaulted. 416-597-8808.

DISTRESS CENTRE 24-hour helpline providing anonymous counselling for anyone experiencing emotional distress.
416-408-4357.

EMERGENCY SHELTER FOR HOMELESS YOUTH STOP 86 shelter for young homeless women, 416-922-3271. Street Helpline, 416-392-3777. Covenant House, with a health clinic, 416-593-4849.

PARENT HELP PHONE Professional counselors and recorded messages to advise parents and caregivers on child-related issues. 1-888-603-9100.

STREETHAVEN AT THE CROSS-ROADS Takes in women on an emergency basis at no cost. 87 Pembroke, 416-967-6060.

TRAVELLERS' AID SOCIETY Emergency service for travellers having financial and other difficulties. Volunteer-operated booths. Wkdays and Sat 9:30 am-6 pm. Union Station, Bay-Dundas Bus Terminal and the Airport. 416-366-7788.

VETERINARY EMERGENCY CLINIC Emergency pet care 24 hrs daily. 920 Yonge, 416-920-2002.

MEDICAL

Access Alliance Multicultural community health centre provides medical care for immigrants, newcomers and refugees. Mon-Wed 9 am-7:30 pm, Thu-Fri 9 am-5 pm.
340 College, ste 500. 416-324-8677, www.accessalliance.ca.
Aids and Sexual Health Infoline 1-800-668-2437, 416-392-2437, www.toronto.ca/health.
Anishnawbe Health Toronto Health and cultural centre for First Nations people. Provides counselling, referrals and medical care. Wkdays 9 am-5 pm. Times vary with special events.
225 Queen E, 416-360-0486.
Bay Centre for Birth Control Free birth control and abortion counselling, by appointment. Mon and Fri 9 am-5 pm, Tue-Thu 9 am-8 pm, Sat 9 am-12:30 pm. Closed holiday wkends.
790 Bay, 8th floor, 416-351-3700.
Birth Control and STD Information Centre Birth control, pregnancy counselling, and VD and anonymous HIV testing. Mon, Wed-Fri 10 am-5 pm, Tue 10 am-6 pm, Thu 10 am-7 pm. Closed holiday wkends. By appointment only. 2828 Bathurst, ste 501, 416-789-4541.
Cabbagetown Women's Clinic Free-standing abortion clinic. Open Mon-Fri 8 am-4 pm. 302 Gerrard E, 416-323-0642.
Centre for Addiction and Mental Health Alcohol and drug addiction counselling and out-patient referrals. 33 Russell, 416-595-6000, 416-535-8501, www.camh.net.
211-Community Info Toronto Community info line for social and health service referrals. Directory of over 20,000 community, social, health and government services. 24 hrs. 416-392-0505, www.211toronto.ca.
Hassle Free Clinic Anonymous

HIV and STD tests, women's health services. Mon-Sat. Call for appt. 66 Gerrard E. Men, 416-922-0603; women, 416-922-0566; www.hasslefree-clinic.org.
Mclaughlin Addiction and Mental Health Information Centre Automated response line 24 hours a day (staffed 9 am-9 pm daily) 416-595-6111, 1-800-463-6273.
Ontario Problem Gambling Helpline 1-888-230-3505.
Parkdale Community Health Clinic Medical care for Parkdale residents. By appointment only. Times vary. 1229 Queen W, 416-537-2455.
Scott Clinic Free-standing abortion clinic. 157 Gerrard E, 416-962-4108, for appointments 416-962-5771.
Telehealth Ontario Get health advice from a registered nurse by phone. Free. 1-866-797-0000.
The Works Hassle-free needle exchange. Clean hypodermic needles are traded for used ones to protect intravenous drug users from exposure to AIDS. Van hours Mon-Sat 6-11:30 pm (call for locations). 277 Victoria, 416-392-0520.
Youthlink Inner City Drop-in resource centre for street-involved and homeless youth. Mon-Fri 9 am-noon and 1-4 pm (closed Tue afternoon, open until 3 pm Fri), drop-in Thu 6:30 pm-9 pm. 7 Vanauley, 416-703-3361, www.youthlink.ca.

DENTAL

Dental Emergency Clinic 1650 Yonge, 416-485-7121.
Ontario Dental Association 416-922-3900, www.dental.oda.on.ca.
U of T Patient Clinic 101 Elm, 416-979-4927.

PHARMACIES & PRESCRIPTIONS

Guardian Drugs 1881 Yonge, other locations, 416-480-1340.
Pharma Plus Drugmart 552 Church, other locations, 416-922-5816.
Shoppers Drug Mart 360 Bloor W, other locations, 416-961-2121.

LEGAL

Aborginal Legal Services Toronto Legal services and counselling for First Nations people. Wkdays 9 am-5 pm. 415 Yonge, ste 803, 416-408-3967.
Downtown Legal Services Free legal help for low-income neighbourhood residents, operated by

resources

faculty of law at U of T. By appointment only.
655 Spadina, 416-934-4535.
Parkdale Community Legal Services Free legal help for low-income clients and Parkdale residents. Mon 2-6 pm, Tue and Thu 2-7 pm, Fri 10 am-1 pm and 2-5 pm. 1266 Queen W, 416-531-2411.

BANKS
BMO Nesbitt Burns (Bank of Montreal)
1 First Canadian Place, other locations, 1-800-363-9992, www.bmo.com.
CIBC (Canadian Imperial Bank of Commerce)
199 Bay, other locations, 1-800-465-2422, www.cibc.com.
Hong Kong Bank of Canada
222 Spadina Ave, 1-888-310-4722, www.hsbc.ca.
Royal Bank
200 Bay, other locations, 1-800-769-2511, www.royalbank.com.
Scotiabank
40 King W, other locations, 1-800-4-SCOTIA (1-800-472-6842), www.scotiabank.com.
Toronto-Dominion Bank/Canada Trust
66 Wellington W, other locations, 1-866-222-3456, www.tdcanadatrust.com.

LIBRARIES
Toronto Public Library
The library has 98 branches and nearly 10.5 million books, videos, CDs, DVDs, magazines and other items in more than 100 languages. Free library cards, electronic databases, high speed Internet access and e-mail at all branches, 416-393-7131, www.tpl.toronto.on.ca.

PARLEZ-VOUS FRANÇAIS?

Canada is officially a bilingual country yet, in Toronto, French culture can seem invisible because there's no geographic region in the city to anchor the 300,000-strong community. The **Alliance Française de Toronto** (24 Spadina Road, 416-922-2014, www.alliance-francaise.ca) acts as the de facto cultural hub of Franco-Ontarian cultural activities, offering art shows, event listings and French lessons designed to make you feel smarter than you did in high school. It has a hand in organizing events on French holidays such as Saint-Jean-Baptiste Day (June 24) and the Semaine de la Francophonie (mid-March).
Toronto-Franco (www.toronto-

franco.com) is a fairly new organization dedicated to bringing together Franco-Ontarians on the Web. The only French-language Toronto newspaper is **L'Express** (www.lexpress.to), while TV needs are served by **TFO** (www.tfo.org), screening a selection of kids' shows, educational programs and documentaries. French films are often screened at **Cinematheque Ontario** (www.e.bell.ca/filmfest/cinematheque), while the **National Film Board** (www.nfb.ca) screens films from France and Quebec on the first Thursday of the month at its **Mediatheque** (150 John) as part of the Ciné Jeudi series (www.onf.ca).

If you're looking for a good French book to read (or a good book en français), then check out **Librairie Champlain** (468 Queen E, 416-364-4345, www.librairiechamplain.com). It stocks more than 100,000 French-language books, from reference texts to fiction best-sellers, as well as CDs (from pop to Edith Piaf) and DVDs, including French and French-Canadian films and Hollywood films dubbed in French.

There's a healthy selection of live theatre in French, offered by the **Théâtre Français de Toronto** (www.theatrefrancais.com) and **Théâtre la Tangente de Toronto** (www.theatrelatangente.ca). For kids, the **Harbourfront Centre** (www.harbourfrontcentre.com) provides art workshops in French, as well as a few plays staged as part of the superb **Milk Festival** (see **Festivals**, page 162). The **Royal Ontario Museum** (www.rom.on.ca; see **Sightseeing**, page 24) has succeeded in spawning Les Amis Francophile du ROM.

For a more informal scene, check out the Wednesday-night parties at the **Bedford Academy** (36 Prince Arthur, 416-921-4600) and practice your best French bar talk.

Toronto is a city of film festivals, and each spring it hosts **Cinéfranco** (www.cinefranco.com), a 10-day feast of French-language cinema from around the world. All films include English subtitles, and many of them (particularly the comedies) won't receive a commercial release in North American theatres. Almost as much fun as the films themselves is watching the double- and triple-cheek kissing in the queues to get in.

Finally, if you need a place to stay, the **French Connection B&B** (102 Burnside, 416-537-7741, www.thefrenchconnection.com) will meet all of votre besoins et désirs.

CULTURAL ORGS
AFRICAN-CANADIAN

African National Congress
292-A Danforth, 416-461-4255.
African Resource Centre
366 Adelaide E, 416-863-6240.
Ontario Black History Society
10 Adelaide E, 416-867-9420.

ARAB & MIDDLE EASTERN
Afghan Association of Ontario
29 Pemican, 416-744-9289, 1200 Markham, 416-438-0808.
Arab Community Centre 5298 Dundas W, 416-231-7746.
Canadian Arab Federation 5298 Dundas W, 416-231-7524.
Iranian Community Association of Ontario 1110 Finch W, 416-736-4090.

CHINESE
Cecil Community Centre
58 Cecil, 416-598-2403.
Chinese Community Centre of Ontario 84 Augusta, 416-365-0917.

SOUTH ASIAN
Hindu Cultural Society
1 Morningview, 416-284-6282.
Islamic Centre of Toronto/Jami Mosque 56 Boustead, 416-769-1192.
Islamic Foundation of Toronto
441 Nugget, 416-321-0909.
Pakistani Canada Cultural Association 54 Bartlett, 416-532-7556.
Sikh Foundation 40 King W, 416-777-6697.

SOUTHEAST ASIAN
Canadian Cambodian Association of Ontario
1111 Finch W 416-736-0832.
Culture Philippines
2687 Kingsberry, 416-276-9199.
Indonesian Association
4294 Fieldgate, 905-828-2550.
Japanese Canadian Cultural Centre 123 Wynford, 416-441-2345.
Korean Community Information Centre
146 Hallam, 416-533-1111.
Korean Cultural Association of Metro Toronto 20 Mobile, 416-755-9288.
Lao Association of Ontario
1111 Finch W, 416-665-3872.
Silayan Filipino Community Centre 418-B Parliament, 416-926-9505.
Vietnamese Association of Toronto 565 College, 416-535-5241.

NATIVE CANADIAN
Native Canadian Centre of Toronto 16 Spadina Road, 416-964-9087, 416-922-2014.

resources

SPIRITUAL RESOURCES

Agonshu Toronto Buddhist Association
1225 Yonge, 416-922-1272, www.japansocietycanada.com.

Baps Shree Swaminarayan Mandir One of the city's foremost mandirs, inspired by His Divine Holiness Pramukh Swami Maharaj.
61 Clairville, 416-798-2277.

Congregation Knesseth Israel Established in 1911, this is the city's oldest synagogue still in use as a place of worship.
54-56 Maria, 416 961-5556.

Dharma Centre of Canada A converted residence with a shrine room/sitting room where classes and meditation take place.
153 Riverdale, 416-778-8193, www.torontodharmacentre.org.

Diamond Way Buddhist Centre Introduction to Buddhism Mon and Wed 8 pm, with meditation Mon and Wed 8:30 pm. By donation. 25 St. Nicholas,
416-925-4494, www.diamondway.org/toronto.

Hindu Cultural Society 1940 Ellesmere #17, 416-438-6661.

Hindu Prathana Samaj Daily prayer services and weekly lectures. 62 Fern, 416-536-9229.

Holy Blossom Temple Reform congregation offers daily worship services and schooling.
1950 Bathurst, 416-789-3291, www.holyblossom.org.

Iskcon/Hare Krishna Temple Offering daily worship, Sunday feasts and, for out-of-towners, a modest room (first come, first served) in the ashram.
243 Avenue Rd, 416-922-5415, www.iskcon.ca.

Islamic Foundation of Toronto Originating in 1969, it's one of the oldest Muslim organizations in Canada, offering classrooms, prayer halls, a library, gymnasium and a Hifz school.
441 Nugget, 416-321-0909, www.islamicfoundation.ca.

Jami Mosque Toronto's first mosque, established in 1968, offering regular services.
56 Boustead, 416-769-1192, www.jamimosque.com.

Karma Sonam Dargye Ling Tibetan Buddhist centre in the St. Clair-Bathurst neighbourhood, offering weekly practice.
86 Vaughan, 416-653-5371.

Korean Buddhist Society of Ontario 6 Wildwood,
416-463-8998.

Nichiren Shoshu Canada 636 King W, 416-368-0123, www.buddhismcanada.com.

Q-AGE A queer spiritual network for women and men holds retreats, workshops, potlucks and brunches. 416-925-9872 ext 2990

Richmond Hill Hindu Temple The largest Hindu temple in

North America, built and run under the Agama Sastra traditions. 10865 Bayview, Richmond Hill, 905-883-9109, www.thehindutemple.ca.

Salaam Toronto A supportive community for gay, lesbian, bisexual, transsexual, transgendered and questioning Muslims and their friends.
416-925-9872 ext 2209, salaam@salaamcanada.com, www.salaamcanada.com.

Shromini Sikh Society Temple 269 Pape, 416-463-3132.

Tengye Ling Tibetan Buddhist Temple This temple holds weekly dharma discourse Tue 7:30 pm. 11 Madison. 416-966-4656, www.tengyeling.ca.

Toronto Buddhist Church Holds religious services, as well as cultural activities, such as ikebana, minyo and karaoke.
1011 Sheppard W, 416-534-4302, www.tbc.on.ca.

Toronto Shambhala Meditation Centre This Tibetan Buddhist centre offers free open meditation sessions Mon and Wed 7-8 pm as well as free instruction. 670 Bloor W, 416-588-6465, www.shambhala.org/centre/toronto.

Toronto Zen Centre Full practice supports, activities and ceremonies for members, plus public workshops. 33 High Park Gardens, 416-766-3400, torontozen.org.

University of Toronto Buddhist Community Located on the downtown campus, this centre offers Buddhist meditation. http://buddhist.sa.utoronto.ca.

Vishnu Temple/Voices of Vedas 8640 Yonge, 905-886-1724.

Wiccan Church of Canada This church holds rituals celebrating pagan spirituality.
109 Vaughan. 416-656-6564, tamarraj@sympatico.ca, www.wcc.on.ca.

Zainabia Muhammadi Mosque 7340 Bayview, 905-881-1763.

Zen Buddhist Temple Meditation services are held Sun 9:30 am and 4 pm and they offer medication courses and retreats. 297 College, 416-658-0137, www. zenbuddhisttemple.org.

TORONTO MEDIA
PRINT

Toronto is the largest media market in the country and one of the most competitive in all of North America.

Toronto's essential and only truly alternative news and entertainment weekly is the independent **NOW Magazine** (www.nowtoronto.com). A new issue is available free every Thursday and can be found in the distinctive green and red street boxes and on racks in

thousands of shops, restaurants and bars. NOW is required reading, as it provides the city's most complete event listings, a kick-ass look at news and arts writing that discovers and uncovers. The megacorp daily the Toronto Star produces the alt-weekly wannabe Eye, while Xtra! and Fab service the queer community.

Toronto also has four paid dailies – the right-wing upstart National Post, slightly less right-wing (but a bit more stuffy) Globe and Mail, city paper Toronto Star and tits-and-trash tabloid Toronto Sun – waging an ongoing newspaper war. Nabbing a free copy of any one of them is a matter of hitting the right street corner on the right day. Toronto subway stations are also littered with stacks of the city's two free daily commuter papers, Metro and Toronto 24 Hours, which provide snapshots of yesterday's events.

Among the numerous monthly and bimonthly magazines published, the glossy city mag Toronto Life is the most notable (and useful to visitors), although it does read a lot like Lifestyles of the Rich and Boring. There are also several weekly and biweekly papers serving Toronto's various ethnic communities, including Greek, Spanish and Ukrainian weeklies, a Portuguese biweekly and three Chinese daily papers.

TELEVISION

Because of our close proximity, our TV offerings look pretty much like what you'd find in the U.S., including the four major U.S. networks and countless digital specialty channels.

But for a bit of Canadian flavour there are a few stations worth tuning into. Foremost is the venerable Canadian Broadcast Corporation (CBC), which operates both the CBC and all-news CBC Newsworld channels with a mandate to cover Canadian news, sports (hello Hockey Night in Canada!) and social issues.

Bell Globemedia, owner of CTV, is the largest private broadcaster, although much of its schedule is devoted to American imports like CSI and American Idol. Likewise with Global TV. Bell Globemedia also purchased CHUM, which includes Citytv, MuchMusic, Star TV and Bravo and which also have a strong community voice, with a good mix of local news, sports, entertainment and lifestyle programming as well as American imports and Hollywood movies.

Much like PBS, Ontario public broadcaster TVO is heavy on highbrow arts programming, while Rogers community television relies on exactly that – news, sports and lifestyle programming produced within and about the GTA, including extensive live coverage of the Toronto International Film Festival press conferences.

As Canada's first free multilingual-and-multicultural TV broadcaster, Omni and its sister station, Omni 2, provide the most ethnically diverse content. They devote 60 per cent of their airtime to cultural programming, in no less than 15 languages, including 22 hours of original multilingual programming produced each week, from a one-hour Italian-language newscast on weeknights to a Portuguese-language newscast that airs each weekday.

RADIO

There are more than 30 radio stations in Toronto, from rock to talk to classical to Ukrainian.

On the AM dial, catch the Blue Jays on the Fan 590, the Maple Leafs on AM 640, all news on 680 News, talk radio on CFRB 1010 and oldies on 1050 CHUM.

Flip over to FM and you'll find the usual suspects: top 40 (CHUM 104.5, Z103.5), hiphop and R&B (flow 93.5), classic rock (Q107), light rock (97.3 EZRock, CHFI 98.1), any kind of pop-rock (Mix 99.9), alternative (The Edge 102.1), cock rock (92.5 Jack FM), classical (Classical 96.3), and jazz (JazzFM 91.1).

Then there's the handful of stations that serve various ethnic communities, including CHIN (AM 1540/FM 100.7), which provides programming in over 30 languages, CIRV (88.9 FM), which serves the Russian, Portuguese, Punjabi, Ukrainian, Chinese and Caribbean communities, and Aboriginal Voices Radio (106.5 FM), which is geared toward the city's more than 40,000 Native Canadians.

Public broadcaster the CBC has three stations: Radio One (99.1 FM) is predominantly talk-oriented and has become part of the Canadian identity; Radio 2 (94.1 FM) plays jazz, classical, celtic/traditional and opera; CBC Radio 3 (channel 94) features Canadian performers in every genre from rock, pop and hiphop to electronica and alt-country, and is available only on the Sirius Satellite Radio network, one of two satellite radio services in the city, the other being XM Satellite Radio.

Finally, but perhaps most importantly, there's the college campus radio stations, which is where all the best, coolest new music from around the world can be heard: U of T's CIUT 89.5, Ryerson's CKIN 88.1 and York U's CHRY 105.5.

ONLINE

The place to start is **www.nowtoronto.com**, the website for altweekly NOW Magazine (and the people behind this guide book). The site is jam-packed with news and lifestyle stories, reviews of movies, CDs, concerts, recitals, stage plays, books, art shows and everything pop-cultural in T.O., including extensive coverage of all of Toronto's major festivals (TIFF, NXNE, Fringe, Caribana, Pride, etc.) as well as Cannes, Sundance and SXSW. NOW provides complete events listings and classified ads and also boasts an excellent restaurant guide, with reviews of eateries that you can sort by food genre, area and cost.

Once you've exhausted what www.nowtoronto.com has to offer, click on over to the popular and easy-to-navigate **www.toronto.com**. Run by TorStar (the folks behind the Toronto Star newspaper), the listings are expansive, but be warned: this site functions more like a Yellow Pages, generating income from ads and listings rather than offering discriminating suggestions.

People post just because they love the city on **www.torontoist.com**. More structured and less rant-filled than a traditional blog, Torontoist is a pleasurable browse that doesn't feel like a news site. Instead of the ravings of one lonely typist, editorial duties are dispersed among a handful of people, keeping it fresh and eclectic. Like all good blogs, it has a theme: the landscape of Toronto and all the weird and wonderful things that take place therein. Entries range from shout-outs to the visiting Olsen twins to commentary on the plight of Kensington's beleaguered St. Stephen-in-the-Fields Church.

Also worthy is **www.beatnikpad.com**, a beautifully designed and written blog. Entries about living in High Park, technical geekery and love all make for inspiring reading. Local hipsters post on everything from concert details to the lineup of their next kickball game at (www.stillepost.ca/boards/index.php?board=7.0) and the listings section has just about everything you'd want for a night out, from cheap beer nights to local shows.

URBAN SPACE

Spacing Magazine, dedicated to the urban fabric of Toronto, has often been credited with ushering in a renaissance of interest in Toronto's cultural history. The **Spacing Wire** (www.spacing.ca/wire) has "daily dispatches from across the city and around the world." The photoblog section (www.spacing.ca/photoblog) offers a great cross-section of photos taken in our town's public spaces. Rannie Turingan, an excellent local photographer, founded the **PhotoJunkie** collective; its site (www.photojunkie.ca) truly captures the character of Toronto.

DEEP INSIDE TORONTO

For history and nature lovers, the unique **www.lostrivers.ca** lets locals trace the paths of dozens of old rivers long buried by the city's expansion. Join this group for one of its meandering Lost River Walks that trace the path of the buried bodies of water. For walks that follow only the whims of the participants, hook up with the folks at the **Toronto Psychogeography Society** (www.psychogeography.ca).

Last but not least, there's the website www.infiltration.org, the zine about going places you're not supposed to go. It will astonish you with secrets from our city's underbelly. And you thought the mole people were a myth!

WIRELESS IN THE CITY

While Toronto is working toward unfettered wireless Internet access city-wide – a goal announced by Toronto Hydro Telecom in early 2006 – implementation can be a bitch. So you might want to look to community groups that are already offering free wireless in a growing number of hot spots around the city. Check out **Wireless Bandit**'s site at http://wirelessbandit.nerdsunderglass.com for a comprehensive list.

Wireless Toronto (www.wirelesstoronto.com) has done much to champion the cause of free wireless and is growing by the day, hooking up dozens of locations. A favourite is the glorious St. Lawrence Market (www.stlawrencemarket.com; see **Sightseeing**, page 17). Do your weekly shopping at the market, then find a comfy corner to sip a coffee and get some work done on your laptop online for free.

Wireless Nomad (www.wirelessnomad.com) uses a co-op model to offer wireless Internet access to members in neighbourhoods around the city, like Hillcrest and Bickford Park. Wireless Nomad also teamed up with Wireless Toronto to provide access in Dufferin Grove Park (on Dufferin, S of Bloor, www.dufferinpark.ca; see **Sightseeing**, page 38).

Oh yeah, the **NOW Lounge** (189 Church, at Dundas, 416-364-1301), in the NOW Magazine office building where this book was written, is also a free wireless hot spot. It's usually quiet, and there's plenty of seating (the lunch specials are pretty reasonable, too!).

Or you could just try wandering the streets with your PDA to find open, unsecure hot spots beaming out from people's houses. Don't worry, it's not illegal (yet).

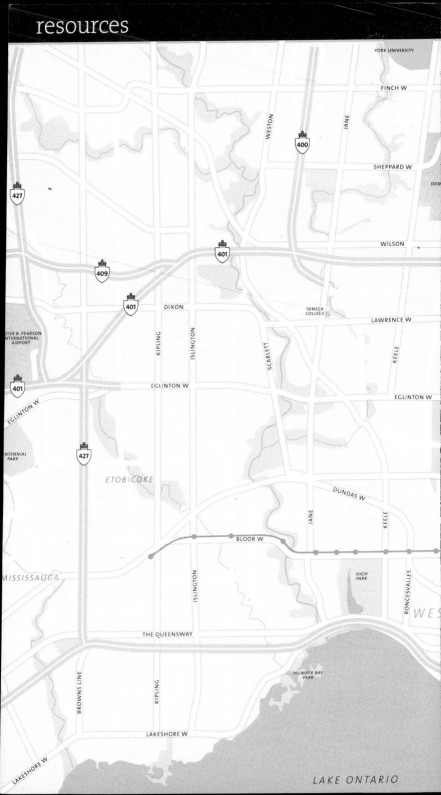

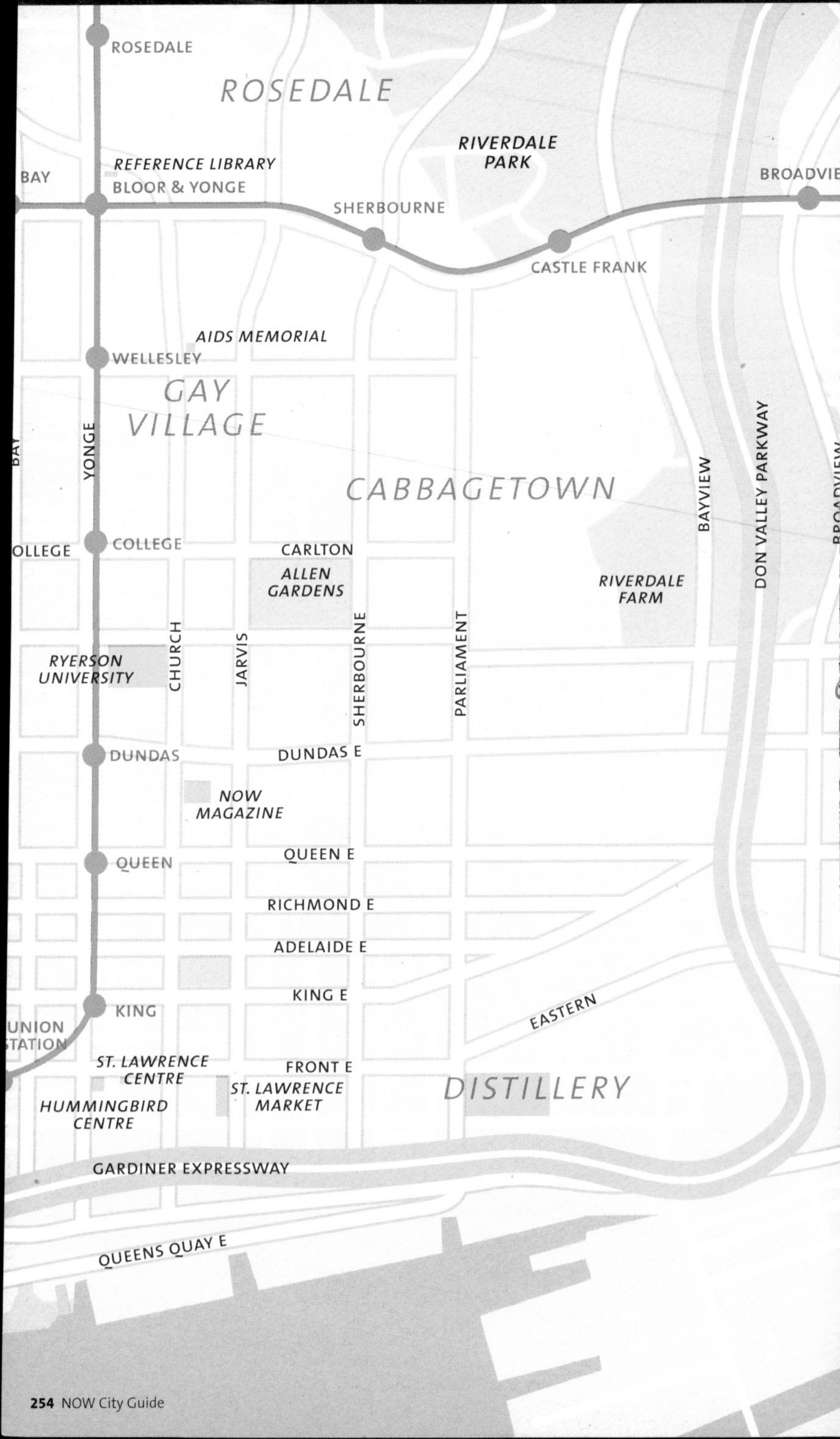

ROSEDALE

ROSEDALE

BAY

REFERENCE LIBRARY
BLOOR & YONGE

RIVERDALE PARK

SHERBOURNE

BROADVIE

CASTLE FRANK

AIDS MEMORIAL

WELLESLEY

GAY VILLAGE

YONGE

BAY

CABBAGETOWN

COLLEGE

OLLEGE

CARLTON

ALLEN GARDENS

BAYVIEW

DON VALLEY PARKWAY

BROADVIEW

RIVERDALE FARM

CHURCH

JARVIS

SHERBOURNE

PARLIAMENT

RYERSON UNIVERSITY

DUNDAS

DUNDAS E

NOW MAGAZINE

QUEEN

QUEEN E

RICHMOND E

ADELAIDE E

KING E

UNION STATION

KING

EASTERN

ST. LAWRENCE CENTRE

FRONT E

DISTILLERY

HUMMINGBIRD CENTRE

ST. LAWRENCE MARKET

GARDINER EXPRESSWAY

QUEENS QUAY E

THE DANFORTH

PAPE

GREENWOOD

CHESTER

DANFORTH

DONLANDS

COXWELL

RIVERDALE

LOGAN

PAPE

JONES

GREENWOOD

COXWELL

GERRARD E

LITTLE
INDIA

GERRARD E

ATOWN E

CARLAW

PAPE

DUNDAS E

QUEEN E

EASTERN

THE BEACH

LAKESHORE E

ASHBRIDGES BAY
PARK

LESLIE

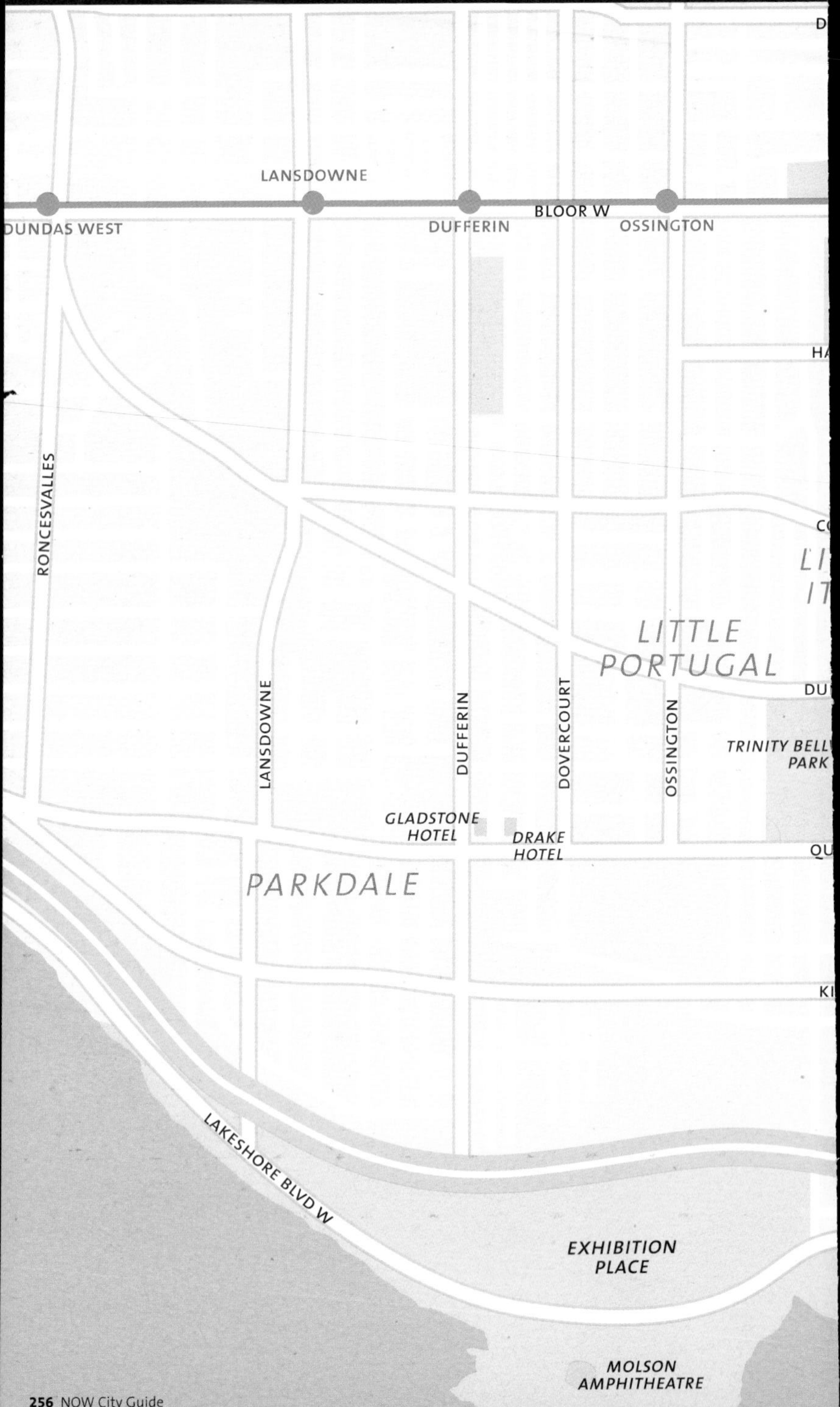

LANSDOWNE

DUNDAS WEST

BLOOR W

DUFFERIN

OSSINGTON

RONCESVALLES

D

HA

C

LITTLE
IT

LITTLE
PORTUGAL

LANSDOWNE

DUFFERIN

DOVERCOURT

OSSINGTON

DU

TRINITY BELL
PARK

GLADSTONE
HOTEL

DRAKE
HOTEL

QU

PARKDALE

KI

LAKESHORE BLVD W

EXHIBITION
PLACE

MOLSON
AMPHITHEATRE

ONTARIO PLACE

DUPONT

ROSEDA

NATIVE CANADIAN CENTRE

YORKVILLE

ANNEX

ST. GEORGE

BAY

BATHURST

SPADINA

ROYAL ONTARIO MUSEUM

BLOOR
YONGE

MUSEUM

HOSKIN

WELLESL

UNIVERSITY OF TORONTO

WELLESLEY

PROVINCIAL LEGISLATURE

COLLEG

QUEEN'S PARK

*KENSINGTON
MARKET
CHINATOWN*

UNIVERSITY

BAY

YONGE

BUS
TERMINAL

BATHURST

*ART
GALLERY
OF ONTARIO*

ST. PATRICK

ST. PATRICK

EATON
CENTRE

DUNDA

*GRANGE
PARK*

*ONTARIO COLLEGE
OF ART AND DESIGN*

CITY
HALL

QUEEN WEST

OSGOODE

QUEE

ADELAIDE W

*FINANCIAL
DISTRICT*

RICHMOND W

CLUBLAND

SPADINA AVE

ST. ANDREW

YORK

KING

FRONT

HISTORIC
FORT YORK

CN TOWER

UNION STATION

*AIR CANADA
CENTRE*

*ROGERS
CENTRE*

GARDINER EXPRESSWAY

QUEENS QUAY W

*YORK QUAY
CENTRE*

*QUEENS QUAY
TERMINAL*

*TORONTO ISLAN
FERRY
TERMINAL*

HARBOURFRONT